150 YEARS OF GLOUCESTER RUGBY 1873 – 2023

A Season-by-Season Record of Every Match

CHRIS COLLIER

with MALC KING and DICK WILLIAMS

GLOUCESTER RUGBY
HERITAGE

First published in 2023
for Gloucester Rugby Heritage
www.gloucesterrugbyheritage.org.uk

by The Hobnob Press, 8 Lock Warehouse, Severn Rd, Gloucester GL1 2GA
www.hobnobpress.co.uk

British Library Cataloguing in Publication Data
A catalogue record for this book is available from the British Library

ISBN 978-1-914907-63-5

Typeset in Octavian 10/11.5 pt. Typesetting and origination by John Chandler

This book has been sponsored by the Gloucester Rugby Foundation

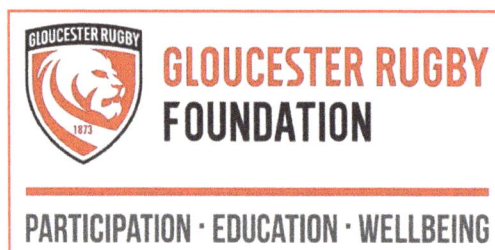

Foreword by Alex Brown
CEO, Gloucester Rugby

As we come together to celebrate Gloucester Rugby's remarkable 150-year journey, I'm filled with a mix of humility and excitement. This isn't just another date on the calendar; it's a powerful testament to the enduring legacy, the profound traditions, and the indelible impact of a Club that's deeply cherished by countless fans and our community. In this foreword, I want to share why I believe it's crucial to acknowledge and celebrate this significant milestone, what makes our Club so exceptional, and some personal moments that fill me with pride.

Gloucester Rugby isn't simply a rugby club; it's a way of life for many. It embodies unwavering passion, loyalty, and a unique sense of togetherness that transcends backgrounds, and brings people together. What distinguishes our Club is not solely the victories on the field, but also the rich tapestry of moments woven into its history. Kingsholm, with its iconic Shed, is not just a stadium; it's an exceptional place where history permeates every aspect of the Club and its community. The raucous cheers of the crowd, the sea of Cherry and White, and the resounding chants that resonate from the Shed to the main stand create an atmosphere which is truly unparalleled.

Having had the privilege of both playing for and against Gloucester Rugby, I can attest to the unique character of Kingsholm. Warming up in front of the Shed, with the crowd's boundless passion charging the air, is an experience that leaves an indelible mark on your memory. Some of my most cherished memories during my playing time at Gloucester are from extraordinary matches; the 2012 Champions Cup victory against Toulouse, while not affecting tournament progression, meant the world to the team and the Club. Lifting the Challenge Cup trophy in 2006, after an epic battle culminating in extra time, is an experience I will never forget. These are the moments that epitomize the unwavering spirit of Gloucester Rugby, stories that will be passed down through generations.

Over the past two decades, in my various roles at Gloucester Rugby, from my early days as a player in 2003 to my current position as CEO, I have had the privilege of being a custodian of the Club's heritage. My journey has been marked by highs and lows, but it has always been accompanied by an overwhelming sense of pride in being a part of this incredible institution. It has instilled in me a profound sense of responsibility to uphold and pass on the greatness of Gloucester Rugby to the next generation.

I should like to express my sincere gratitude to Gloucester Rugby Heritage for their unwavering commitment to researching and preserving the Club's rich history. Their books, talks, displays and website have all played a pivotal role in ensuring that Gloucester Rugby's vast history and heritage is celebrated and preserved, and passed on. A special mention must go to Chris Collier, our esteemed statistician, who has painstakingly compiled the details of every match ever played by the Club and has been the driving force behind this book. His unwavering dedication to preserving our history, along with the hard work of Malc King and Dick Williams, has truly brought this book to life.

Under the leadership of George Skivington, our Director of Rugby, the heritage of Gloucester Rugby has been embraced and instilled as a source of inspiration in the current squad. He reminds them daily that they are part of something truly special; a Club with 150 years of history, a Club that has weathered challenges and celebrated triumphs, and a Club that continues to inspire. I hope that Gloucester Rugby's legacy continues to inspire generations to come.

In celebrating 150 years of Gloucester Rugby, we honour the past, celebrate the present, and look forward to the future with unwavering hope and pride. This book serves as a tribute to the Club's remarkable journey and the equally remarkable individuals who have contributed to its extraordinary history. May the legacy and future of the Cherry and Whites endure and flourish.

Introduction

From the mid nineteenth century a form of primitive rugby appeared which allowed players to handle and run with the ball when caught on the full or after one bounce. This had evolved from the game known as football. In 1863 the Football Association was formed, in order to formulate a set of rules. It also set to distance itself from the new running game. As a result, football outlawed handling the ball.

By this time, informal games of rugby were being played on the Spa in Gloucester, but as yet there were no organised clubs in Gloucester. The developing game of rugby had no set of rules, "hacking", or kicking, was allowed, and any matches had to be played under conditions agreed between the participating teams. As the sport became more popular, especially in the universities, it became clear that this anarchic approach had to end. In January 1871 delegates from 21 clubs, almost all from London, came together to form the Rugby Football Union. One of those on the first RFU committee, charged with producing a standardised set of rules, was Frank Hartley, who was opposed to hacking, and it was abolished, much to the disgust of some die-hards.

A couple of years later, Hartley came to work in Gloucester, and on 15 September 1873 the Gloucester Journal reported, "At a meeting at the Spread Eagle Hotel, Gloucester, for the purpose of enrolling Members of a Football Club for the City, about forty-five gentlemen joined. Mr Frank Hartley was elected Captain and Mr J.P.Riddiford, Hon Sec." The Gloucester Rugby journey had begun.

The game at this time was hardly a spectacle. Many matches consisted of prolonged scrummages, with very little handling, and as one observer put it, "forwards wasted their strength in protracted shoving matches, and backs neglected dropping almost entirely." Note the reference to "dropping" or going for a drop goal which was one of the ways of scoring a "goal". Only a goal could win a game. A try merely gave the opportunity to score a goal if the conversion kick was successful.

Nevertheless, Rugby became more popular and spread across the country, becoming especially popular with working class men in South Wales and the West Country. Elsewhere in England and Scotland a large proportion of rugby players were drawn from the middle classes. Indeed, in the early days the rules of the Gloucester Club were designed to ensure it remained a middle-class preserve. But A.W.Vears, who became the Gloucester Club Chairman, was determined to strengthen the team by opening selection to a wider base of players. Very soon, in the early 1880s two labourers at the Wagon Works, George Coates in 1882 and his friend Tommy Bagwell in 1883,

broke into the team. Coates was the outstanding player in the unbeaten "Invincibles" team of 1882-83, and Bagwell was Club captain from 1890-92. From then on it became obvious that locals of all classes aspired to play for Gloucester and did. This was crucial in establishing Gloucester as one of the leading clubs in the country, a status which has been retained throughout the subsequent history of the Club, and which it enjoyed before the Gloucester Association Football Club was founded in 1883. Gloucester has remained primarily a Rugby City ever since.

Gloucester's early home was the Spa, but in 1891, in order to ensure a game against Swansea went ahead, a too liberal scattering of salt killed the grass, and ruined the pitch for the subsequent cricket season. The Gloucester Cricket Club held the lease to the Spa, and the rugby club were sub-tenants in the winter. The rugby club had to leave and found a new home at Kingsholm.

All the while Gloucester's fixture list steadily became stronger with the inclusion of the major Welsh clubs like Cardiff, Newport, Swansea and Llanelli. It became the measure of the success or otherwise of a season to assess how results against the Welsh "big four" had gone. There were many seasons of outstanding success against other English clubs, but dismal failure against the Welsh. Northern clubs also featured on the fixture list. Huddersfield, Wigan, Dewsbury and Wakefield Trinity were all played before the schism in 1895, when the Northern Union severed links with the RFU and went their own way, eventually changing some rules and creating the sport of Rugby League.

A steady stream of Gloucester players won international honours, most notably Frank Stout who captained the British Lions to a series win in Australia in 1899, Arthur Hudson who scored four tries for England in Paris in 1906, and Tom Voyce, one of Gloucester's finest players who won 27 England caps between 1920 and 1926, and revolutionised the role of wing forward.

In the 1930s Gloucester went through a golden age. There were outstanding wins and doubles over the Welsh giants, but all was cut short by the intrusion of war again in 1939. The decades after the war were mixed in terms of success, until in 1972 Gloucester won the inaugural National Knock-out Competition. Much of the credit for this triumph could be put down to the inspiring captaincy of Mike Nicholls, arguably the best captain the Club ever had. The Knock-out Competition, later titled a cup, was also won by the Club in 1978, 1982 (shared) and 2003.

Since Rugby Union became a professional sport in 1995, the Club has welcomed international players from all over the world and some have become "Shed" favourites, such as Terry Fanolua, Ian Jones, Ollie Azam, Jake Boer and Junior Paramore. This also saw the advent of European cup competitions, and the Club won European Challenge cups in 2006 and 2015.

In the last decade, women's rugby has grown in both participation and popularity. In association with Hartpury University, Gloucester Rugby formed the Gloucester-Hartpury Women's RFC in 2014, and their results are included in this book. Some of their matches are played at Kingsholm, most notably the league final in 2023, which attracted nearly 10,000 spectators to see Gloucester-Hartpury beat Exeter.

In this book the reader will find the details of all Gloucester's games (both men and women) season by season from 1873 to 2023. Each season is summarised followed by the details of each game. In a few cases in the early seasons, the scorers are unknown, and in even fewer the result remains a mystery. Over the years, there have been alterations to scoring values, and these changes are recorded in the seasons when they first took effect.

Chris Collier
Gloucester Rugby Heritage Statistician

Acknowledgements

This book is largely the work of Chris Collier, statistician for Gloucester Rugby Heritage. It represents the culmination of many years of work by him to meticulously research and record every match played by Gloucester Rugby in the 150 years since they played their first on 4th October 1873. Most of the information was drawn from records in the Gloucestershire Archives (now known as the Heritage Hub) in Alvin Street, just round the corner from the home of Gloucester Rugby at Kingsholm. The principal sources were match reports in The Citizen, which was first published in 1876 and has given extensive coverage to Gloucester Rugby ever since, and the notebooks produced by WB (Bill Bailey) that paper's rugby correspondent for some 60 years.

Chris has been assisted on this book by Malc King, who has contributed the season summaries up to the Second World War, and by Dick Williams, who has overseen all the images in the book, including photo processing to improve the quality of many of the team photos. We are grateful to Martin Bennett, Club photographer since 2008, for the team photos for many of the more recent seasons. We have also been fortunate to benefit from the skills of John Chandler for the design and type-setting of the book, and for overseeing the printing of the book by Lightning Source.

Gloucester Rugby Heritage has now been operating for 16 years, following the unearthing of many old records when the old stand at Kingsholm was demolished in 2007, and throughout has enjoyed the support and encouragement of the Club, the Archives and the Former Players, for which we have been very grateful. I am particularly pleased that Alex Brown, former player and now CEO of the Club has kindly contributed the Foreword for this book.

We also owe thanks to the Gloucester Rugby Foundation, and its CEO, Rob Webber, for generously sponsoring this book. Gloucester Rugby Heritage is a non-profit charity committed to educate people in the history of the Club, but this funding has enabled us to meet this purpose by reducing the price of the book to a very reasonable level. It will also enable us to donate copies to local libraries.

Malc King
Chairman, Gloucester Rugby Heritage

1873-74

Played 5 Won 2 Drawn 3
For 3 goals Against nil
Captain: Frank Hartley

Frank Hartley, captain of the Flamingoes, a team based at Battersea in London, represented his club at the meeting which set up the Rugby Football Union in 1871. He became a member of the first RFU committee, charged with organising the game and drawing up the laws, as well as becoming an England selector. He was a solicitor and joined a Gloucester law firm in 1873, where he worked alongside John Riddiford. The two of them met with other rugby enthusiasts and organised a meeting at the Spread Eagle in Gloucester on 15th September 1873, which resulted in the formation of the Gloucester (Rugby) Football Club.

Frank Hartley was elected as captain and John Riddiford as secretary. Frank was described as a useful half-back and a good runner. As captain he also coached the team and is credited with influencing the early development of Gloucester as a side skilled in the "short-passing game". The members of the Club were in professional and commercial employment, and the costs and rules of membership, and the timing of practice sessions, effectively excluded working class men.

Home matches and training sessions were held on the Spa ground, which was leased to Gloucester Cricket Club by the Gloucester Corporation. The Club colours in this first season were recorded 50 years later as black and blue. At the end of the season, the balance sheet showed that there were 35 members, and that the Club was in the black to the tune of £11.

At this time only goals counted in deciding the result of a match – a try merely presented the opportunity to take a conversion kick to turn it into a goal. Consequently, a high proportion of games ended as a draw. It may be that additional games were played of which no record has been found, so there is doubt about declaring this as an unbeaten season.

Oct 4 College (King's School) 0
Gloucester 2 goals 6 tries
Tries: F.Hartley (3), J.F.Riddiford (3), W.A.Lucy, A.King;
Conversions: W.A.Lucy, W.A.Boughton
Gloucester had 10 players against 15 for College School

Oct 22 Gloucester 1 goal 4 tries
College (King's School) 0
Tries: J.F.Riddiford (2), F.Hartley, H.Jewesbury, W.Haines;
Conversion: W.A.Lucy
Gloucester had 13 players against 20 for College School

Nov 4 Gloucester 0 Hereford 0

Nov 21 Frampton 0 Gloucester 0
Gloucester scored 3 tries to nil, but kicked no conversions

Nov 26 Gloucester 0 Cirencester 0
Gloucester had 14 players against 15 for Cirencester

1874-75

Played 5 Won 0 Lost 1 Drawn 4
For nil Against 1 goal
Captain: Frank Hartley

By the start of this season a more formal arrangement had been reached whereby the Club was a sub-tenant of Gloucester Cricket Club for the use of the Spa ground and the pavilion for spectator seating, teas and changing rooms. The pitch had a "Beaufort end" and a "Railway Line end".

Only goals counted towards the result of a match, and Gloucester had six tries at goal and their opponents five, but none of the attempted conversions succeeded. So, every match ended as a scoreless draw, except when a dropped goal was kicked by Hereford. However, results were expressed as draws in favour of one team or the other according to the number of tries at goal, so Gloucester's record included two draws in their favour and two draws in favour of their opponents.

The most important match of the season was against Western Counties, which was played as a trial for the Western Counties side due to play Oxford University the following month. Both William Boughton and John Riddiford of Gloucester are known to have played for the West of England; Frank Hartley was selected but unable to play, but no record of the match itself has been found. Gloucester were also due to join with Hereford and Worcester players in a combined team against Western Counties, but no evidence has been found of this match taking place, and the match between Gloucester and Hereford may have been played instead.

The first match of the season at Cirencester was played in Earl Bathurst's Park, and the second was played in snow at Hereford, where, owing to a misunderstanding, Gloucester had only ten players against their opponent's twelve. Gloucester only managed to field eleven players for their final match against Newnham, but nevertheless had the better of it.

Indeed, the Club realised that if they were going to compete successfully against the likes of "Hereford, Worcester and elsewhere," the number of playing members needed to increase. In order to encourage this, the 5s joining fee for membership was abolished and only the annual subscription of 5s remained. In the absence of a match against another club, a match between members was played on the Spa every Friday. In all but the last game, the Gloucester scorers are not known

Nov 6 Cirencester 0 Gloucester 0
Cirencester scored one try but failed to kick the goal to convert it

Nov 27 Hereford 0 Gloucester 0
Gloucester scored one try but failed to kick the goal to convert it

Feb 5 Gloucester 0 Western Counties 0
Gloucester scored a try and W Counties scored 4 tries, but none were converted

Feb 12 Gloucester 0 Hereford 1 drop goal
Gloucester had only 10 players

Mar 12 Newnham 0 Gloucester 0
Gloucester scored 4 tries but failed to convert any of them
Tries: F.Hartley (2), W.Boughton, W.F.Brown
Gloucester had only 11 players

1875-76

Played 8 Won 4 Lost 3 Drawn 1
For 5 goals, 9 tries Against 1 goal, 1 try
Captain: Frank Hartley

Prior to November 1875 games could only be won by scoring a goal, but thereafter, if both sides scored the same number of goals or no goals were scored, the number of tries scored decided the winner.

The formation of the team varied between matches. When Gloucester played Ross-on-Wye in December, both teams played with ten forwards, two backs, one three-quarter-back and two half-backs. The Chronicle reported that "few runs were made, and long and fierce scrimmages were the order of the day" and the result was a scoreless draw.

In February the Club played its first match against a London team, the Flamingoes. There were admission charges for the first time at a Gloucester match. Frank Hartley, as captain of Gloucester and ex-captain of the Flamingoes, made his former teammates very welcome. The match was played on a Saturday, and the post-match socialising then started at the Ram Inn, and seems to have gone well. Although one of the Flamingoes players made it back to London on the Saturday night, the rest did not make it home until Tuesday.

In March a serious injury occurred for the first time soon after the start of the match against Ross-on-Wye, when Sydney Lane sustained a bad fracture of his thigh. The following week's fixture was cancelled, and the injury was reported to have "had a serious effect on the attendance at matches for some time, the ladies particularly absenting themselves from matches".

Nov 5 Gloucester 4 goals Newnham 0
Tries: F.Hartley (2), H.J.Boughton, E.J.Gardom, R.Edwards;
Conversions: E.J.Gardom (2);
Drop goals: J.Brown, F.Hartley

Dec 17 Ross-on-Wye 0 Gloucester 0

Dec 21 Painswick Institute 2 tries Gloucester 0

Dec 27 Hereford 1 goal Gloucester 0
Gloucester fielded 13 players

Feb 12 Gloucester 1 goal 2 tries Flamingoes 0
Tries: F.O.Stephens, W.A.Boughton, F.Molyneux;
Conversion: J.Brown

Feb 18 Newnham 0 Gloucester 1 try
Scorer unknown

Feb 25 Gloucester 3 tries Painswick Institute 0
Scorers unknown

Mar 11 Gloucester 0 Ross-on-Wye 1 try
Sydney Lane broke his leg soon after kick-off and was replaced by Ward.

Mar 17 Gloucester v Hereford - cancelled

1876-77

Played 11 Won 6 Lost 3 Drawn 2
For 8 goals, 6 tries
Against 8 goals, 7 tries
Captain: Frank Brown

Most appearances: W.A.Boughton, P.B.Cooke, W.Brown, J.F.Grimes, 10, J.F.Brown, H.J.Boughton 9
Most tries: H.J.Boughton, J.F.Brown 2
Most conversions: J.F.Brown 4

On the departure of Frank Hartley, Frank Brown took over the captaincy at the age of 19. He recruited his older brother, William, to play alongside him in his first game in charge. He played in at least nine of the eleven fixtures, but in several different positions, although almost always in the backs. His main contributions were in organising the training and tactics of the team, as well as leading the team during matches, but he also took on most of the goal-kicking duties and organised the Gloucester Thursday and Post Office teams.

There was no referee to make binding decisions, and disputes had to be resolved between the captains, which sometimes proved impossible. Against Ross-on-Wye, "the game throughout was greatly marred by the frequent exchanges of anything but compliments," and when "the play was taken right up to the Gloucester goal, the ball forced over the line, and touch-down — by whom it is not quite clear — a Ross and a Gloucester man each claiming it. The Gloucester man certainly had the ball first and declared he touched it down, but as Ross would not give way the try was allowed under protest." However, the return match "proved one of the best-contested and most amicable games this season".

A full complement of players was not always available, and therefore formations varied somewhat, but most commonly the line-up was two backs, one three-quarter, two half-backs and ten forwards. Most noteworthy amongst the forwards were G. A. Ward, P. B. Cooke and J. F. Grimes. Frank Brown may have been the star of the team, but amongst the backs, William Boughton was reported to be playing better than ever, missed only one game, and his "play being very fine" when he stood in as captain against R.A.C. Cirencester. His younger brother, Hubert "Jimmy" Boughton, emerged as a "most conspicuous" talent.

Oct 21 Gloucester 1 goal 1 try Stroud 0
Tries: H.J.Boughton, W.Snushall;
Conversion: J.Bennett

Nov 4 R.A.C. Cirencester 4 goals 3 tries Gloucester 0

Dec 1 Gloucester 1 try 2 disputed tries Hereford 0
Try: W.A.Boughton; scorers of disputed tries not known

Dec 9 Gloucester 1 goal, 1 try Druids (Bristol) 0
Tries: J.Cadle, J.F.Brown;
Conversion: J.F.Brown

Dec 16 Ross-on-Wye 1 goal Gloucester 2 goals, 1 try
Tries: H.J.Boughton, Ward, unknown;
Conversions: H.J.Boughton (2)

Jan 20 Gloucester 1 goal Swindon Rangers 0
Try: J.Barker;
Conversion: J.F.Brown

Jan 27 Gloucester 1 goal, 1 try Ross-on-Wye 0
Tries: J.Bennett, J.F.Brown;
Conversion: J.F.Brown

Feb 10 Gloucester 1 goal

Cheltenham White Cross 1 goal
Try: J.Barnett;
Conversion: J.F.Brown

Feb 17 Hereford 1 try Gloucester 1 try
Try: J.F.Grimes

Mar 3 Cheltenham White Cross 1 drop goal 3 tries Gloucester 1 goal
Scorers unknown

Mar 7 Gloucester 0
R.A.C. Cirencester 1 goal

1877-78

J.W.Bayley J.Bennett W.A.Boughton P.B.Cooke unidentified H.J.Berry F.Billett H.J.Boughton
J.F.Brown(Capt) W.Snushall F.Tandy L.Bubb
G.J.Dewey W.Brown J.F.Grimes

Played 15 Won 10 Lost 3 Drawn 2
For 31 goals, 21 tries
Against 2 goals, 7 tries
Captain: Frank Brown

Most appearances: H.J.Boughton, J.F.Brown, G.W.Dewey, F.O.Stephens, F.Tandy 14, W.A.Boughton, W.Brown, J.F.Grimes 13
Most tries: H.J.Boughton 8, J.F.Brown 7
Most conversions: H.J.Boughton 19
One game where team and scorers are not known

In September 1877, £15 rent was paid to the Cricket Club for the use of the Spa ground and pavilion. Admission charges to matches were made both to cover the Club's costs, which rose as the fixture list was strengthened, and to pay the financial guarantees which were the norm for visiting teams. The pitch was surrounded by canvas screening, but there were problems in collecting admission money from all the spectators.

This was another very successful season with only three defeats, and two goals and seven tries conceded, against 31 goals and 21 tries scored. The main criticism of the team was that they tended to start slowly.

For the first time, Gloucester played against a club which more than a century later would become an opponent in the Premiership. Away to Worcester on 17th November 1877, captain Frank Brown led the way with four tries as Gloucester romped home by eight goals and four tries to nil, the conversions being kicked by Jimmy Boughton. Worcester had only recently resumed playing after a break of a couple of seasons. Painswick Institute were on the receiving end of an even bigger drubbing, by seven goals and nine tries to nil on the Spa.

For most of the season, Gloucester used a

formation of one back, two three-quarters, two half-backs (sometimes referred to as quarter-backs) and ten forwards. There was a permanent pairing at half/quarter-back of the captain, Frank Brown, and William Boughton, the most influential players in the team, along with Jimmy Boughton, who played at three-quarter unless standing in for K. Smith at back. W. Snushall was most commonly the other three-quarter. Most prominent amongst the forwards, who did not have specialist positions within the pack, were William Brown, F. Tandy, G. Dewey, and J. F. Grimes.

In three games at the end of the season, a different formation was used with a back, two three-quarter backs, two quarter-backs, one half-back and nine forwards. In the final game of the season at Handsworth, there was a crowd of more than 1,500.

**Oct 20 R.A.C. Cirencester 2 tries
Gloucester 0**

**Oct 27 Gloucester 1 goal 2 drop goals
Cheltenham Training College 0**
Try: J.Bennett;
Conversion: H.J.Boughton;

Drop goals: H.J.Boughton, W.A.Boughton

**Nov 10 Cheltenham White Cross 0
Gloucester 1 try**
Try: J.Bennett

**Nov 17 Worcester 0
Gloucester 8 goals 4 tries**
Tries: J.F.Brown (4), W.A.Boughton (3), H.J.Boughton, Ward, W.Brown, G.W.Dewey, F.O.Stephens
Conversions: H.J.Boughton (8)

**Dec 8 Gloucester 2 goals 2 tries
Stroud 0**
Tries: H.J.Boughton (3), E.F.Wright;
Conversions: H.J.Boughton (2)

**Dec 22 Gloucester 1 goal 1 try
Ross-on-Wye 2 tries**
Try: W.A.Boughton;
Drop goal: Cazalet

Jan 5 Ross-on-Wye 1 try Gloucester 0

**Jan 12 Gloucester 7 goals 9 tries
Painswick Institute 0**
Scorers unknown

**Jan 26 Gloucester 1 goal 3 tries
Cheltenham White Cross 1 try**
Tries: J.F.Brown (2), W.Snushall, H.J.Boughton;
Conversion: E.F.Wright

Feb 2 Stroud 0 Gloucester 0

**Feb 16 Gloucester 2 goals 1 drop goal
Handsworth 0**
Tries: W.Snushall, H.J.Boughton;
Conversions: H.J.Boughton (2);
Drop goal: H.J.Boughton

**Feb 23 Cheltenham College 1 try
Gloucester 0**

**Mar 2 Cheltenham Training College 0
Gloucester 4 goals 1 try**
Tries: W.A.Boughton (2), W.Brown, T.Humpidge, J.F.Grimes;
Conversions: H.J.Boughton (4)

**Mar 9 Gloucester 2 goals 1 try
R.A.C. Cirencester 2 goals**
Tries: W.F.Evans, J.F.Brown, W.Snushall;
Conversions: H.J.Boughton (2)

Mar 23 Handsworth 0 Gloucester 0

1878-79

**Played 16 Won 12 Lost 1 Drawn 3
For 28 goals, 31 tries Against 2 tries
Captain: Frank Brown**

Gloucester Second XV
Played 5 Won 2 Lost 2 Drawn 1
For 3 goals, 2 tries Against 3 goals, 5 tries

Most appearances: H.J.Boughton 16, H.J.Berry, J.F.Brown, F.Tandy 15, W.A. Boughton, J.F.Bennett, J.F.Grimes 14, G.J.Dewey 13
Most tries: J.F.Bennett 11, J.F.Brown 10, E.F.Wright, H.J.Boughton, W.A.Boughton 7
Most conversions: H.J.Boughton 21

The highlight of the season was a floodlit match on the Spa on 30th January 1879. Four electric floodlights were erected, but only three worked simultaneously and one of those flickered on and off. In the prevailing gloom, Gloucester managed a good win against Rockleaze from Bristol, and the event was such a novelty that it attracted several thousand spectators, who stumbled around the park in the dark and damaged the shrubbery. This eventually resulted in the Club being banned from the Spa by the Parks Committee, and the last match of the season was played at Dean's Walk.

However, the Club rallied support and the full Council rescinded the ban in time for the start of the following season. The next floodlit match was staged in 1967. In the return match against Rockleaze on the Downs at Clifton, a strong wind blew the ball over the cliffs, 150 yards from the pitch.

On 7th December 1878, Gloucester played a Welsh side for the first time, drawing 0-0 at Newport, in front of 2-3,000 spectators, both teams thus remaining unbeaten. Newport was also the first Welsh club to play at Gloucester, winning in controversial circumstances on 15th February 1879– "Ponsford, a Newport forward, crying out so lustily he was hurt, the Gloucester men all stopped playing. Ponsford, however, getting up, rushed quickly out with the ball, relieving his side when in a critical position by a very shady piece of play".

Herbert Berry was usually the rock at back, but two backs were occasionally played. Jimmy Boughton and James Bennett most frequently played as the three-quarters, but sometimes there were three. Frank Brown the captain usually controlled the game as the sole half-back, but sometimes there were two or three. William Boughton and W. Snushall were invariably the

two quarter-backs. The norm was to play nine forwards, but it varied from eight to ten.

Frank Brown and Jimmy Boughton were prime movers in the formation of a County Club, and Frank and Herbert Berry played against Somerset in the first Gloucestershire match. They were joined by J.Bennett and J.Cadle in the first County match on the Spa against Wiltshire.

Jan 15 Gloucestershire 4 goals, 3 tries
Wiltshire 0 (The Spa)
Tries: H.L.Evans (2), T.R.Packenham, M.Cartwright, J.Bennett, J.F.Brown, F.Winterbotham
Conversions: E.J.Lamb (3), J.D.Miller
Gloucester players: H.J.Berry, J.F.Brown, J.Bennett, J.Cadle

**Oct 19 Gloucester 1 goal 5 tries
Cheltenham White Cross 0**
Tries: H.J.Boughton (2), W.A.Boughton, E.F.Wright, J.Bennett;
Conversion: H.J.Boughton

**Oct 26 Stroud 1 try
Gloucester 3 goals 1 try**
Tries: F.Tandy, H.J.Boughton, J.F.Brown,

J.Bennett;
Conversions: H.J.Boughton (3)

Nov 2 R.A.C. Cirencester 0
Gloucester 3 goals 1 try
Tries: W.A.Boughton, W.Snushall, E.F.Wright,
J.F.Brown;
Conversions: H.J.Boughton (3)

Nov 23 Gloucester 7 goals 3 tries
Cheltenham Training College 0
Tries: J.F.Bennett (3), W.Snushall (2),
W.A.Boughton, J.F.Grimes, F.Tandy,
H.J.Boughton, E.F.Wright
Conversions: H.J.Boughton (3), H.J.Berry (2),
J.F.Bennett, E.F.Wright

Nov 30 Gloucester 2 goals 5 tries 1
drop goal Rockleaze 0
Tries: E.F.Wright (4), J.F.Bennett,
H.J.Boughton, J.F.Brown;
Conversions: H.J.Boughton, H.J.Berry;
Drop goal: J.F.Brown

Dec 7 Newport 0 Gloucester 0

Jan 11 Gloucester v Stroud - cancelled due to
frost

Jan 18 Gloucester 3 goals 4 tries
Ross-on-Wye 0
Tries: J.F.Bennett (2), W.A.Boughton (2),
J.F.Grimes, G.J.Dewey, H.J.Boughton;
Conversions: H.J.Boughton (3)

Jan 30 Gloucester 4 goals 4 tries
Rockleaze 0
Tries: J.F.Brown (3), W.A.Boughton (2),
F.Winterbothan (2), J.F.Bennett;
Conversions: H.J.Boughton (4)

Feb 1 Ross-on-Wye 0 Gloucester 1 try
Try: H.J.Berry

Feb 8 Gloucester 3 goals 4 tries
Handsworth 0

Tries: J.F.Brown (2), J.F.Bennett (2),
F.Winterbotham, W.Snushall;
Conversions: H.J.Boughton (2);
Drop goal: M.Cartwright

Feb 15 Gloucester 0 Newport 1 try

Feb 22 Cheltenham College 0
Gloucester 0

Mar 1 Gloucester 2 tries Stroud 0
Tries: J.F.Brown, J.Bennett

Mar 15 Gloucester 1 goal
Cheltenham Training College 0
Try: F.W.Billett;
Conversion: H.J.Boughton

Mar 22 Rockleaze 0 Gloucester 0

Mar 29 Handsworth 0
Gloucester 1 try
Try scorer unknown

1879-80

Played 16, Won 14, Lost 2;
For 28 goals, 27 tries
Against 1 goal, 9 tries
Captain: Frank Brown

Gloucester Second XV
Played 8 Won 7 Lost 1
For 4 goals, 20 tries Against 1 try
Captain: F.W.Wood

Most appearances: W.Brown, W.J.Bayley
16, J.F.Bennett, J.F.Grimes 15, W.Snushall,
P.B.Cooke, G.J.Dewey 14, J.F.Brown 13
Most tries: J.F.Bennett 16, H.J.Boughton,
W.Snushall 5
Conversions: H.J.Boughton 17, J.F.Bennett 4,
H.J.Berry, J.R.Cowan 1
Drop goals: J.F.Bennett, J.F.Brown 2,
F.Winterbotham 1

Another very successful season under the
captaincy of Frank Brown, with only two
losses, home and away to Clifton, and an
overwhelmingly positive margin in the scores.
The team benefited from fairly settled selection
and formation. Frank Brown, frequently
reported to be the outstanding player, led by
example at half-back, where he was normally
partnered by W. Snushall and one other. The
regular three-quarters were James Bennett and
either Jimmy Boughton or Ronald Grist. At
back was Herbert Berry and sometimes J.Fisher.
Most prominent amongst the nine forwards
were William Brown, W.Beaumont, "Down

'Em" Bayley, G.J.Dewey, P.B.Cooke, J.F.Grimes,
H.Williams and H.Birks. Five players were
capped by Gloucestershire.

New to the fixture list was Moseley, who had
not lost a match the previous season, and
was reckoned to be the strongest side in the
Midlands. But they were beaten, home and
away, in what was to become a long series of
matches between the clubs. The first game was
played over 80 minutes, longer than normal at
that time.

The try of the season was scored at Swindon
Rangers, when "Snushall got the ball and
passed to Frank Brown, who in turn handed it to
Jimmy Boughton, the latter making a splendid
run, and successfully eluding the numerous
attempts of the Rangers to hold him, grounded
the ball behind the posts. This run was the
great feature of the match, and, as it deserved,
brought down the house".

Rockleaze, who were trounced by six goals
and eight tries to nil, were "completely beaten
by the fast forward play of the home team, who
fairly surpassed themselves by their splendid
dribbling, the ball frequently being taken the
length of the ground". Indeed, this skill at
dribbling was a feature of Gloucester's play
throughout the season.

Five players won County caps

Oct 18 Gloucester 3 goals
Cheltenham White Cross 1 try
Tries: J.F.Bennett, W. Brown, M.G.Cartwright;
Conversions: H.J. Boughton (3)

Oct 25 Swindon Rangers 0
Gloucester 1 goal
Try: H.J. Boughton;
Conversion: H.J. Boughton

Nov 1 Gloucester 1 try Moseley 0
Try: W.Snushall

Nov 8 Clifton 1 goal 3 tries
Gloucester 0

Nov 15 Gloucester 3 goals 3 tries
Cheltenham Training College 0
Tries; J. F. Brown, J. Bennett, J. Bayley, W.
Snushall;
Conversion: H.J. Boughton;
Drop goals: J.F. Brown (2)

Nov 29 Gloucester 6 Goals 7 Tries
Rockleaze (Bristol) 0
Tries: H.Williams (3), J.F.Bennett (3), H
Boughton (2), W.Snushall (2), F.Winterbotham,
W.Brown;
Conversions: H.Boughton (5);
Drop goal: F.Winterbotham

Jan 3 Stroud 0
Gloucester 3 goals 2 tries
Tries: J.F.Bennett(3), J.F.Brown, H. Boughton;

Conversions: H. Boughton (3)

Jan 10 Ross 0
Gloucester 2 goals 3 tries
Tries: Bubb, H. Boughton, G.J.Dewey,
J.F.Bennett;
Conversion: H. Boughton;
Drop goal: J.F.Bennett

Jan 17 Gloucester 4 goals 1 try
Cheltenham White Cross 0
Tries: L.R.Grist, H.Boughton, F.Winterbotham,
J.Clark;
Conversions: H. Boughton (3);
Drop goal: J.F.Bennett

Feb 7 Gloucester 1 try Stroud 0
Try: W.Snushall

Feb 14 Cheltenham College 1 try
Gloucester 1 goal
Try: R.L.Grist;
Conversion: H.J.Berry

Feb 21 Gloucester 3 tries
Swindon Rangers 1 try
Tries: J.F.Bennett (3)

Feb 28 Gloucester 0 Clifton 4 tries

Mar 6 Cheltenham Training College 0
Gloucester 2 goals 2 tries
Tries: J.F.Grimes (2), J.F.Bennett (2);
Conversions: J.F.Bennett (2)

Mar 13 Gloucester 2 goals 1 try
RAC Cirencester 0
Tries: J.F.Grimes, J.F.Brown, W.Brown;
Conversions: J.F.Bennett (2)

Mar 20 Moseley 1 disputed try
Gloucester 1 goal 1 try
Tries: J.F.Bennett (2);
Conversion: J.R.Cowan

1880-81

Played 13, Won 6, Lost 4 Drawn 3
For 17 goals, 24 tries
Against 2 goals, 8 tries
Captain: Frank Brown

Gloucester Second XV
Played 6 Won 2 Lost 2 Drawn 1 (one result
unknown)
For 3 goals, 10 tries Against 1 goal, 1 try
Captain: H.Cadenne

Most appearances: H.J.Berry, R.C.Grist,
W.A.Boughton, J.F.Brown 12, W.Snushall,
W.J.Bayley 11, P.B.Cooke, G.J.Dewey,
J.F.Grimes, H.Birks, W.Brown 9
Most tries: W.A.Boughton 6, W.F.Evans,
J.F.Brown 5, H.C.Buck, W.Brown 4
Conversions: H.J.Berry 11, H.C.Buck,
W.A.Boughton, H.J.Boughton 1
Drop goals: H.J.Berry, H.C.Buck, W.F.Evans

Results, although still on the positive side, took
a bit of a dip compared with previous seasons,
most notably against Moseley, who achieved
the double over Gloucester. Their match on the
Spa attracted over 3,000 spectators, and the
visit of Newport attracted a crowd of "several
thousand".

The norm was to play nine forwards, and,
although starring at half-back in previous
seasons, Frank Brown, the captain, played as a
forward in every match except for the last. He
was ably supported by W. Brimmell ,"Down
'Em" Bayley, P. B. Cooke, William Brown,
who scored a hat trick against Rockleaze, Tom
Graves Smith, H. Birks and G. J. Dewey, as
those amongst the forwards most frequently
mentioned in dispatches. Many games were
played almost entirely amongst the forwards,
and the skill of the Gloucester pack in dribbling
the ball was outstanding.

There were usually three half-backs – W.
Snushall, William Boughton, who kicked off
with a hat trick in the first match, and W. F.
Evans, who was a tricky runner – he scored a
hat trick against Newent, and against Clifton
"Evans made one of his own peculiar runs,
eluding many of the Clifton men, and slipping
from the grasp of others when apparently quite
settled".

R. L. Grist played throughout at three-quarter,
and scored a hat trick against Swindon Rangers,
but his partner was continually changing.
Jimmy Boughton was missed, working in
London for most of the season, so only available
for the last two games of the season.

At back in all but one game was Herbert Berry,
who kicked his first dropped goal at the start
of the season, and seven conversions in two
successive games – a notable feat in an era when
most kicks were unsuccessful; he was selected
for all five County matches. The backs in general
were criticised for repeatedly "attempting to
tackle round the neck rather than the waist".

A County trial was played at the Spa with all
16 players in the North of County side from
Gloucester, and ten of them won County caps
at some stage during the season, with games
against Somerset and Surrey, both of them won,
being played on the Spa.

Oct 20 Gloucester 1 goal 5 tries 1
drop goal
Cheltenham Training College 0
Tries: W.A.Boughton (3), W.F.Evans (2),
J.F.Grimes;
Conversion: H.J.Berry;
Drop goal: Hojer

Oct 23 Swindon Rangers 0
Gloucester 1 drop goal
Drop goal: H.C.Buck

Oct 30 R.A.C. Cirencester 1 try
Gloucester 2 goals 2 tries
Tries: W.Snushall, H.Buck, W.A.Boughton,
J.F.Brown;
Conversions: H.J.Berry (2)

Nov 6 Gloucester 0 Moseley 1 Try

Nov 13 Cheltenham College 1 drop
goal Gloucester 1 try 1 drop goal
Try: H.C.Buck;
Drop goal: W.F.Evans
Game declared a draw even though both sides
scored drop goals but Gloucester scored a try
as well – perhaps played under old rules?

Nov 20 Rockleaze 0
Gloucester 5 goals 4 tries
Tries: W.Brown (3), H.C.Buck (2), J.F.Brown
(2), H.J.Berry, W.A.Boughton;
Conversions: H.J.Berry (3), W.A.Boughton,
H.C.Buck

Nov 25 Gloucester 4 goals 6 tries
Newent 0
Tries: W.F.Evans (3), J.F.Brown (2),
W.Brimmell, J.Fisher, W.A.Boughton,
J.F.Grimes, .Brown;
Conversions: H.J.Berry (4)

Dec 4 Gloucester 0 Newport 0

Dec 11 Clifton 0 Gloucester 0

Jan 1 Newport 3 tries Gloucester 0

Feb 19 Cheltenham College 1 try 1 drop goal Gloucester 1 goal
Try: R.L.Grist;
Conversion: H.J.Boughton

Feb 26 Gloucester 1 goal 6 tries Swindon Rangers 0
Tries: H.J.Boughton (3), R.L.Grist (2), W.Snushall, H.Birks;

Conversion: H.J.Berry

Mar 12 Moseley 2 tries Gloucester 0
Gloucester played one short

1881-82

Played 19 Won 14 Lost 5
For 26 goals, 23 tries
Against 8 goals, 10 tries
Captain: Frank Brown

Gloucester Second XV
Played 15 Won 12 Lost 2 Drawn 1
For 27 goals, 35 tries Against 3 goals, 4 tries

Most appearances: H.J.Berry, H.E.Taylor 19, P.B.Cooke 18, R.L.Grist, W.Bayley 16, H.J.Boughton, J.F.Brown, H.A.Martin, A.C.Seymour 15
Most tries: H.E.Taylor 11, W.F.Evans 8, H.J.Boughton, R.L.Grist 5
Conversions: H.J.Berry 17, H.J.Boughton 6, P.C.Adams, H.V.Jones 1
Drop goal: H.J.Boughton 1

Frank Brown, the captain reverted to playing at half-back in a formation consisting of one back, two or three half-backs, two or three three-quarters, one back and nine forwards for much of the season. But later games saw three half-backs, three three-quarters, one back and eight forwards.

A reasonably successful season was based on the strength of the forwards, especially in the loose, whilst the backs were criticised early on for "feeble tackling" and "a lack of combined play". They improved later, especially after H.V.Jones made an immediate impact at half-back following his debut against Cheltenham College.

The fixture list was strengthened again, most notably with a match on a Monday against a touring side, Irish Rovers. Gloucester had a good first half and scored when "Grist out-paced his opponents in fine style". The heavier Irish team fought back in the second half and were credited with two tries although one was registered "under protest, as the umpires differed in their opinions - The Rovers afterwards virtually acknowledged that the try was not legal".

The matches against Worcester were also controversial. Gloucester won away, but the Worcester crowd invaded the pitch several times and prevented Gloucester from attempting a conversion. Worcester failed to turn up for the return fixture and Gloucester records say "Not

played; Worcester funked". The clubs did not meet again at 1st XV level until 1999.

Controversy continued to the last match of the season at Moseley, with the Citizen reporting "the rules of off-side do not appear to be well understood by the umpires around Birmingham".

However, there was huge satisfaction taken from winning home and away against Newport, now regarded as "old opponents", especially since Newport lost only three games that season, the other being to the Irish Rovers. The try of the season secured the win at Newport, when "H.V.Jones seized the ball from a scrimmage and made off, passed to Boughton, who passed to Taylor, who made a magnificent run, and placed a try".

Ten Gloucester players were capped by the County.

Oct 1 Gloucester 3 goals Colts XX 1 goal
Tries: H.E.Taylor, J.F.Brown, R.Graves;

Conversions: H.J.Boughton (3)

Oct 15 Swindon Rangers 1 goal 1 try
Gloucester 2 goals
Tries: J.F.Brown, R.L.Grist;
Conversions: H.J.Berry (2)
Gloucester fielded 14 players

Oct 22 Gloucester 2 goals 3 tries
Newent 0
Tries: W.F.Evans (2), J.F.Brown, F.Wood,
H.E.Taylor;
Conversions: H.J.Berry (2)

Oct 29 R.A.C. Cirencester 0
Gloucester 4 goals 4 tries
Tries: W.F.Evans (5), P.C.Adams, H.J.Berry,
W.Brown;
Conversions: H.J.Berry (2), H.J.Boughton,
P.C.Adams

Nov 5 Cheltenham College 2 tries
Gloucester 0

Nov 7 Gloucester 1 try
Irish Rovers 2 tries
Try: R.L.Grist

Nov 12 Worcester 0
Gloucester 1 goal 2 tries
Tries: H.V.Jones, H.E.Taylor, other try scorer

unknown;
Conversion: H.J.Berry

Nov 19 Gloucester 1 goal
Moseley 1 try
Try: R.L.Grist;
Conversion: H.J.Berry (disputed)

Dec 3 Gloucester 1 goal, 2 tries
Newport 1 goal
Tries: W.F.Evans, H.J.Boughton, R.L.Grist;
Conversion: H.J.Berry

Dec 10 Gloucester 1 goal Colts XX 0
Try: H.E.Taylor;
Conversion: H.J.Berry

Dec 12 Gloucester 1 goal
Old Monmouthians 1 try
Try: J.A.Preen;
Conversion: H.J.Berry

Dec 17 Clifton v Gloucester - cancelled due to
"inclement weather"
Jan 7 Gloucester v Worcester - cancelled
because Worcester could not raise a team.

Jan 21 Gloucester 2 goals 4 tries
Cheltenham 0
Tries: H.J.Boughton (3), H.E.Taylor (2);
Conversion: H.J.Berry;
Drop goal: H.J.Boughton

Jan 28 Gloucester 0
Clifton 1 goal 1 try

Feb 4 Newport 0 Gloucester 1 try
Try: H.E.Taylor

Feb 8 Cheltenham College 1 goal 1 try
Gloucester 1 goal
Try: H.V.Jones;
Conversion: H.J.Berry

Feb 18 Gloucester 2 goals 2 tries
Swindon Rangers 1 goal
Tries: H.V.Jones, J.F.Brown, H.E.Taylor,
R.L.Grist;
Conversions: H.J.Berry (2)

Mar 4 Gloucester 5 goals 2 tries
R.A.C. Cirencester 0
Tries: H.E.Taylor (2), A.C.Seymour,
W.M.Jenkins, H.V.Jones, H.J.Berry,
H.J.Boughton;
Conversions: H.J.Berry (2), H.J.Boughton (2),
H.V.Jones

Mar 11 Newent 0 Gloucester 1 try
Try: H.E.Taylor

Mar 18 Moseley 2 goals 1 try
Gloucester 1 try
Try: W.A.Boughton

1882-83

Played 14 Won 11 Lost 0 Drawn 3
For 16 goals, 35 tries
Against 1 goal, 6 tries
Captain: Frank Brown

Gloucester Second XV
Played 11 Won 6 Lost 2 Drawn 3
For 9 goals, 19 tries Against 2 goals, 2 tries
Captain: Jimmy Boughton

Most appearances: H.J.Berry, H.V.Jones,
W.Brown 14, H.J.Boughton, H.E.Taylor,
W.A.Boughton, W.J.Bayley 13, G.J.Dewey,
P.B.Cooke, H.B.Sloman 12, G.Coates 11
Most tries: G.Coates 11, H.J.Boughton 10,
H.E.Taylor 8, H.V.Jones 7
Conversions: H.J.Berry 8, H.V.Jones 5,
H.J.Boughton 3

The only season in the Club's history in which
all games played are known to have been
recorded and in which Gloucester have boasted
an unbeaten record; the team was dubbed "The
Invincibles". Frank Brown led the team in his
seventh and last full season as captain, during

which time the Club played 104 matches, won
73, drew 13 and lost 18, whilst scoring 321 tries
and conceding only 71.

The captain also acted as coach, and the
attractive and effective style of play which
Frank introduced increased Club membership
tenfold, and raised Gloucester's status to one of
the leading clubs in the country. The formation
adopted towards the end of the previous season,
with seven backs (three half-backs, three three-
quarters and a full-back) and eight forwards,
continued to be used in most but not all matches.

George Coates was selected for the match at
Swindon Rangers, the first working class man
to play for the Club – he was a labourer at the
Wagon Works. He made an immediate impact as
leading try scorer, and ensured that recruitment
to the Club was open to all in future.

Cardiff and Bath were added to the fixture list. In
the first match against Cardiff, Gloucester gave
their opponents an object lesson in "the passing
game" and "the seven backs" formation, and

won by one goal and seven tries to nil. Cardiff
soon followed the Gloucester example and
reduced to eight forwards, but adopted a backs
formation with four three-quarters, which would
be adopted throughout the game ten years later.

There were other highlights in this record-
breaking season. Newport, playing eight
current Welsh internationals, were defeated
away, the double was achieved in the first home
and away fixtures against Bath, and Clifton
were beaten for the first time at the sixth time
of asking.

Ten players were capped by Gloucestershire.

Sep 30 Gloucester 1 goal Colts XX 0
Try: H.V.Jones;
Conversion: H.J.Berry

Oct 7 Gloucester 1 goal 2 tries
Cheltenham 2 tries
Tries: H.E.Taylor (2), H.V.Jones;
Conversion: H.J.Berry

A.W.Vears H.J.Boughton W.A.Boughton G.Coates H.J.Berry J.F.Brown(Capt) H.E.Taylor H.V.Jones
B.Sloman T.G.Smith P.B.Cooke J.W.Bayley A.C.Seymour (or H.T.Birks) W.Brimmell W.Brown
H.Fream G.J.Dewey

**Oct 14 Swindon Rangers 0
Gloucester 3 goals 2 tries**
Tries: H.V.Jones (3), G.Barnard (2);
Conversions: H.J.Berry (2), H.V.Jones

**Oct 21 Gloucester 1 goal 7 tries
Cardiff 0**
Tries: W.H.Fream (2), H.E.Taylor (2), J.F.Brown,
G.J.Dewey, H.J.Boughton, G.Coates;
Conversion: H.J.Boughton

**Oct 28 R.A.C. Cirencester 1 goal
Gloucester 2 goals 2 tries**
Tries: G.Coates (3), H.E.Taylor;
Conversions: H.J.Berry, H.J.Boughton

Nov 4 Gloucester 0 Newport 0

**Nov 18 Cheltenham College 0
Gloucester 1 goal 4 tries**

Tries: G.Coates (2), H.Sloman, J.F.Brown,
H.J.Boughton;
Conversion: H.V.Jones

**Dec 2 Gloucester 3 goals 3 tries
Bath 0**
Tries: G.Coates (3), G.J.Dewey, H.Sloman,
H.J.Boughton;
Conversions: H.J.Berry,   H.V.Jones,
H.J.Boughton

**Dec 16 Bath 1 try
Gloucester 1 goal 2 tries**
Tries: H.J.Boughton (2), G.Coates;
Conversion: H.J.Berry

**Jan 6 Newport 1 try
Gloucester 1 goal 1 try**
Tries: G.Coates, H.J.Boughton;
Conversion: H.V.Jones

**Jan 20 Gloucester 1 try
Swindon Rangers 1 try**
Try: W.Brimmell

**Feb 3 Gloucester 1 goal 4 tries
Clifton 0**
Tries: H.J.Boughton (3), H.V.Jones, H.E.Taylor;
Conversion: H.J.Berry

Feb 24 Cardiff 1 try Gloucester 1 try
Try: H.V.Jones

**Mar 3 Gloucester 1 goal 6 tries
R.A.C. Cirencester 0**
Tries: H.E.Taylor (2), W.Brimmell, H.Sloman,
T.Smith, W.A.Boughton, H.J.Boughton;
Conversion: H.V.Jones

1883-84

**Played 19 Won 15 Lost 2 Drawn 2
For 21 goals, 61 tries
Against 2 goals, 4 tries
Captain: Jimmy Boughton**

Gloucester Second XV
Played 15 Won 10 Lost 5

For 7 goals, 39 tries Against 6 goals, 12 tries
Captain: H.Moffat

Most appearances: W.A.Boughton, W.H.Fream
19, H.V.Jones, W.Brown, E.D.Tandy 18,
T.G.Smith 17, H.J.Boughton 16
Most tries: G.Coates 14, H.E.Taylor 10,

H.V.Jones 8, H.J.Boughton 7
Conversions: H.V.Jones 10, H.J.Berry 4,
H.J.Boughton 3, W.A.Boughton 1
Drop goals: H.J.Boughton 2, H.J.Berry 1

At the end of the previous season, the old
pavilion at the Spa was torn down and a new

H.E.Cadenne H.J.Boughton (Capt) G.Coates W.A.Boughton H.V.Jones
A.W.Vears(Umpire) H.L.Broughton H.E.Taylor J.W.Bayley H.J.Berry E.D.Tandy
B.Sloman H.Fream T.G.Smith H.A.Sanders W.Brown G.J.Dewey

one built to serve both Cricket and Rugby clubs, with home and "strangers" dressing rooms and bathrooms.

Frank Brown started this season as captain, but early on his work took him to London, and Jimmy Boughton took over, but not before the season kicked off at Bath, where Gloucester displayed "machine-like passing, fast and loose play, quick following up, and safe tackling," in scoring 17 tries, a Club record. During Frank's lengthy tenure as captain and coach, he had revolutionised the style of play and led the Club to national prominence in losing only 19 and winning 78 of 110 matches.

This season ended with one of the best records in the country. Membership increased from 277 to 350, and gate money from £65 to £134. However, Gloucester were criticised by their own supporters for rarely being ready to start a game on time, and for the discourtesy of leaving opposition teams standing around waiting.

In previous seasons, there had been a lengthy break in fixtures over the Christmas period, but a new tradition started on Boxing Day 1883. A representative London team, the first to visit Gloucester since the Flamingoes, and including the famous England rugby and cricket player, A.E.Stoddart, drew the biggest crowd yet at the Spa, and £40 was taken on the gate. Before the match a gold watch was presented to Frank Brown, who had recently left Gloucester, but was instrumental in arranging this fixture and returned to captain the team.

Results against Welsh clubs were better than usual. The presence of seven backs on each side against Swansea was criticised for reducing the pace of the game, but it didn't stop Gloucester scoring three tries for a famous victory, and they soon had another fine win against Cardiff, but the bad feeling which was usually simmering with Newport came to a head. The first match played at Newport should have resulted in a victory for Gloucester, but all the scores were disputed, so it was declared a draw. At this time the referee's decision was not final – it could be overruled by the captains, but they often failed to agree. In the return match at Gloucester, Rowland Hill, Secretary of the Rugby Union, refereed, and Newport won, but Gloucester claimed the moral high ground for not disputing the winning try.

Gloucester normally played with one back, three three-quarters, three half-backs and eight forwards, but the formation varied occasionally. Ten players were capped by the County.

Oct 4 Gloucester 1 goal 2 tries
20 Colts of City Clubs 1 goal
Tries: W Boughton (2), H.E.Cadenne;
Conversion: H.Boughton

Oct 13 Bath 0
Gloucester 5 goals 12 tries
Tries: H.J.Boughton (2), H.Taylor (2), H.V.Jones (2), W.H.Fream (2), H.L.Broughton (2), J.F.Brown, W.Brown, E.D.Tandy, H.B.Sloman, A.Cromwell, W.Boughton, T.Smith;
Conversions: H.J.Boughton (2), W.Boughton, H.J.Berry, H.V.Jones

Oct 20 Gloucester 3 tries Swansea 0
Tries: Sloman (2), E.D.Tandy

Oct 27 Cheltenham College 1 goal
Gloucester 2 tries
Tries: G.Coates, J.W.Bayley
Cheltenham College won

Oct 31 R.A.C. Cirencester 0
Gloucester 1 goal 2 tries
Tries: H.B.Sloman, A.Cromwell;
Drop goal: H.J.Boughton

Nov 3 Gloucester 1 goal 5 tries
Weston-super-Mare 0
Tries: H.E.Taylor (2), C.J.Dewey, H.V.Jones, W.H.Fream;
Drop goal: H.J.Boughton

Nov 17 Newport 0 Gloucester 0
Try: E.D.Tandy;
Conversion: H.V.Jones

Newport scored two tries and Gloucester one, which was converted, but all 3 tries were disputed, so the game was declared a draw

Nov 24 Gloucester 1 goal 1 try
Cardiff 0
Tries: H.J.Boughton, H.Berry;
Conversion: H.V.Jones

Nov 29 Gloucester 1 goal 6 tries
Bristol Medicals 0
Tries: H.E.Taylor (2), H.V.Jones (2), H.E.Cadenne, H.J.Boughton, E.D.Tandy;
Conversion: H.V.Jones

Dec 1 Swindon Rangers 0
Gloucester 3 goals 6 tries
Tries: E.D.Tandy (2), G.Coates, H.E.Taylor, G.Freeth, H.A.Sanders, H.V.Jones, T.Bagwell;
Conversions: H.V.Jones, H.J.Berry;
Drop goal: H.J.Berry

Dec 26 Gloucester 2 tries
London Team 0
Tries: T.Bagwell (2)

Dec 29 Redland Park 0
Gloucester 2 goals 5 tries
Tries: G.Coates (2), W.A.Boughton, H.V.Jones, T.Bagwell, H.A.Sanders, B.Holtham;
Conversions: H.J.Berry (2)

Jan 12 Gloucester 2 goals 6 tries
Bath 0
Tries: G.Coates (5), H.Taylor, H.A.Sanders, E.D.Tandy;
Conversions: H.V.Jones (2)

Jan 19 Gloucester 0 Newport 1 try

Feb 2 Gloucester 2 tries Clifton 0
Tries: G.Coates (2)

Feb 16 Gloucester 1 goal 4 tries
Swindon Rangers 0
Tries: H.J.Boughton (3), G.Coates (2);
Conversion: H.V.Jones

Feb 23 Cardiff 0 Gloucester 0

Mar 1 Gloucester 1 goal 1 try 1
disputed try R.A.C. Cirencester 0
Tries: G.Coates, H.V.Jones (disputed try): H.B.Sloman;
Conversion: H.V.Jones

Mar 8 Cheltenham College 0
Gloucester 1 goal 2 tries
Tries: H.E.Taylor (2), F.Jackson;
Conversion: H.V.Jones

1884-85

Played 20 Won 11 Lost 7 Drawn 2
For 16 goals, 16 tries
Against 10 goals, 8 tries
Captain: Jimmy Boughton

Gloucester Second XV
Played 15 Won 11 Lost 2 Drawn 2
For 13 goals, 23 tries Against 2 goals, 7 tries
Captain: O.H.Jones

Most appearances: W.H.Fream, H.L.Broughton 20, G.Coates, 19, T.Bagwell 18, H.E.Cadenne, H.V.Jones, A.Gorin 17, H.E.Taylor, W.Brown, H.J.Boughton 14
Most tries: G.Coates 9, H.J.Boughton 4
Conversions: H.V.Jones 9, O.Phillips 6, H.J.Boughton 1

Overall this season was disappointing when compared with the previous two. The main reason was continual changes to the team and consequent lack of cohesion, caused in part by injuries - both the captain, Jimmy Boughton, and the best defensive player, Harry Taylor, were missing for several matches. Jimmy gave up the captaincy at the end of the season, and soon ended his playing career after 114 appearances, but continued as the Club's solicitor, organizing the acquisition of the Kingsholm ground; he was also instrumental in the formation of the County Club and of the Gloucestershire Referees Society. This season also saw the retirement of William Brown, a hard and fast forward, with 119 appearances.

It came as a shock that the Royal Agricultural College, Cirencester, won so decisively in the first club match, Gloucester lacking organisation and fitness. There was a positive response in the following match against Swindon Rangers, but Newport soon brought a dose of reality, and presaged a season in which there was no success against the Welsh.

On Boxing Day, Frank Brown returned to Gloucester to captain the team against a strong London XV, and it was like old times as "the forwards were quick on the ball, and the passing of the backs was superb and every man seemed impelled with a desire to do his very utmost". There followed comfortable victories over new opponents in Queen's College, Cork, and the Civil Service, who were captained and coached by Frank Brown, who brought his new club to Gloucester when a fixture against Blackheath fell through.

George Coates was the outstanding player, and by now had been joined in the team by another gifted player, Tommy Bagwell, his friend and fellow labourer at the Wagon Works. There was some improvement in the goal kicking, with H.V.Jones leading the way, and the tries of the season were scored by Jimmy Boughton in successive games, "executing a capital dodgy run, ending by his gaining a try" to win the second match against Clifton, and "by undoubtedly the best run seen on the Spa this season, gained a try right behind the posts" against Swindon.

Eight players were capped by the County, and Harry Taylor played for Western Counties against London. The 2nd XV lost only two of their 15 matches, and the Juniors XV, "a kind of third team", lost only one of their eight matches.

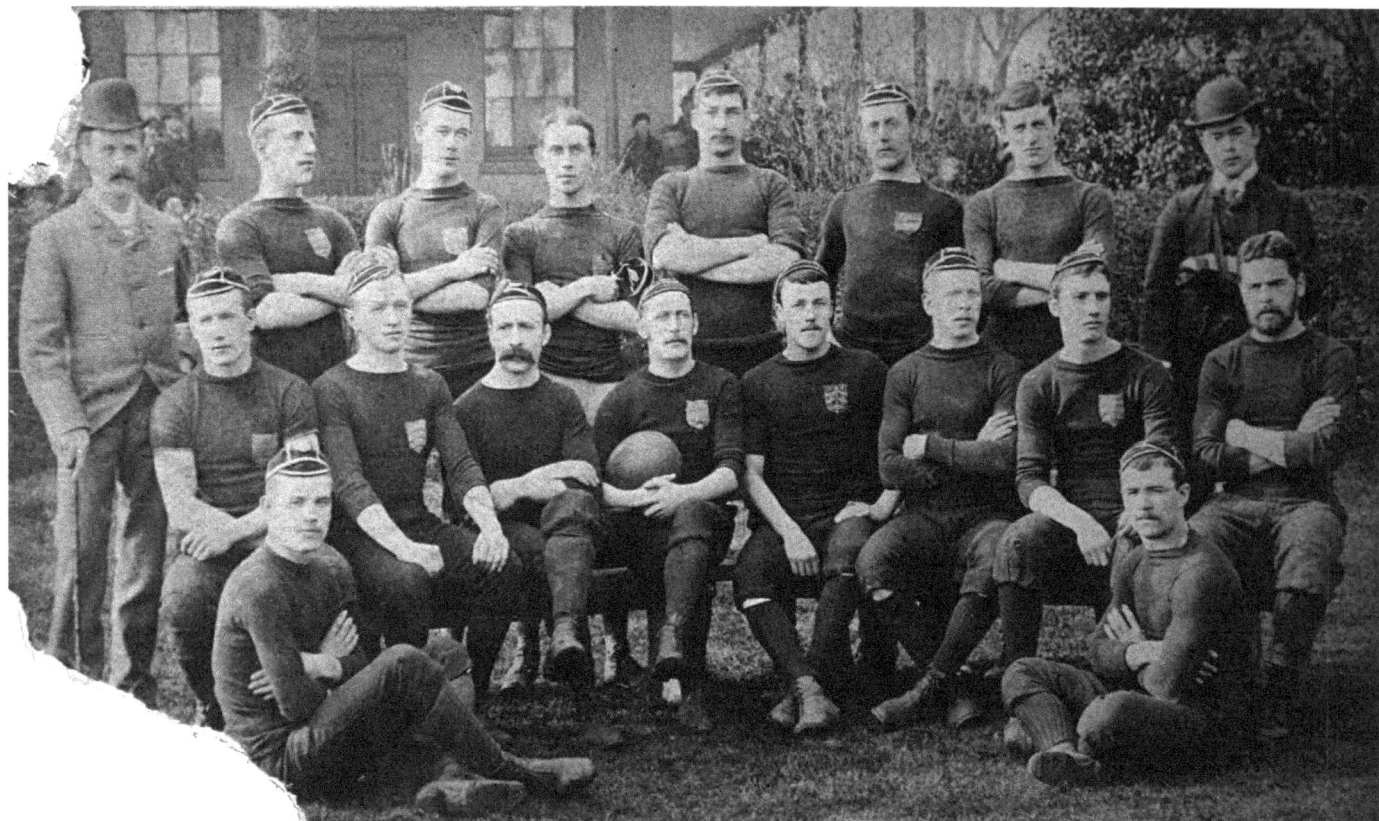

Oct 11 Gloucester 1 goal 2 tries
Colts XX 0
Tries: H.A.Sanders, W.Brimmell, T.G.Smith;
Conversion: H.V.Jones

Oct 25 R.A.C. Cirencester 2 goals 2
tries Gloucester 0

Nov 8 Swindon Rangers 0
Gloucester 2 goals
Tries: G.Coates (2);
Conversions: H.V.Jones (2)

Nov 15 Gloucester 0
Newport 1 drop goal 2 tries

Nov 29 Bath 0 Gloucester 3 goals
Tries: T.Bagwell, H.E.Taylor, G.Coates;
Conversions: O.Phillips (3)

Dec 3 Gloucester 2 goals 1 try
Bristol Medicals 0
Tries: H.J.Boughton, G.Coates, H.E.Taylor;
Conversions: O.Phillips (2)

Dec 13 Gloucester 0 Cardiff 2 tries

Dec 20 Clifton 1 goal Gloucester 0

Dec 26 Gloucester 1 goal
London Team 0
Try: H.E.Taylor;
Conversion: H.J.Boughton

Jan 3 Redland Park 1 try
Gloucester 1 goal 4 tries
Tries: H.Bailey, T.Bagwell, G.Coates,
H.L.Griffiths, J.W.Bayley;
Conversion: O.Phillips

Jan 12 Gloucester 2 goals 2 tries
Queen's College, Cork 0
Tries: H.V.Jones, G.Coates, H.D.Hay,
H.J.Boughton;
Conversions: H.V.Jones (2)

Jan 17 Gloucester 1 goal 4 tries
Bath 0
Tries: A.H.Brown (2), G.Coates, W.G.Moore,
T.Bagwell;
Conversion: H.V.Jones

Jan 24 Newport 2 goals 1 try
Gloucester 0

Jan 31 Gloucester 1 try Civil Service 0
Try: H.V.Jones

Feb 7 Gloucester 2 goals 1 try
Redland Park 0
Tries: G.Coates (2), H.L.Griffiths;
Conversions: H.V.Jones (2)

Feb 12 Bristol Medicals 0 Gloucester 0

Feb 14 Gloucester 1try Clifton 0
Try: H.J.Boughton

Feb 21 Gloucester 1 goal
Swindon Rangers 2 goals
Try: H.J.Boughton;
Conversion: H.V.Jones

Feb 28 Cardiff 4 goals Gloucester 0

Mar 7 Gloucester 0
R.A.C. Cirencester 0

1885-86

Played 17 Won 13 Lost 3 Drawn 1
For 27 goals, 32 tries
Against 8 goals, 9 tries
Captain: Tom Smith

Gloucester Second XV
Played 15 Won 11 Lost 0 Drawn 4
For 6 goals, 26 tries Against 1 goal, 4 tries
Captain: O.H.Jones

Most appearances: T.Bagwell, H.L.Broughton, E.D.Tandy 17, J.Oswell, G.Coates, T.Smith, 16, H.V.Jones, H.A.Sanders 15, W.H.Fream 14
Most tries: G.Coates 18, H.V.Jones 10, E.W.Urquhart 7, T.Bagwell 6
Conversions: H.V.Jones 20, H.A.Sanders 6, H.Payne 1

Some critics rated this the best team yet to turn out for the Club when judged against an ever-stronger fixture list. The team played in a new strip – red, yellow and black jerseys and stockings, and dark blue knickerbockers. During a very successful season, only Cardiff (twice), who went through the season unbeaten, and the London team, inflicted defeats. This was despite a fair amount of turbulence in selection with 33 players used.

The outstanding backs were James Oswell at full-back, who had a prodigious kick and showed a cool head in moments of crisis; H.V.Jones who successfully switched from half-back to three-quarter and was a reliable goal-kicker; Tommy Bagwell, small of stature, but a live wire at half-back, renowned for his collaring and dodging runs; and George Coates, who contributed lots of dash and 18 tries, a record for the Club. Harry Taylor was the best in defence, but decided that he needed a break from the game towards the end of the season. A very able substitute was found in an old boy of Cheltenham College, E.W.Urquhart, a strong runner who appeared five times and scored seven tries.

First and foremost, in a good set of forwards, was Tom Graves Smith, the captain, much respected and admired, who led by example in hard work and focus. But the forwards had a

tendency to hold on to the ball and be reluctant to let it out quickly to a back line whose brilliant passing regularly baffled opponents.

Frank Brown returned for one appearance against the London team on Boxing Day, and Jimmy Boughton played only twice. The 2nd XV were unbeaten. The season was rounded off with a charity match when the players divided according to political affiliations, and the Liberals beat the Conservatives.

Ten Gloucester players were selected for Gloucestershire during the season. Harry Taylor and Richard Bankes represented Western Counties against London, and Harry also played for London against Oxford and Cambridge.

Oct 3 Gloucester 1 goal 3 tries
Twenty Colts of City Clubs 1 try
Tries: G.Coates (2), E.Tandy, Moore;
Conversion: H.V.Jones

Oct 10 Gloucester 3 goals 5 tries
Kidderminster 0
Tries: H.V.Jones (3), T.Bagwell (3), H.Cadenne (2);
Conversions: H.V.Jones (3)

Oct 17 Gloucester 3 goals Bath 0
Tries: G.Coates (2), H.Taylor;
Conversion: H.V.Jones (3)

Oct 24 R.A.C. Cirencester 0
Gloucester 1 goal 1 try
Tries: T.Bagwell, W.G.Roberts;
Conversion: H.V.Jones

Nov 21 Cardiff 4 goals 4 tries
Gloucester 0

Nov 28 Gloucester 2 goals 5 tries
Swindon Rangers 0
Tries: G.Coates (4), R.Bankes, H.V.Jones, H Taylor;
Conversions: H.V.Jones (2)

Dec 3 Bristol Medicals 0
Gloucester 1 goal

Try: W.G.Moore;
Conversion: H.Payne

Dec 19 Clifton 1 try Gloucester 1 goal
Try: G.Coates;
Conversion: H.V.Jones

Dec 26 Gloucester 1 goal 1 try
R James' London Team 2 goals
Tries: G.Coates, H.Cadenne;
Conversions: H.V.Jones

Jan 2 Gloucester 1 try Cardiff 2 tries
Try: H.E.Taylor

Jan 14 Bath 1 try Gloucester 1 try
Try: G.Coates

Jan 30 Gloucester 2 tries Clifton 0
Tries: H.E.Taylor, A.Gorin

Feb 6 Gloucester 5 goals 4 tries
Old Edwardians 0
Tries: H.V.Jones (4), E.W.Urquhart (2), G.Coates, T.Bagwell, H.A.Sanders
Conversions: H.A.Sanders (3), H.V.Jones (2)

Feb 13 Gloucester 5 goals 2 tries
Redland Park 0
Tries: G.Coates (2,) E.W.Urquhart (2), E.O.Tandy (2), H.V.Jones
Conversions: H.A.Sanders (3), H.V.Jones (2)

Feb 20 Swindon Rangers 1 drop goal
Gloucester 2 goals 4 tries
Tries: G.Coates (2), T.Bagwell (2), E.W.Urquhart, E.D.Tandy;
Conversions: H.V.Jones (2)

Mar 6 Gloucester 2 tries
R.A.C. Cirencester 0
Tries: G.Coates, E.W.Urquhart

Mar 13 Gloucester 2 goals 2 tries
Civil Service (London) 1 goal
Tries: G.Coates, E.W.Urquhart, H.E.Taylor, H.V.Jones;
Conversions: H.V.Jones (2)

1886-87

Played 19 Won 10 Lost 7 Drawn 2
For 12 goals, 25 tries
Against 9 goals, 11 tries
Captain: Tom Smith

Gloucester Second XV

Played 17 Won 13 Lost 0 Drawn 4
For 14 goals, 36 tries Against 1 goal, 3 tries
Captain: W.G.Roberts

Most appearances: J.N.Oswell, S.A.Ball, H.L.Broughton, H.A.Sanders 19, T.Bagwell 18, G.Coates, T.Smith, E.D.Tandy 17, C.E.Brown,

W.H.Fream 16
Most tries: G.Coates 12, T.Bagwell, H.E.Taylor 4
Conversions: T.Smith 5, T.Bagwell 3, H.A.Sanders, H.Payne 1
Drop goals: J.N.Oswell 1, T.Smith 1 from a mark

New this season was the appointment of impartial referees, sufficiently empowered to prevent the unseemly wrangles and disputes which had plagued many earlier matches. There were few changes to the personnel from the previous season, but the results were not as good, and the points scoring was much reduced. Home and away matches with Llanelly and Swansea were played for the first time, fixtures with Newport were resumed, and not a single victory was registered against a Welsh club. On the other hand, the London XV was the only non-Welsh team to inflict a defeat.

Oswell at full-back was as sure as ever, often relieving pressure with his huge kicking. George Coates and Harry Taylor were a fine pair of wings, but it was unfortunate that H.V.Jones departed Gloucester, leaving the Club without a reliable goal kicker, which proved to be the major weakness in the team. E.W.Urquhart proved a good replacement in the three-quarters when available, but C.E.Brown less so and he was switched to the forwards. Hughes the second team full-back proved a better bet.

The half-backs, Tommy Bagwell and Sammy Ball formed an effective partnership, and the smartness of Bagwell's kicking, running, dodging, and tackling got even better as the season wore on. The forwards, ably led by the captain, Tom Graves Smith, regularly proved their mettle.

The most exciting match of the season was the visit to the Spa of the "Invincibles" of Cardiff, played in front of 5,000 spectators. Cardiff scored in the first half, and Gloucester only equalised on the stroke of time, when "Brown secured the ball and passed to Stoddart, who judiciously transferred to Coates, and the latter, warding off his opponents in fine style, dashed over the line and scored a try" - the crowd went wild. But the largest crowd of the season was for the Boxing Day match against a London XV, which had rapidly become a treasured tradition.

Nine Gloucester players appeared in the County's draw with Somerset, and ten in the defeat of Devon. Richard Bankes played for Western Counties against London, and for London against Oxford & Cambridge. For the second season in succession the 2nd XV went through the season unbeaten.

**Oct 9 Gloucester 1 try
Twenty Colts of City Clubs 0**
Try: G.Coates

**Oct 16 R.A.C. Cirencester 0
Gloucester 1 goal 3 tries**
Tries: E.Tandy (2), G.Coates, H.Payne;
Conversion: H.Payne

Oct 23 Bath 1 try Gloucester 4 tries
Tries: G. Coates (3), E.Tandy

**Oct 30 Gloucester 1 try
Swansea 1 goal 2 tries**
Try: W.G.Moore

**Nov 6 Swindon Rangers 0
Gloucester 1 goal 2 tries**
Tries: C.E.Brown, G.Coates, H.E.Taylor;
Conversion: H.Sanders

**Nov 20 Newport 1 drop goal 2 tries
Gloucester 0**

Nov 27 Gloucester 1 try Cardiff 1 try
Try: G.Coates

**Dec 4 Llanelly 2 goals 1 try
Gloucester 0**

**Dec 11 Gloucester 3 goals 1 try
R.A.C.Cirencester 0**
Tries: H.Taylor, R.Stoddart, R.Grist, R.Bankes;
Conversions: T.Smith (3)

Dec 18 Clifton 0 Gloucester 4 tries
Tries: G.Coates (3), S.Ball

**Dec 26 Gloucester 0
R James' London Team 1 try**

**Jan 15 Gloucester 1 goal
Swindon Rangers 0**
Goal: T.G.Smith from a mark

Jan 22 Gloucester 0 Llanelly 0

**Jan 29 Gloucester 0
Newport 1 goal 1 try**

Feb 5 Gloucester 2 goals 5 tries Clifton 0
Tries: T.Bagwell (3), E.W.Erquhart, T.Smith, S.Ball, T.Taylor;
Conversions: T.Smith, T.Bagwell

Feb 10 Gloucester 1 goal 3 tries Willesden (London) 1 try

Tries: G.Coates, H.Taylor, T.Bagwell, C.E.Brown;
Conversions: T.Bagwell

Feb 19 Cardiff 1 try Gloucester 0

Mar 5 Gloucester 1 goal 1 try

Civil Service (London) 1 drop goal
Tries: G.Coates, T.Smith;
Conversion: T.Bagwell

Mar 19 Swansea 2 goals 1 try Gloucester 1 drop goal
Drop Goal: T.Oswell

1887-88

Played 19 Won 10 Lost 6 Drawn 3
For 12 goals, 28 tries
Against 3 goals, 17 tries
Captain: Tom Smith

Gloucester Second XV
Played 16 Won 10 Lost 4 Drawn 2
For 21 goals, 41 tries Against 9 goals, 10 tries
Captain: W.G.Roberts

Most appearances: H.E.Taylor, A.F.Hughes, S.A.Ball 18, W.H.Fream, T.Bagwell 16, T.Smith, H.L.Broughton, E.D.Tandy, T.Taylor, G.W.Coates 15
Most tries: H.E.Taylor 11, G.W.Coates 7, S.A.Ball 5, C.E.Brown 4
Conversions: T.Smith 10, A.F.Hughes 2

The Club's rent for the Spa ground was reduced from £15 to £9, but admission prices were unchanged at 5s and 2s 6d for season tickets, and 6d and 2d for individual matches. The Club accounts showed a balance of less than £3 at the end of the season.

Gloucester's form during the season was inconsistent, largely because of a lack of accuracy in the passing amongst the backs. There was also some difficulty in persuading players to travel for away matches, so 34 players were used, and the results reflected these problems, but a more settled side emerged towards the end of the season. Teams were selected by the Club committee, chaired by the captain, a few days in advance of a match.

"Barley" Hughes, a strong defender, performed well at full-back, but his place kicking was poor, so the captain took over those duties. Harry Taylor and George Coates were as good as ever on the wings, and Walter George came in to the side and performed very well at half-back outside Sammy Ball, which allowed Tommy Bagwell to move out to centre.

Amongst the forwards, Tom Graves Smith coached the team well and was a popular and painstaking captain. Joe Cromwell, the old warhorse, had lost none of his dash, and George

Witcomb proved to be one of the best players to join the Club for many years, with A.E.Healing another useful acquisition.

The season finished on a high with victory against a Cardiff side which had lost only once previously. Both sides played a formation of one back, four three-quarters, two half-backs and eight forwards. Gloucester had switched to this formation, which would become the norm across the game a few years later, in mid-season, having used nine forwards until the New Year. This match was rated one of the finest played at the Spa, and Gloucester's victory as the best of the season. Harry Taylor was the hero, scoring both Gloucester tries, and at the end of the game he was borne off along Brunswick Road on the shoulders of ecstatic supporters. Often standing in as captain, this was his last full season; he finished with 52 tries from 108 appearances.

Twelve players were capped by Gloucestershire. Harry Taylor played for Western Counties against London.

Oct 1 Gloucester 2 tries Gloucester Next XVIII 1 try
Tries: E.Tandy, C.Brown;

Oct 15 R.A.C. Cirencester 0 Gloucester 3 goals 1 try
Tries: H.Taylor (2), G.Coates, A.Cromwell;
Conversions: T.Smith (3)

Oct 22 Gloucester 0 Newport 3 tries

Oct 29 Cardiff 1 goal 2 tries Gloucester 0

Nov 12 Gloucester 0 Swindon Rangers 1 try

Nov 24 Gloucester 1 goal Willesden (London) 0
Try: H.E.Taylor;
Conversion: T.Smith

Nov 26 Swansea 2 tries Gloucester 0

Dec 10 Gloucester 1 try Moseley 1 goal
Try: H.E.Taylor

Dec 17 Clifton 0 Gloucester 4 tries
Tries: C.Brown, H.Taylor, W.George, R.Stoddart

Dec 24 Gloucester 0 P C Adams' XV 0

Dec 26 Gloucester 1 try Kensington 0
Try: H.E.Taylor

Dec 31 Newport 6 tries Gloucester 2 tries
Tries: G.Coates, A.H.Brown

Jan 7 Gloucester 1 try Bath 1 try
Try: A.H.Brown

Jan 14 Swindon Rangers 0 Gloucester 1 goal
Try: C.E.Brown;
Conversion: T.G.Smith

Jan 21 Gloucester 0 Swansea 0

Jan 28 Gloucester 4 tries Clifton 1 try
Tries: G.Coates, S.Ball, H.E.Taylor, G.Witcomb

Feb 4 Bath 0 Gloucester 3 goals 5 tries
Tries: G.Coates (2), S.Ball (2), W.George, C.E.Brown, H.Taylor, E.Tandy
Conversions: A.F.Hughes (2), T.G.Smith

Mar 3 Gloucester 3 goals, 6 tries R.A.C. Cirencester 0
Tries: G.Coates (2), S.Ball (2), H.Taylor (2), W.George, E.Tandy, A.H.Brown;
Conversions: T.G.Smith (3)

Mar 10 Gloucester 1 goal 1 try Cardiff 1 drop goal
Tries: H.E.Taylor (2);
Conversion: T.G.Smith

A.W.Vears E.D.Tandy G.J.Witcomb A.Cromwell unidentified G.Coates R.C.Jenkins
C.E.Brown T.Taylor R.Grist T.G.Smith(Capt) T.Bagwell W.Brown T.Collins
J.Williams W.George A.F.Hughes S.A.Ball R.Dere

Played 23 Won 15 Lost 3 Drawn 5
For 22 goals 46 tries
Against 3 goals 11 tries
Captain: Tom Smith

Gloucester Second XV
Played 19 Won 12 Lost 4 Drawn 3
For 22 goals 24 tries Against 8 goals, 10 tries
Captain: W.G.Roberts

Most appearances: W.George, T.Collins 23,
S.Ball, A.H.Brown 22, R.C.Jenkins,
E.D.Tandy 21
Most tries: T.Bagwell 10, R.Grist, S.Ball 9,
G.W.Coates 7
Conversions: T.G.Smith 9, A.F.Hughes 6,
T.Collins, E.Smith 2
Drop goals: R.Dere 2

There were more thrilling matches than usual, with fewer dominated by forward play, and consistency of selection with only 26 players used. Results improved despite a stronger fixture list. The Citizen reported that "the Gloucester players have made themselves masters of the science of the game to such a degree that in this lies the secret of their success". Overall, opponents were heavily outscored, but goal kicking remained a problem with only 18 successes out of 65 attempts.

The play of the forwards was markedly improved as they "adopted to perfection the latest manoeuvres in wheeling tight scrimmages, and heeling-out," and their dribbling and fast following up were real strengths. At the end of the season, Tom Graves Smith stood down as captain and player – he had made 124 appearances, and during his four seasons as captain only 19 of 78 matches were lost. This was also the last full season played by Ernest Tandy, a stalwart of the pack with 100 appearances. But newcomers William Taylor, Charlie Jenkins, and Jack Williams helped bolster a formidable pack, which was responsible for much of the Club's success.

Amongst the backs, the experienced George Coates and Tommy Bagwell, played better than ever, but this was George's last season, bowing out with 78 tries in 107 appearances; he had broken the mould as the first working man to represent the Club, and he did it magnificently. The passing and defence of Charles Brown was much improved, and the speed and dodging running of Ronald Grist frequently perplexed opponents - he made the most brilliant run of the season when he slipped through half the Swansea side during a magnificent win to round off the programme.

Highlights were the victories over Cardiff, Newport and Swansea, as well as two within a week against Moseley. Of the four matches against Cardiff, the first three were drawn, and it took a determined effort to win the fourth, the first time Gloucester had won in Cardiff. With ten minutes left, "Barley" Hughes tried a drop kick from the touchline at half-way, which only just dropped short, and Dere following up seized the ball and scored. A special train had taken a thousand Gloucester supporters to the match; they were exultant, and even more turned out to celebrate when the team returned to Gloucester.

The highlight of the County season was the visit of the first international touring team, the New Zealand Maoris, to the Spa, where 11 Gloucester players in the County side helped constrain the visitors to victory by a goal and a try to a try. During the season 15 players were capped by Gloucestershire.

Oct 6 Gloucester 1 goal 1 drop goal 1 try Colts XX 0
Tries: W.Taylor, S.Ball;
Conversion: K.Smith;
Drop goal: R.Dere

Oct 13 Gloucester 2 goals 4 tries R.A.C. Cirencester 0
Tries: R.Grist (2), S.Ball, G.Coates, A.Cromwell, T.Bagwell;
Conversions: T.G.Smith (2)

Oct 20 Gloucester 1 goal 1 try Clifton 0
Tries: S.Ball (2);
Conversion: A.F.Hughes

Oct 27 Moseley 1 drop goal 1 try Gloucester 2 goals
Tries: S.Ball (2);
Conversion: A.F.Hughes (2)

Nov 3 Gloucester 1 goal Moseley 0
Try: T.Bagwell;
Conversion: A.F.Hughes

Nov 10 Swindon Rangers 0 Gloucester 1 goal
Try: R.C.Jenkins;
Conversion: A.F.Hughes

Nov 17 Gloucester 0 Cardiff 0

Nov 24 Swansea 1 try Gloucester 0

Dec 1 Gloucester 1 goal 9 tries Rest of County 1 try

Tries: T.Bagwell (2), G.Witcomb (2), E.D.Tandy (2), G.Coates, R.Grist, R.C.Jenkins, A.Cromwell
Conversion: T.Smith

Dec 8 Cardiff 1 try Gloucester 1 try
Try: S.Ball

Dec 22 Newport 1 try Gloucester 1 try
Try: Scorer unknown

Dec 26 Gloucester 1 try London Team 1 try
Try: Scorer unknown

Dec 29 Gloucester 5 tries Bath 0
Tries: E.D.Tandy (2), G.Coates, S.Ball, G.Witcomb

 Jan 5 Gloucester v Swansea - cancelled due to frost

Jan 19 Gloucester 1 try Newport 0
Try: W.George

Jan 26 Clifton 1 try Gloucester 1 goal 3 tries
Tries: G.Coates (3), T.Bagwell;
Conversion: A.F.Hughes

Feb 9 Llanelly 1 try Gloucester 0

Feb 16 Gloucester 1 try Llanelly 1 goal
Try: A.H.Brown

Feb 23 Gloucester 0 Cardiff 0

Feb 25 Gloucester 2 goals 1 try Civil Service 0
Tries: R.C.Jenkins, C.E.Brown, R.Grist;
Conversions: T.Collins (2)

Mar 2 Gloucester 1 goal 10 tries Swindon Rangers 0
Tries: G.Witcomb (3), T.Bagwell (2), A.H.Brown, A.Cromwell, T.Collins, R.W.Stoddart, S.Ball, R.Grist
Conversion: T.Smith

Mar 9 Gloucester v Willesden - cancelled due to floods

Mar 16 Cardiff 1 goal 2 tries Gloucester 1 goal, 1 try, 1 penalty goal
Tries: R.Grist, R.Dere;
Conversion: T.Smith;
Penalty: T.Smith

Mar 23 R.A.C. Cirencester 0 Gloucester 3 goals 4 tries
Tries: R.Grist (2), E.D.Tandy, A.Cromwell, T.Bagwell, R.George, C.Brown;
Conversions: T.Smith (3)

Mar 30 Gloucester 3 goals 2 tries Swansea 1 try
Tries: T.Taylor, R.C.Jenkins, R.Grist, R.Dere;
Conversions: E.Smith (2);
Drop Goal: R.Dere

1889-90

Played 25 Won 14 Lost 8 Drawn 3
For 124 Against 45
Captain: Charles Edward Brown

Gloucester Second XV
Played 18 Won 13 Lost 5
For 27 goals, 40 tries Against 1 goal, 7 tries
Captain: Trevor Powell

Most appearances: T.Bagwell 25, W.George, C.Williams 24 C.E.Brown, A.F.Hughes 23, S.A.Ball , R.C.Jenkins 21, J.Williams 20, T.Collins 18
Most tries: T.Bagwell 11 W.George, C.E.Brown 8 T.Powell 7
Conversions: A.F.Hughes 19, H.V.Page 6, T.Bagwell, T.Collins, J.Watts 1

Point scoring first introduced: Try: 1 point;
Conversion: 2 points;

Penalty: 2 points; Field goal: 4 points;
Drop goal: 3 points

There was a run of seven successive wins and a sequence of seven matches in which opponents were prevented from scoring, but a severe tailing off in the last two months of the season detracted from the overall record. A contributing factor was the lack of continuity in selection, with 39 players used. It was against clubs from Wales and the North of England that the record was particularly poor.

Amongst the backs, Charles Brown led the team energetically and was strong in defence. He was ably supported by Tommy Bagwell, with his "characteristic trickiness, pace and pluck". The promotion of Walter Jackson from the 2nd XV was a great success, and the goal kicking of "Barley" Hughes improved. Sammy Ball

and Walter George maintained a high level of performance at half-back.

H.V.Page was a splendid pack leader, particularly well supported by A.E.Healing and George Witcomb. Charlie Jenkins, Joe Cromwell, Tom Collins and Jack Williams provided experience, and Albert Collins and Charlie Williams were able newcomers.

"Barley" Hughes, Tommy Bagwell, Charles Brown, Walter George and George Witcomb were selected for Western Counties against London.

Gloucester were delighted to have their first fixture against a side from Yorkshire, but were humiliated in a very rough match. A player from each side was sent off, and Huddersfield lost three more to injury. The visitors held their own even when it was 11 against 14, treating the Gloucester forwards "as if they were a lot of schoolboys".

Gloucester made their first tour to the North later in the season. They were judged unlucky to lose to Swinton, but there was no argument about Wigan being the better team in the second match. Despite the results, "a black fog hanging over Manchester" throughout, and the Club making a loss financially, the tour was thoroughly enjoyed by the Gloucester players.

For the first time the Club took out insurance on both 1st and 2nd XV players, who had to have paid their membership fees to be selected. There was a continuing problem with visiting teams being on the ground before the home team. The Club made a profit of £55 on the season.

Sep 28 Gloucester 6 Next XX 3
Tries: W.George, T.Bagwell, C.E.Brown, G.F.Dere;
Conversion: J.Watts

Oct 5 Gloucester 22 Colts XX 0
Tries: W.George (4), R.C.Jenkins, A.H.Brown, A.Cromwell, S.A.Ball, E.D.Tandy;
Conversions: A.F.Hughes (5); Field goal: C.F.Brown

Oct 12 Gloucester 7 H.V.Page's XV 0
Tries: W.George, T.Bagwell, A.H.Brown;
Conversions: A.F.Hughes (2)

Oct 16 Gloucester 1 Huddersfield 7
Try: R.C.Jenkins

Oct 19 Gloucester 7 Swindon Rangers 0
Tries: C.E.Brown, T.Bagwell, J.Williams;
Conversions: T.Collins, T.Bagwell

Oct 26 Gloucester v Bristol - cancelled, Bristol unable to raise a side.

Nov 2 Gloucester 0 Llanelly 0

Nov 9 Clifton 0 Gloucester 16
Tries: T.Bagwell (2), H.V.Page, A.Cromwell, G.Witcomb, C.E.Brown;
Conversions: A.F.Hughes (5)

Nov 16 Cardiff 2 Gloucester 1
Try: W.George

Nov 23 Gloucester 8 Bath 0
Tries: C.E.Brown, G.Witcomb, E.J.Ward, R.Grist;
Conversion: A.F.Hughes;
Penalty: A.F.Hughes

Dec 7 Gloucester 0 Swansea 0

Dec 14 Gloucester 0 Cardiff 0

Dec 26 Gloucester 5 Penygraig 0
Tries: A.E.Healing, E.J.Ward, S.A.Ball;
Conversion: A.F.Hughes

Dec 28 Gloucester 1 Moseley 0
Try: W.George

Jan 4 Gloucester 1 Old Merchant Taylors 0
Try: R.C.Jenkins

Jan 18 Moseley 0 Gloucester 12
Tries: W.Jackson (2), G.Witcomb, T.Bagwell;
Conversions: A.F.Hughes (2), H.V.Page (2)

Jan 25 Gloucester 6 Clifton 0
Tries: T.Powell (2), C.E.Brown, T.Bagwell;
Conversion: H.V.Page

Feb 8 Bath 0 Gloucester 15
Tries: T.Bagwell (2), C.E.Brown, G.Witcomb, E.Ellis, T.Powell, A.E.Healing;
Conversions: H.V.Page (3)
Penalty: W.Jackson

Feb 15 Gloucester 0 Cardiff 1

Feb 22 Swinton 6 Gloucester 0

Feb 24 Wigan 5 Gloucester 0

Mar 1 Swindon Rangers 0 Gloucester 8
Tries: T.Powell (3), W.Jackson;
Conversions: A.F.Hughes (2)

Mar 8 Llanelly 2 Gloucester 1
Try: T.Powell

Mar 15 R.A.C. Cirencester 0 Gloucester 7
Tries: C.E.Brown (2), T.Bagwell (2), W.Jackson;
Conversion: A.F.Hughes

Mar 22 Cardiff 15 Gloucester 0

Mar 29 Swansea 4 Gloucester 0

1890-91

Played 26 Won 21 Lost 2 Drawn 3
For 127 Against 28
Captain: Tommy Bagwell

Gloucester Second XV
Played 20 Won 17 Lost 3
For 141 Against 25

Most appearances: T.Bagwell, W.Jackson, W.George, A.Collins 26, A.F.Hughes, C.Williams, A.Cromwell 24, R.C.Jenkins 22, S.A.Ball, J.Williams 21, W.Taylor 20
Most tries: T.Powell, W.Taylor 11, W.Jackson 10, T.Bagwell 9, W.George, A.Collins 6
Conversions: A.F.Hughes 15, H.V.Page 4, W.Jackson 3, C.Williams, T.H.Mugliston 1
Penalty: W.Jackson 1
Drop goal: T.Powell 1

There was a dramatic improvement in the Club's results, despite a stronger fixture list. It was a settled side with the best players appearing in almost every game. The Citizen reported that "never before did the club stand so high in the football world as exponents of the game in its highest and most scientific form".

Much pride was taken from results against Welsh clubs – won seven, drawn two, lost two. The double over Cardiff was achieved for the first time, and when the unbeaten records of Cardiff and Swansea were ended, Gloucester were dubbed the "Record Smashers". Not a single English club was able to lower Gloucester's colours, 13 matches being won and one drawn; the 2nd XV also suffered no defeats by English opponents.

The most significant match of the season took place at the Spa on 10th January 1891. The pitch was frozen in the morning, but cartloads of salt were applied, and a huge crowd saw Swansea defeated. But the pitch became a mudbath, the grass never recovered, and it was agreed that the Rugby and Cricket Clubs could no longer share the Spa ground. So, this was the last season of rugby there, and during the summer the Kingsholm ground was purchased.

Tommy Bagwell, the first blue collar worker to be appointed captain of the Club, worked tirelessly and led an outstanding back division. Walter Jackson was judged the best three-quarter to have played for the Club, with marvelous dodging, beautifully judged and effective kicking, sure collaring, and skill in giving and

S.S.Starr A.Cromwell R.C.Jenkins G.J.Witcomb A.E.Healing C.Williams J.Williams A.Ward T.B.Powell
A.Collins A.F.Hughes W.H.Taylor T.Bagwell(Capt) T.Collins H.V.Page T.G.Smith
W.George S.A.Ball W.Jackson

taking passes. Walter Taylor emerged as a very talented wing with exceptional pace, and the occasional appearances of Charles Hooper were treasured. At full-back, the form and place kicking of "Barley" Hughes was erratic, but occasional outstanding performances kept him in the team.

The skills and mutual understanding of Walter George and Sammy Ball, "The Tigers" at half-back, were rarely equalled by opponents. The forwards showed improvement, the most talented being George Witcomb, ably supported by the old war horse, Joe Cromwell, and Albert Collins who showed up particularly well in loose play. The pack leader was H.V.Page, who also captained the County team.

During the season, 17 Gloucester players represented the County, and 13 of them played in the County Championship semi-final, which was lost in Lancashire. Tommy Bagwell, "Barley" Hughes and Charlie Williams played for Western Counties against London & Midlands.

Sep 20 Gloucester 4 Colts XX 1
Tries: R.C.Jenkins, C.Williams, T.Powell, T.Bagwell

Sep 27 Cardiff Harlequins 3 Gloucester 6
Tries: T.Powell, G.S.S.Marshall;
Conversions: A, F. Hughes (2)

Oct 4 Exeter 3 Gloucester 6
Tries: T.Bagwell, T.Powell;
Conversions: A.F.Hughes (2)

Oct 11 Gloucester 23 Rugby 0
Tries: A.Collins (3), W.Jackson (2), T.Powell (2), H.V.Page, E.Bolton, W.George, G.F.Dere, R.C.Jenkins, T.Bagwell;
Conversions: A.F.Hughes (2), H.V.Page (2), T.H.Mugliston

Oct 18 Swansea 12 Gloucester 4
Try: T.Powell;
Drop goal: T.Powell

Oct 25 Gloucester 3 Moseley 1
Try: T.Bagwell;
Conversion: H.V.Page

Nov 1 Gloucester 3 Penarth 0
Try: W.Taylor;
Conversion: A.F.Hughes

Nov 8 Old Edwardians 0 Gloucester 8
Tries: T.Bagwell (2), G.Witcomb, W.George, T.Powell, W.Taylor;
Conversion: A.F.Hughes

Nov 15 Gloucester 4 Cardiff 0
Tries: C.Williams, T.Bagwell;
Conversion: A.F.Hughes

Nov 22 Coventry 1 Gloucester 4
Tries: W.Taylor, W.Jackson;
Conversion: A.F.Hughes

Nov 29 Gloucester 3 Llanelly 0
Tries: W.George, A.Cromwell, T.Powell

Dec 6 Gloucester 14 Exeter 0
Tries: W.Taylor (4), T.Powell (3), S.A.Ball, W.Jackson, A.Collins;
Conversions: C.Williams, A.F.Hughes

Dec 26 Gloucester 1 Old Merchant Taylors 0
Try: T.Bagwell

Dec 27 Gloucester 9 Clapham Rovers 0
Tries: W.Jackson, A.Cromwell, T.Bagwell, A.F.Hughes, W.Taylor;
Conversions: A.F.Hughes, H.V.Page

Jan 10 Gloucester 4 Swansea 0
Tries: W.George, W.Taylor;
Conversion: A.F.Hughes

Jan 17 Gloucester 0 Penygraig 0

Jan 24 Gloucester 2 Swindon 0
Tries: W.George, R.C.Jenkins

Jan 31 Llanelly 0 Gloucester 0

Feb 7 Gloucester 5 Old Edwardians 1
Tries: W.Jackson, W.George, C.Williams;
Conversion: A.F.Hughes

Feb 9 Gloucester 4 Hull 0
Tries: A.E.Healing, W.Jackson;

Conversion: A.F.Hughes

Feb 14 Moseley 1 Gloucester 1
Try: A.Collins

Feb 21 Gloucester 3 Coventry 0
Try: W.Jackson;
Conversion: W.Jackson;

Feb 28 Cardiff 1 Gloucester 4
Tries: W.Jackson, A.Collins;
Conversion: W.Jackson

**Mar 7 Gloucester 2
Cardiff Harlequins 0**
Tries: G.Witcomb, T.Collins

Mar 21 Penarth 4 Gloucester 3
Penalty: W.Jackson
Played under Welsh scoring: 2 points for a try
and 3 for a penalty. Under the English system
the game would have ended 2-2.

**Mar 30 Gloucester 7
R.N.C. Devonport 0**
Tries: W.Taylor (2), W.Jackson;
Conversions: W.Jackson (2)

1891-92

T.G.Smith(Hon.Sec) W.Taylor H.G.Brown D.Price F.W.Mugliston G.J.Witcomb C.J.Click J.Mayo A.Collins H.W.Bennett(Sec)
S.S.Starr (Treas) D.Phelps G.Jones S.A.Ball T. Bagwell(Capt) W.George W.Jackson C.Jenkins
C.James T.Huggins A.F.Hughes

**Played 34 Won 24 Lost 6 Drawn 4
For 306 Against 96
Captain: Tommy Bagwell**

Gloucester Second XV
Played 23 Won 15 Lost 6 Drawn 2
For 221 Against 119
Captain: A.H.Gorin

All home matches from 10 October 1891 played
at Kingsholm

Most appearances: A.F.Hughes, T.Bagwell,
W.George 32, A.Cromwell 30, W.Jackson 29,

A.Collins 24, W.Taylor, S.A.Ball, R.C.Jenkins
22
Most tries: W.Jackson 17, T.Bagwell 10,
A.Cromwell 8, J.B.Powell, W.Taylor 7
Conversions: W.Jackson 29, J.Watts 4,
A.F.Hughes 2, A.Cromwell 1
Penalties: W.Jackson 3
Drop goals: W.Jackson 2, W.Taylor 1

Point scoring this season: Try: 2 points;
Conversion: 3 points;
Penalty: 3 points;
Drop goal: 4 points

A considerably strengthened fixture list
included northern clubs in St Helens, Dewsbury
and Wakefield, although the Citizen noted that
"the Dewsbury men are unable to maintain that
stolid outward indifference which characterise
Midlands teams – our own for example. Each
time a try was awarded them they held their
hands straight above their heads and indulged
in a succession of jumps and whoo-hoops. It is
only their way, but nevertheless looks rather
funny, dontcherknow."

The Club's level of success was rated as
"exceptionally good", the 24 wins being the

largest number secured up to that season. After a few matches played at Denmark Road, the new ground at Kingsholm was opened on 10ᵗʰ October with a convincing win against Burton. New ground was also broken with a first visit to London, where London Scottish were defeated at Old Deer Park.

Some players were reluctant to travel longer distances for away matches, and the Club took a firm line with a few players who wanted to play together when it suited them, all of which resulted in some weaker teams being selected and 48 players appearing. A supporter had to be brought off the terrace to make up numbers at Cardiff. But a strong finish to the season saw seven successive victories, the first of them being a notable scalp in the Barbarians.

"Barley" Hughes was cool and capable at full-back. Walter Jackson with sure tackling, tricky running, and judicious kicking at centre, led the way in scoring most tries and kicking most goals. He played outside the evergreen captain, Tommy Bagwell. They performed at a consistently high level in a three-quarter line which kept changing around them, except for Walter Taylor, a speedy wing.

Sammy Ball and Walter George provided experience and stability at half-back, but it was Sammy's last full season – he retired after 128 appearances. There was little continuity in the pack. The pick of the forwards were Joe Cromwell in his last full season and eventually finishing with 121 appearances, George Witcomb not available on a regular basis, and Albert Collins. Charles Click was a promising newcomer.

No less than 17 players represented Gloucestershire, including eleven against the Midland Counties. Six – Walter Taylor, Walter Jackson, Walter George, George Witcomb, J.Mayo and A.E.Healing - played for Western Counties against the Midlands, and George Witcomb played for the South against the North.

In addition to the First and Second XVs, for the first time the Club ran a Thursday XV, this being early closing day in Gloucester.

Sep 19 Gloucester 0
Twenty Colts of City Clubs 0

Sep 26 Gloucester 15
Gloucester Next XX 0
Tries: J.B.Powell, C.J. Click, T.Bagwell;
Conversions: W.Jackson(2), A.F.Hughes

Oct 3 Stratford on Avon 10
Gloucester 18
Tries: C.J.Click, J.B.Powell, T.Bagwell, A.Collins (2), A.Price;
Conversions: W.Jackson(2)

Oct 10 Gloucester 18 Burton 0
Tries: J.B.Powell(2), A.E.Henshaw, T.Bagwell, W.George, J.Williams;
Conversions: W.Jackson(2)

Oct 17 London Scottish 4
Gloucester 13
Tries: J.B.Powell, C.A.Hooper;
Penalty: W.Jackson;
Conversions: W.Jackson (2)

Oct 24 Coventry 2 Gloucester 0

Oct 26 Gloucester 6 St Helens 0
Try: W.Jackson;
Drop goal: T.Taylor

Oct 31 Leicester 0 Gloucester 15
Tries: W.Jackson, J.B.Powell, W.Taylor;
Conversions: W.Jackson(3)

Nov 7 Gloucester 28
Old Edwardians 0
Tries: A.Collins(2), T.Bagwell, A.Cromwell, A.E.Henshaw, S.A.Ball, W.George, J.B.Powell;
Penalty: W.Jackson;
Conversions: W.Jackson (3)

Nov 14 Cardiff 4 Gloucester 2
Try: T.Bagwell

Nov 21 Moseley 2 Gloucester 11
Tries: W.Taylor(2);
Conversions: W.Jackson;
Drop Goal: W.Jackson

Nov 28 Gloucester 0 Newport 2

Dec 5 Exeter 0 Gloucester 2
Try: Taylor

Dec 12 Gloucester 5 Swansea 0
Try: W.Jackson;
Conversion: W.Jackson

Dec 19 Gloucester 12 Coventry 0
Tries: C.E.Brown, T.Bagwell, C.Williams;
Conversions: W.Jackson(2)

Dec 26 Gloucester v Old Merchant Taylors - abandoned through frost.

Jan 2 Gloucester 6 Leicester 0
Tries: W.Jackson, W.Taylor, C.Williams

Jan 16 Gloucester v London Scottish - cancelled. London Scottish could not raise a team.

Jan 18 Gloucester 0 Dewsbury 7

Jan 23 Burton 2 Gloucester 12
Tries: T.Bagwell (2), W.Gough;
Conversions: J.Watts (2)

Jan 30 Swansea 10 Gloucester 0

Feb 4 Gloucester 14
Wakefield Trinity 8
Tries: W.Taylor, W.Jackson, T.Bagwell, P.F.Toller;
Conversions: J.Watts (2)

Feb 6 Gloucester 9 Moseley 0
Tries: W.Jackson, W.Gough, G.F.Jones;
Penalty: W.Jackson

Feb 10 Gloucester 0
Oxford University 0

Feb 13 Penarth 0 Gloucester 0

Feb 27 Gloucester 2 Cardiff 0
Try: A.Stephens

Mar 5 Gloucester 13 Exeter 0
Tries: R.C.Jenkins, W.Jackson, A.C.James;
Conversion: A.Cromwell;
Drop goal: W.Jackson from mark

Mar 12 Gloucester 2 Maritime 2
Try: W.Taylor

Mar 19 Newport 24 Gloucester 0

Mar 26 Gloucester 2
London Scottish 0
Try: A.Collins

Mar 28 Gloucester 10 Barbarians 9
Tries: A.Cromwell, W.Jackson;
Conversions: W.Jackson (2)

Apr 9 Gloucester 17
Devonport Albion 2
Tries: G.Jones, A.Collins, W.Jackson, A.Cromwell;
Conversions: W.Jackson (3)

Apr 16 Gloucester 19
Rest of County 6
Tries: A.Cromwell (5), T.Bagwell, W.Jackson,

C.A.Hooper;
Conversion: W.Jackson

**Apr 18 Gloucester 15
Devon Nomads 0**
Tries: W.Jackson (2), C.A.Hooper (2), W.Gough,

F.W.Mugliston;
Conversion: A.F.Hughes

Apr 19 Gloucester 22 Troedyrhiw 2
Tries: W.Jackson (3), W.Gough (2), W.George,
H.G.Brown, J.R.Price;

Conversions: W.Jackson (2)

Apr 23 Gloucester 15 Penarth 0
Tries: W.Jackson (2) G.Jones;
Conversions: W.Jackson (3)

1892-93

**Played 31 Won 16 Lost 12 Drawn 3
For 197 Against 143
Captain: Walter George**

Gloucester Second XV
Played 26 Won 17 Lost 5 Drawn 4
For 239 Against 81
Captain: E.Platt

Most appearances: R.C.Jenkins 30, W.Gough,
C.J.Click 28, W.Jackson 27, W.George 26,
W.Taylor 25, J.R.Price 24, A.F.Hughes 23,
T.Bagwell, A.Wellings, T.Huggins 22
Most tries: W.Taylor 18, W.Jackson 10,
A.Collins 5
Conversions: W.Jackson 18, J.Watts,
A.F.Hughes 1
Penalties: W.Jackson 2, F.O.Poole 1
Drop goals: W.Jackson 2, W.Gough, A.Collins 1

The Club invested in a new set of jerseys,
changing from wool to merino; the red, black
and yellow colours were unchanged, but with
narrower yellow stripes. Although there had
been previous matches against teams from
Bristol, such as Clifton and Rockleaze, the
opening fixture of the season was the first
against the Bristol club at 1st XV level. The
six goals and four tries scored against Burton
were a record for a match at Kingsholm. Frost
interfered with fixtures either side of Christmas,
and the visit of Kent Wanderers could only be
played as an exhibition. Interest was generated
at Easter by the visit of Tyldesley, known as the
"The Mighty Bongers".

There was satisfaction that opponents were
rendered scoreless in eleven matches, but
disappointment that Newport, Cardiff and
Coventry did the double over Gloucester, and
that fewer tries and goals were scored and more
conceded than in the previous season.   The
number of defeats was a record, and reflected
the lack of stability in the team, with young
inexperienced players pressed into service.

Amongst the backs, the captain, Walter George,
and Henshaw played everywhere but full-back.
The best set of three-quarters was Jackson,
Taylor, the leading try scorer, and Gough and
Bartlett, who were solid in defence despite their
youth.

Sammy Ball retired and his absence affected the
form of his half-back partner, Walter George
was captain in his last season, although he made
a couple of guest appearances later to finish with
146 appearances and 26 tries. The problem was
solved by moving Tommy Bagwell to half-back
to pair up with Arthur Stephens, who proved to
be a real success despite being new to the scrum-
half position.

It was a season of transition for the pack,
with George Witcomb not available, H.V.Page
and Hubert Brown rarely available, and Joe
Cromwell, Tom Collins and Jack Williams
dropped after the heavy defeat by Newport,
never to play again. Charlie Jenkins and Albert
Collins soldiered on, but it was Charlie's last
full season – he finished with 120 appearances.
A succession of new players were tried, and
rarely was the same eight played in successive
matches, the outstanding newcomer being
Alfred Wellings.

Nine Gloucester players were capped by the
County.

**Sep 10 Gloucester 26
Gloucester Colts XX 0**
Tries: J.Watts, T.Bagwell, W.H.Taylor,
C.Williams, W.George, J.Williams, A.C.James;
Conversions: W.Jackson (4)

**Sep 17 Gloucester 2
Gloucester Next XX 2**
Try: A Collins

Sep 24 Gloucester 15 Bristol 0
Tries: W.Jackson, A.G.Brown, W.H.Taylor,
A.Collins;
Conversion: J.Watts;
Drop Goal: A.Collins

Oct 1 Old Edwardians 2 Gloucester 9
Try: W.Taylor;
Conversion: W.Jackson;
Drop Goal: W.Jackson

Oct 8 Gloucester 2 Coventry 3
Try: T.Bagwell

Oct 15 Devonport Albion 10

Gloucester 2
Try: A.C.James

Oct 22 Burton 2 Gloucester 5
Try: W.Taylor;
Penalty: W.Jackson

Nov 5 Newport 29 Gloucester 0

Nov 12 Gloucester 2 Cardiff 13
Try: W.Jackson

Nov 19 Leicester 0 Gloucester 16
Tries: W.Taylor (3), W.Jackson (2);
Conversion: W.Jackson (2)

Nov 26 Gloucester 4 Moseley 5
Tries: W.Gough, W.Taylor

Dec 3 Gloucester 11 Penarth 4
Tries: W.Taylor (2), J.R.Price, W.Bartlett;
Conversion: A.F.Hughes

Dec 10 Nottingham v Gloucester - abandoned
due to frost

Dec 17 Gloucester 0 Newport 2

Dec 24 Gloucester 2 Old Edwardians 0
Try: W.Taylor

**Dec 26 Gloucester 7
Old Merchant Taylors 2**
Tries: W.Taylor, W.Jackson;
Conversion: W.Jackson

Dec 27 Gloucester 0 Kent Wanderers 5

Dec 31 Swansea 6 Gloucester 2
Try: W.Taylor

Jan 7 Gloucester v Aberavon - abandoned due
to frost

Jan 14 Gloucester v Penarth - abandoned due
to snow

**Jan 21 Gloucester 10
Cardiff Harlequins 0**
Tries: W.Taylor, W.Jackson;
Conversion: W.Jackson (2)

Jan 28 Moseley 0 Gloucester 7
Tries: W.Taylor, W.Jackson;
Conversion: W.Jackson

Feb 4 Gloucester 36 Burton 0
Tries: W Jackson (2), J.B.Powell, J.R.Price,
W.George, T.Bagwell, H.Bartlett, T.Huggins;
Conversions: W.Jackson (4);
Drop Goals: W.Gough, W.Jackson

Feb 11 Coventry 4 Gloucester 3
Penalty: F.O.Poole

Feb 18 Gloucester 12 Leicester 0
Tries: A.Collins (2), W.Jackson;
Conversions: W.Jackson (2)

**Feb 22 Oxford University 2
Gloucester 5**
Try: A.Collins;
Penalty: W.Jackson

Feb 25 Cardiff 32 Gloucester 0

Mar 11 Bristol 2 Gloucester 2
Try: A.Stephens

**Mar 18 Gloucester 0
Middlesex Wanderers 5**

Mar 25 Gloucester v Nottingham - Nottingham
scratched

**Apr 1 Gloucester 7
Broughton Rangers 6**
Tries: W.Taylor (2);
Conversion: W.Jackson

Apr 3 Gloucester 2 Tyldesley 0
Try: W.Taylor

**Apr 4 Gloucester 2
Hartlepool Rovers 2**
Try: C.J.Click

Apr 8 Gloucester 2 Swansea 0
Try: A.E.Henshaw

Apr 15 Gloucester 4 Stroud 5
Tries: W.Collins H.George

1893-94

Played 30 Won 19 Lost 10 Drawn 1
For 251 Against 196
Captain: John Hanman

Gloucester 'A'
Played 23 Won 12 Lost 8 Drawn 3
For 174 Against 61

Most appearances: C.Williams 30, A.Wellings, A.Collins 28, A.Stephens 26, A.F.Hughes 23, W.Taylor, F.Miller, T.Bagwell 21, A.H.Click 19
Most Tries: W.Taylor 10, A.Collins , C.Williams 6, F.Miller 5
Conversions: F.Watts 9, F.O.Poole 5, F.Abbey 3, J.Hanman, N.Biggs 2, A.Cromwell, A.Collins, A.Stephens, T.Eagles 1
Penalties: F.Watts, T.Eagles 1
Drop goals: A.F.Hughes, H.Bartlett, A.E.Bellingham 1

Point scoring this season: Try: 3 points; Conversion: 2 points; Penalty: 3 points; Drop goal: 4 points

A season famous for both Club and captain, John Hanman, serving bans by the RFU. It started poorly with a badly disorganised team. There were multiple changes every week, and 47 players were used during the season. The best performance against Welsh clubs was a draw against Swansea, and yet Bristol and Old Merchant Taylors were the only English opposition to inflict defeats.

"Barley" Hughes had retired early in the season, but was persuaded to return at full-back. The loss of Walter Jackson was a severe blow, and absences early in the season of Walter Taylor and Albert James, meant that 26 players were tried in a weak three-quarter line. When Taylor returned, he was switched from wing to centre with great success. At half-back, Arthur Stephens showed great improvement, and when his original partner, Frank Watts, was injured, Tommy Bagwell came out of retirement.

The main strength of the team lay in the forwards. Initially a number of veterans were persuaded to resume their careers, but they lacked pace and were soon replaced by more active younger players. Albert Collins, Charlie Williams and Alfred Wellings were to the fore, but John Hanman, J.R.Price, Bill Collins, Charles and Fred Click, J.Mayo and W.Leighton made up a formidable pack.

In December, the Gloucester Thursday team played against Walter Shewell of Stroud, who said he was planning to come to Gloucester to find work and would like to play for Gloucester. The Gloucester captain, John Hanman, said he would try to help and selected Shewell to play at Newport, but he was still registered with Stroud, who complained to the Gloucestershire RFU. Shewell was banned and Gloucester were fined £10.

Gloucester thought they had done no wrong, so appealed to the RFU, who were concerned about professionalism amongst northern clubs and mounted an investigation. They suspended Gloucester for three weeks and Hanman for the rest of the season. The Club was embarrassed, but they and Hanman, regarded as a martyr locally, attempted to make up lost revenue by holding boxing and soccer matches during the ban, and additional rugby matches after. Emerging straight into the Easter programme from the suspension, three games in four days were all won.

Eight players represented Gloucestershire, and Walter George played for Western Counties against the Midlands.

Sep 16 Gloucester 11 Colts XX 0
Tries: H.Bartlett, W.Gough, C.Williams;
Conversion: F.Watts

Sep 23 Gloucester 6   Next XVI 11
Tries: C.J.Click, J.Hanman

Sep 30 Gloucester 3 Bristol 7
Try: A.Collins

Oct 7 Leicester 3 Gloucester 8
Tries: J.B.Powell, J.Price;
Conversion: A.Cromwell

Oct 14 Gloucester 22
Burton-on Trent 0
Tries: J.B.Powell, G.Page, A.Collins, H.George;
Conversions: F.Abbey (3);
Drop goal: H.Bartlett

Oct 21 Gloucester 3 Swansea 3
Try: C.Williams

Nov 4 Gloucester 3 Newport 19

Try: J.Williams

Nov 25 Cardiff 33 Gloucester 3
Try: C.Rose

Dec 9 Gloucester 9 Old Edwardians 0
Try: A.Stephens;
Conversion: J.Hanman;
Drop goal: A.E.Bellingham

Dec 16 Gloucester 5 Penarth 16
Try: A.Wellings;
Conversion: J.Hanman

Dec 23 Coventry 0 Gloucester 5
Try: C.A.Hooper;
Conversion: A.Stephens

Dec 26 Gloucester 0
Old Merchant Taylors 11

Dec 27 Gloucester 14
Kent Wanderers 0
Tries: F.Watts (2), T.Bagwell;
Conversion: F.Watts;
Penalty: F.Watts

Dec 30 Newport 26 Gloucester 0

Jan 6 Gloucester v Leicester - cancelled due to frost

Jan 13 Moseley 0 Gloucester 5
Try: W.Taylor;
Conversion: F.Watts

Jan 20 Old Edwardians 3 Gloucester 7
Try: F.Miller;
Drop goal: A.F.Hughes

Jan 27 Gloucester 6 Coventry 4
Tries: F.Miller, G.Page

Feb 3 Burton-on-Trent 0
Gloucester 13
Tries: W.Taylor (2), A.Wellings;
Conversions: F.Watts (2)

Feb 10 Bridgwater 5 Gloucester 13
Tries: W.Taylor, A.H.Click, C.J.Click;
Conversions: F.Watts (2)

Feb 17 Gloucester 16 Derby 0
Tries: C.Williams (2), F.Miller, W.Collins;
Conversions: F.Watts (2)

Feb 24 Old Merchant Taylors 0 Gloucester 3
Try: W.Collins

Mar 3 Bristol 7 Gloucester 0

Mar 26 Gloucester 11 Lennox 5
Tries: W.Taylor, D.Phelps, A.Collins;
Conversion: F.Poole

Mar 27 Gloucester 8 Runcorn 4
Try: A.Stephens;
Conversion: T.Eagles;
Penalty: T.Eagles

Mar 29 Gloucester 22 Devon Nomads 0
Tries: W.Taylor (2), F.Miller (2), C.Williams, A.Wellings;
Conversions: F.Poole (2)

Mar 31 Penarth 13 Gloucester 5
Try: A.Stephens;
Conversion: A.Collins

Apr 7 Swansea 18 Gloucester 3
Try: W.Taylor

Apr 14 Gloucester 16 Bridgwater 0
Tries: A.Collins (2), F.Poole, E.Tymms;
Conversions: F.Poole (2)

Apr 21 Gloucester 15 E.Fenner's XV (Bristol) 0
Tries: A.Collins, C.Williams, A.Wellings, T.Bagwell, W.Pitt

Apr 28 Gloucester 16 Castleford 8
Tries: W.Taylor (2), N.Biggs (2);
Conversions: N.Biggs (2)

1894-95

Played 28 Won 14 Lost 11 Drawn 3
For 252 Against 155
Captain: John Hanman

Gloucester 'A'
Played 22 Won 8 Lost 8 Drawn 6
For 91 Against 83
Captain: James Oswell

Most appearances: G.T.Bourne, C.Hall 28, A.Wellings, W.Leighton 27, W.Pitt 26, C.Williams 25, F.Miller 24, T.Bagwell 23, W.Taylor, J.Hanman, J.R.Price 21,
Most tries: W.Taylor 13, G.T.Bourne 6, F.Miller, A.Collins, W.Pitt 5
Conversions: F.Watts 19, J.Hanman 6, E.Marsh 1
Penalties: F.Watts 2, J.Hanman 1
Drop goals: W.Taylor 2

One of the worst seasons in the Club's history included not a single victory against a Welsh club for the second season in succession, and Old Edwardians was the only Midlands club defeated. There was more consistency of selection with 33 players used, but all too often the team under-preformed. Defence was far from flawless, but the main weakness was in attack.

There was some controversy over the fixture at Stroud, which coincided with an outbreak of smallpox in Gloucester – more than one thousand supporters travelled, to be greeted by posters advising the citizens of "Gotham" not to mix with them, but all passed off satisfactorily. The last two games of the season were against Salford and Wigan, both of whom became professional Rugby League clubs that summer, as did Morecambe, played in the first game.

After a few games, a young Frank Watts was thrown in at the deep end against Newport, promoted from the A team at full-back. He kicked 20 of 33 conversion attempts, a high ratio for that era, but showed defensive frailties, and was eventually replaced by F.Miller, switched from centre. The three-quarter line never functioned smoothly and lacked aggression, but Walter Taylor stood out as by far the most accomplished player. G.T.Bourne, a youngster on the left wing, showed pace and pluck. Gorin Morgan, small in stature but agile and clever with a useful screw punt, was the pick of the half-backs, but the form of Arthur Stephens and Tommy Bagwell was in decline, and Tommy called it a day at the end of the season after 247 appearances and 63 tries, but continued to serve and inspire the Club for the rest of his life.

At their best and with first-choice players available, the pack looked very good in both scrums and loose play. Twice they played heroically against the might of Newport, but their form dropped off alarmingly in other matches. In the loose, J.R.Price, Albert Collins, William Pitt, "Nobby" Hall and Alfred Wellings were the most prominent, whilst the hardest workers in the tight were Charlie Williams, W.Leighton and the captain, John Hanman, who received much praise for his enthusiastic leadership, often in adversity. Injury to Albert Collins in March ended his career after 131 appearances.

Eight players were chosen to represent Gloucestershire. Walter Taylor, W.H.Devonshire and Albert Collins played for Western Counties against Midland Counties, and Walter Taylor also played in an England trial for London & Western Counties against Oxford and Cambridge.

Sep 15 Gloucester 20 Colts XX 0
Tries: W.Pitt, W.Leighton, A.Morgan, G.T.Bourne, G.Page, A.Stephens;
Conversion: J.Hanman

Sep 22 Gloucester 23 Next XVI 0
Tries: M.Thornett, A.Collins, C.Hall, A.Wellings, W.Pitt;
Conversions: J.Hanman (4)

Sep 24 Gloucester 14 Morecambe 3
Tries: A.Wellings, W.Pitt, C.Hall;
Conversion: J.Hanman;
Penalty: J.Hanman

Sep 29 Gloucester 9 Cardiff and District 5
Tries: W.Pitt, W.Devonshire, F.Miller

Oct 6 Penarth 9 Gloucester 6
Tries: W.Taylor (2)

Oct 13 Coventry 5 Gloucester 3
Try: W.Taylor

Oct 20 Swansea 4 Gloucester 4
Drop Goal: W.Taylor

Nov 3 Newport 8 Gloucester 0

Nov 10 Gloucester 3 Cardiff 14
Penalty: F.Watts

Nov 17 Bath v Gloucester - cancelled due to flooded pitch

Nov 24 Gloucester 16 Bristol 3
Tries: F.Miller (2), W.Taylor, G.T.Bourne;
Drop goal: W.Taylor

Dec 1 Moseley 4 Gloucester 3
Try: W.Taylor

Dec 15 Gloucester 0 Leicester 0

Dec 22 Old Edwardians 0 Gloucester 8
Tries: W.Taylor (2);
Conversion: F.Watts

Dec 26 Gloucester 10
Old Merchant Taylors 0
Tries: W.Taylor, F.Miller;
Conversions: F.Watts (2)

Dec 27 Gloucester 36
Kent Wanderers 5
Tries: W.Taylor (2), C.Williams, W.Leighton,
A.Collins, W.George, T.Bagwell, G.T.Bourne;
Conversions: F.Watts (6)

Dec 29 Gloucester 18 Clifton 0
Tries: A.Collins (3), C.Williams;
Conversions: F.Watts (3)

Jan 5 Gloucester v Derby - cancelled due to frost
Jan 12 Gloucester v Moseley - cancelled due to frost

Jan 19 Clifton 3 Gloucester 22
Tries: C.Williams, J.R.Price, A.Wellings,
W.Taylor, A.Cummings, G.T.Bourne
Conversions: F.Watts (2)

Feb 2 Coventry v Gloucester - cancelled due to frost
Feb 9 Gloucester v Bath - cancelled due to frost

Feb 16 Leicester 9 Gloucester 0

Feb 23 Gloucester 23
Old Edwardians 0
Tries: J.R.Price (2), C.Williams, T.Collins,
A.Stephens;
Conversions: F.Watts (4)

Mar 2 Bristol 0 Gloucester 0

Mar 9 Gloucester 3 Newport 12
Penalty: F.Watts

Mar 16 Gloucester 11
Weston-super-Mare 0
Tries: J.Hanman, G.T.Bourne, F.Miller;
Conversion: F.Watts

Mar 23 Cardiff 32 Gloucester 0

Mar 30 Gloucester 12
Middlesex Wanderers 10
Tries: W.Taylor (2), W.Pitt, D.Phelps

Apr 6 Gloucester 0 Swansea 9

Apr 13 Gloucester 3 Penarth 12
Try: G.T.Bourne

Apr 15 Gloucester 0 Salford 8

Apr 16 Gloucester 5 Wigan 0
Try: A.Cummings;
Conversion: E.Marsh

1895-96

Played 26 Won 8 Lost 12 Drawn 6
For 116 Against 165
Captain: Charlie Williams

Gloucester 'A'
Played 29 Won 13 Lost 13 Drawn 3
For 136 Against 108
Captain: A.D.Lansley

Most appearances: C.Williams 26, A.Morgan
C.Rose 25, F.Stout, C.Hall 24, A.Stephens 23,
A.F.Hughes, A.Wellings 22, W.Beard 20
Most tries: W.Taylor 10, A.Wellings 6,
W.H.Devonshire 4
Conversions: W.Taylor 4, A.Cummings 2,
W.Leighton 1
Penalty: J.Stephens 1

This was rated the most disastrous season experienced by the Club to date, with more losses than wins registered for the first time, and more points against than for. A miserly 33 tries were scored, and only seven were converted. This continued a decline which had been apparent for the previous three seasons, and disheartening results early on seemed to engender a continuing lack of belief amongst the team. The selection committee tried multiple combinations, using 43 players, but better results did not follow. A clique of players amongst the forwards decided to make themselves available only if all of them were selected, but their bluff was called by the selection committee, and the revolt lasted for only a few games.

There were no wins against Welsh opponents,

and The Citizen declared "the team has rarely risen above what one would expect from a decent second-class combination … the attack and defence have alike been exceptionally poor at times". And the season came to an abrupt end with the last six games cancelled because of an outbreak of smallpox.

The loyal veteran Arthur "Barley" Hughes was wheeled out of retirement at full-back and tried manfully, but eventually had to give way, retiring after 186 appearances. A successful combination could not be found at three-quarter. The form and availability of the best players, Walter Taylor and W.H.Devonshire, was inconsistent, William Pitt was dropped for refusal to train regularly, and G.T.Bourne left to join Cheltenham. But the appearance of new talent in George Clutterbuck and Percy Stout in the second half of the season offered future promise.

Arthur Stephens played outstandingly well at half-back, but received poor support from his partner, Gorin Morgan, and his three-quarters. He was tempted by an offer from a Rugby League club, but declined to sign professional forms.

Charlie Williams, the captain, appeared in every fixture and showed untiring energy in a pack, in which Charlie Williams, "Nobby" Hall and Alfred Wellings also stood out, but Alfred retired part way through the season after 111 appearances. Charlie Rose and Frank Stout were useful acquisitions.

Eight players won caps for Gloucestershire, and "Nobby" Hall played for Western Counties against Midland Counties.

Sep 21 Gloucester 0
Cardiff & District 3

Sep 28 Leicester 6 Gloucester 0

Oct 5 Gloucester 22
Weston-super-Mare 0
Tries: W.H.Devonshire, W.Pitt, A.Cummings,
A.Wellings, G.J.Bourne, C.Rose;
Conversions: A.Cummings (2)

Oct 12 Cardiff 5 Gloucester 3
Try: W.H.Devonshire

Oct 19 Gloucester 9 Old Edwardians 3
Tries: A.Wellings (2);
Penalty: J.Stephens

Oct 26 Bristol 8 Gloucester 0

Nov 2 Gloucester 3 Newport 30
Try: W.Taylor

Nov 16 Gloucester 6 Stroud 0
Tries: W.Taylor, W.H.Devonshire

Nov 23 Coventry 6 Gloucester 0

Dec 7 Gloucester 0 Swansea 0

Dec 14 Bath 3 Gloucester 3

Try: A.Wellings

Dec 21 Gloucester 3 Moseley 3
Try: W.Taylor

**Dec 26 Gloucester 0
Old Merchant Taylors 0**

Dec 28 Gloucester 0 Llanelly 17

Jan 4 Gloucester 20 Leicester 12
Tries: A.Wellings (2), W.Taylor (2), P.Stout,
F.Miller;
Conversion: W.Leighton

**Jan 11 Devonport Albion 3
Gloucester 3**
Try: W.Taylor

Jan 18 Gloucester 14 Coventry 3
Tries: P.Stout (2), W.Taylor, F.Stout;
Conversion: W.Taylor

Jan 25 Old Edwardians 3 Gloucester 8
Tries: W.Taylor, W.Spiers;
Conversion: W.Taylor

Feb 1 Gloucester 6 Forest of Dean 8
Tries: W.Taylor, A.Stephens

Feb 8 Swansea 30 Gloucester 0

Feb 15 Gloucester 0 Bristol 6

Feb 22 Gloucester 0 Cardiff 8

Feb 29 Stroud 0 Gloucester 5
Try: W.H.Devonshire;
Conversion: W.Taylor

Mar 7 Gloucester 0 Bath 0

**Mar 14 Weston-super-Mare 3
Gloucester 8**
Tries: Taylor, J.Stephens;
Conversion: W.Taylor

Mar 21 Gloucester 3 Penarth 5
Try: C.Rose

Mar 28 Gloucester v Newport – cancelled owing to smallpox, as were the later matches against Llanelly, Skipton, Devonport Albion, Moseley and Penarth

1896-97

**Played 31 Won 18 Lost 8 Drawn 5
For 250 Against 131
Captain: Walter Taylor**

Gloucester 'A'
Played 26 For 15 Lost 4 Drawn 7
For 150 Against 91

Most appearances: C.Williams, A.H.Click 30, W.Taylor, C.Hall, C.Rose 28, A.Stephens 26, G.Clutterbuck 23, F.Stout, W.Spiers 22, P.Stout 21, C.Cummings 20
Most tries: G.Clutterbuck 9, W.Taylor 8, P.Stout 7, J.Barnes 6
Conversions: P.Stout 17, W.Taylor 5, G.Clutterbuck, A.Stephens, W.Spiers 1
Penalty: P.Stout 1
Drop goals: P.Stout, W.Taylor 2, C.Cummings 1

There was a welcome improvement in results compared with several previous seasons. The 18 wins were an improvement of eight over the previous season, and 59 tries were scored, up from 33. Results of the A team also improved despite having to call on 70 players during the season.

As usual there was a huge disparity between results against English teams and those against the Welsh. Only two defeats were suffered at the hands of English clubs, Moseley and Devonport Services – Gloucester lost two players during a very rough match against Moseley, which caused the fixtures for the following season to be cancelled. Two victories were achieved against Welsh opponents, and the triumph against the Welsh champions, Llanelly, was undoubtedly the highlight of the season.

The Scarlets arrived at Kingsholm on 3rd April 1897 with an unbeaten record and only a couple more fixtures left in the season. It was a thrilling match in which the Gloucester pack excelled. One of those forwards, Charles "Nobby" Hall, the eldest of seven brothers who played for Gloucester, "taking every advantage of a grand opening, scored a try near the posts amidst tumultuous cheering". Percy Stout kicked the conversion, but Llanelly replied with a try for Gloucester to lead 5-3 at half-time. Llanelly strained every nerve to save their record during the second half, but the Gloucester defence stood firm. Their captain, Walter Taylor, was carried shoulder-high from the field after the final whistle, and a smoking concert was held to celebrate the victory.

Seven players won County caps, and Frank Stout, in only his second season of rugby at the age of 20, was selected for three England trials and then became the first current Gloucester player to be capped by England, when he played against Wales on 9th January 1897. He retained his place against Ireland, and made his first appearance for the Barbarians.

Sep 26 Gloucester 12 Cheltenham 0
Tries: W.Taylor, G.Clutterbuck;
Conversion: W.Taylor;
Drop goal: C.Cummings

Oct 3 Gloucester 11 Old Edwardians 6
Tries: W.Taylor (2), W.Pitt;
Conversion: W.Taylor

Oct 10 Stroud 0 Gloucester 14
Tries: A.Stephens, W.Taylor, C.Cummings, C.Gamble;

Conversion: W.Taylor

Oct 17 Gloucester 8 Bristol 3
Tries: G.Clutterbuck (2);
Conversion: G.Clutterbuck

Oct 24 Gloucester 0 Cardiff 9

Oct 31 Cinderford 3 Gloucester 3
Try: W.Taylor

Nov 14 Penarth 0 Gloucester 0

Nov 21 Gloucester 8 Moseley 0
Tries: A.Finch (2);
Conversion: P.Stout

**Nov 28 Gloucester 5
Devonport Albion 5**
Try: C.Hall;
Conversion: P.Stout

Dec 5 Bath 0 Gloucester 14
Tries: P.Stout, C.Williams, G.Barton, A.Robbins;
Conversion: P.Stout

Dec 12 Gloucester 4 Swansea 5
Drop goal: W.Taylor

Dec 19 Newport 26 Gloucester 5
Try: J.G.Howarth;
Conversion: W.Taylor

**Dec 26 Gloucester 3
Old Merchant Taylors 0**
Try: B.Hough

Dec 28 Coventry 0 Gloucester 0

Jan 2 Old Edwardians 0 Gloucester 12
Tries: A.Stephens, C.Cummings;
Conversion: P.Stout;
Drop goal: P.Stout

Jan 9 Gloucester 0 Cinderford 0

Jan 16 Gloucester 25 Clifton 0
Tries: F.Stout (2), J.G.Howarth, A.H.Click,
G.Clutterbuck;
Conversion: P.Stout
Drop goals: P.Stout, W.Taylor

Jan 23 Gloucester v Coventry – cancelled due
to frost

Jan 30 Llanelly 12 Gloucester 3
Try: G.Clutterbuck

Feb 6 Gloucester 5 Penarth 0
Try: T.Hatherall;
Conversion: W.Taylor

Feb 13 Moseley 12 Gloucester 0

Feb 20 Cheltenham 0 Gloucester 14
Tries: P.Stout, A.H.Click, J.Barnes,
G.Clutterbuck;
Conversion: P.Stout

Feb 27 Swansea 20 Gloucester 5
Try: P.Stout;
Conversion: P.Stout

Mar 6 Gloucester 0 Newport 3

Mar 13 Bristol 0 Gloucester 3
Try: J.Barnes

Mar 20 Gloucester 11 Stroud 3
Tries: C.Cummings, J.Barnes, F.Stout;
Conversion: W.Spires

Mar 27 Cardiff v Gloucester - cancelled. Cardiff
ground suspended.

Apr 3 Gloucester 5 Llanelly 3
Try: C.Hall;
Conversion: P.Stout

Apr 10 Devonport Albion 13 Gloucester 3
Try: G.Clutterbuck

Apr 16 Gloucester 10 Manchester 5
Tries: T.Hatherall, A.H.Click;
Conversions: P.Stout (2)

Apr 17 Gloucester 27 Bath 0
Tries: P.Stout (2), W.Taylor, J.Barnes, A.Pitt,
A.H.Click, A.Stephens;
Conversions: P.Stout (3)

Apr 19 Gloucester 15 Broughton 3
Tries: J.Barnes, W.Taylor, G.Clutterbuck;
Conversions: P.Stout (3)

**Apr 24 Gloucester 25
North Gloucester Combination 0**
Tries: P.Stout (2), J.Barnes, G.Clutterbuck,
W.Taylor, Lewis Smith;
Conversions: P.Stout, A.Stephens;
Drop goal (from a mark): P.Stout

1897-98

H.W.Grimes (Hon.Sec) F.M.Stout C.Hall P.W.Stout C.Rose A.H.Click B.W.Bingle(Treas) F.W.Lovesy (Sec)
H.Haines(Trainer) F.Goulding G.Smith W.H.Taylor(Capt) F.M.Luce B.L.Watkins B.Hipwood
G.F.Clutterbuck A.Stephens C.Williams (C.Cummings - absent)

**Played 35 Won 24 Lost 5 Drawn 6
For 335 Against 120
Captain: Walter Taylor**

Gloucester 'A'
Played 25 Won 21 Lost 2 Drawn 2
For 473 Against 53
Captain: Ben Hough

Most appearances: C.Williams 33,
C.Rose W.Taylor 32, A.H.Click 31, C.Hall
G.Clutterbuck L.Watkins 29, F.Goulding,
C.Cummings 27
Most tries: W.Taylor 16, G.Clutterbuck 12,
P.Stout 11, F.Stout, L.Watkins 5
Conversions: P.Stout 27, G.Romans 4, W.Taylor

2, F.Stout, A.Stephens, G.Clutterbuck 1
Penalties: P.Stout 5, W.Taylor, G.Clutterbuck 1
Drop goals: P.Stout, G.Clutterbuck 2,
W.Taylor 1

One of the best seasons in its history restored
the Club to a position as one of the strongest
in the country. No other club kept an unbeaten

record into the New Year. And Gloucester was the only English club to go through the season unbeaten by another English club. The record against Welsh clubs was much improved with four wins, five losses, and four drawn games. Cardiff was the only Welsh club to win at Kingsholm, but there was sweet revenge in the return fixture in Cardiff, when the hosts were denied their unbeaten ground record.

The number of tries scored rose to 74, and the goal-kicking improved with Percy Stout converting 27 out of 53 attempts. Success on the pitch attracted large crowds and record gate receipts, which left Club finances in a very healthy state. And the A team lost only two of 25 fixtures.

Ben Hipwood started the season as the regular full-back, but a promising newcomer was found in George Romans. Walter Taylor was a unifying captain, the leading try-scorer and led a very strong three-quarter line. George Clutterbuck added strength, and latterly Frank Luce fresh impetus. But Percy Stout at centre emerged as the star of the team - a strong runner, a sensational kicker, and a fearless and sure tackler, he was rated as the finest three-quarter ever to have played for the Club. He had a field day against Weston with 32 points from four tries, five conversions, two penalties and a dropped goal.

Arthur Stephens and Car Cummings were a capable pairing at half-back. This was Arthur's swan song – he retired early in the following season after 144 appearances. The forwards pack outshone opponents in the loose and lineouts, although sometimes bettered in scrums. The core of the pack – Frank Stout, "Nobby" Hall, Fred Goolding, Fred Click, Albert Pitt and Lewis Watkins – also formed the heart of a more successful County side.

Frank and Percy Stout won England caps, Frank first playing against Ireland and then Percy joining him to play against Scotland and Wales. Both scored tries against Wales, the first time that brothers had scored in the same match for England. Fred Goolding had an England trial for the South against the North. Twelve players won caps for Gloucestershire.

Sep 18 Goucester 14 Clifton 0
Tries: G.Clutterbuck (2), F.Stout, J.Stephens;
Conversion: A.Stephens

Sep 25 Gloucester 26 Cheltenham 0
Tries: W.Taylor (2), P.Stout (2),
G.Clutterbuck (2);
Conversions: P.Stout (4)

Oct 2 Gloucester 21 Coventry 0
Tries: J.Roberts (2), W.Taylor, G.Clutterbuck;
Conversions: P.Stout (4);
Penalty: P.Stout

Oct 9 Gloucester 18 Old Edwardians 0
Tries: F.Stout, F.Goolding, W.Taylor, J.Cook;
Conversions: P.Stout (3)

Oct 16 Stroud 0 Gloucester 3
Try: C.Williams

Oct 23 Bristol 0 Gloucester 3
Penalty: P.Stout

Oct 30 Gloucester 6 Penarth 0
Tries: A.H.Click, W.Taylor

Nov 6 Clifton 3 Gloucester 13
Tries: C.Rose, A.H.Click, G.Clutterbuck;
Conversions: G.Romans (2)

Nov 13 Cinderford 0 Gloucester 14
Tries: F.Stout (2), L.Watkins, G.Clutterbuck;
Conversion: P.Stout

Nov 20 Cheltenham 0 Gloucester 3
Penalty: W.Taylor

Nov 27 Gloucester 0 Llanelly 0

Dec 4 Bath 0 Gloucester 11
Tries: C.Williams, F.Oswell, W.Taylor;
Conversion: G.Romans

Dec 11 Gloucester 0 Newport 0

Dec 18 Gloucester 3 Swansea 3
Try: H.Broady

**Dec 27 Gloucester 21
Old Merchant Taylors 0**
Tries: C.Williams, F.Stout, W.Taylor, P.Stout,
G.Clutterbuck;
Conversions: P.Stout (2), F.Stout

**Jan 1 Devonport Albion 0
Gloucester 0**

Jan 8 Gloucester 11 Bath 0
Tries: C.Williams, A.Stephens, J.Cook;
Conversion: G.Romans

Jan 15 Swansea 19 Gloucester 3
Try: W.Taylor

Jan 22 Gloucester 5 Old Edwardians 0
Try: W.Taylor;
Conversion: G.Clutterbuck

Jan 29 Llwynypia 6 Gloucester 5
Try: C.Hall;

Conversion: P.Stout

Feb 5 Gloucester 0 Cardiff 10

Feb 12 Llanelly 18 Gloucester 0

**Feb 19 Gloucester 3
Devonport Albion 0**
Try: W.Taylor

Feb 26 Stroud 3 Gloucester 20
Tries: W.Taylor, G.Clutterbuck, C.Smith;
Penalty: G.Clutterbuck;
Drop goals: W.Taylor, G.Clutterbuck

Mar 5 Gloucester 5 Bristol 0
Try: L.Watkins;
Conversion: W.Taylor

Mar 12 Newport 24 Gloucester 0

Mar 16 Plymouth 4 Gloucester 12
Tries: G.Clutterbuck, W.Taylor;
Conversion: P.Stout;
Drop goal: P.Stout

**Mar 19 Gloucester 50
Weston-super-Mare 0**
Tries: P.Stout (4); F.M.Luce (2), C.Smith,
W.Dovey, L.Watkins, F.Oswell;
Conversions: P.Stout (5);
Penalties: P.Stout (2);
Drop goal: P.Stout

Mar 26 Gloucester 3 Cinderford 0
Penalty: P.Stout

Apr 2 Cardiff 5 Gloucester 9
Try: G.Clutterbuck;
Conversion: W.Taylor;
Drop goal: G.Clutterbuck

Apr 8 Gloucester 8 Rockcliff 8
Tries: W.Taylor (2);
Conversion: P.Stout

Apr 9 Gloucester 8 Llwynypia 3
Tries: P.Stout, L.Watkins;
Conversion: P.Stout

Apr 11 Gloucester 8 Penygraig 5
Tries: P.Stout, A.Stephens;
Conversion: P.Stout

**Apr 12 Weston-super-Mare 3
Gloucester 23**
Tries: F.Stout, P.Stout, L.Watkins, F.M.Luce;
Conversions: P.Stout (4)

Apr 16 Penarth 6 Gloucester 6
Tries: W.Taylor, G.Clutterbuck

1898-99

Played 34 Won 27 Lost 6 Drawn 1
For 300 Against 116
Captain: Walter Taylor

Gloucester 'A'
Played 29 Won 17 Lost 7 Drawn 5
For 292 Against 100
Captain: Ben Hough

There are six games in mid-season, for which the teams and scorers are not known, so appearances, top try scorers etc. are taken from the season summary published in the Citizen on 18th April 1899.

Most appearances: G.Romans 34, F.Click 32, W.Taylor 31, G.Hall 30, G.Smith 29, C.Hall 25, J.Lewis 24, F.Stout, F.Goolding 23
Most tries: W.Taylor 14, P.Stout 7
Conversions: P.Stout 13, G.Collett, J.Cook 5, G.Romans 4, G.Clutterbuck, W.Taylor 2, F.Stout 1
Drop goals: J.Cook 2, G.Romans, P.Stout, W.Taylor 1

A team united under the captaincy of the popular Walter Taylor achieved a record total of 27 victories, with a series of notable triumphs in the second half of the season, against both English and Welsh clubs. Swansea, Cardiff and Newport were all vanquished at Kingsholm, but the highlight was the first win at Llanelly. When the team arrived back at Gloucester late that night they were greeted by a large crowd and a band, and were carried through a City celebrating with coloured lights and fireworks.

The only losses to English clubs came against Blackheath and Leicester. Gloucester could also lay claim to being champions of Gloucestershire with nine wins and a draw, including a comprehensive double over Bristol. Consistency of selection helped, with 34 players used, significantly fewer than in previous seasons. Club finances benefited from consistently large gates.

George Romans developed into a fine full-back, performing particularly well under intense pressure from Welsh opponents. Walter Taylor led the line well, produced some sensational runs, was top try scorer for the eighth time in nine seasons, and went past the milestone of 100 tries. The brilliant Percy Stout was available for fewer than half of the matches, but his defence in particular received rave reviews. Coming back from injury later in the season, George Clutterbuck was dangerous in attack and a determined tackler, paired in the centre with Jim Cook, who was a "box of tricks".

The retirement of Arthur Stephens early on gave Dicky Goddard the opportunity to establish himself as partner to George Hall at half-back.

Gloucester had a pack which could perform splendidly, but was inconsistent. Charlie Rose retired mid-season after 114 appearances, and Charlie Williams later with 224 appearances. Fresh blood was introduced in the New Year with great success, particularly against Welsh opposition. Fred Goolding was the pick of the forwards, hard in the scrum, fast and clever in the loose, and an enthusiastic tackler. Experienced players who did well were "Nobby" Hall, Frank Stout and Fred Click, and promising newcomers included Fred Oswell and Harry Manley.

Sixteen players represented Gloucestershire. Fred Goolding earned an England trial for South versus North, and Percy and Frank Stout each played in three trials, before they both won further England caps against Ireland and Scotland, and Percy another against Wales. In the summer Frank toured Australia with the British Lions, played in all 21 matches and was captain for the three Tests which were won. Percy left the country to work in Egypt.

Sep 17 Gloucester 18 Clifton 0
Tries: F.Stout (2), G.Smith, F.Goolding;
Conversions: P.Stout (3)

Sep 24 Gloucester 16 Coventry 0
Tries: P.Stout, W.Taylor, G.Clutterbuck, L.Watkins;
Conversions: P.Stout (2)

Oct 1 Gloucester 14 Old Edwardians 0
Tries: P.Stout, F.M.Luce, G.Smith, C.Williams;
Conversion: P.Stout

Oct 8 Gloucester 5 Blackheath 6
Try: P.Stout;
Conversion: P.Stout

Oct 15 Cardiff 14 Gloucester 5
Try: P.Stout;
Conversion: P.Stout

Oct 22 Gloucester 6 Exeter 0
Tries: W.Taylor, H.Manley

Oct 29 Gloucester 18 Bristol 0
Tries: W.Taylor (2), P.Stout, J.Lewis;
Conversions: P.Stout (3)

Nov 5 Cheltenham 0 Gloucester 8
Scorers unknown

Nov 12 Gloucester 3 Aberavon 0
Try: F.Click

Nov 19 Clifton 4 Gloucester 6
Tries: F.Oswell, W.Taylor

Nov 26 Bath 0 Gloucester 18
Scorers unknown

Dec 3 Gloucester 5 Llanelly 14
Scorers unknown

Dec 10 Swansea 26 Gloucester 0

Dec 17 Gloucester 17 Stroud 5
Scorers unknown

Dec 24 Old Edwardians 3 Gloucester 5
Scorers unknown

Dec 26 Gloucester 5
Old Merchant Taylors 4
Try: G.F.Collett;
Conversion: G.F.Collett

Dec 27 Gloucester 5 Cinderford 3
Try: W.Taylor;
Conversion: G.F.Collett

Dec 31 Gloucester 11 Cheltenham 0
Try: W.Taylor (other scorers unknown)

Jan 7 Coventry 0 Gloucester 8
Tries: C.Hall, F.Click;
Conversion: G.Collett

Jan 14 Llanelly 3 Gloucester 6
Tries: P.Stout, R.Goddard

Jan 21 Newport 4 Gloucester 0

Jan 28 Gloucester 8 Bath 0
Tries: W.Dovey, W.Taylor;
Conversion: G.Romans

Feb 4 Gloucester 4 Swansea 3
Drop goal: J.Cook

Feb 11 Exeter 0 Gloucester 4
Drop goal: P.Stout

Feb 18 Gloucester 5 Cardiff 3
Try: B.Parham;
Conversion: P.Stout

Feb 25 Stroud 0 Gloucester 10
Tries: C.Smith, G.Clutterbuck;
Drop goal: W.Taylor

Mar 4 Gloucester 6 Leicester 5
Tries: G.Clutterbuck, W.Taylor

Mar 11 Gloucester 11 Newport 0
Tries: H.Manley, W.Taylor, J.Lewis;
Conversion: G.Clutterbuck

Mar 18 Bristol 5 Gloucester 9
Tries: P.Stout, G.Clutterbuck, G.Hall

Mar 25 Gloucester 5 Llwynypia 0
Try: F.Stout;
Conversion: P.Stout

Apr 1 Gloucester 18 Northampton 8
Tries: J.Lewis (2), C.Hall, W.Taylor;
Conversion: J.Cook;

Drop goal: J.Cook

Apr 3 Gloucester 37 Ashford House 0
Tries: C.Smith (2), G.Hall (2), B.Parham,
W.Dovey, F.Stout, C.Hall, W.Taylor;
Conversions: W.Taylor (3), J.Cook (2)

Apr 8 Cinderford 0 Gloucester 0

Apr 15 Leicester 6 Gloucester 4
Drop goal: G.Romans

1899-1900

Played 32 Won 23 Lost 7 Drawn 2
For 406 Against 110
Captain: Walter Taylor

Gloucester 'A'
Played 24 Won 17 Lost 4 Drawn 3
For 341 Against 90
Captain: Ben Hough

Most appearances: H.Manly 31, A.H.Click,
G.Hall 30, G.Romans, F.Oswell, J.Lewis 29,
C.Smith 28, R.Goddard, G.H.Smith 27, C.Hall,
A.Hawker 24
Most tries: W.Taylor 15, J.Cook, C.Smith 9,
J.Lewis, Lewis Smith 8
Conversions: G.Romans 41, J.Cook 8,
R.Goddard, J.Stephens 1
Penalty: G.Romans 1
Drop goals: G.Clutterbuck 3, J.Cook 1

Gloucester were unbeaten by any other English
club, with a points difference of 322-21 from
19 games, and could therefore rightly claim
to be the strongest in the country. Blackheath
and Leicester lowered Gloucester colours the
previous season, so satisfaction was taken
from beating both away from home, with the
defensive performance at Blackheath judged the
best of the season. There was a large increase
in try scoring with 72, and, with two narrow
victories over Bristol, Gloucester again claimed
the title of champion club of the County. As so
often it was the Welsh who proved much more
troublesome.

The playing strength took a hit with the
retirement of the Stout brothers, and with Fred
Goolding being called up to serve in the Boer
War. With some supporters also being called up,
gate receipts were down. However, a successful
season was underpinned by continuity of
selection with only 33 players used, and by the
goal kicking of George Romans, who landed 41
kicks from 70 attempts, thought to be the best
ratio in the country.

Romans was consistently brilliant at full-
back. Walter Taylor was yet again the pick of
the back line, well supported by "Whacker"
Smith, an extraordinarily strong right wing
and destructive tackler, George Clutterbuck,
dashing and resourceful, and "Jummer"
Stephens, a clever new recruit. Dicky Goddard
and George Hall were a first-class pairing at
half-back, never bettered by their opponents.

The forwards were not quite as strong as
previously, principally because of the loss of
Fred Goolding. Although they lacked a little
in weight, there was a solid base of experience
with "Nobby" Hall, Fred Click, Harry Manley,
Fred Oswell, George Smith and Jack Lewis, who
was the best of them, his play in the loose being
immense.

Much pride was taken in the allocation of
an international match, England v Wales, to
Kingsholm for the first time in January 1900,
but no Gloucester players were involved, and it
was a financial disaster for the Club. By way of
compensation a match against the Barbarians
was arranged.

Twelve players represented Gloucestershire,
and George Romans and "Nobby" Hall were
selected to play for the South in an England trial.

Sep 16 Gloucester 30 Clifton 8
Tries: W.H.Taylor (3), F.Goolding (2),
G.Clutterbuck (2), J.Lewis;
Conversions: J.Cook (3)

Sep 23 Gloucester 21 Bath 0
Tries: J.Cook (2), W.H.Taylor, R.Goddard,
Lewis Smith;
Conversions: 3 (kicker not recorded, but
probably J.Cook)

Sep 30 Gloucester 14
Old Edwardians 0
Tries: A.H.Click, W.H.Taylor, H.Manley,
F.Goolding;

Conversion: J.Cook

Oct 7 Blackheath 4 Gloucester 5
Try: J.Cook;
Conversion: R.Goddard

Oct 14 Gloucester 4 Cinderford 0
Drop goal from mark: J.Cook

Oct 21 Gloucester 0 Swansea 10

Oct 28 Bristol 0 Gloucester 3
Try: W.Hayward

Nov 4 Gloucester 10 Cheltenham 0
Tries: J.Cook, J.Stephens;
Conversions: G.Romans (2)

Nov 11 Gloucester 0 Cardiff 5

Nov 18 Bath 0 Gloucester 20
Tries: Lewis Smith (2), J.Lewis, A.Hawker;
Conversions: G.Romans (4)

Nov 25 Gloucester 22 Stroud 0
Tries: Lewis Smith (2), J.Cook, G.H.Smith,
G.Hall, J.Lewis;
Conversions: J.Cook, J.Stephens

Dec 2 Coventry 0 Gloucester 0

Dec 9 Newport 8 Gloucester 0

Dec 23 Clifton 0 Gloucester 27
Tries: J.Cook (2), R.Goddard (2), C.Smith,
A.Hawker, B.Hough;
Conversions: G.Romans (3)

Dec 26 Gloucester 16
Old Merchant Taylors 3
Tries: R.Goddard, G.H.Smith, Lewis Smith,
C.Hall;
Conversions: G.Romans (2)

Dec 27 Gloucester 21 Cinderford 0
Tries: J.Cook (2), C.E.Miller, C.Smith, J.Lewis;

Conversions: 3 [kicker not recorded, but probably G.Romans]

Dec 30 Gloucester 26 Penarth 0
Tries: C.Smith (2), C.Hall, R.Goddard, G.Romans, F.Oswell;
Conversions: G.Romans (4)

Jan 13 Swansea 27 Gloucester 4
Drop goal: G.Clutterbuck

Jan 20 Gloucester 7 Llanelly 3
Try: Lewis Smith;
Drop goal: G.Clutterbuck

Jan 27 Leicester 3 Gloucester 10
Tries: A.Hawker, Lewis Smith;
Drop goal: G.Clutterbuck

Feb 3 Northampton v Gloucester – abandoned
Feb 10 Gloucester v Coventry – abandoned

Feb 17 Cheltenham 0 Gloucester 21
Tries: C.Smith, T.Spiers, G.Clutterbuck, J.Lewis, W.H.Taylor;
Conversions: G.Romans (3)

Feb 24 Gloucester 0 Leicester 0

Mar 3 Cardiff 16 Gloucester 0

Mar 10 Gloucester 5 Newport 8
Try: W.Spiers;
Conversion: G.Romans

Mar 17 Stroud 3 Gloucester 43
Tries: W.Taylor (4), G.Hall (3), C.Smith (2), A.H.Click, F.Westbury;
Conversions: G.Romans (5)

Mar 24 Gloucester 3 Bristol 0
Try: C.Hill

Mar 31 Penarth 4 Gloucester 16
Tries: A.Hawker, G.Smith, G.Clutterbuck;

Conversions: G.Romans (2);
Penalty: G.Romans

Apr 7 Cinderford 0 Gloucester 21
Tries: W.Taylor, G.Clutterbuck, J.Gough, C.Hall, J.Stephens;
Conversions: G.Romans (3)

Apr 12 Gloucester 13 Barbarians 0
Tries: C.Smith, A.H.Click, J.Lewis;
Conversions: G.Romans (2)

Apr 14 Gloucester 26 Treherbert 0
Tries: W.Taylor (2), C.Smith, R.Goddard, G.Hall, G.Clutterbuck;
Conversions: G.Romans (4)

Apr 16 Gloucester 18 Carlisle 0
Tries: W.H.Taylor (2), J.Lewis (2);
Conversions: G.Romans (3)

Apr 17 Llanelly 8 Gloucester 0

1900-01

S.Bingle(Sec) H.W.Grimes(Hon.Sec) T.Spiers F.Oswell A.Hawker C.Hall J.Lewis F.Click C.N.Dancey(Hon.Treas) T.Bagwell(Trainer)
J.Gough C.Smith J.Cook G.Romans(Capt) J.Stephens G.F.Clutterbuck C.Miller
R.Goddard G.Hall

Played 34 Won 24 Lost 5 Drawn 5
For 522 Against 75
Captain: George Romans

Gloucester 'A'
Played 25 Won 16 Lost 7 Drawn 2
For 205 Against 73
Captain: George Barnes

Most appearances: J.Cook, R.Goddard 33, G.Hall 32, F.Oswell 30, T.Spiers 29, J.Stephens, J.Lewis 27, G.Romans, A.Hawker 26, G.Clutterbuck, J.Gough 25
Most tries: G.Clutterbuck 23, J.Cook 19, C "Whacker" Smith 15, J.Lewis 12, R.Goddard 10
Conversions: G.Romans 55, R.Goddard 6, W.Gardner 5
Penalties: G.Romans 2, W.Gardner 1
Drop goals: G.Romans, R.Goddard, S.S.Harris 1

The finances of the Club were still in a parlous state as a result of the losses made on the international match staged at Kingsholm earlier in 1900, but three members came to the rescue by guaranteeing the Club's overdraft. In an attempt to restore the Club's finances, three matches were made all-pay, but this caused a drop in membership. The best gate was from the match against Newport, and the Club made a profit of £191 on the season.

The two most successful clubs in England this

season were Gloucester and Devon Albion. Gloucester set a number of Club records. For the first time they went through a season unbeaten at Kingsholm with 17 wins and two draws, and of the five defeats away, four were in Wales and only one in England, to Richmond. This was the culmination of a very successful 4-season period against other English clubs, during which Gloucester won 78, lost 3 and drew 7.

George Clutterbuck broke the Club's individual try scoring record with 23, and Jim Cook with 19 also beat the previous record of 18 set by George Coates and Walter Taylor. In total 123 tries were scored and 522 points scored – also new Club records.

Highlights of the season were the home wins against Llanelly, Cardiff and Swansea, although a draw against Newport prevented a clean sweep against the best of the Welsh. The defeat of Llanelly was perhaps the most notable, including a hat trick of tries by Lewis Smith.

Important elements in the success of the Club were the kicking of George Romans and the three-quarter quartet of George Clutterbuck, Jimmy "Jummer" Stephens, Jim Cook and "Whacker" Smith, who played exceptionally well in combination, not just with attacking flair and pace, but also scything opponents down with deadly tackling.

The half-back pairing of Dicky Goddard and George Hall, affectionately known as "the midgets", were effective in opening out the game and were supplied with plenty of ball by a pack which was outstanding in the loose but occasionally struggled in the set scrum. They were led by "Nobby" Hall, but also prominent were Fred Click, a veteran, and Bill Spiers, a newcomer.

England caps were won by "Nobby" Hall against Ireland and Scotland and by "Whacker" Smith against Wales; George Romans had a trial and was reserve for two England matches, and Dicky Goddard and "Jummer" Stephens also had trials.

Sep 15 Gloucester 66 Clifton 0
Tries: G.Clutterbuck (6), J.Lewis (3), C.Smith (2), F.Stout (2), J.Cook, R.Goddard, J.Stephens;
Conversions: G.Romans (9)

Sep 22 Penarth 0 Gloucester 0

**Sep 29 Gloucester 27
Old Edwardians 0**
Tries: C.Smith (3), G.Clutterbuck (2), J.Cook;
Conversions: G.Romans (3);
Penalty: G.Romans

Oct 6 Stroud 0 Gloucester 33
Tries: G.Clutterbuck (3), J.Cook, R.Goddard, G.Romans, J.Lewis;
Conversions: G.Romans (4)
Drop goal: G.Romans

Oct 13 Gloucester 35 Coventry 0
Tries: J.Cook (3), C.Hall (2), G.Clutterbuck, C.Smith;
Conversions: G.Romans (5);
Drop goal from mark: G.Romans

Oct 20 Swansea 13 Gloucester 3
Penalty: G. Romans

Oct 27 Gloucester 14 Bristol 0
Tries: C.Smith, A.Hawker;
Conversions: G.Romans (2);
Drop goal: R.Goddard

Nov 3 Gloucester 34 Stroud 3
Tries: S.S.Harris (2), T.Spiers (2), E.T.James, J.Stephens, W.Taylor, J.Lewis;
Conversions: W.Gardner (3);
Field goal: S.S.Harris

Nov 10 Richmond 3 Gloucester 0

Nov 17 Cardiff 3 Gloucester 0

Nov 24 Bath 0 Gloucester 10
Tries: J.Cook, W.Taylor;
Conversions: W.Gardner (2)

Dec 1 Gloucester 9 Cheltenham 5
Tries: R.Goddard, J.Cook, J.Gough

Dec 8 Gloucester 0 Newport 0

Dec 15 Gloucester 17 Northampton 0
Tries: Lewis Smith (2), J.Cook, W.Taylor, R.Goddard;
Conversion: G.Romans

Dec 22 Gloucester 10 Blackheath 0
Tries: J.Cook, C.E.Miller;
Conversions: G.Romans (2)

**Dec 26 Gloucester 0
Old Merchant Taylors 0**

Dec 29 Gloucester 25 Treorchy 0
Tries: Lewis Smith (2), C.E.Miller, G.H.Smith, A.Hawker, F.Luce, G.Clutterbuck;
Conversions: G.Romans (2)

Jan 5 Old Edwardians 0 Gloucester 23
Tries: J.Lewis (2), R.Goddard, G.Hall, J.Stephens;
Conversions: R.Goddard (4)

Jan 12 Gloucester 33 Bath 0
Tries: G.Clutterbuck (2), J.Cook (2), C.Hall, A.Hawker, R.Goddard;
Conversions: G.Romans (6)

Jan 19 Leicester 0 Gloucester 5
Try: C Smith;
Conversion: G.Romans

Feb 9 Clifton 3 Gloucester 64
Tries: G.Clutterbuck (3), J.Lewis (3), G.Hall (2), J.Gough, C.E.Miller, R.Goddard, F.Oswell, A.Hawker, J.Cook;
Conversions: G.Romans (11)

Feb 16 Gloucester 15 Llanelly 0
Tries: Lewis Smith (3), J.Cook, G.Clutterbuck

Feb 23 Llanelly 8 Gloucester 0

Mar 2 Gloucester 11 Cardiff 3
Tries: G.Clutterbuck, J.Cook (2);
Conversion: G.Romans

Mar 9 Newport 9 Gloucester 0

Mar 16 Gloucester 19 Penarth 0
Tries: C.Smith (2), G.Hall, G.Clutterbuck, C.E.Miller;
Conversions: G.Romans (2)

Mar 23 Bristol 3 Gloucester 3
Try: C.Smith

Mar 30 Cheltenham 0 Gloucester 16
Tries: G.Clutterbuck (2); R.Goddard, J.Lewis;
Conversions: G.Romans (2)

Apr 5 Gloucester 14 Rockcliff 3
Tries: G.Smith, C.Hall, C.Smith (2);
Conversion: G.Romans

Apr 6 Gloucester 6 Leicester 0
Tries: J.Cook, R.Goddard

Apr 8 Gloucester 5 Treherbert 3
Try: C.Smith;
Conversion: G.Romans

Apr 13 Gloucester 6 Swansea 3
Tries: J.Lewis, R.Goddard

Apr 20 Treherbert 3 Gloucester 3
Try: J.Cook

**Apr 27 Northampton 10
Gloucester 16**
Tries: C.Smith, C.Hall, J.Cook;
Conversions: R.Goddard (2); Penalty: W.Gardner

A.Purton J.Jewell A.H.Click W.Essex G.F.Collett F.Westbury T.Spiers T.Bagwell(Trainer) C.H.Dancey(Treas)
L.Smith R.Goddard F.Oswell C.Hall G.Romans(Capt) G.H.Smith G.Hall B.Parham
J.Stephens C.Smith

Played 34 Won 24 Lost 7 Drawn 3
For 542 Against 103
Captain: George Romans

Gloucester 'A'
Played 19 Won 15 Lost 4
For 204 Against 70
Captain: George Barnes

Most appearances: J.Steohens, G.Hall 31,
A.H.Click F.Westbury 30, G.Romans 29,
F.Oswell 28, C. Hall, C."Whacker" Smith 27
Most tries: C."Whacker" Smith 29, Lewis
Smith 10, G.Hall, C.Hall, F.Oswell 9
Conversions: G.Romans 52, W.H.Taylor,
L.Vears 2, W.Gardner 1
Penalties: G.Romans 4, G.F.Collett 1
Drop goals: G.Romans, L.F.Morgan 1

Although not quite as successful as the previous
season, the results were remarkably good in view
of a succession of injuries. George Clutterbuck
was injured early in the season, which proved
his last after 131 appearances. "Whacker" Smith,
Lewis Smith, Dicky Goddard and Bill Spiers were
all injured for significant periods. With Jim Cook
falling out with the committee for a while, and
the loss of Jack Lewis to Bristol and Cecil Miller
to Richmond, there was plenty of chopping and
changing with team selections. The veteran
Walter Taylor gallantly came out of retirement on
four occasions in the Club's hour of need.

Yet only one game was lost in the first half
of the season. A disrupted team and a poor
performance led to the loss of the long-standing
ground record to Leicester. But over five seasons
only six games out of 112 had been lost to
English opponents, with a points difference of
1,751 - 169.

Receipts for the Bristol match beat the record for
any Club match. New Club records for a single
match were set in the first game of the season
with the score of 74 and "Whacker's" eight tries.
Although defence had always been "Whacker's"
forte, this season he showed how formidable he
could be in attack as he set a new Club record
with 29 tries. Further Club records were broken
with the season points total of 542 and the tally
of 135 tries

Dicky Goddard, good at making openings, and
George Hall, snappy at the heels of the pack,
formed a brilliant combination at half-back. But
by the start of the following season both had left
Gloucester to go north to play Rugby League for
Hull.

"Nobby" Hall, who captained Gloucestershire
in their first County Championship final, acted
as vice-captain for his Club, and led a pack,
which was often out-weighted, but fast and
skilful in the loose. He retired at the end of the
season after 210 appearances. The experience

of Fred Click and Fred Oswell and the vigour
of a young Bert Parham frequently came to the
fore, whilst J.Jewell and F.Westbury established
places in the team.

The victory over Pontypridd was particularly
hard-earned - in a rough match, Gloucester lost
one player to injury early on and a second later,
so finished with 13 players. And one of the best
exhibitions of rugby brought success against
a strong London Welsh side led by the Welsh
international, Willie Llewellyn.

Gloucestershire reached the final of the County
Championship, which was lost 3-9 to Durham
at Kingsholm. Gloucester provided seven
players – "Nobby" Hall (captain), George
Romans, "Whacker" Smith, Lewis Smith,
Dicky Goddard, F.Westbury and Cecil Miller –
and 14 during the season as a whole.

George Romans, "Whacker" Smith, Jim Cook,
Dicky Goddard, George Hall and "Nobby" Hall
played for the Rest of South against London &
Varsities, "Nobby" played for South v North,
and George Romans and Dicky Goddard played
for the Rest against England

Sep 21 Gloucester 74 Clifton 0
Tries: C.Smith (8), F.Westbury (3), C.E.Miller
(2), F.Oswell (2), T.Spiers, G.Hall, J.Lewis;
Conversions: G.Romans (10)

**Sep 28 Gloucester 44
Old Edwardians 3**
Tries: G.Clutterbuck (3), C.Smith (2), T.Spiers
(2), F.Westbury, C.Hall, C.E.Miller;
Conversions: G.Romans (5); Goal from Mark:
G.Romans

Oct 5 Northampton 0 Gloucester 9
Tries: R.Cook, C.Smith, R.Goddard

Oct 12 Gloucester 0 Newport 0

Oct 19 Bristol 7 Gloucester 3
Try: C.E.Miller

Oct 26 Gloucester 14 Pontypridd 8
Tries: Lewis Smith (2), J.Stephens;
Conversion: G.Romans;
Penalty: G.Romans

Nov 2 Stroud 4 Gloucester 7
Drop goal: L.F.Morgan;
Penalty: G.F.Collett

Nov 9 Gloucester 8 Richmond 0
Tries: C.Smith, R.Goddard;
Conversion: G.Romans

Nov 16 Gloucester v Cardiff – cancelled to frost

Nov 23 Cheltenham 0 Gloucester 3
Try: W.Taylor

Nov 30 Gloucester 21 Bath 3
Tries: F.Oswell, A.H.Click, F.Rooke, G.Hall,
W.Taylor;
Conversions: W.Taylor (2), W.Gardner,

**Dec 4 Cambridge University 3
Gloucester 12**
Tries: Lewis Smith, J.Cook, F.Oswell, C.E.Miller

Dec 7 Gloucester 27 Coventry 5
Tries: J.Cook (2), C.Smith (2), L.Smith, G.Hall,
J.Stephens;
Conversions: G.Romans (3)

Dec 14 Gloucester 19 Penycraig 0
Tries: J.Merchant, A.James, L.Smith,
J.Stephens, T.Spiers;
Conversions: G.Romans (2)

Dec 21 Swansea v Gloucester – cancelled due
to hard ground

**Dec 26 Gloucester 5
Old Merchant Taylors 5**
Try: J.Cook;
Conversion: G.Romans

Dec 27 Bath 0 Gloucester 26
Tries; C.Smith (2), J.Jewell, F.Rooke, G.Hall;
Conversions: G.Romans (4);
Penalty: G.Romans

Dec 28 Gloucester 11 Penarth 3
Tries: C.Smith (2), G.Romans;
Conversion: G.Romans

Jan 4 Gloucester 11 Bridgwater 0
Tries: G.Romans (2);
Conversion: G.Romans;
Penalty: G.Romans

Jan 11 Clifton 3 Gloucester 20
Tries: C Hall, F.Westbury, B.Parham,
G.Romans, A.H.Click, A.S.F.Pruen;
Conversion: G.Romans

**Jan 18 Old Edwardians 0
Gloucester 30**
Tries: G.Clutterbuck, G.F.Collett, F.Rooke,
G.Hall, C.Hall (2), T.Spiers, F.Westbury;
Conversions: G.Romans (3)

Jan 25 Gloucester 0 Leicester 3

Feb 1 Gloucester 22 Lydney 0
Tries: G.F.Collett, C.Hall, G.Hall, F.Westbury,
J.Stephens, B.Parham;
Conversions: G.Romans (2)

Feb 8 Newport 18 Gloucester 0

Feb 18 Cardiff v Gloucester – cancelled due to

frost

Feb 22 Gloucester 44 Stroud 0
Tries: C.Smith (4), C.Hall (2), B.Parham,
G.F.Collett, G.Hall, F.Oswell;
Conversions: G.Romans (7)

Mar 1 Leicester 6 Gloucester 0

Mar 5 Cardiff 5 Gloucester 0

Mar 8 Gloucester 27 Northampton 0
Tries: C.Hall (2), L.Smith (2), G.Hall, F.Oswell,
C.Smith;
Conversions: G.Romans (3)

Mar 15 Gloucester 11 Bristol 6
Tries: G.Smith, L.Smith, R.Goddard;
Conversion: G.Romans

Mar 22 Coventry 0 Gloucester 22
Tries: C.Smith (2), A.H.Click, G.Smith,
R.Goddard, L.Smith;
Conversions: G.Romans (2)

Mar 28 Gloucester 14 London Welsh 3
Tries: C.Smith (2), A.Purton, B.Parham;
Conversion: G.Romans

Mar 29   Gloucester v Treherbert – cancelled
due to funeral of H.J.Boughton

Mar 31 Gloucester 24 Penarth 0
Tries: F.Oswell (3), C.Smith (2), G.Hall;
Conversions: G.Romans (3)

Apr 1 Plymouth 6 Gloucester 6
Try: A.Purton;
Penalty: G.Romans

Apr 12 Gloucester 0 Swansea 9

Apr 17 Gloucester 28 Cheltenham 0
Tries: F.Rooke (2), C.Smith, J.Stephens,
G.F.Collett, W.Johns, W.Essex, L.Vears
Conversions: L.Vears (2)

Apr 19 Gloucester 0 Cardiff 3

1902-03

**Played 35 Won 19 Lost 15 Drawn 1
For 381 Against 193
Captain: George Romans**

Gloucester 'A'
Played 26 Won 15 Lost 8 Drawn 3
For 185 Against 75
Captain: George Barnes

Most Appearances: B.Parham 33, C.Smith
G.Smith 32, A.Purton 29, G.Romans 28,
J.Stephens F.Keys A.Click 27, G.Collett
F.Westbury 25
Most tries: C.Smith 14, L.Smith B.Parham 8,
G.Collett F.Keys 7
Penalties: G.Romans 2, G.Collett 1
Conversions: G.Romans 30, A.Purton 4,
L.Vears 3, G.Collett, F.Pugh 1

Drop goals: G.Collett 2, G.Romans 1

After a succession of very successful seasons,
this one came as a considerable disappointment,
with not a single victory against any of the
leading Welsh clubs. Even worse perhaps were
the nine defeats suffered at the hands of English
clubs, more than the total lost in the previous
five years. The 15 defeats in total was a Club

T.Bagwell(Trainer) F.Westbury W.Johns A.Purton A.H.Click F.Pegler H.Harris H.Collins S.W.Bingle(Sec)
B.Parham F.Oswell L.Vears G.Romans(Capt) G.H.Smith A.Hudson F.Rooke
C.Smith F.Keys (A.Hawker J.Stephens J.Jewell G.F.Collett L.Morgan C.H.Dancey(Treas) — absent)

record, the previous worst being 12 in 1895-96.

The title of Champion Club of the County went to Bristol for the first time since that 1895-96 season, but their narrow victory on Easter Monday was tarnished by their recruitment of "strange players" from Swansea in order to strengthen their team for this crucial match. Gloucester were equally short of first team regulars, but chose to make up numbers with local players.

Throughout the season, the main problem was the inability to field a settled team. As a result many players had to be asked to play out of their normal position. Much of this stemmed from the loss of "Nobby" Hall as pack leader, George Hall and Dicky Goddard at half-back, and Jim Cook from the three-quarters, the latter three having signed for Rugby League clubs. Walter Taylor made his final appearance during this season, bringing his total to 249. It proved impossible to replace that wealth of experience and ability. Fred Click retired at the end of the season after 226 appearances, as did Fred Oswell with 133. But there was some hope for the future with new players coming through, most notably Arthur Hudson, who played his first game for the Club on 27th December, marking his debut with two tries in the victory over Cheltenham.

The most thrilling match of the season was against Cambridge University, when Gloucester

snatched victory at the last gasp. The Chronicle described the winning try: "some tricky play on the part of Stephens and "Whacker" Smith ending in the latter going over right under the posts, and a mighty cheer went up when Romans steered the oval through the legitimate aperture".

Sep 20 Gloucester 45 Clifton 0
Tries: L.Smith (4), F.Keys (2), G.Smith,
F.Goolding, W.Johns, G.Collett, F.Rooke
Conversions: G.Romans (6)

**Sep 27 Gloucester 48
Old Edwardians 0**
Tries: C.Smith (4), F.Westbury (2), J.Stephens (2), F.Goolding, F.Oswell, G.Smith, B.Parham;
Conversions: G.Romans (6)

Oct 4 Blackheath 10 Gloucester 3
Try: F.Westbury

Oct 11 Newport 16 Gloucester 0

Oct 18 Gloucester 3 Swansea 9
Try: B.Parham

Oct 25 Gloucester 6 Bristol 4
Penalty try;
Penalty: G.Romans

Nov 1 Gloucester 11 Stroud 0
Tries: F.Pyart, C.Smith, F.Rooke;

Conversion: L.Vears

Nov 8 Richmond 9 Gloucester 5
Try: G.Smith;
Conversion: G.Romans

Nov 15 Cardiff 6 Gloucester 0

Nov 22 Gloucester 22 Bath 3
Tries: G.Collett (3), C.Smith, B.Parham, F.Keys;
Conversions: A.Purton (2)

Nov 29 Clifton 0 Gloucester 8
Tries: L.Vears, C.Smith;
Conversion: A.Purton

6 Dec 6 Gloucester v Penarth - cancelled due to heavy frost

Dec 13 Gloucester 28 Bridgwater 3
Tries: F.Oswell (2), J.Stephens, A.Purton,
A.Hawker, L.Smith;
Conversions: G.Romans (3);
Drop goal: G.Collett

**15 Dec 15 Gloucester 5
Cambridge University 3**
Try: C.Smith;
Conversion: G.Romans

Dec 20 Bristol 14 Gloucester 5
Try: F.Keys;
Conversion: G.Romans

**Dec 26 Gloucester 8
Old Merchant Taylors 5**
Tries: L.Smith, B.Parham;
Conversion: G.Romans

Dec 27 Gloucester 14 Cheltenham 11
Tries: A.Hudson (2), B.Parham, L.Morgan;
Conversion: G.Romans

Jan 3 Gloucester 36 Coventry 0
Tries: L.Smith (2), F.Rooke (2), C.Smith (2),
G.Collett, J.Jewell, G.Smith, B.Parham;
Conversions: G.Collett, A.Purton, F.Pugh

Jan 10 Leicester 6 Gloucester 3
Try: A.Purton

17 Jan Old Edwardians v Gloucester - cancelled
due to frost

Jan 24 Coventry 0 Gloucester 5
Try: C.Smith;
Conversion: G.Romans

Jan 31 Gloucester 0 Newport 8

Feb 7 Gloucester 3 Bristol 5
Try: F.Oswell

Feb 13 Stroud 0 Gloucester 6
Tries: J.Stephens (2)

Feb 20 Swansea 32 Gloucester 3
Try: A.Hudson

Feb 25 Gloucester 7 Cardiff 16
Try: C.Smith;
Drop goal from mark: G.Collett

Mar 7 Gloucester 5 Leicester 9
Try: A.Click;
Conversion: G.Romans

Mar 14 Northampton 8 Gloucester 3
Penalty: G.Romans

Mar 21 Gloucester 14 Pontypridd 0
Tries: G.Collett (2), A.Hudson, L.Morgan;
Conversion: G.Romans

Mar 25 Cheltenham 6 Gloucester 6
Try: C.Smith;

Penalty: G.Collett

Apr 3 Gloucester 6 Northampton 0
Tries: L.Vears, F.Westbury

Apr 10 Gloucester 16 London Welsh 0
Tries: G.Williams (2), A.Purton, W.Johns;
Conversions; L.Vears (2)

Apr 11 Gloucester 11 Penygraig 0
Tries: H.Harris, B.Parham, F.Westbury;
Conversion: G.Romans

Apr 13 Bristol 5 Gloucester 0

Apr 14 Bath 0 Gloucester 26
Tries: F.Keys (2), B.Parham, C.Smith, F.Peglar,
G.Romans;
Conversions: G.Romans (4)

Apr 15 Plymouth 8 Gloucester 0

Apr 18 Penarth 3 Gloucester 20
Tries: F.Keys, F.Peglar, L.Vears, G.Williams;
Conversions: G.Romans (2);
Drop goal: G.Romans

1903-04

S.W.Bingle(Sec) J.Cromwell(Trainer) C.Smith F.Goulding G.Vears A.Hawker J.Gough A.Pegler T.Bagwell(Trainer) C.H.Dancey(Treas)
L.Vears G.Williams J.Harrison G.Romans(Capt) J.Stephens G.H.Smith B.Parham
W.Johns D.R.Gent (A.Purton — absent)

**Played 34, Won 18, Lost 14 Drawn 2
For 416 Against 200
Captain: George Romans**

Gloucester 'A'
Played 26 Won 11 Lost 8 Drawn 7

For 159 Against 130

Most appearances: J.Stephens 33, W.Johns 31,
C "Whacker" Smith 30, G.Romans 29, G.Vears,
B.Parham 28, F.Goolding, A.Purton, A.Hawker,
F.Pegler 27

Most tries: C "Whacker" Smith 19, J.Harrison
11, A.Hudson, J.Stephens, B.Parham,
G.Williams 8
Conversions: G.Romans 43, L.Vears 3, F.Pugh 2
Penalties: G.Romans 3
Drop goals: J.Harrison 2, O.Burgum 1

A moderate season started poorly, improved considerably in the New Year, and ended with a brilliant victory at Northampton. The improvement came when Jimmy Harrison, a centre from Lydney, G.Williams, a fly-half from Chepstow, and Dai Gent, a scrum-half from Cheltenham Training College, joined the Club and greatly strengthened the back division. As in many seasons the Welsh proved the most difficult opponents, and Penarth was the only Welsh side to be defeated. Generally, results against English clubs were much better, although the losses to Clifton and Cheltenham were regarded as low points, and only once previously had the Club suffered more than twelve defeats in a season.

A total of 47 players were selected, which reflected difficulties in finding players of adequate quality. The second season of indifferent performances affected attendances, so it was also a tough season financially. The Gloucester A side suffered a similarly poor season.

Jimmy "Jummer" Stephens was almost ever-present, but his position varied between centre, stand-off and scrum-half as required, and he was reliant on skill and experience rather than speed. "Whacker" Smith remained a threat and enjoyed a purple patch mid-season, but the lack of real speed merchants on the wings was a handicap. Arthur Hudson was tried but dropped, a surprise in view of his later successes. George Romans continued to captain the side and turn in good performances at full-back, but his powers were starting to wane as his long career was drawing to an end. However, one bright feature was the emergence of Ernie Hall as a young centre of real promise.

The pack was comprised mainly of old and experienced hands, led by Bert Parham, but a young Gordon Vears won a regular place. Although performing creditably as individuals, the forwards sometimes lacked cohesion and they were frequently beaten in the scrums. The resulting lack of possession lost a number of games.

Six players were capped by the County, and Fred Goolding played for the West against the Rest of the South.

Sep 12 Gloucester 5 Stroud 0
Try: F.Oswell;
Conversion: H Romans
Sep 19 Coventry 6 Gloucester 18
Tries: A.Hudson (2), C.Smith, B.Parham;
Conversions: L.Vears (3)

Sep 26 Gloucester 3 Clifton 5
Try: F.Westbury

Oct 3 Old Edwardians 3 Gloucester 13
Tries: L.Vears, A.Purton, J.Stephens;
Conversions: F.Pugh (2)

Oct 10 Gloucester 3 Newport 19
Try: B.Parham

Oct 17 Gloucester 0 Swansea 23

Oct 24 Gloucester 8 Bristol 10
Tries: C.Smith, W.John;
Conversion: G.Romans

**Oct 31 Devonport Albion 0
Gloucester 0**

Nov 14 Gloucester 0 Cardiff 18

Nov 21 Gloucester 25 Bath 0
Tries: G.Foulkes (2), F.Keys (2), C.Smith,
J.Gough;
Conversions: G.Romans (2);
Penalty: G.Romans

Nov 28 Cheltenham 8 Gloucester 3
Try: L.Vears

Dec 5 Gloucester 36 Old Edwardians 0
Tries: A.Hudson (3), B.Parham (2), C.Smith (2),
G.Williams (2), J.Stephens
Conversions: G.Romans (3)

Dec 12 Bristol 7 Gloucester 0

Dec 19 Gloucester 0 Blackheath 8

**Dec 26 Gloucester 11
Old Merchant Taylors 0**
Tries: G.H.Smith, L.Vears, J.Gough;
Conversion: G.Romans

Jan 2 Gloucester 23 Cheltenham 5
Tries: J.Harrison (2), G.H.Smith, G.Williams,
J.Stephens;
Conversions: G.Romans (4)

Jan 9 Clifton 0 Gloucester 49
Tries: C.Smith (6), F.Pegler, A.Hawker, D.Gent,
J.Stephens, A.Hudson;
Conversions: G.Romans (6);
Drop goal: J.Harrison

Jan 16 Gloucester 21 Leicester 0
Tries: C.Smith, G.Williams, W.Johns, J.Gough,
B.Parham;
Conversions: G.Romans (3)

Jan 23 Gloucester 59 Coventry 0

Tries: C.Smith (5), J.Harrison (3), A.Hudson
(2), G.Williams (2), J.Stephens
Conversions: G.Romans (10)

Jan 30 Newport 5 Gloucester 4
Drop Goal: J.Harrison

Feb 6 Gloucester 11 Bristol 0
Tries: F.Goolding, J.Harrison;
Conversion: G.Romans;
Penalty: G.Romans

**Feb 13 Gloucester 0
Devonport Albion 6**

Feb 20 Swansea 24 Gloucester 0

Feb 27 Cardiff 7 Gloucester 3
Try: L.Vears

Mar 5 Leicester 3 Gloucester 0

**Mar 12 Gloucester 11
Northampton 10**
Tries: G.H.Smith, M.Mills;
Conversion: G.Romans;
Penalty: G.Romans

Mar 19 Gloucester 17 Richmond 0
Tries: J.Harrison (2), G.Williams, C.Smith,
A.Hawker;
Conversion: G.Romans

Mar 26 Stroud 5 Gloucester 26
Tries: T.Leonard (4), J.Stephens, B.Parham;
Conversion: G.Romans (4)

Apr 1 Gloucester 14 London Welsh 3
Tries: O.Burgum, J.Harrison, B.Parham,
L.Vears;
Conversion: G.Romans

Apr 2 Gloucester 23 Penarth 5
Tries: G.Smith, G.Williams, J.Harrison,
G.Matthews, L.Vears;
Conversions: G.Romans (2);
Drop goal: O.Burgum

Apr 4 Bristol 0 Gloucester 6
Tries: C.Smith, J.Stephens

Apr 5 Gloucester 8 Bath 8
Tries: Cecil Biggs, D.Gent;
Conversion: G.Romans

Apr 9 Penarth 12 Gloucester 0

Apr 16 Gloucester 16 Northampton 0
Tries: B.Parham, J.Harrison, F.Goolding,
J.Stephens;
Conversions: G.Romans (2)

S.W.Bingle(Sec) W.H.Rasbach(Committee) F.Pegler W.Johns G.Vears A.Hawker F.Oswell G.Matthews A.Cromwell(Trainer) W.H.Worth(Treas)
T.Bagwell(Trainer) L.Vears F.Goulding J.Harrison G.Romans(Capt) C.Smith J.Stephens T.Leonard B.Parham G.H.Smith
D.R.Gent C.H.Robinson

**Played 36 Won 23 Lost 11 Drawn 2
For 499 Against 155
Captains: George Romans and Billy
Johns**

Gloucester 'A'
Played 27 Won 16 Lost 8 Drawn 3
For 337 Against 110
Captain: F.Pyart

Most Appearances: B.Parham 35, G.Romans,
A.Hawker 33, C.Smith 32, G.Matthews
A.Hudson 31, J.Harrison W.Johns F.Pegler
G.Vears 30
Most tries: A.Hudson 35, C.Smith 16, E.Hall,
J.Harrison 13, B.Parham 10
Conversions: G.Romans 44, E.Hall 4, L.Vears 2
Penalties: G.Romans 7
Drop Goals: D.Gent 2, J.Harrison 1

Following two poor seasons, this one started badly as well, and it was recognised that change was needed. George Romans stood down as captain mid-season and the players elected Billy Johns as his successor, who quickly proved to be an inspiring and popular leader. A problem at stand-off was solved when "Jummer" Stephens was moved from centre and quickly formed an effective half-back pairing with Dai Gent. "Whacker" Smith, Ernie Hall, Jimmy Harrison and Arthur Hudson settled down as one of the best three-quarter combinations ever fielded by

the Club. Hudson's prolific scoring saw him set a new Club record with 35 tries, including seven and six in individual matches, and Harrison scored seven in the first match of the season.

Two stalwarts of the pack retired early in the season – George Smith with 150 appearances and Fred Goolding with 104. Billy Johns led a light pack by shining example, and they were often dashing in loose play. In addition, their heeling improved and they provided a better supply of ball to the backs. Overall, there was more stability in the side with 35 players used during the season, and this trickled down to the A team, who also enjoyed a more successful season.

Around the turn of the year six successive games were won and this proved to be the turning point; there was a splendid double over a strong London Welsh team, and notable victories over Northampton and Leicester.

The toughest opponents were the invincible Swansea team, who did the double over Gloucester but only by a try to nil at Kingsholm and by a dropped goal to nil at St Helens. However, this was one of only two games lost at Kingsholm during the season. And the icing on the cake was winning the County Cup - Cheltenham and Stroud were seen off in earlier rounds before Bristol were defeated 12-0 in the final, for which the Gloucester players received

gold medals.

Eleven players were capped by Gloucestershire, and George Matthews played for London & Varsities against Rest of the South,

**Sep 24 Gloucester 45
Old Edwardians 0**
Tries: J.Harrison (7), F.Oswell (2), L.Vears (2),
C.Smith (2);
Conversions: G.Romans (3)

Oct 1 Northampton 10 Gloucester 4
Drop goal: D.Gent

Oct 8 Gloucester 0 Swansea 3

Oct 15 Gloucester 9 Penarth 3
Try: E.Hall;
Penalties: G.Romans (2)

Oct 22 Bristol 17 Gloucester 6
Try: C.Smith;
Penalty: G.Romans

Oct 29 Gloucester 18 Stroud 8
Tries: F.Pegler, A.Hudson, C.Robinson;
Conversions: G.Romans (3);
Penalty: G.Romans

Nov 5 Cardiff 12 Gloucester 3
Try: A.Hudson

Nov 12 Cheltenham 3 Gloucester 0

**Nov 19 Gloucester 0
Devonport Albion 0**

Nov 26 Penarth 8 Gloucester 0

Dec 3 Gloucester 8 Bath 5
Tries: W.Hyam, E.Hall;
Conversion: G.Romans

Dec 10 Gloucester 6 Lydney 8
Tries: W.Hyam, E.Hall

**Dec 17 Old Edwardians 0
Gloucester 40**
Tries: A.Hudson (4), W.Hyam (2), A.Hall (2),
B.Parham, C.Smith;
Conversions: G.Romans (5)

Dec 24 Gloucester 5 Bristol 0
Try: A.Hudson;
Conversion: G.Romans

**Dec 26 Gloucester 27
Old Merchant Taylors 0**
Tries: A.Hudson (2), G.Matthews, J.Harrison,
H.Collins, B.Parham, A.Hawker;
Conversions: G.Romans (3)

Dec 27 Gloucester 13 London Welsh 3
Tries: C.Smith, A.Hawker, J.Stephens;
G.Romans (2)

Dec 31 Gloucester 3 Cheltenham 0
Penalty: G.Romans

Jan 7 London Welsh 5 Gloucester 8
Tries: E.Hall, A.Hudson;

Conversion: G.Romans

Jan 14 Cinderford 3 Gloucester 0

Jan 21 Lydney 0 Gloucester 22
Tries: C.Smith (2), A.Hudson, J.Jewell, F.Pegler,
A.Hall;
Conversions: G.Romans (2)

Jan 28 Leicester 6 Gloucester 3
Try: F.Pegler

Feb 4 Gloucester 40 Clifton 0
Tries: C.Smith (3), A.Hudson (2), B.Parham (2),
F.Pegler, A.Hall, E.Hall;
Conversions: G.Romans (5)

**Feb 11 Devonport Albion 18
Gloucester 3**
Try: D.Gent

Feb 18 Clifton 8 Gloucester 19
Tries: A.Hudson (3), C.Smith (2);
Conversions: G.Romans (2)

**Feb 22 Gloucester 14 Cheltenham 5
(County Cup)**
Tries: B.Parham, W.Johns, A.Hudson;
Conversion: G.Romans;
Penalty: G.Romans

Mar 4 Gloucester 3 Cardiff 3
Try: A.Hudson

**Mar 11 Gloucester 13 Stroud 0
(County Cup)**
Tries: W.Johns, A.Hudson, B.Parham;
Conversions: G.Romans (2)

Mar 18 Gloucester 29 Northampton 3

Tries: A.Hudson (2), J.Harrison (2),
G.Matthews, C.Smith, E.Hall;
Conversions: G.Romans (4)

**Mar 25 Gloucester 12 Bristol 0
(County Cup Final)**
Tries: E.Hall (2), J.Jewell;
Penalty: G.Romans

**Apr 1 Gloucester 51 United Services
3**
Tries: A.Hudson (6), J.Harrison (3),
G.Matthews, C.Smith, F.Pegler, E.Hall;
Conversions: G.Romans (6)

Apr 8 Swansea 4 Gloucester 0

Apr 15 Stroud 6 Gloucester 16
Tries: F.Pegler (2), L.Vears, E.Hall;
Drop goal: J.Harrison

**Apr 21 Gloucester 51
Broughton Park 0**
Tries: A.Hudson (7), E.Hall (3), B.Parham (2),
J.Stephens;
Conversions: L.Vears (2), E.Hall (4)

Apr 22 Gloucester 9 Leicester 0
Try: C.Smith;
Conversion: G.Romans;
Drop goal: D.Gent

Apr 24 Gloucester 8 Cinderford 5
Tries: B.Parham (2);
Conversion: G.Romans

Apr 25 Bath 6 Gloucester 11
Tries: C.Smith, A.Hudson, W.Johns;
Conversion: G.Romans

1905-06

**Played 37 Won 26 Lost 8 Drawn 3
For 661 Against 165
Captain: Billy Johns**

Gloucester 'A'
Played 27 Won 18 Lost 7 Drawn 2
For 340 Against 103
Captain: F.Pyart

Most appearances: B.Parham 36, G.Matthews
35, C."Whacker" Smith 33, E.Hall A.Hawker
H.Collins 32, G.Romans 31, J.Harrison
W.Johns 30
Most tries: A.Hudson 41, C.Smith 27, E.Hall
19, J.Harrison 12, L.Vears 11
Conversions: G.Romans 70, L Vears 5,
A.Wood 1

Penalties: G.Romans 4, L.Vears 1
Drop goals: E.Hall, J.Harrison, A.Hawker
H.Ewers, W.Holder 1

The season started with the opening of the
gymnasium, including changing rooms and
tea room; now known as the Lions Den, it is the
oldest building still standing at Kingsholm.

A very successful season, with the team at its
best when attacking, produced a new points
scoring record of 661. The touring All Blacks
was the only side in the country to score more
points. Arthur Hudson broke the try scoring
record with 41 in 26 games, a total which has
never been exceeded. "Whacker" Smith's 27
tries would have been outstanding in any other
season. The kicking of George Romans at full-

back was as good as ever, and the flood of tries
gave him the opportunity to kick 70 conversions,
but the emphasis on try scoring is illustrated by
his meagre return of one goal from a mark and
three penalties.

The first choice back division gave some brilliant
displays, and the Citizen reckoned that "as a
combination they were as near perfection one
could wish for in a rugby XV", but selections
for representative sides and injuries reduced
their availability. The half-backs, "Jummer"
Stephens and Dai Gent, showed such wonderful
form that it was recognised at national level.
Ernie Hall and Jimmy Harrison benefited from
their excellent service to produce a stream of
openings for the strength of "Whacker"Smith
and the speed of Arthur Hudson outside them.

S.W.Bingle(Sec) B.Parham F.Pegler G.Matthews A.Hawker G.Vears H.Collins W.Holder J.Jewell W.H.Worth(Treas)
G.Romans J.Harrison A.Hudson W.Johns(Capt) C.Smith E.Hall A.Hall T.Bagwell(Trainer)
D.R.Gent J.Stephens (J.Merchant – absent)

Billy Johns captained the side and "no more genuine worker has put his head down in the pack," which also benefited from the experience of Bert Hawker, Bert Parham, and George Matthews. "The forwards did their work manfully and triumphed in the one main object, to get the ball as often as possible to the outsiders. They were a grand all-round pack, scrummaging well and equally effective in the lines out and loose footwork."

The biggest game of the season was against New Zealand. Gloucester went down 0-44, seriously outgunned and weakened by injuries. But the game produced a handsome profit for the Club's coffers. Against other clubs, victory over Newport and a draw with Cardiff were rated very highly.

There were England caps for Arthur Hudson against Ireland, Wales (1 try) and France (4 tries), and for Dai Gent against New Zealand, Ireland and Wales; "Jummer" Stephens was called up as a reserve. Thirteen players were capped by Gloucestershire.

Sep 23 Gloucester 29 Clifton 0
Tries: A.Wood (3), A.Hudson (2), D.Gent, J.Harrison, B.Parham, F.Pegler;
Conversion: G.Romans

Sep 30 Gloucester 17 Bristol 6
Tries: A.Wood (2), W.Johns, A.Hudson, J.Merchant;
Conversion: A.Wood

Oct 7 Gloucester 0 Swansea 3

Oct 14 Northampton 3 Gloucester 9
Tries: A.Hudson (2), A.Wood

Oct 19 Gloucester 0 New Zealand 44

Oct 21 Cheltenham 3 Gloucester 3
Try: A.Hudson

Oct 28 Gloucester 3 Cardiff 3
Try: B.Parham

Nov 4 London Welsh 5 Gloucester 0

Nov 11 Gloucester 31 Stroud 3
Tries: L.Vears (2), W.Johns (2), A.Hawker, H.Ewers;
Conversions: G.Romans (5);
Penalty: G.Romans

Nov 18 Lydney 0 Gloucester 11
Tries: A.Hudson (2), C.Smith;
Conversion: G.Romans

Nov 25 Gloucester 52 Bedford 5
Tries: A.Hudson (4), E.Hall (3), B.Parham (2), C.Smith (2), J.Harrison;
Conversions: G.Romans (8)

Dec 2 Torquay Athletic 4 Gloucester 0

Dec 4 Plymouth 8 Gloucester 10
Tries: A.Hudson, J.Harrison;
Conversions: G.Romans (2)

Dec 9 Gloucester 16 Bath 0

Tries: C.Smith, J.Jewell, C.Goddard, H.Hughes,
Conversions: L.Vears (2)

Dec 16 Stroud 0 Gloucester 12
Tries: C.Smith, E.Hall;
Conversion: G.Romans;
Drop goal: J.Harrison

Dec 23 Gloucester 20 Cheltenham 0
Tries: C.Smith (2), A.Hudson (2), J.Harrison;
Conversion: G.Romans;
Penalty: G.Romans

**Dec 26 Gloucester 36
Old Merchant Taylors 5**
Tries: A.Hudson (3), C.Smith (2), G.Matthews, A.Hawker, E.Hall;
Conversions: G.Romans (6)

Dec 27 Gloucester 7 London Welsh 0
Try: C.Smith;
Drop goal: E.Hall

Dec 30 Bristol 3 Gloucester 5
Try: A.Hudson;
Conversion: G.Romans

Jan 6 Clifton 3 Gloucester 28
Tries: H.Hughes (4), L.Vears (2), W.Pitt, J.Merchant;
Drop goal: H.Ewers

Jan 13 Gloucester 20 Leicester 0
Tries: J.Harrison (3), C.Smith (2), H.Collins;
Conversion: G.Romans

Jan 20 Newport 9 Gloucester 5

Try: E.Hall;
Conversion: G.Romans

Jan 27 Gloucester 29 Cinderford 0
Tries: C.Smith (2), E.Hall (2), J.Harrison,
J.Merchant, B.Parham;
Conversions: G.Romans (4)

Feb 3 Gloucester 24 Lydney 5
Tries: E.Hall (2), D.Gent, H.Collins, L.Vears;
Conversions: L.Vears (3);
Penalty: L.Vears

Feb 10 Swansea 5 Gloucester 0

Feb 17 Gloucester 48 Penylan 3
Tries: A.Hudson (5), C.Smith (3), E.Hall (2),
B.Parham;
Conversions: G.Romans (6);
Penalty: G.Romans

Feb 24 Gloucester 68 Bream 0
(County Cup)

Tries: A.Hudson (6), C.Smith (3), E.Hall (3),
J.Harrison (2), B.Parham, F.Pegler;
Conversions: G.Romans (10)

Mar 3 Cinderford 0 Gloucester 0

Mar 10 Cinderford 0 Gloucester 9
(County Cup)
Tries: A.Hudson, H.Collins;
Penalty: G.Romans

Mar 17 Gloucester 71 Plymouth 0
Tries: L.Vears (6), C.Smith (5), E.Hall (2),
G.Vears, B.Parham, A.Hawker,
J.Harrison;
Conversions: G.Romans (10)

Mar 24 Gloucester 3 Bristol 8
(County Cup Final)
Try: A.Wood

Mar 31 Cardiff 15 Gloucester 0
Apr 7 Gloucester 5 Newport 0

Try: A.Hudson;
Conversion: G.Romans

**Apr 13 Gloucester 37
Hartlepool OB 3**
Tries: A.Hudson (5), E.Hall, J.Merchant;
Conversions: G.Romans (6);
Drop goal: A.Hawker

Apr 14 Gloucester 30 Lennox 13
Tries: A.Hudson (2), E.Hall, C.Smith,
J.Harrison, H.Collins, B.Parham, A.Hall;
Conversions: G.Romans (3)

Apr 16 Gloucester 20 Northampton 6
Tries: A.Hudson (2), C.Smith, F.Smith;
Conversions: G.Romans (2);
Drop goal: W.Holder

April 21 Bath 0 Gloucester 3
Try: F.Smith

1906-07

H.Collins W.Johns F.Pegler G.Vears A.Hawker W.Holder B.Parham A.Purton
W.H.Worth(Treas) J.Stephens F.Smith A.Hudson D.R.Gent(Capt) A.Wood C.Smith H.Smith T.Bagwell(Trainer) (G.Matthews and A.Hall – absent)

**Played 34 Won 21 Lost 11 Drawn 2
For 363 For 205
Captain: Dai Gent**

Gloucester 'A'
Played 25 Won 13 Lost 9 Drawn 3
For 266 Against 99

Most Appearances: H.Collins 32, J.Stephens,
B.Parham 29, G.Vears F.Smith 28, F.Pegler
W.Johns W.Holder 27, H.Smith A.Hawker 24,
A.Purton 23
Most tries: F.Smith 17, A.Hudson 14,
B.Parham, H.Smith, F.Bloxsome 6
Conversions: A.Wood 24, G.Romans 11,

F.Perry 7, A.Holder 1
Penalties: A.Wood 2, G.Romans 2
Dropped Goal: C.Smith 1

Results did not live up to the high standards set in
the previous record-breaking season. Things did
not go well from the start, with the loss of Jimmy

Harrison to rugby league, Ernie Hall being rarely available, and Dai Gent out with injury almost as soon as he had been elected captain. Adequate replacements were never found, but, with Gent back, results improved around the turn of the year, until a further batch of injuries seriously weakened the team after Easter.

George Romans, no longer in his prime, fell out with the Club halfway through the season, and so ended a long and distinguished career as full-back and place kicker after 269 appearances. In this case an excellent replacement was found in Alfie Wood, a magnificent kicker with either foot, fearless in stopping rushes, and a deadly tackler. The Club were also fortunate to find a new wing, Frank Smith, whose speed and guile more than made up for his small stature. This allowed Arthur Hudson to be switched into the centre, where he saw more of the ball but scored fewer tries.

There were some capable individuals amongst the forwards, but overall they were lightweight compared with most opposition packs, and consequently the talented half-backs, Gent and Stephens, were all too often having to play going backwards. Bert Hawker played his last full season before retiring with 198 appearances and becoming captain of the 2nd XV.

Not a single victory was registered against any of the big four Welsh clubs. Victory at Stroud came in such a savage match that four players were sent off and future fixtures were cancelled. Bristol dumped Gloucester out of the County Cup, and other losses to local opponents hurt at the hands of Cinderford, Bristol for a second time, and Cheltenham, who recorded their first ever victory at Kingsholm.

This indifferent form soon led to diminishing attendances, and the Club finances started to suffer, so the committee resorted to other sources of income – benefit theatrical performances and sports meetings – to try to help shore up the books.

Arthur Hudson was called up as a reserve for England, and eight players were capped by Gloucestershire.

Sep 22 Gloucester 6 Lydney 0
Tries: A.Wood, W.Johns

Sep 29 Gloucester 27 Clifton 3
Tries: A.Hudson (2), G.Matthews (2), E.Hall, B.Parham, A.Wood;
Conversions: A.Wood (2), G.Romans

Oct 6 Swansea 13 Gloucester 0

Oct 13 Gloucester 18 Penylan 0
Tries: W.Holder (2), J.Merchant, A.Hudson;
Conversions: G.Romans (3)

Oct 20 Gloucester 0 Cheltenham 3

Oct 27 Cardiff 13 Gloucester 0

Nov 3 Northampton 9 Gloucester 11
Tries: F.Smith, A.Purton;
Conversion: G.Romans;
Penalty: G.Romans

Nov 10 Gloucester 11 Stroud 5
Tries: H.Collins, F.Smith;
Conversion: G.Romans;
Penalty: G.Romans

Nov 17 London Welsh 0 Gloucester 3
Try: H.Collins

Nov 24 Gloucester 9 Newport 17
Tries: H.Smith, J.Stephens, B.Parham

**Dec 1 Gloucester 13
London Hospital 3**
Tries: A.Hudson, J.Stephens, A.Hall;
Conversions: G.Romans (2)

Dec 8 Stroud 3 Gloucester 10
Tries: L.Vears, F.Smith;
Drop goal: C.Smith

Dec 15 Bristol 8 Gloucester 0

Dec 22 Newport 24 Gloucester 5
Try: A.Hudson;
Conversion: G.Romans

**Dec 26 Gloucester 12
Old Merchant Taylors 0**
Tries: F.Smith (2), A.Hudson, C.Smith

Dec 27 Gloucester 17 London Welsh 5
Tries: H.Smith (2), F.Smith, E.Butler, D.Gent;
Conversion: G.Romans

Jan 5 Clifton 6 Gloucester 11
Tries: F.Bloxsome, D.Gent, F.Pegler;
Conversion: G.Romans

Jan 12 Gloucester 16 Bristol 0
Tries: F.Bloxsome (2), W.Holder, D.Gent;
Conversions: A.Wood (2)

Jan 19 Gloucester 16 Exeter 0
Tries: F.Smith (2), A.Hawker;
Conversions: A.Wood (2);
Penalty: A.Wood

Jan 26 Gloucester v Swansea - cancelled due to frost

Feb 2 Cheltenham 8 Gloucester 12
Tries: F.Smith (3), H.Collins

Feb 9 Plymouth 8 Gloucester 3
Try: B.Parham

Feb 16 Exeter 6 Gloucester 6
Tries: A.Hudson, F.Smith

**Feb 23 Gloucester 20 Lydney 0
(County Cup)**
Tries: A.Hudson (2), B.Parham, W.Holder;
Conversions: A.Wood (4)

Mar 2 Leicester 17 Gloucester 5
Try: A.Purton;
Conversion: A.Wood

**Mar 9 Gloucester 5 Bristol 7
(County Cup)**
Try: F.Smith;
Conversion: A.Wood

Mar 16 Gloucester 13 Plymouth 3
Tries: W.Johns, A.Hudson, F.Bloxsome;
Conversions: A.Wood (2)

Mar 23 Cheltenham 3 Gloucester 3
Penalty: A.Wood

Mar 29 Gloucester 19 Abertillery 5
Tries: H.Smith, F.Bloxsome, D.Gent, F.Smith, B.Parham;
Conversions: A.Wood (2)

Mar 30 Gloucester 49 Percy Park 5
Tries: T.West (4), H.Smith (2), D.Gent, F.Bloxsome, W.Holder, F.Smith, J.Stephens;
Conversions: H.Perry (7), W.Holder

Apr 1 Gloucester 15 Cinderford 3
Tries: A.Hudson (2), T.West;
Conversions: A.Wood (3)

Apr 2 Gloucester 15 Northampton 0
Tries: A.Hudson, F.Smith, H.Collins;
Conversions: A.Wood (3)

Apr 6 Gloucester 5 Cardiff 16
Try: A.Hudson;
Conversion: A.Wood

Apr 13 Cinderford 12 Gloucester 0

Apr 20 Lydney 0 Gloucester 8
Tries: B.Parham, F.Smith;
Conversion: A.Wood

1907-08

H.A.Dancey G.H.Bland N.D.Haines(Hon.Sec.) C.E.Brown(Pres) E.T.Huggins J.T.Brookes J.J.Little S.W.Bingle C.H.Dancey(Vice-Pres)
L.Vears A.W.Vears R.Craddock C.Smith D.Hollands G.Halford F.Pegler H.Quixley C.Williams Rev O.E.Hayden
H.M.Taynton H.G.Brown(Sec) W.Johns F.Smith G.Cook G.Vears(Capt) A.Hudson F.Welshman B.Parham T.Bagwell(Trainer) W.H.Worth(Treas)
W.Dix J.Stephens (D.R.Gent and G.Matthews – absent)

Played 35 Won 24 Lost 9 Drawn 2
For 360 Against 233
Captain: Gordon Vears

Gloucester 'A'
Played 29 Won 27 Lost 2
For 539 Against 80
Captain: F.Arthur

Most appearances: J.Stephens, B.Parham, H.Quixley, D.Hollands 31, G.Vears 30, W.Johns, R.Craddock, G.Cook 28
Most tries: A.Hudson 25, G.Cook 9, F.Smith 7, C "Whacker" Smith, W. Johns 6
Conversions: A.Wood 14, R.Welshman 11, G.Cook 7, F.Stout 1
Penalties: R.Welshman 4, A.Wood 2, G.Cook 1
Drop goals: E.Hall, G.Cook, W.Dix 1

Whilst not a record-breaking season, the Club looked back on this campaign with a good deal of satisfaction. First, and foremost, were the victories gained over Swansea and Newport, the former being won by one of the tries of the season – Alfie Wood gathered the ball behind his own line, but refused to touch down and kicked out, Billy Johns followed up and his tackle knocked the ball loose, Dave Hollands regained possession and passed inside to Arthur Hudson, who ran half the length of the ground to touch down behind the posts.

There was also much pleasure taken in the comprehensive defeat of Plymouth in December, this being the first setback the Devonians had suffered against an English club. There was an unbeaten record against other Gloucestershire teams, with nine wins and two draws. And only two matches were lost at Kingsholm, by two points to Cardiff and by ten to Coventry, when Gloucester had a "wretched game".

Several players retired during this season, most notably "Whacker" Smith, who received a public testimonial and a gold watch and chain from the Club for his long and distinguished service with 270 appearances. Representative calls regularly weakened the team, but plenty of useful reserves came through. In particular, the frequent absence of Dai Gent with injury saw the emergence of a bright young talent in "Father" Dix at scrum-half.

The forwards lacked weight, but turned in some sterling performances, especially in the first half of the season. They were enthusiastically led by Gordon Vears, and the vice-captain, Billy Johns, was the finest amongst them. George Matthews (107 appearances) and Harry Collins (99 appearances) retired during the season after distinguished careers, but their loss was balanced by the emergence of Harry Berry and George Griffiths, each of whom joined the Club having completed military service. The strength of the reserves was illustrated by the results achieved by the Gloucester A team, which won 27 of 29 fixtures.

Arthur Hudson played for England against France (1 try), Wales, Ireland (2 tries) and Scotland. Alfie Wood won England caps against France, Wales (2 conversions) and Ireland (2 conversions), immediately before joining Cheltenham and then going to play professional rugby for Oldham. Wood, Dai Gent and A.Teague played for Western Counties against London. Nine players put in 26 appearances for the County.

Sep 21 Gloucester 38 Clifton 10
Tries: A.Hudson (5), W.Johns (2), G.Vears, H.Smith;
Conversions: A.Wood (4)
Penalty: A.Wood

Sep 28 Northampton 19 Gloucester 9
Tries: A.Hudson, C.Smith, B.Parham

Sep 30 Gloucester 9 Cinderford 5
Try: D.Hollands;
Conversion: A.Wood;
Drop goal: E.Hall

Oct 5 Gloucester 8 Swansea 3
Tries: E.Hall, A.Hudson;
Conversion: A.Wood

Oct 12 Cinderford 3 Gloucester 3
Try: E.Hall

Oct 19 Bristol 3 Gloucester 5
Try: A.Hudson;
Conversion: F.Welshman

Oct 26 Gloucester 9 Cardiff 11
Tries: A.Hudson (2);
Penalty: A.Wood

Nov 2 Gloucester 11 Lydney 3
Tries: G.Matthews, C.Smith, W.Johns;
Conversion: A.Wood

Nov 9   Exeter 6   Gloucester 13
Tries: C.Smith, W.Dix, G.Cook;
Conversions: F.Welshman (2)

Nov 16   Cheltenham 5   Gloucester 15
Tries: A.Hudson, G.Cook, F.Quixley;
Conversions: A.Wood (3)

Nov 23   Newport 16   Gloucester 3
Try: A.Hudson

Nov 30   Gloucester 5   Pontypool 0
Try: F.Quixley;
Conversion: A.Wood

Dec 7   Gloucester 6   Exeter 0
Tries: J.Stephens, C.Smith

Dec 14   Gloucester 8   Leicester 6
Try: D.Hollands;
Conversion: F.Welshman;
Penalty: F.Welshman

Dec 21   Gloucester 12   Plymouth 5
Tries: C.Smith, W.Dix, J.Beard, F.M.Stout

**Dec 26   Gloucester 22
Old Merchant Taylors 8**
Tries: A.Hudson (5), E.Hall;
Conversions: F.M.Stout, G.Cook

**Dec 27   Gloucester 24
Old Edwardians 11**
Tries: H.Smith (2), G.Cook, A.Hudson, J.Beard,
G.Matthews;

Conversions: A.Wood (3)
Dec 28   Gloucester 3   Cheltenham 0
Try: F.M.Stout

Jan 4   Clifton v Gloucester - abandoned due to
frost
Jan 11   Coventry v Gloucester - abandoned due
to frost

Jan 18   London Welsh 3   Gloucester 7
Try: C.Smith;
Drop goal: W.Dix

Jan 25   Swansea 11   Gloucester 3
Penalty: F.Welshman

Feb 1   Gloucester 0   Coventry 10

Feb 8   Leicester 11   Gloucester 0

Feb 15   Gloucester 6   Bristol 0
Tries: B.Parham, D.Hollands

Feb 22   Pontypool 14   Gloucester 0

Feb 29   Gloucester 19   Pill Harriers 3
Tries: G.Cook (2), A.Hudson, G.Griffiths;
Conversions: F.Welshman (2);
Penalty: F.Welshman

Mar 7   Gloucester 11   Northampton 9
Tries: A.Hudson (2), G.Cook;
Conversion: F.Welshman

Mar 14   Plymouth 9   Gloucester 3

Try: F.Smith
Mar 21   Gloucester 11   Cheltenham 0
Tries: G.Cook, F.Smith, D.Hollands;
Conversion: F.Welshman

Mar 28   Gloucester 9   Newport 3
Tries: A.Hudson, F.Smith;
Penalty: F.Welshman

Apr 4   Cardiff 16   Gloucester 8
Tries: A.Hudson (2);
Conversion: F.Welshman

Apr 11   Lydney 3   Gloucester 3
Try: A.Hudson

**Apr 17   Gloucester 16
London Welsh 14**
Tries: W.Johns (2), G.Holford, F.Smith;
Conversions: F.Welshman (2)

Apr 18   Gloucester 27   Lennox 10
Tries: W.Dix (3), G.Cook (2), J.Stephens;
Conversions: G.Cook (3);
Penalty: G.Cook

Apr 20   Gloucester 20   Cinderford 0
Tries: B.Parham (2), F.Smith, A.Hall;
Conversions: G.Cook (2);
Drop goal: G.Cook

Apr 25   Gloucester 14   Bristol 3
Tries: F.Smith (2), D.Hollands, W.Johns;
Conversion: G.Cook

1908-09

**Played 36 Won 22 Lost 10 Drawn 4
For 437 Against 236
Captain: Arthur Hudson**

Gloucester 'A'
Played 28 Won 24 Lost 3 Drawn 1
For 406 Against 64
Captain: Bert Hawker

Most appearances: G.Holford 35, F.Smith,
B.Parham, G.Griffiths 31, J.Wyburn, W.Hall 30,
H.Berry 29, J.Stephens, W.Johns, G.Vears 27
Most tries: F.Smith 18, W.Hall 12, H.Smith,
B.Parham, H.Berry 6
Conversions: F.Welshman 27, C.Cook 20,
S.Hayward 1
Penalties: F Welshman, C Cook 4
Drop goals: F.Smith, W.Dix, A.Hall, A.Pegler,
C.Cook 1

A disappointing season started with bright

prospects, which were dented by the early loss of Arthur Hudson to injury. This meant that Gordon Vears had to stand in as captain for most of the season and earned praise for his enthusiastic leadership. At Kingsholm there was only one defeat, at the hands of Newport, in seven months, before results fell away towards the end of the season. Not a single victory was achieved against any of the big four Welsh clubs.

Results against English clubs were much better, with only three losses. In the County League, Gloucester only lost one game, and finished at the top of the competition, but these games attracted little interest and Gloucester decided not to enter the following season. Attendances fell away, so the Club suffered financially, which caused renewed grumbling about the level of rent for Kingsholm set by the Ground Company.

Dai Gent and "Jummer" Stephens played

like clockwork at half-back, with a reverse pass between them regularly bamboozling the opposition, but the three-quarter line was consistently weak and lacking in pace, except for Frank Smith on the wing.

Most of the successes achieved were down to the forwards. A mobile if light pack developed well as the season wore on, and they were credited with fine displays against the might of Welsh opponents. Billy Johns was brilliant in the loose and lineouts. "Biddy" Halford looked set to play in every game only to miss the very last of the season, which saw the retirement of Bert Parham after ten years of sterling service and 265 appearances.

At Easter, four games were played in five days, including a 75-5 demolition of Castleford, which set a record team score and a record for a kicker with Charley Cook kicking twelve conversions

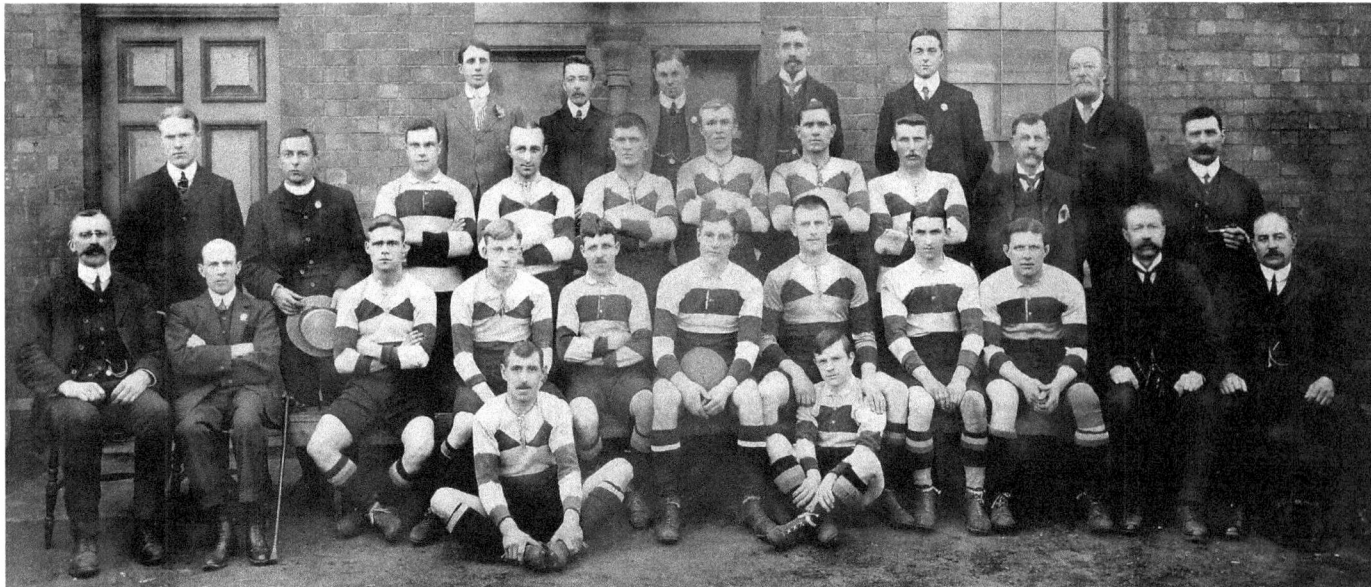

A.F.Fielding J.J.Little W.H.Rasbach G.H.Bland J.T.Brookes C.H.Dancey(Vice-Pres)
A.H.Harris O.E.Hayden G.Griffiths W.Johns J.Wyburn G.Halford H.Berry B.Parham A.W.Vears A.C.Williams
H.G.Brown(Sec) H.M.Taynton(Chairman) F.Smith W.Hall H.Smith A.Hudson(Capt) G.Vears C.Cook D.Hollands W.H.Worth(Treas) T.Bagwell(Trainer)
J.Stephens D.R.Gent

and a penalty. Two days later the largest crowd of the season saw Cinderford take away Gloucester's unbeaten record against English clubs at Kingsholm, and the following day five Cinderford players turned out for Gloucester to complete the double over Northampton.

Billy Johns became a fixture in the England side with caps against Wales, Ireland, Scotland and France (1 try). Harry Berry was first reserve for the Wales game. Thirteen players were selected for Gloucestershire during the season, including eleven in the County side which beat Racing Club de France 39-0, and Arthur Hudson captained the County against Australia, both matches played at Kingsholm.

Sep 19 Plymouth 9 Gloucester 21
Tries: F.Smith (2), H.Smith, T.Elliot, D.Gent;
Conversions: F.Welshman (3)

Sep 26 Gloucester 8 Abertillery 8
Tries: M.Neale (2);
Conversion: F.Welshman

Sept 28 Gloucester 3 Cinderford 3
Penalty: F.Welshman

Oct 3 Swansea 11 Gloucester 0

**Oct 8 Stroud 5 Gloucester 28
(County League)**
Tries: J.Baldwin (2), W.Dix, A.Pegler, W.Hall, A.Hall;
Conversions : F.Welshman (3);
Drop goal: A.Hall

Oct 10 Cinderford 7 Gloucester 9
Tries: F.Smith (2), G.Holford

Oct 17 Gloucester 8 Pontypool 6
Tries: A.Hudson (2);
Conversion: F.Welshman

Oct 24 Cardiff 14 Gloucester 8
Tries: F.Smith (2);
Conversion: F.Welshman

Oct 31 Gloucester 25 Lydney 7
Tries: A.Hudson (3), W.Hall, F.Smith, B.Parham;
Conversions: F.Welshman (2)
Penalty: F.Welshman

Nov 7 Northampton 3 Gloucester 11
Tries: W.Dix, F.Pegler, B.Parham;
Conversion: F.Welshman

Nov 14 Gloucester 16 Cheltenham 3
Tries: W.Hall, J.Hamblin, F.Smith;
Conversions: F.Welshman (2);
Penalty: F.Welshman

Nov 21 Gloucester 3 Newport 8
Try: W.Hall

Nov 28 Gloucester 14 Coventry 0
Tries: L.Vears (2), F.Smith, J.Hamblin;
Conversion: F.Welshman

Dec 5 Clifton 8 Gloucester 19
Tries: D.Hollands (2), W.Dix, H.Smith,

A.Pegler;
Conversions: C.Cook (2)

Dec 12 Gloucester 13 Leicester 3
Tries: W..Hall (2), D.Hollands;
Conversions: F.Welshman (2)

Dec 19 Pontypool 6 Gloucester 0

**Dec 26 Gloucester 14
Old Merchant Taylors 13**
Tries: F.Smith, L.Vears, H.Berry, B.Parham;
Conversion: F.Welshman

Dec 28 Gloucester 17 Stroud 0
Tries: D.Hollands, J.Stephens, J.Hamblin, W.Dix, B.Parham;
Conversion: F.Welshman

Jan 2 Cheltenham 8 Gloucester 13
Tries: G.Holford, B.Parham, W.Dix;
Conversion: F.Welshman (2)

Jan 16 Gloucester 19 Clifton 9
Tries: T.Elliot (2), F.Smith, R.Craddock, J.Wyburn;
Conversions: F.Welshman (2)

**Jan 23 Gloucester 12
London Hospital 12**
Try: H.Berry;
Conversion: F.Welshman;
Penalty: F.Welshman;
Drop goal: A.Pegler

Jan 30 Coventry 9 Gloucester 8
Tries: W.Hall, H.Smith;

Conversion: F.Welshman

Feb 6 Gloucester 16 Pill Harriers 6
Tries: J.Hall, G.Halford, F.Smith, B.Parham;
Conversions: F.Welshman (2)

Feb 13 Bristol 3 Gloucester 8
(County League)
Tries: R.Craddock, F.Smith;
Penalty: C.Cook

Feb 20 Cheltenham 6 Gloucester 11
Tries: H.Smith, H.Berry;
Conversion: C.Cook;
Penalty: C.Cook

Feb 27 Leicester 23 Gloucester 11
Try: H.Berry;
Drop goals: C.Cook, F.Smith

Mar 6 Gloucester 0 Swansea 0

Mar 13 Gloucester 12 Plymouth 6
Tries: T.Elliot, G.Halford;
Conversion: C.Cook;
Drop goal: W.Dix

Mar 20 Newport 5 Gloucester 0

Mar 27 Gloucester 13 Bristol 3
(County League)
Tries: F.Smith, W.Hall;
Penalty: C.Cook;
Conversions: C.Cook (2)

April 3 Gloucester 0 Cardiff 6

Apr 9 Gloucester 11 London Welsh 15
Tries: H.Berry, G.Halford;

Penalty: C.Cook;
Conversion: C.Cook

Apr 10 Gloucester 75 Castleford 5
Tries: W.Hall (4), H.Smith (3), F.Smith (3),
H.Barnes (2), W.Johns, J.Wyburn, D.Hollands,
H.Berry;
Conversions: C.Cook (12);
Penalty: C.Cook

Apr 12 Gloucester 0 Cinderford 6
(County League)

Apr 13 Gloucester 3 Northampton 0
Try: W.Nelmes

Apr 17 Lydney 0 Gloucester 8
Tries: T.Elliot, D.Gent;
Conversion: S.Hayward

1909-10

W.H.Rasbach C.J.Hall A.C.Williams J.J.Little J.T.Brookes A.F.Fielding
C.E.Hayden A.W.Vears J.Stephens G.Griffiths G.Halford H.Berry F.Pegler J.Wyburn G.H.Bland G.Romans N.D.Haines(Hon.Sec) H.G.Brown(Sec)
H.M.Taynton(Chairman) D.Hollands W.Egerton W.Washbourne H.Barnes W.Johns A.Hudson G.Vears W.Hall W.J.Pearce W.Dix T.Bagwell(Trainer)
W.H.Worth(Treas) (D.R.Gent – absent)

Played 38 Won 23 Lost 8 Drawn 7
For 401 Against 203
Captain: Arthur Hudson

Gloucester 'A'
Played 24 Won 18 Lost 5 Drawn 1
For 302 Against 86

Most appearances: W.Hall 35, G.Vears,
D.Hollands 34, G.Halford 32, J.Stephens,
W.Egerton 30, H.Berry 29, W.J.Pearce, F.Pegler
27
Most tries: A.Hudson 11, W.J.Vance 10, F.Smith
9, W.Hall 8, D.Hollands, W.J.Pearce 7
Conversions: W.Egerton 33, J.Hall 3, C.Cook,
D.Hollands, H.Hancock 1

Penalties: W.Egerton 5, C.Cook, J.Hall 1
Drop goals: H.Barnes 2

Given that the Club regularly had to call on numerous replacements, because of a high level of representative calls and injuries, a good deal of satisfaction was taken from the results achieved. There was more success than usual against Welsh clubs, most notably a brilliant win against Swansea, when Billy Johns played his first game of the season and Arthur Hudson returned after almost a year out injured. Pride was also taken in draws home and away against Newport when Gloucester fielded seven and eight reserves.

Only two matches were lost at Kingsholm, to Cardiff and Headingly, Gloucester being unable to field a representative team against the latter. The County Cup was won when Lydney were defeated in the last game of the season.

The strength of the team was in the forwards and the half-backs. The pace and footballing skills of the pack, led by Gordon Vears, more than made up for their relative lack of weight. The internationals, Billy Johns and Harry Berry were to the fore, along with "Biddy" Halford, James Wyburn and Dave Holland, although Holland transferred to Devon Albion at the end of the season after 98 appearances.

The veteran "Jummer" Stephens passed the previous record number of appearances for the Club, and would retire early in the following season with 323. He and Dai Gent were again outstanding at half-back. Although work took Gent away from the Club in March, he returned for the odd game and finished with 146 appearances. Fortunately there was an able replacement in "Father" Dix. The long absences of Hudson and Vance on the wings weakened the back line, which under-performed for much of the season, despite Willie Hall shining in the centre.

The Club was proud to set a new record with four players representing their country – Harry Berry (Wales, Ireland, France, Scotland), Billy Johns (Wales, Ireland, France), Dai Gent (Wales, Ireland) and Arthur Hudson (France) – as England beat Wales for the first time since 1898, and won the International Championship for the first time in 18 years.

Thirteen Gloucester players were selected for the County during the season, and seven of them - Dai Gent (captain), Arthur Hudson (2 tries), "Jummer Stephens, Billy Johns, Harry Berry, Dave Hollands and "Biddy" Holford - played in the 23-0 victory over Yorkshire in the final, when Gloucestershire became County Champions for the first time.

Sep 11 Gloucester 11 Penarth 6
Tries: G.Halford, F.Smith;
Conversion: C.Cook;
Goal from Mark: C.Cook

Sep 18 Abertillery 3 Gloucester 3
Try: H.Berry

Sep 23 Pontypool 14 Gloucester 0

Oct 2 Gloucester 8 Swansea 5
Tries: W.Hall, A.Hudson;
Conversion: W.Egerton

Oct 4 Gloucester 3 Cinderford 0
Try: H.Barnes

Oct 9 Northampton 12 Gloucester 4
Drop goal: H.Barnes

Oct 16 Lydney 0 Gloucester 3
Penalty: W.Egerton

Oct 23 Gloucester 8 Cardiff 20
Tries: J.Stephens (2);
Conversion: W.Egerton

Oct 30 Cinderford 0 Gloucester 0

Nov 6 Clifton 5 Gloucester 23
Tries: W.Hall, D.Hollands, W.J.Vance, W.Dix;
Conversions: W.Egerton (4);
Penalty: W.Egerton

Nov 13 Cheltenham 0 Gloucester 24
Tries: A.Hudson (2), F.Smith (2), H.Berry, W.J.Pearce;
Conversions: W.Egerton (3)

Nov 20 Gloucester 29 Stroud 6
Tries: W.J.Vance (2), W.Hall (2), F.Smith (2), G.Griffiths;
Conversions: W.Egerton (4)

Nov 27 Gloucester 8 Bristol 6
Tries: J.Wyburn, W.J.Pearce;
Conversion: W.Egerton

Dec 4 Gloucester 24 Clifton 0
Tries: W.J.Vance (3), W.Hall, G.Halford, J.Baldwin;
Conversion: W.Egerton (3)

Dec 11 Gloucester 14 Lydney 3
Tries: F.Smith (2), D.Hollands, W.Johns;
Conversion: W.Egerton

Dec 18 Newport 3 Gloucester 3
Try: W.J.Vance

Dec 25 Gloucester 9 Abertillery 5
Tries: F.Smith (2), J.Baldwin.

**Dec 27 Gloucester 14
Old Merchant Taylors 9**
Tries: D.Hollands (2), W.Hall, W.J.Pearce;
Conversion: W.Egerton

**Dec 28 Gloucester 27
Bridgwater Albion 0**
Tries: A.Hudson (4), W.J.Pearce (2), W.J.Vance;
Conversion: W.Egerton (3)

Jan 1 Gloucester 31 Cheltenham 0
Tries: W.J.Vance (2), H.Barnes, D.Gent, H.Berry, A.Hudson, G.Halford;
Conversions: W.Egerton (5)

Jan 8 Stroud 0 Gloucester 10
Tries: J.Baldwin, H.Barnes;
Drop goal: H.Barnes

Jan 15 Leicester 0 Gloucester 0

Jan 22 Gloucester 19 Pontypool 3
Tries: D.Gent, W.J.Pearce, G.Halford, J.Hamblin, J.Wyburn;
Conversions: W.Egerton (2)

Jan 29 Gloucester 17 Cheltenham 0

Tries: W.Washbourne (2), J.Baldwin, H.Barnes, G.Vears;
Conversion: H.Hancock

Feb 5 Bristol 10 Gloucester 6
Try: W.Washbourne;
Penalty: W.Egerton

Feb 12 Neath 14 Gloucester 3
Try: W.Dix

Feb 19 Plymouth 6 Gloucester 6
Tries: D.Hollands, H.Berry

**Feb 26 Gloucester 14
2nd Glo'ster's Regt 0**
Tries: D.Hollands (2), W.Washbourne, E.Hall;
Conversion: W.Egerton

March 5 Swansea 31 Gloucester 0

**March 12 Gloucester 11 Cinderford 5
(County Cup)**
Try: F.Pegler;
Conversion: W.Egerton;
Penalties: W.Egerton (2)

March 19 Gloucester 3 Newport 3
Try: W.Dix

March 25 Gloucester 8 Headingley 15
Tries: E.Hall, W.Jones;
Conversion: W.Egerton

March 26 Gloucester 0 Neath 0

March 28 Gloucester 8 Cinderford 0
Try: W.Dix;
Conversion: E.Hall;
Penalty: E.Hall

**March 29 Gloucester 10
Northampton 8**
Tries: W.J.Pearce, W Hall;
Conversion: E.Hall (2)

April 2 Cardiff 11 Gloucester 8
Tries: F.Pegler, H.Berry;
Conversion: W.Egerton

April 16 Gloucester 14 Leicester 0
Tries: A.Hudson, H.Barnes, H.Berry, W.Washbourne;
Conversion: D.Hollands

**April 23 Gloucester 18 Lydney 0
(County Cup Final)**
Tries: A.Hudson (2), H.Barnes, W.Hall, W.Washbourne, W.Dix

1910-11

C.J.Woolf J.Hanman(Chairman) C.Hall A.C.Williams A.F.Fielding G.Romans W.H.Rasbach
H.Barnes G.Griffiths W.Johns N.L.Hayes G.Halford G.Vears(Sub Capt) Lieut C.Carleton F.Pegler W.H.Worth (Treas)
H.G.Brown(Sec) J.T.Brookes(Hon.Match Sec) T.Bagwell(Trainer) H.Berry W.Washbourne J.Hamblin A.Hudson(Capt) F.Yates C.Cook A.Lodge J.Wyburn
C.E.Brown(Pres)

Played 40 Won 25 Lost 13 Drawn 2
For 483 Against 187
Captain: Arthur Hudson

Gloucester 'A'
Played 28 Won 21 Lost 7
For 464 Against 104
Captain: Fred Pegler

Most appearances: C.Cook 37, W.Hall, W.Dix 36, G.Halford 34, A.Lodge 33, A.Hudson 32, W.Washbourne, H.Berry 30
Most tries: A.Hudson 32, W.Washbourne 15, W.Dix, G.Halford 9, H.Berry 8
Conversions: C.Cook 46, W.Egerton 2
Penalties: C.Cook 5
Drop goals: W.Hall 3, C.Cook 2, W.Dix 1

The fixture list of 40 matches was a record, and 50 players were called upon to represent the Club. The highlight of the season was the demolition of Cardiff by four tries and a penalty to nil. Kingsholm was ecstatic that day, and the Citizen reckoned it to be the Club's best ever performance – "the standard of excellence surprised even their most enthusiastic supporters".

There were also memorable triumphs over Llanelly, who had not visited Kingsholm since 1901, and Swansea, achieved a couple of days after the team returned from a six-day trip to Toulouse, where they registered a famous victory over Stade Toulousain. The double was completed over a Northampton side which was otherwise enjoying a very successful season. However, a number of matches were lost by frustratingly narrow margins, one of which was by a single point against Dai Gent's Plymouth, and there were four defeats at Kingsholm.

At full-back, Charley Cook was very consistent, played a notable part in the wins over Swansea and Cardiff, and was rated as "one of the best custodians in the country". Indeed, the three-quarters formed a good defensive unit, but were not as effective in attack, although Arthur Hudson, who appeared far more regularly than in the previous two seasons, resumed his try scoring feats. Early in the season "Jummer" Stephens finally brought a long and distinguished career to a close and he was accorded a public testimonial. Willie Hall replaced him at fly-half and soon stood out as the classiest player in the team, and "Father" Dix developed further as a clever scrum-half.

There was some turnover in the pack, but they continued to produce fine and consistent performances, with Gordon Vears, Billy Johns, "Biddy" Holford, Harry Berry, James Wyburn, Fred Pegler and George Griffiths providing a wealth of experience, and Norman Hayes, Ernest "Fatty" Yates and Allen Lodge introducing exciting fresh talent. The Club offered to supply "pumps" to any who would go running in the summer.

There were England trials for Harry Berry, Dave Hollands and Dai Gent, but no international caps for Gloucester players, although ten represented Gloucestershire.

Sep 3 Gloucester 30 Bream 5
Tries: A.Hudson (3), W.Washbourne (2), H.Berry (2), G.Holford;
Conversions: C.Cook (3)

Sep 10 Gloucester 61 Stroud 0
Tries: A.Hudson (4), W.Washbourne (3), W.Hall (2), A.Lewis, W.Dix, H.Berry, G.Griffiths, J.Wyburn, W.J.Pearce;
Conversions: C.Cook (8)

Sep 17 Cinderford 0 Gloucester 3
Try: A.Hudson

Sep 24 Gloucester 52 Clifton 0
Tries: A.Hudson (5), W.Washbourne (2), J.Wyburn (2), A.Lewis (2), G.Halford, W.Dix, H.Berry;
Conversions: C.Cook (3);
Drop goal: W.Hall

Oct 1 Swansea 12 Gloucester 0

Oct 3 Gloucester 3 Cinderford 11
Try: H.Berry

Oct 8 Gloucester 8 Northampton 3
Tries: W.Dix, H.Rudge;
Conversion: C.Cook

Oct 15 Gloucester 11 Cheltenham 0
Tries: J.Wyburn, A.Hudson (2);

Conversion: C.Cook

Oct 22 Cardiff 5 Gloucester 0

Oct 29 Bristol 8 Gloucester 0

Nov 5 Clifton 3 Gloucester 22
Tries: W.Washbourne (2); H.W.Clock (2),
F.Yates, C.Cook;
Conversions: W.Egerton (2)

Nov 12 Gloucester 19 Llanelly 6
Tries: W.J.Pearce, W.Hall, S.Cook, A.Hudson;
Conversions: C.Cook 2;
Penalty: C.Cook

Nov 19 Lydney 0 Gloucester 3
Try: H.Rudge

Nov 26 Gloucester 16 Pontypool 3
Tries: W.Washbourne, A.Hudson, J.Wyburn,
G.Nelmes;
Conversions: C.Cook (2)

Dec 3 Stroud 3 Gloucester 8
Try: H.W.Clock;
Conversion: C.Cook;
Penalty: C.Cook

Dec 10 Gloucester 0 Newport 5

Dec 17   Neath v Gloucester - cancelled due to
flooding on railway

Dec 24 Pontypool 13 Gloucester 3
Try: G.Halford

**Dec 26 Gloucester 10
Old Merchant Taylors 5**
Tries: K.H.Soutar, A.Hudson;
Drop goal: W.Hall

Dec 27 Gloucester 5 Abertillery 4
Try: W.Dix;
Conversion: C.Cook

Dec 31 Cheltenham 0 Gloucester 8
Tries: W.Dix, K.H.Soutar;
Conversion: C.Cook

Jan 7 Gloucester 3 Neath 5
Try: F.Yates

Jan 14 Leicester 3 Gloucester 0

Jan 21 Plymouth 9 Gloucester 8
Tries: A.Hudson, H.Barnes;
Conversion: C.Cook

Jan 28 Gloucester 39 Lydney 0
Tries: A.Hudson (3), H.Berry (2), H.Barnes,
W.Dix, G.Halford, J.Hamblin;
Conversions: C.Cook (6)

Feb 4 Cheltenham 5 Gloucester 23
Tries: A.Hudson (3), W.Dix (2), H.Barnes;
Conversion: C.Cook;
Penalty: C.Cook

Feb 11 Cinderford 3 Gloucester 8
Tries: W.Washbourne, G.Halford;
Conversion: C.Cook

Feb 18 Gloucester 23 Bristol 6
Tries: H.Barnes, W.Hall, W.Washbourne,
G.Halford, A.Hudson;
Conversions: C.Cook (2);
Drop goal: W.Dix

Feb 25 Abertillery 14 Gloucester 3
Try: J.Harris

Feb 28 Stade Toulousain 13

Gloucester 18
Tries: G.Holford, F.Pegler, W.Hall;
Conversion: C.Cook;
Penalty: C.Cook

Mar 4 Gloucester 13 Swansea 6
Tries: W.Johns, A.Hudson, F.Yates;
Conversions: C.Cook (2)

Mar 11 Bristol 0 Gloucester 0

Mar 18 Newport 8 Gloucester 0

Mar 23 Gloucester 29 Bream 3
Tries: A.Hudson (3), W.Hall, N.Hayes, H.Berry,
J.Meadows;
Conversions: C.Cook (4)

Mar 25 Gloucester 10 Plymouth 0
Tries: G.Halford, A.Lodge;
Drop goal: C.Cook

Apr 1 Gloucester 15 Cardiff 0
Tries: W.Washbourne, G.Halford, A.Hudson,
H.Barnes;
Penalty: C.Cook

Apr 8 Northampton 3 Gloucester 4
Drop goal: W.Hall

Apr 14 Gloucester 4 Aberavon 12
Drop goal: C.Cook

Apr 15 Gloucester 5 Leicester 5
Try: W.Dix;
Conversion: C.Cook

Apr 17 Gloucester 13 Cinderford 0
Tries: A.Hudson, W.Washbourne, J.Hamblin;
Conversions: C.Cook (2)

Apr 18 Llanelly 6 Gloucester 3
Try: W.Washbourne

1911-12

**Played 40 Won 24 Lost 12 Drawn 4
For 359 Against 208
Captain: Arthur Hudson**

Gloucester 'A'
Played 27 Won 20 Lost 5 Drawn 2
For 407 Against 93
Captain: Joe Harris

Most appearances: W.Washbourne 34,
J.Meadows 33, W.Dix, S.Smart L.Hamblin 32,
A.Hudson, G.Vears, 31, H.Berry 30, C.Cook
29, A.Lodge 28
Most tries: A.Hudson 23, W.Washbourne 16,
W.Dix, J.Hamblin 6

Conversions: L.Hamblin 22, W.Hall, C.Cook 3,
F.Hayward 2
Penalties: L.Hamblin 3, H.Hancock, W.Dix 1
Drop goals: W.Dix, W.Hall 1

Although results were mixed, Gloucester went
through the season unbeaten at home by any
Welsh team, a unique achievement amongst
English clubs. Arthur Hudson again made a
specialty of scoring against the Welsh, and a
record of seven wins and two draws, with a
points aggregate of 116-25, was to be savoured,
including victories over Cardiff, Swansea and
Llanelly. The record in the return games in Wales
was very different.

The most exhilarating rugby came in the
matches against Watsonians and Old Merchant
Taylors at Christmas. Gloucester travelled
to Oxford University for the first time for 18
years, and came away well beaten, which was
regarded as a real disappointment, although
injury robbed them of Willie Hall for much of
the game. He was a reserve for England against
France, but that was the closest any Gloucester
player came to an international cap. Thirteen
Gloucester players appeared for Gloucestershire
during the season, but Sid Smart was alone in
playing in all seven fixtures.

The highlight for the players was a second trip to

G.Leaver C.J.Hall A.C.Williams A.W.Vears A.L.Lane J.Hanman(Chairman) P.M.Chance G.Romans W.H.Rasbach
N.Hayes H.Berry G.Halford F.Pegler G.Vears A.Lodge S.Smart J.Meadows
H.G.Brown(Sec) C.J.Woolf J.T.Brookes L.Hamblin S.Cook A.Hudson(Capt) C.Cook F.E.Chapman T.Bagwell(Trainer) W.H.Worth(Treas)
W.Hall W.Dix

France, where they not only beat Stade Francais in Paris, but were also entertained to a splendid banquet – "the boys had a great time".

As usual the strength of the team lay forward, where Gordon Vears again led a pack which was full of talent and experience and never played a poor game. Billy Johns was talked out of retirement, Sid Smart quickly jumped to the front rank, and Norman Hayes came on as the season progressed. "Biddy" Halford was fancied for higher honours, but did not make it beyond England trials, whilst Harry Berry recovered his best form.

Willie Hall and "Father" Dix were as good a pair of half-backs as any in the country at their best, but both suffered injuries. Charley Cook again offered a solid final line of defence, but there was a lack of pace amongst many of the three-quarters, although the wings, Arthur Hudson and William Washbourne were deadly but inconsistent try scorers. Stanley Cook injected dash and a solid defence into the centre in the dozen games for which he was available, and Fred Webb, aged 16, a schoolboy international with a try on debut, offered promise for the future.

Sep 9 Gloucester v Bream - cancelled owing to hardness of ground

Sep 16 Gloucester 27 Penycraig 0
Tries: A.Hudson (3), W.Hall, W.Staunton, W.Washbourne;

Conversion: W.Hall;
Drop goal: W.Hall;
Penalty: H.Hancock

Sep 23 Gloucester 3 Devon Albion 0
Try: W.Hall

Sep 30 London Welsh 0 Gloucester 13
Tries: W.Dix. W.Johns, A.Hudson;
Conversions: W.Hall (2)

Oct 2 Gloucester 8 Cinderford 10
Tries: J.Hamblin, S.Smart;
Conversion: F.Hayward

Oct 7 Northampton 3 Gloucester 3
Try: W.Washbourne

Oct 14 Gloucester 15 Cheltenham 3
Tries: W.Washbourne (3), W.Staunton, J Hamblin

Oct 21 Gloucester 11 Cardiff 0
Tries: A.Hudson (2), W.Washbourne;
Conversion: C.Cook

Oct 28 Cinderford 3 Gloucester 8
Tries: A.Hudson, W.Washbourne;
Conversion: C.Cook

Nov 2 Gloucester 20 Stroud 16
Tries: A.Hudson (2), W.Dix, W.Washbourne, W.Staunton, L.Hamblin;
Conversion: C.Cook

Nov 4 Gloucester 25 Clifton 8
Tries: H.Berry, L.Hamblin, F.Yates, F.Bloxsome, W.Washbourne, J.Hamblin, J.Meadows;
Conversions: L.Hamblin (2)

Nov 11 Oxford University 18 Gloucester 0

Nov 18 Clifton 3 Gloucester 10
Tries: W.Washbourne, H.Berry;
Conversions: L.Hamblin (2)

Nov 25 Gloucester 8 Swansea 3
Tries; A.Hudson, W.Staunton;
Conversion: C.Cook

Dec 2 Gloucester 5 Pontypool 5
Try: A.Hudson;
Conversion: L.Hamblin

Dec 9 Gloucester 14 Penylan 5
Tries: A.Hudson (2), F.Bloxsome (2);
Conversion: L Hamblin

Dec 16 Newport 19 Gloucester 5
Try: J.Hamblin;
Conversion: L.Hamblin

Dec 23 Gloucester 11 Watsonians 11
Tries: A.Hudson, W.Johns;
Conversion: L.Hamblin;
Penalty: L.Hamblin

Dec 26 Gloucester 0 Old Merchant Taylors 5

Dec 27 Gloucester 23 Abertillery 3
Tries: F.E.Chapman (2), S.Cook, J.Meadows,
A.Hudson; Conversions: L.Hamblin (4)

Dec 30 Llanelly 14 Gloucester 0

Jan 6 Gloucester 8 Llanelly 3
Tries: A.Hudson, G.Holford;
Conversion: L.Hamblin

Jan 13 Leicester 0 Gloucester 7
Try: W.Washbourne;
Drop goal: W.Dix

Jan 20 Pontypool 12 Gloucester 3
Try: J.Hamblin

Jan 27 Gloucester 16 Bristol 8
Tries: H.Berry, S.Smart, W.Dix, N.Hayes;
Conversions: L.Hamblin (2)

Feb 3 Gloucester v Leicester - abandoned due
to frost

Feb 10 Cheltenham 0 Gloucester 6
Tries: W.Washbourne, J Hamblin

Feb 17 Bristol 3 Gloucester 8
Tries: S.Smart, W.Washbourne;
Conversion: L.Hamblin

Feb 24 Gloucester 14 Northampton 3
Tries: A.Hudson (2), W.Washbourne,
L.Hamblin;
Conversion: L.Hamblin

Mar 2 Swansea 11 Gloucester 5
Try: N.Hayes;
Conversion: L.Hamblin

Mar 4 Neath 3 Gloucester 0

Mar 9 Gloucester 9 Bristol 0
Tries: A.Hudson, N.Hayes, W.Washbourne

Mar 14 Stade Francais 3 Gloucester 13
Tries: W.Dix, A.Hudson;
Conversions: L.Hamblin (2);
Penalty: L.Hamblin

Mar 16 Cinderford 3 Gloucester 0

Mar 23 Cardiff 6 Gloucester 0

Mar 30 Gloucester 6 Newport 6
Try: W.Washbourne;
Penalty: L.Hamblin

Apr 5 Gloucester 14 London Welsh 0
Tries: W.Dix, W.Hall, A.Cook, F.Yates;
Conversion: L Hamblin

Apr 6 Gloucester v Neath - cancelled by Neath

Apr 6 Gloucester 12 Bream 3
Tries: A.Hudson (2), L.Hamblin;
Penalty: W.Dix

Apr 8 Gloucester 12 Cinderford 5
Tries: S.Smart, A.Lodge, N.Hayes, L.Hamblin

Apr 9 Stroud 0 Gloucester 14
Tries: F.Webb, W.Dix, A.Hudson, A.Lodge;
Conversion: F.Hayward

Apr 13 Abertillery 9 Gloucester 0

Apr 20 Devon Albion 7 Gloucester 3
Try: Stanley Cook

1912-13

Played 39 Won 21 Lost 14 Drawn 4
For 369 Against 224
Captain: Arthur Hudson/George Halford

Gloucester 'A'
Played 23 Won 15 Lost 4 Drawn 4
For 257 Against 82
Captain: Fred Bloxsome

Most appearances: W.Dix 37, S.Millard 36,
A.Lewis 33, L.Hamblin 32, W.Dovey 31,
N.Hayes 29, C.Cook, G.Halford 28, A.Cook,
W.Wilkes 27
Most tries: A.Hudson 14, G.Bowen 13,
L.Hamblin, W.Washbourne 10
Conversions: C.Cook, L.Hamblin 8,
F.Hayward 3, W.Dix 2
Penalties: C.Cook 6, F.Hayward 2, L.Hamblin 1
Drop goals: A.Lewis 2, W.Dix 1

The best performances of the season were
described as supreme examples of the team
showing lots of "Glawster Dawg". On the
same day as the County Championship final,
Gloucester, with nine reserves, entertained
a full-strength and high-flying Cardiff at
Kingsholm and displayed "pluck, resolution,
hard work and tenacity" to earn a remarkable
draw. The team was also short of several
leading players when they travelled to Leicester
and pulled off an unexpected win to take
away Leicester's unbeaten home record, and

the double was completed a month later. But
perhaps best of all was the late-season draw
against a Newport side who had only lost twice
and whose ferocious approach was matched not
only on the field of play but also amongst the
spectators on the Tump.

Of the four fixtures against Cinderford, one
was cancelled for frost, one was drawn, and
Gloucester won the other two, but they were all
the usual hard-fought contests, the first resulting
in three Gloucester players retiring injured. An
oddity was the match against Bristol which had
to be abandoned before half-time, such was the
severity of the storm which struck Kingsholm.
Indeed, the Club operated at a loss, ascribed
principally to the most attractive fixtures being
rained on, but also the 14 defeats were the most
sustained in a season for ten years.

The team was workmanlike rather than clever,
and there was a lack of pace among the backs,
although Charley Cook was solid at full-back.
Injuries disrupted the three-quarters, most
notably to Arthur Hudson, who was able to play
in less than half of the fixtures and surrendered
the captaincy. Lionel Hamblin stood out at
centre. "Father" Dix and Willie Hall played well
at half-back until Hall fell out with the Club and
left mid-season after 139 appearances.

The pack was weakened when Harry Berry

(136 appearances) and George Griffiths (112
appearances) retired after a few games, and Billy
Johns was not regularly available, but "Biddy"
Halford led the pack well, ably supported by
Gordon Vears, Norman Hayes, Sid Smart and
Syd Millard.

Sid Smart played in all of England's matches as
they won their first Grand Slam, and against
South Africa. Stanley Cook and Cornelius
Carleton featured in England trials. Eight
Gloucester players represented Gloucestershire
during the season, and seven - Lionel Hamblin
(try, conversion, penalty), Stanley Cook,
William Washbourne, Billy Johns, Sid Smart,
Norman Hayes and Gordon Vears -played in the
County Championship final at Carlisle, where
Cumberland were beaten 14-3 to secure the
County's second title.

Sep 14 Gloucester 29 Bream 0
Tries: L.Hamblin (2), N.Hayes (2), A.Hudson,
W.Washbourne, S.Smart, A.Lewis;
Conversion: A.Dix;
Penalty: L.Hamblin

Sep 21 Gloucester 8 Llanelly 0
Tries: W.Washbourne, A.Lewis;
Conversion: L.Hamblin

Sep 28 Gloucester 12 Cinderford 5
Tries: A.Hudson, L.Hamblin, H.Berry, A.Lewis

J.T.Brookes(Hon.Sec) A.C.Williams G.Romans A.W.Vears A.L.Lane P.M.Chance A.F.Fielding C.J.Woolf
W.H.Worth(Treas) A.Cook S.Millard C.Mumford G.Halford N.Hayes F.Pegler W.Dovey S.Smart
T.Bagwell(Trainer) C.Cook L.Hamblin W.Washbourne A.Hudson(Capt) W.Wilks E.Bowen G.Vears H.G.Brown(Sec)
A.Lewis W.Dix

Sep 30 Gloucester 6 Northampton 3
Tries: W.Sysum, W.Johns

Oct 5 Swansea 16 Gloucester 0

Oct 12 Gloucester 7 Neath 3
Try: L.Hamblin;
Drop goal: A.Lewis

Oct 19 Devon Albion 17 Gloucester 0

Oct 26 Cardiff 6 Gloucester 4
Drop goal: W.Dix

Nov 2 Gloucester 36 Clifton 0
Tries: E.Bowen (4), A.Hudson (3), A.Cook (2),
A.Saunders;
Conversions: F.Hayward (3)

Nov 9 Gloucester 3 Newport 11
Try: W.Hall

Nov 16 Stroud 0 Gloucester 20
Tries: A.Lewis, E.Bowen, F.Webb, W.Dix,
G.Halford, W.Hall;
Conversion: W.Dix

Nov 23 Gloucester 3
Oxford University 12
Try: J.Meadows

Nov 30 Cinderford v Gloucester - abandoned
due to frost

Dec 7 Gloucester 32 Stroud 0
Tries: F.Webb (3), W.Dix (2), W.Wilkes,
A.Hudson, G.D.Bottomley;
Conversions: C.Cook (4)

Dec 14 Clifton 3 Gloucester 9
Tries: E.Bowen, F.Webb;
Penalty: F.Hayward

Dec 21 Gloucester 8 Pontypool 12
Try: A.Hudson;
Conversion: C.Cook;
Penalty: C.Cook

Dec 26 Gloucester 3
Old Merchant Taylors 0
Penalty: C.Cook

Dec 27 Gloucester 15
1ˢᵗ Gloucester Regiment 3
Tries: J.Harris (2), E.Bowen, C.Mumford,
F.Bloxsome

Dec 28 Gloucester 9 Watsonians 9
Tries: W.Dix, E.Bowen, R.A.Clarke

Jan 4 Leicester 8 Gloucester 13
Tries: W.Wilkes, L.Hamblin, E.Nash;
Drop goal: A.Lewis

Jan 11 Gloucester 14 Cheltenham 0
Tries: W.Wilkes (2), W.Dix, Lieut.Carleton;
Conversion: C.Cook

Jan 18 Bristol 0 Gloucester 3
Try: A.Hudson

Jan 25 Abertillery 7 Gloucester 0

Feb 1 Gloucester 11 Leicester 3
Tries: L.Hamblin, A.Cook;
Conversion: L.Hamblin;
Penalty: C.Cook

Feb 8 Pontypool 19 Gloucester 0

Feb 15 Gloucester 6 Devon Albion 8
Try: A.Hudson;
Penalty: C.Cook

Feb 20 Gloucester 25 Cheltenham 4
Tries: A.Hudson (4), E.Bowen (2), G.Vears;
Conversions: L.Hamblin (2)

Feb 22 Northampton 8 Gloucester 6
Tries: E.Bowen, W.Washbourne

Mar 1 Gloucester 3 Cardiff 3
Penalty: F.W.Hayward

Mar 8 Cheltenham 6 Gloucester 8
Try: L.Hamblin;
Conversion: C.Cook;
Penalty: C.Cook

Mar 15 Cinderford 3 Gloucester 9
Tries: W.Washbourne, E.Bowen, G.Halford

Mar 21 Gloucester 6 Abertillery 0
Tries: W.Washbourne, J.Harris

Mar 22 Gloucester 9 Bristol 0 -
abandoned at half time due to storm
Tries: W.Washbourne (2), E.Bowen

Mar 24 Gloucester 26 Cinderford 0
Tries: L.Hamblin (2), W.Washbourne, W.Wilkes,
A.Cook, A.Lewis;

Conversions: L.Hamblin (3), C.Cook,

Mar 29 Gloucester 8 Harlequins 8
Tries: L.Hamblin, A.Hudson;
Conversion: L.Hamblin

Apr 2 Cheltenham 3 Gloucester 12
Tries: W.Sysum (2), G.Halford, W.Washbourne

Apr 5 Newport 15 Gloucester 6

Try: W.Washbourne;
Penalty: C.Cook

Apr 12 Gloucester 0 Swansea 8

Apr 19 Neath 18 Gloucester 0

Apr 21 Llanelly 3 Gloucester 0

Apr 26 Cinderford 0 Gloucester 0

1913-1914

**Played 37 Won 25 Lost 10 Drawn 2
For 357 Against 167
Captain: George Halford**

Gloucester 'A'
Played 27 Won 19 Lost 5 Drawn 3
For 295 Against 107
Captain: Fred Bloxsome

Most appearances: W.Parham 35, C.Cook 32,
J.Baker 30, G.Halford 29, N.Hayes 28
Most tries: F.Webb 23, W.Washbourne 12,
L.Hamblin 8, S.Sysum 7
Conversions: C.Cook 18, L.Hamblin,
S.Sysum 5, T.Burns 1
Penalties: C.Cook 3, L.Hamblin 2, F.Hayward,
S.Sysum 1
Drop goals: L.Hamblin 3, F.Ruck, A.Lewis 1

The prospects for the season were not good with
the huge loss of experience with Billy Johns
(266 appearances), Gordon Vears (287) and Fred
Pegler (239) retiring at the end of the previous
season. This was exacerbated by Arthur
Hudson and "Father" Dix being available for
very few games. But "Biddy" Halford was an
effective captain, and the whole season turned
out well, both in terms of results and financially.

Powerful sides were beaten in Harlequins,
Oxford University, Cardiff, Swansea,
Pontypool, Old Merchant Taylors, and Leicester
(twice), and only two defeats were sustained at
Kingsholm. The overall record against English
clubs was excellent, but as so often visits to
Wales ended in disappointment. Pontypool were
so violent on their visit to Kingsholm that future
fixtures were cancelled.

Gloucester played for the first time at
Twickenham, where the forwards had their best
game of the season, and two dropped goals by
Lionel Hamblin were too much for a Harlequins
side led by Adrian Stoop and rated as the best
in the country. The following week in heavy

rain against Swansea, "the passing movements
were positively thrilling and bewildering in
execution", and the pack "worked in perfect
unity with dash, skill, cleverness and resource",
the first half being described as the best rugby
the Club had ever played.

Charley Cook continued to reign supreme at
full-back. William Washbourne scored five
tries in the first three games of the season, Fred
Webb scored eight tries in three matches in
September, and together with Alec Lewis and
Lionel Hamblin they formed the first choice
three-quarter line. "Tart" Hall joined the Club
as an established County player, and formed
an effective half-back partnership with Joseph
Baker.

The backbone of a very fine pack of fast, dashing
and clever forwards was "Biddy" Halford, Sid
Smart, Norman Hayes, Syd Millard and Arthur

Saunders, supported by promising new recruits
in Joe Lawson, Frank Ayliffe and William
Parham.

Sid Smart retained his position as No8
throughout the season for England as they
recorded their second successive Grand Slam.
"Biddy" Halford and Lionel Hamblin were
selected for England trials, and ten Gloucester
players represented Gloucestershire.

Sep 6 Gloucester 7 Bream 3
Try: W.Washbourne;
Drop goal: F.Ruck

**Sep 13 Gloucester 56 1st
Gloucester Regiment 0**
Tries: F.Webb (5), W.Washbourne (3),
L.Hamblin (3), N.Hayes;
Conversions: C.Cook (8);
Drop goal: A.Lewis

The Gloucester Team driving off from Oxford station

Sep 20 Gloucester 14 Moseley 0
Tries: F.Webb (2), W.Washbourne, N.Hayes;
Conversion: C.Cook

Sep 27 Northampton 9 Gloucester 3
Try: F.Webb

Sep 29 Gloucester 3 Cinderford 3
Penalty: F.Hayward

Oct 4 Harlequins 0 Gloucester 8
Drop goals: L.Hamblin (2)

Oct 11 Gloucester 9 Swansea 0
Tries: F.Webb (2), W.Washbourne

Oct 18 Pontypool 15 Gloucester 3
Try: W.Washbourne

Oct 25 Gloucester 9 Bristol 0
Tries: F.Webb, W.Washbourne, N.Hayes

Nov 1 Clifton 0 Gloucester 16
Tries: H.Wager, O.T.Powell, S.Sysum;
Conversions: C.Cook (2);
Penalty: C.Cook

Nov 8 Gloucester 6 Cardiff 4
Try: L.Hamblin;
Penalty: L.Hamblin

Nov 15 Stroud 3 Gloucester 17
Tries: A.Hudson (3), S.Sysum, F.Bloxsome;
Conversion: C.Cook

Nov 22 Oxford University 6
Gloucester 9
Tries: F.Webb (2);
Penalty: C.Cook

Nov 29 Gloucester 19 Bath 0

Tries: A.Hudson (3), J.Meadows, S.Sysum;
Conversions: C.Cook (2)

Dec 6 Cheltenham 0 Gloucester 0

Dec 13 Gloucester 8 Stroud 6
Tries: O.T.Powell (2);
Conversion: S.Sysum

Dec 20 Llanelly 3 Gloucester 0

Dec 26 Gloucester 12
Old Merchant Taylors 6
Tries: F.Webb, A.Lewis, J.Baker, J.F.Lawson

Dec 27 Gloucester 8 Cheltenham 5
Try: L.Hamblin;
Conversion: L.Hamblin;
Penalty: L.Hamblin

Jan 3 Gloucester 3 Leicester 0
Try: F.Webb

Jan 10 Abertillery 14 Gloucester 3
Try: F.Webb

Jan 17 Bristol 0 Gloucester 5
Try: F.Webb;
Conversion: T.Burns

Jan 24 Gloucester 31 Cheltenham 0
Tries: W.Washbourne (4), A.Hall (2), G.Halford,
S.Sysum;
Conversion: C.Cook (2);
Penalty: S.Sysum

Jan 31 Newport 19 Gloucester 0

Feb 7 Gloucester 8 Pontypool 0
Tries: F.Webb (2);
Conversion: S.Sysum

Feb 14 Gloucester 30 Llanhilleth 3
Tries: F.Webb (3), A.Lewis (2), L.Hamblin,
S.Sysum, F.Ayliffe;
Conversions: S.Sysum (2), L.Hamblin

Feb 21 Gloucester 0 Newport 10

Feb 28 Cardiff 3 Gloucester 0

Mar 7 Gloucester 11 Llanelly 0
Tries: A.Lewis, J.Lawson;
Conversion: C.Cook;
Penalty: C.Cook

Mar 14 Leicester 3 Gloucester 6
Tries: W.Dovey (2)

Mar 21 Swansea 22 Gloucester 5
Try: T.B.Powell;
Conversion: L.Hamblin

Mar 28 Gloucester 16 Northampton 0
Tries: L.Hamblin, A.Lewis, G.Halford,
R.A.Clarke;
Conversions: L.Hamblin, S.Sysum

Apr 4 Cinderford 7 Gloucester 6
Tries: G.Halford, S.Sysum

Apr 10 Gloucester 4 Headingley 17
Drop goal: L.Hamblin

Apr 11 Gloucester 6 Abertillery 3
Tries: S.Sysum, F.Bloxsome

Apr 13 Gloucester 6 Cinderford 0
Tries: L.Hamblin, C.Mumford

Apr 18 Bath 3 Gloucester 10
Tries: F.Webb, F.Ayliffe;
Conversions: L.Hamblin, C.Cook

~ ~ 1918-1941 ~ ~

1918-19

Played 11 Won 4 Lost 6 Drawn 1
For 88 Against 127

Most appearances: A.Hall, A.Redding 10,
L.Robbins, Sgt.Maj.Pugh 8
Most tries: A.Hudson 7, L.Hamblin 3
Conversions: L.Hamblin 7, N.Hayes, Sgt.Maj.
Pugh 1
Drop goal: L.Hamblin 1

At the time of the armistice which ended the
Great War on 11th November 1918, the Club had
debts of £536, but committee members acted
as guarantors with the bank. The Club was
brought back to life mainly through the efforts
of Arthur Fielding, John Brookes, Frank Ayliffe
and Arthur Hudson.

During the war, 30 men who had played for
Gloucester before the outbreak of hostilities,
died, whilst many others were wounded, and
it took time for the survivors to be demobbed
and return home. With all clubs experiencing
trouble finding sufficient players, early games
were played against military sides. The first
match was arranged for 21st December, when
only 1,200 spectators came through the gates,
but the second match on Boxing Day attracted
some 2,800. The first matches since 1914 against
another club were away and then home against
Cardiff.

Whilst soldiers were awaiting repatriation
to New Zealand and Canada, they formed
rugby teams, and both came to Kingsholm, the
Canadians attracting the biggest crowd of the
season of more than 3,000. However, the try of
the season came against the New Zealanders
when "well inside the home half Dix opened
out; the ball in turn was handled by all the
backs. Hudson was the last to receive, and
the Old International putting on his best pace,
raced away in fine style. He cut inside the full
back beautifully, and beating another opponent
who had come across the field finished up a
great effort by scoring behind the posts." These
matches helped to wipe out the overdraft and
put the Club's bank account into the black by
the end of the season to the tune of £274.

Dec 21 Gloucester 9 3rd Gloucesters 6
Tries: A.Hudson (2), F.W.Hayward

Dec 26 Gloucester 17
4th Reserve Gloucestershire Regiment 3
Tries: A.Hudson (2), N.Hayes, J.Webb,
J.Daniells;
Conversion: N.Hayes

Jan 25 Cardiff 3 Gloucester 3
Try: A.Redding

Feb 8 Leicester 15 Gloucester 0

Feb 15 Gloucester 5
R.N.Depot (Devonport) 14
Try: L.Hamblin;
Conversion: Sgt.Maj.Pugh

Mar 8 Gloucester 5 Cardiff 17
Try: L.Robbins;
Conversion: L.Hamblin

Mar 22 Gloucester 12
New Zealand Army 15
Tries: A.Hudson, L.Hamblin;
Conversion: L.Hamblin;
Drop goal: L.Hamblin

Apr 5 Gloucester 8 RAF 18
Tries: L.Hamblin, W.L.Stone;
Conversion: L.Hamblin

Apr 19 Gloucester 21 Canadians 6
Tries: F.Mansell, A.Hudson, L.Robbins,
S.Smart, penalty try;
Conversions: L.Hamblin (3)

Apr 21 Gloucester 8 Cross Keys 0
Tries: A.Hudson, J.Harris;
Conversion: L.Hamblin

Apr 26 Pill Harriers 30 Gloucester 0

1919-20

Played 33 Won 19 Lost 12 Drawn 2
For 384 Against 222
Captain: George "Biddy" Halford

Gloucester 'A'
Played 26 Won 14 Lost 10 Drawn 2
For 228 Against 123
Captain: F.Bloxsome

Most appearances: F.Ayliffe 30, F.Webb,
A.Hudson, W.Dix, A.Hall 26, N.Hayes 23,
J.H.Webb 21, G.Welshman, T.Millington 20
Most tries: A.Hudson, F.Webb 17,
W.Washbourne 12, S.A.Brown 9, W.Dix 8
Conversions: L.Hamblin 14, G.Welshman 13,
W.Dix 3, T.Millington 2, F.Webb, H.Stone 1
Penalties: L.Hamblin 5, G.Welshman,
T.Millington 1
Drop goal: W.Dix 1

In the first full season following the end of
the Great War, a lot of fresh faces appeared
for the Club. Four players went north to play
professional rugby, the greatest loss being Billy
Stone, a brilliant centre, who signed for Hull and
soon earned international honours in Rugby
League. Selections were regularly disrupted by
injuries, most notably keeping Sid Brown out for
much of the season. Of the remaining players,
many were called upon to play representative
rugby. This meant that there were few occasions
on which the first choice team made it onto the
field, and 50 players were used, but the results
achieved were regarded as reasonably good.

There were some old players who loyally
responded to the Club's need – for example,
Norman Hayes came out of retirement to play
the whole season, but then finally retired after
144 appearances. Lionel Hamblin scored heavily

with his boot in the first half of the season, but
then lost his place for both Club and County and
finished his career with 113 appearances.

Amongst the highlights of the season were doing
the double over both Bristol and Bath. Victory
over Cardiff included a brilliant try when Sid
Brown beat several opponents with a tricky run,
Frank Ayliffe carried on powerfully, and Arthur
Hudson finished it off with a sprint behind the
posts. The visit of Newport attracted the largest
crowd of the season, close to 10,000, but a rail
strike prevented fixtures against Harlequins
and Northampton being fulfilled.

Arthur Hudson retained his position as leading
try scorer but broke his collarbone during the
County Championship final, which ended his
playing career after 268 appearances. At the end
of the season, he became Secretary of the Club,

Match v Cardiff, 18 Oct 1919
N.Hayes J.F.Lawson F.Ayliffe J.Harris A.Ward A.Hall T.Bagwell(Trainer)
F.W.Hayward F.Webb A.Hudson G.Halford(Capt) W.Davis S.Brown T.Voyce
L.Hamblin W.Dix

at a salary of £120 per annum, a position he was to retain for 42 years.

In order to put the Club into a sound financial position, it was felt necessary to double the membership fees for the season to 2gns for patrons, £1 for the grandstand (10s for ladies), 10s for ground admission, and 5s for juveniles; admission charges for non-members for individual games were increased to grandstand 2s 6d, Worcester Street 2s, Dean's Walk 1s and boys 6d. This enabled the Club to make a profit of £587 on the season, and raise the bank balance to £1,037. An additional 380 shares in the Ground Company were purchased to bring the Club's holding to 1391 (out of 3150 in total).

Much pride was taken from the representative honours earned. Fifteen players were capped by Gloucestershire, and nine played in the County Championship final, when Yorkshire were defeated 27-3 at Bradford; they were Fred Webb (2 tries), Frank Ayliffe (try), Arthur Hudson, Tom Millington (conversion), "Father" Dix, Arthur Hall, Sid Smart, "Biddy" Halford and A.Ward. Three players were capped by England – Sid Smart against Wales, Ireland & Scotland, "Biddy" Halford against Wales & France, and Tom Voyce against Ireland & Scotland – and "Father" Dix and "Tart" Hall had trials.

13 Sep Gloucester 13 Lydney 3

Tries: F.Webb (3);
Conversions: L.Hamblin (2)

20 Sep Gloucester 13 Abertillery 0
Tries: S.Brown (2), A.Hudson;
Conversions; L.Hamblin (2)

4 Oct Gloucester 21 Cheltenham 6
Tries: S.Brown (2), A.Hudson, J.F.Lawson, W.Stone;
Conversions: L.Hamblin (2), W.Stone

6 Oct Gloucester 14 Forest XV 11
Tries: F.Webb, A.Hudson;
Conversions: L.Hamblin (2);
Drop goal: W.Dix

11 Oct Bristol 0 Gloucester 10
Tries: W.Dix, J.Harris;
Conversions: L.Hamblin (2)

18 Oct Gloucester 10 Cardiff 3
Tries: J.Harris, A.Hudson;
Conversions: L.Hamblin (2)

25 Oct Swansea 12 Gloucester 5
Try: S.Smart;
Conversion: L.Hamblin

8 Nov Gloucester 9 Oxford University 5
Try: T.Millington;

Penalties: L.Hamblin (2)

15 Nov Cross Keys 11 Gloucester 0

22 Nov Gloucester 12 Pontypool 3
Tries: F.Webb, W.Dix;
Penalties: L.Hamblin (2)

6 Dec Gloucester 33 Cheltenham 3
Tries: F.Ayliffe (3), A.Lewis (2), W.Washbourn (2), F.Webb, J.F.Lawson;
Conversions: W.Dix (2), L.Hamblin

13 Dec Northampton 15 Gloucester 8
Tries: F.Ayliffe, J.F.Lawson;
Conversion: G.Welshman

20 Dec Stroud 0 Gloucester 28
Tries: A.Hudson (2), W.Washbourn (2), W.Dix (2), F.Mansell, F.Webb;
Conversions: F.Webb, W.Dix

26 Dec Gloucester 15 Old Merchant Taylors 0
Tries: F.Webb, L.Hamblin, T.Voyce, W.Dix, J.Harris

27 Dec Gloucester 9 Llanelly 13
Tries: W.Washbourn, F.Webb;
Penalty: L.Hamblin

3 Jan Leicester 14 Gloucester 9

Tries: F.Webb (2), W.Washbourn

10 Jan Bath 0 Gloucester 24
Tries: A.Hudson (4), W.Washbourn (3), W.Dix

17 Jan Gloucester 25 Moseley 0
Tries: W.Washbourn (3), A.Hudson (2),
T.Millington, S.Brown;
Conversions: W.Washbourn (2)

24 Jan Lydney 0 Gloucester 0

31 Jan Gloucester 3 Newport 18
Try: S.Brown

7 Feb Cheltenham 0 Gloucester 10
Tries: N.Daniell, penalty try;
Conversions: G.Welshman (2)

14 Feb Cardiff 9 Gloucester 6

Tries: S.Brown, F.Ayliffe

21 Feb Gloucester 42 Stroud 0
Tries: F.Webb (2), W.Dix (2), J.Webb,
T.Millington, F.Ward, J.Brown, S.Brown,
A.Hudson;
Conversions: T.Millington (2), G.Welshman;
Penalties: T.Millington, G.Welshman

28 Feb Pontypool 12 Gloucester 0

6 Mar Gloucester 6 Bristol 3
Tries: F.Webb, J.Webb

13 Mar Gloucester 0 Leicester 3

20 Mar Llanelly 29 Gloucester 5
Try: F.Webb;
Conversion: G.Welshman

27 Mar Gloucester 16 Bath 6
Tries: J.Humphries (3), A.Hudson;
Conversions: G.Welshman (2)

3 Apr Newport 23 Gloucester 3
Try: F.Mansell

5 Apr Gloucester 6 Cross Keys 6
Tries: F.Webb (2)

6 Apr Gloucester 23 Cheltenham 5
Tries: A.Hudson (3), S.Brown, J.Humphries;
Conversions: G.Welshman (4)

10 Apr Gloucester 3 Swansea 0
Try: T.Millington

17 Apr Abertillery 9 Gloucester 3
Try: T.Voyce

F.A.Abbey A.Cromwell A.Brown G.Leaver A.F.Fielding(Chairman) H.C.Williams E.J.Baldwin G.J.Collingbourne(Hon.Treas)
J.Harris F.Mansell T.Voyce N.L.Hayes J.Webb S.Smart C.Mumford J.F.Lawson Rev O.E.Hayden F.Pegler
J.T.Brookes(Hon.Sec) G.Welshman W.Washbourne A.Hall A.Hudson(Asst.Sec) G.Halford(Capt) F.W.Webb S.A.Brown F.W.Ayliffe F.Ward
T.Bagwell(Trainer)
W.Dix T.Millington

1920-21

Played 37 Won 25 Lost 10 Drawn 2
For 453 Against 262
Captain: Fred Webb

Gloucester 'A'
Played 23 Won 22 Lost 1 Drawn 0
For 402 Against 89

Most appearances: T.Millington 34, F.Ayliffe 33, G.Halford 32, W.Dix, A.Hall 31, S.Smart 30, N.Daniell, J.F.Lawson 28

Most tries: S.Brown 20, N.Daniell 18, F.Webb 12, A.Robbins 7
Most conversions: A.Robbins 13, T.Burns 9, T.Voyce 5, T.Millington, S.Cook 4
Penalties: A.Robbins 5, T.Voyce 2, T.Millington 1
Drop goals: A.Robbins 3, W.Dix 1

The season at Kingsholm started with a new stand, built during the summer at a cost of £1,113. It was all standing, but the roof provided protection from the weather for the first time on the south side of the ground, and this probably contributed to the membership increasing substantially to 1,978.

The biggest crowd of the season, about 12,000, with a record £768 taken on the gate, was again attracted by the visit of Newport, who arrived unbeaten after 25 matches. It was a game full of incident, played at high speed, and described as the most exciting match since the visit of New Zealand in 1905. A.Robbins had a wonderful game at outside half, and his half-back partner,

A.Cromwell G.Collingbourne A.Brown N.Hayes G.Leaver A.F.Fielding J.T.Brookes G.Romans E.J.Baldwin
F.Pegler J.F.Lawson F.W.Warde F.Mansell J.H.Webb Sir J.Bruton M.P.(Pres) S.Smart G.Halford T.Voyce J.Harris G.Fox
A.Hudson(Sec) F.Abbey N.Daniell S.Brown F.W.Ayliffe C.F.Webb(Capt) T.Millington A.Hall C.Mumford C.Cook T.Bagwell
A.Robbins W.Dix

"Father" Dix, nipped in for a try which sent the ground into raptures. Gloucester's 12-9 victory was their first over these opponents since 1908.

Against Llanelly, Gloucester lost a forward to injury in the first half, and were 0-8 down well into the second half. The remaining seven in the pack responded magnificently, Robbins again played a blinder at outside half, and "Father" Dix again raised the roof with a try. The 11-8 victory meant that Gloucester had beaten the four big Welsh clubs in one season, a feat which they had accomplished only once before, in 1898-99, and which had only ever been achieved by one other English club, Devon Albion.

This season saw the retirement of winger William Washbourne after 169 appearances, and full-back Charley Cook after 157.

Spectators forgot what it was like to see their team defeated at Kingsholm, with the 1st XV, the A team, and the County all going through the season without having their colours lowered there. The Citizen declared it the finest season in the history of the Club, and presented the players with inscribed silver cigarette cases; the Club gave them blazers.

Ten players were capped by Gloucestershire and nine of them - Stanley Cook (2 tries), "Father" Dix, Tom Millington, "Biddy" Halford, Tom Voyce, Sid Smart, Frank Ayliffe, Arthur Hall and Joe Harris - played in the County Championship final at Kingsholm, where Leicestershire were

thrashed 31-4, in front of 10,700 spectators who paid a record amount for a match at Kingsholm of £1,011. The Club only saw £40 of it for the hire of the ground, but made a profit of £906 for the season as a whole.

Tom Voyce was a fixture in the England side which won the Grand Slam by defeating Wales, Ireland, Scotland and France, and "Father" Dix was a reserve for all of these games; Sid Smart had a trial.

Sep 11 Gloucester 17 Lydney 0
Tries: S.Brown (2), T.Millington, N.Daniell;
Conversion: T.Voyce;
Penalty: T.Voyce

Sep 18 Gloucester 9 Bath 6
Tries: J.Webb, A.Hall;
Penalty: T.Voyce

Sep 25 Gloucester 14 Northampton 8
Tries: F.Webb (2), T.Voyce (2);
Conversion: G.Smith

Oct 2 Harlequins 8 Gloucester 10
Tries: T.Millington, S.Smart;
Conversions: G.Smith, T.Voyce

Oct 4 Gloucester 5 Cinderford 0
Try: S.Brown;
Conversion: T.Voyce

Oct 9 Gloucester 6 Bristol 3
Tries: S.Brown (2)

Oct 16 Gloucester 6 Guy's Hospital 3
Tries: G.Thomas, J.Webb

Oct 23 Cardiff 10 Gloucester 0

Oct 30 Northampton 11 Gloucester 5
Try: W.Washbourn;
Conversion: T.Voyce

Nov 6 Coventry 6 Gloucester 3
Try: N.Daniell

Nov 13 Cheltenham 3 Gloucester 24
Tries: S.Brown (2), N.Daniell (2), T.Voyce, W.Dix;
Conversions: T.Burns (3)

Nov 20 Pontypool 20 Gloucester 8
Try: S.Brown (2);
Conversion: T.Burns

Nov 27 Gloucester 29 Moseley 0
Tries: S.Brown (4), N.Daniell (2), A.Robbins, W.Washbourn, A.Wright;
Conversion: T.Burns

Dec 4 Gloucester 10 Swansea 0
Tries: S.Brown, N.Daniell;
Drop goal: W.Dix

Dec 11 Gloucester 24 Stroud 0
Tries: N.Daniell (2), W.Collins (2), D.Brown, N.Wright;
Conversions: T.Burns (3)

Dec 27 Gloucester 16
Old Merchant Taylors 3
Tries: F.Webb (2), S.Brown, T.Voyce;
Drop goal: A.Robbins

Dec 28 Gloucester 18 Bridgwater 8
Tries: S.Brown (2), N.Daniell, T.Voyce,
A.Robbins, J.F.Lawson

Jan 1 United Services Portsmouth 5
Gloucester 5
Try: F.Webb;
Conversion: T.Burns

Jan 8 Gloucester 12 Leicester 3
Tries: F.Ayliffe, S.Cook;
Conversion: C.Cook;
Drop goal: A.Robbins

Jan 15 Moseley 11 Gloucester 24
Tries: F.Webb (2), J.Webb, W.Collins,
A.Robbins;
Conversions: A.Robbins (3);
Penalty: A.Robbins

Jan 22 Gloucester 16
United Services Portsmouth 3
Tries: G.Holford, N.Daniell, T.Millington,
A.Robbins;
Conversions: A.Robbins, T.Voyce

Jan 29 Gloucester 12 Newport 9

Tries: W.Dix, J.Harris;
Conversion: A.Robbins;
Drop goal: A.Robbins

Feb 5 Gloucester 18 Cheltenham 11
Tries: G.Halford, J.Harris, N.Daniell, S.Brown;
Conversions: C.Cook (3)

Feb 12 Gloucester 16 Cardiff 11
Tries: N.Daniell, F.Webb, G.Halford, J.Harris;
Conversions: A.Robbins (2)

Feb 19 Guy's Hospital 14 Gloucester 8
Try: F.Webb;
Conversion: A.Robbins;
Penalty: A.Robbins

Feb 26 Gloucester 5 Pontypool 5
Try: F.Webb;
Conversion: A.Robbins

Mar 5 Gloucester 25 Coventry 6
Tries: F.Webb (2), F.Ayliffe(2), S.Brown;
Conversions: A.Robbins (2);
Penalties: A.Robbins (2)

Mar 12 Bristol 10 Gloucester 3
Penalty: A.Robbins

Mar 19 Gloucester 11 Llanelly 8
Tries: A.Robbins, D.Brown, W.Dix;

Conversion: A.Robbins

Mar 26 Newport 24 Gloucester 3
Try: F.Ayliffe

Mar 28 Gloucester 20 Manchester 3
Tries: N.Daniell (3), F.Webb, J.Harris,
S.Langston;
Conversion: T.Millington

Mar 29 Bridgwater 6 Gloucester 24
Tries: N.Daniell (2), S.Brown, C.Mumford,
A.Hall;
Conversions: T.Millington (3);
Penalty: T.Millington

Apr 2 Leicester 3 Gloucester 0

Apr 9 Swansea 16 Gloucester 0

Apr 11 Llanelly 18 Gloucester 9
Tries: J.Phelps (3)

Apr 16 Manchester 9 Gloucester 30
Tries: J.Phelps (3), F.Ayliffe, F.Burford, A.Hall,
E.Curtis, F Webb;
Conversions: W.Dix (3)

Apr 23 Bath 0 Gloucester 8
Tries: A.Robbins (2);
Conversion: A.Robbins

1921-22

F.Rust A.Cromwell J.T.Brookes G.Leaver F.Pegler
A.Hall G.Halford S.Bayliss R.James M.Evans H.Collier Maj Roderick J.Harris G.Fox
A.Hudson F.Abbey G.Hughes S.Brown S.Crowther N.Daniell S.Smart(Capt) F.Webb A.Wright F.Ayliffe T.Voyce T.Bagwell
T.Millington W.Dix

Played 41 Won 24 Lost 14 Drawn 3
For 500 Against 322
Captain: Sid Smart

Gloucester 'A'
Played 30 Won 18 Lost 10 Drawn 2
For 366 Against 191
Captain: Tommy Burns

Most appearances: S.Smart 35, A.Hall 34, F.Ayliffe, J.Harris 33, T.Millington 31, N.Daniell 30, T.Voyce 28, E.H.Hughes 27, Major Roderick 26
Most tries: N.Daniell 19, T.Millington 13, S.Brown 12, J.Harris 8
Most conversions: T.Millington 37
Most penalties: T.Millington 11
Most drop goals: T.Millington, H.R.James 2

The Club was in a healthy position financially, and improved the accommodation at Kingsholm for the start of the season, with additional seating in the pavilion, a new terrace at the Worcester Street end, and renewed terracing on the south side. For the first time ladies were not offered reduced rates, and car parking at Kingsholm was charged, but there was a big increase in membership to 2,734 and a profit on the season of £1,355.

In December 1921, a Gloucester Rugby Supporters Club was started with an initial membership of 150 which soon soared over 500. Chaired by the Mayor; it supported not only the Gloucester Club, but also local clubs and schools' rugby.

The season was moderately successful, with ten of the 14 defeats inflicted by Welsh clubs. Highlights were doing the double over Bristol, Leicester and United Services (Portsmouth), and away wins at Northampton and Bath. At Kingsholm the most notable wins were against Cardiff (seen by the largest crowd), Llanelly, Harlequins and Guy's Hospital, regarded as the strongest Club team in England, with a strong South African contingent.

Sid Smart, with legendary status already, worked untiringly both on and off the field as captain and played in more games than anyone. He had wonderful support in the pack from "Biddy" Halford, Tom Voyce, Frank Ayliffe, Joe Harris and Arthur Hall.

Tom Millington, vice-captain, directed operations from fly-half, did the kicking, set a new Club record with 154 points, and had a wonderful understanding with his scrum-half, "Father" Dix. There were two outstanding speedsters on the wings - Norman Daniell and Sid Brown.

There were two candidates for try of the season. Against Cross Keys – "Inside their own half Gloucester opened out, and one of the finest combined movements possible to imagine followed. Millington, Hughes, Robbins, Dix, Millington (again), Webb and Daniell all took part, ending in the right wing scoring a great try in the corner". Against Leicester – "From a kick out Brown fielded, and with admirable judgment punted across to the opposite wing. Here Dix secured, and passed to Crowther. The latter was tackled a few yards outside, but he managed to get the ball away to Millington, who crossed the line amidst great cheering."

Tom Voyce again played in all four England internationals; "Biddy" Halford and "Father" Dix had trials. Thirteen players were capped by Gloucestershire, nine of whom played in the County Championship final, when North Midlands were beaten 19-0 at Villa Park. – "Biddy" Halford (captain), "Father" Dix (try), Frank Ayliffe (try), Tom Millington (conversion), Stanley Cook, Tom Voyce, Arthur Hall, Sid Smart and Major Roderick.

Sep 10 Gloucester 23 Lydney 0
Tries: N.Daniell (2), S.Brown, W.Dix, J.Webb;
Conversions: Millington (4)

Sep 17 Gloucester 9 Bath 9
Tries: T.Millington, A.Wright;
Penalty: T.Millington

Sep 24 Northampton 8 Gloucester 24
Tries: T.Millington (2), D.Brown, W.Washbourn;
Conversions: T.Millington (4);
Drop goal: D.Brown

Oct 1 Gloucester 6 Harlequins 0
Tries: T.Millington, G.Halford

Oct 3 Gloucester 32 Devonport Services 3
Tries: N.Daniell (3), E.H.Hughes, S.C.Cook, S.Brown;
Conversions: T.Millington (4);
Penalties: T.Millington (2)

Oct 8 Bristol 6 Gloucester 14
Tries: N.Daniell, W.Dix, E.H.Hughes;
Conversion: T.Millington;
Penalty: T.Millington

Oct 15 Gloucester 13 Guy's Hospital 0
Tries: T.Voyce, W.Dix, N.Daniell;
Conversions: T.Millington (2)

Oct 22 Gloucester 5 Cardiff 3
Try: N.Daniell;
Conversion: T.Millington

Oct 26 Oxford University 33 Gloucester 3
Try: J.Harris

Oct 29 United Services Portsmouth 5 Gloucester 6
Tries: S.Brown, T.Millington

Nov 5 Gloucester 16 Coventry 3
Tries: S.R.Allen, A.Wright;
Conversion: J.Harris;
Drop goals: W.Washbourne, S.Brown

Nov 12 Gloucester 0 Pontypool 3

Nov 19 Newport 13 Gloucester 6
Tries: W.Washbourne, E.H.Hughes

Nov 26 Moseley 6 Gloucester 6
Tries: W.Washbourne, E.H.Hughes

Dec 3 Gloucester 6 Llanelly 3
Penalties: T.Millington (2)

Dec 10 Coventry 11 Gloucester 3
Try: E.H.Hughes

Dec 17 Gloucester 22 Cheltenham 0
Tries: S.Brown (2), E.H.Hughes, A.Robbins, S.Bayliss,
Conversions: A.Robbins (2);
Penalty: A.Robbins

Dec 24 Gloucester 6 Cross Keys 8
Try: N.Daniell;
Penalty: T.Millington

Dec 26 Gloucester 28 Old Merchant Taylors 0
Tries: T.Voyce (2), N.Daniell(2), F.Ayliffe, J.Harris, F.Webb, S.Smart;
Conversions: T.Millington (2)

Dec 27 Bath 3 Gloucester 13
Tries: T.Millington, W.Washbourne, J.Harris;
Drop goal: T.Millington

Dec 31 Gloucester 26 Northampton 3
Tries: T.Millington, T.Voyce, F.Webb, J.Harris, N.Daniell;
Conversions: T.Millington (4);
Penalty: T.Millington

Jan 7 Leicester 9 Gloucester 10
Tries: S.Smart, N.Daniell;
Conversions: T.Millington (2)

Jan 14 Gloucester 20 Moseley 0

Tries: F.Meadows (3), N.Daniell, F.Ayliffe, G.Poole;
Conversion: H.R.James

Jan 21 Gloucester 0 Swansea 0

Jan 28 Guy's Hospital 20 Gloucester 5
Try: T.Millington;
Conversion: T.Millington

Feb 4 Swansea 16 Gloucester 0

Feb 11 Cardiff 22 Gloucester 8
Tries: W.Dix, M.Evans;
Conversion: T.Millington

Feb 18 Gloucester 3 Newport 9
Try: N.Daniell

Feb 25 Cheltenham 12 Gloucester 8
Tries: Maj.Roderick, N.Daniell;
Conversion: T.Burns

Mar 4 Gloucester 31 London Welsh 5
Tries: T.Gough(3), N.Daniell (2), Stanley Budd, J.Harris;

Conversions: Stanley Budd (3);
Drop goal: R.H.James

Mar 11 Gloucester 15 Bristol 9
Tries: S.R.Crowther, J.Harris, W.Dix;
Conversion: T.Millington;
Drop goal: R.H.James

Mar 16 Gloucester 40 Clifton 6
Tries: S.Brown (3), F.Meadows (2), M.Evans, S.R.Crowther, T.Millington, S.Bayliss, H.W.Collier;
Conversions; T.Millington (5)

Mar 18 Pontypool 23 Gloucester 3
Penalty: T.Millington

Mar 25 Gloucester 17 Leicester 3
Tries: T.Millington (2), S.Brown, E.H.Hughes;
Conversion: T.Millington;
Penalty: T.Millington

Apr 1 Gloucester 19 United Services 0
Tries: T.Millington, T.Voyce, W.Dix, J.Harris, H.W.Collier;

Conversions: T.Millington (2)

Apr 8 Llanelly 28 Gloucester 7
Drop Goal: T.Millington;
Goal from Mark: T.Millington

Apr 10 Neath 7 Gloucester 4
Drop goal: G.Thomas

Apr 15 Gloucester 14 Headingley 13
Tries: S.Brown (3), N.Daniell;
Conversion: W.Dix

Apr 17 Gloucester 21 Bradford 7
Tries: T.Millington, T.Voyce, S.R.Crowther, J.Harris;
Conversion: T.Millington;
Drop Goal: W.Dix;
Penalty: T.Millington

Apr 18 Lydney 3 Gloucester 5
Try: T.Voyce;
Conversion: T.Millington

Apr 22 Cross Keys 12 Gloucester 3
Try: G.Halford

1922-23

G.F.Clutterbuck G.J.Collingbourne A.Brown A.Cromwell E.Keys F.Abbey
J. Harris H.J.Balchin F.Pegler A.Hall S.Bayliss G.Halford A.Rea H.Collier S.Smart G.R.Fox
A.Hudson(Sec) T.Bagwell T.Coulson J.C.Collett T.Millington S.Stone F.W.Ayliffe(Capt) N.W.Daniell S.Brown M.Evans T.Voyce J.T.Brookes(Chairman)
W.Collins E.H.Hughes

Played 43 Won 27 Lost 13 Drawn 3
For 516 Against 273
Captain: Frank Ayliffe

Gloucester 'A'
Played 28 Won 20 Lost 5 Drawn 3
For 329 Against 177
Captain: Frank Mansell

Most appearances: A.Hall 37, T.Coulson 36, S.Brown, G.Halford 35, S.Smart 34, E.H.Hughes 33, F.Ayliffe, S.Bayliss 32, T.Millington 31, N.Daniell, J.C.Collett 30
Most tries: S.Brown 22, T.Voyce 12, N.Daniell 11, E.H.Hughes, S.Stone 10
Most conversions: T.Millington 32, F.Ayliffe 7, R.H.James, T.Voyce 5
Penalties: T.Millington 3, J.C.Collett 1

Drop goals: J.C.Collett 2, T.Millington, C.A.Watkins 1

The results were a marginal improvement on the previous season and regarded as satisfactory, but overall performances were thought to have slipped. The selectors found it difficult to find the right combination in the backs, and the centres had a habit of running across the field, which often wasted the threat of Sid Brown and Norman Daniell on the wings. John Collett made a positive impact at full-back with sound defence based on reliable tackling and mammoth kicking, including two magnificent dropped goals against Newport and Plymouth, but he played his county rugby for Kent and transferred away from Gloucester at the end of the season to Blackheath. Before the end of the season Fred Webb left for Carmarthen after 115 appearances in the thee-quarters.

The retirement of "Father" Dix fairly early in the season, after 243 appearances, was a great loss at scrum-half. He received a substantial testimonial, but his partner at half-back, Tom Millington missed his service and particularly his masterpiece reverse pass, lost some of his form, and was tried in other positions. The pack missed "Father's" very vocal advice when they needed some encouragement, but were still powerful when at full strength, which was the case all too rarely. Tom Voyce managed to play in only half the games due to representative commitments; Frank Ayliffe, "Biddy" Halford, "Tart" Hall and Sid Smart were the other leading lights despite their veteran status., but a lot of experience was lost when Joe Harris retired early in the season with 104 appearances, and "Biddy" at Christmas with 326.

Results against English clubs were good, the four losses were all away but reversed in the return fixtures at Kingsholm. The highlights were beating Harlequins at Twickenham, Gloucester having yet to be defeated by them, and a stirring victory over Guy's Hospital at Kingsholm. The results were very different against the Welsh clubs - three wins and nine losses.

Ten players turned out for Gloucestershire. Tom Voyce was again ever present for England as they beat Wales, Ireland, Scotland and France to secure a Grand Slam. Tom Millington appeared in the final trial.

Support held up well, membership rose to 2,504, and gate takings were good, so the Club's finances were healthy with a profit of over £1,000. Thoughts turned as to where next to invest, some favouring acquiring the ground by buying the remaining shares in the Ground Company, whilst others favoured the construction of a new grandstand, and the latter eventually prevailed.

Sep 9 Gloucester 11 Lydney 0
Tries: N.Daniell (2), T.Voyce;
Conversion: T.Millington

Sep 16 Gloucester 17 Bath 5
Tries: W.Dix (2), T.Voyce, J.Harris, A.M.David;
Conversion: W.Dix

Sep 21 Stroud 6 Gloucester 34
Tries: T.Voyce (2), N.Daniell (2), M.Evans, S.Brown, A.Hall, Maj.Roderick;
Conversions: T.Millington (4), R.James

Sep 23 Gloucester 3 Cross Keys 16
Try: S.R.Crowther

Sep 30 Harlequins 0 Gloucester 11
Tries: T.Millington, Maj.Roderick, S.Bayliss;
Conversion:T.Millington

Oct 2 Gloucester 7 Plymouth Albion 3
Penalty: T.Millington;
Drop goal: J.C.Collett

Oct 7 Gloucester 8 Bristol 4
Tries: S.R.Crowther, F.Meadows;
Conversion: T.Millington

**Oct 14 Gloucester 16
Guy's Hospital 0**
Tries: A.Hall, N.Daniell, S.Brown, T.Millington;
Conversions: T.Millington (2)

Oct 21 Cardiff 11 Gloucester 8
Tries: S.Stone, N.Daniell;
Conversion: T.Millington

**Oct 28 Gloucester 21
United Services (Portsmouth) 5**
Tries: F.Ayliffe, S.Bayliss, A.Hall. N.Daniell, T.Voyce;
Conversions: T.Millington (2), T.Voyce

Nov 4 Cheltenham 6 Gloucester 15
Tries: S.Brown (3), E.H.Hughes, H.W.Collier

**Nov 9 Gloucester 11
Oxford University 3**
Tries: F.Meadows, E.H.Hughes, N.Daniell;
Conversion: T.Voyce

**Nov 11 Gloucester 8
Devonport Services 5**
Tries: H.W.Collier, S.R.Crowther;
Conversion: F.Ayliffe

Nov 18 Newport 14 Gloucester 6
Try: S.Stone;
Penalty: T.Millington

Nov 25 Gloucester 22 Moseley 5
Tries: E.H.Hughes (2), S.Stone (2), J.C.Collett, S.R.Crowther;
Conversions: R.James (2)

**Dec 2 United Services (Portsmouth) 5
Gloucester 8**
Try: T.Gough;
Conversion: T.Millington;
Penalty: T.Millington

Dec 9 Gloucester 13 Cheltenham 3
Tries: J.W.Gibbs, S.R.Crowther, S.Smart;
Conversions: R.James (2)

Dec 16 Gloucester 13 Llanelly 0
Tries: S.Smart, F.Ayliffe, E.H.Hughes;
Drop goal: T.Millington

Dec 23 Gloucester 0 Swansea 6

**Dec 26 Gloucester 26
Old Merchant Taylors 3**
Tries: S.Brown (2), T.Millington (2), S.Stone, T.Coulson,
Conversions: T.Millington (4)

Dec 27 Bath 9 Gloucester 6
Tries: S.Brown, S.Stone

Dec 30 Coventry 9 Gloucester 21
Tries: E.H.Hughes (2), A.M.David, H.W.Collier, F.Meadows;
Conversions: T.Millington (3)

Jan 6 Gloucester 39 Old Blues 8
Tries: S.Brown (2), S.R.Crowther (2), A.M.David, A.Hall, A.Rea, T.Coulson, E.H.Hughes;
Conversions: F.Ayliffe (6)

Jan 13 Pontypool 10 Gloucester 0

Jan 20 Gloucester 5 Neath 3
Try: T.Gough;
Conversion: T.Millington

Jan 27 Guy's Hospital 6 Gloucester 3
Try: T.Voyce

Feb 3 Gloucester 23 Cinderford 6
Tries: S.Brown (2), T.Voyce, N.Daniell, S.Bayliss;
Conversions: T.Millington (4)

Feb 10 Gloucester 5 Cardiff 5
Try: S.Brown;
Conversion: T.Millington

Feb 17 Llanelly 24 Gloucester 3
Try: S.Bayliss

Feb 24 Gloucester 23 Coventry 5
Tries: T.Voyce (2), M.Evans, S.Stone, E.H.Hughes;
Conversions: T.Voyce (3), J.C.Collett

Mar 3 Swansea 13 Gloucester 0

Mar 10 Bristol 3 Gloucester 3
Try: S.Brown

Mar 17 Gloucester 10 Newport 14
Try: S.R.Crowther;
Penalty: J.C.Collett;
Drop goal: J.C.Collett

Mar 22 Gloucester 23 Clifton 0
Tries: S.Brown (2), T.Voyce (2), T.Coulson,
W.Clements, W.Collins;
Conversion: G.Holford

Mar 24 Cheltenham 3 Gloucester 21
Tries: G.Halford, S.Stone, W.Collins,
E.H.Hughes, S.Bayliss;
Conversions: G.Holford (2), J.C.Collett,

Mar 31 Gloucester 14 Abertillery 3
Tries: S.Brown, N.Daniell, S.Smart, P.Carter;
Conversion: T.Millington

Apr 2 Gloucester 11 London Welsh 8
Tries: S.Brown, T.Coulson, W.Collins;
Conversion: T.Millington

Apr 3 Lydney 12 Gloucester 16
Tries: J.C.Collett (2), S.Brown, S.Stone;
Drop goal: C.A.Watkins

Apr 7 Gloucester 0 Pontypool 0

**Apr 14 Devonport Services 11
Gloucester 6**
Tries: T.Voyce, N.Daniell

**Apr 16 Plymouth Albion 6
Gloucester 0**

Apr 17 Sidmouth 6 Gloucester 21
Tries: S.Brown (2), S.R.Crowther, S.Stone,
F.Mansell;
Conversions: T.Millington (3)

Apr 21 Cross Keys 9 Gloucester 5
Try: S.Brown;
Conversion: T.Millington

1923-24

G.F.Clutterbuck E.Keys A.Brown J.T.Brookes(Chairman) A.Cromwell G.J.Collingbourne
H.J.Balchin F.Pegler W.Collins N.Daniell F.W.Ayliffe J.Merry F.Ford H.W.Collier F.J.Seabrook G.Halford G.Fox
T.Bagwell F.Meadows T.Coulson S.A.Brown A.Hall(Vice-Capt) T.Millington(Capt) R.H.James S.R.Crowther S.Bayliss P.Carter A.Hudson(Sec)
E.H.Hughes G.Poole (T.Voyce - absent)

**Played 39 Won 24 Lost 14 Drawn 1
For 426 Against 310
Captain: Tom Millington**

Gloucester 'A'
Played 31 Won 21 Lost 10 Drawn 0
For 448 Against 155
Captain: Frank Mansell

Most appearances: R.H.James 36, T.Millington
35, J.Merry 32, S.Brown, F.Ayliffe, P.Carter,
F.Meadows 31, E.H.Hughes, A.Hall,
H.W.Collier 29
Most tries: S.Brown 18, S.Crowther 11,
T.Voyce, R.B.Miller 9

Conversions: T.Millington 26, R.H.James 7,
F.Ayliffe 4, S.Williams 1
Penalties: T.Millington 12, F.Ayliffe 1
Drop goals: T.Voyce 2

The season opened with a new stand on the south
side accommodating 1,750, all covered. Now
holding 2,129 of the 3,150 shares in the Ground
Company, and the Club having paid £2,343 for
this stand, the previous arrangement whereby
all buildings on the ground became the property
of the Ground Company, was overthrown – from
now on the Club retained ownership. The Club
reached its jubilee this season, but did not realise
in time, and celebration was left to the following

season. Despite a drop in admission prices in
response to the state of the country's economy,
membership numbers dropped slightly.

Gloucester finished the season as they started
it, in brilliant fashion, winning seven and
drawing one of their first eight matches, and
all six in the final month, but went through a
lengthy bad patch through the middle of the
season. Highlights were doing the double over
Bristol, Northampton and Plymouth Albion,
and the defeats of Harlequins, Guy's Hospital,
Newport, Llanelly and Pontypool at home.
Devonport Services won at Kingsholm in
November, which was the first loss at home to

an English club since Leicester in March 1920, more than 3½ years previously.

As ever, the Welsh clubs offered the greatest challenges – Cross Keys and Abertillery won at Kingsholm, both completing the double over Gloucester, and not a single win was recorded in Wales. The worst blunder was against Cardiff at Kingsholm when Gloucester thought the ball would go dead and allowed Cardiff to steal in for the equalising try. The greatest pleasure was taken from the 8-6 defeat of Newport at Kingsholm, which featured a spectacular try by Tom Voyce, who was passed the ball in his own half and "getting his head back, Voyce put on his fastest and best and, though hotly chased, was never caught, and finished up a truly great run with a try, which Millington converted."

Overall, the backs were judged to lack sufficient thrust, although Sid Brown was always a threat on the wing. Towards the end of the season Norman Daniell was injured and never played again after 116 appearances. In line with tradition, the pack was the backbone of the side, but they missed "Biddy" Halford and Sid Smart, who bowed out early in the season after 196 appearances.

Eleven players won County caps. Tom Voyce scored the winning try for England and Wales against Scotland and Ireland in a match to celebrate the centenary of the game of rugby, and then played for England as they beat Wales, Scotland, Ireland and France to secure another Grand Slam. He went to South Africa with the British Isles (Lions) team in summer 1924 and won two Test caps.

Sep 8 Gloucester 43 Lydney 12
Tries: N.Daniell (3), T.Voyce (2), F.Ayliffe, S.Brown, E.H.Hughes;
Conversions: T.Millington (4), R.James (2);
Penalty: T.Millington;
Drop goal: T.Voyce

Sep 15 Gloucester 18 Bath 8
Tries: H.W.Collier, T.Millington;
Conversion: T.Millington;
Penalties: T.Millington (2);
Drop goal: T.Voyce

Sep 22 Northampton 0 Gloucester 3
Try: S.Brown

Sep 29 Gloucester 14 Harlequins 10
Tries: T.Millington (2), N.Daniell, T.Voyce;
Conversion: T.Millington

Oct 6 Bristol 0 Gloucester 3
Penalty: T.Millington

Oct 13 Gloucester 6 Guys Hospital 4
Try: F.Ayliffe;
Penalty: T.Millington

Oct 20 Gloucester 8 Cardiff 8
Tries: A.M.David, A.Hall;
Conversion: T.Millington

Oct 27 Gloucester 31 Clifton 0
Tries: R.Miller (2), E.H.Hughes (2), F.Meadows, S.Crowther, T.Coulson, R.Loveridge, G.Poole;
Conversions: R.James (2)

Nov 3 Abertillery 13 Gloucester 6
Try: A.M.David;
Penalty: T.Millington

Nov 8 Oxford University 28 Gloucester 11
Tries: S.Brown (2), A.M.David;
Conversion: T.Millington

Nov 10 Gloucester 8 Devonport Services 13
Tries: G.Poole, J.Merry;
Conversion: T.Millington

Nov 17 Gloucester 8 Newport 6
Tries: T.Coulson, T.Voyce;
Conversion: T.Millington

Nov 24 Cheltenham 0 Gloucester 8
Tries: E.H.Hughes, R.Miller;
Conversion: R.James

Dec 1 United Services (Portsmouth) 6 Gloucester 3
Try: W.Collins

Dec 8 Clifton 8 Gloucester 20
Tries: R.Miller (3), S.Crowther, R.Loveridge;
Conversion: S.Williams;
Penalty: F.Ayliffe

Dec 15 Gloucester 13 Plymouth Albion 0
Tries: R.Miller, R.Loveridge, E.H.Hughes;
Conversions: T.Millington (2)

Dec 22 Gloucester 3 Abertillery 7
Try: R.Miller

Dec 26 Gloucester 9 Old Merchant Taylors 8
Tries: S.Brown, R.Miller, P.Carter

Dec 27 Bath 12 Gloucester 5
Try: F.Meadows;
Conversion: T.Millington

Dec 29 Llanelly 22 Gloucester 5

Try: G.Hogg; Converson: T.Millington

Jan 5 Gloucester 14 Old Blues 9
Tries: S.Brown (2), F.Ayliffe, H.W.Collier;
Conversion: T.Millington

Jan 14 Cross Keys 8 Gloucester 6
Tries: S.Brown, F.J.Seabrook

Jan 19 Gloucester 5 Pontypool 0
Try: S.Bayliss;
Conversion: T.Millington

Jan 26 Guy's Hospital 12 Gloucester 0

Feb 2 Gloucester 20 United Services 6
Tries: S.Brown (4), H.W.Collier, J.Merry;
Conversion: T.Millington

Feb 9 Cardiff 26 Gloucester 3
Try: S.Brown

Feb 16 Gloucester 11 Llanelly 8
Tries: F.Ayliffe, T.Voyce, S.Brown;
Conversion: T.Millington

Feb 23 Richmond 6 Gloucester 0

Mar 1 Gloucester 6 Cross Keys 9
Try: S.Bayliss;
Penalty: T.Millington

Mar 8 Gloucester 11 Bristol 6
Try: T.Voyce;
Conversion: T.Millington;
Penalties: T.Millington (2)

Mar 15 Newport 9 Gloucester 0

Mar 22 Gloucester 6 St Bart's Hospital 5
Tries: F.Meadows, S.Crowther

Mar 29 Pontypool 8 Gloucester 0

Apr 5 Gloucester 31 Cheltenham 6
Tries: F.Ford (2), S.Crowther, T.Voyce, L.E.Saxby, T.Coulson, T.Millington;
Conversions: T.Millington, F.Ayliffe (4)

Apr 12 Plymouth Albion 8 Gloucester 9
Tries: L.E.Saxby, S.Crowther;
Goal from Mark: T.Millington

Apr 14 Devonport Services 3 Gloucester 6
Tries: S.Crowther, S.Brown

Apr 19 Gloucester 28 Northampton 3
Tries: S.Crowther (3), F.Ayliffe (2), S.Brown,

T.Coulson;
Conversions: T.Millington, R.James;
Penalty: T.Millington

Apr 21 Gloucester 30 London Welsh 8
Tries; T.Voyce (2), E.Triggs-Herbert,
S.Crowther, E.H.Hughes, T.Millington,
F.Ayliffe;
Conversions: T.Millington (2), R.James;

Penalty: T.Millington

Apr 22 Lydney 5 Gloucester 15
Tries: S.Brown (2), S.Crowther;
Conversions: T.Millington (3)

1924-25

G.F.Clutterbuck A.Brown F.Abbey
H.J.Balchin F.W.Ayliffe E.Triggs-Herbert T.Millington S.Duberley W.Prior J.Rea M.Short Lt W.H. Wood G.R.Fox
A.Hudson(Sec) S.Crowther G.Hughes H.Roberts S.Brown(Acting Capt) J.Hemmings F.Ford A.Hall T.Bagwell A.Cromwell
G.Thomas R.Milliner (T.Voyce(Capt) Dr G.C.C.Taylor – absent)

Played 40 Won 24 Lost 15 Drawn 1
For 430 Against 308
Captain: Tom Voyce

Gloucester 'A'
Played 24 Won 16 Lost 5 Drawn 3
For 306 Against 117
Captain: Albert Rea

Most appearances: F.Ford 36, J.Hemmings 34,
F.Ayliffe 33, S.Crowther, T.Millington, A.Hall
31, S.Brown 29
Most tries: S.Crowther 18, S.Brown 14,
E.H.Hughes 9, J.Hemmings 8
Conversions: T.Millington 28, S.Williams 9,
Dr.G.Taylor 2, P.Hogg, T.Voyce 1
Penalties: T.Millington 3, T.Voyce 2
Drop goals: G.Thomas, Dr.G.Taylor,
G.R.James 1

The season started with "Doc" Alcock as
President in place of Sir James Bruton, who
presented the Club with a clock to go on the
gymnasium (now the Lions Den). The price of

the 10s season ticket was reduced to 8s 6d, but
times were tight and membership numbers still
dropped further.

The two biggest matches of the season at
Kingsholm were the Club's Jubilee match
and the visit of the All Blacks. The President
of the RFU, Capt Donne, brought a team of
international and county players to Kingsholm
for the Jubilee match on 13th November, which
was "one of the finest exhibitions of the
handling code ever witnessed in Gloucester". A
fast and open game was won in the last minute
when C.E.Macintosh scored a try in the corner
in his only game for Gloucester. Eleven days
later, the All Blacks took on Gloucestershire,
and prevailed 6-0 in conditions described as
"a Taranaki cow-yard, old style, and everyone
splished, splashed and sploshed after the ball".

Ahead of the match against Old Blues on 17th
January 1925, it was decided to donate the
proceeds to the Gloucester Royal Infirmary,
which seemed all the more appropriate when

tragedy struck. Stan Bayliss, a forward who
had played 102 games for Gloucester, broke his
neck during the first half and was taken to the
Infirmary where he died three days later. The
following match against Guy's Hospital was
cancelled because of Stan's funeral. An appeal
raised £1,500 for Stan's widow and son.

In a moderately successful season, the Club
suffered its first defeat by Harlequins, its first
defeat at Kingsholm by Guy's Hospital, and the
first there to Bristol since 1907. But there were
some highlights other than the Jubilee match,
and things improved in the second half of the
season when Tom Voyce was more regularly
available. The double was achieved against
Coventry, and there were wins at Kingsholm
against Cardiff, Llanelly and Newport. And the
best was left for the Easter period with a good
performance against Northern followed by
"their most entertaining display of the season,"
and biggest victory, over London Welsh, when
"the whole team shared in the triumph. The
forwards kept things moving all the time, and

there was not a man in the pack who did not do something special," while the backs combined well to score eight of the ten tries.

Eleven players won County caps, and eight - Tom Millington, Dr.G.C.Taylor, S.Duberley, Tom Voyce, Frank Ayliffe, Fred Ford, E.H.Hughes and Dick Milliner - played in the final of the Championship, which was lost to Leicestershire. Tom Voyce played for England against New Zealand, Wales, Ireland, Scotland and France. Dr.G.C.Taylor was reserve for two England games, and Tom Millington had a trial.

Sep 13 Gloucester 0 Lydney 0

Sep 18 Gloucester 24 Moseley 14
Tries: S.Bayliss, G.Thomas, J.Hemmings, F.Ayliffe (2), F.Ford;
Conversions: T.Millington (2), S.Williams (1)

Sep 20 Gloucester 12 Coventry 6
Tries: W.Collins (2), H.W.Collier, G.Thomas

Sep 27 Bath 16 Gloucester 7
Try: S.Brown;
Drop goal: Dr.Taylor

Sep 29 Gloucester 8 Cinderford 7
Tries: F.Ayliffe, J.Hemmings;
Conversion: T.Millington

Oct 4 Gloucester 10 Bristol 12
Tries: Dr.Taylor, S.Brown;
Conversions: T.Millington (2)

Oct 11 Gloucester 0 Guy's Hospital 5

Oct 18 Cardiff 19 Gloucester 0

Oct 25 Lydney 3 Gloucester 5
Try: A.Hall;
Conversion: P.Hogg

**Nov 1 Gloucester 11
Plymouth Albion 3**
Tries: T.Voyce (2), S.Crowther;
Conversion: T.Millington

**Nov 6 Gloucester 23
Oxford University 16**
Tries: S.Duberley, R.Milliner, T.Voyce, M.Short, W.Hemmings;
Conversions: T.Millington (2);
Drop goal: G.Thomas

**Nov 8 Gloucester 0
Devonport Services 8**

Nov 13 Gloucester 11

Capt Donne's Team 9
Tries: F.Ford, T.Voyce, C.E.Macintosh;
Conversion: T.Millington

Nov 15 Newport 25 Gloucester 12
Tries: F.Ayliffe, W.Prior;
Penalties: T.Millington, T.Voyce

Nov 22 Gloucester 26 Cheltenham 0
Tries: W.Print, R.Loveridge, W.Prior, G.Thomas, S.Bayliss, S.Crowther;
Conversions: S.Williams (4)

Nov 29 Harlequins 17 Gloucester 6
Tries: J.Bruce-Jones, G.Thomas

**Dec 6 Gloucester 0
Combined Services 21**

Dec 13 Cheltenham 0 Gloucester 9
Tries: H.Roberts, E.Comley, A.Rea

Dec 20 Gloucester 8 Pontypool 6
Tries: W.Prior, S.Brown;
Conversion: T.Millington

**Dec 26 Gloucester 0
Old Merchant Taylor's 3**

Dec 27 Gloucester 21 Bath 0
Tries: S.Brown (2), E.H.Hughes (2), Dr.Taylor, J.Hemmings;
Penalty: T.Millington

Jan 3 Llanelly v Gloucester - cancelled

Jan 10 Coventry 3 Gloucester 8
Try: S.Crowther;
Conversion: T.Voyce;
Penalty: T.Voyce

Jan 17 Gloucester 25 Old Blues 9
Tries: S.Crowther (4), S.Brown, F.Ford, F.Ayliffe;
Conversions: Dr.Taylor (2)

Jan 24 Gloucester v Guy's Hospital - cancelled owing to funeral of Stan Bayliss

Jan 31 Gloucester 11 Swansea 13
Tries: R.Milliner, S.Duberley, Dr.Taylor;
Conversion: T.Millington

**Feb 7 United Services Portsmouth 13
Gloucester 10**
Tries: H.Roberts, J.Hemmings;
Drop goal: R.James

Feb 14 Gloucester 8 Cardiff 6
Tries: S.Crowther, R.Loveridge;
Conversion: T.Millington

Feb 21 Gloucester 25 Richmond 3
Tries: E.H.Hughes (2), F.Ayliffe, J.Hemmings, R.Loveridge, S.Crowther, A.Hall;
Conversions: T.Millington (2)

Feb 28 Swansea 6 Gloucester 3
Penalty: T.Millington

Mar 2 Llanelly 9 Gloucester 3
Try: G.Thomas

Mar 7 Bristol 0 Gloucester 5
Try; G.Thomas;
Conversion: T.Millington

Mar 14 Gloucester 8 Llanelly 5
Tries: E.H.Hughes, N.Macdonald;
Conversion: Millington

Mar 21 Gloucester 8 Newport 0
Tries: S.Brown (2);
Conversion: T.Millington

**Mar 28 Gloucester 26
St Bart's Hospital 5**
Tries: S.Crowther (2), J.Bartlett, S.Brown, J.Hemmings, W.Prior;
Conversions: S.Williams (4)

Apr 4 Pontypool 13 Gloucester 6
Tries: E.H.Hughes, S.Crowther

Apr 11 Gloucester 18 Northern 3
Tries: S.Crowther, H.Roberts, W.H.Wood, E.H.Hughes;
Conversions: T.Millington (3)

Apr 13 Gloucester 40 London Welsh 8
Tries: S.Brown (3), W.H.Wood (2), S.Crowther (2), R.Milliner, E.H.Hughes, E.Triggs-Herbert;
Conversions: T.Millington (5)

Apr 14 Cinderford 3 Gloucester 5
Try: T.Millington;
Conversion: T.Millington

**Apr 18 Devonport Services 6
Gloucester 8**
Tries: T.Voyce, E.H.Hughes;
Conversion: T.Millington

**Apr 19 Plymouth Albion 13
Gloucester 8**
Tries: S.Brown, S.Crowther;
Conversion: T.Millington

Apr 20 Sidmouth 0 Gloucester 12
Tries: S.Crowther (2), S.Brown, T.Voyce

1925-26

Played 37 Won 19 Lost 17 Drawn 1
For 430 Against 283
Captain: Tom Voyce

Gloucester 'A'
Played 25 Won 17 Lost 6 Drawn 1 Abandoned 1
For 306 Against 117
Captain: Albert Rea

Most appearances: T.Millington, R.Milliner
35, J.Hemming 33, F.Ayliffe 31, H.Roberts 28,
E.H.Hughes 27
Most Tries: S.A.Brown 21, R.N.Loveridge,
S.R.Crowther 10, T.Voyce 7
Conversions: T.Millington 46, T.Voyce 2,
Penalties: T.Millington 11, T.Voyce 2,
S.Williams, A.E.Hopcroft 1
Drop goal: Dr.G.Taylor 1

A moderate season as regards results still had
some highlights. There were few in the first half
of the season, when Gloucester lost to Bristol,
their first ever defeat on the Memorial Ground.
However, a terrific match against Swansea at
Kingsholm saw Gloucester triumph by a single
point, but only because Swansea scored a late
try and then missed the conversion.

Results improved somewhat after Sid Brown
scored a hat trick to beat Old Blues in the benefit
match for the Royal Infirmary at the end of
January, with Tom Millington converting eight
of the nine tries. The return fixture against Bristol
was won in March at Kingsholm in front of a
record crowd for the season of 7-8,000. However,
although there was no mention of rough play in
the match reports, the Bristol players insisted
that their club cancel future fixtures after 34
years of matches with Gloucester, and their
committee did so. Sid Brown scored two tries as
Bath were beaten comfortably, but the following
week and for the second season in succession,
tragedy struck at Kingsholm.

During the match against Aberavon on Easter
Saturday, Sid Brown, the Gloucester vice-
captain in his 185th appearance, was injured. It
did not seem serious at first, but in the evening
he was taken to the Royal Infirmary, where he
was found to be haemorrhaging from badly
ruptured kidneys, and he died the following
morning. He had already scored 21 tries, more
than twice as many as any other player that
season, some featuring exhilarating bursts of
speed. A fund on behalf of Sid's widow and son
was set up and raised £1,645. The Bayliss and
Brown funds were wound up in 1946, when both
widows had remarried, and the residues were
paid to the sons. From then on the Club insured

players against death.

The two remaining matches of the Easter
programme and the following Saturday's match
were cancelled. Play resumed with the West
Country tour, when Frank Ayliffe made the last
of his 239 appearances and all three fixtures
were won, but then Lydney ended the season by
winning at home to Gloucester for the first time.

Eleven players represented Gloucestershire.
Tom Voyce was again selected for every England
game, playing against Wales, Ireland, Scotland
and France in what would prove to be his last
season for his country; Dr.G.C.Taylor was
reserve for two matches.

Sep 10 Stroud 3 Gloucester 19
Tries: S.A.Brown, R.Loveridge, E.Pope,
T.Voyce; Conversions: T.Millington (2);
Penalty: T.Millington

Sep 12 Gloucester 28 Lydney 6
Tries: R.Loveridge (2), S.A.Brown, Dr G Taylor,
T.Voyce, F.Ayliffe;
Conversions: T.Millington (5)

Sep 17 Gloucester 14
Old Edwardians 3
Tries: R.Milliner, T.Voyce, S.A.Brown, F.Ford;
Conversion: T.Millington

Sep 19 Gloucester 13 Coventry 3
Tries: E.H.Hughes, J.Reed, S.Crowther;
Conversions: T.Millington (2)

Sep 26 Gloucester 9 Moseley 7
Tries: E.L.Saxby, R.Loveridge;
Penalty: T.Millington

Sep 28 Gloucester 6 Cinderford 0
Try: S.A.Brown;
Penalty: T.Millington

Oct 3 Bristol 9 Gloucester 5
Try: E.H.Hughes;
Conversion: T.Millington

Oct 10 Gloucester 11 Guy's Hospital 8
Tries: R.Milliner, J.Hemming;
Conversion: T.Millington;
Penalty: T.Millington

Oct 17 Gloucester 8 Cardiff 8
Tries: T.Voyce (2);
Conversion: T.Millington

Oct 24 Llanelly 8 Gloucester 6
Tries: S.A.Brown, A.Hopcroft

Oct 31 Cheltenham 5 Gloucester 19
Tries: S.A.Brown (4), Dr. G.Taylor;
Conversions: T.Millington (2)

Nov 4 Oxford University 17
Gloucester 11
Tries: T.Voyce (2), A.E.Hopcroft;
Conversion: T.Millington

Nov 7 Gloucester 15 Swansea 14
Tries: Dr.G.Taylor, S.A.Brown;
Conversion: T.Millington;
Penalty: T.Millington;
Drop goal: Dr.G.Taylor

Nov 14 Gloucester 0
Devonport Services 9

Nov 21 Gloucester 3 Newport 17
Penalty: T.Voyce

Nov 28 Lydney v Gloucester - cancelled due to
frost
Dec 5 United Services (Portsmouth) v
Gloucester - cancelled due to frost

Dec 12 Gloucester 6 Cheltenham 7
Try: H.Roberts;
Penalty: S.Williams

Dec 19 Gloucester 10 Harlequins 14
Tries: S.A.Brown, G.McIlwaine;
Conversions: T.Millington (2)

Dec 24 Gloucester v Abertillery - cancelled due
to snow

Dec 26 Gloucester 39
Old Merchant Taylors 10
Tries: S.A.Brown (2), R.H.Hamilton-Wickes
(2), Dr.G.Taylor, M.Short, E.H.Hughes;
Conversions: T.Millington (6);
Penalties: T.Millington, T.Voyce

Jan 2 Swansea 11 Gloucester 3
Try: E.H.Hughes

Jan 9 Coventry 9 Gloucester 6
Tries: R.C.Thompson (2)

Jan 14 Gloucester 6
London Hospital 8
Tries: A.Hopcroft, G.Foulkes

Jan 16 Gloucester v Plymouth Albion - cancelled
due to snow and frost.

Jan 23 Guy's Hospital 6 Gloucester 3
Try: H.Roberts

Jan 30 Gloucester 39 Old Blues 13
Tries: S.A.Brown (3), S.R.Crowther (2),
R.Milliner, E.H.Hughes;
Conversions: T.Millington (6)
Penalties: T.Millington (2)

**Feb 6 Gloucester 12
United Services (Portsmouth) 5**
Tries: G.McIlwaine, S.A.Brown, R.C.Thompson,
S.R.Crowther

Feb 13 Cardiff 12 Gloucester 5
Try: R.Milliner;
Conversion: T.Millington

Feb 20 Gloucester 6 Llanelly 11
Try: H.Roberts;
Penalty: A.Hopcroft

Feb 27 Bath 3 Gloucester 0

Mar 6 Gloucester 8 Bristol 3
Tries: R.C.Thompson, S.R.Crowther;
Conversion: T.Millington

Mar 13 Newport 16 Gloucester 10
Tries: S.A.Brown, S.R.Crowther;
Conversions: T.Millington (2)

Mar 18 Gloucester 21 R.A.F. 3
Tries: R.N.Loveridge (2), S.R.Crowther,
S.A.Brown, E.H.Hughes;
Conversions: T.Millington (3)

Mar 20 Gloucester 17 Bath 3
Tries: S.A.Brown (2), R.C.Thompson,
S.R.Crowther;
Conversion: T.Millington;
Penalty: T.Millington

**Mar 27 Gloucester 21
St.Bart's Hospital 3**
Tries: R.N.Loveridge (2), S.R.Crowther (2),
J.Hemming;
Conversions: T.Voyce (2), T.Millington

Apr 3 Gloucester 8 Aberavon 9
Try: H.Roberts;
Conversion: T.Millington;

Penalty: T.Millington

Apr 5 Gloucester v London Welsh
Apr 6 Gloucester v Cinderford
Apr 10 Gloucester v Moseley
All cancelled owing to the death of Sid Brown.

**Apr 17 Plymouth Albion 6
Gloucester 11**
Tries: L.Abbey, T.Millington, S.Weaver;
Conversion: T.Millington

**Apr 19 Devonport Services 9
Gloucester 16**
Tries: R.N.Loveridge (2), G.Foulkes, R.Milliner;
Conversions: T.Millington (2)

Apr 20 Sidmouth 3 Gloucester 13
Tries: G.Foulkes, R.C.Thompson, F.Ayliffe;
Conversions: T.Millington (2)

Apr 24 Lydney 5 Gloucester 3
Penalty: T.Millington

1926-27

H.J.Balchin F.Pegler S.Smart J.T.Brookes E.Keys J.F.Scoon G.F.Clutterbuck G.J.Collingbourne
H.Ferris G.Foulkes H.Pitt F.Russell R.N.Loveridge M.Short T.Wadley J.Hatton E.H.Hughes
A.Hudson(Sec) S.Crowther S.J.Stephens J.Hemmings T.Millington A.T.Voyce(Capt) L.E.Saxby G.Shaw E.Comley L.Abbey T.Bagwell
G.Thomas R.James R.Milliner

**Played 40 Won 23, Lost 17
For 413 Against 398
Captain: Tom Voyce**

Gloucester 'A'
Played 27 Won 23 Lost 3 Drawn 1

For 422 Against 80
Captain: Albert Rea

Most appearances: M.Short, G.Foulkes 36,
R.Milliner, T.Millington 33, J.Hemming 31,
G.Thomas, R.James 30, J.Stephens 27

Most tries: R.N.Loveridge, T.Millington,
S.R.Crowther 11, J.Stephens 9
Conversions: T.Millington 28, R.James 2,
R.Milliner, T.Voyce, Dr.G.Taylor 1
Penalties: T.Millington 9, R.James 1
Drop goals: T.Millington 2, G.Thomas,

R.N.Loveridge, R.James 1

Membership fell again to 1,926, the first time it had dropped below 2,000 since 1920-21. But the Club now owned 3,017 of 3,150 shares in the Ground Company.

Gloucester players refused to play alongside Bristol players in the County side if they continued to refuse to play a club game, which they did, so the County selected no Bristol players for their first County game against Yorkshire at Kingsholm. On the other hand, fixtures with Leicester were reinstated.

The Gloucester side were going through a period of rebuilding, injury kept the captain, Tom Voyce, out of action for more than half of the fixtures, and the vice-captain, Richard Loveridge was absent almost as often. Consequently, results overall were disappointing, and there were occasions on which the team was outclassed, particularly amongst the backs where they displayed weak defence with a lack of speed, cohesion, and quickness of thought. There was some improvement as the season wore on, mainly through new recruits amongst the forwards, but there was never a settled back division.

There were some notable triumphs at Kingsholm over Newport, Llanelly, Swansea, Northampton, Devonport Services, United Services, Guy's Hospital, and Leicester. But successes in away matches were few and far between, the best performances being the defeats of Bath and the United Services.

The player of the season was Tom Millington, restored to outside half, where he was the brains of the team in attack, showing finesse and skill, and the team relied heavily on his experience and sound judgement to get them out of difficulties. It was his swan song – he retired at the end of the season after 250 appearances, as did E.H.Hughes after 163 appearances, mostly as a centre. Sidney Crowther's powers on the wing were declining and he soon retired after 120 appearances. A 16-year-old Harold Boughton was given a run at full-back towards the end of the season and showed plenty of promise.

The forwards often lacked a leader, and "Tart" Hall was only available occasionally before retiring after 237 appearances, but the transfer of Les Saxby from centre to back row forward was a great success, and Miles Short showed up well.

The players probably regarded a day when they didn't play as the highlight of the season.

Travelling to London to meet Guy's Hospital, they found the ground frozen. But Arthur Bourchier, an actor and the prospective Labour candidate for Gloucester stepped in. He was playing John Silver in "Treasure Island" at the Strand Theatre, where the players were his guests at a matinee performance. He hosted dinner afterwards at Simpson's, took them to the evening show at the Hippodrome and back to the Strand Theatre for refreshments until it was time to make for Paddington and home.

Sep 9 Stroud 3 Gloucester 8
Tries: R.Loveridge (2);
Conversion: T Millington

Sep 11 Gloucester 6 Lydney 3
Try: T.Voyce;
Penalty: T.Millington

Sep 18 Gloucester 6 Northampton 3
Tries: R.James, T.Voyce

Sep 25 Gloucester 13 Moseley 8
Tries: R.Loveridge (2), G.Foulkes;
Drop goal: T.Millington

Sep 28 Gloucester 23 Cinderford 15
Tries: G.McIlvaine (2), R.Loveridge, R.Thompson, R.James, E.H.Hughes, L.Bartlett;
Conversion: R.Milliner

**Oct 2 Gloucester 20
St Thomas Hospital 14**
Tries: R.Thompson (3), G.Foulkes, R.Milliner, L.Bartlett;
Conversion: Dr.G.Taylor

Oct 9 Gloucester 19 Guys Hospital 3
Tries: S.Crowther (2), R.Thompson, T.Voyce, T.Millington;
Conversions: T.Voyce, T.Millington

Oct 16 Cardiff 15 Gloucester 8
Tries: M.Short; T.Voyce;
Conversion: T Millington

Oct 23 Lydney 6 Gloucester 5
Try: E.Goodwin;
Conversion: R.James

Oct 30 Gloucester 6 Aberavon 13
Try: J.Stephens;
Penalty: T.Millington

**Nov 4 Gloucester 3
Oxford University 13**
Try: J.Stephens

Nov 6 Swansea 19 Gloucester 3
Try: R.James

**Nov 13 Gloucester 12
Devonport Services 3**
Tries: H.Roberts, T.Millington;
Conversion: T.Millington;
Drop goal: R.James

Nov 20 Newport 18 Gloucester 6
Try: T.Millington;
Penalty: T.Millington

Nov 27 Cheltenham 14 Gloucester 3
Try: R.Loveridge

Dec 4 Gloucester 11 United Services 5
Tries: J.Stephens, E.Hughes, T.Millington;
Conversion: T.Millington

Dec 11 Gloucester 10 Cheltenham 5
Tries: R.Loveridge, J.Stephens;
Drop goal: R.Loveridge

Dec 18 Harlequins 36 Gloucester 7
Try: R.Loveridge;
Drop goal: G.Thomas

**Dec 27 Gloucester 8
Old Merchant Taylors 21**
Tries: T.Millington, J.Stephens;
Conversion: T.Millington

Dec 28 Bath 6 Gloucester 13
Tries: T.Millington, R.Loveridge, E.Comley;
Conversions: T.Millington (2)

Jan 1 Gloucester 11 Swansea 0
Tries: G.McIlwane (2), S.Crowther;
Conversion: T.Millington

Jan 8 Gloucester 11 Llanelly 6
Tries: G.McIlwane, J.Stephens;
Conversion: T.Millington;
Penalty: T.Millington

Jan 15 Leicester 11 Gloucester 3
Try: R.Milliner

Jan 22 Guys Hospital v Gloucester - cancelled

Jan 29 Gloucester 14 Old Blues 7
Tries: E.Hughes, J.Hemmings, S.Crowther;
Conversion: T.Millington;
Penalty: T. Millington

**Feb 5 United Services (Portsmouth) 5
Gloucester 9**
Tries; T.Millington, H.Pitt;
Penalty: T.Millington

Feb 12 Gloucester 8 Cardiff 22
Tries: T.Voyce, S.Crowther;

Conversion: T.Millington

Feb 19 Aberavon 10 Gloucester 3
Try: T.Voyce

Feb 26 Gloucester 6 Bath 5
Tries: M.Short, S.Crowther

Mar 5 Gloucester 18 UCS Old Boys 8
Tries: S.Crowther, J.Stephens, H.Pitt,
E.Comley;
Conversions: T.Millington (3)

Mar 12 Gloucester 5 Newport 4
Try: R.Loveridge;
Conversion: T.Millington

Mar 17 Gloucester 28 RAF 11
Tries: M.Short, R.Loveridge, J.Stephens, A.Rea,
T.Millington, E.Goodwin, L.Saxby;
Conversion: T.Millington (2);

Penalty: T.Millington

Mar 19 Llanelly 12 Gloucester 0

**Mar 26 Gloucester 17
St Barts Hospital 6**
Tries: S.Crowther, H.Pitt, R.James, G.Foulkes;
Conversion: T.Millington;
Penalty: R.James

Mar 30 Moseley 9 Gloucester 6
Tries: L.Franklin, J.Stephens

Apr 2 Gloucester 12 Leicester 3
Try: F.Russell;
Conversion: T.Millington;
Penalty: T.Millington;
Drop goal: T.Millington

Apr 9 Plymouth 14 Gloucester 8
Tries: R.James, E.Comley;

Conversion: T.Millington

**Apr 11 Devonport Services 14
Gloucester 11**
Tries: S.Crowther, T.Millington, L.Saxby;
Conversion: T.Millington

Apr 16 Gloucester 31 Northern 9
Tries: S.Crowther (2), L.Abbey, J.Hemming,
E.Comley, T.Millington, L.Wadley;
Conversions: T.Millington (5)

**Apr 18 Gloucester 19
London Welsh 8**
Tries: L.Saxby, T.Millington, L.Abbey, R.James;
Conversions: T.Millington, R.James;
Penalty: T.Millington

Apr 19 Cinderford 11 Gloucester 3
Try: F.Beard

1927-28

**Played 44 Won 25 Lost 16 Drawn 3
For 477 Against 293
Captain: Les Saxby**

Gloucester 'A'
Played 27 Won 20 Lost 5 Drawn 2
For 455 Against 137
Captain: Albert Rea

Most appearances: E.Comley 42, R.James,
F.Wadley 37, L.Saxby 36, J.Stephens, G.Foulkes
34, L.Abbey, H.Boughton 32, A.Hough,
R.Milliner 31
Most tries: R.James 20, A.Hough 17,
J.Stephens 15, E.Comley 7
Conversions: H.Boughton 38, J.Stephens 4,
R.James 3, E.Comley, L.Saxby 1
Penalties: H.Boughton 6, J.Stephens 2,
L.Saxby 1
Drop goals: R.James 2, J.Stephens, A.W.Lewis,
E.Stephens 1

Club membership was again down to 1,864, but
the holding in the Ground Company was up to
3,047 shares. The number of fixtures, 44, was a
record, and fortunes varied, but the Club turned
a profit of £441. There were few outstanding
performances, perhaps the best being a
wonderful exhibition of grit against Oxford
University, and the capture of Torquay's ground
record during the end-of-season tour, but the
13-0 victory over Swansea was the only one
against a premier Welsh club. The Club were no
longer invincible at Kingsholm, and the worst
spell was in March with five successive defeats.

All through the season the Selection Committee

were forced to resort to numerous experiments
in many positions, with the inevitable result
that individual form and team work suffered.
For example, seven different players appeared at
full-back, and 51 players in all. The Club was
fortunate to have such an enthusiastic leader
as Les Saxby - popular with the players and
an eternal optimist, he got the very best out
of his ever-changing and often youthful team.
The back division was the youngest that ever
represented the Club.

Harold Boughton's kicking, both place and
out-of-hand, remained a strength. The best
of the backs regularly available was Jack
Stephens, with Arthur Hough, Roy James, and
Les Abbey the optimum formation alongside
him, but for eleven matches the Club benefited
from the experience and class of A.M.David, a
former Oxford Blue, home on leave from India.
Dick Milliner brought plenty of experience
and stability in his final season at scrum-half,
playing his final and 122nd game on the end-of-
season tour. There was never a settled outside-
half, the best being Dick Stephens, but he was
more focused on his first-class cricket career.

The pack became a settled unit only towards the
end of the season, and were at their best in the
loose, but often beaten in gaining possession.
Tom Voyce played the last of his 171 games in
November in the memorable win at Oxford
University. Les Saxby was ably assisted by
Ernest Comley and George Fowke (or Foulkes),
and Fred Wadley was the find of the season,
with Joe Davies another useful recruit.

Only four players were selected for a County side
which failed to win a game, but Les Saxby and
George McIlwaine played for Gloucestershire &
Somerset against New South Wales Waratahs.

Sep 8 Stroud 0 Gloucester 8
Tries: J.Stephens, R.N.Loveridge;
Conversion: J.Stephens

Sep 10 Gloucester 3 Lydney 0
Penalty: L.Saxby

Sep 17 Gloucester 9 Northampton 3
Tries: J.Stephens (2), R.C.Thompson

Sep 22 Gloucester 8 Bristol 5
Tries: J.Stephens, R.Milliner;
Conversion: H.Boughton

Sep 24 Gloucester 14 Moseley 5
Tries: R.James (2), R.C.Thompson, L.Abbey;
Conversion: J.Stephens

Sep 28 Gloucester 20 Cinderford 0
Tries: L.Abbey, J.Hemming, R.James,
D.Meadows;
Conversions: H.Boughton (2);
Drop goal: R.James

Oct 1 Guy's Hospital 8 Gloucester 8
Try: J.Hemming;
Conversion: H.Boughton;
Penalty: H.Boughton

Oct 8 Gloucester 3 Cardiff 20
Try: A.M.David

**Oct 15 Gloucester 22
St Thomas's Hospital 8**
Tries: R.James (3), T.Voyce, N.East;
Conversions: H.Boughton (2);
Penalty: H.Boughton

Oct 22 Cheltenham 0 Gloucester 3
Try: E.Comley

Oct 29 Gloucester 3 Harlequins 11
Try: R.James

**Nov 3 Oxford University 11
Gloucester 22**
Tries: T.Wadley, L.Saxby, R.Loveridge,
R.Milliner;
Conversions: J.Stephens (2);
Penalties: J.Stephens (2)

Nov 5 Swansea 12 Gloucester 0

**Nov 12 Gloucester 5
Devonport Services 11**
Try: T.Wadley;
Conversion: E.Comley

Nov 19 Gloucester 3 Newport 24
Try: R.James

**Nov 26 Gloucester 25
Oxford University Greyhounds 13**
Tries: J.Hemming(2), R.James (2),
R.Loveridge (2), T.Wadley;
Conversion: R.James (2)

**Dec 3 United Services (Portsmouth) 3
Gloucester 23**
Tries: J Stephens (2), R.Milliner, A.Hough,
A.W.Lewis;
Conversions: H.Boughton (4)

**Dec 10 Gloucester 14
St Bart's Hospital 0**
Tries: S.Short, A.Hough, E.Comley, L.Abbey;
Conversion: L.Saxby

Dec 17 Lydney 0 Gloucester 0

Dec 24 Gloucester 20 Cheltenham 0
Tries: E.Comley(2), T.Wadley, A.Hough,

J.Davies, L.Saxby;
Conversion: H.Boughton

**Dec 26 Gloucester 18
Old Merchant Taylors 3**
Tries: E.Comley, J.Davies, A.Hough, R.Milliner;
Conversion: H.Boughton;
Drop goal: J.Stephens

Dec 27 Gloucester 8 Bath 5
Tries: L.Abbey, J.Hemming;
Conversion: H.Boughton

Dec 31 Moseley v Gloucester - cancelled due to
frost

Jan 7 Llanelly 9 Gloucester 0

Jan 14 Gloucester 6 Leicester 3
Tries: L.Saxby (2)

Jan 21 Northampton 4 Gloucester 0

Jan 28 Gloucester 3 Guy's Hospital 6
Try: L.Abbey

**Feb 4 Gloucester 29
United Services (Portsmouth) 3**
Tries: A.Hough (3), L.Abbey, E.Stephens,
R.James, E.Comley;
Conversions: H.Boughton (4)

**Feb 11 Gloucester 22
Plymouth Albion 3**
Tries: A.Hough (2), J.Stephens, G.Foulkes,
T.Wadley;
Conversions: H.Boughton (2);
Penalty: H.Boughton

Feb 18 Gloucester 26 Old Blues 5
Tries: A.Hough, R.James, J.Davies, L.Franklin,
L.Saxby, J.Stephens;
Conversions: H.Boughton (4)

**Feb 23 Gloucester 35
5ᵗʰ Royal Tank Corps 0**
Tries: L.Saxby, R.James, E.Comley, F.Russell,
F.Benbow, A.Hough, A.W.Lewis;
Conversions: H.Boughton (3);
Drop goals: R.James, E.Stephens

Feb 25 Newport 22 Gloucester 0

Mar 3 Gloucester 13 Swansea 0
Tries: A.Hough, T.Wadley, H.Pitt;
Conversions: H.Boughton (2)

Mar 7 Bristol 6 Gloucester 5
Try: J.Stephens;
Conversion: H.Boughton

Mar 10 Gloucester 6 Llanelly 7
Penalties: H.Boughton (2)

Mar 17 Cardiff 8 Gloucester 0

Mar 24 Gloucester 5 Torquay 6
Try: J.Stephens;
Conversion: H.Boughton

Mar 31 Leicester 18 Gloucester 6
Tries: A.Hough (2)

**Apr 7 Gloucester 28
Welsh Universities 5**
Tries: J.Stephens (2), A.Hough, J.Davies,
F.Russell, R.James;
Conversions: H.Boughton (5)

Apr 9 Gloucester 9 London Welsh 8
Tries: F.Russell, J.Stephens, R.James

Apr 10 Cinderford 6 Gloucester 18
Tries: A.Hough (2), R James (2);
Conversion: R.James;
Drop goal: A.W.Lewis

**Apr 14 Devonport Services 3
Gloucester 3**
Try: J.Hemming

**Apr 16 Plymouth Albion 11
Gloucester 3**
Penalty: H.Boughton

Apr 17 Torquay 8 Gloucester 13
Tries: J.Stephens (2), R.James;
Conversions: H.Boughton (2)

Apr 21 Bath 10 Gloucester 8
Tries: R.James (2);
Conversion: H.Boughton

1928-29

**Played 42 Won 21 Lost 17 Drawn 4
For 456 Against 295
Captain: Les Saxby**

Gloucester 'A'
Played 25 Won 16 Lost 6 Drawn 3
For 284 Against 134
Captain: Albert Rea

N.B All results are included, but there are 11
games where the team sheets are incomplete, or
rely on the selected team printed in the Citizen,
and there are two games where the scorers are
unknown. Consequently appearances and
leading scorers are not comprehensive.

Most appearances: H.Boughton 36, L.Abbey
35, F.Wadley 35, E.Comley 34, R.James
32   E.L.Saxby 31, J.Stephens 32, J.Davies 29,
J.Hemming 28, T.Hiam 27, A.Carpenter 26
Most tries: J.Stephens 21, R.James 14,
A.Hough 8
Most conversions: H.Boughton 42

Most penalties: H.Boughton 15
Dropped goals: J.Stephens 2, H.Boughton 1

These remained hard economic times and membership slipped a bit further to 1,824, but the hard line taken by the Secretary, Arthur Hudson, resulted in an overall profit of £405. This was after grants to local clubs and donations to charities, nearly all health-related, including £75 to the Royal Infirmary.

The Club scored a lot more points than it conceded, and remained amongst the leading clubs in the country, but there were too many holes in the walls of Castle Grim by way of home defeats to make the season memorable. The strength of the team remained amongst the forwards, and the captain of Harlequins declared the Gloucester pack to be the finest they had come up against. Les Saxby's "vigour and enthusiasm breathed success in the side" as captain and pack leader, very well supported up front by Joe Davies, "Bumps" Carpenter and Fred Wadley.

At full-back, Harold Boughton was the outstanding back and ever dependable with his kicking. The back division was stronger when Maurice McCanlis was available in the centre, and he scored the try of the season against Guy's Hospital when "the ball came out to McCanlis, who took it at full speed. The Old Oxford Blue cut between the two opposing centres, and rounding Kennedy finished a glorious run over half the length of the field by scoring in a good position."

The best performances of the season were kept for Newport. In a great away game, Gloucester came storming back from a 6-19 deficit, scoring three tries and equalising in the last two minutes, their best result at Newport since 1900. They won fair and square at Kingsholm, with "rousing football between the forwards – too much vigour, perhaps, at times. In the loose the City players hung together splendidly, the backing up was excellent, and all tackled relentlessly. The City's greatest work was in defence, and in this respect Jack Stephens tackling was of such a character as to put fear into the hearts of the visitors." It was his final season before going north after 93 appearances.

There were other fine victories over Llanelly, Harlequins, Guy's Hospital, Leicester, Northampton, and Devonport Services. Against Cheltenham the referee abandoned the game seven minutes early when several players engaged in a "free fight," but when fixtures against Bristol were reinstated, "hard knocks were given and taken in the true sporting spirit".

Eight players were capped by Gloucestershire.

Sep 6 Stroud 0 Gloucester 18
Tries: A.Hough (3), G.Foulkes, J.Stephens;
Penalty: H.Boughton

Sep 8 Gloucester 9 Lydney 8
Tries: A.Hough, E.L.Saxby, R.James

Sep 15 Gloucester 28 Old Edwardians 3
Tries: A.Hough (3), J.Stephens (2), R.James;
Conversions: H.Boughton (5)

Sep 22 Gloucester 8 Torquay 0
Try: A.Hough;
Conversion: H.Boughton;
Penalty: H.Boughton

Sep 29 Cardiff 9 Gloucester 7
Try: J.Stephens;
Drop goal: J.Stephens

Oct 1 Gloucester 36 Cinderford 6
Tries: J.Stephens (4), A.W.Lewis (2), L.Franklin, R.James;
Conversions: H.Boughton (6)

Oct 6 Bristol 19 Gloucester 3
Penalty: H.Boughton

**Oct 13 Gloucester 30
Guy's Hospital 6**
Tries: R.James (4), J.Stephens, J.Hemming, M.McCanlis, J.Davies;
Conversions: Boughton (3)

Oct 20 Gloucester 6 Bath 0
Tries: R.James, L.Abbey

Oct 27 Moseley 3 Gloucester 8
Tries: E.Comley, L.Meadows;
Conversion: H.Boughton

**Nov 1 Gloucester 0
Oxford University 9**

Nov 3 Gloucester 0 Swansea 8

Nov 10 Cheltenham 0 Gloucester 9
Try: J.Stephens;
Penalties: H.Boughton (2)

Nov 17 Newport 19 Gloucester 19
Tries: L.C.Meadows (2), Roy James, J.Stephens, E.Comley;
Conversions: H.Boughton (2)

**Nov 22 Oxford University
Greyhounds 19 Gloucester 6**
Tries: J.M.F.Edmiston, L.E.Saxby

**Nov 24 Gloucester 3
Plymouth Albion 9**
Penalty: H.Boughton

Dec 1 Gloucester 18 United Services 8
Tries: J.Stephens (2), I.Storrie;
Penalties: J.Stephens (3)

**Dec 8 Gloucester 18
Devonport Services 20**
Tries: F.Russell, E.L.Saxby, L.Abbey, penalty try;
Conversions: H.Boughton (3)

Dec 15 Gloucester 13 Llanelly 3
Tries: E.Comley, E.L.Saxby, I.Storrie;
Conversions: H.Boughton (2)

Dec 22 Harlequins 0 Gloucester 3
Try: F.Wadley

**Dec 26 Gloucester 0
Old Merchant Taylors 3**

Dec 27 Bath 3 Gloucester 3
Try: S.Weaver

Dec 29 Gloucester 9 Cheltenham 3
Tries: F.Russell, I.Storrie;
Penalty: H.Boughton

Jan 5 Llanelly 6 Gloucester 0

Jan 12 Gloucester 11 Leicester 3
Tries: W.Cuffe, J.Stephens;
Conversion: H.Boughton;
Penalty: H.Boughton

Jan 19 Gloucester 11 Northampton 3
Try: J.Stephens;
Conversion: H.Boughton;
Penalties: H.Boughton (2)

Jan 26 Guy's Hospital 14 Gloucester 0

Feb 2 United Services 9 Gloucester 0

Feb 9 Gloucester 28 Old Blues 6
Tries: J.Stephens (3), R.James (2), G.Foulkes;
Conversions: H.Boughton (5)

Feb 16 Northampton v Gloucester - cancelled

Feb 23 Gloucester 15 Newport 5
Tries: M.McCanlis, R.James;
Conversion: H.Boughton;
Penalty: H.Boughton;
Drop goal: H.Boughton

Mar 2 Swansea 9 Gloucester 6

Tries: G.Foulkes, J.Hemming

Mar 9 Gloucester 11 Bristol 11
Tries: L.Abbey, J.Davies;
Conversion: H.Boughton;
Penalty: H.Boughton

Mar 16 Gloucester 5 Cardiff 10
Try: A.Carpenter;
Conversion: H.Boughton

Mar 23 Leicester 12 Gloucester 3
Penalty: H.Boughton

Mar 30 Gloucester 22 Moseley 3
Tries: F.Wadley (2), J.Davies, E.Comley,

E.L.Saxby;
Conversions: H.Boughton (2);
Penalty: H.Boughton

Apr 1 Gloucester 8 London Welsh 14
Try: G.Foulkes;
Conversion: H.Boughton;
Penalty: H.Boughton

Apr 2 Cinderford 3 Gloucester 16
Tries: R.Hook (2), I.Storrie, W.N.Hoare;
Conversions: R.James (2)

Apr 6 Gloucester 35 U.C.S Old Boys 0
Scorers unknown

**Apr 13 Plymouth Albion 12
Gloucester 9**
Scorers unknown

**Apr 15 Devonport Services 8
Gloucester 16**
Tries: W.Cuffe (2), L.Abbey;
Conversions: H.Boughton (2);
Drop goal from a mark: E.L.Saxby

Apr 16 Torquay 3 Gloucester 3
Try: I.Storrie

Apr 20 Lydney 6 Gloucester 3
Try: R.Loveridge

1929-30

A.T.Voyce S.Smart F.Abbey E.Keys E.J.James J.T.Brookes(Chairman) Rev. H.J.Hensman   J.F.Scoon
F.W.Ayliffe T.H.Millington G.Foulkes K.Smith L.Abbey E.Stephens H.Boughton F.Wadley F.Russell H.J.Balchin
A.Hudson(Sec) R.N.Loveridge M.A.McCanlis E.Comley A.Carpenter G.R.James L.E.Saxby(Capt) J.Hemming A.Hough R.L.Baker D.Crichton-Miller
J.Davis G.F.Clutterbuck
F.Price D.Meadows

**Played 41 Won 23 Lost 12 Drawn 6
For 427 Against 273
Captain: Les Saxby**

Gloucester 'A'
Played 23 Won 11 Lost 11 Drawn 1
For 274 Against 168
Captain: Albert Rea

Most appearances: G.Foulkes 40, E.Comley,
F.Price 39, F.Wadley 34, J.Hemming 33,
H.Boughton 32, R.James 30, A.Carpenter 28
Most tries: R.James 14, M.McCanlis 11,
G.Foulkes 8, J.Davies, R.L.Baker 6
Conversions: H.Boughton 44, R.James 2,
W.Ash 1
Penalties: H.Boughton 11, R.L.Baker 1
Drop goals: D.Meadows 4, E.Stephens 2,

R.James, R.N.Loveridge, R.L.Baker 1

The playing record was the best for ten years,
and was as usual based on the strength of the
pack, which was enhanced further by the former
Oxford blue, Donald Crichton-Miller, who
offered his services when he took up a teaching
post at Monmouth. He quickly became a crowd
favourite as a dynamic flanker, who was fast
onto the ball, a deadly tackler and effective
dribbler.

The best result of the season was the victory
at Cardiff, the first for 33 years. Roy James
captained the side in the absence of Saxby.
Maurice McCanlis deservedly scored both tries,
but it was the kicking of 19-year-old Harold
Boughton, which made the difference between

the sides. A band and a large crowd greeted
the players on their return to Gloucester and
the conquering heroes were carried shoulder-
high through the City. When Roy James again
deputised as captain against United Services
(Portsmouth), he led the way in every sense,
scoring two brilliant tries and converting them
both for a 10-8 win.

The success of the season was judged
principally by victories over each of the Welsh
big four, the finest game of the season reckoned
to be against Swansea, with Crichton-Miller
man-of-the-match, and a very high standard
of play throughout. Several matches were won
thanks to Boughton's kicking, none more so
than against Oxford University, when he kicked
two penalties and three conversions. The two

penalty kicks were from near half-way and against a strong wind. Both were magnificent efforts, and the second was described by Tom Voyce as one of the finest he had ever seen.

The Club hosted an England trial, which attracted a crowd of more than 7,000 to Kingsholm, despite the absence of Gloucester players. Maurice McCanlis, Joe Davies and Fred Wadley were selected as reserves, but the nearest any of them came to the pitch was McCanlis, who was handed a flag and asked to act as touch judge. Season ticket holder numbers were again down, to 1,588, but successes on the field of play kept crowds up to the point where a profit of £490 was made.

Ten players represented Gloucestershire, and eight of them - Harold Boughton, Roy James, Maurice McCanlis, Fred Wadley, "Bumps" Carpenter, Ernest Comley, Les Saxby and Joe Davies – were in the team which defeated Lancashire at Blundellsands 13-7 to win the County Championship. Harold Boughton and Joe Davies had England trials.

Sep 12 Stroud 6 Gloucester 18
Tries: L.Abbey (2), F.Price, L.Franklin;
Conversions: H.Boughton (3)

Sep 14 Gloucester 13 Lydney 0
Tries: E.Stephens, J.Davies;
Penalty: H.Boughton;
Conversions: H.Boughton (2)

**Sep 21 Gloucester 18
Old Edwardians 3**
Tries: G.Foulkes (2), F.Price, J.Davies;
Conversions: H.Boughton (3)

Sep 28 Bath 3 Gloucester 3
Try: Roy James

Sep 30 Torquay 9 Gloucester 4
Drop goal: E.Stephens

Oct 5 Gloucester 5 Bristol 7
Try: L.Saxby;
Conversion: H.Boughton

Oct 12 Gloucester 20 Leicester 11
Tries: L.Meadows, J.Davies, L.Abbey, F.Price;
Conversions: H.Boughton (2);
Drop goal: R.Loveridge

Oct 19 Cardiff 9 Gloucester 10
Tries: M.McCanlis (2);
Conversions: H.Boughton (2)

Oct 26 Gloucester 8 Moseley 9
Try: G.Foulkes;

Conversion: H.Boughton;
Penalty: H.Boughton

**Oct 30 Oxford University 14
Gloucester 24**
Tries: S.Weaver (2), J.Davies, M.McCanlis;
Conversions: H.Boughton (3);
Penalties: H.Boughton (2)

Nov 2 Swansea 9 Gloucester 3
Try: D.Crichton-Miller

Nov 9 Old Edwardians 0 Gloucester 11
Tries: R.Loveridge (2), J.Hemming;
Conversion: W.Ash

**Nov 14 Gloucester 19
Oxford University Greyhounds 16**
Tries: F.Wadley, R.Loveridge, J.Davies;
Conversion: H.Boughton;
Drop goals: R.James, E.Stephens

Nov 16 Gloucester 3 Cheltenham 3
Try: G.Foulkes

Nov 23 Gloucester 8 Newport 6
Tries: E.Comley, F.Price;
Conversion: H.Boughton

**Nov 30 Gloucester 19
Guy's Hospital 3**
Tries: R.James (2), M.McCanlis, F.Price;
Conversions: H.Boughton (2);
Penalty: H.Boughton

Dec 7 United Services 8 Gloucester 10
Tries: R.James (2);
Conversions: R.James (2);

**Dec 14 Gloucester 30
Devonport Services 3**
Tries: M.McCanlis (3), E.Stephens, E.Comley, R.James;
Conversions: H.Boughton (4);
Drop goal: D.Meadows

Dec 21 Northampton 10 Gloucester 5
Try: R.James;
Conversion: H.Boughton

**Dec 26 Gloucester 22
Old Merchant Taylors 8**
Tries: M.McCanlis (2), D.Meadows, R.Loveridge, E.Stephens, L.Saxby;
Conversions: H.Boughton (2)

Dec 27 Gloucester 3 Bath 3
Try: H.Boughton

Dec 28 Moseley 11 Gloucester 3
Try: F.Russell

Jan 4 Llanelly 16 Gloucester 0

Jan 11 Cheltenham 3 Gloucester 0

**Jan 18 Gloucester 11
St Bartholomew's Hospital 5**
Try: R.Baker;
Conversion: H.Boughton;
Penalties: H.Boughton (2)

Jan 25 Guy's Hospital 0 Gloucester 14
Tries: D.Crichton-Miller, R.James;
Conversion: H.Boughton;
Penalties: H.Boughton (2)

Feb 1 Gloucester 10 United Services 3
Tries: A.Hough (2);
Drop goal: D.Meadows

Feb 8 Gloucester 3 Cardiff 3
Try: R.James

Feb 15 Gloucester 5 Llanelly 3
Try: D.Meadows;
Conversion: H.Boughton

Feb 22 Newport 6 Gloucester 0

Mar 1 Gloucester 15 Swansea 6
Tries: J.Hemming, G.Foulkes, D.Crichton-Miller;
Conversion: H.Boughton;
Drop goal: D.Meadows

Mar 8 Bristol 6 Gloucester 0

Mar 15 Gloucester 6 Old Blues 6
Tries: G.Foulkes, R.James

Mar 22 Gloucester 12 Northampton 6
Tries: A.Hough, M.McCanlis, G.Foulkes;
Drop goal from mark: R.Baker

Mar 29 Leicester 16 Gloucester 5
Try: R.Baker;
Conversion: H.Boughton

Apr 5 Gloucester 11 Harlequins 8
Tries: R.James, M.McCanlis;
Conversion: H.Boughton;
Penalty: H.Boughton

**Apr   12   Devonport   Services   6
Gloucester 11**
Tries: R.James, P.Hordern;
Conversion: H.Boughton;
Penalty: H.Boughton

Apr 14 Camborne 6 Gloucester 21
Tries: R.Baker (2), D.Meadows, L.Abbey,

I.C.Bendall;
Conversions: H.Boughton (3)

**Apr 19 Gloucester 27
U.C.S Old Boys 5**

Tries: R.Baker (2), R.James, L.Abbey, A.Hough;
Conversions: H.Boughton (4);
Drop goal: R.Baker

Apr 21 Gloucester 8 London Welsh 8
Tries: R.James, G.Foulkes;

Conversion: H.Boughton

Apr 22 Lydney 12 Gloucester 9
Try: J.Davies;
Conversion: H.Boughton;
Drop goal: D.Meadows

1930-31

E.T.James J.F.Scoon Rev.H.J.Hensman A.T.Voyce G.F.Clutterbuck S.Smart
H.J.Balchin L.E.Saxby Dr.Steel-Perkins J.Hemming K.Smith V.Sheppard L.Abbey W.N.Hoare T.Millington
A.Hudson(Sec) G.Davies A.Carpenter H.Boughton G.R.James(Capt) F.Wadley F.Russell J.Davies J.T.Brookes(Chairman)
F.Price(inset) E.Comley F.Fifield D.Meadows L.Franklin M.A.McCanlis(inset)

**Played 38 Won 17 Lost 16 Drawn 5
For 321 Against 293
Captain: Roy James**

Gloucester United
Played 27 Won 14 Lost 9 Drawn 4
For 233 Against 143
Captain: Arthur Webb

Most appearances: E.Comley, F.Wadley
34, R.James, D.Meadows, J.Hemming 33,
L.Franklin 32, F.Price 30
Most tries: R.James 9, D.Meadows, L.Franklin
6, L.Abbey 5, M.McCanlis 5
Penalties: H.Boughton 9, R.James 2
Conversions: H.Boughton 15, R.James 13,
R.N.Loveridge 2, Dr.Steele-Perkins 1
Drop goals: T.Stephens 2, F.Price,
H.Boughton 1

The Club remained in profit by £288, despite membership dropping to 1,488, although Bristol was the only other club in the country with a membership this large. With considerable reluctance the name of the second team was changed from A to United, the Club feeling compelled to do this because some other clubs refused to accept fixtures against an A team.

The highlight of the season was doing the double over Cardiff, only previously achieved in 1890-91. The try of the season was scored against Leicester at Kingsholm, when "Meadows seized the ball, and McCanlis and James in turn handled. McCanlis again received, and cross-kicking Wadley took the ball and broke clear. Franklin positioned himself ready for the pass, and with a sharp run scored near the posts – a brilliant try, covering three-parts the length of the ground."

But the lack of a settled team led to many disappointing results. More games were won than lost only because of victory over Plymouth Albion in the final game of the West Country tour and a surprise win against Harlequins at Twickenham on the last day of the season.

The main handicap was the use of 21 different players in the three-quarters, where the strongest combination was Roy James, Maurice McCanlis, John Brookes and Kit Tanner, but they were never all available together. Roy James, the captain, played at wing, centre, outside half and full-back. The loss of Jack Stephens to Rugby League was keenly felt, but Vernon Sheppard made his debut and proved to be a strong resolute runner.

Don Meadows at stand-off had "no superior

as an individualist who made wonderful side-stepping runs, but he was a difficult player to combine with". At full-back, Harold Boughton had a fine season, his kicking being a great strength for Club and County.

The pack was disrupted early in the season, and George Foulkes (Fowke) was no longer able to command a regular place, but ended with 157 appearances and then captained the United for four seasons. Things improved after Les Saxby returned at the end of October, and provided plenty of ball for the backs, who often failed to take advantage. The front row of Fred Wadley, "Bumps" Carpenter and Ernest Comley, was outstanding.

During the season, 13 players represented Gloucestershire, who won the County Championship by rather luckily defeating Warwickshire 10-9 in the final at Kingsholm, when the Gloucester contingent was Harold Boughton (2 conversions), Maurice McCanlis (try), Frank Wadley, "Bumps" Carpenter, Les Saxby (try) and Joe Davies.

For England, Maurice McCanlis won caps against Wales and Ireland, and Harold Boughton was twice a reserve; Joe Davies, "Bumps" Carpenter, and Fred Wadley played in England trials. Donald Crichton-Miller made his debut for Scotland against Wales and scored two tries; he added further caps against Ireland and England.

Sep 11 Stroud 3 Gloucester 26
Tries: R.Loveridge (2), Don Meadows,
L.Franklin, G.Foulkes, Roy James;
Drop goals: T.Stephens (2)

Sep 13 Gloucester 0 Lydney 0

Sep 20 Gloucester 23 Moseley 0
Tries: R.Loveridge, L.Franklin, E.Stephens,
J.Davies, E.Comley, F.Price;
Conversion: H.Boughton;
Penalty: H.Boughton

Sep 25 Gloucester 13 Bath 0
Tries: P.Hordern (2), D.Crichton-Miller;
Conversions: H.Boughton (2)

Sep 27 Gloucester 8 Northampton 11
Tries: Roy James, A.Hough;
Conversion: H.Boughton

Oct 4 Bristol 13 Gloucester 0

Oct 11 Leicester 27 Gloucester 8
Tries: D.Meadows, J.Davies;
Conversion: Roy James

Oct 18 Gloucester 17 Cardiff 10
Tries: J.Davies, F.Wadley;
Conversions: H.Boughton (2);
Penalty: H.Boughton;
Drop goal: F.Price

Oct 25 Moseley 6 Gloucester 6
Tries: L.E.Saxby, N.Powell

Nov 1 Gloucester 0 Llanelly 0

**Nov 8 Gloucester 26
Oxford University Greyhounds 8**
Tries: D.Meadows, F.Price, T.Hiam,
J.T.Andrews, Roy James;
Conversions: Roy James (4);
Penalty: Roy James

Nov 15 Newport 6 Gloucester 3
Penalty: H.Boughton

**Nov 22 Gloucester 6
Devonport Services 5**
Try: Roy James;
Penalty: Roy James

**Nov 27 Gloucester 10
Oxford University 13**
Tries: L.E.Saxby, M.McCanlis;
Conversions: R.Loveridge (2)

Nov 29 Gloucester 10 Swansea 11
Tries: F.Price, M.McCanlis;
Conversions: Roy James (2)

Dec 6 Gloucester 9 United Services 3
Try: F.Price;
Penalties H.Boughton (2)

Dec 13 Cheltenham 0 Gloucester 0

Dec 20 Northampton 3 Gloucester 8
Tries: L.Abbey, A.Spackman;
Conversion: H.Boughton

**Dec 26 Gloucester 8
Old Merchant Taylors 13**
Tries: A.Spackman, A.G.Cridlan;
Conversion: H.Boughton

Dec 27 Gloucester 3 Cheltenham 8
Try: L.Abbey

Jan 3 Llanelly 9 Gloucester 3
Try: L.Abbey

Jan 10 Gloucester 8 R.A.F 3
Tries: Roy James, Graham Davies;
Conversion: H.Boughton

Jan 17 Bath 9 Gloucester 3
Try: D.Meadows

Jan 24 Guy's Hospital 9 Gloucester 3
Try: J.Hemming

Jan 31 Gloucester 15 Old Blues 0
Tries: L.Franklin, L.E.Saxby, M.McCanlis;
Conversions: Roy James (3)

**Feb 7 United Services 11
Gloucester 13**
Tries: M.McCanlis, L.Abbey, Dr.Steele-Perkins;
Conversions: Dr.Steele-Perkins, Roy James

Feb 14 Cardiff 4 Gloucester 6
Tries: F.Wadley, Roy James

**Feb 21 Gloucester 12
Plymouth Albion 3**
Tries: E.Comley, L.Abbey;
Penalties: H.Boughton (2)

Feb 28 Gloucester 5 Guy's Hospital 7
Try: Dr.Steele-Perkins;
Conversion: H.Boughton

Mar 7 Swansea 6 Gloucester 0

Mar 21 Gloucester 0 Newport 8

Mar 28 Gloucester 16 Leicester 8
Tries: M.McCanlis, Dr.Steele-Perkins,
L.Franklin, G.Davies;
Conversions: H.Boughton (2)

**Apr 4 Gloucester 19
U.C.S Old Boys 13**
Tries: Roy James (2), L.Franklin, D.Meadows;
Conversions; H.Boughton, Roy James;
Penalty: H.Boughton

Apr 6 Gloucester 0 London Welsh 6

Apr 7 Lydney 8 Gloucester 8
Tries: R.Loveridge, D.Meadows;
Conversion: Roy James

**Apr 11 Devonport Services 31
Gloucester 0**

**Apr 13 Plymouth Albion 8
Gloucester 13**
Tries: W.V.Sheppard, Roy James;
Penalty: H.Boughton;
Drop goal: H.Boughton

Apr 18 Harlequins 10 Gloucester 13
Tries: W.V.Sheppard, G.Davies, L.Franklin;
Conversions: H.Boughton (2)

J.T.Brookes(Chairman) H.G.Kingscott Rev.H.J.Hensman G.F.Clutterbuck E.T.James S.Smart F.Abbey
H.J.Balchin F.W.Ayliffe L.Franklin J.Hyett K.Smith R.James A.Welshman Dr.R.N.Williams E.Comley J.C.Brooks T.Millington A.T.Voyce
H.Boughton W.V.Sheppard C.C.Tanner G.W.Parker Dr.A.Alcock(Pres) L.E.Saxby(Capt) F.Wadley A.Carpenter J.Hemming A.Hudson(Sec) T.Bagwell
C.Fifield D.Meadows M.A.McCanlis(absent)

**Played 38 Won 19 Lost 16 Drawn 3
For 287 Against 269
Captain: Les Saxby**

Gloucester United
Played 25 Won 21 Lost 4 Drawn 0
For 399 Against 103
Captain: George Fowke

Most Appearances: F.Wadley 33, E.Comley,
A.Welshman 31, J.Hemming 30, G.W.Parker,
J.C.Brooks 27, H.Boughton 26, K.Smith,
L.Franklin 25
Most tries: W.V.Sheppard 7, L.E.Saxby,
G.W.Parker 6, R.James, J.T.Andrews 4
Conversions: H.Boughton 23, G.W.Parker 7,
R.James 2
Penalties: H.Boughton 9, G.W.Parker 3
Dropped goals: R.James 3, D.Meadows 1

Although the season ended with slightly more wins than losses, the points scored total was the lowest for 35 years, and the points conceded was the lowest for 11 years, with only 57 tries scored. Les Saxby in his fourth and final season as captain may have been disappointed with these results, but for him personally the season was a triumph as he was capped by England, led Gloucestershire to the County Championship and went on the Barbarians Easter tour, before retiring after 169 appearances.

However, numerous representative honours with England and Gloucestershire and injuries frequently weakened the team and contributed to the moderate results. Lydney completed their first ever double over Gloucester, and their first win at Kingsholm since 1904-05. First Saturday fixtures were played against Blackheath and Oxford University, both of which were lost.

But there were highlights. Leicester arrived at Kingsholm having won their first six games without conceding a point, but Gloucester came from behind at half-time to win. Harold Boughton kicked a fine penalty in the first minute against Cardiff and it proved enough to win the match thanks to a stirring display by the pack and ferocious tackling thereafter. Swansea were also narrowly defeated at Kingsholm after another strenuous arm-wrestle.

Most of the successes were down to the forwards, especially the formidable front row of Fred Wadley, Bumps Carpenter and Ernest Comley, backed up by the excellent Les Saxby and Jack Hemming. The backs were better individually than in combination, and their handling was a real weakness. The best three-quarter line was Kit Tanner, Maurice McCanlis, Roy James and Vernon Sheppard, but they never played together, and 18 players were tried at various times. Les Abbey had lost pace on the wing and played his last and 147th game mid-season.

The overall record was improved by a sequence of three victories in four days over Easter against Wakefield, London Welsh and Bradford. Two fine tries led to victory against Harlequins – first "the ball came across to Sheppard, who handed off Pattison, and raced up to Block. Giving an inside pass to Brooks, the latter completed the effort by scoring a capital try," and the second "was a Meadows' effort almost entirely. Breaking through, he fed Sheppard, and receiving a re-pass beat Block easily and scored a fine try".

Fifteen players turned out for Gloucestershire in the course of the season, and nine of them - Les Saxby (captain), Kit Tanner, Maurice McCanlis, Vincent Sheppard, Roy James (drop goal), Ernest Comley, "Bumps" Carpenter, Fred Wadley and Jack Hemming – played in the final of the County Championship, which was won 9-3 against Durham at Blaydon. Saxby(captain), McCanlis, Carpenter and Wadley played for Gloucestershire & Somerset against South Africa.

For England, Les Saxby was capped and made pack leader against South Africa and Wales, Kit Tanner was capped against South Africa, Wales, Ireland and Scotland, and "Bumps" Carpenter against South Africa; Roy James was reserve for four internationals.

It was noted that in the ten years since 1920 charities had received £1,650 and local clubs £550 from the Club.

Sep 10 Stroud 3 Gloucester 9
Tries: R.James, C.Fifield, A.Welshman

Sep 12 Gloucester 3 Lydney 5
Try: F.Wadley

Sep 19 Gloucester 8 Moseley 3
Tries: H.Applin, L.E.Saxby;
Conversion: H.Boughton

Sep 26 Gloucester 10 Northampton 8
Tries: L.E.Saxby, E.Comley;
Conversions: H.Boughton (2)

Oct 1 Gloucester 8 Bristol 6
Tries: R.James, J.Hemming;
Conversion: H.Boughton

Oct 3 Llanelly 12 Gloucester 3
Penalty: G.W.Parker

Oct 10 Gloucester 12 Leicester 6
Try: R.N.Loveridge;
Penalty: H.Boughton;
Conversion: H.Boughton;
Drop goal: R.James

Oct 17 Cardiff 17 Gloucester 0

**Oct 24 Gloucester 15
U.C.S Old Boys 8**
Tries: L.Franklin (2), H.J.Hyett;
Conversions: G.W.Parker (3)

**Oct 31 Gloucester 13
Devonport Services 6**
Tries: J.T.Andrews, R.James;
Conversions: H.Boughton (2);
Penalty: H.Boughton

**Nov 5 Gloucester 18
Oxford Greyhounds 3**
Tries: J.T.Andrews (2), R.N.Loveridge,
Dr.Steele-Perkins;
Conversions: H.Boughton (3)

Nov 7 Swansea 13 Gloucester 3
Try: L.Franklin

Nov 14 Gloucester 11

St.Bart's Hospital 8
Tries: H.Applin, J.T.Andrews;
Conversion: H.Boughton;
Penalty: H.Boughton

Nov 21 Gloucester 0 Newport 5

**Nov 28 Gloucester 6
Oxford University 17**
Tries: C.C.Tanner, Dr.Steele-Perkins

Dec 5 Blackheath 10 Gloucester 3
Try: J.Hemming

Dec 12 Lydney 7 Gloucester 5
Try: J.C.Brooks;
Conversion: G.W.Parker

Dec 19 Northampton 3 Gloucester 0

**Dec 26 Gloucester 5
Old Merchant Taylors 5**
Try: W.V.Sheppard;
Conversion: H.Boughton

Jan 2 Cheltenham 0 Gloucester 0

Jan 9 Gloucester 7 Plymouth Albion 0
Try: G.W.Parker;
Drop goal: R.James

Jan 16 Gloucester 8 Bath 3
Try: G.W.Parker;
Conversion: H.Boughton;
Penalty: H.Boughton

Jan 23 Gloucester 16 Guy's Hospital 6
Tries: K.Smith, F.Wadley, G.W.Parker;
Conversions: H.Boughton (2);
Penalty: H.Boughton

Jan 30 Gloucester 9 Old Blues 10
Tries: C.C.Tanner, E.Comley;
Penalty: H.Boughton

Feb 13 Gloucester 3 Cardiff 0
Penalty: H.Boughton

Feb 20 Leicester 7 Gloucester 5
Try: W.V.Sheppard;

Conversion: H.Boughton

Feb 27 Gloucester 9 Cheltenham 8
Tries: W.V.Sheppard (2);
Penalty: H.Boughton

Mar 5 Gloucester 5 Swansea 3
Try: L.E.Saxby;
Conversion: H.Boughton

Mar 12 Bristol 6 Gloucester 5
Try: T.Hiam;
Conversion: H.Boughton

Mar 19 Newport 24 Gloucester 0

Mar 26 Gloucester 18 Wakefield 3
Tries: C.Fifield, W.V.Sheppard, G.W.Parker,
H.J.Hyett;
Conversion: G.W.Parker;
Drop goal: R.James

**Mar 28 Gloucester 23
London Welsh 11**
Tries: W.V.Sheppard (2), R.James;
Conversion: G.W.Parker (2);
Penalties: G.W.Parker (2);
Drop goal: D.Meadows

Mar 29 Gloucester 13 Bradford 3
Tries: L.E.Saxby (2), H.J.Hyett;
Conversions: R.James (2)

Apr 2 Gloucester 18 Harlequins 13
Tries: J.C.Brooks (2), D.Meadows, E.Comley;
Conversions: H.Boughton (3)

Apr 9 Gloucester 3 Llanelly 6
Try: J.Hemming

**Apr 16 Plymouth Albion 3
Gloucester 0**

**Apr 18 Devonport Services 10
Gloucester 10**
Tries: G.W.Parker, L.E.Saxby;
Conversions: H.Boughton (2)

Apr 19 Bath 8 Gloucester 3
Penalty: H.Boughton

1932-33

**Played 37 Won 24 Lost 10 Drawn 3
For 423 Against 259
Captain: Fred Wadley**

Gloucester United
Played 27 Won 21 Lost 3 Drawn 3
For 336 Against 142
Captain: George Fowke

Season records are incomplete. There are ten games where team sheets are incomplete and six games where scorers are either unknown or incomplete. Appearances and season's scorers are taken from the season summary in the "Citizen."

Most appearances: C.Fifield, R.Morris 36, W.V.Sheppard, D.Meadows, A.Carpenter,

E.Comley 32, F.Wadley 31, R.James 28, J.C.Brooks 26
Most tries: W.V.Sheppard 18, C.C.Tanner 17, R.James, J.C.Brooks, R.McKay 8, R.Hook 7
Most conversions: H.Boughton 26, R.James 10
Penalties: H.Boughton 4, D.Meadows 2, G.Parker 1
Drop goals: D.Meadows 3, W.V.Sheppard, P.Hordern 1

T.Voyce J.F.Scoon G.F.Clutterbuck S.Smart E.T.James Rev.H.J.Hensman A.Brown
F.W.Ayliffe J.Hemmings G.R.James I.Williams A.Welshman W.V.Sheppard J.C.Brooks T.Hiam T.Millington H.J.Balchin
J.T.Brookes R.Morris E.Comley H.Boughton F.Wadley(Capt) Dr.Alcock(Pres) K.Smith F.G.Edwards A.Carpenter R.B.McKay A.Hudson(Sec)
C.Fifield C.C.Tanner P.Hordern D.Meadows.

The results and the attractive style of play on the field led to larger crowds and left the Club in a healthy position financially. A fresh agreement was reached with local clubs, with Gloucester making a £5 annual grant to each club plus a 1s capitation fee per player per match for those who played occasionally but not regularly for the City club.

The highlights of a very successful season were the two victories over Newport, the first time this had been achieved for 50 years. Also of note were the defeats of Blackheath and Harlequins. The end-of-season tour of Devon was judged a great success, with victories over Devonport Services and Torquay, and more generally results away from Kingsholm were a marked improvement on previous seasons.

Amongst the backs, illness compelled Maurice McCanlis to miss the whole season at centre, and on the wing injuries to Dick Loveridge restricted his availability and led to his retirement after 126 appearances. Without them, the first choice back division was Harold Boughton; Kit Tanner, John Brooks, Roy James, Vernon Sheppard; and Don Meadows and Connie Fifield. With Meadows pulling the strings, there were times when this combination played brilliant football. Although Meadows sometimes eluded his colleagues as well as opponents, the forceful running of Sheppard and the sheer class and speed of Tanner on the wings

ensured that advantage was taken of the many opportunities created inside, and there were some breath-taking solo runs. Boughton did the kicking with James deputising as necessary. The most promising newcomer was Francis Edwards in the centre.

Fred Wadley was a fine leader of an experienced pack and a well-balanced side in his first season as captain. The pack kept up the best traditions of uncompromising Gloucester forward play, and supplied a steady stream of ball. Wadley himself, "Bumps" Carpenter and Ernest Comley formed a very strong front row. "Digger" Morris came through as a strong presence in the second row, preferably paired with Ken Smith. Peter Hordern showed his international class as the star of the back row, and formed a very effective combination with Albert Welshman and Ivor Williams, a recruit from Cardiff. Consequently, Jack Hemming was unable to keep his place in the side and retired with 267 appearances.

During the season, nine players were selected for a Gloucestershire side which lost all its matches. Kit Tanner played in two England trials, and scored a try in each, but illness denied him the chance of international honours.

Sep 8 Stroud 0 Gloucester 9
Tries: R.Hook (2), D.Meadows

Sep 10 Gloucester 12 Lydney 0
Tries: D.Meadows, W.V.Sheppard; other scorers

unknown.

Sep 17 Gloucester 17 Moseley 6
Tries: R.Hook (2), F.Wadley, D.Meadows, E.Comley;
Conversion: R.James

Sep 24 Gloucester 17 Northampton 3
1 goal and 4 tries; scorers unknown

Oct 1 Bristol 14 Gloucester 0

Oct 8 Gloucester 3 Llanelly 18
Penalty: D.Meadows (by drop kick)

Oct 15 Cardiff 18 Gloucester 0

Oct 22 Moseley 3 Gloucester 8
Tries: P.Hordern, J.Hemming;
Conversion: R.Hook

Oct 29 Leicester 6 Gloucester 3
Try: R.B.McKay

Nov 5 Gloucester 8 Swansea 8
Scorers unknown

**Nov 10 Gloucester 21
Oxford University Greyhounds 0**
Tries: R.B.McKay (2), J.C.Brooks, H.J.Hyett, F.Ford;
Conversions: T.Stephens (3)

Nov 12 Gloucester 3

Old Cranleighans 0
Try: W.V.Sheppard

Nov 19 Bath 3 Gloucester 0

**Nov 26 Oxford University 3
Gloucester 3**
Try: C.C.Tanner

Dec 3 Gloucester 18 Blackheath 6
Tries: W.V.Sheppard, J.C.Brooks, R.James,
R.B.McKay;
Conversions: R.James (3)

Dec 10 Lydney 0 Gloucester 0

**Dec 17 Gloucester 12
Devonport Services 4**
Tries: R.B.McKay (2), D.Meadows, R.James

Dec 24 Northampton 8 Gloucester 18
Try: J.C.Brooks; other scorers unknown

**Dec 26 Gloucester 11
Old Merchant Taylors 3**
Tries: C.C.Tanner, W.V.Sheppard;
Conversion: G.W.Parker;
Penalty; G.W.Parker

Dec 27 Gloucester 21 Old Blues 9
Tries: R.James, C.C.Tanner, A.Carpenter,
J.C.Brooks, W.V.Sheppard;
Conversion: G.W.Parker;
Drop goal; D.Meadows

Dec 31 Llanelly 4 Gloucester 0

Jan 7 Cheltenham 4 Gloucester 8

Try: K.Smith; other scorers unknown

Jan 14 Newport 6 Gloucester 10
Tries: W.V.Sheppard, J.C.Brooks;
Conversions: R.Hook (2)

Jan 21 Gloucester 17 Bristol 11
Tries: C.C.Tanner (2), W.V.Sheppard;
Conversions: R.James (2);
Drop goal: D.Meadows

Jan 28 Guy's Hospital v Gloucester - cancelled
due to frost

Feb 4 Gloucester 34 United Services 8
Tries: C.C.Tanner (4), J.C.Brooks (2),
A.Welshman, D.Meadows;
Conversions: H.Boughton (5)

Feb 11 Gloucester 3 Cardiff 15
Try: R.Hook

Feb 18 Gloucester 9 Leicester 11
Tries: C.C.Tanner (2);
Penalty: H.Boughton

Feb 25 Gloucester v R.A.F. - cancelled due to
snow

Mar 4 Swansea 21 Gloucester 3
Penalty: H.Boughton

Mar 11 Gloucester 17 Bath 3
Tries: P.Hordern, C.C.Tanner, R.James;
Conversions: H.Boughton (2);
Drop goal: P.Hordern

Mar 18 Gloucester 10 Newport 0
Tries: R.B.McKay, P.Hordern;
Conversions: H.Boughton (2)

Mar 25 Gloucester 35 Cheltenham 4
Tries: W.V.Sheppard (2), F.Edwards,
C.C.Tanner, R.Morris, R.B.McKay, P.Hordern;
Conversions: H.Boughton (5), D.Meadows (2)

Apr 1 Harlequins 21 Gloucester 28
Tries: C.C.Tanner (2), R.James (2), P.Hordern,
T.Hiam;
Conversions: H.Boughton (3);
Drop goal: D.Meadows

**Apr 8 Devonport Services 5
Gloucester 10**
Tries: A.Welshman, R.James;
Conversions: H.Boughton (2)

Apr 10 Torquay 3 Gloucester 5
Try: W.V.Sheppard;
Conversion: H.Boughton

Apr 15 Gloucester 18 Sale 7
Tries: W.V.Sheppard (2);
Conversion: H.Boughton;
Penalties: H.Boughton (2);
Drop goal: R.James

**Apr 17 Gloucester 14
London Welsh 19**
Tries: A.E.Brookes (3); other scorers unknown

Apr 18 Gloucester 18 Halifax 5
Tries: W.V.Sheppard (3), A.Carpenter;
Conversions: H.Boughton (3)

1933-34

**Played 39 Won 29 Lost 8 Drawn 2
For 556 Against 205
Captain: Fred Wadley**

Gloucester United
Played 27 Won 22 Lost 5 Drawn 0
For 428 Against 136
Captain: George Fowke

Most Appearances: F.Wadley 39, R.Morris 37,
C.Fifield, A.Welshman 34, A.Carpenter 33,
D.Meadows, I.Williams 31, E.Comley 28,
Most tries: W.V.Sheppard 17, R.James 11,
C.C.Tanner 10, J.C.Brooks 9
Most conversions: H.Boughton 39, G.Parker 9,
R.Hook 8, R.James 7
Penalties: H.Boughton 8, R.Hook, G.Parker 1
Most drop goals: D.Meadows 4, R.James 2,
H.Boughton 2,

The first match of the season on 9th September
was cancelled because of a hard-baked pitch,
but Bertram Mills circus continued in the
car park. A fire broke out at the back of the
main stand, which burnt down, and terrified
animals, including tigers and elephants, had to
be evacuated. The Club's insurance claim was
settled quickly, and matches continued during
the construction of a new and larger stand. This
opened only nine weeks later and remained in
place until 2007.

In this diamond jubilee season, the number of
wins was the most achieved in a season, and
the points aggregate was the second best in
the Club's history. The captain, Fred Wadley,
appeared in every match. The London press
declared Gloucester the best English club side of

the season, and indeed every London opponent
was vanquished.

In addition, Newport, Swansea and Llanelly
were all defeated at Kingsholm, and the double
was recorded over Swansea. Gloucester came
from behind to secure their first ever win at
St Helens in 50 years of trying. In the return
match at Kingsholm, Harold Boughton kicked
a goal from near half-way, Roy James dropped
a lovely goal from a difficult angle, and Vernon
Sheppard scored a spectacular try plunging
into the corner. However, defeat was suffered
at the hands of Cardiff, both home and away,
that being the only loss at Kingsholm, where
Gloucester United were undefeated for the third
season in succession.

The win over Oxford University was rated as

S.H.Budd H.Berry H.Boughton G.F.Clutterbuck A.T.Voyce J.T.Brookes(Chairman) S.Smart E.T.James
H.J.Balchin E.Compley T.Hiam L.Franklin A.D.Carpenter P.Hordern W.V.Sheppard T.Millington F.W.Ayliffe F.Abbey
A.Hudson(Sec) R.Morris R.James I.Williams J.C.Brooks(Vice-Capt) Dr.Alcock(Pres) F.Wadley (Capt) A.Welshman F.Edwards C.C.Tanner J.G.A'Bear
C.Fifield D.Meadows

one of the best matches ever seen at Kingsholm, but just before the end, Shaun Waide, the Oxford and Ireland wing fell awkwardly and had to be carried off. He had damaged his spleen, but Dr Arnold Alcock, the Gloucester President, was a surgeon and performed a successful operation on him at the Royal Infirmary.

The double against Leicester included a massive win at Kingsholm with Sheppard scoring a hat trick, and he repeated the dose against Bradford, when Kit Tanner and Ivor Williams also scored hat tricks. The double against Guy's Hospital included an immaculate display of siege gun kicking by Boughton which caused The Times to report "Boughton was just Boughton - how the Guy's forwards must have hated the sight of him long before the finish!"

On their debut in the Middlesex Sevens, Gloucester lost 8-10 to Edgware in the first round.

Fifteen players received the call from Gloucestershire, who reached the County Championship final, for which nine Gloucester players were selected - Harold Boughton, Kit Tanner, John Brooks, Roy James, Conway Fifield, Don Meadows, Ernest Comley, "Bumps" Carpenter and Ivor Williams - but they lost 0-10 to East Midlands at Northampton. This was the last season for Comley, who made 272 appearances

Peter Hordern played for England against Wales; both Don Meadows and Roy James were reserves against Ireland; Kit Tanner had two

trials but missed out on a cap through illness: John Brooks and Ernest Comley also had trials.

Sep 16 Gloucester 16 Moseley 5
Tries: A.Welshman, R.James, W.V.Sheppard;
Conversions: H.Boughton (2);
Penalty: H.Boughton

Sep 21 Gloucester 16 Lydney 0
Tries: R.Hook (2), R.James;
Conversions: R.Hook (2);
Penalty: R.Hook

Sep 23 Leicester 4 Gloucester 18
Tries: R.James, D.Meadows;
Conversions: H.Boughton (2);
Drop goals: C.Fifield, R.James

Sep 30 Gloucester 16 Bristol 0
Tries: R.James, J.C.Brooks, C.C.Tanner, D.Meadows;
Conversions: H.Boughton (2)

Oct 7 Gloucester 5 Northampton 0
Try: C.C.Tanner;
Conversion: H.Boughton

Oct 14 Gloucester 0 Cardiff 6

Oct 21 Guy's Hospital 3 Gloucester 17
Tries: A.Welshman (2), R.James;
Conversions: H.Boughton (2);
Drop goal: H.Boughton

Oct 28 Gloucester 18 Old Blues 5
Tries: M.McCanlis (2), T.Hiam, L.Franklin;

Conversions: H.Boughton (3)

Nov 4 Swansea 6 Gloucester 8
Tries: F.Wadley, L.Franklin;
Conversion: H.Boughton

**Nov 9 Gloucester 38
Oxford University Greyhounds 0**
Tries: R.Mackay (3), M.McCanlis, R.Hook, P.Hordern, D.Meadows, L.Franklin;
Conversions: R.Hook (5);
Drop goal: D.Meadows

Nov 11 Moseley 8 Gloucester 17
Tries: R.Hook (2), R.Mackay (2), W.V.Sheppard;
Conversion: R.Hook

Nov 18 Gloucester 23 Bath 8
Tries: P.Hordern (2), R.James, C.C.Tanner;
Conversions: H.Boughton (4);
Penalty: H.Boughton

**Nov 25 Gloucester 10
Oxford University 7**
Tries: L.Franklin, C.C.Tanner;
Conversions: H.Boughton (2)

Dec 2 Blackheath 3 Gloucester 8
Try: R.Hook;
Conversion: H.Boughton;
Penalty: H.Boughton

Dec 9 Lydney v Gloucester - cancelled due to frost

Dec 16 Gloucester 17 Cheltenham 0
Tries: R.Mackay (2), J.C.Brooks, R.Hook;

Conversion: H.Boughton;
Penalty: H.Boughton

Dec 23 Northampton 17 Gloucester 3
Try: R.Hook

**Dec 26 Gloucester 18
Old Merchant Taylors 3**
Tries: F.Edwards (2), J.C.Brooks, L.Franklin;
Conversions: R.James (3)

Dec 27 Gloucester 41 Old Paulines 11
Tries: C.C.Tanner (2), L.Franklin (2), R.James,
M.McCanlis, D.Meadows, G.Parker,
J.C.Brooks;
Conversions: G.Parker (5), R.James (2)

Dec 30 Llanelly 12 Gloucester 5
Try: J.C.Brooks;
Conversion: G.Parker

**Jan 6 Gloucester 16
Devonport Services 3**
Tries: R.James (2), L.C.Watkins;
Conversions: G.Parker (2);
Penalty: G.Parker

Jan 13 Gloucester 9 Newport 0
Try: C.Fifield;
Conversion: G.Parker;
Drop goal: L.C.Watkins

Jan 20 Bristol 5 Gloucester 0

**Jan 27 Gloucester 28
Guy's Hospital 11**

Tries: M.McCanlis (2), F.Wadley, L.Franklin,
P.Hordern, R.James;
Conversions: H.Boughton (3);
Drop goal: D.Meadows

**Feb 3 United Services (Portsmouth) 11
Gloucester 14**
Tries: F.Edwards (2), K.Voyce, W.V.Sheppard;
Conversion: L.C.Watkins

Feb 10 Cardiff 12 Gloucester 7
Try: L.C.Watkins;
Drop goal: R.Mackaay

Feb 17 Gloucester 35 Leicester 7
Tries: W.V.Sheppard (3), C.Fifield, M.McCanlis,
R.Mackay, J.C.Brooks;
Conversions: H.Boughton (5);
Drop goal: D.Meadows

Feb 24 Gloucester 24 R.A.F. 3
Tries: W.V.Sheppard (2), C.C.Tanner,
M.McCanlis;
Conversion: H.Boughton;
Penalties: H.Boughton (2);
Drop goal: D.Meadows

Mar 3 Gloucester 10 Swansea 3
Try: W.V.Sheppard;
Penalty: H.Boughton;
Drop goal: R.James

Mar 10 Bath 13 Gloucester 8
Tries: F.Edwards, W.V.Sheppard;
Conversion: L.C.Watkins

Mar 17 Newport 8 Gloucester 0

Mar 24 Gloucester 11 Llanelly 6
Tries: Ivor Williams, W.V.Sheppard, F.Edwards;
Conversion: R.James

Mar 31 Gloucester 27 London Welsh 3
Tries: W.V.Sheppard (3), C.Fifield (2),
F.Edwards, J.C.Brooks;
Conversions: W.V.Sheppard,   J.C.Brooks,
R.James

Apr 2 Gloucester 6 Headingley 6
Tries: L.C.Watkins, J.C.Brooks

Apr 3 Gloucester 47 Bradford 3
Tries: W.V.Sheppard (3), Ivor Williams (3),
C.C.Tanner (3), R.James, J.C.Brooks;
Conversions: H.Boughton (7)

**Apr 7 Devonport Services 0
Gloucester 0**

Apr 9 Torquay 5 Gloucester 9
Try: Lewis (Devonport Services player);
Conversion: H.Boughton;
Drop goal: H.Boughton

Apr 14 Gloucester 8 Harlequins 0
Tries: C.Fifield, F.Edwards;
Conversion: H.Boughton

Apr 19 Lydney 8 Gloucester 0

Apr 21 Cheltenham 0 Gloucester 3
Penalty: H.Boughton

1934-35

**Played 39 Won 25 Lost 14
For 550 Against 315
Captain: Fred Wadley**

Gloucester United
Played 31 Won 25 Lost 5 Drawn 1
For 528 Against 178
Captain: George Fowke

Most appearances: F.Wadley 39, A.Carpenter
35, A.Welshman 33, D.Meadows, K.Smith,
L.Franklin 32, F.Edwards 31, R.James 30
Most tries: F.Edwards 21, I.Williams 15,
R.James 13, C.Tanner 10, L.Franklin 9
Most conversions: H.Boughton 48,
D.Meadows, T.Stephens 4
Penalties: H.Boughton 10
Drop goals: D.Meadows 6, R.James 3,
H.Boughton 2

Before the season started, the old pavilion, built
in 1892, was taken down, and a new covered

terrace accommodating 3,000 was constructed
on the north side of the ground (the first part
of what would later be known as the Shed).
In October, electric light was installed on the
front of the Worcester Street stand in order to
illuminate training, although the committee
proved reluctant to turn them on for reasons of
economy.

The Club was in fine fettle with a profit of £360,
a membership of 1,983, and a good season on the
pitch. Fred Wadley, the captain, again appeared
in every match, and the other most influential
players were Harold Boughton, Francis
Edwards, Don Meadows, Ivor Williams, Peter
Hordern and Roy James.

The greatest satisfaction was taken from the
victories in Wales over Newport and Cardiff
– both were closely fought but well-deserved
triumphs. Gloucester coped better with the
gale blowing at Newport, while the Gloucester

Supporters Club chose Cardiff for their annual
outing, thoroughly enjoying Gloucester's
recovery from 0-6 down at half-time to snatch
victory with a dropped goal by Don Meadows
on the stroke of time. However, Cardiff and
Newport had narrow wins at Kingsholm, and
overall honours were even against the big Welsh
clubs.

The best performances in matches with English
clubs were against Torquay and Leicester. The
Gloucester backs had too much pace for Torquay
and this, combined with slick passing, produced
eleven tries, including hat tricks for both Francis
Edwards and Kit Tanner, and eight conversions
by Harold Boughton. "The match with Leicester
was one of scintillating and brilliant play … the
City backs dazzled at times with brilliant solo
and combined movements," – with Gloucester
running up a 24-0 lead by half-time.

Fred Wadley retired at the end of the season

after three years as captain and 287 appearances at prop. From the back row, Trevor Hiam stood down after 130 appearances and became captain of the United, Les Franklin finished early in the next season with 153 appearances, as did Ivor Williams when he moved to Cardiff after 100 appearances. Connie Fifield played only a few more games before finishing with 142 appearances at scrum half.

The Club was invited to make a second appearance at the Middlesex Sevens, but were again eliminated in the first round, and had to wait until 1973 for another invitation. For the fourth season in succession the United XV was undefeated at Kingsholm, and the 1st and United teams together aggregated more than 1,000 points.

Boughton's excellent kicking for Gloucester earned him international honours. He kicked a penalty on debut to earn England a draw against Wales, and then kicked a conversion and three penalties in a 14-0 defeat of Ireland, before winning a third cap against Scotland. Ivor Williams had a trial for Wales. Twelve players represented the County.

Sep 8   Gloucester 22 Lydney 6
Tries: L.Watkins (2,) L.Morris (2), R.James, F.Edwards;
Conversions: D.Meadows (2)

Sep 15 Gloucester 20 Moseley 10
Tries: I.Williams, R.James, F.Wadley;
Conversions: H.Boughton (2);
Penalty: H.Boughton;
Drop goal: D.Meadows

**Sep 22 Gloucester 37
Guys Hospital 11**
Tries: I.Williams (2), L.Franklin (2), P.Hordern, R.James, C.Fifield, A.Welshman;
Conversions: H.Boughton (3)
Penalty: H.Boughton;
Drop goal: R.James

Sep 29 Bristol 7 Gloucester 13
Tries: F.Edwards (2), L.Watkins;
Conversions: H.Boughton (2)

**Oct 6   Gloucester 22
St Barts Hospital 5**
Tries: F.Edwards, P.Hordern, C.Tanner, I.Williams, L.Watkins, C.Fifield;
Conversions: H.Boughton (2)

Oct 13 Gloucester 0 Cardiff 3

Oct 20 Richmond 6 Gloucester 9
Tries: I.Williams, F.Edwards, L.Watkins

Oct 27 Gloucester 13 Old Blues 3
Tries: T.Pugsley, A.Welshman (2);
Conversions: T.Pugsley (2)

**Nov 3   Gloucester 24
Old Cranleighans 8**
Tries: R.James (2), F.Edwards (2), L.Franklin, D.Meadows;
Conversions: H.Boughton (3)

Nov 10 Northampton 13 Gloucester 0

**Nov 15 Gloucester 18
Oxford University Greyhounds 9**
Tries: H.J.Hyett (2), D.Meadows, J.G.A'Bear;
Conversions: H.Boughton (3)

Nov 17 Gloucester 17 Bath 0
Tries: A.Welshman, F.Edwards, C.Tanner, L.Watkins;
Conversion: H.Boughton;
Penalty: H.Boughton

Nov 24 Gloucester 49 Torquay 11
Tries: F.Edwards (3), C.Tanner (3), L.Franklin (2), I.Williams (2), J.C.Brooks;
Conversions: H.Boughton (8)

**Nov 29 Oxford University 12
Gloucester 8**
Tries: L.Franklin, F.Edwards;
Conversion: H.Boughton

Dec 1   Gloucester 8 Blackheath 3
Tries: L.Franklin, C.Tanner;
Conversion: H.Boughton

Dec 8   Cheltenham 3 Gloucester 5
Try: Penalty try;
Conversion: R.Hook

**Dec 15 Gloucester 16
Devonport Services 8**
Tries: F.Edwards (2), I.Williams, L.Franklin;
Conversions: H.Boughton (2)

Dec 22 Gloucester 5 Northampton 6
Try: K.Smith;
Conversion: H.Boughton

**Dec 26 Gloucester 26
Old Merchant Taylors 5**
Tries: C.Tanner, F.Edwards, V.Sheppard, A.Welshman;
Conversions: H.Boughton (2);
Penalties: H.Boughton (2);
Drop goal: D.Meadows

Dec 29 Leicester 27 Gloucester 0

Jan 5   Gloucester 29 London Scottish 5
Tries: I.Williams, F.Wadley, T.Pugsley, R.James, C.Tanner;
Conversions: H.Boughton (4);
Penalties: H.Boughton (2)

Jan 12 Newport 3 Gloucester 8
Tries: I.Williams, R.James;
Conversion: G.W.Parker

Jan 19 Gloucester 3 Bristol 8
Try: C.Tanner

Jan 26 Guys Hospital 18 Gloucester 8
Try: L.Franklin;
Conversion: H.Boughton;
Penalty: H.Boughton

Feb 2   Gloucester 10 United Services 0
Try: R.Hook;
Drop Goal: D.Meadows;
Penalty: H.Boughton

Feb 9   Cardiff 6 Gloucester 9
Try: F.Edwards;
Conversion: D.Meadows;
Drop goal: D.Meadows

Feb 16 Bath 3 Gloucester 0

Feb 23 Gloucester 38 R.A.F. 8
Tries: C.Fifield (2), F.Edwards (2), L.Williams (2), F.Wadley, R.Hook;
Conversions: H.Boughton (5);
Drop goal: D.Meadows

Mar 2   Gloucester 25 Cheltenham 3
Tries: R.James (2), F.Edwards, P.Hordern;
Conversions: H.Boughton (3);
Penalty: H.Boughton;
Drop goal: H.Boughton;

Mar 9   Llanelly 9 Gloucester 0

Mar 16 Gloucester 8 Newport 11
Tries: J.C.Brooks, R.James;
Conversion: D.Meadows

Mar 23 Gloucester 32 Leicester 0
Tries: I.Williams, P.Hordern, R.James, A.Carpenter, D.Meadows, J.C.Brooks;
Conversions: H.Boughton (3);
Drop goals: H.Boughton, R.James

Mar 30 Harlequins 31 Gloucester 10
Tries: J.C.Brooks (2);
Drop goal: R.James

Apr 6   Gloucester 10 Llanelly 3
Tries: C.Tanner, J.R.Haines;
Conversions: T.Stephens (2)

Apr 13 Devonport Services 18 Gloucester 9
Tries: F.Edwards (2), R.James

Apr 15 Torquay 11 Gloucester 5
Try: R.Hook;
Conversion: R.Hook

Apr 20 Gloucester 13 London Welsh 0
Tries: R.James, K.Voyce, R.Hook;
Conversions: T.Stephens (2)

Apr 22 Gloucester 17 Sale 6
Tries: R.Hook (2), I.Williams, T.Stephens,
K.Smith;

Conversion: H.Boughton

Apr 23 Lydney 16 Gloucester 4
Drop goal: D.Meadows

1935-36

H.J.Balchin S.T.Davies A.T.Voyce H.H.Berry R.L.Loveridge J.F.Scoon E.T.James S.Smart
A.Hudson(Sec) N.F.McGrath T.Stephens J.G.A'Bear R.Morris A.Welshman I.Williams T.Price G.R.James T.Millington R.I.Scorer(Ref)
J.T.Brookes(Chairman) E.L.Phillips R.E.Hook F.G.Edwards J.C.Brooks(Capt) Dr.Alcock(Pres) D.Meadows A.Carpenter C.Harris H.Boughton T.Bagwell
E.R.Day R.E.Early

Played 37 Won 23 Lost 9 Drawn 5
For 402 Against 233
Captain: John Brooks

Gloucester United
Played 21 Won 12 Lost 8 Drawn 1
For 253 Against 112
Captain: Trevor Hiam

This season's records are incomplete. Team sheets are incomplete for seven games. Appearances are taken from the "Citizen" records.

Most appearances: D.Meadows 37, R.Morris, J.A'Bear 35, C.Harris, T.Price, A.Welshman 33, A.Carpenter 31, R.Hook 30, J.C.Brooks 28
Most tries: R.Hook 19, F.Edwards 13, J.C.Brooks 9
Conversions: H.Boughton 35, G.W.Parker 3, R.Hook 2, D.Meadows, T.Stephens 1
Penalties: H.Boughton 11, R.Hook, T.Stephens 1
Drop goals: H.Boughton, R.Hook, C.Fifield, D.Meadows, T.Pugsley, Dr.J.M.Dick 1

After a slow start to the season with three successive losses in October, the tide was turned when Bill Phillips at centre and Eddie Day at scrum-half were recruited. Thereafter, Day's quick passing created time for periodic brilliance from Don Meadows at fly-half, and performances improved markedly. The team was well led by John Brooks and Meadows as captain and vice-captain respectively. Brooks retired at the end of the season after 126 appearances. The centres, Bob Hook and Francis Edwards finished as top try-scorers; Edwards injured an ankle against London Welsh, so was moved out to the wing, where he proceeded to score a hat trick.

The forwards maintained consistently good form and were dominant in scrums, with the veteran "Bumps" Carpenter acting as the team's enforcer. Tom Price and Cyril Harris propped for Carpenter – a new combination which was rarely beaten in the scrums. Peter Hordern was the star of the back row, and joined the Barbarians for their Easter tour. This was the last full season for his back row partner, Albert Welshman, who retired with 185 appearances.

The team was unbeaten in February and March, when they "just missed being a really great side". An attractive style of rugby and good results brought the crowds out, and the Club did well financially, despite bad weather causing the cancellation of four fixtures. The membership reached 2,123, the first time it had gone above 2,000 for ten years, and the Club turned a profit of £508.

The highlights of what finished as a very good season were doing the double over Leicester, by a combined margin of 37-13, and Guy's Hospital, and the defeat of three leading Welsh teams, Cardiff, Newport, and Llanelly. This included only the second triumph at Stradey Park, 37 years after the first. Despite the Llanelly pack including three internationals, the Gloucester forwards established a clear dominance, with Carpenter and Hordern leading the way, although Gloucester had to defend heroically under severe pressure in the latter stages. The win at Cardiff was also based on winning the scrums and rattling the Welsh in the loose.

Harold Boughton topped 100 points with his goal-kicking for the fifth time, and during the season passed 1,000 points, which was thought to be the first time this landmark had been reached by any rugby player. In three successive games his goal-kicking saved Gloucester from defeat, he won the match against Llanelly with a successful conversion from near the touch line, and the game against Cardiff with a penalty.

Nine players were capped by the County; Boughton, Edwards and Carpenter played for Gloucestershire & Somerset against New Zealand; and Peter Hordern had an England trial.

Sep 14 Gloucester 21 Lydney 3
Tries: F.Edwards (2), L.Franklin, R.Hook;
Conversions: H.Boughton (3;
Penalty: H.Boughton

Sep 21 Gloucester 18 Moseley 4
Tries: C.Harris, I.Williams, T.Pugsley, C.Fifield;
Conversion: H.Boughton;
Drop goal: C.Fifield

Sep 28 Gloucester 3 Bristol 3
Try: P.Hordern

Oct 5 Northampton 3 Gloucester 0

Oct 12 Cardiff 0 Gloucester 3
Penalty: H.Boughton

Oct 19 Gloucester 14 Llanelly 19
Tries: I.Williams, C.Harris;
Conversions: H.Boughton (2);
Drop goal: H.Boughton

Oct 26 Cheltenham 6 Gloucester 7
Drop goal: T.Pugsley;
Penalty: R.Hook

Nov 2 Newport 9 Gloucester 0

Nov 9 Gloucester 10 Old Blues 15
Tries: Dr.J.M.Dick, R.Hook;
Drop goal: Dr.J.M.Dick

**Nov 14 Gloucester 14
Oxford University Greyhounds 6**
Tries: B.Cook (2), H.Edwards, J.C.Brooks;
Conversion: D.Meadows

Nov 16 Gloucester 6 Bath 3
Try: R.Hook;
Penalty: H.Boughton

**Nov 23 Guy's Hospital 11
Gloucester 18**
Tries: D.Meadows, J.C.Brooks, T.Price, W.Cale;
Conversions: H.Boughton (3)

**Nov 30 Gloucester 13
Oxford University 15**
Tries: J.C.Brooks, P.Hordern, R.Hook;
Conversions: H.Boughton (2)

Dec 7 Blackheath v Gloucester - cancelled due to fog

Dec 14 Moseley 5 Gloucester 13
Tries: R.Hook (2), A.Welshman;
Drop goal: R.Hook

Dec 21 Gloucester v Northampton - cancelled due to frost

**Dec 26 Gloucester 23
Old Merchant Taylors 0**
Tries: R.Hook (2), F.Edwards (2), G.Parker;
Conversions: G.Parker (2);
Drop goal: D.Meadows

**Dec 28 Gloucester 9
Devonport Services 3**
Tries: F.Edwards, K.Smith, J.H.Bown

Jan 4 London Scottish v Gloucester - cancelled due to international

Jan 11 Leicester 6 Gloucester 16
Tries: F.Edwards, J.C.Brooks, R.Hook, P.Hordern;
Conversions: R.Hook (2)

Jan 18 Bristol 14 Gloucester 3
Try: F.Edwards

Jan 25 Gloucester v Guy's Hospital - cancelled

Feb 1 Royal Navy 8 Gloucester 8
Try: F.Edwards;
Conversion: H.Boughton;
Penalty: H.Boughton

Feb 8 Gloucester 6 Cardiff 6
Try: E.Day;
Penalty: H.Boughton

Feb 15 Bath 3 Gloucester 3
Penalty: H.Boughton

**Feb 22 Gloucester 16
Oxford University 6**
Tries: R.Hook (2), J.C.Brooks;
Conversions: H.Boughton (2);
Penalty: H.Boughton

Feb 29 Gloucester 16 Richmond 3
Tries: F.Edwards, J.C.Brooks, J.A'Bear;
Conversions: H.Boughton (2);
Penalty: H.Boughton

Mar 7 Llanelly 3 Gloucester 5
Try: R.Morris;
Conversion: H.Boughton

Mar 14 Gloucester 21 Leicester 7
Tries: R.Hook (2), T.Price, E.L.Phillips;
Conversions: H.Boughton (3);
Penalty: H.Boughton

Mar 21 Gloucester 13 Newport 3
Tries: J.C.Brooks(2), I.Williams;
Conversions: H.Boughton (2)

**Mar 26 Gloucester 27
Guy's Hospital 5**
Tries: C.Harris, E.L.Phillips, D.Meadows, T.Price, J.A'Bear, R.E.Early, K.Smith;
Conversions: H.Boughton (3)

Mar 28 Gloucester 10 Cheltenham 3
Tries: J.C.Brooks, C.Harris;
Conversions: H.Boughton (2)

**Apr 4 Devonport Services 11
Gloucester 8**
Try: R.Hook;
Conversion: T.Stephens;
Penalty: T.Stephens

Apr 6 Torquay 3 Gloucester 16
Tries: F.Edwards, R.Hook, J.A'Bear;
Conversions: H.Boughton (2);
Penalty: H.Boughton

**Apr 11 Gloucester 32
London Welsh 13**
Tries: F.Edwards (3), J.A'Bear, E.L.Phillips, T.Price, R.Hook;
Conversions: H.Boughton (4);
Penalty: H.Boughton

Apr 13 Gloucester 5 Headingley 3
Try: D.Meadows;
Conversion: H.Boughton

Apr 14 Lydney 3 Gloucester 3
Try: R.E.Early

Apr 18 Gloucester 5 Harlequins 10
Try: R.Hook;
Conversion: H.Boughton

Apr 25 Gloucester 6 Bristol 0
Tries: J.A'Bear, G.Parker

Apr 27 Stroud 5 Gloucester 11
Tries: R.Hook (2), R.James;
Conversion: G.Parker

May 2 Bristol 13 Gloucester 0

1936-37

S.T.Davies J.H.A'Bear E.T.James J.F.Scoon S.Smart T.Millington
H.J.Balchin E.Bayliss P.C.Hordern A.Welshman T.Price R.Morris G.R.James K.Smith F.Abbey
A.Hudson(Sec) F.G.Edwards E.L.Phillips R.E.Early D.Meadows(Capt) Dr.A.Alcock(Pres) J.G.A'Bear C.Harris R.E.Hook A.D.Carpenter
J.T.Brookes(Chairman)
E.R.Day G.W.Parker

Played 36 Won 20 Lost 14 Drawn 2
For 342 Against 274
Captain: Don Meadows

Gloucester United
Played 16 Won 10 Lost 5 Drawn 1
For 102 Against 114
Captain: Tom Stephens

Most appearances: K.Smith 32, D.Meadows 31, A.Welshman 30, J.A'Bear 29, R.Hook 28, C.Harris 27, E.Bayliss 26, A.Carpenter, E.A.Day 25
Most tries: R.Hook 18, F.Edwards 7, A.L.Warr 6, E.Bayliss 5
Conversions: G.Parker 19, H.Boughton 11, T.Stephens 4
Penalties: G.Parker 9, H.Boughton 5, T.Stephens 2
Drop goals: D.Meadows, R.James 2

A season of mixed results started with an extension of the covered stand at the Deans Walk end of the north side, which completed what would become known as the Shed — entry charges were 5s per season or 6d per game. There was some cause for celebration with victories over the two top teams in Wales, Cardiff and Llanelly, at Kingsholm, but the season finished with a whimper as the last three fixtures were all lost.

The best match of the season was the fine victory over Cardiff and their internationals Wooller, Bassett and Cliff Jones. The visitors possessed the more dangerous back division, but "Cliff Jones did more retreating than he cared for" as "those indomitable Gloucester forwards" allowed them no space or time with "speedy rushes and vigorous tackling," and Grahame Parker, down from Cambridge, gave a fine exhibition at full-back. Gloucester came from behind to win the game in the last seven minutes with a dropped goal from Don Meadows and a brilliant try started in his own 25 by Meadows and scored in the corner by Kit Tanner.

The match against Llanelly was won by a beautiful Gloucester try. The move started when Roy James intercepted and passed on to Bob Hook, who gave an easy run in under the posts to Warr. Roy James had wanted to retire in 1935, but turned out for two more seasons when required, and finished with 298 appearances. Ken Smith also retired at the end of the season after 163 appearances.

Against London Scottish, Bob Hook scored a hat trick of tries in the first half, and added a fourth later. The following week, the England selectors used the game against Leicester as an international trial and inserted the dangerous Prince Obolensky amongst the Leicester three-quarters, but Gloucester never gave him an opening, and won a fine victory.

One of the finest tries of the season was scored against London Welsh, when Grahame Parker fielded near his own 25, punted ahead, and, getting to the ball before the Welsh full-back, gathered to score under the posts; he converted his own try.

The outstanding players across the season were Roy James and the everlasting "Bumps" Carpenter, who was selected for the Barbarians Easter tour, a rare honour for a working class player, and judged by "Bumps" himself to be a greater honour than his England cap.

Eleven players appeared for Gloucestershire, seven of them - Graham Parker (conversion), Rev."Bill" Phillips, Francis Edwards, Bob Hook, "Bumps" Carpenter, Cyril Harris and John A'Bear - in the County Championship final, when East Midlands were beaten 5-0 at Bristol. Parker and Edwards had England trials.

Sep 12 Gloucester 16 Lydney 3
Tries: R.Hook, G.Parker, C.Fifield, K.Smith;
Conversions: G.Parker (2)

Sep 19 Gloucester 3 Coventry 0

Try: G.Parker

Sep 24 Gloucester 5 Moseley 8
Try: T.Price;
Conversion: T.Stephens

Sep 26 Bristol 0 Gloucester 11
Tries: C.Fifield, E.L.Phillips;
Conversion: G.Parker; Penalty: G.Parker

Oct 3 Gloucester 11 Old Cranleighans 10
Tries: R.Hook, R.James, F.Edwards;
Conversion: H.Boughton

Oct 10 Gloucester 13 Cardiff 9
Try: C.Tanner; Penalties: G.Parker (2);
Drop goal: D.Meadows

Oct 17 Gloucester 40 Guy's Hospital 11
Tries: F.Edwards (2), M.McCanlis (2), R.Hook (2), E.Day, I.Williams, T.Price;
Conversions: H.Boughton (5);
Penalty: H.Boughton

Oct 24 Lydney 13 Gloucester 6
Penalties: H.Boughton (2)

Oct 31 Richmond 3 Gloucester 9
Try: I.Jones;
Penalties: G.Parker (2)

Nov 7 Leicester 7 Gloucester 3
Try: I.Jones

Nov 14 Gloucester 7 Old Blues 11
Try: I.Jones;
Drop goal: R.James

**Nov 19 Gloucester 6
Oxford University Greyhounds 8**
Tries: E.L.Phillips (2)

Nov 21 Bath 11 Gloucester 5
Try: E.Bayliss; Conversion: H.Boughton

**Nov 28 Oxford University 3
Gloucester 15**
Tries: T.Price, E.Day, E.L.Phillips;
Conversions: G.Parker (3)

Dec 5 Gloucester 14 Blackheath 0
Tries: F.Edwards, E.Bayliss (2);
Conversion: H.Boughton;
Penalty: H.Boughton

Dec 12 Cheltenham 0 Gloucester 0

Dec 19 Gloucester 8 Newport 22
Tries: R.Hook (2);
Conversion: G.Parker

**Dec 26 Gloucester 13
Old Merchant Taylors 6**
Tries: R.Hook(2), F.Edwards;
Conversions: G.Parker(2)

Jan 2 Gloucester 29 London Scottish 13
Tries: R.Hook (5), A.L.Warr (2);
Conversions: G.Parker (4)

Jan 9 Gloucester 14 Leicester 12
Tries: P.Hordern, E.Bayliss, F.Edwards,
A.L.Warr; Conversion: G.Parker

Jan 16 Coventry 3 Gloucester 8
Tries: E.Bayliss, R.Hook;
Conversion: G.Parker

Jan 23 Gloucester 0 Bristol 0

Jan 30 Guy's Hospital 6 Gloucester 8
Tries: I.Jones, D.Meadows;
Conversion: H.Boughton

**Feb 6 Gloucester 0
United Services (Portsmouth) 12**

Feb 13 Cardiff 14 Gloucester 0

Feb 20 Gloucester 7 Bath 3

Try: J.H.Bown;
Drop goal: D.Meadows

Feb 27 Newport v Gloucester - cancelled due to unfit state of ground

Mar 6 Gloucester 19 Cheltenham 0
Tries: R.E.Early (3), A.Carpenter;
Conversions: H.Boughton (2);
Penalty: H.Boughton

Mar 13 Llanelly 29 Gloucester 0

Mar 20 Gloucester 9 R.A.F. 0
Tries; A.Welshman, F.Edwards, R.Hook

Mar 27 Gloucester 15 London Welsh 0
Tries: R.Morris, G.Parker, R.Hook;
Conversions: G.Parker (3)

Mar 29 Gloucester 13 Sale 14
Tries: A.L.Warr, A.Welshman;
Conversions: T.Stephens (2);
Penalty: T.Stephens

**Mar 30 Gloucester 11
Universities Athletic Union 3**
Tries: A.L.Warr, R.Hook:
Conversion: T.Stephens;
Penalty: T.Stephens

Apr 3 Gloucester 8 Llanelly 6
Try: A.L.Warr;
Conversion: G.Parker;
Penalty: G.Parker

Apr 10 Harlequins 16 Gloucester 6
Penalties: G.Parker (2)

Apr 12 Torquay 9 Gloucester 4
Drop goal: R.James

Apr 17 Gloucester 6 Bedford 9
Try: R.Hook;
Penalty: G.Parker

1937-38

**Played 36 Won 29 Lost 6 Drawn 1
For 413 Against 228
Captain: John A'Bear**

Gloucester United
Played 28 Won 20 Lost 6 Drawn 2
For 242 Against 122
Captain: Tom Stephens

Most appearances: D.Meadows 35,
C.Harris, J.A'Bear 33, R.Morris 32, E.Day 31,
C.J.Dibden, A.Carpenter 29, H.Boughton 27,
T.Price 26

Most tries: R.Hook 19, W.H.Hopkin 7,
J.H.Bown, J.A'Bear 6
Conversions: H.Boughton 28, R.Hook,
T.Stephens 3
Penalties: H.Boughton 21, T.Stephens 4,
W.Hook 3, R.Hook 2
Drop goals: D.Meadows 3, C.B.Dibden 2,
H.Boughton 1

John A'Bear took over as captain at the age of 24,
one of the youngest ever. He was enthusiastic and
popular, and engendered a happy team spirit. He
led from the front, no more so than at Llanelly

where he scored a try in a famous win. He had
a splendid physique and speed, and formed a
very powerful second row alongside Roy Morris.
The loss of Peter Hordern in the back row was
compensated for by the brilliant displays of Rev
Mervyn Hughes in his first season.

The 29 victories equalled the Club record,
these successes being largely down to a pack of
experienced and consistent forwards, the goal
kicking of Harold Boughton, who continued
to rack up points with monotonous regularity,
the brilliance of Don Meadows at stand-

H.J.Balchin J.H.A'Bear F.W.Ayliffe A.T.Voyce E.T.James J.F.Scoon S.Smart R.N.Loveridge
J.H.Bown Rev.E.L.Phillips R.E.Hook W.Barrow S.Mabbett H.Edwards E.L.Manning Rev.H.M.Hughes R.E.Burke R.Morris Canon H.J.Hensman
A.Hudson(Sec) T.Price A.Carpenter H.Boughton(Vice-Capt) Dr.Alcock(Pres) J.G.A'Bear(Capt) C.Harris F.Mustoe J.T.Brookes(Chairman)
D.Meadows E.R.Day Dr.J.Mackay-Dick (inset)

off and the finishing ability of Bob Hook on the wing, who headed the try scorers for the third season in succession. W.H.Hopkin, the Welsh international wing, joined at the start of the season, romped in for a hat trick in the first game, and scored seven tries in his eight appearances before returning to Newport.

Home and away victories were achieved against Llanelly, for the first time, Bristol, Bedford, Torquay Athletic, Devonport Services and Lydney. There was plenty of success against London clubs with eight wins and only one loss. After seven successive victories at Kingsholm, the ground record was lost to Newport, but later in the season revenge was taken at Rodney Parade.

The match of the season was against Oxford University on their last outing before the Varsity match. Bob Hook found himself marking Prince Obolensky, who scored a try, but Harold Boughton dropped a goal at the death to earn Gloucester victory in a brilliant and exciting display.

The try of the season was scored against Leicester — "on the Gloucester 25 Meadows gathered in the loose and opened out to Bown, who short-punted for Phillips to race up and collect the ball on the bounce. The old Oxford Blue ran up to Barr, and then yielded to Hook on the centre line. Putting on his best pace, Hook kept his lead over Fox and finished a great run

by scoring behind the posts."

In the penultimate game, Bill Hook, a 16-year-old schoolboy at Sir Thomas Rich's and Bob's brother, made a memorable debut at full-back, kicking three penalties to win the game against U.A.U.

Ten players were capped by Gloucestershire.

Sep 11 Gloucester 30 Lydney 3
Tries: W.H.Hopkin (3), R.Hook (2),
A.Welshman, T.Price, R.Morris;
Conversions: H.Boughton (3)

Sep 18 Gloucester 9 Moseley 0
Try: W.H.Hopkin;
Penalties: H.Boughton (2)

Sep 25 Gloucester 6 Bristol 3
Try: R.Hook;
Penalty: H.Boughton

Oct 2 Gloucester 5 Old Cranleighans 0
Try: W.H.Hopkin;
Conversion: H.Boughton

Oct 9 Cardiff 20 Gloucester 6
Penalties: H.Boughton (2)

Oct 16 Gloucester 23 Torquay 0
Tries: E.L.Phillips (2), J.A'Bear;
Conversion: H.Boughton;
Penalties: H.Boughton (4)

Oct 23 Bedford 5 Gloucester 9
Tries: W.H.Hopkin (2);
Penalty: H.Boughton

Oct 30 Gloucester 3 Richmond 0
Try: C.Tanner

Nov 6 Gloucester 14 Leicester 9
Tries: C.Harris, R.Hook, J.Bown;
Conversion: H.Boughton;
Penalty: H.Boughton

Nov 13 Gloucester 23 Old Blues 3
Tries: H.M.Hughes (2), C.Tanner, C.J.Dibden,
J.A'Bear, J.Bown;
Conversion: H.Boughton;
Penalty: H.Boughton

Nov 20 Bath 3 Gloucester 0

**Nov 27 Gloucester 10
Oxford University 8**
Tries: W.Barrow, E.Day;
Drop goal: H.Boughton

Dec 4 Blackheath 11 Gloucester 13
Tries: J.G.A'Bear, J.Bown, R.Hook;
Conversions: H.Boughton (2)

Dec 11 Cheltenham 8 Gloucester 3
Penalty: T.Stephens

Dec 18 Gloucester 5 Newport 8

Try: Dr.Dick;
Conversion: H.Boughton

**Dec 27 Gloucester 29
Old Merchant Taylors 3**
Tries: F.Edwards (3), E.L.Philips,
Rev.H.M.Hughes, J.G.A'Bear, T.Price;
Conversions: H.Boughton (4)

Dec 28 Gloucester 3 Cheltenham 0
Penalty: T.Stephens

Jan 1 London Scottish 15 Gloucester 3
Try: R.Hook

Jan 8 Leicester 6 Gloucester 6
Try: R.Early;
Penalty: T.Stephens

Jan 15 Gloucester 9 Bedford 8
Try: R.Hook; Convertion: T.Stephens;
Drop goal: C.J.Dibden

Jan 22 Bristol 0 Gloucester 3
Penalty: H.Boughton

**Jan 29 Gloucester 11
Guy's Hospital 3**
Tries: R.Hook, J.G. A' Bear;
Conversion: H.Boughton;
Penalty: H.Boughton

Feb 5 United Services (Portsmouth) 7

Gloucester 8
Try: R.Morris;
Conversion: H.Boughton;
Penalty: H.Boughton

Feb 12 Gloucester 9 Cardiff 11
Tries: E.L.Phillips, R.Hook;
Penalty: H.Boughton

Feb 19 Gloucester 10 Bath 0
Tries: R.Hook, E.L.Phillips; Convertions:
R.Hook (2)

**Feb 26 Gloucester 17
Devonport Services 4**
Tries: R.Hook (3), E.V.Manning, E.Bayliss;
Conversion: R.Hook

Mar 5 Llanelly 11 Gloucester 13
Tries: R.Burke, J.G.A'Bear;
Conversions: T.Stephens (2);
Penalty: T.Stephens

Mar 12 Gloucester 6 R.A.F. 0
Tries: R.Morris, Rev.H.M.Hughes

Mar 19 Newport 6 Gloucester 8
Tries: R.Hook (2);
Conversions: H.Boughton

Mar 26 Gloucester 14 Llanelly 5
Tries: J.H.Bown (2);

Conversions: H.Boughton (2);
Drop goal: C.J.Dibden

**April 2 Devonport Services 13
Gloucester 18**
Tries: R.E.Burke (2), R.Hook, D.Meadows;
Conversions: H.Boughton (3)

April 4 Torquay 9 Gloucester 10
Penalties: R.Hook (2)
Drop goal: D.Meadows;

April 9 Gloucester 14 Harlequins 13
Tries: R.E.Burke, R.Hook, S.Mabbett;
Conversion: H.Boughton;
Penalty: H.Boughton

**April 16 Gloucester 24
London Welsh 16**
Tries: E.V.Manning, S.Mabbett;
Conversions: H.Boughton (2);
Penalties: H.Boughton (2);
Drop goals: D.Meadows (2)

**April 18 Gloucester 12
Universities Athletic Union 11**
Try: C.J.Dibden;
Penalties: W.Hook (3)

April 19 Lydney 6 Gloucester 27
Tries: R.Hook (2), R.E.Burke, J.Bown, C.Harris;
Conversions: H.Boughton (3);
Penalties: H.Boughton (2)

1938-39

**Played 38 Won 19 Lost 14 Drawn 5
For 325 Against 296
Captain: John A'Bear**

Gloucester United
Played 14 Won 12 Lost 1 Drawn 1
For 206 Against 59
Captain: H.Edwards

There are two games where not all the scorers are known, and two games where the full teams are not known.

Most appearances: A.G.Hudson 31, J.A'Bear, J.Bown 30, R.Morris 28, S.Mabbett 27, A.Carpenter 26, H.Boughton 25
Leading scorers: Tries: R.Hook 10, R.Upham 8, J.Bown 7, R.Morris 6
Conversions: H.Boughton 15, T.Price 3, J.Berry, T.Stephens 2
Penalties: H.Boughton 14, D.Meadows 3, T.Stephens 2
Drop goals: D.Meadows 3, R.Hook, N.A.Gidney, W.D.C.Hughes 1

This was a season of only moderate success,

in striking contrast to the previous year. Only an improvement in the last couple of months ensured more wins than losses. John A'Bear found his second season as captain much more difficult than his first with 45 players used, rumours of war, bad weather and a lack of star players.

Gloucester's best performances came against the Welsh clubs at Kingsholm. Cardiff, the Welsh champions, and Newport were both defeated, and the game with Llanelly was drawn. The double was achieved against Leicester, coming from 13 points down at half-time in the away game, and there was a good win over Sale at Easter. Amongst the many disappointments were four losses to London clubs, and defeat by Bath at Kingsholm for the first time, which meant Bath completed the double, as did Bedford.

The strength of the team lay in the forwards, where "Bumps" Carpenter at age 39 was as powerful as ever, and they were rarely beaten in the scrums. However, Cyril Harris broke his

leg half way through the season which ended his career after 121 appearances, and broke up a very successful front row, although Tom Day came through to start a long and distinguished career at prop. A'Bear and "Digger" Morris were a formidable pair in the second row. Gordon Hudson and Johnny Thornton were two more young players who came through to make a good impression in the back row.

The main problem lay with the backs, where quality players were hard to find. The exception was Don Meadows, who was regularly present, although he retired at the end of the season with 305 appearances. He had to work with a variety of scrum-halves when Ernie Day dropped out with illness. At full-back, Harold Boughton suffered injury and Bill Hook was rarely available. Bill Phillips had departed at centre, and Bob Hook was only available for half the games, and played little more before finishing with 156 appearances. The selection committee made frequent experiments amongst the three-quarters but with little positive effect - there was a lack of cohesion, speed, cleverness and thrust,

F.Abbey   T.H.Millington   E.T.James   S.Smart   F.W.Ayliffe
A.Hudson(Sec)   J.H.Bown   A.G.Hudson   J.Thornton   S.Mabbett   Rev.H.M.Hughes   F.Mustoe   R.Morris   H.J.Balchin
J.H.A'Bear   A.Carpenter   S.Walden   H.Boughton   J.G.A'Bear(Capt)   D.Meadows   T.Price   R.E.Hook   C.Harris
E.J.Parfitt   W.D.C.Hughes

and far too many dropped passes.

Nine players were selected by the County. "Digger" Morris and Tom Price had England trials.

The Club suffered a terrible loss mid-season when John Brookes, the Chairman, died suddenly. At the 1939 AGM the Club reported assets of £11,000 which were compared with £11 at the end of the first season in 1874.

Sep 10   Gloucester 18   Lydney 5
Tries: R.Morris, F.Gough, R.Hook, T.Price;
Conversion: H.Boughton;
Drop goal: R.Hook

Sep 15   Stroud 11   Gloucester 6
Tries: J.Bown, R.Upham

Sep 17   Gloucester 17   Moseley 3
Tries: F.Gough, S.Mabbett, R.Hook,
E.Manning;
Conversion: R.Hook;
Penalty: H.Boughton

Sep 24   Bristol 0   Gloucester 6
Tries: R.Hook (2)

Oct 1   Gloucester 7   Bedford 12
Try: R.Morris;

Drop goal: D.Meadows

Oct 8   Gloucester 8   Cardiff 6
Try: R.Hook;
Conversion: H.Boughton;
Penalty: H.Boughton

Oct 15   Gloucester 7   Northampton 3
Penalty: H.Boughton;
Drop goal: D.Meadows

**Oct 19   Oxford University 14
Gloucester 3**
Try: E.Manning

Oct 22   Gloucester 19   Old Blues 5
Tries: E.L.Phillips (2), E.J.Parfitt, D.Meadows,
E.V.Manning;
Conversions: J.Berry (2)

Oct 29   Richmond 11   Gloucester 3
Penalty: H.Boughton

Nov 5   Leicester 13   Gloucester 17
Tries: S.Walden, R.Morris, J.Bown;
Conversions: H.Boughton (2);
Drop goal: D.Meadows

**Nov 12   Gloucester 3
St.Mary's Hospital 11**
Penalty: D.Meadows

Nov 19   Gloucester 3   Bath 5
Penalty: H.Boughton

Nov 26   Guy's Hospital 9   Gloucester 17
Tries: J.A'Bear, E.L.Phillips, unknown;
Conversion: H.Boughton;
Penalties: H.Boughton (2)

Dec 3   Gloucester 3   Blackheath 16
Penalty: H.Boughton

Dec 10   Moseley 8   Gloucester 8
Try: W.Barrow;
Conversion: H.Boughton;
Penalty: H.Boughton

Dec 17   Newport 10   Gloucester 3
Penalty: H.Boughton

Dec 24   Cheltenham v Gloucester - cancelled due to frozen pitch
Dec 26   Gloucester v Old Merchant Taylors - cancelled due to snow and frost

**Dec 27   Gloucester 15
Universities Athletic Union 11**
Tries: H.M.Hughes, R.Upham, R.Morris;
Conversions: H.Boughton (3)

Dec 31   Llanelly 24   Gloucester 0

Jan 7 Gloucester 3 London Scottish 13
Try: C.Harris

Jan 14 Gloucester 8 Leicester 3
Tries: F.Mustoe, R.Upham;
Conversion: H.Boughton

Jan 21 Bedford 11 Gloucester 6
Tries: R.Morris (2)

Jan 28 Gloucester 3 Bristol 3
Try: R.Hook

**Feb 4 Gloucester 13
United Sevices (Portsmouth) 0**
Tries: C.J.Howe, R.Hook, R.Upham;
Conversions: H.Boughton (2)

Feb 11 Cardiff 13 Gloucester 5
Try: S.Walden;
Conversion: T.Price

**Feb 16 Gloucester 26
Oxford University Greyhounds 11**
Tries: W.Jones (3), R.G.Vincent, T.Price,

A.Carpenter, R.Upham, T.Cowan;
Conversion: T.Price

Feb 18 Bath 6 Gloucester 5
Try: J.Bown;
Conversion: T.Stephens

Feb 25 Gloucester 0 Llanelly 0

Mar 4 Gloucester 13 Cheltenham 6
Tries: R.Hook (2), T.Day;
Drop goal: N.Gidney

Mar 11 Northampton 8 Gloucester 8
Tries: E.Manning, R.Upham;
Conversion: T.Stephens

Mar 18 Gloucester 12 Newport 5
Tries: R.Upham, F.Mustoe;
Penalties: T.Stephens (2)

**Mar 25 Gloucester 13
Guy's Hospital 8**
Tries: R.Hook, J.Bown, unknown;
Conversions: H.Boughton (2)

**Apr 1 Devonport Services 11
Gloucester 11**
Tries: W.D.C.Hughes, R.Upham;
Conversion: H.Boughton;
Penalty: H.Boughton

Apr 3 Sidmouth 0 Gloucester 6
Try: H.Edwards;
Penalty: H.Boughton

Apr 8 Gloucester 10 London Welsh 6
Try: J.Thornton;
Penalty: H.Boughton;
Drop goal: W.D.C.Hughes

Apr 10 Gloucester 6 Sale 0
Penalties: D.Meadows (2)

Apr 11 Lydney 9 Gloucester 11
Tries: J.Bown (2), W.Jones;
Conversion: T.Price

Apr 15 Harlequins 6 Gloucester 3
Penalty: H.Boughton

1939-40

**Played 21 Won 11 Lost 5 Drawn 5
For 307 Against 199
Captain: Various**

There are four games where the full teams are not known. However, all scores and scorers are complete.

Most Appearances: T.Day 20, A.G.Hudson 20, J.A'Bear 19, Rev.H.M.Hughes 18, A.Carpenter 17, W.D.Kear 17, H.Boughton 16
Most tries: A.G.Hudson 9, Rev.H.M.Hughes 7, P.Brown 6, R.C.Upham 5
Conversions: H.Boughton 25, T.Stephens 4, W.Hook 3
Penalties: T.Stephens 6, H.Boughton 3, W.Hook 1
Drop goals: W.D.Kear 2, T.Stephens 2, E.J.Parfitt, R.Hook 1

A full fixture list, the strongest yet, had been arranged for the season, but, when war was declared on 3rd September 1939, the Government immediately banned all sporting activities, and the Club cancelled all fixtures. However, the Government quickly thought again, the ban on sporting activities was lifted, and games were actively encouraged to sustain morale.

The Club then organised a revised list of matches against a mixture of military and club sides. Admission charges were lowered and

most of the proceeds went to charities, whilst entry was free for members of the Armed Forces. Players stationed in the area were recruited to replace players posted elsewhere, so a third of the players representing the Club during this season had not made an appearance for the Club before the war.

The buildings and stands at Kingsholm were commandeered by the Local Authority for Civil Defence purposes, the wooden seats and steps were removed, and ambulances and buses were stationed on the ground. The Club committee met at the New Inn.

It was agreed that international matches should be played between England and Wales in aid of the Red Cross, and the England home game was at Kingsholm on 13th April 1940, organised entirely by Gloucester Club officials. The Chief Constable stipulated that the 16,000 spectators had to be evenly dispersed around the ground in order to minimise casualties in the event of an air raid. Prince Obolensky was selected to play but was killed when his Spitfire crashed a few days before. Francis Edwards of Gloucester was in the centre for England, and delighted the crowd when he cut through to put Unwin in for a try; England won 17-3.

**Oct 14 Gloucester 29
Fifth Gloucestershire Regiment 9**

Tries: J.A'Bear (2), P.Brown (2), A.G.Hudson, H.M.Hughes, T.Price;
Conversions: H.Boughton (4)

Oct 21 Gloucester 6 Stroud 11
Tries: J.H.Bown (2)

**Oct 28 Oxford University 21
Gloucester 9**
Tries: R.Upham, T.Price, P.Brown

**Nov 4 Gloucester 13
Welsh Army XV 8**
Tries: D.Kear, T.Price, H.M.Hughes;
Conversions: H.Boughton (2)

**Nov 11 Gloucester 28
Oxford University 14**
Tries: R.Morris, F.Edwards, A.G.Hudson, P.Brown, J.A'Bear;
Conversions: W.Hook (3);
Penalty: W.Hook;
Drop goal: E.J.Parfitt

**Nov 18 Gloucester 6
Weston-super-Mare 6**
Tries: A.G.Hudson, P.Brown

**Dec 2 Gloucester 23
East Yorkshire Regiment 14**
Tries: A.G.Hudson (2), J.Bown, R.Cook, E.J.Parfitt;

Conversions: H.Boughton (4)

Dec 9 Gloucester 3 Bath 3
Penalty: H.Boughton

Dec 16 Gloucester 3 Bridgend 3
Try: T.Day

Dec 23 Stroud 11 Gloucester 7
Try: T.Day;
Drop goal: W.D.Kear

Dec 26 Gloucester 16 Cheltenham 3
Tries: J.Bown, F.Edwards, R.Upham,
A.G.Hudson;
Conversions: H.Boughton (2)

Jan 6 Bristol 15 Gloucester 0

**Feb 10 Gloucester 13
Welsh Army XV 16**
Tries: W.D.Kear, H.M.Hughes, P.Brown;
Conversions: H.Boughton (2)

**Feb 24 Gloucester 16
South Wales Borderers 0**
Tries: T.Day, A.G.Hudson, W.Hook;
Conversions: H.Boughton (2);
Penalty: H.Boughton

Mar 2 Gloucester 11 Bristol 11
Try: M.J.Daly;
Conversion: T.Stephens;
Penalties: T.Stephens (2)

**Mar 9 Gloucester 24
Royal Artillery Officer Cadets 9**
Tries: H.M.Hughes, R.Hook, J.A'Bear;
Conversions: T.Stephens (3);
Penalties: T.Stephens (3)

**Mar 16 Gloucester 17
Universities Athletic Union 17**
Tries: R.Hook, Dr.G.W.Balfour, W.Hook;
Conversions: H.Boughton (2);
Drop goal: W.D.Kear

**Mar 23 Gloucester 19
Guy's Hospital 6**
Tries: A.G.Hudson (2), J.Bown, J.Thornton,
W.Moreland;
Drop goal: T.Stephens

**Mar 25 Gloucester 24
St.Mary's Hospital 0**
Tries: R.Upham (3), R.Morris, W.Hook;
Conversions: H.Boughton (3);
Penalty: T.Stephens

Mar 30 Gloucester 18 Bridgend 13
Tries: H.M.Hughes (2), R.Hook;
Conversion: H.Boughton;
Penalty: H.Boughton;
Drop goal: T.Stephens

**Apr 6 Gloucester 22
Somerset Police 9**
Tries: H.Ricketts, H.M.Hughes, T.Day,
R.Hook;
Conversions: H.Boughton (3);
Drop goal: R.Hook

1940-41

**Played 26 Won 18 Lost 6 Drawn 2
For 402 Against 215
Captain: Various**

There are eight games where the complete teams are not known. However, all scorers are known.

Most appearances: R.Upham, J.A'Bear 25, J.Robbins 24, A.Carpenter 22, H.Boughton 21
Mos tries: R.Upham 25, W.S.Collinson 9, N.J.Herbert 8, J.A'Bear, P.N.Walker 7
Conversions: H.Boughton 41, W.Hook 5, J.A'Bear 3
Penalties: H.Boughton 8, W.Hook 2, D.Walters 1
Drop goal: F.Gough

In September 1940, the Club was given permission to continue to use Kingsholm for matches, and a decision was made to carry on. However, it was decided not to play fixtures before October, since many players had joined the Forces, and it would take time to recruit other players from Service Units in the district. The fixtures which were arranged pitted Gloucester against a variety of military and civilian sides. Even fewer Gloucester players from before the war were available, and the number of imports grew to two-thirds this season.

A special match was organised at Kingsholm in November 1940 as part of Gloucester's War Weapons Week. Wavell Wakefield persuaded

several internationals to turn out for his XV against Tom Voyce's XV, and they won an exciting game 18-11. Spectators were asked to contribute by throwing pennies onto a blanket carried round the ground – the target of a ton was exceeded.

Oct 12 Gloucester 11 R.A.F. XV 6
Tries: R.Upham, F.Gough, J.Jackson;
Conversion: H.Boughton

**Oct 19 Gloucester 12
New Zealand Forestry XV 12**
Try: R.Upham;
Conversion: H.Boughton;
Penalty: H.Boughton;
Drop goal: F.Gough

**Oct 26 Gloucester 13
Welsh Army XV 13**
Tries: F.Gough, A.G.Hudson;
Conversions: H.Boughton (2);
Penalty: H.Boughton

**Nov 2 Gloucester 16
Bristol University 3**
Tries: S.Walden, J.A'Bear, G.Birch;
Conversions: H.Boughton (2);
Penalty: H.Boughton

Nov 9 Stroud 6 Gloucester 3
Try: Hanks

Nov 30 Gloucester 19

Officer Cadet Training Unit 13
Tries: A/C Daniell (2), R.Upham (2), S.Walden;
Conversions: H.Boughton (2)

**Dec 7 Gloucester 22
Army XV (London Scots) 6**
Tries: R.Upham (2), B.Davies, S.Mabbett,
W.S.Collinson, J.A'Bear;
Conversions: H.Boughton (2)

Dec 14 Gloucester 6 Stroud 0
Tries: R.Upham, Rev.H.M.Hughes

**Dec 21 Gloucester 12
Army XV (Depot) 5**
Tries: H.M.Hughes, R.Upham, W.S.Collinson;
Penalty: H.Boughton

**Dec 26 Gloucester 26
Army XV (5ᵗʰ Glosters) 3**
Tries: R.Upham (2), W.S.Collinson, J.A'Bear,
P.N.Walker;
Conversions: H.Boughton (4);
Penalty: H.Boughton

**Dec 28 Gloucester 33
New Zealand Forestry XV 8**
Tries: R.Upham (4), F.Edwards, P.N.Walker,
W.S.Collinson;
Conversions: H.Boughton (6)

Jan 11 Gloucester 16 R.A.F. XV 8
Tries: W.Burrows, W.S.Collinson, J.A'Bear,
T.Day;

Conversions: H.Boughton (2)

Jan 25 Gloucester 36 Hereford XV 6
Tries: W.S.Collinson (4), P.N.Walker,
W.J.Oakley, B.Davies, R.Upham;
Conversions: H.Boughton (6)

Feb 1 Gloucester 9 Welsh Army XV 6
Tries: P.Brown, R.Upham;
Penalty: H.Boughton

Feb 8 Gloucester 11 Hereford XV 3
Tries: R.Upham (2), J.A'Bear;
Conversion: J.A'Bear

**Feb 15 Gloucester 21
Officer Cadet Training Unit 17**
Tries: G.Birch, J.Robbins, B.Davies,
A.Carpenter;
Conversions: H.Boughton (3);
Penalty: H.Boughton

Feb 22 Gloucester 3 Rotol Works 5
Try: R.Upham

**Mar 1 Gloucester 19
Army XV (Depot) 0**
Tries: D.Walters, R.Upham, W.Burrows,

J.Davis, J.A'Bear;
Conversions: H.Boughton (2)

**Mar 8 Gloucester 10
Birmingham University 12**
Tries: F.L.Stubbs, J.Davis;
Conversions: H.Boughton (2)

**Mar 15 Gloucester 15
Oxford University 13**
Tries: N.J.Herbert, J.A'Bear, J.Thornton;
Conversions: H.Boughton (3)

**Mar 22 Gloucester 8
St.Mary's Hospital 31**
Try: T.Day;
Conversion: H.Boughton;
Penalty: H.Boughton

**Mar 29 Gloucester 26
New Zealand Army XV 6**
Tries: R.Upham (2), N.J.Herbert (2),
P.N.Walker, W.Hook;
Conversions: W.Hook (4)

**Apr 5 Gloucester 17
R.A.F. XV (Rissington) 8**
Tries: R.Upham, P.N.Walker, N.J.Herbert;

Conversion: W.Hook;
Penalties: W.Hook (2)

**Apr 12 Gloucester 6
Officer Cadet Training Unit 8**
Try: R.Upham;
Penalty: D.Walters

**Apr 14 Gloucester 13
Birmingham Old Edwardians 14**
Tries: N.J.Herbert, P.N.Walker, R.Upham;
Conversions: H.Boughton (2)

**Apr 19 Gloucester 19
R.A.F. XV (Innsworth) 3**
Tries: N.J.Herbert (3), A.G.Hudson, P.N.Walker;
Conversions: J.A'Bear (2)

The steady diminution of players who could be
regarded as truly representative of Gloucester,
and of opponents who would have traditionally
appeared on a Gloucester fixture list, finally
brought Gloucester Club matches to a halt.
By the start of the 1941-42 season, it had been
decided that matches should cease. However,
Services Internationals between England and
Wales were played at Kingsholm each year,
1942-45.

~ ~ 1945-1965 ~ ~

1945-46

F.Wadley R.N.Loveridge L.Middleditch T.Millington F.Abbey R.E.Hook S.Smart
H.J.Balchin J.Walkley R.Morris T.Day G.Hudson W.Hogg S.Smart C.Dunn C.H.Gadney(Ref) T.Williams
A.T.Voyce(Chairman) C.Crabtree E.Horsfall H.Boughton(Capt) Dr.Alcock(Pres) S.Davies S.Dangerfield B.Davies A.Hudson(Hon.Sec)
H.Rickards K.Daniell (T.Price W.D.Kerr J.Hopson J.W.Thornton — absent)

Played 31 Won 21 Lost 5 Drawn 5
For 481 Against 248
Captain: Harold Boughton

Most appearances: H.Boughton, T.Day
29, R.Morris, W.Hogg 26, G.Hudson 25,
J.Hopson, C.Dunn 24, S.Smart 23
Most tries: C.Crabtree 16, W.D.Kear 12,
S.Dangerfield 11, G.Hudson 10
Conversions: H.Boughton 35, W.E.Jones 9
Penalties: H.Boughton 17, T.Price 2, W.E.Jones 1
Drop goals: W.E.Jones 10, D.D.Evans,
S.H.Davies 1

The first post WW2 season started brightly
with a convincing win over old rivals Bristol,
but in the third game Gloucester were crushed
by ten-try Cardiff. The Cardiff team was clearly
fitter and had been playing competitive games
for some time. This was the first time ten tries
had been conceded to a club team. However, in
general terms the season was a success with
only five games ending in defeat. The double
was achieved over Leicester, bringing the total
to eight successive victories over the Tigers.
Bath were beaten away for the first time since
the 1926-27 season. There was also a double

over Moseley, and good wins against Neath,
Coventry, Northampton and Harlequins.

Several players who played before the outbreak
of war returned, including Harold Boughton,
who posted 121 points. Others who returned
were Bob and Bill Hook, Gordon Hudson, Roy
"Digger" Morris, Tom Day, Tom Price and John
Thornton. Boughton was persuaded to postpone
retirement and captain the team at the age of 35.
Bob Hook only played in three games before
retiring having made 156 appearances in his
career.

Of the new generation Charlie Crabtree had a
very productive time on the wing, and scored
a hat-trick of tries against Pontypool. In the
forwards Gordon Hudson was soon back to his
form of old. He was ably supported by Tom Day,
Joe Hopson, "Digger" Morris, John Thornton
and Charlie Dunn who all had a good season.

John Thornton, Tom Price and Gordon Hudson
played for England in "Victory" Internationals.
No caps were awarded. Sid Dangerfield,
"Digger" Morris and Joe Hopson played for
Gloucestershire/Somerset against the New

Zealand Army Touring Team. John Thornton
played for Combined Services against the New
Zealand Army XV and for the RAF against the
Kiwis.

Sep 29 Gloucester 18 Bristol 0
Tries: C.Crabtree (2), W.D.Kear, S.Dangerfield;
Conversions: H.Boughton (3)

Oct 6 Gloucester 9
Richmond & Blackheath 5
Tries: C.Crabtree (2), W.D.Kear

Oct 13 Cardiff 40 Gloucester 9
Try: J.Thornton;
Penalties: T.Price (2)

Oct 20 Gloucester 6 Cheltenham 6
Try: S.Dangerfield;
Penalty: H.Boughton

Oct 27 Stroud 6 Gloucester 9
Tries: C.Crabtree, C.Dunn;
Penalty: H.Boughton

Nov 3 Gloucester 27 Leicester 0
Tries: G.Hudson (2), W.D.Kear, S.Dangerfield,

T.Price;
Conversions: H.Boughton (3);
Penalties: H.Boughton (2)

Nov 10   Gloucester 15   Old Blues 8
Tries: W.Hogg(2), W.G.Thomas, J.Hopson,
T.Price

Nov 17   Bath 8   Gloucester 27
Tries: W.G.Bailey, G.Hudson, W.D.Kear,
D.D.Evans, A.Buckley;
Conversions: H.Boughton (2), W E Jones (2);
Drop goal: D.D.Evans

Nov 24   Gloucester 3   Newport 11
Penalty: H.Boughton

Dec 1   Gloucester 6   Neath 5
Penalties: H.Boughton (2)

Dec 8   Moseley 14   Gloucester 14
Tries: I.B.Edwards, R.Parham, A.Buckley;
Conversion: H.Boughton;
Penalty: H.Boughton

Dec 15   Gloucester 15   Coventry 3
Tries: W.D.Kear, penalty try;
Conversion: H.Boughton;
Penalty: W.E.Jones;
Drop goal: W.E.Jones

Dec 22   Gloucester 26   Moseley 3
Tries: T.Price (2), C.Dunn (2), W.G.Thomas;
Conversions: H.Boughton (2);
Penalty: H.Boughton;
Drop goal: W.E.Jones

Dec 26   Gloucester 30
Old Merchant Taylors 3
Tries: W.G.Thomas (2), S.Dangerfield (2),
K.Daniell, I.B.Edwards, W.E.Jones, T.Day;
Conversions: W.E.Jones (3)

Dec 27   Gloucester 32
Universities Athletic Union 8

Tries: S.Dangerfield (2), G.Hudson (2), C.Dunn,
C.Crabtree, W.G.Thomas, W.Hogg;
Conversions: H.Boughton (4)

Dec 29   Gloucester 12   Stroud 0
Try: I.B.Edwards;
Conversion: H.Boughton;
Penalty: H.Boughton;
Drop goal: W.E.Jones

Jan 5 London Scottish v Gloucester cancelled –
ground too hard

Jan 12   Leicester 11   Gloucester 12
Try: W.G.Thomas;
Conversion: H.Boughton;
Penalty: H.Boughton;
Drop goal: W.E.Jones

Jan 19   Gloucester v Lydney cancelled – severe
frost

Jan 26   Bristol 4   Gloucester 4
Drop goal: W.E.Jones

Feb 2   Cheltenham 0   Gloucester 7
Try: S.Dangerfield;
Drop goal: W.E.Jones

Feb 9   Gloucester 3   Cardiff 18
Penalty: H.Boughton

Feb 16   Gloucester 11   Bath 13
Tries: G.Hudson, T.Price;
Conversion: H.Boughton;
Penalty: H.Boughton

Feb 23   Lydney 3   Gloucester 18
Tries: W.D.Kear (2), C.Crabtree, C.Dunn;
Conversions: H.Boughton (3)

Mar 2   Gloucester 13   Northampton 7
Tries: W.D.Kear, R.Morris, S.Dangerfield;
Drop goal: W.E.Jones

Mar 9   Gloucester 29   Pontypool 7
Tries: C.Crabtree (3), W.D.Kear, B.Davies,
C.Dunn, G.Hudson;
Conversions: H.Boughton, W.E.Jones;
Drop goal: W.E.Jones

Mar 16   Neath 9   Gloucester 8
Tries: E.Horsfall, C.Dunn;
Conversion: H.Boughton

Mar 23   Gloucester 27
Guy's Hospital 5
Tries: K.Daniell (2), S.Smart, C.Crabtree,
J.Thornton;
Conversions: W.E.Jones (3), H.Boughton;
Drop goal: W.E.Jones

Mar 30   Gloucester 25
St Mary's Hospital 9
Tries: W.D.Kear (2), S.Dangerfield, K.Daniell;
Conversion: H.Boughton;
Penalty: H.Boughton;
Drop goals: W.E.Jones, S.H.Davies

Apr 6   Newport 21   Gloucester 21
Tries: G.Hudson (2), C.Crabtree, T.Day;
Conversions: H.Boughton (3);
Penalty: H.Boughton

Apr 13   Gloucester 11   Harlequins 5
Tries: W.D.Kear, S.Dangerfield;
Conversion: H.Boughton;
Penalty: H.Boughton

Apr 20   Gloucester 8   London Welsh 8
Try: C.Crabtree;
Conversion: H.Boughton;
Penalty: H.Boughton

Apr 22   Gloucester 26
London Hospital 8
Tries: C.Crabtree (2), A.L.Davies, G.Hudson,
C.Dunn, K.Daniell;
Conversions: H.Boughton (4)

1946-47

**Played 30 Won 19 Lost 10 Drawn 0
Abandoned 1
For 365 Against 235
Captains: Tom Price & Roy Morris**

Gloucester United
Played 19 Won 7 Lost 9 Drawn 3
For 115 Against 137

Most appearances: S.Smart 26, C.Dunn 24,
R.Morris 23, W.E.Jones, T.Day, D.D.Evans 22,
G.Hudson 21, K.Daniell 20

Most tries: K.Daniell 11, G.Hudson 9,
C.Crabtree 7
Conversions: W.E.Jones 27, W.Hook 4,
H.Boughton 1
Penalties: W.E.Jones 17, W.Hook 2,
H.Boughton 1
Drop goals: W.E.Jones 11, W.Hook,
D.D.Evans 1

Willie Jones scored 158 points, which broke the
Club record established by Tom Millington in
1922. He even kicked a hat-trick of drop goals

against Bedford. Following the Leicester game
in January Tom Price resigned the captaincy
due to sciatica, and "Digger" Morris took
over. The winter of 1947 was one of the coldest
in living memory, and a series of games was
called off. This caused a severe financial loss to
the Club. Only one game was possible between
late January and early March. This was against
Cardiff, and was only possible due to a lavish
covering of straw over the playing surface.
When this was removed it was found that the
ground underneath was frozen. Nevertheless,

F.Abbey S.F.Taylor T.Millington R.N.Loveridge T.Burns H.Boughton L.H.Middleditch
J.Barnes F.Wadley K.Watkins A.G.Hudson J.Thornton H.Meadows S.Smart G.Collier C.Dunn R.E.Hook S.Smart
H.J.Balchin T.Day C.Crabtree K.Daniell Dr.Alcock R.Morris S.H.Davies W.Hook A.Hudson
D.D.Evans W.E.Jones

both teams agreed to go ahead with the game.

Gloucester lost all their games to Cardiff and Newport, the only Welsh clubs played. The number of injuries affected the playing record, and only a few major clubs were beaten. There were victories over Leicester, Moseley, Wasps, and Richmond (away). The injury problem was so acute that Harold Boughton came out of retirement in October to play one final game against Cardiff. He had made 372 appearances and scored 1423 points. Ken Daniell, elusive and fast on the wing, topped the try scorers. The forwards were always competitive, with consistent displays from Gordon Hudson, Charlie Dunn, Tom Day and Sid Smart.

Gloucestershire reached the final of the County Championship. This resulted in a draw with Lancashire. The replay at Kingsholm was won by Lancashire, 14-3. Gloucester players involved were Stephen Davies, Ken Daniell, Willie Jones, Tom Day, "Digger" Morris, who captained the team, Gordon Hudson and John Thornton. Thornton also played in an England Trial game.

Sep 14 Gloucester 30 Lydney 3
Tries: C.Crabtree (2), W.D.Kear, S.Dangerfield, W.Jones;
Conversions: W.Jones (4);
Penalty: W.Jones;
Drop goal: W.Hook

Sep 18 Gloucester 25 Moseley 12
Tries: G.Hudson (2), H.Rickards, S.Dangerfield;
Conversions: W.Jones (3);
Penalty: W.Jones;
Drop goal: W.Jones

Sep 28 Bristol 11 Gloucester 5
Try: W.Jones;
Conversion: W.Jones

Oct 5 Gloucester 12 Exeter 6
Tries: W.D.Kear (2);
Conversion: W.Jones;
Drop goal: W.Jones

Oct 12 Cardiff 20 Gloucester 8
Try: K.Daniell;
Conversion: H.Boughton;
Penalty: H.Boughton

Oct 19 Gloucester 8 Wasps 5
Tries: C. Crabtree, K.Daniell;
Conversion: W.Hook

Oct 26 Gloucester 24 Old Blues 8
Tries: G.Collier (2), D.Gladwin, C.Crabtree;
Conversion: W.Hook (3);
Penalty: W.Hook   (other scorer unknown)

Nov 2 Leicester 16 Gloucester 3
Penalty: W.Jones

Nov 9 Moseley 16 Gloucester 4
Drop goal: W.Jones

Nov 16 Gloucester 27 Bath 9
Tries: G.Hudson (2), K.Daniell, Capt.F.Farmer, S.Dangerfield;
Conversions: W.Jones (3);
Penalties: W.Jones (2)

Nov 23 Newport 3 Gloucester 0
abandoned in second half due to waterlogged ground

Nov 30 Richmond 3 Gloucester 15
Tries: S.H.Davies, K.Daniell;
Conversion: W.Jones;
Penalty: W.Jones;
Drop goal: W.Jones

Dec 7 Gloucester 21 Blackheath 0
Tries: G.Hudson, Capt.F.Farmer, K.Daniell, S.H.Davies;
Conversions: W.Jones (3);
Penalty: W.Jones

Dec 14 Gloucester 6 Old Paulines 8
Tries: D.P.Parsons, S.H. Davies

Dec 21 Gloucester v Coventry – cancelled due to frost

Dec 26 Gloucester 6

Old Merchant Taylors 3
Tries: K.Daniell, C.Dunn

**Dec 28 Gloucester 21
Universities Athletic Union 14**
Tries: K.Daniell (2), C.Crabtree;
Conversion: W.Jones;
Penalty: W.Jones (2);
Drop goal: W.Jones

Jan 4 Gloucester 19 London Scottish 3
Tries: St.Maj.Beaven, G.Hudson, K.Daniell;
Conversions: W.Jones (3);
Drop goal: W.Jones

Jan 11 Gloucester 10 Leicester 5
Try: G.Collier;
Penalty: W.Jones;
Drop Goal: W.Jones

Jan 18 Stroud 0 Gloucester 6
Try: C.Crabtree;
Penalty: W.Jones

Jan 25 Gloucester v Bristol – cancelled due to frost

Feb 1 Gloucester v United Services – cancelled due to frost

Feb 8 Gloucester 11 Cardiff 12
Try: G.Hudson;
Conversion: W.Jones;
Penalties: W.Jones (2)

The following games were all cancelled due to severe frosts and snow:

Feb 15   Bath v Gloucester
Feb 22   Gloucester v Stroud
Mar 1   Northampton v Gloucester
Mar 8   Gloucester v R.A.F.

**Mar 15 Gloucester 11
Guy's Hospital 3**
Tries: C.Crabtree, G.Hudson;
Conversion: W.Jones;
Penalty: W.Jones

Mar 22 Newport 14 Gloucester 0

Mar 29 Gloucester 27 R.A.F. 8
Tries: W.Dix (3), T.Day (2), S.H.Davies, D.D.Evans;
Conversions: W.Jones (3)

Apr 5 Gloucester 6 London Welsh 5
Try: C.Dunn;

Penalty: W.Jones

Apr 7 Gloucester 10 Sale 6
Penalties: W.Jones (2);
Drop goal: W.Jones

Apr 8 Lydney v Gloucester - cancelled

Apr 12 Gloucester 7 Harlequins 17
Try: W.Dix;
Drop goal: D.D.Evans

Apr 19 Gloucester 26 Bedford 6
Tries: W.Jones, C.Dunn, K.Daniell, T.Day;
Conversion: W.Jones;
Drop goals: W.Jones (3)

Apr 24 Gloucester 3 Stroud 8
Penalty: W.Hook

Apr 26 Gloucester v Bristol - cancelled

May 1 Lydney 3 Gloucester 11
Tries: S.H.Davies, G.Hudson, K.Daniell;
Conversion: W.Jones

May 3 Bath 8 Gloucester 3
Try: N.Wickham

1947-48

**Played 40 Won 29 Lost 10 Drawn 1
For 588 Against 294
Captain: Gordon Hudson**

Gloucester United
Played 21 Won 13 Lost 6 Drawn 2
For 268 Against 138
Captain: Bill Moreland

Most appearances: R.Morris 40, W.Hook 34, G.Hudson, J.Watkins, T.Day 33, C.Dunn 32, S.Dangerfield 31, W.Jones, D.D.Evans 30
Most tries: K.Daniell 19, S.Dangerfield 11, G.Hudson 9, C.Crabtree, C.Dunn 8
Conversions: W.Jones 42, W.Hook 15, T.Price 1
Penalties: W.Jones 18, W.Hook 11, T.Price 1
Drop goals: W.Jones: 17, W.Hook 2, T.Price, W.Burrows, D.D.Evans 1

Tom Voyce resigned as Chairman of the Club Committee and was replaced by Tom Millington.

An excellent season. The number of wins equalled the club record. Perhaps the form was better in the first half of the season, when there were some scintillating displays. In the New Year the standard dropped slightly. Swansea

returned to the fixture list for the first time since 1934 and were beaten. Newport were beaten at Kingsholm. There were doubles over Leicester, Bristol and Bath.

For the second season running Willie Jones broke the club points record; this time posting 212. The fly-half consistently made breaks leading to tries, and tackled well. He also broke the club record for drop goals. Jones and fellow Welshman Dan Evans formed an effective half-back partnership. Bill Hook was a tower of strength at full-back. In the forwards, Tom Price was rewarded for consistent performances with two England caps, against Scotland and France. From the 1948-49 season he played for Cheltenham. For the second season running Ken Daniell was the top try scorer. The fact that on the other wing Sid Dangerfield was also scoring a lot of tries, demonstrated that the backs were a potent force.

The forwards were very powerful, being well led by captain Gordon Hudson. He was ably supported by "Digger" Morris, Jack Watkins, Charlie Dunn and Tom Day. "Digger" Morris played in every game, and at the age of 37 it was a remarkable feat. He then decided to retire. He

had first played in 1931 and appeared 317 times. A Gloucestershire/Somerset team played the touring Australians at Kingsholm in front of 15,000 spectators. Steve Davies, John Thornton and Gordon Hudson were the Gloucester representatives.

Sep 11 Stroud v Gloucester - cancelled due to hard ground

Sep 13 Gloucester 23 Lydney 8
Tries: C.Crabtree (2), R.Morris, F.Walden;
Conversions: W.Hook (2);
Penalty: W.Hook;
Drop goal: W.Hook

Sep 20 Moseley 6 Gloucester 7
Try: W.Dix;
Drop goal: D.D.Evans

Sep 27 Gloucester 9 Bristol 8
Try: T.Price;
Penalties: W.Jones (2)

Oct 4 Bedford 22 Gloucester 6
Try: C.Dunn;
Penalty: W.Jones

Oct 11 Gloucester 6 Cardiff 12
Penalties: W.Jones (2)

Oct 18 Wasps 0 Gloucester 17
Tries: C.Crabtree, K.Daniell, W.Jones;
Conversions: W.Jones (2);
Drop goal: W.Jones

Oct 25 Gloucester 10 Old Blues 5
Tries: K.Daniell (2);
Drop goal: W.Burrows

Nov 1 Gloucester 20 Leicester 6
Tries: K.Daniell (2), S.Dangerfield;
Conversions: W.Jones (2);
Penalty: W.Jones,
Drop goal: W.Jones

Nov 8 Gloucester 27 Moseley 3
Tries: Sgt.Maj.Beaven, S.Smart, W.Burrows,
F.Daniels, J.Thornton;
Conversions: W.Hook (3);
Penalties; W.Hook (2)

Nov 15 Bath 8 Gloucester 14
Tries: K.Daniell (2);
Conversion: W.Jones;
Penalties; W.Jones (2)

Nov 22 Gloucester 7 Newport 3
Try: K.Daniell;
Drop goal; W.Jones

Nov 29 Gloucester 29 Richmond 3
Tries: K.Daniell (2), S.H.Davies (2), G.Hudson,
J.Wilson, T.Price;
Conversions: W.Jones (4)

Dec 6 Blackheath 13 Gloucester 32
Tries: K.Daniell (2), S.Dangerfield (2), J.Wilson,
C.Dunn, R.Nicholls;
Conversions; W.Jones (2);
Penalty: W.Jones;
Drop goal: W.Jones

Dec 13 Gloucester 6 Old Paulines 8
Tries: C.Crabtree, J.Wilson

Dec 20 Gloucester 20 Coventry 6
Tries: K.Daniell, S.H.Davies, G.Hudson;
Conversions: W.Jones (2);
Penalty: W.Jones;
Drop goal: W.Jones

**Dec 26 Gloucester 51
Old Merchant Taylors 3**
Tries: G.Hudson (3), C.Dunn (2), J.Wilson,
S.Dangerfield, W.Moreland, C.Crabtree;
Conversions: W.Jones (4), W.Hook (4);
Drop goals: W.Jones (2)

**Dec 27 Gloucester 18
Universities Athletic Union 5**
Tries: C.Dunn, G.Hudson, D.D.Evans;
Conversions: W.Jones (3);
Penalty: W.Jones

Jan 3 London Scottish 14 Gloucester 3
Penalty: W.Jones

Jan 8 Gloucester 25 Army 9
Tries: S.H.Davies, K.Daniell, T.Price,
W.Moreland;
Conversions: W.Jones (3);
Penalty: W.Jones;
Drop goal: W.Jones

Jan 10 Leicester 6 Gloucester 13
Tries: K.Daniell (2), Sgt.Maj.Beaven;
Conversions: W.Jones (2)

**Jan 17 Gloucester 24
Devonport Services 0**
Tries: T.Price (2), T.Day, S.Dangerfield;
Conversions: W.Jones (2);
Drop goals: T.Price, W.Jones

Jan 24 Bristol 8 Gloucester 17
Tries: Price, Daniell;
Conversions: Jones (2);
Penalty: W.Jones;
Drop goal: W.Jones

Jan 31 Gloucester 3 Swansea 0
Try: S.Dangerfield

**Feb 7 United Services (Portsmouth) 20
Gloucester 8**
Try: C.Dunn;
Conversion: T.Price;
Penalty: T.Price

Feb 14 Gloucester 15 Bath 0
Tries: S.Dangerfield, G.Hudson, R.Jones;
Conversion: W.Jones;
Drop goal: W.Jones

Feb 21 Cardiff v Gloucester – cancelled due to
unfit ground

**Feb 28 Gloucester 7
Oxford University 18**
Penalty: W.Jones;
Drop goal: W.Jones

Mar 6 Northampton 7 Gloucester 5
Try: K.Daniell;
Conversion: W.Jones

Mar 13 Gloucester 18 R.A.F. 6
Tries: S.Smart, C.Crabtree, W.Jones;
Conversions: W.Jones (3);
Penalty: W.Jones

**Mar 20 Guy's Hospital 10
Gloucester 3**
Try: J.Watkins

Mar 27 Gloucester 8 London Welsh 6
Drop goals: W.Jones (2)

**Mar 29 Gloucester 31
London Hospital 3**
Tries: K.Daniell, S.Dangerfield, G.Hudson,
C.Dunn, S.H.Davies;
Conversions: W.Jones (5);
Penalties: W.Jones (2)

Mar 30 Lydney 6 Gloucester 33
Tries: W.Moreland (2), C.Dunn, R.Nicholls,
S.Dangerfield, T.Day, G.Hudson;
Conversions: W.Jones (3), W.Hook;
Drop goal: W.Jones

Apr 3 Newport 8 Gloucester 3
Try: J.Wilson

Apr 7 Stroud 0 Gloucester 10
Penalties: W.Hook (2);
Drop goal: W.Hook

Apr 10 Gloucester 16 Harlequins 3
Tries: S.Smart, J.Wilson;
Penalties: W.Hook (2);
Drop goal: W.Jones

Apr 17 Exeter 6 Gloucester 6
Penalties: W.Hook (2)

**Apr 19 Penzance & Newlyn 3
Gloucester 15**
Tries: D.D.Evans, S.Dangerfield, C.Crabtree;
Conversions: W.Hook (3)

**Apr 20 Devonport Services 6
Gloucester 8**
Try: S.Dangerfield;
Conversion: W.Hook;
Penalty: W.Hook

Apr 24 Cheltenham 3 Gloucester 12
Try: C.Crabtree;
Conversion: W.Hook;
Penalty: W.Hook;
Drop goal: W.Jones

Apr 28 Cardiff 33 Gloucester 3
Try: R.Mitchell

J.Barnes F.Wadley Rev.Hughes R.Loveridge T.Millington(Chairman) S.Smart L.M.Middleditch R.James S.Taylor
T.Burns C.Dunn M.Fletcher J.Watkins R.Hodge H.J.Meadows S.Smart R.Parry W.Hook F.Daniells A.T.Voyce
H.J.Balchin R.Weston R.Sutton A.G.Hudson(Capt) Dr.A.Alcock(Pres) S.Dangerfield C.Crabtree T.Day A.Hudson
R.Mitchell W.Burrows

Played 43 Won 23 Lost 15 Drawn 5
For 431 Against 288
Captain: Gordon Hudson

Gloucester United
Played 31 Won 16 Lost 13 Drawn 2
For 303 Against 238
Captain: Steve Davies

Most appearances: C.Dunn 40, C.Crabtree 38, R.Sutton 37, R.Hodge, S.Smart 36, G.Hudson 35, J.Watkins 33, T.Day 32, S.Dangerfield 31
Most tries: C.Crabtree 18, S.Dangerfield 15, R.Sutton 9, G.Hudson 8, C.Dunn 6
Most conversions: W.Hook 16, P.Nicholls 12, R.Western 9
Most penalties: W.Hook, P.Nicholls 7, W.Jones 6
Drop goals: W.Burrows 2, R.Sutton 1

A reasonable season, but the playing record suffered through the success of Gloucestershire in the Championship. The Club supplied the majority of the players, (16 through the whole campaign), putting a strain on resources, and severely weakened teams played on several occasions. There was a sweeping win over Llanelly. Other good results were wins over Leicester and Newport, and a fine victory away to Harlequins.

Bill Hook's form throughout was excellent and he was unlucky to be only a reserve for England,

after appearing in all three trial games. Charlie Crabtree and Sid Dangerfield were prolific try scorers on the wings. Willie Jones was injured early in the season, but Wally Burrows took over at fly-half to good effect. The pack was as strong as ever. In the front row Tom Day and newcomers George Hastings and Roy Parry were outstanding. Sid Smart performed admirably in the second row, whilst the back row of Jack Watkins, Bob Hodge and Gordon Hudson was probably the best in the country. Hodge was playing in his first season and made an immediate impact. "Digger" Morris played his final game on 12 December against Coventry. He had made 317 appearances in a career stretching back to 1931. Willie Jones also played his final game, against Cardiff on 26 February.

In December Roy Parry started a sequence of 69 consecutive appearances, not ending until September 1950. It would have been longer, had he not injured himself playing in a charity game!

Captained by Gordon Hudson the County reached the final of the Championship, losing to Lancashire. Gloucester players in the team were: Bill Hook, Jack Watkins, Gordon Hudson, Sid Dangerfield, Bob Hodge and Wally Burrows.

Sep 11 Gloucester 29 Lydney 12
Tries: R.Sutton, C.Dunn, C.Crabtree,
W.Burrows, K.Daniell, S.Dangerfield;
Conversions: W.Hook (4);
Penalty: W.Hook

Sep 16 Stroud 3 Gloucester 3
Penalty: W.Hook

Sep 18 Gloucester 9 Moseley 9
Tries: S.Dangerfield (2);
Penalty: W.Hook

Sep 25 Bristol 16 Gloucester 9
Tries: S.Dangerfield, K.Daniell (2)

Oct 2 Gloucester 6 Bedford 6
Tries: J.Wilson (2)

Oct 9 Cardiff 20 Gloucester 6
Penalties: W.Jones (2)

Oct 13 Cheltenham 8 Gloucester 14
Tries: G.Hudson, S.Dangerfield (2);
Conversion: W.Jones;
Penalty: W.Jones

Oct 16 Gloucester 6 Wasps 0
Tries: C.Crabtree (2)

Oct 23 Clifton 6 Gloucester 18
Tries: B.Knight, R.Beamish, C.Crabtree,
R.Morris;
Conversions: P.Nicholls (3)

Oct 30 Richmond 12 Gloucester 22
Tries: R.Hodge (2), K.Daniell;
Conversions: W.Jones (2);
Penalties: W Jones (3)

Nov 6 Gloucester 18 Leicester 16
Tries: B.Knight (2), S.Dangerfield, C.Crabtree;
Conversions: W.Hook (3)

Nov 13 Moseley 6 Gloucester 3
Penalty: P.Nicholls

Nov 20 Gloucester 5 Bath 0
Try: C.Crabtree;
Conversion: W.Jones

**Nov 23 Oxford University 11
Gloucester 6**
Try: J.Watkins;
Penalty: P.Nicholls

Nov 27 Newport 16 Gloucester 6
Try: B.Knight;
Penalty: P.Nicholls

Dec 4 Gloucester 23 Llanelly 8
Tries: R.Sutton, G.Hudson, R.Hodge, C.Crabtree;
Conversions: W.Hook (4);
Penalty: W.Hook

Dec 11 Gloucester 6 Stroud 0
Tries: R.Beamish, B.Wilkes

Dec 18 Coventry 5 Gloucester 3
Penalty: G.Hudson

**Dec 27 Gloucester 13
Old Merchant Taylors 3**
Tries: R.Sutton, C.Dunn;
Conversions: W.Hook (2);
Penalty: W.Hook

**Dec 28 Gloucester 30
Universities Athletic Union 5**
Tries: C.Dunn (2), R.Beamish, W.Burrows, T.Day, G.Hudson, C.Crabtree;
Conversions: P.Nicholls (2), G.Hudson;

Penalty: P.Nicholls

Jan 1 Gloucester 13 London Scottish 0
Tries: C.Crabtree (2), G.Hudson;
Conversions: P.Nicholls (2)

Jan 6 Gloucester 6 Army 6
Try: C.Crabtree;
Penalty: P.Nicholls

Jan 8 Leicester 6 Gloucester 3
Penalty: G.Hudson

Jan 15 Gloucester 15 Neath 9
Tries: S.Dangerfield, K.Daniell, G.Hudson;
Conversions: P.Nicholls (3)

Jan 22 Gloucester 11 Bristol 3
Tries: R.Sutton, C.Crabtree;
Conversion: W.Hook;
Penalty: W.Hook

Jan 29 Swansea 14 Gloucester 8
Try: K.Daniell;
Conversion: W.Hook;
Penalty: W.Hook

**Feb 5 Gloucester 6
United Services (Portsmouth) 8**
Try: C.Crabtree;
Penalty: P.Nicholls

Feb 12 Bath 13 Gloucester 5
Try: S.Dangerfield;
Conversion: W.Hook

Feb 19 Gloucester v Exeter – cancelled

Feb 26 Gloucester 0 Cardiff 8

Mar 5 Gloucester 0 Northampton 0

Mar 12 Gloucester 3 R.A.F. 5
Try: C.Crabtree

**Mar 19 Gloucester 14
Guy's Hospital 3**

Tries; R.Hodge, C.Crabtree, S.Dangerfield;
Conversion: P.Nicholls;
Drop goal: W.Burrows

Mar 26 Gloucester 6 Newport 3
Drop goal: W.Burrows;
Penalty: P.Nicholls

Mar 31 Gloucester 22 Blackheath 3
Tries: S.Dangerfield (2), G.Hudson (2), C.Dunn, R.Parry;
Conversions: P.Nicholls, S.Dangerfield

Apr 2 Llanelly 9 Gloucester 0

Apr 7 Gloucester 5 Cheltenham 0
Try: T.Day;
Conversion: R.Western

Apr 9 Harlequins 3 Gloucester 5
Try: R.Sutton;
Conversion: R.Western

Apr 16 Gloucester 22 London Welsh 0
Tries: C.Crabtree (2), R.Mitchell, S.Dangerfield, W.Burrows: Conversions: R.Western (2);
Drop goal: R.Sutton

Apr 18 Gloucester 26 Sale 3
Tries: W.Burrows (2), H.Meadows, S.Dangerfield, R.Sutton;
Conversions: B.Western (4);
Penalty: R.Western

Apr 19 Lydney 8 Gloucester 0

**Apr 23 Devonport Services 5
Gloucester 17**
Tries: R.Sutton (2), S.Smart, C.Dunn, G.Hudson;
Conversion: R.Western

Apr 25 Torquay 12 Gloucester 0

Apr 26 Teignmouth 5 Gloucester 9
Tries: S.Dangerfield, R.Sutton, C.Crabtree

1949-50

**Played 43 Won 19 Lost 17 Drawn 7
For 295 Against 277
Captain: Gordon Hudson**

Gloucester United
Played 24 Won 14 Lost 9 Drawn 1
For 256 Against 190
Captain: Steve Davies

Most appearances: R.Parry 43, T.Day 41,

G.Hastings 38, R.Sutton 37, C.Dunn, G.Hudson 36, W.Burrows 27, S.Smart, M.Baker 26
Most tries: G.Hudson 8, C.Dunn 6, M.Baker 5
Most conversions: W.Hook 10, M.Baker 8
Most penalties: W.Hook 12, M.Baker, G.Hudson 4
Drop goals: W.Hook, M.Baker, J.Teakle 1

With 17 defeats this was the worst playing

record since 1928-29. The situation was not helped by a string of injuries to key players. Bill Hook was injured against Cardiff in December and did not play again for 11 weeks. In addition, Ken Daniell, Charlie Crabtree, Roy Mitchell, Jack Watkins and Bob Hodge all missed half the season due to injuries. On the bright side, in October a win at Neath was the first victory in Wales since the War, and in November Leicester were beaten at Kingsholm. A late flourish of wins, notably on the annual south-west tour, at

J.Barnes H.J.Meadows R.H.James S.F.Taylor T.Millington L.H.Middleditch R.N.Loveridge Rev.H.M.Hughes S.H.Davies
A.T.Voyce C.Dunn R.Parry M.Baker J.Watkins R.Hodge R.Chamberlayne D.Ibbotson G.Hastings R.A.Beattie(Ref) T.Burns(Hon.Fixture Sec)
H.J.Balchin(Hon.Treas) T.Day R.Sutton A.G.Hudson(Capt) Dr.Arnold Alcock(Pres) S.F.Dangerfield W.Burrows W.G.Hook A.Hudson(Hon.Sec)
V.Davies J.A.Teakle

least ensured that wins outnumbered defeats. At full-back, in the absence of Hook, Pat Nicholls proved to be a good substitute. Although playing with spirit the three-quarters lacked speed and physique. However, at half-back, Vivian Davies a recruit from Swansea, was a splendid scrum-half, and with John Teakle, the Somerset fly-half, formed a sound partnership.

The forwards played well, but there was some lack of weight and height, which led to problems in the scrum and line-out. Gordon Hudson (who also led the County team) was an enthusiastic captain. Young forwards George Hastings and Dennis Ibbotson showed promise for the future. Michael Baker, a 17-year-old schoolboy made his mark at full-back and wing, retained his place for most of the season, and proved to be a good place kicker. Sid Smart retired at the end of the season after playing in 133 games.

Jack Watkins played in an England Trial game.

Sep 10 Gloucester 3 Lydney 3
Penalty: W.Hook

Sep 15 Gloucester 22 Stroud 0
Tries: G.Hudson (2), C.Crabtree, C.Dunn;
Conversions: W.Hook (2);
Penalty: W.Hook;
Drop goal: M.Baker

Sep 17 Moseley 13 Gloucester 9
Penalties: W.Hook (3)

Sep 24 Gloucester 11 Bristol 11
Try: C.Dunn;
Conversion: W.Hook;
Penalties: W.Hook (2)

Sep 28 Cheltenham 9 Gloucester 9
Try: M.Fletcher;
Penalties: W.Hook (2)

Oct 1 Bedford 28 Gloucester 0

Oct 8 Gloucester 24 Old Paulines 6
Tries: C.Dunn, W.Burrows, G.Hastings,
S.Smart, B.Knight, W.Evans;
Conversions: R.Western (3)

Oct 15 Neath 8 Gloucester 10
Tries: W.Burrows, V.Davies;
Conversions: W.Hook (2)

Oct 22 Gloucester 19 Old Blues 0
Tries: G.Hastings, C.Dunn, W.Burrows,
K.Daniell;
Conversions: R.Western, M.Baker;
Penalty: R.Western

Oct 29 Gloucester 12 Richmond 0
Tries: V.Davies, R.Sutton, M.Baker;
Penalty: W.Hook

Nov 5 Gloucester 18 Leicester 6
Tries: C.Crabtree (2), M.Baker, G.Hudson;
Conversions: W.Hook (3)

Nov 12 Gloucester 5 Moseley 5
Try: V.Davies;
Conversion: R.Western

Nov 19 Llanelly 3 Gloucester 0

Dec 3 Blackheath 3 Gloucester 8
Try: M.Baker;
Conversion: M.Baker;
Penalty: M.Baker

Dec 10 Gloucester 0 Cardiff 11

Dec 17 Coventry 11 Gloucester 0

Dec 24 Bath 14 Gloucester 11
Tries: C.Dunn, V.Davies;
Conversion: P.Nicholls;
Penalty: G.Hudson

**Dec 26 Gloucester 8
Old Merchant Taylors 5**
Tries: S.Dangerfield, R.Sutton;
Conversion: S.Dangerfield

**Dec 27 Gloucester 6
Universities Athletic Union 3**
Try: S.Dangerfield;

Penalty: M.Baker

Dec 31 Newport 11 Gloucester 0

Jan 7 London Scottish 6 Gloucester 3
Penalty: M.Baker

Jan 12 Gloucester 5 Army 26
Try: T.Day;
Conversion: M.Baker

Jan 14 Leicester 6 Gloucester 3
Try: G.Hudson

Jan 21 Gloucester 3 Neath 11
Penalty: G.Hudson

Jan 28 Bristol v Gloucester – cancelled due to frost

Feb 4 United Services (Portsmouth) 3 Gloucester 6
Penalties: Nicholls (2)

Feb 11 Gloucester 3 Bath 0
Penalty: G.Hudson

Feb 16 Gloucester 5 Oxford University 0

Try: G.Hudson:
Conversion: P.Nicholls

Feb 18 Gloucester 3 Swansea 5
Penalty: P.Nicholls

Feb 25 Cardiff 11 Gloucester 3
Try: B.Knight

Mar 4 Northampton 6 Gloucester 0

Mar 11 Gloucester 0 R.A.F. 3

Mar 18 Guy's Hospital 17 Gloucester 3
Penalty: G.Hudson

Mar 25 Gloucester 3 Newport 3
Try: D.Ibbotson

Mar 30 Gloucester 3 Stroud 5
Penalty: W.Hook

Apr 1 Gloucester 6 Cheltenham 5
Try: M.Baker;
Penalty: M.Baker

Apr 8 Gloucester 8 London Welsh 0
Try: S.Dangerfield;

Conversion: M.Baker;
Drop goal: J.Teakle

Apr 10 Gloucester 18 Headingley 3
Tries: R.Parry, W.Burrows, G.Hudson;
Conversions: M.Baker (3);
Drop goal: W.Hook

Apr 11 Lydney 3 Gloucester 3
Try: R.Chamberlayne

Apr 15 Gloucester 0 Llanelly 0

Apr 22 Exeter 0 Gloucester 11
Tries: D.Ibbotson (2), C.Dunn;
Conversion: M.Baker

Apr 24 Penzance & Newlyn 3 Gloucester 9
Tries: M.Baker, G.Hudson, T.Day

Apr 25 Teignmouth 8 Gloucester 16
Tries: E.Turner (2), R.Sutton, S.Dangerfield;
Conversions: W.Hook (2)

Apr 29 Gloucester 6 Devonport Services 3
Try: G.Hudson;
Penalty: W.Hook

1950-51

Rev.H.M.Hughes S.F.Taylor R.H.James T.Millington S.H.Davies L.H.Middleditch S.Smart T.Burns(Fixture Sec)
A.T.Voyce F.Wadley W.Cartmell H.Wells A.G.Hudson R.Hodge I.Ryder G.Hastings C.Crabtree W.Cale R.Morris
H.J.Balchin(Hon.Treas) W.G.Hook E.Turner R.Sutton T.Day(Capt) Dr.A.Alcock(Pres) R.Parry D.Ibbotson R.Chamberlayne M.Baker A.Hudson(Hon.Sec)
H.L.Terrington D.Humphris

Played 45 Won 23 Lost 16 Drawn 6
For 373 Against 248
Captain: Tom Day

Gloucester United
Played 20 Won 13 Lost 7
For 231 Against 131
Captain: Ivor Jones

Most appearances: T.Day 45,
R.Chamberlayne, R.Hodge 43, D.Ibbotson 42,
R.Parry 37, R.Sutton, G.Hudson 35, H.Wells
34, E.Turner 32, C.Crabtree 31
Most tries: C.Crabtree, D.Ibbotson 10,
R.Sutton, S.Troughton 9, E.Turner 7
Conversions: W.Hook 13, M.Baker 10, T.Halls 9
Penalties: W.Hook 11, M.Baker 6, T.Halls 2
Drop goals: H.Terrington 5, J.Teakle 2,
W,Hook, W.Burrows 1

For the second season running, injuries and
County calls weakened the team on several
occasions. However, there were good wins over
Blackheath, Bristol (away), Llanelly, Bath, Wasps
(away), Oxford University, Northampton and
Coventry. The win against Llanelly was achieved
despite the team being reduced to 14 men through
injury in the first half. Just before this Gloucester
had scored a fine try through Roy Sutton, who
took full advantage of a searing break from John
Teakle. Then Henry Wells had to go off with a
leg injury, but Gloucester dominated for most of
the second half to gain an outstanding victory. A
sparkling display of running rugby accounted for
a powerful Northampton team. It was the first
win over "The Saints" for five years. In April, the
Newport game attracted a crowd of over 12,000.

The forwards were strong, and well led by captain
Tom Day, in his final season. He first played
in 1936 and made 267 appearances. Day had
fine support from hooker Reg Chamberlayne,
George Hastings, Roy Parry, Bob Hodge,
Dennis Ibbotson, who was equal highest try
scorer, and evergreen Gordon Hudson. Scrum-
half David Humphris made great progress, but
lacked a regular partner at fly-half. John Teakle,
Howard Terrington and Bill Cartmell all played
at various times, but were not always available.

There was a continuing lack of physique in
the backs, especially at centre, with the result
that wings Charlie Crabtree, Ernie Turner and
Michael Baker were given few chances. At full-
back Bill Hook was at last awarded an England
cap against Scotland. He kicked the conversion
which won the game.

Sid Dangerfield and Charlie Dunn both made
one appearance, before retiring. Dangerfield
had played in 116 games and Dunn 157.

Sep 9 Gloucester 3 Lydney 8
Try: C.Crabtree

Sep 14 Gloucester 23 Stroud 6
Tries: D.Ibbotson (3), R.Sutton;
Conversions: W.Hook (4);
Penalty: W.Hook

Sep 16 Gloucester 14 Moseley 5
Tries: C.Crabtree, R.Sutton;
Conversion: M Baker;
Penalty: M Baker;
Drop goal: H.Terrington

Sep 23 Bristol 3 Gloucester 9
Penalties: W Hook (2);
Drop goal: H.Terrington

Sep 28 Gloucester 14 Blackheath 8
Tries: H.Wells, D.Ibbotson;
Conversion: W.Hook;
Penalty: W.Hook;
Drop goal: W.Hook

Sep 30 Newport 6 Gloucester 0

Oct 5 Gloucester 0 Cheltenham 0

Oct 7 Gloucester 8 Bedford 0
Try: D.Ibbotson;
Conversion: M.Baker;
Penalty: M.Baker

Oct 14 Gloucester 22 Old Paulines 3
Tries: R.Hodge, T.Day, E.Turner, C.Crabtree,
H.Terrington, G.Hastings;
Conversions: T.Halls, M.Baker

Oct 21 Gloucester 14 Exeter 0
Tries: C.Crabtree, M.Baker;
Conversion: M.Baker;
Penalty: M.Baker;
Drop goal: H.Terrington

Oct 28 Clifton 0 Gloucester 5
Try: E.Turner;
Conversion: M.Baker

Nov 4 Leicester 19 Gloucester 14
Tries: G.Hudson, S.Troughton, J.Teakle;
Conversion: W.Hook;
Penalty: W.Hook

Nov 11 Moseley 8 Gloucester 3
Try: B.Ash

Nov 18 Gloucester 5 Llanelly 3
Try: R.Sutton;
Conversion: W.Hook

Nov 25 Gloucester 9
Birkenhead Park 6
Tries: T.Day, E.Turner;
Penalty: M.Baker

Dec 2 Cardiff 16 Gloucester 9
Tries: R.Sutton, D.Ibbotson;
Penalty: W.Hook

Dec 9 Gloucester 22 Old Blues 0
Tries: C.Crabtree (2), D.Ibbotson, S.Troughton;
Conversions: T.Halls (2);
Penalty: T.Halls;
Drop goal: W.Burrows

Dec 16 Coventry v Gloucester – cancelled –
frost

Dec 23 Gloucester 27 Bath 3
Tries: S.Troughton, R.Sutton, M.Baker,
R.Hodge, D.Ibbotson;
Conversions: T.Halls (3);
Penalty: T.Halls;
Drop goal: J.Teakle

Dec 26 Gloucester 11
Old Merchant Taylors 0
Tries: S.Troughton, G.Hastings, R.Parry;
Conversion: T.Halls

Dec 27 Gloucester 8
Universities Athletic Union 6
Try: M.Baker;
Conversion: T.Halls;
Penalty: M.Baker

Dec 30 Richmond v Gloucester – cancelled due
to frost

Jan 6 Gloucester 0 London Scottish 8

Jan 11 Gloucester 11 Army 11
Tries: R.Hodge, C.Crabtree, H.Wells;
Conversion: T.Halls

Jan 13 Gloucester 3 Leicester 8
Try: T.Day

Jan 20 Wasps 0 Gloucester 3
Try: D.Ibbotson

Jan 27 Gloucester 0 Bristol 0

Feb 3 United Services (Portsmouth) 0
Gloucester 0

Feb 10 Bath 8 Gloucester 3
Penalty: W.Hook

Feb 17 Swansea 9 Gloucester 6
Tries: E.Turner, J.Watkins

Feb 24 Gloucester 3 Cardiff 6
Penalty: W.Hook

**Mar 1 Gloucester 12
Oxford University 8**
Tries: S.Troughton (2), R.Chamberlayne,
E.Turner

Mar 3 Gloucester 21 Northampton 0
Tries: G.Hudson (2), D.Hill, R.Hodge;
Conversions: W.Hook (3);
Drop goal: J.Teakle

Mar 10 Gloucester 8 R.A.F. 0
Try: C.Crabtree;
Conversion: M.Baker;
Penalty: M.Baker

Mar 17 Gloucester 25 Guys Hospital 8
Tries: S.Troughton (3), R.Sutton (3), G.Hudson;
Conversions: M.Baker (2)

Mar 24 Gloucester 10 London Welsh 8
Tries: G.Hudson, R.Sutton;
Conversions: W.Hook (2)

Mar 26 Gloucester 6 Sale 11
Penalties: W.Hook (2)

Mar 27 Lydney 0 Gloucester 0

Mar 31 Llanelly 15 Gloucester 3
Try: C.Crabtree

Apr 5 Gloucester 3 Stroud 0
Try: W.Cartmell

Apr 7 Gloucester 3 Harlequins 3
Try: D.Ibbotson

Apr 11 Cheltenham 3 Gloucester 0

Apr 14 Gloucester 3 Newport 11
Drop goal: H.Terrington

**Apr 21 Devonport Services 12
Gloucester 0**

**Apr 23 Penzance & Newlyn 6
Gloucester 8**
Try: G.Hudson;
Conversion: M.Baker;
Drop goal: H.Terrington

Apr 24 Teignmouth 13 Gloucester 8
Tries: E.Turner (2);
Conversion: M.Baker

Apr 28 Gloucester 14 Coventry 0
Tries: C.Crabtree, R.Hodge, H.Terrington;
Conversion: W.Hook;
Penalty: W.Hook,

1951-52

F.Wadley T.Millington R.H.James Rev.H.M.Hughes(Chairman) S.F.Taylor R.N.Loveridge L.M.Middleditch
T.Burns(Hon.Fixture Sec) R.Blair A.Wadley C.Crabtree W.G.Hook J.A.Teakle G.Hastings C.Thomas R.Hodge A.G.Hudson P.Ford H.Wells
S.H.Davies W.Cale
H.J.Balchin T.Hall R.Parry R.Sutton J.Watkins(Capt) Dr.A.Alcock H.L.Terrington M.Baker J.Taylor D.Ibbotson A.Hudson(Hon.Sec)
V.Davies W.Cartmell

**Played 45 Won 30 Lost 11 Drawn 4
For 563 Against 317
Captain: Jack Watkins**

Gloucester United
Played 32 Won 26 Lost 5 Drawn 1
For 434 Against 152
Captain: Ivor Jones

Most appearances: H.Wells 44, R.Hodge,
J.Watkins 43, C.Thomas 41, W.Cartmell,

G.Hudson 37, G.Hastings 36, J.Taylor 34, P.Ford
31, T.Halls 30
Most tries: C.Crabtree 16, J.Taylor 15,
G.Hudson 11, V.Davies 9
Conversions: T.Halls 45, W.Hook 11, M.Baker 3
Penalties: T.Halls 13, W.Hook 12, M.Baker 3,
G.Hudson 1
Drop goals: M.Baker 4, W.Hook,
H.Terrington 1

It was fitting that in the Diamond Jubilee year

of the opening of Kingsholm that the Club
should post a record season of 30 wins. The
Jubilee was also celebrated at a dinner attended
by the President of the Rugby Football Union
and representatives of clubs from all over the
country. Charlie Williams and Walter Taylor the
only surviving players from the first game at
Kingsholm against Burton, sixty years before,
were present.

The backs formed a brilliant attacking force.

Howard Terrington and John Teakle in the centre, and John Taylor and Charlie Crabtree on the wings were outstanding. The half-backs, with Vivian Davies at scrum-half and Bill Cartmell at fly-half, made sure the backs received plenty of ball to exploit. Bill Hook at full-back made only 15 appearances due to injury, but still won two England caps, against Wales and South Africa. He retired at the end of the season. Trevor Halls proved to be a sound substitute when Hook was unavailable, and as a place kicker scored 129 points.

The forwards formed one of the strongest packs in the country, and were well led by captain Jack Watkins. Bob Hodge was in fine form all season, and Gordon Hudson, as ever, performed superbly on the flank. Peter Ford, an extremely promising flanker, made his debut against Stroud in September, and retained his place for the rest of the season. Young Dennis Ibbotson continued to make good progress.

A highlight of the season was the first win over Cardiff since 1938, in front of a crowd of 12,000. The "Citizen" stated: "The whole Gloucester XV played like heroes" and, "Ibbotson was here, there and everywhere". There was also a cherished double over old rivals Bristol. In December Coventry suffered their first defeat by an English club. In the match against Leicester, at Kingsholm, there was a rare hat-trick of tries from a forward, Henry Wells. The defeat of Llanelly in April was the first they had suffered against an English club.

Western Counties played the South Africans. Howard Terrington and Gordon Hudson (try) were the Gloucester players.

Honorary Club Secretary, Arthur Hudson completed fifty years of loyal service, both as a player and official.

Sep 8 Gloucester 11 Lydney 3
Tries: C.Crabtree, G.Hastings, J.Syme;
Conversion: W.Hook

Sep 13 Stroud 3 Gloucester 3
Drop goal: W.Hook

Sep 15 Gloucester 11 Moseley 6
Try: D.Ibbotson;
Conversion: W.Hook;
Penalties: W.Hook (2)

Sep 17 Gloucester 11 Waterloo 6
Tries: J.Taylor, D.Ibbotson, R.Beamish;
Conversion: W.Halls

Sep 22 Gloucester 11 Neath 11
Try: R.Beamish;
Conversion: W.Hook;
Penalties: W.Hook (2)

Sep 27 Gloucester 14 Blackheath 8
Tries: J.Taylor, J.Teakle;
Conversion: T.Halls;
Penalties: T.Halls (2)

Sep 29 Gloucester 11 Bristol 6
Try: G.Hudson;
Conversion: W.Hook;
Penalties: W.Hook (2)

Oct 3 Cheltenham 3 Gloucester 6
Try: R.Beamish;
Penalty: G.Hudson

Oct 6 Bedford 19 Gloucester 9
Penalties: W.Hook (3)

Oct 10 Cardiff 24 Gloucester 3
Penalty: T.Halls

Oct 13 Gloucester 21 Old Paulines 5
Tries: P.Ford (2), G.Hudson, H.Wells, R.Beamish;
Conversions: T.Halls (3)

Oct 20 Birkenhead Park 3 Gloucester 9
Try: P.Ford;
Penalties: T.Halls (2)

Oct 27 Gloucester 56 Old Blues 3
Tries: H.Terrington (2), C.Crabtree (2), R.Beamish (2), W.Cartmell (2), H.Wells (2), V.Davies, R.Hodge, P.Ford, D.Ibbotson;
Conversions: T.Halls (7)

Nov 3 Gloucester 16 Leicester 8
Tries: H.Wells (3), V.Davies;
Conversions: T.Halls (2)

Nov 10 Newport 15 Gloucester 0

Nov 17 Gloucester 32 Devonport Services 8
Tries: C.Crabtree (3), J.Taylor (2), G.Hudson (2);
Conversions: T.Halls (4);
Penalty: T.Halls

Nov 24 Gloucester 0 Stroud 0

Dec 1 Gloucester 24 Oxford University 21
Tries: C.Crabtree (2), G.Hudson, J.Taylor, G.Hastings;
Conversions: T.Halls (3);
Penalty: T.Halls

Dec 15 Gloucester 16 Coventry 8
Tries: H.Terrington, V.Davies;
Conversions: T.Halls (2);
Penalties: T.Halls (2)

Dec 22 Bath 3 Gloucester 0

Dec 26 Gloucester 12 Old Merchant Taylors 6
Tries: G.Hudson (2), C.Thomas, C.Crabtree

Dec 27 Gloucester 3 Universities Athletic Union 5
Try: R.Hodge

Dec 29 Gloucester 15 Richmond 8
Tries: J.Taylor, P.Ford, H.Wells;
Conversions: W.Hook (3)

Jan 5 London Scottish 3 Gloucester 5
Try: R Hodge;
Conversion: T Hallls

Jan 10 Gloucester 0 Army 5

Jan 12 Leicester 9 Gloucester 5
Try: D.Gladwin;
Conversion: T.Halls

Jan 19 Gloucester 27 Wasps 12
Tries: C.Crabtree (3), C.Thomas, J.Teakle, Penalty Try;
Conversions: T.Halls (3);
Drop goal: H.Terrington

Jan 26 Bristol 6 Gloucester 11
Tries: V.Davies, H.Terrington;
Conversion: W.Hook;
Penalty: W.Hook

Feb 7 Gloucester 29 United Services (Portsmouth) 11
Tries: R.Hodge (2), J.Taylor (2), G.Hudson, V.Davies;
Conversions: T.Halls (4);
Penalty: T.Halls

Feb 9 Gloucester v Bath – cancelled due to death of King George VI

Feb 16 Gloucester 8 Swansea 8
Penalty Try;
Conversion: W.Hook;
Penalty: W.Hook

Feb 23 Gloucester 14 Cardiff 0
Tries: J.Taylor, W.Cartmell;
Conversion: W.Hook;
Penalty: W.Hook;
Drop goal: M.Baker

Mar 1 Northampton 5 Gloucester 3
Penalty: M.Baker

Mar 8 Gloucester 14 R.A.F. 3
Tries: R.Hodge, J.Taylor, V.Davies, R.Sutton;
Conversion: W.Hook

**Mar 15 Guy's Hospital 3
Gloucester 18**
Tries: G.Hudson, V.Davies, R.Sutton;
Conversions: T.Halls (3);
Penalty: T.Halls

Mar 22 Coventry 19 Gloucester 16
Tries: W.Cartmell (2), C.Thomas;
Conversions: T.Halls (2);
Penalty: T.Halls

Mar 29 Gloucester 0 Newport 6

Apr 5 Gloucester 21 Harlequins 5
Tries: V.Davies (2), D.Ibbotson, J.Taylor,
C.Thomas, G.Hudson;
Penalty: T.Halls

Apr 10 Gloucester 5 Cheltenham 0
Try: C.Crabtree;
Conversion: M.Baker

Apr 12 Gloucester 12 London Welsh 8
Tries: R.Blair (2);
Penalties: M.Baker (2)

Apr 14 Gloucester 30 Bradford 0
Tries: M.Baker (2), R.Hodge, R.Blair,
C.Crabtree, P.Ford, D.Ibbotson;
Conversions: T.Halls (2), M.Baker;
Drop goal: M.Baker

Apr 15 Lydney 10 Gloucester 5

Try: C.Crabtree;
Conversion: T.Halls

Apr 19 Gloucester 8 Llanelly 5
Try: G.Hudson;
Conversion: M.Baker;
Drop goal: M.Baker

Apr 26 Exeter 8 Gloucester 13
Tries: J.Taylor (2), D.Ibbotson;
Conversions: T.Halls (2)

Apr 28 Penzance 6 Gloucester 8
Tries: R.Beamish, R.Hodge;
Conversion: T.Halls

Apr 29 Teignmouth 3 Gloucester 19
Tries: J.Taylor (2), P.Ford, A.Wadley;
Conversions: T.Halls (2);
Drop goal: M.Baker

1952-53

C.N.Smith F.H.James T.Millington R.N.Loveridge S.H.Davies L.H.Middleditch S.F.Taylor A.T.Voyce Rev.H.M.Hughes(Chairman)
F.Wadley R.Morris R.Parry M.Burford T.Halls J.Gwilliam P.Ford H.Wells M.Baker W.Cale T.Burns(Fixture Sec)
H.J.Balchin(Hon.Treas) E.Turner R.Sutton J.Taylor Dr.A.Alcock(Pres) R.Hodge(Capt) G.Hastings D.Ibbotson A.Hudson(Hon.Sec)
H.L.Terrington J.Hobbs

**Played 42 Won 23 Lost 15 Drawn 4
For 416 Against 317
Captain: Bob Hodge**

Gloucester United
Played 32 Won 26 Lost 5 Drawn 1
For 381 Against 148
Captain: Ivor Jones

Most appearances: P.Ford 42, R.Parry 37,
H.Wells 36, D.Ibbotson, H.Terrington 35,

E.Turner 34, J.Taylor 33, R.Hodge 31
Most tries: P.Ford 15, E.Turner 14, J.Taylor 11,
C.Crabtree 6
Conversions: M.Baker 16, T.Halls 10, W.Smith
4, H.Terrington 3, H.Wells 1
Penalties: M.Baker 15, T.Halls 5, W.Smith 2,
H.Wells, G.Hudson 1
Drop goals: H.Terrington, D.Ibbotson,
M.Baker, L.Morgan 1

The strength of the side was in the forwards,

especially in the loose. Hooker, Cyril Thomas
made many strikes against the head. The Welsh
international John Gwilliam proved to be a
great asset, his skill and resourcefulness was of
immense help to the team. Captain Bob Hodge,
as well as being a splendid leader, thoroughly
deserved his recognition by the England
selectors that he was on the brink of winning a
cap. Peter Ford played in every game, and was
also top try scorer.

The back division proved to be a problem and

many experimental selections were made. Vivian Davies, scrum-half, who returned to Swansea, was sorely missed. John Hobbs looked a promising replacement. John Taylor and Ernie Turner looked dangerous on the wings when given the chance, which was not often enough. Michael Baker made further progress and his place kicking was dependable. Bill Smith, doing his National Service at RAF Innsworth, and ex Crypt Grammar schoolboy, played 22 games at full-back, and seemed a promising talent.

John Gwilliam played for Wales in three internationals, captaining the team against England. Bob Hodge played in two England trial games, and was reserve in attendance for all England's games.

The double was achieved over Leicester. Cardiff were beaten for the second season running, with Peter Ford, Dennis Ibbotson, John Gwilliam and Cyril Thomas playing blinders. There was an outstanding win at Swansea; only the second time that had been achieved. Indeed, it appeared that Swansea would win the game when with only minutes left, Wales International winger, Horace Phillips broke clean away, but in dogged pursuit John Taylor tackled him just short of the line and Gloucester hung on to win.

Charlie Crabtree who had been a regular since the end of WW2, played in only nine games and retired after making 171 appearances. Former club captain Jack Watkins also made only a handful of appearances and returned to his old club, Lydney. He had played in 157 games.

Sep 13 Gloucester 11 Lydney 17
Tries: J.Taylor, D.Jones;
Conversion: T.Halls;
Penalty: T.Halls

Sep 18 Stroud 11 Gloucester 11
Tries: J.Gwilliam, R.Sutton;
Conversion: T.Halls;
Penalty: T.Halls

Sep 20 Gloucester 14 Exeter 8
Tries: G.Bevan, D.Ibbotson, P.Ford, W.Nield;
Conversion: T.Halls

Sep 27 Bristol 6 Gloucester 9
Tries: C.Thomas, D.Ibbotson;
Penalty: T.Halls

Oct 2 Cheltenham 6 Gloucester 3
Penalty: T.Halls

Oct 4 Gloucester 6 Bedford 14
Penalties: M.Baker (2)

Oct 11 Gloucester 30 Old Paulines 0
Tries: E.Turner (2), D.Jones (2), H.Terrington, C.Crabtree, P.Ford, H.Wells;
Conversions: H.Terrington (2), H.Wells

Oct 18 Cardiff 8 Gloucester 0

Oct 25 Gloucester 24 Old Blues 3
Tries: P.Ford (3), A.Bainbridge, C.Thomas, C.Crabtree;
Conversions: W.Smith (3)

Nov 1 Leicester 3 Gloucester 6
Tries: J.Taylor, C.Crabtree

Nov 8 Llanelly 22 Gloucester 6
Penalties: W.Smith (2)

Nov 15 Newport 8 Gloucester 3
Drop goal: D.Ibbotson

Nov 22 Gloucester 20 Clifton 0
Tries: J.Taylor (2), C.Crabtree (2), D.Ibbotson, P.Ford;
Conversion: W.Smith

Nov 29 Oxford University v Gloucester – cancelled due to frost & snow
Dec 6 Gloucester v Neath – cancelled due to frost & snow

Dec 13 Gloucester 11 Bath 3
Tries: C.Crabtree, M.Baker, R.Parry;
Conversion: M.Baker

Dec 20 Coventry 3 Gloucester 3
Penalty: M.Baker

**Dec 26 Gloucester 10
Old Merchant Taylors 8**
Tries: E.Turner (2);
Conversions: M.Baker (2)

**Dec 27 Gloucester 11
Universities Athletic Union 5**
Try: P.Ford,
Conversion: M.Baker;
Penalties: M.Baker (2)

Jan 3 Gloucester 23 London Scottish 3
Tries: J.Taylor (2), P.Ford (2), M.Baker;
Conversion: M.Baker;
Drop goals: M.Baker, H.Terrington

Jan 8 Gloucester 13 Army 6
Tries: D.Ibbotson, M.Baker;
Conversions: M.Baker (2);
Penalty: M.Baker

Jan 10 Gloucester 10 Leicester 6
Tries: H.Terrington, E.Turner;

Conversions: M.Baker (2)

Jan 17 Wasps 11 Gloucester 3
Penalty: M.Baker

Jan 24 Gloucester 6 Bristol 12
Try: J.Taylor;
Penalty: M.Baker

Jan 31 Neath 8 Gloucester 5
Penalty Try;
Conversion: H.Terrington

**Feb 7 Gloucester 17
United Services (Portsmouth) 11**
Tries: J.Gwilliam, J.Taylor, E.Turner;
Conversion: M.Baker: Penalties: M.Baker (2)

**Feb 14 Gloucester 11
Cambridge University 9**
Tries: J.Hobbs, E.Turner, M.Baker;
Conversion: T.Halls

Feb 21 Swansea 8 Gloucester 10
Tries: E.Turner, H.Terrington;
Conversions: M.Baker (2)

Feb 28 Gloucester 14 Cardiff 9
Tries: J.Hobbs, E.Turner;
Conversion: M.Baker;
Penalties: M Baker (2)

Mar 7 Gloucester 6 Northampton 6
Try: P.Ford;
Drop goal: L.Morgan

Mar 14 Gloucester 6 R.A.F. 5
Try: P.Ford;
Penalty: M.Baker

**Mar 21 Gloucester 20
Guy's Hospital 10**
Tries: W.Cartmell (2), J.Taylor, G.Hastings;
Conversions: T.Halls (4)

Mar 28 Gloucester 6 Newport 14
Try: R.Stower;
Penalty: M.Baker

Apr 2 Gloucester 14 Stroud 9
Tries: E.Turner (2), R.Hodge;
Conversion: T.Halls;
Penalty: T.Halls

Apr 4 Gloucester 3 London Welsh 3
Try: E.Turner

Apr 6 Gloucester 9 Sale 0
Tries: J.Taylor, P.Ford, R.Parry

Apr 7 Lydney 6 Gloucester 3

Try: E.Turner

Apr 11 Gloucester 11 Blackheath 3
Tries: R.Sutton (2), R.Hodge;
Conversion: M.Baker

Apr 16 Gloucester 8 Cheltenham 0
Tries: G.Hastings, P.Ford;
Conversion: M.Baker

Apr 18 Harlequins 13 Gloucester 11
Tries: J.Bowdler, J.Gwilliam:
Conversion: M.Baker;
Penalty: M.Baker

Apr 23 Bath 11 Gloucester 0

**Apr 25 Devonport Services 13
Gloucester 9**

Tries: P.Ford, M.Burford;
Penalty: H.Wells

Apr 27 Penzance 3 Gloucester 14
Tries: P.Ford, D.Ibbotson, J.Taylor;
Conversion: T.Halls;
Penalty: G.Hudson

Apr 28 Teignmouth 13 Gloucester 6
Tries: E.Turner, A.Bainbridge

1953-54

J.Gwilliam(inset) R.Morris F.Wadley T.Day T.Millington R.N.Loveridge I.Jones L.H.Middeditch G.J.Dance R.Hodge(inset)
Rev.H.M.Hughes(Chairman) C.N.Smith E.Turner R.Parry T.Halls A.G.Hudson H.Wells J.Varney M.Baker L.Morgan W.Cale T.Burns(Hon.Fixture Sec)
H.J.Balchin(Hon.Treas) D.Ibbotson R.Sutton P.Ford Dr.Alcock(Pres) J.Taylor(Capt) C.Thomas G.Hastings A.Hudson(Hon.Sec)
D.Jones J.Hobbs (W.Cartmell - absent)

**Played 42 Won 31 Lost 10 Drawn 1
For 430 Against 280
Captain: John Taylor**

Gloucester United
Played 28 Won 19 Lost 8 Drawn 1
For 362 Against 217
Captain: Ivor Jones

Most appearances: T.Halls 38, D.Ibbotson 36,
P.Ford 35, E.Turner, G.Hastings 34, J.Taylor,
J.Hobbs, H.Wells, C.Thomas 33, R.Parry 32,
R.Sutton 31, M.Baker 30
Most tries: J.Taylor 13, E.Turner 12,
D.Ibbotson, P.Ford 9, G.Hastimgs 6
Conversions: T.Halls 23, M.Baker 12,
L.Morgan 3
Penalties: T.Halls 13, M.Baker 8, L.Morgan 2
Drop goals: L.Morgan 4, J.Hobbs, R.Sutton,
W.Cartmell 1

This was a record season with regard to number

of wins. Well led by John Taylor the team played
an attacking brand of rugby leading to a number
of good away wins over Bath, Wasps, London
Scottish and Moseley, whilst at Kingsholm there
were victories over Newport, Swansea, Llanelly,
Neath, Bristol, Leicester, Northampton,
Coventry and Oxford University. The season
started with eight straight wins, before the
first defeat at Coventry, when the team was
weakened due to a County game taking five
players. The same thing happened later against
Leicester and Cardiff.

Skipper John Taylor was a dashing wing, and
scored the most tries. Taylor left Gloucester
at the end of the season to play for Leicester
where he lived. Ernie Turner on the other wing
also showed resource and speed. John Hobbs at
scrum-half had a fine season, whilst at fly-half,
Lewis Morgan in his second season had a run
of good displays late on. In the forwards Peter
Ford was outstanding and other forwards who

had an excellent season were Cyril Thomas who
out-hooked most opponents, winning countless
scrums against the head, Roy Parry at prop,
second row Henry Wells and Dennis Ibbotson
in the back row.

At the end of the season Gordon Hudson finally
drew down the curtain on a distinguished
career, which had started in 1935. He played
in 320 Gloucester games, won nine War Time
international and one "Victory" international
caps. He would later become Club Chairman.
Wing Ernie Turner and full-back Trevor Halls
also announced their retirements.

John Gwilliam won four Wales caps against
England, Ireland, France and New Zealand.
Pater Ford was a reserve for the England v
France game, and Bob Hodge played in an
England Trial game. Western Counties played
the touring All Blacks at Bristol. John Taylor,
George Hastings, Bob Hodge and Dennis

Ibbotson were in the Counties team.

Sep 12 Gloucester 24 Lydney 0
Tries: E.Turner (2), H.Wells, J.Hobbs,
G.Hastings, P.Ford;
Conversions: T.Halls (3)

Sep 17 Stroud 0 Gloucester 15
Tries: E.Turner, J.Taylor, P.Ford, A.Baimbridge;
Drop goal: L.Morgan

Sep 19 Gloucester 13 Moseley 0
Tries: E.Turner, D.Ibbotson, P.Ford;
Conversions: T.Halls (2)

Sep 23 Cheltenham 9 Gloucester 11
Try: E.Turner;
Conversion: T.Halls;
Penalties: T.Halls (2)

Sep 26 Gloucester 11 Bristol 3
Tries: G.Hastings, S.Troughton;
Conversion: T.Halls;
Penalty: T.Halls

Oct 3 Bedford 6 Gloucester 13
Tries: E.Turner, M.Baker;
Conversions: T.Halls (2);
Penalty: T.Halls

Oct 10 Gloucester 11 Old Blues 6
Tries: R.Hodge, S.Troughton, D.Meadows;
Conversion: T.Halls

Oct 17 Gloucester 8 Newport 3
Try: E.Turner;
Conversion: T.Halls;
Penalty: T.Halls

Oct 24 Coventry 9 Gloucester 6
Penalties: T.Halls (2)

Oct 31 Gloucester 9
Oxford University 8
Tries: J.Taylor (2);
Penalty: T.Halls

Nov 7 Leicester 13 Gloucester 8
Tries: S.Troughton, D.Meadows;
Conversion: T.Halls

Nov 14 Moseley 0 Gloucester 3
Drop goal: R.Sutton

Nov 21 Gloucester 13 Blackheath 5
Tries: J.Taylor. P.Ford, D.Ibbotson;
Conversions: T.Halls (2)

Nov 28 Gloucester 3 Cardiff 19
Drop goal: W.Cartmell

Dec 5 Neath 20 Gloucester 3
Try: R.Sutton

Dec 12 Bath 6 Gloucester 9
Tries: J.Taylor, C.Thomas, M.Baker

Dec 19 Gloucester 14 Coventry 3
Tries: D.Ibbotson, R.Sutton, G.Hudson;
Conversion: M.Baker;
Drop goal: J.Hobbs

Dec 26 Gloucester 9
Old Merchant Taylors 6
Tries: M.Baker, C.Thomas, H.Wells

Dec 28 Gloucester 12
Universities Athletic Union 8
Try: G.Hastings;
Penalties: T.Halls (3)

Jan 2 London Scottish 0 Gloucester 10
Tries: G.Hastings, J.Taylor;
Conversions: T.Halls (2)

Jan 7 Gloucester v Army – cancelled due to frost

Jan 9 Gloucester 19 Leicester 0
Tries: E.Turner (2), J.Taylor, G.Hastings, P.Ford;
Conversions: T.Halls, M.Baker

Jan 16 Gloucester 14 Wasps 8
Try: C.Thomas;
Conversion: M.Baker;
Penalties: T.Halls (2), M.Baker

Jan 23 Bristol 3 Gloucester 3
Penalty: M.Baker

Jan 30 Gloucester v Neath – cancelled due to
snow and frost
Feb 6 United Services (Portsmouth) v
Gloucester - cancelled due to snow and frost.

Feb 13 Gloucester 14 Bath 5
Tries: R.Sutton, D.Ibbotson;
Conversion: M.Baker;
Penalties: M.Baker (2)

Feb 20 Gloucester 8 Swansea 0
Tries: J.Taylor (2);
Conversion: M.Baker

Feb 27 Cardiff 17 Gloucester 5
Try: D.Ibbotson;
Conversion: T.Halls

Mar 6 Gloucester 15 Llanelly 13
Tries: D.Ibbotson, E.Turner, P.Ford;
Conversions: T.Halls (3)
Mar 13 Gloucester 6 R.A.F. 14

Try: R.Redman;
Penalty: M.Baker

Mar 20 Guys Hospital 14 Gloucester 8
Tries: J.Taylor, M.Burford;
Conversion: T.Halls

Mar 27 Newport 6 Gloucester 0

Apr 3 Gloucester 5 Northampton 3
Try: R.Sutton;
Conversion: M.Baker

Apr 8 Gloucester 6 Cheltenham 9
Try: P.Ford;
Drop goal: L.Morgan

Apr 10 Gloucester 12 Harlequins 8
Tries: R.Amos, G.Hastings, D.Jones;
Penalty: L.Morgan

Apr 15 Gloucester 6 Stroud 3
Try: P.Ford;
Drop goal: L.Morgan

Apr 17 Gloucester 15
Birkenhead Park 5
Tries: C.Thomas (2), D.Ibbotson;
Conversions: L.Morgan (3)

Apr 19 Gloucester 3 Bradford 8
Penalty: L.Morgan

Apr 20 Lydney 3 Gloucester 12
Tries: P.Ford, J.Taylor, T.Halls;
Penalty: M.Baker

Apr 24 Exeter 9 Gloucester 13
Tries: R.Perks (2), G.Hudson;
Conversions: M.Baker (2)

Apr 26 Torquay Athletic 13
Gloucester 19
Tries: M.Baker (2), J.Gwilliam, D.Jones,
D.Ibbotson;
Conversions: M.Baker (2)

Apr 27 Teignmouth 0 Gloucester 8
Tries: J.Taylor, J.Hobbs;
Conversion: M.Baker

Apr 29 Gloucester 8 Neath 0
Tries: G.Hudson, D.Ibbotson;
Conversion: M.Baker

May 1 Gloucester 26
Devonport Services 18
Tries: L.Morgan (2), J.Taylor, E.Turner, D.Jones;
Conversion: M.Baker;
Penalties: M.Baker (2);
Drop goal: L.Morgan

1954-55

R.Sutton F.Wadley T.Day T.Voyce L.H.Middleditch T.Millington R.N.Loveridge G.J.Dance
R.Morris R.Parry R.Blair J.Green J.Varney R.Hodge P.Ford D.A.Jones B.Sibery M.Baker S.H.Davies T.Burns(Fixture Sec)
H.J.Balchin(Hon.Treas) C.Thomas D.Ibbotson Dr.Alcock(Pres) G.W.Hastings(Capt) L.Morgan I.Sheen D.Perks A.Hudson(Hon.Sec)
J.Hobbs D.Jones

Played 41 Won 19 Lost 19 Drawn 3
For 391 Against 402
Captain: George Hastings

Gloucester United
Played 28 Won 8 Lost 17 Drawn 3
For 215 Against 240
Captain: Ivor Jones

Most appearances: R.Hodge 40, P.Ford 37,
R.Parry 36, D.Ibbotson 35, J.Hobbs 32,
R.Blair, D.Jones 31, C.Thomas 29, J.Varney 28
Most tries: P.Ford 14, R.Blair 11, M.Baker,
D.Ibbotson 7
Most conversions: M.Baker 25, L.Morgan 5,
R.Blair 4
Most penalties: M.Baker 12, T.Jones 5
Drop goals: M.Baker, H.Terrington 1

A refurbished Worcester Street stand welcomed
fans for the start of the season.

Following the record breaking 1953-54 season,
this campaign was hugely disappointing.
However, a large part of the decline could be
explained by the fact that several players had
retired before the start of the season. John
Taylor, John Gwilliam, Gordon Hudson, Ernie
Turner, Bill Cartmell and Trevor Halls were
no longer available, and their replacements

were largely inexperienced and took a long
time to adjust to the rigours of top-class rugby.
After early promise there was a depressing
run of nine defeats on the trot, and 12 out of
13. From February there was a welcome rally
which included wins over Leicester, Newport,
Harlequins and Swansea, which gave hope for
the future. The forwards fought nobly. Hastings,
Peter Ford, Dennis Ibbotson and Bob Hodge all
led by example. The backs were inexperienced,
but Roy Blair scored some exciting tries, and
so did Michael Baker, who, together with
successful kicks, scored 110 points.

In the victory over Newport, there was an all too
rare example of flair from the backs: "Centre
Lewis Morgan went through with a beautiful
run, sent out a perfectly timed pass to David
Jones, and the outside half scored near the posts,
after a characteristic burst". Making his debut
in the Newport game was Ieuan Sheen, playing
in the centre, although he would be soon known,
and for several seasons, as a dependable full-
back. The win over Harlequins who played six
capped players, was very satisfying, and reports
of the Swansea game praised the performances
of the back row of Hodge, Ford and Ibbotson.

It fell to George Hastings as captain to try and
keep everything together which he did manfully,
although being regularly absent on England
duty. He played in all four of England's games in

the International Championship, scoring a try
against Ireland.

A worrying sign for the future was that the
Kingsholm crowd for the Bristol game was only
3,000, with the England v Wales game being
televised live at the same time.

Sep 11 Gloucester 11 Lydney 0
Tries: R.Amos, D.Ibbotson;
Conversion: M.Baker ;
Drop goal: M.Baker

Sep 18 Gloucester 32 Moseley 0
Tries: R.Blair (2), M.Baker, D.Ibbotson,
R.Sutton, P.Ford ;
Conversions: M.Baker (3), R.Blair;
Penalties: M.Baker (2)

Sep 23 Gloucester 5 Cheltenham 3
Try: D.Jones ;
Conversion: T.Jones

Sep 25 Bristol 20 Gloucester 22
Tries: D.Ibbotson, R.Blair, D.Hill;
Conversions: T.Jones (2);
Penalties: T.Jones (3)

Sep 30 Gloucester 11 Stroud 8
Tries: C.Thomas, R.Sutton;
Conversion: M.Baker ;
Penalty: M.Baker

Oct 2 Gloucester 6 Bedford 6
Try: P.Ford ;
Penalty: T.Jones

Oct 9 Gloucester 6 Richmond 18
Tries: R.Blair;
Penalty: T.Jones

Oct 16 Newport 16 Gloucester 0

Oct 23 Gloucester 5 Coventry 31
Try: G.Counsell ;
Conversion: M.Baker

**Oct 30 Oxford University 27
Gloucester 3**
Penalty: R.Blair

Nov 6 Leicester 12 Gloucester 6
Try: D.Jones ;
Penalty: D.Jones

Nov 13 Moseley 21 Gloucester 11
Try: G.Williams, R.Blair;
Conversion: R.Blair;
Drop goal: H.Terrington

Nov 20 Gloucester 3 Aberavon 16
Try: G.Hastings

Nov 27 Cardiff 9 Gloucester 8
Tries: R.Sutton, P.Ford ;
Conversion: M.Baker

Dec 4 Gloucester 3 Neath 6
Penalty: M.Baker

Dec 13 Gloucester 11 Bath 3
Tries: D.Ibbotson, M.Baker ;
Conversion: M.Baker ;
Penalty: M.Baker

Dec 20 Coventry 14 Gloucester 8
Tries: R.Sutton, P.Ford ;
Conversion: M.Baker

**Dec 26 Gloucester 13
Old Merchant Taylors 19**
Tries: D.Perks, D.Ibbotson, A.Hollingsworth ;
Conversions: M.Baker (2)

Dec 28 Gloucester 3

Universities Athletic Union 14
Try: H.Wells

Jan 1 Gloucester 8 London Scottish 12
Try: P.Ford ;
Conversion: D.Jones ;
Penalty: D.Jones

Jan 6 Gloucester v Army - cancelled due to snow

Jan 8 Gloucester 11 Leicester 9
Tries: A.Hollinsworth, M.Baker ;
Conversion: M.Baker;
Penalty: M.Baker

Jan 15 Wasps v Gloucester - cancelled due to snow

Jan 22 Gloucester 3 Bristol 3
Try: R.Parry

Jan 29 Neath 26 Gloucester 6
Tries: P.Ford, R.Blair

Feb 5 Gloucester 11 Civil Service 3
Try: R.Blair ;
Conversion: I.Sheen ;
Penalties: Sheen (2)

Feb 12 Bath 0 Gloucester 21
Tries: M.Baker, R.Blair, E.Lewis, P.Ford,
A.Meek ;
Conversions: M.Baker (3)

Feb 19 Swansea v Gloucester - cancelled due to snow
Feb 26 Gloucester v Cardiff - cancelled due to snow

Mar 5 Northampton 11 Gloucester 6
Tries: A.Hollingsworth, P.Ford

Mar 12 Gloucester 19 R.A.F. 8
Tries: M.Baker, D.Jones ;
Conversions: M.Baker (2) ;
Penalties: M.Baker (3)

**Mar 19 Gloucester 18
Guy's Hospital 0**
Tries: P.Ford, D.Ibbotson, R.Parry, R.Blair ;
Conversions: R.Blair (2), D.Jones

Mar 26 Gloucester 11 Newport 3
Tries: P.Ford, D.Jones, M.Baker ;
Conversion: M.Baker

Mar 31 Stroud 3 Gloucester 13
Tries: P.Ford, J.Varney;
Conversions: M.Baker (2);
Penalty: M.Baker

April 2 Gloucester 10 Harlequins 5
Tries: R.Blair, R.Hodge ;
Conversions: M.Baker (2)

April 4 Gloucester 6 Swansea 3
Try: P.Ford ;
Penalty: M.Baker

April 6 Cheltenham 3 Gloucester 11
Tries: P.Lewis, P.Ford ;
Conversion: M.Baker;
Penalty: M.Baker

April 9 Gloucester 11 New Brighton 6
Tries: P.Lewis, R.Sutton ;
Conversion: I.Sheen;
Penalty I.Sheen

April 11 Gloucester 16 Sale 19
Tries: C.Thomas (2), A.Hollingsworth;
Conversions: L.Morgan (2);
Penalty: L.Morgan

April 12 Gloucester 0 Lydney 3

April 16 Gloucester 3 Ebbw Vale 3
Try: G.Hastings

**April 23 Gloucester 10
Devonport Services 6**
Tries: L.Morgan, R.Hodge ;
Conversions: L.Morgan (2)

April 25 Redruth 11 Gloucester 3
Penalty: L.Morgan

April 26 Teignmouth 14 Gloucester 11
Tries: R.Blair, D.Perks ;
Conversion: L.Morgan;
Penalty: L.Morgan

April 30 Gloucester 16 Exeter 3
Tries: D.Jones, M.Baker, P.Ford, D.Ibbotson ;
Conversions: M.Baker (2)

1955-56

S.H.Davies F.Wadley A.T.Voyce T.H.Millington T.Day R.N.Loveridge W.Burrows

T.Burns(Sec) R.Morris H.Cale R.Sutton R.Parry M.Baker R.A.Clark B.Green R.Long D.A. Jones D.Solomon I.Jones Rev.H.M.Hughes(Chairman)

A.Hudson(Hon.Sec) P.Lewis I.Sheen R.Blair P.Ford(Capt) Dr.A.Alcock(Pres) D.Ibbotson G.W.Hastings C.Thomas D.Perks H.J.Balchin(Hon.Treas)

B.Reade A.Holder

Played 43 Won 16 Lost 23 Drawn 4
For 376 Against 390
Captain: Peter Ford

Gloucester United
Played 28 Won 11 Lost 14 Drawn 3
For 243 Against 290
Captain: Johnny Lowe

Most appearances: P.Ford, D.Ibbotson 41, B.Reade 38, R.Parry 37, R.Blair, B.Green 35, C.Thomas 32, A.Holder 31, M.Baker 30, G.Hastings 29, J.Wills, P.Lewis 28
Most tries: R.Blair 13, P.Lewis 11, G.Hastings 7, P.Ford 6
Conversions: M.Baker 16, A.Holder 9, R.Smart 2, I.Sheen, B.Sibery 1
Penalties: M.Baker 19, A.Holder, R.Smart 6, B.Sibery 1
Drop goal: M.Baker 1

A poor season. The number of losses was the highest in the Club's history. It was the more frustrating because the season started well with three straight wins. But after that form was very erratic. There were very good wins over Newport and Leicester, and then over the Christmas period the four games, including a 20-5 win over Neath, netted a total of 104 points. The Newport victory was indeed outstanding. The Welsh side fielded six internationals. The following match programme, singled out for special attention, "Roy Sutton, whose calm and polished display must have given heart to younger and less experienced team mates behind the scrum".

These though were the highlights accompanied by a large number of undistinguished performances. None of this detracted from the consistent endeavour of Peter Ford, who led the side by example, and his form never faltered. Much of the problem lay with the backs who lost confidence in attack and developed a leaky defence, which led to several matches being thrown away. Roy Blair and Peter Lewis topped the try scorers, but were given few opportunities in attack. For the second season running Michael Baker topped one hundred points with 104.

By and large the forwards remained a strong unit, holding their own against most sides, with Ford providing the inspiration. A lot of the pack were young and would perform better with experience. Bob Hodge playing in his final season provided stout support. He ended up playing in 258 games. Roy Parry also retired having made 270 appearances.

Having given up the Club captaincy, George Hastings was made County captain, although the season was a poor one. He also played in three England trial games.

Towards the end of the season a new social club was opened at the Worcester Street end of the ground beside the Grandstand.

Sep 10 Gloucester 16 Lydney 6
Tries: J.Wills, L.Morgan;
Conversions: M.Baker (2);
Penalties: M.Baker (2)

Sep 13 Gloucester 12
Dublin Wanderers 3
Tries: P.Ford, G.Hastings;
Penalties: M.Baker (2)

Sep 17 Gloucester 13 Moseley 6
Tries: R.Sutton (2);
Conversions: M.Baker (2);
Penalty: M Baker

Sep 21 Cheltenham 3 Gloucester 0

Sep 24 Gloucester 6 Bristol 14
Try: G.Hastings;
Penalty: M Baker

Sep 29 Stroud 3 Gloucester 8
Tries: D.Solomon, R.Sutton;
Conversion: R.Smart

Oct 1 Bedford 5 Gloucester 3
Try: J.Wills

Oct 8 Gloucester 6 Old Blues 14
Penalties: M.Baker (2)

Oct 15 Gloucester 11 Newport 6
Try: R.Blair;
Conversion: R.Smart;
Penalties: R Smart (2)

Oct 22 Coventry 28 Gloucester 9
Penalties: R.Smart (3)

**Oct 29 Gloucester 6
Oxford University 0**
Tries: R.Sutton, C.Thomas

Nov 5 Gloucester 22 Leicester 11
Tries: P.Lewis (2), B.Green, J.Wills;
Conversions: A.Holder (2);
Penalties: R Smart, A.Holder

Nov 12 Moseley 20 Gloucester 0

**Nov 16 Cambridge University 37
Gloucester 3**
Try: N.Creese

Nov 19 Aberavon 6 Gloucester 6
Tries: P.Lewis, J.Wills

Nov 26 Gloucester 3 Llanelly 6
Penalty: A Holder

Dec 3 Neath 6 Gloucester 3
Try: R.Blair

Dec 10 Gloucester 11 Bath 3
Try: R.Blair;
Conversion: M.Baker;
Penalty: M.Baker (2)

Dec 17 Gloucester 0 Coventry 3

Dec 24 Gloucester 40 Stroud 5
Tries: R.Blair (3), P.Lewis (2), D.Ibbotson,
A.Holder, G.Hastings, I.Sheen;
Conversions: M.Baker (2), A.Holder (2),
I.Sheen;
Drop goal: M.Baker

**Dec 26 Gloucester 22
Old Merchant Taylors 0**
Tries: P.Hawker (2), A.Holder, R.Blair, R.Parry;
Conversions: A.Holder (2);
Penalty: M.Baker

Dec 27 Gloucester 22

Universities Athletic Union 0
Tries: A.Holder (2), G.Hastings, M.Baker,
P.Ford, I.Sheen;
Conversions: A.Holder, M.Baker

Dec 31 Gloucester 20 Neath 5
Tries: R.Blair (3), C.Thomas (2), R.Sutton;
Conversion: A.Holder

Jan 7 London Scottish 9 Gloucester 3
Penalty: A.Holder

Jan 14 Leicester 9 Gloucester 5
Try: P.Lewis;
Conversion: M.Baker

Jan 21 Gloucester 18 Wasps 3
Tries: M.Baker, P.Lewis, R.Blair, G.Hastings,
P.Ford;
Penalty: M.Baker

Jan 28 Gloucester 3 Army 19
Penalty: M.Baker

Feb 4   Gloucester v Cardiff - cancelled due to
frozen ground
Feb 11   Gloucester v Bath - cancelled due to
frozen ground

Feb 18 Gloucester 0 Swansea 0

Feb 25 Guys Hospital v Gloucester - cancelled
due to frozen ground

Mar 3 Northampton 19 Gloucester 6
Tries: M.Baker, P.Hawker

Mar 10 Gloucester 3 R.A.F. 22
Try: P.Ford

Mar 17 Cardiff 17 Gloucester 10
Tries: C.Thomas, R.Blair;
Conversions: M.Baker (2)

Mar 24 Newport 15 Gloucester 3
Penalty: M.Baker

Mar 31 Gloucester 8 Bradford 8
Try: P.Lewis;
Conversion: M.Baker;
Penalty: M.Baker

**Apr 2 Gloucester 14
Birkenhead Park 3**
Tries: D.Ibbotson (2), P.Ford;
Conversion: B.Sibery;
Penalty: M.Baker;

Apr 3 Gloucester 8 Lydney 0
Try: B.Green;
Conversion: A.Holder;
Penalty: A.Holder

Apr 7 Gloucester 6 Harlequins 8
Try: P Lewis;
Penalty: A Holder

Apr 12 Gloucester 3 Cheltenham 3
Penalty: A.Holder

Apr 14 Bristol 11 Gloucester 0

Apr 19 Gloucester 3 Cardiff 11
Penalty: M.Baker

Apr 21 Exeter 6 Gloucester 16
Tries: G.Hastings (2); P.Lewis;
Conversions: M.Baker (2);
Penalty: M.Baker

**Apr 23 Penzance & Newlyn 14
Gloucester 9**
Tries: P.Ford, M.Baker;
Penalty: B.Sibery

Apr 24 Teignmouth 5   Gloucester 3
Penalty: M.Baker

**Apr 28 Gloucester 13
Devonport Services 10**
Tries: P.Lewis, R.Blair;
Conversion: M.Baker (2);
Penalty: M.Baker;

1956-57

**Played 44 Won 21 Lost 17 Drawn 6
For 380 Against 326
Captain: Peter Ford**

Gloucester United
Played 28 Won 18 Lost 9 Drawn 1
For 309 Against 204
Captain: Roy Sutton

Most appearances: A.Holder 38, B.Green 37,
V.Leadbetter 36, C.Thomas 35, I.Sheen 34,
B.Lane 33

Most tries: R.Blair, B.Lane 9, A.Holder,
D.Jones 6, P.Hawker, P.Ford 5
Conversions: A.Holder 12, I.Sheen 5,
G.Hastings, M.Jenkin, M.Baker 2, D.Jones 1
Penalties: A.Holder 8, G.Hastings, S.Ingram 3,
K.Ibbotson 2, M.Jenkin 1
Drop goals: D.Jones 7, K.Ibbotson, M.Jenkin 2,
A.Holder, S.Ingram, M.Booth, J.Corbett 1

The playing record showed an improvement
on the previous season, and more games were
won than lost. It was a great handicap that

Peter Ford was absent for a long period of the
season through illness, and his leadership was
sorely missed. The standard of play did not
come up to expectation as a whole, but there
was an outstanding double (the first since 1932-
33) over Newport; the win at Newport being
the first since 1938. Bristol and Northampton
were beaten at Kingsholm, whilst there were
wins over Harlequins and Coventry away, and
a draw at Swansea. The win at Coventry was
particularly satisfying as there was a clash with
the County playing on the same day, to which

T.Day R.Parry T.H.Millington(Vice-Pres) R.N.Loveridge R.Hodge I.Jones W.Burrows G.J.Dance
T.Burns(Gen.Sec) J.Herbert B.J.Lane R.Long V.H.Leadbetter B.J.Green R.A.Clark D.Solomon B.Jones C.Thomas S.H.Davies R.Morris
H.J.Balchin(Hon.Treas) J.M.Jenkin S.Ingram I.Sheen(Vice-Capt) P.Ford(Capt) E.Wakefield A.Holder R.A.Blair A.Hudson(Hon.Sec)
M.Booth D.Ibbotson

the club supplied five players.

As normal the strength of the team lay with the forwards. Cyril Thomas was outstanding at hooker. He was ably supported by the ex-Northampton player Vic Leadbetter and George Hastings. Hastings was restored to the England team and played in all four of England's Championship games, and toured Canada with the Barbarians.

Yet again the backs were not penetrative, and several combinations were tried without a lot of success. Playing in his second season, a young back, Alan Holder, showed enough to suggest he would be a valuable asset to the club in future seasons, as did debutant Mickey Booth at scrum-half.

South-West Counties played South African Universities at Kingsholm. Ieuan Sheen and Cyril Thomas played for Counties.

Sep 8 Gloucester 15 Lydney 8
Tries: R.Blair (2), D.Perks;
Penalties: G.Hastings (2)

Sep 15 Gloucester 6 Bucharest 10
Penalty: A.Holder;
Drop goal: A.Holder

Sep 20 Gloucester 3 Moseley 6
Drop goal: M.Jenkin

Sep 22 Gloucester 28 Exeter 5
Tries: P.Ford (2), M.Craig, I.Sheen, M.Jenkin, R.Blair;
Conversions: A.Holder, M.Jenkin;
Penalty: A.Holder;
Drop goal: D.Jones

Sep 27 Gloucester 0 Cheltenham 0

Sep 29 Bristol 29 Gloucester 17
Tries: D.Jones, D.A.Jones;
Conversion: G.Hastings;
Penalties: G.Hastings, A.Holder;
Drop goal: D.Jones

Oct 6 Gloucester 6 Bedford 3
Tries: P.Lewis (2)

Oct 13 Gloucester 16 Old Blues 3
Tries: P.Lewis, J.Corbett, K.Ibbotson;
Conversions: M.Baker (2);
Drop goal: J.Corbett

Oct 20 Newport 6 Gloucester 8
Try: C.Thomas;
Conversion: I.Sheen;
Drop goal: D.Jones

Oct 27 Coventry 9 Gloucester 11
Tries: A.Holder, V.Leadbetter;
Conversion: M.Jenkin;
Penalty: M.Jenkin

Nov 3 Leicester 14 Gloucester 8

Scorers unknown

Nov 10 Moseley 12 Gloucester 3
Drop goal: M.Jenkin

Nov 17 Gloucester 9 Aberavon 9
Tries: M.Jenkin, G.Hastings, B.Lane

Nov 24 Llanelly 31 Gloucester 3
Try: R.Blair

Dec 1 Oxford University 14 Gloucester 8
Try: B.Lane;
Conversion: A.Holder;
Penalty: A.Holder

Dec 8 Gloucester 27 Bath 6
Tries: R.Blair (2), M.Jenkin (2), M.Booth;
Conversions: I.Sheen (3);
Penalties: I.Sheen (2)

Dec 15 Gloucester 3 Coventry 3
Try: D.Jones

Dec 22 Stroud 3 Gloucester 0

Dec 29 Neath 0 Gloucester 3
Penalty: A.Holder

Jan 5 Gloucester 3 London Scottish 3
Try: M.Booth

Jan 10 Gloucester 3 Army 6

Penalty: A.Holder

Jan 12 Gloucester 0 Leicester 6

Jan 19 Wasps 22 Gloucester 6
Try: A.Holder;
Drop goal: S.Ingram

Jan 26   Gloucester 11   Cambridge University 0
Tries: D.Jones, B.Jones, P.Hawker;
Conversion: A.Holder

Jan 31 Gloucester 10 Royal Navy 0
Tries: R.Blair, P.Hawker;
Conversions: A.Holder (2)

Feb 2 Gloucester 21 Bristol 3
Tries: P.Hawker (2), D.Jones, G.Hastings;
Conversions: A.Holder (3);
Penalty: A.Holder

Feb 9 Bath 11 Gloucester 0

Feb 16 Swansea 0 Gloucester 0

Feb 23 Gloucester 3 Neath 3
Penalty: A.Holder

Mar 2 Gloucester 12 Northampton 6
Try: B.Lane;
Drop goals: D.Jones (3)

Mar 9 Gloucester 6 R.A.F. 8
Tries: P.Ford, B.Lane

Mar 16 Gloucester 17 Guy's Hospital 0
Tries: B.Lane, M.Craig, A.Holder, P.Hawker;
Conversion: D.Jones;
Drop goal: D.Jones

Mar 23 Cardiff 6 Gloucester 3
Penalty: S.Ingram

Mar 30 Gloucester 12 Newport 6
Tries: D.Jones (2), V.Leadbetter, I.Sheen

Apr 6 Harlequins 16 Gloucester 19
Tries: A.Holder, B.Lane, R.Blair, R.Craig;
Conversions: A.Holder, G.Hastings;
Drop goal: M.Booth

Apr 10 Cheltenham 0 Gloucester 11
Tries: A.Holder, E.Wakefield, B.Lane;
Conversion: A.Holder

Apr 13 Gloucester 0 Cardiff 11

Apr 16 Gloucester 6 Stroud 0
Try: E.Wakefield;
Penalty: S.Ingram

Apr 20 Gloucester 9 New Brighton 11
Tries: B.Lane, J.Hart, J.Hancock

Apr 22 Gloucester 12 Sale 31
Try: J.Hart;
Penalties: K.Ibbotson, S.Ingram;
Drop goal: K.Ibbotson

Apr 23 Lydney 0 Gloucester 14
Tries: P.Ford, J.Hancock;
Conversion: I.Sheen;
Penalty: K.Ibbotson;
Drop goal: K.Ibbotson

Apr 27 Gloucester 11 Devonport Services 0
Tries: E.Wakefield, B.Lane, R.Blair;
Conversion: A.Holder

Apr 29 Teignmouth 3 Gloucester 11
Tries: P.Ford, I.Sheen, E.Wakefield;
Conversion: A.Holder

Apr 30 Weston-S-Mare 3 Gloucester 6
Tries: A.Holder, I.Oakes

1957-58

G.J.Dance R.Parry T.Day A.T.Voyce(Vice-Pres) A.G.Hudson T.H.Millington(Vice-Pres) R.N.Loveridge R.C.Upham R.Sutton
S.H.Davies B.Hudson L.King V.H.Leadbetter J.Sainsbury B.J.Green J.Herbert P.Hawker D.Haine R.Smith
Rev.H.M.Hughes(Chairman) H.J.Balchin(Hon.Treas) D.Ibbotson B.J.Lane I.Sheen P.Ford(Capt) Arnold Alcock(Pres) C.Thomas A.Holder K.Ibbotson
A.Hudson(Hon.Sec) T.Burns(Gen.Sec)
M.Booth D.Phelps

Played 44 Won 26 Lost 15 Drawn 3
For 382 Against 335
Captain: Peter Ford

Gloucester United
Played 29 Won 16 Lost 10 Drawn 3
For 281 Against 203
Captain: Les King

Most appearances: A.Holder 40, M.Booth 39, C.Thomas, D.Ibbotson 36, Bob Smith 35, J.Herbert 34, P.Hawker, D.Phelps 32, B.Lane 31, V.Leadbetter 29
Most tries: Bob Smith 13, A.Holder 9, P.Ford 8, D.Ibbotson 7
Conversions: P.Hawker 7, S.Ingram 6, A.Holder, I.Sheen, G.Hastings 4, D.Haine 1
Penalties: A.Holder, I.Sheen 6, S.Ingram 5, A.Holder 4, G.Hastings 1
Drop goals: K.Ibbotson 3, S.Ingram, P.Lewis, M.Booth, D.Phelps 1

A mixed season. It started well including a remarkable win at Coventry when the team was six short of its best players who were playing for Gloucestershire on the same day. In the next game Leicester were defeated at Kingsholm. However, there followed a run of six consecutive defeats. In late December Cardiff visited Kingsholm having only lost two games, whilst Gloucester had been defeated in eight of their last ten. The Cherry and Whites pulled off a famous win, when, in the only score of the game Alan Holder kicked a penalty from 40 yards. This success seemed to inspire the team, for in the second half of the season 17 out of 23 games were won. This included an away win at Northampton, and the completion of the double over Leicester.

In his second season as captain, Peter Ford was as inspirational as before, and received strong support from Cyril Thomas, Vic Leadbetter and Dennis Ibbotson. George Hastings only played in 17 games due to England calls. He won caps against Wales, Ireland, Scotland (penalty), France (penalty and conversion) and Australia.

The backs were again erratic. Bob Smith scored 13 tries on the wing, but place kicking was a weakness. Stan Ingram, Peter Hawker, Alan Holder, Ieuan Sheen and George Hastings were all tried, but found to be inconsistent. This weakness led to the loss of several games. Winger Roy Blair only played in two early season games, before moving on to Cinderford. He had scored 36 tries in 106 appearances

Western Counties played Australia at Bristol. Ieuan Sheen, Peter Ford and George Hastings played for Counties.

Sep 9 Gloucester 11 Waterloo 3
Tries: P.Ford, D.Jones, P.Hawker;
Conversion: S.Ingram

Sep 14 Gloucester 3 Lydney 0
Penalty: S.Ingram

Sep 19 Newport 24 Gloucester 6
Penalties: S.Ingram (2)

Sep 21 Gloucester 16 Moseley 3
Tries: M.Jenkin (2), M.Craig, P.Ford;
Conversions: S.Ingram (2)

Sep 25 Cheltenham 5 Gloucester 3
Try: P.Ford

Sep 28 Gloucester 9 Bristol 3
Try: I.Sheen;
Penalty: I.Sheen;
Drop goal: P.Lewis

Oct 5 Bedford 9 Gloucester 9
Tries: P.Lewis, D.Ibbotson;
Penalty: S.Ingram

Oct 12 Gloucester 22 Old Blues 0
Tries: R.Long, B.Jones, R.Sutton, D.Ibbotson;
Conversions: P.Hawker (2);
Penalties: P.Hawker (2)

Oct 19 Gloucester 18 Civil Service 18
Tries: A.Holder (3), B.Green ;
Conversions: P.Hawker (3)

Oct 26 Coventry 3 Gloucester 6
Try: C.Lynch ;
Drop goal: S.Ingram

Nov 2 Gloucester 12 Leicester 8
Tries: A.Holder, P.Ford, P.Hawker ;
Penalty: P.Hawker

Nov 9 Moseley 17 Gloucester 11
Tries: D.Ibbotson, D.Soloman, B.Lane ;
Conversion: D.Haine

Nov 16 Aberavon 11 Gloucester 3
Penalty: P.Hawker

Nov 20 Gloucester 8
Cambridge University 13
Tries: A.Holder, P.Ford ;
Conversion: S.Ingram

Nov 23 Cardiff 12 Gloucester 0

Nov 30 Gloucester 6
Oxford University 8
Try: G.Hastings;
Penalty: I.Sheen

Dec 3 Neath 11 Gloucester 3
Try: Bob Smith

Dec 14 Bath 6 Gloucester 9
Tries: B.Lane, Bob Smith, B.Green

Dec 21 Gloucester 10 Coventry 18
Tries: P.Hawker, B.Lane;
Conversions: P.Hawker (2)

Dec 26 Gloucester 12
Old Merchant Taylors 9
Tries: Bob Smith (2), P.Hawker ;
Penalty: A.Holder

Dec 27 Gloucester 3
Universities Athletic Union 19
Try: D.Ibbotson

Dec 28 Gloucester 3 Cardiff 0
Penalty: A.Holder

Jan 4 London Scottish 6 Gloucester 9
Tries: Bob Smith, P.Hawker, M.Jenkin

Jan 11 Leicester 0 Gloucester 11
Tries: P.Ford, D.Ibbotson, G.Hastings ;
Conversion: S.Ingram

Jan 18 Gloucester 17 Wasps 0
Tries: V.Leadbetter, Bob Smith, P.Ford ;
Conversion: S.Ingram;
Penalty: S.Ingram;
Drop goal: K.Ibbotson

Jan 25 Gloucester v Army - cancelled

Feb 1 Bristol 17 Gloucester 11
Tries: D.Ibbotson, B.Lane, P.Ford ;
Conversion: A.Holder

Feb 6 Gloucester 0 Royal Navy 21

Feb 8 Gloucester 15 Bath 3
Tries: Bob Smith, V.Leadbetter, C.Thomas ;
Penalty: A.Holder;
Drop goal: K.Ibbotson

Feb 15 Gloucester 0 Swansea 3

Feb 22 Gloucester 11
Devonport Services 0
Tries: Bob Smith, B.Green;
Conversion: A.Holder;
Penalty: A.Holder

Mar 1 Northampton 5 Gloucester 9
Tries: B.Jones, A.Holder ;
Drop goal: D.Phelps

Mar 8 Gloucester 10 R.A.F. 6

Tries: I.Sheen, P.Hawker ;
Conversions: G.Hastings (2)

**Mar 15   Guy's Hospital 14
Gloucester 3**
Try: J.Hancock

Mar 22   Gloucester 6   Newport 8
Try: B.Lane;
Penalty: G.Hastings

Mar 29   Stroud 3   Gloucester 8
Tries: Bob Smith, K.Ibbotson;
Conversion: G.Hastings

April 5   Gloucester 11   Headingley 9
Tries: Bob Smith, D.Phelps;
Conversion: I.Sheen;

Penalty: I.Sheen

**April 7   Gloucester 14
Birkenhead Park 8**
Tries: Bob Smith, M.Booth ;
Conversion: I.Sheen;
Penalty: I.Sheen;
Drop goal: M.Booth

April 8   Lydney 3   Gloucester 13
Tries: A.Holder (2), B.Lane;
Conversions: I.Sheen, A.Holder

April 12   Gloucester 5   Neath 3
Try: D.Ibbotson;
Conversion: G.Hastings

April 17   Gloucester 9   Cheltenham 6

Try: Bob Smith;
Penalty: I.Sheen;
Drop goal: D.Ibbotson

April 19   Gloucester 12   Stroud 0
Tries: D.Haine, V.Leadbetter, B.Green
Penalty: I.Sheen

April 26   Exeter 11   Gloucester 13
Tries: A.Holder, M.Booth, Bob Smith ;
Conversions: I.Sheen, A.Holder

April 28   Torquay 6   Gloucester 9
Try: D.Haine, Penalties: A.Holder (2)

**April 29   Weston-S-Mare 3
Gloucester 3**
Try: K.Ibbotson

1958-59

T.Day E.Martin G.Dance T.H.Millington R.Upham(Hon.Treas)
R.Morris T.Lewis A.Ricketts R.Timms B.Hudson L.King W.M.Patterson R.Smith(Dick) R.Smith(Bob) R.Chamberlayne S.Davies
H.J.Balchin(Gen.Sec) A.T.Voyce B.Green P.Ford C.Thomas(Capt) A.Alcock Esq(Pres) A.Holder G.Hastings D.Ibbotson Rev.H.M.Hughes(Chairman)
A.Hudson(Hon.Sec)
K.Ibbotson M.Booth

**Played 42 Won 17 Lost 21 Drawn 4
For 361 Against 431
Captain: Cyril Thomas**

Gloucester United
Played 29 Won 14 Lost 12 Drawn 3
For 358 Against 218
Captain: Les King

Most appearances: P.Ford 38, D.Ibbotson 35,
A.Holder 34, B.Green 33, C.Thomas 31

Most tries: P.Ford 16, M.Booth 6, D.Phelps,
D.Ibbotson, A.Ricketts, R.Timms,
W.Patterson 5
Most conversions: G.Hastings 9, I.Sheen 6
Penalties: I.Sheen 7, M.Booth 6, A.Holder 3,
B.Sibery 1
Drop goals: D.Phelps, M.Booth 2, A.Holder 1

A poor season, where losses easily outnumbered
victories. The first four games were won, but
soon a pattern of narrow defeats was established,

although there were some heavy losses to
Newport and Swansea, plus a thrashing by
Northampton. at Kingsholm. There was a good
win at Leicester, and one at home against Neath,
(when legend Dick Smith played his first game),
but these were exceptions. Place kicking again
was a weakness, making it even harder to close
games out.

As in former seasons the backs lacked
penetration. The problem was so acute that on

occasions Dick Smith was removed from the forwards to play in the centre or on the wing. What could be achieved by a class back was demonstrated in the seven games Bill Patterson played in the centre. The Sale and British Lion scored five tries, displaying flair and initiative to thrill the Kingsholm faithful.

The forwards as ever were strong. Cyril Thomas led the team well, and the pack was seldom outplayed. That this was the Club's strength was shown by the fact that Peter Ford, by a distance, was top try scorer. George Hastings (who retired at the end of the season after 260 games, and 13 England caps), Dennis Ibbotson, Brian Green and Dick Smith were also outstanding. Roy Sutton played in only one game and retired after making 224 appearances. Michael Baker left Gloucester after 180 appearances, and went on to play for, and captain, Weston-super-Mare.

George Hastings played in three England trial games, and Mickey Booth in one. Gloucestershire reached the final of the Championship, before losing to Warwickshire at Bristol. Gloucester players were Ieuan Sheen, Alan Holder, Mickey Booth, George Hastings and Brian Green.

Sep 13 Gloucester 40 Lydney 8
Tries: P.Ford (3), V.Leadbetter, D.Ibbotson, M.Booth, D.Phelps;
Conversions: G.Hastings (5);
Penalties: G.Hastings (3)

Sep 18 Gloucester 23 Milan 9
Tries: M.Booth, P.Ford, D.Phelps, A.Holder, V.Leadbetter, D.Ibbotson;
Conversion: I.Sheen;
Penalty: A.Holder

Sep 20 Gloucester 9 Moseley 6
Tries: J.Hart (2), D.Phelps

Sep 25 Gloucester 9 Cheltenham 5
Tries: P Ford (2);
Drop goal: M.Booth

Sep 27 Gloucester 3 Bristol 13
Penalty: G.Hastings

Oct 1 Pontypool 14 Gloucester 3
Try: J.Hart

Oct 4 Gloucester 13 Bedford 3
Tries: D.Ibbotson, D.Phelps, C.Thomas;
Conversions: G.Hastings (2)

Oct 11 Gloucester 9 Old Blues 6
Tries: P.Ford (2), J.Herbert

Oct 18 Newport 30 Gloucester 3
Penalty: G.Hastings

Oct 25 Coventry 3 Gloucester 0

Nov 1 Leicester 6 Gloucester 12
Tries: J.Buckland, A.Ricketts;
Penalties: A.Holder (2)

Nov 8 Moseley 14 Gloucester 11
Tries: A.Ricketts, T.Preedy, P.Ford;
Conversion: P.Hawker

Nov 15 Gloucester 8 Aberavon 15
Try: J.Buckland;
Conversion: G.Hastings;
Penalty: G.Hastings

Nov 22 Gloucester 5 Cardiff 11
Try: A.Ricketts; Conversion: A.Holder

Nov 29 Oxford University 16 Gloucester 8
Tries: C.Thomas, P.Ford;
Conversion: A.Holder

Dec 6 Gloucester 10 Neath 8
Tries: P.Ford (2);
Conversions: I.Sheen (2)

Dec 13 Gloucester 8 Bath 8
Tries: Dick Smith, V.Leadbetter;
Conversion: A.Ricketts

Dec 20 Gloucester 3 Coventry 3
Try: P.Hawker

Dec 26 Gloucester 20 Old Merchant Taylors 3
Tries: Dick Smith, P.Hawker, D.Phelps, J.King, M.Booth ;
Conversion: M.Baker;
Drop goal: D.Phelps

Dec 27 Gloucester 3 Universities Athletic Union 14
Try: G.Hastings

Jan 3 Gloucester 3 London Scottish 0
Try: M.Booth

Jan 10 Gloucester v Leicester - cancelled due to frost
Jan 17 Wasps v Gloucester - cancelled due to frost

Jan 24 Gloucester 3 Cambridge University 22
Try: P.Ford

Jan 31 Gloucester 0 Army 3

Feb 5 Gloucester 12 Royal Navy 20
Tries: P.Ford (2), D.Ibbotson, A.Ricketts

Feb 7 Gloucester 6 Bristol 19
Try: G.Hastings; Penalty: I.Sheen

Feb 14 Bath 3 Gloucester 3
Try: A.Ricketts

Feb 21 Swansea 25 Gloucester 3
Try: C.Thomas

Feb 28 Gloucester 14 Pontypool 21
Tries: G.Hastings, A.Holder, W.Patterson;
Conversion: I.Sheen;
Penalty: I.Sheen

Mar 7 Gloucester 3 Northampton 33
Drop goal: M.Booth

Mar 14 Gloucester 16 R.A.F. 19
Tries: I.Sheen, W.Patterson, R.Long;
Conversions: K.Ibbottson (2);
Penalty: I.Sheen

Mar 21 Gloucester 14 Guy's Hospital 11
Tries: W.Patterson (2), Dick Smith (2);
Conversion: G.Hastings

Mar 28 Gloucester 22 New Brighton 11
Tries: A.Holder, Bob Smith;
Conversions: I.Sheen (2);
Penalties: I.Sheen (3);
Drop goal: D Phelps

Mar 30 Gloucester 12 Sale 16
Tries: A.Holder, P.Ford, G.Mace;
Penalty: B.Sibery

Mar 31 Lydney 0 Gloucester 3
Penalty: I.Sheen

April 4 Gloucester 3 Llanelli 3
Try: J.King

April 11 Cardiff 8 Gloucester 3
Try: Bob Smith

April 15 Cheltenham 0 Gloucester 6
Tries: K.Ibbotson, R.Timms

April 18 Gloucester 0 Newport 8

Apr 23 Gloucester 17 Stroud 0
Tries: R.Timms (2), G.Wells, I.Oakes, W.Patterson;
Conversion: S.Ingram

April 25 Devonport Services 6

Gloucester 9
Tries: R.Timms, M.Booth;
Drop goal: A.Holder

Tries: R.Timms, D.Ibbotson, M.Booth

1959-60

R.Morris J.A'Bear R.B.Brett G.Dance R.Sutton E.Day
F.D.H.Dawe(Hon.Treas) R.Fowke J.Taylor D.Owen R.Timms R.Long A.Townsend B.Green P.Meadows B.Kear I.Sheen J.Lowe
H.J.Balchin(Gen.Sec) T.Millington D.Ibbotson C.Thomas P.Ford(Capt) A.Alcock (Pres) A.Holder D.Smith(Dick) R.Smith(Bob) T.Day
Rev.H.M.Hughes(Chairman)
M.Booth G.Mace T.Hopson

Played 42 Won 26 Lost 14 Drawn 2
For 521 Against 377
Captain: Peter Ford

Gloucester United
Played 29 Won 19 Lost 9 Drawn 1
For 479 Against 214
Captain: Les King

Most Appearances: T.Hopson 41, Dick
Smith 40, A.Townsend 40, B.Kear 38, P.Ford
38, R.Fowke 38, A.Holder 37, R.Timms 35,
M.Booth 35, R.Long 34, C.Thomas 34
Most Tries: Bob Smith 12, R.Timms 11,
T.Hopson 10, P.Ford 9
Conversions: J.Taylor 21, A.Holder 10
Penalties: J.Taylor 18
Dropped goals: M.Booth 10, T.Hopson 3

A season when there were remarkably few
injuries, meant that the same fifteen was able
to turn out week after week. The resulting
stability fired confidence, and there was a run
of 13 successive wins, which established a
Club record. All this would have seemed highly
unlikely after the first game of the season
resulted in a loss to Stroud at Kingsholm.

However, as the team bedded down, some
very stylish rugby was played. Terry Hopson,
a recruit from Bath, immediately made the
fly-half position his own and an outstanding
partnership was developed with Mickey Booth
at scrum-half. Booth was the perfect foil to the
mercurial Hopson. Alan Holder was solid at
full-back. On the wings Bob Smith and Bob
Timms were the top try scorers, receiving good
service from centres Jeremy Taylor and Brian
Kear. That excellent club man, full-back Ieuan
Sheen, who would, when required, also turn out
at centre or fly-half, retired after making 117
appearances.

As always, the forwards were formidable. Cyril
Thomas, who won a long overdue England trial
game, yet again out-hooked all-comers, and
was ably propped by Roy Fowke and Allan
Townsend. In the second row Roy Long and
Tony Ricketts gave sterling service, whilst the
back-row of Peter Ford, Dick Smith and Dave
Morris was one of the best in the country.
Dennis Ibbotson played in only nine games and
retired at the end of the season, having played
since 1949 and made 337 appearances.

The 13-game winning sequence included
doubles over Coventry and Bath, with other
victories over Aberavon, and away at Neath. The
second half of the season was less successful,
with as many defeats as wins. But in April there
was a fine win over Cardiff at Kingsholm.

Jeremy Taylor brought a very welcome solution
to the perennial place-kicking problems and
scored 111 points. Mickey Booth chipped away
all season with drop goals, scoring ten in all.

Sep 10 Gloucester 14 Stroud 17
Tries: B.Kear, G.Mace;
Conversion: I.Sheen;
Penalties: I.Sheen (2)

Sep 12 Gloucester 28 Lydney 15
Tries: D.Ibbotson (2), R.Timms (2), P.Ford,
R.Fowke;
Conversions: I.Sheen (2);
Drop goals: M.Booth (2)

Sep 16 Cheltenham 5 Gloucester 8
Tries: M.Booth, B.Green;
Conversion: A.Holder

Sep 19   Gloucester 14   Moseley 6
Tries: M.Booth, D.Ibbotson, R.Timms;
Conversion: J.Taylor;
Penalty: J.Taylor

Sep 23   Cardiff 17   Gloucester 9
Try: R.Timms;
Penalty: G.Hale;
Drop goal: A.Holder

Sep 26   Gloucester 11   Bristol 25
Tries: P.Ford, B.Green;
Conversion: A.Holder;
Penalty: A.Holder

Sep 30   Pontypool 25   Gloucester 6
Try: R.Fowke;
Drop goal: M.Booth

Oct 3   Bedford 8   Gloucester 8
Try: L.King;
Conversion: I.Sheen;
Penalty: A.Holder

Oct 10   Gloucester 13   Old Blues 0
Tries: T.Hopson (2), Bob Smith;
Conversions: G.Hale (2)

Oct 17   Gloucester 6   Newport 11
Try: A.Holder;
Penalty: J.Taylor

Oct 24   Gloucester 20   Coventry 9
Tries: T.Hopson (2), A.Ricketts, R.Timms;
Conversion: J.Taylor;
Penalties: J.Taylor (2)

Oct 31   Gloucester 5
Oxford University 3
Try: P.Ford;
Conversion: G.Hale

Nov 7   Gloucester 18   Leicester 3
Tries: R.Timms, A.Holder, P.Ford, D.Morris,
T.Hopson;
Penalty: G.Hale

Nov 14   Moseley 3   Gloucester 18
Tries: D.Morris, T.Hopson, J.King;
Conversions: G.Hastings (3);
Drop goal: T.Hopson

Nov 18   Cambridge University 6
Gloucester 10
Tries: B.Kear, J.Taylor;
Conversions: J.Taylor (2)

Nov 21   Gloucester 16   Aberavon 6
Tries: C.Thomas, Bob Smith;
Conversions: J.Taylor (2);
Penalty: J.Taylor;

Drop goal: M.Booth

Nov 28   Gloucester 9   Bath 3
Tries: P.Ford, D.Morris, Bob Smith

Dec 5   Neath 3   Gloucester 12
Try: Bob Smith;
Penalties: J.Taylor (2);
Drop goal: M.Booth

Dec 12   Bath 8   Gloucester 26
Tries: D.Morris (2), A.Ricketts, Dick Smith,
J.Taylor, R.Fowke;
Conversions: J.Taylor (4)

Dec 19   Coventry 0   Gloucester 5
Try: T.Hopson;
Conversion: J.Taylor

Dec 26   Gloucester 23
Old Merchant Taylors 11
Tries: Bob Smith, J.Taylor, C.Thomas,
T.Hopson;
Conversions: J.Taylor (3), A.Holder;
Drop goal: M.Booth

Dec 28   Gloucester 17
Universities Athletic Union 11
Tries: P.Ford, R.Timms;
Conversion: J.Taylor;
Drop goals: B.Kear, Bob Smith, M.Booth

Jan 2   London Scottish 0   Gloucester 11
Tries: B.Kear, M.Booth;
Conversion: J.Taylor;
Drop goal: M.Booth

Jan 9   Leicester 6   Gloucester 3
Penalty: J.Taylor

Jan 16   Gloucester v Wasps - cancelled due to snow

Jan 23   Aberavon 11   Gloucester 6
Try: D.Morris;
Penalty: J.Taylor

Jan 30   Gloucester 16   Army 3
Tries: J.Taylor, D.Morris;
Conversions: J.Taylor (2);
Penalties: J.Taylor (2)

Feb 6   Bristol 11   Gloucester 0

Feb 13   Gloucester v Bath - cancelled due to snow

Feb 20   Gloucester 6   Swansea 6
Tries: R.Fowke, P.Ford

Feb 27   Gloucester 9   Pontypool 18

Tries: J.Bellamy, C.Ravenhill;
Penalty: J.Taylor

Mar 5   Northampton 28   Gloucester 9
Penalties: J.Taylor (2);
Drop goal: T.Hopson

Mar 12   Gloucester 14   R.A.F. 8
Tries: R.Timms (2), R.Long;
Conversion: J.Taylor;
Penalty: J.Taylor

Mar 19   Llanelly 16   Gloucester 6
Try: G.Mace;
Penalty: J.Taylor

Mar 26   Newport 11   Gloucester 10
Tries: A.Townsend, J.Taylor;
Conversions: J.Taylor (2)

Apr 2   Gloucester 9   Richmond 5
Penalty: J.Taylor;
Drop goals: T.Hopson, M.Booth

Apr 7   Gloucester 11   Cheltenham 6
Tries: J.Fowke, Dick Smith;
Conversion: J.Taylor;
Penalty: J.Taylor

Apr 9   Gloucester 10   Cardiff 6
Tries: T.Hopson, Dick Smith;
Conversions: I.Sheen (2)

Apr 16   Gloucester 5   Headingley 10
Try: D.Owen;
Conversion: I.Sheen

Apr 18   Gloucester 38
Birkenhead Park 8
Tries: Bob Smith (4), P.Meadows, T.Hopson,
Dick Smith, R.Timms, G.Mace, A.Holder
Conversions: A.Holder (3), P.Meadows

Apr 19   Lydney 0   Gloucester 15
Tries: Bob Smith, R.Timms, R.Fowke,
C.Thomas;
Drop goal: M.Booth

Apr 23   New Brighton 8   Gloucester 14
Tries: P.Ford, Bob Smith, R.Fowke;
Conversion: A.Holder;
Penalty: A.Holder

Apr 25   Sale 10   Gloucester 3
Try: A.Holder

Apr 30   Gloucester 30
Devonport Services 11
Tries: J.Lowe (2), Bob Smith, Dick Smith,
P.Meadows, M.Booth, P.Ford, B.Green
Conversions: A.Holder (3)

1960-61

G.Dance J.Hickie T.Day R.Morris R.B.Brett J.Reid A.Beattie T.Millington(Vice-Pres)

H.J.Balchin(Gen.Sec) R.Chamberlayne F.Smith R.Long B.Hudson A.Townsend A.Brinn T.Davies H.Symonds R.Smith K.Taylor R.Sutton Rev.H.M.Hughes

F.D.Dawe(Hon.Treas) J.Taylor R.Timms J.King P.Ford(Capt) A.Alcock (Pres) A.Holder R.J.Hillier P.Hole P.Meadows A.Hudson(Hon.Sec) G.Mace T.Hopson

Played 48 Won 18 Lost 22 Drawn 8
For 409 Against 439
Captain: Peter Ford

Gloucester United
Played 28 Won 19 Lost 6 Drawn 3
For 344 Against 137
Captain: Les King

Most appearances: A.Holder 48, T.Hopson 43, A.Townsend 41, P.Ford 40, Dick Smith 40, A.Brinn 37, R.Long 36, J.Fowke 35, G.Mace 34
Most tries: T.Hopson 16, Bob Smith 13, P.Ford 12, Dick Smith 9, J.King 8
Conversions: J.Taylor 15, R.Hillier 9, A.Holder 2, P.Ford, P.Meadows, G.Hale 1
Penalties: A.Holder 7, J.Taylor 4, R.Hillier 2, P.Ford 1
Drop goals: T.Hopson 2, A.Holder, M.Booth 1

Following the previous season which showed so much promise, this campaign was very disappointing. More games were lost than won. The lack of a dependable goal-kicker again led to many losses. Under 30% of the tries scored were converted, and only 14 penalties were scored all season. The defeat against Coventry in December was particularly galling. Gloucester played all the rugby, scored three tries to one, but still lost, because in George Cole, Coventry had a good kicker. In the Plymouth Albion game at Kingsholm, Peter Ford scored a try to square the score with

time about up. He was obviously frustrated by the number of missed kicks during the game and decided to take the conversion kick from the touchline himself. The kick hit one post, bounced on the cross bar and went over!

In April a match was played against an International XV including 12 England and Wales capped players. The proceeds went towards changing quarters at the Memorial Ground in Tuffley Avenue, which had been a longstanding project to provide pitches and facilities for local clubs.

Although a disappointing season, there were, however, some good days, including a thrilling victory over a very in-form Northampton. Neath were also beaten, and there was a very creditable draw at Moseley, when the team was depleted by County commitments.

Terry Hopson (the top try scorer) and Gary Mace formed an effective half-back pairing. Mickey Booth was only available on occasions due to commitments with the RAF. The backs lacked penetration, although Bob Smith and Jim King had their moments. As usual the forwards were the backbone of the team, with an outstanding back-row in Peter Ford, Dave Owen and Dick Smith. Brian Green played a few games early in the season and then moved on to Lydney after 172 appearances. Longstanding hooker, Cyril Thomas, whose

career had started in 1948, played until the end of 1960, and retired from top class rugby to play for Gloucestershire Police. He had appeared in 357 games. Peter Ford said of him: "the best hooker I ever played with".

There was mounting concern over falling gates, due to the televising of sport on Saturday afternoons.

Peter Ford played for Western Counties against South Africa at Kingsholm.

Sep 5 Gloucester 26 Waterloo 14
Tries: Bob Smith (4), T.Hopson, Dick Smith, J.Taylor;
Conversion: J.Taylor;
Drop goal: A.Holder

Sep 7 Cardiff 14 Gloucester 0

Sep 10 Gloucester 14 Lydney 14
Tries: Bob Smith (2), J.Bellamy, T.Hopson;
Conversion: J.Taylor

Sep 15 Stroud 0 Gloucester 8
Tries: J.Taylor, penalty try;
Conversion: J.Taylor

Sep 17 Gloucester 10 Moseley 5
Tries: T.Hopson, Bob Smith;
Conversions: J.Taylor (2)

Sep 22 Gloucester 3 Cheltenham 3
Penalty: J.Taylor

Sep 24 Bristol 16 Gloucester 13
Tries: T.Hopson, P.Ford;
Conversions: J.Taylor (2);
Penalty: J.Taylor

Sep 28 Pontypool v Gloucester - cancelled due to flooded pitch

Oct 1 Gloucester 11 Bedford 6
Tries: Bob Smith, T.Hopson, H.Symonds;
Conversion: J.Taylor

Oct 8 Gloucester 6 Neath 0
Penalty: J.Taylor;
Drop goal: T.Hopson

Oct 15 Newport 15 Gloucester 14
Tries: T.Hopson, Bob Smith, C.Thomas,
R.Timms;
Conversion: J.Taylor

Oct 22 Coventry 12 Gloucester 3
Try: T.Hopson

**Oct 29 Oxford University 11
Gloucester 6**
Try: P.Ford;
Penalty: A.Holder

Nov 5 Gloucester 11 Leicester 8
Tries: A.Holder, Bob Smith, J.Bayliss;
Conversion: P.Meadows

Nov 12 Moseley 6 Gloucester 6
Tries: T.Hopson (2)

Nov 19 Gloucester 3 Aberavon 13
Try: J.Fowke

Nov 26 Gloucester 0 Old Blues 0

Dec 3 Gloucester 8 Plymouth Albion 6
Tries: P.Ford, Dick Smith;
Conversion: P.Ford

Dec 10 Gloucester v Bath - cancelled due to flooded pitch

Dec 17 Gloucester 15 Coventry 17
Tries: Dick Smith (2), C.Thomas;
Penalty: P.Ford;
Drop goal: M.Booth

Dec 24 Gloucester 11 Pontypool 19
Tries: M.Booth, D.Smith;

Conversion: J.Taylor;
Penalty: J.Taylor

**Dec 26 Gloucester 9
Old Merchant Taylors 6**
Tries: J.Taylor, T.Hopson, M.Booth

**Dec 27 Gloucester 5
Universities Athletic Union 8**
Try: M.Booth;
Conversion: J.Taylor

Dec 31 Gloucester 8 Newbridge 3
Tries: P.Meadows, R.Fowke;
Conversion: J.Taylor

Jan 7 Gloucester 8 London Scottish 8
Tries: T.Hopson, P.Ford;
Conversion: G.Hale

Jan 14 Leicester 21 Gloucester 3
Try: P.Ford

Jan 21 Wasps 10 Gloucester 6
Tries: P.Ford (2)

Jan 26 Gloucester 16 Army 9
Tries: J.King (2), G.Mace;
Conversions: R.Hillier (2);
Penalty: R.Hillier

**Jan 28 Gloucester 3
Cambridge University 3**
Try: T.Hopson

Feb 4 Gloucester 6 Bristol 13
Penalties: A.Holder (2)

Feb 11 Gloucester 17 Bath 8
Tries: H.Symonds, A.Townsend, T.Hopson,
Dick Smith, R.Timms;
Conversion: R.Hillier

Feb 18 Swansea 10 Gloucester 6
Try: P.Ford;
Drop goal: T.Hopson

Feb 25 Aberavon 18 Gloucester 0

Mar 4 Gloucester 14 Northampton 11
Tries: R.Timms, Dick Smith, Bob Smith,
A.Holder;
Conversion: R.Hillier

Mar 11 Gloucester 8 R.A.F. 6
Tries: Bob Smith, T.Hopson;
Conversion: R.Hillier

**Mar 18 Gloucester 14
Guy's Hospital 6**
Tries: T.Hopson, A.Davies, H.Symonds;
Conversion: R.Hillier;
Penalty: R.Hillier

Mar 25 Gloucester 6 Newport 14
Try: P.Ford;
Penalty: A.Holder

Mar 28 Bath 3 Gloucester 8
Tries: G.Mace, P.Hole;
Conversion: R.Hillier

Apr 1 Gloucester 13 New Brighton 21
Tries: Bob Smith, Dick Smith;
Conversions: A.Holder (2);
Penalty: A.Holder

Apr 3 Gloucester 9 Sale 11
Try: A.Holder;
Penalties: A.Holder (2)

Apr 4 Lydney 0 Gloucester 0

**Apr 8 Gloucester 34
Devonport Services 0**
Tries: P.Ford (2), R.Timms (2), J.King (2),
H.Symonds, Dick Smith, A.Holder, T.Hopson
Conversions: R.Hillier (2)

Apr 12 Cheltenham 11 Gloucester 3
Try: L.King

Apr 15 Gloucester 3 Cardiff 14
Try: K.Taylor

**Apr 18 Gloucester 6
International XV 12**
Tries: J.King (2)

Apr 20 Gloucester 6 Stroud 3
Tries: L.King, J.King

**Apr 22 Plymouth Albion 9
Gloucester 13**
Tries: P.Ford, P.Meadows, A.Holder;
Conversions: J.Taylor (2)

Apr 24 Teignmouth 8 Gloucester 6
Tries: J.Bayliss (2)

Apr 25 Taunton 3 Gloucester 0

Apr 29 Gloucester 11 Llanelly 11
Tries: J.King, J.Taylor, R.Timms;
Conversion: J.Taylor

R.Parry T.Day J.G.A'Bear A.Beattie R.B.Brett J.Reid T.Millington N.H.B.Duncalfe R.Sutton
W.Cale P.Lane B.Hudson K.Taylor R.(Dick)Smith T.Davis A.Brinn J.Herbert J.Spalding A.Hopson Rev.H.M.Hughes(Chairman)
F.D.H.Dawe(Hon.Treas) R.Long R.Hillier R.Timms A.Townsend(Capt) Dr.A.Alcock(Pres) A.Holder P.Meadows J.Bayliss P.Ford A.Hudson(Hon.Sec)
M.Booth J.Lowe

Played 43 Won 22 Lost 18 Drawn 3
For 496 Against 468
Captain: Allan Townsend

Gloucester United
Played 29 Won 17 Lost 11 Drawn 1
For 257 Against 228

Most appearances: A.Townsend, P.Ford,
P.Meadows 38, A.Holder 36, T.Hopson 33,
R.Hillier, R.Long, A.Davies 31, Dick Smith 29
Most tries: P.Meadows 13, P.Ford 12, J.Bayliss,
Dick Smith, T.Hopson 10
Most conversions: M.Booth 20, R.Hillier 18,
S.Ingram 7
Penalties: R.Hillier 22, M.Booth 5
Drop goals: T.Hopson 3, A.Holder 2, P.Hawker,
S.Ingram 1

There was a slight improvement in the playing
record over the previous season, in that wins
outnumbered losses. The campaign started with
great promise. There was only one defeat in the
first seven games, including a sweeping win
over Bristol, in a thrilling game, which showed
what the team was capable of. Terry Hopson
scored a fine try running in from the half-way
line. The team for that game included a very
young Mike Nicholls. There was also a good
win at Bedford. But six of the following eight
games were lost, although there was a fine win
at Moseley, when the team was missing eight
players due to County calls. Later there were

wins at Kingsholm against Leicester, Coventry,
Swansea, and a coveted success against Cardiff.
Away form was poor, and there was only one
win in Wales, against Newbridge.

Of the backs, John Bayliss was the most
penetrative, and was a regular for the County.
Alan Holder partnered Bayliss in the centre,
but of necessity had to play many games at full-
back. Pete Meadows on the wing demonstrated
his speed to be the top try scorer. Terry Hopson
and Mickie Booth were the regular half-backs,
but when Booth was unavailable on County
duty, newcomer John Spalding ably deputised.
As ever there were few teams which could
master the Gloucester forwards. Peter Ford,
Tony Davies and Dick Smith formed a back-row
which performed consistently over the whole
season. They were backed up by Roy Long in
the second row and Allan Townsend at prop.
Russell Hillier was dependable at full-back, and
scored 102 points from place kicks.

Concern grew over the continued fall in gates,
due to the televising of international games, and
other sporting events, on Saturday afternoons.

Sep 9 Gloucester 26 Lydney 3
Tries: R.Long, R.Timms, P.Ford, Dick Smith,
B.Hudson;
Conversions: M.Booth (3), R.Hillier;
Penalty: M.Booth

Sep 13 Cheltenham 6 Gloucester 18
Tries: J.King, P.Ford, B.Hudson, J.Bayliss;
Conversions: M.Booth (3)

Sep 16 Gloucester 3 Moseley 3
Try: A.Osman

Sep 20 Cardiff 10 Gloucester 6
Tries: P.Meadows, R.Long

Sep 23 Gloucester 15 Bristol 3
Tries: J.Bayliss (2), Dick Smith;
Conversions: M.Booth (3)

Sep 28 Gloucester 35 Stroud 0
Tries: R.Timms (2), J.Bayliss (2), A.Holder,
T.Hopson, P.Meadows, Dick Smith;
Conversions: M.Booth (4);
Penalty: M.Booth

Sep 30 Bedford 11 Gloucester 17
Tries: P.Ford, J.Bayliss, A.Brinn;
Conversion: M.Booth;
Penalties: M.Booth (2)

Oct 7 Llanelly 10 Gloucester 8
Tries: Dick Smith, P.Meadows;
Conversion: M.Booth

Oct 14 Neath 12 Gloucester 3
Try: P.Ford

Oct 21 Gloucester 11 Newport 23
Tries: P.Meadows (3);
Conversion: M.Booth

Oct 28 Coventry 26 Gloucester 8
Tries: T.Hopson, E.Stephens;
Conversion: R.Chamberlayne

Nov 4 Gloucester 26 Leicester 11
Tries: M.Booth (2), J.Bayliss (2), R.Timms;
Conversions: R.Hillier (2), M.Booth (2);
Penalty: M.Booth

Nov 11 Moseley 5 Gloucester 13
Tries: T.Hopson, R.Timms;
Conversions: A.Ricketts, A.Holder:
Drop goal: P.Hawker

**Nov 15 Cambridge University 14
Gloucester 0**

Nov 18 Gloucester 13 Aberavon 19
Tries: P.Meadows, Dick Smith;
Conversions: R.Hillier, M.Booth;
Penalty: R.Hillier

Nov 25 Gloucester 40 Old Blues 3
Tries: Dick Smith (2), E.Stephens (2), D.Gilbert-
Smith (2), R.Timms, T.Hopson;
Conversions: S.Ingram (4), R.Chamberlayne;
Drop goals: T.Hopson, S.Ingram

**Dec 2 Gloucester 8
Oxford University 39**
Tries: A.Ricketts, Dick Smith;
Conversion: A.Ricketts

Dec 9 Gloucester 9 Bath 3
Tries: P.Meadows (2), Dick Smith

Dec 16 Gloucester 14 Coventry 8
Tries: P.Ford (2), P.Hawker, T.Hopson;
Conversion: M.Booth

Dec 23 Newbridge 8 Gloucester 13
Tries: Dick Smith, B.Hudson, T.Hopson;
Conversions: S.Ingram (2)

Dec 26 Gloucester v Old Merchant Taylors -
cancelled due to snow & frost

Dec 27 Gloucester v Pontypool - cancelled due
to snow & frost
Dec 30 Gloucester v Neath - cancelled due to
unfit ground

Jan 6 London Scottish 36 Gloucester 5
Try: A.Holder;
Conversion: S.Ingram

Jan 13 Leicester 16 Gloucester 3
Try: T.Hopson

Jan 20 Gloucester 19 Wasps 0
Tries: D.Gilbert-Smith, P.Ford, T.Hopson;
Conversions: R.Hillier (2);
Penalty: R.Hillier;
Drop goal: T.Hopson

Jan 27 Gloucester 16 Army 8
Tries: A.Osman, P.Taylor, P.Meadows,
T.Hopson;
Conversions: R.Hillier (2)

Feb 3 Bristol 23 Gloucester 0

Feb 10 Bath 8 Gloucester 8
Try: P.Ford;
Conversion: R.Hillier;
Penalty: R.Hillier

Feb 17 Gloucester 5 Swansea 3
Try: A.Holder;
Conversion: R.Hillier

Feb 24 Aberavon 24 Gloucester 6
Penalties: R.Hillier (2)

Mar 3 Northampton 17 Gloucester 10
Tries: A.Osman, A.Holder;
Conversions: R.Hillier (2)

Mar 10 Gloucester 14 Richmond 10
Tries: H.Symonds, P.Ford, T.Hopson,
A.Ricketts;
Conversion: R.Hillier

Mar 15 Gloucester 9 R.A.F. 6
Try: H.Symonds;
Penalties: R.Hillier (2)

**Mar 17 Guy's Hospital 9
Gloucester 21**
Tries: P.Meadows, A.Osman, J.Spalding,
A.Townsend;
Penalties: R.Hillier (3)

Mar 24 Newport 9 Gloucester 0

Mar 29 Stroud 6 Gloucester 14
Tries: P.Meadows, R.Timms, P.Ford;
Conversion: R.Hillier;
Penalty: R.Hillier

Mar 31 Gloucester 14 Harlequins 17
Tries: P.Ford, R.Timms;
Conversion: R.Hillier, Penalties: R.Hillier (2)

Apr 7 Gloucester 6 Cardiff 0
Penalties: R.Hillier (2)

Apr 12 Gloucester 17 Cheltenham 3
Tries: P.Ford, R.Timms, A.Holder;
Conversion: R.Hillier;
Penalty: R.Hillier;
Drop goal: A.Holder

Apr 14 Pontypool 19 Gloucester 6
Penalty: R.Hillier;
Drop goal: T.Hopson

Apr 19 Lydney 6 Gloucester 6
Try: P.Meadows;
Penalty: R.Hillier

Apr 21 Gloucester 3 Headingley 0
Penalty: R.Hillier

**Apr 23 Gloucester 5
Birkenhead Park 9**
Try: J.Bayliss;
Conversion: R.Hillier

**Apr 28 Devonport Services 18
Gloucester 3**
Penalty: R.Hillier

Apr 30 Teignmouth 3 Gloucester 20
Tries: J.Lowe (2), J.Bayliss;
Conversion: R.Hillier;
Penalties: R.Hillier (2);
Drop goal: A.Holder

1962-63

**Played 38 Won 21 Lost 15 Drawn 2
For 456 Against 318
Captain: Mickey Booth**

Gloucester United
Played 24 Won 16 Lost 6 Drawn 2
For 318 Against 158

Captain: Pete Hawker

Most appearances: M.Booth 36, A.Osman 31,
A.Holder, A.Townsend 30, J.Fowke, B.Hudson
29, P.Ford 27, R.Pitt, J.Bayliss, A.Brinn 25
Most tries: G.White 15, A.Osman 14, P.Ford 10,
T.Hopson 9, A.Brinn 7

Most conversions: M.Booth, R.Hillier 15,
A.Holder 6, G.White 5
Penalties: R.Hillier 4, M.Booth, G.White 2,
A.Holder, J.Taylor 1
Drop goals: T.Hopson 5, M.Booth 3

In November, a building programme for

T.Tandy A.G.Hudson A.Beattie N.H.B.Duncalfe J.Hickie V.B.Clarke(Hon.Treas)
T.Day P.Meadows R.Hillier R.Pitt A.Osman D.Owen A.Brinn R.Timms R.(Dick)Smith K.Taylor J.Bayliss J.Fowke W.Cale
A.Hudson Rev.H.M.Hughes(Chairman) B.Hudson A.Townsend M.Booth(Capt) Dr.A.Alcock(Pres) A.Holder P.Ford G.White M.Wetson T.H.Millington
J.Lowe T.Hopson

Kingsholm was launched. A new club house was envisaged between the Grandstand and Worcester Street. It would be 1966 before the club house was opened. The winter was the coldest in living memory and ten games were lost to frost or snow.

On the field it was another patchy season, and the playing record was only made respectable by a run of 12 wins from 13 games towards the end of the campaign. There was plenty of talent available but games too often inexplicably slipped away. Place kicking was again a problem. Mickey Booth, Alan Holder, Russell Hillier, Gary White, and even Peter Ford were all tried without any consistent success.

The season started badly, when, in the opening home game, Lydney won at Kingsholm for the first time in ten years. There were, however, a few outstanding wins. In October the team travelled to Newport and brought off an astonishing 16-0 win. With five minutes to go the Cherry and Whites led 8-0, and could be forgiven for closing the game down. But skipper Mickey Booth had other ideas. He broke across field to give a sweet pass to Dick Smith playing on the wing, who stormed over. Booth converted and there was still time for him to drop a goal before the end. The Citizen enthused that, "the forwards displayed a fast and furious exhibition of open rugby." The return game at Kingsholm was a more sober affair which was won 8-3, with Peter Ford playing a blinder.

Cardiff were beaten at Kingsholm, largely due to a fiery display by the pack, and the hard tackling of centres John Bayliss and Ron Pitt. In an amazing display Pontypool were beaten, 30-8. Gloucester kicked off, and Alan Brinn following up, took advantage of dithering defence to dive on the ball for a try. He touched down another later, as the team scored six tries.

As well as having another storming season for Gloucester, Peter Ford captained the County to the semi-final of the County Championship. He was accompanied by team mates John Bayliss, Dick Smith, Ken Wilson and Brian "Baggy" Hudson. Ken "Tug" Wilson won an England cap against France and promptly signed professional terms to play for Oldham.

Sep 6 Torquay Athletic 9 Gloucester 21
Tries: J.Bayliss (2), P.Ford (2), R.Clutterbuck;
Conversions: R.Hillier (3)

Sep 8 Gloucester 12 Lydney 13
Tries: P.Meadows, A. Brinn: Penalties: R.Hillier (2)

Sep 13 Gloucester 14 Cheltenham 0
Tries: R.Pitt, M.Booth, Dick Smith, R.Timms;
Conversion: M.Booth

Sep 15 Gloucester 15 Moseley 8
Tries: H.Symonds, A.Osman, B.Hudson;
Conversions: A.Holder (3)

Sep 18 Gloucester 22 Universities Athletic Union 9
Tries: G.Mace, R.Pitt, P.Meadows, R.Clutterbuck, H.Symonds, A.Osman;
Conversions: A.Holder (2)

Sep 22 Bristol 10 Gloucester 3
Try: H.Symonds

Sep 27 Stroud 9 Gloucester 6
Tries: A.Osman (2)

Sep 29 Gloucester 17 Bedford 13
Tries: K.Wilson (2), A.Osman, P.Ford;
Conversion: A.Holder;
Penalty: A.Holder

Oct 6 Gloucester 6 Neath 6
Penalty: M.Booth;
Drop goal: M.Booth

Oct 13 Pontypool 9 Gloucester 8
Tries: G.White, B.Hudson;
Conversion: M.Booth

Oct 20 Newport 0 Gloucester 16
Tries: T.Hopson, P.Ford, Dick Smith;
Conversions: M. Booth (2);
Drop goal: M.Booth

Oct 27 Coventry 34 Gloucester 0

Nov 3 Gloucester 6 Leicester 8
Tries: T.Hopson, R.Pitt

Nov 10 Moseley 0 Gloucester 5
Try: A.Holder;
Conversion: R.Hillier

Nov 17 Aberavon 6 Gloucester 3
Try: K.Wilson

Nov 24 Gloucester 46 Old Blues 3
Tries: G.White (5), J.Taylor, B.Jackson,
A.Osman, A.Brinn, T.Hopson ;
Conversions: M.Booth (8)

Dec 1   Gloucester v Oxford University –
cancelled due to fog

Dec 8 Gloucester 19 Bath 3
Tries: D.Gilbert-Smith, T.Hopson, A.Osman,
D.Owen, G.White;
Conversions: M.Booth, J.Taylor

Dec 14 Gloucester 3 Coventry 6
Try: P.Meadows

Dec 22 Neath 22 Gloucester 3
Penalty: J.Taylor

Dec 26 Gloucester v Old Merchant Taylors –
cancelled
Dec 27 Gloucester v Pontypool – cancelled

Dec 29 Cardiff 11 Gloucester 0

Jan 5 Gloucester v London Scottish – cancelled
Jan 12 Leicester v Gloucester – cancelled
Jan 17 Gloucester v Army- cancelled
Jan 19 Wasps v Gloucester – cancelled
Jan 26 Gloucester v Cambridge University –
cancelled
Jan 28 Gloucester v Bristol – cancelled
Feb 9 Bath v Gloucester - cancelled

Feb 16 Swansea 17 Gloucester 6

Penalty: M.Booth;
Drop goal: M.Booth

Feb 24 Gloucester 8 Aberavon 16
Tries: D.Owen, Dick Smith;
Conversion: M.Booth

Mar 2 Gloucester 3 Northampton 6
Try: A.Osman

Mar 9 Gloucester 17 R.A.F. 0
Tries: J.Bayliss (2), A.Osman (2), M. Booth;
Conversion: R.Hillier

Mar 16 Gloucester 16 Guys Hospital 3
Tries: P.Ford, D.Owen, A.Osman, J.Taylor;
Conversions: R.Hillier (2)

Mar 23 Gloucester 8 Newport 3
Tries: J.Taylor, P.Ford;
Conversion: R.Hillier

Mar 28 Gloucester 19 Stroud 3
Tries: T.Hopson (2), A.Brinn, A.Holder,
G.White;
Conversions: R.Hillier (2)

Mar 30 Harlequins 30 Gloucester 11
Tries: G.White, D.Owen;
Conversion: R.Hillier;
Penalty: R.Hillier

Apr 6 Gloucester 6 Cardiff 3
Tries: P.Ford, B.Hudson

Apr 10 Cheltenham 0 Gloucester 6
Tries: A.Osman (2)

Apr 13 Gloucester 14 New Brighton 5
Tries: T.Hopson (2), M.Booth, R.Pitt;
Conversion: P Ford

Apr 15 Gloucester 19 Sale 6
Tries: G.White, A.Brinn;
Conversions: G.White (2);
Penalty: G.White;
Drop goals: T.Hopson (2)

Apr 16 Lydney 3 Gloucester 14
Tries: E.Stephens, R.Timms, A.Osman;
Conversion: G.White;
Penalty: G.White

Apr 20 Gloucester 22 Cheltenham 8
Tries: G.White (2), R.Timms, J.Bayliss,
A.Brinn, D.Owen;
Conversions: P.Ford (2)

Apr 22 Gloucester 30 Pontypool 8
Tries: A.Brinn (2), R.Timms (2), G.White (2);
Conversions: G.White (2), M.Booth;
Drop goals: T.Hopson (2)

Apr 27 Redruth 9 Gloucester 15
Tries: P.Ford (2), G.Mace;
Conversions: R.Hillier (3)

Apr 29 Exeter 5 Gloucester 3
Try: P.Ford

**May 2 Gloucester 14
County Presidents XV 14**
Tries: T.Hopson, G.White;
Conversion: R.Hillier;
Penalty: R.Hillier;
Drop goal: T.Hopson

1963-64

**Played 44 Won 27 Lost 14 Drawn 3
For 507 Against 343
Captain: Alan Holder**

Gloucester United
Played 32 Won 8 Lost 20 Drawn 4
For 206 Against 385
Captain: Peter Hawker

Most appearances: A.Holder 43, A.Townsend
43, A.Brinn 40, Dick Smith 38, Bob Smith 37,
T.Hopson, M.Booth, P.Ford 32.
Most tries: Bob Smith 19, P.Ford 16, G.White 12,
T.Hopson 11
Conversions: G.White 27, D.Ainge 15, P.Ford 3,
M.Booth 2, J.Taylor 1
Penalties: G.White 13, D.Ainge 7, J.Taylor,
M.Booth 1
Drop Goals: T.Hopson 5, D.Ainge 2, A.Holder 1

In March, local company, Fielding and Platt Ltd,
donated a set of steel goal-posts to the Club. It
was claimed that they would not sway in strong
winds. It proved to be true and the posts survived
for 50 years, until the prodigious kicking of
Ludovic Mercier necessitated extensions to the
posts, to help officials decide whether kicks
were good or not. They were finally removed
in 2015, still in good condition, to conform with
Rugby World Cup requirements.

The season as a whole was mixed. Doubles were
achieved over Pontypool and Bath. There were
home wins over Aberavon, Neath, Newport and
Bristol. Away form was uneven, but there were
wins at Leicester and Northampton, and a draw
at Aberavon. Results were not helped by the
success of the County, when five or six players
were selected for each game, and the Club had to

play big matches with a high number of reserves
in the starting fifteen.

Bob Smith scored lots of tries, starting the
season with eight in the first eight games. The
top try scoring forward was Peter Ford. Other
forwards who had a good season were
AllanTownsend, Alan Brinn, Dick Smith and
Gary White, the latter proving to be the most
reliable place kicker for several seasons, and
added to the number of tries he scored, totalled
129 points. Terry Hopson and Mickie Booth
were the usual intelligent half-backs again. At
full-back, captain Alan Holder played in all but
one game, and led by example. Holder retired at
the end of the season having played 337 times
and scored 341 points. He would return to play
one more game in the 1964-65 season. Ron Pitt
and John Bayliss formed a very hard tackling
pairing in the centre. David Ainge, a promising

Dr.A.Alcock(Pres)(inset) W.Cale T.Day A.G.Hudson A.Beattie N.H.B.Dincalfe J.Bayliss(inset)
J.Fowke A.Osman A.Townsend B.Hudson D.Owen A.Brinn R.Timms R.(Bob)Smith K.Taylor M.Nicholls P.Meadows
A.T.Voyce T.Millington R.Pitt R.(Dick)Smith A.Holder(Capt) Rev.H.M.Hughes P.Ford G.White D.Ainge T.R.Tandy(Hon.Sec) A.Hudson
M.Booth T.Hopson

centre or fly-half emerged during the season. He was also a useful place kicker.

The most satisfying aspect of the season was the long overdue recognition of Peter Ford at international level. He played in all four of England's Championship games. He also captained the County team. Brian Hudson played in an England trial game. Western Counties played New Zealand at Bristol. Terry Hopson, Mickey Booth, Peter Ford and Dick Smith were in the team. The tourists said that Booth and Hopson were the best half-backs they played on the tour. Gloucestershire reached the semi-final of the Championship. Peter Ford, Allan Townsend, Dick Smith, John Bayliss and Mickey Booth were in the team.

Sep 7   Neath 6   Gloucester 0

Sep 12   Stroud 3   Gloucester 35
Tries: Bob Smith (2), P.Ford (2), A.Osman, T.Hopson;
Conversions: G.White (4);
Penalties: G.White, J.Taylor;
Drop goal: T.Hopson

Sep 14   Gloucester 22   Lydney 6
Tries: Bob Smith (3), P.Ford (3);
Conversions: G.White (2)

Sep 18   Cheltenham 3   Gloucester 20
Tries: P.Ford, G.White, A.Osman;

Conversion: G.White;
Penalty: G.White;
Drop goals: T.Hopson (2)

Sep 21   Gloucester 13   Moseley 6
Tries: J.Bayliss, Dick Smith;
Conversions: G.White (2);
Penalty: G.White

Sep 25   Newport 6   Gloucester 3
Try: Bob Smith

Sep 28   Gloucester 16   Bristol 6
Tries: Bob Smith, T.Hopson, G.White;
Conversions: G.White (2);
Penalty: G.White

Oct 5   Bedford 6   Gloucester 14
Tries: Bob Smith, G.White;
Conversion: G.White;
Penalties: G.White (2)

Oct 9   Pontypool 6   Gloucester 10
Tries: A.Osman, penalty try;
Conversions: G.White (2)

Oct 12   Harlequins 9   Gloucester 6
Try: A.Osman;
Penalty: G.White

Oct 19   Gloucester 14   Newport 3
Tries: P.Ford, M.Nicholls, Bob Smith;
Conversion: G.White;

Penalty: M.Booth

Oct 26   Gloucester 13   Coventry 15
Tries: G.Mace, R.Pitt;
Conversions: J.Taylor, D.Ainge;
Penalty: D.Ainge

Nov 2   Leicester 3   Gloucester 9
Tries: G.White (2), Bob Smith

Nov 9   Moseley 6   Gloucester 3
Try: Bob Smith

Nov 16   Gloucester 14   Aberavon 9
Tries: Bob Smith (2), P.Ford;
Conversion: G.White;
Penalty: G.White

**Nov 20   Cambridge University 8
Gloucester 8**
Tries: P.Ford, T.Hopson;
Conversion: G.White

Nov 23   Gloucester 10   Old Blues 8
Tries: A.Brinn, Bob Smith;
Conversions: D.Ainge (2)

**Nov 30   Gloucester 0
Oxford University 28**

Dec 7   Gloucester 3   Llanelly 9
Try: G.White

Dec 14 Gloucester v Bath - cancelled due to frost

Dec 21 Coventry v Gloucester - cancelled due to frost

Dec 26 Gloucester 18 Old Merchant Taylors 0
Tries: M.Wetson, G.White, A.Brinn;
Conversions: D.Ainge (3);
Penalty: D.Ainge

Dec 27 Gloucester 9 Pontypool 3
Tries: Bob Smith, T.Hopson;
Penalty: G.White

Dec 28 Gloucester 3 Cardiff 14
Drop goal: T.Hopson

Jan 4 London Scottish 20 Gloucester 19
Tries: T.Hopson (2), A.Holder;
Conversions: D.Ainge (2);
Penalty: D.Ainge;
Drop goal: D.Ainge

Jan 11 Gloucester 0 Leicester 11

Jan 18 Gloucester v Wasps - cancelled due to frost

Jan 25 Gloucester 6 Army 19
Try: D.Owen;
Penalty: D.Ainge

Feb 1 Bristol v Gloucester - cancelled due to County semi-final on the same day

Feb 8 Bath 11 Gloucester 19
Tries: G.White (2), D.Owen, J.Bayliss,

R.Timms;
Conversions: G.White (2)

Feb 15 Gloucester 14 Swansea 14
Tries: D.Owen, P.Ford, J.Bayliss;
Conversion: M.Booth;
Drop goal: A.Holder

Feb 22 Gloucester 17 Neath 8
Tries: A.Holder, Bob Smith;
Conversion: G.White;
Penalties: G.White (3)

Feb 29 Gloucester 6 Exeter 0
Tries: J.Bayliss, T.Hopson

Mar 7 Northampton 3 Gloucester 6
Try: R.Pitt;
Drop goal: T.Hopson

Mar 14 Gloucester 14 R.A.F. 5
Tries: P.Ford (2), R.Timms, J.Bayliss;
Conversion: P.Ford

Mar 21 Guy's Hospital 0 Gloucester 3
Try: D.Owen

Mar 26 Lydney 0 Gloucester 11
Tries: R.Timms (2), D.Owen;
Conversion: G.White

Mar 28 Gloucester 16 Headingley 11
Tries: R.Timms, A.Osman, G.White, R.Long;
Conversions: G.White, P.Ford

Mar 30 Gloucester 26 Birkenhead Park 6
Tries: T.Hopson (2), P.Ford (2), M.Booth, Bob Smith, G.Wright, D.Owen;

Conversion: P.Ford

Apr 4 Aberavon 11 Gloucester 11
Tries: G.White, Bob Smith, T.Hopson;
Conversion: G.White

Apr 9 Gloucester 23 Cheltenham 3
Tries: T.Hopson, Dick Smith, R.Long, J.Bayliss, R.Timms;
Conversions: G.White (4)

Apr 11 Cardiff 19 Gloucester 6
Try: Bob Smith;
Penalty: G.White

Apr 16 Bristol 12 Gloucester 0

Apr 18 Gloucester 6 Newbridge 13
Try: D.Ainge;
Penalty: D.Ainge

Apr 22 Gloucester 14 Bath 0
Tries: Dick Smith (2), A.Holder, J.Bayliss;
Conversion: M.Booth

Apr 25 Penzance & Newlyn 3 Gloucester 15
Tries: A.Brinn, R.Timms, P.Ford;
Conversions: D.Ainge (3)

Apr 27 Exeter 8 Gloucester 11
Try: R.Pitt;
Conversion: D.Ainge;
Penalties: D.Ainge (2)

Apr 30 Gloucester 21 Stroud 3
Tries: A.Townsend, P.Ford, G.White, R.Timms;
Conversions: D.Ainge (3);
Drop goal: D.Ainge

1964-65

Played 44 Won 28 Lost 15 Drawn 1
For 562 Against 468
Captain: Mickey Booth

Gloucester United
Played 28 Won 10 Lost 15 Drawn 3
For 268 Against 353
Captain: Bob Timms

Most appearances: N.Foice 44, R.Long 42, D.Owen 41, P.Ford 40, M.Booth 38,
Most tries: N.Foice, P.Ford 13, J.Bayliss, T.Hopson, Dick Smith 10, R.Morris 9
Conversions: D.Rutherford 39, D.Ainge 10, M.Teague 1
Penalties: D.Rutherford 27, D.Ainge 7
Drop goals: T.Hopson 7, D.Rutherford, D.Ainge 5, M.Booth 4

With the arrival of full-back Don Rutherford, at a stroke Gloucester had solved the perennial place-kicking problem. Rutherford scored 180 points, all but six of them from the boot. He also played for England in all four of the International Championship games, kicking three penalties.

It took the team a long time to settle, and in the first half of the season there were more games lost than won. However, in November there was a thrilling display to defeat Leicester. John Bayliss had an outstanding game. The Citizen reporter wrote, "Bayliss was determined and evasive, contributing a number of splendid runs, which cut the Leicester defence to ribbons and set up two of the best tries". In December there was a heart-breaking defeat to Coventry. Gloucester, without Rutherford who was

appearing in an England trial game, played all the rugby and scored four tries. None were converted. Coventry had a star kicker in George Cole, who kicked three penalties and converted Coventry's only try, to win 14-12.

But from mid-January the team found its feet, and there were only three more defeats. This pattern was illustrated by matches against Welsh clubs. There was not a single victory until Aberavon were beaten in February. Thereafter there were wins over Cardiff and Newport in successive weeks, and Pontypool. The Cardiff victory was the biggest ever against them since the introduction of points scoring.

In his debut season, winger Nick Foice played in every game, and was joint top try scorer with

T.Day L.Keck P.Hawker R.Morris S.Dangerfield A.G.Hudson G.Dance J.Dancey
T.R.Tandy(Hon.Sec) T.Hopson J.Bayliss N.Foice R.Long P.Ford D.Owen M.Burton M.Nicholls J.Milner K.Taylor R.Morris
Rev.H.M.Hughes(Chairman)
A.T.Voyce T.Millington R.Smith R.Pitt M.Booth(Capt) Dr.A.Alcock(Pres) A.Brinn R.Timms D.Rutherford A.Hudson F.D.H.Dawe(Hon.Fixture Sec)
J.Fowke D.Ainge

Peter Ford, who again captained the County team. John Bayliss and Ron Pitt put together a promising centre partnership, but injuries to both hampered their development. As always, the forwards did not take a backward step; the back-row of Ford, Dick Smith and Dave Owen, being one of the best in the country. Smith played in an England trial game, but deserved more recognition than that. The back-row was ably supported by Roy Long, "Baggy" Hudson and a young Mike Burton.

Old campaigners Allan Townsend and Bob Smith only played in a few games each and retired. Townsend had appeared 196 times and captained the Club in 1961-62. Winger Smith made 163 appearances and scored 60 tries.

Sep 5 Gloucester 9 Waterloo 3
Penalty: D.Rutherford;
Drop goals: D.Rutherford, T.Hopson

Sep 12 Gloucester 33 Lydney 0
Tries: J.Bayliss (2), N.Foice (2), P.Ford, H.Symonds, D.Rutherford;
Conversions: D.Rutherford (3);
Penalty: D.Rutherford;
Drop goal: T.Hopson

Sep 17 Gloucester 16 Cheltenham 0
Tries: N.Foice (2), J.Bayliss;
Conversions: D.Rutherford (2);
Penalty: D.Rutherford

Sep 19 Gloucester 20 Moseley 0
Tries: P.Ford (2);
Conversion: D.Rutherford;
Penalties: D.Rutherford (2);
Drop goals: T.Hopson (2)

Sep 23 Cardiff 16 Gloucester 9
Penalty: D.Rutherford;
Drop goals: T.Hopson, M.Booth

Sep 26 Bristol 10 Gloucester 6
Try: A.Osman;
Penalty: D.Rutherford

Sep 30 Pontypool 13 Gloucester 8
Tries: D.Owen, P.Ford;
Conversion: D.Rutherford

Oct 3 Gloucester 19 Bedford 9
Tries: N.Foice (2), K.Taylor, A.Brinn;
Conversions: D.Rutherford (2);
Penalty: D.Rutherford

Oct 7 Stroud 0 Gloucester 6
Try: P.Ford;
Penalty: D.Rutherford

Oct 10 Gloucester 19 Harlequins 16
Tries: Dick Smith, B.Hudson;
Conversions: D.Rutherford (2);
Penalties: D.Rutherford (2)
Drop goal: D.Ainge

Oct 17 Newport 18 Gloucester 6
Try: Bob Smith;
Penalty: D.Rutherford

Oct 24 Coventry 45 Gloucester 0

Oct 31 Oxford University 12 Gloucester 13
Tries: P.Ford, Dick Smith;
Conversions: D.Rutherford (2);
Penalty: D.Rutherford

Nov 7 Gloucester 22 Leicester 9
Tries: D.Owen, J.Bayliss, R.Pitt, Dick Smith, D.Rutherford;
Conversions: D.Rutherford (2);
Drop goal: M.Booth

Nov 14 Moseley 26 Gloucester 12
Penalties: D.Ainge (4)

Nov 21 Aberavon 18 Gloucester 8
Try: J.Bayliss;
Conversion: D.Rutherford;
Drop goal: D.Ainge

Nov 28 Newbridge 42 Gloucester 0

Dec 5 Gloucester 3 Neath 6
Drop goal: D.Ainge

Dec 12 Gloucester 13 Bath 3
Tries: J.Groves (2), R.Morris;
Conversions: D.Rutherford (2)

Dec 19   Gloucester 12   Coventry 14
Tries: T.Hopson, B.Hudson, N.Foice, P.Ford

**Dec 26   Gloucester 12
Old Merchant Taylors 3**
Tries: M.Booth, R.Morris, R.Timms;
Penalty: D.Rutherford

Dec 28 Gloucester v Pontypool - cancelled due
to snow

Jan 2   Gloucester 0   London Scottish 26

Jan 9   Leicester 21   Gloucester 0

Jan 16   Wasps 8   Gloucester 9
Try: J.Groves;
Penalty: D.Ainge;
Drop goal: T.Hopson

**Jan 23   Gloucester 20
Cambridge University 8**
Tries: T.Hopson, J.Bayliss;
Conversion: D.Rutherford;
Penalties: D.Rutherford (3);
Drop goal: T.Hopson

Jan 30   Gloucester 29   Army 11
Tries: Dick Smith (3), J.Bayliss, P.Ford,
T.Hopson, K.Taylor;
Conversions: D.Rutherford (4)

Feb 6   Gloucester 9   Bristol 5
Penalty: D.Rutherford;
Drop goals: D.Rutherford, M.Booth

Feb 13   Bath 6   Gloucester 8
Tries: N.Foice, J.Groves;
Conversion: M.Teague

Feb 20   Swansea 14   Gloucester 3
Try: Dick Smith

Feb 27   Gloucester 10   Aberavon 8
Tries: R.Morris, T.Hopson;
Conversions: D.Ainge (2)

Mar 6 Gloucester v Northampton – cancelled
due to snow

Mar 13   Gloucester 36   R.A.F. 3
Tries: P.Ford (2), N.Foice (2), J.Bayliss (2),
T.Hopson (2);
Conversions: D.Rutherford (6)

Mar 18   Gloucester 13   Royal Navy 12
Tries: J.Bayliss, N.Foice, R.Morris;
Conversions: D.Ainge (2)

**Mar 20   Gloucester 16
Guy's Hospital 5**
Tries: R.Morris (2), P.Ford;
Conversions: D.Ainge (2);
Drop goal: D.Ainge

Mar 27   Gloucester 14   Newport 11
Tries: R.Pitt, T.Hopson, R.Morris;
Conversion: D.Rutherford;
Penalty: D.Rutherford

Apr 3   Gloucester 23   Cardiff 3
Tries: R.Timms (2), T.Hopson, R.Morris;
Conversions: D.Rutherford (4);
Penalty: D.Rutherford

Apr 7   Cheltenham 3   Gloucester 14
Tries: T.Hopson, N.Foice;
Conversion: D.Rutherford;
Penalty: D.Rutherford;

Drop goal: M.Booth

Apr 10   Neath 13   Gloucester 3
Drop goal: D.Rutherford

Apr 15   Lydney 6   Gloucester 6
Tries: T.Hopson, R.Timms

Apr 17   Gloucester 25   New Brighton 5
Tries: Dick Smith (2), D.Owen, R.Pitt,
M.Teague;
Conversions: D.Ainge (2);
Penalty: D.Ainge;
Drop goal: D.Ainge

Apr 19   Gloucester 8   Sale 6
Try: R.Morris;
Conversion: D.Ainge;
Penalty: D.Ainge

Apr 22   Gloucester 18   Pontypool 5
Tries: D.Owen (2), R.Pitt, R.Long;
Conversions: D.Rutherford (3)

**Apr 24   Penzance-Newlyn 3
Gloucester 12**
Try: P.Ford;
Penalties: D.Rutherford (2);
Drop goal: D.Rutherford

Apr 26   Exeter 15   Gloucester 9
Penalties: D.Rutherford (3)

Apr 29   Gloucester 31   Stroud 8
Tries: R.Long, A.Brinn, R.Timms, Dick Smith,
N.Foice, P.Ford, D.Ainge;
Conversions: D.Ainge, D.Rutherford;
Penalty: D.Rutherford;
Drop goal: D.Rutherford

1965-66

E.Lane J.Hickie C.H.Sibery N.H.B.Duncalfe P.K.Hawker R.R.Morris T.Day E.Cale G.J.Dance R.B.Brett
G.Redding D.Christopher J.C.Milner C.Hannaford M.Nicholls R.G.Long D.Owen N.J.Foice C.N.Teague A.Osman R.Morris C.Wheatman T.R.Tandy(Hon.Sec)
T.H.Millington(Vice-Pres) F.D.H.Dawe(Hon.Fixture Sec) A.Brinn R.(Dick)Smith M.H.Booth(Capt) Dr.A.Alcock(Pres) D.B.W.Ainge J.Bayliss G.G.White
A.T.Voyce(Vice-Pres) Rev.H.M.Hughes(Chairman)
J.T.Hopson J.Groves

Played 49 Won 23 Lost 20 Drawn 6
For 444 Against 421
Captain: Mickey Booth

Gloucester United
Played 28 Won 14 Lost 12 Drawn 2
For 270 Against 311
Captain: Bob Timms

Most appearances: M.Nicholls 44, M.Booth 43,
A.Brinn, R.Long, D.Owen 41, J.Bayliss, N.Foice
39, G.White 38, T.Hopson 37, Dick Smith 36
Most tries: N.Foice 13, T.Hopson 12, J.Bayliss,
G.White 7, G.Redding 5
Conversions: D.Rutherford 12, D.Ainge 11,
M.Booth, G.White, P.Meadows 2, B.Mace 1
Penalties: D.Rutherford 20, D.Ainge 18,
G.White 4, M.Teague, P.Meadows 1
Drop goals: T.Hopson 6, M.Booth, D.Ainge,
D.Rutherford 1

Not a very successful season. Wins only just
outnumbered defeats. Part of the problem
stemmed from an inability to turn pressure
into points. Only 75 tries were scored. There
were some very good performances including
draws home and away against Cardiff. Oxford

University were beaten at Kingsholm on a
day when the County were playing and so
Gloucester had six replacements. Even more
creditable was the win at Leicester on another
County day when five players were missing.
Bristol, Newport and Swansea were defeated at
Kingsholm.

Nick Foice who had appeared in every game the
previous season continued his run until March.
He had made 80 consecutive appearances, a
club record which still stands, and it is unlikely
to be beaten. Don Rutherford again played in all
four of England's games, and he also captained
the County team. He was selected for the British
Lions tour of Australia and New Zealand,
appearing in one test against Australia.

Although the season was disappointing, there
were hopeful signs. John Bayliss and Roy
Morris forged a solid centre partnership, but too
often the forwards set up a platform which was
not exploited often enough by the backs. The
back row of Gary White, Dave Owen and Dick
Smith was particularly effective, and the second
row of Alan Brinn and Roy Long never let the
side down.

Bob Timms captained the United, but made
two more first team appearances before retiring,
making a total of 150 during which he scored 49
tries.

Sep 2 Gloucester 12 Broughton Park 14
Tries: N.Foice, G.Moore;
Penalties: G.White (2)

Sep 4 Gloucester 11 Lydney 0
Tries: R.Pitt, T.Hopson, N.Foice;
Conversion: D.Rutherford

Sep 8 Gloucester 3 Cardiff 3
Penalty: D.Rutherford

Sep 11 Gloucester 3 Neath 8
Penalty: G.White

Sep 15 Cheltenham 0 Gloucester 6
Penalties: D.Rutherford (2)

Sep 18 Moseley 8 Gloucester 16
Tries: G.White (2), T.Hopson, N.Foice;
Conversions: D.Rutherford (2)

Sep 22 Gloucester 14 Wolfhounds 18

Try: T.Hopson;
Conversion: D.Rutherford;
Penalties: D.Rutherford (2);
Drop goal: T.Hopson

Sep 25 Gloucester 9 Bristol 3
Tries: T.Hopson, A.Osman;
Drop goal: T.Hopson

Sep 28 Gloucester 16 Stroud 6
Tries: D.Owen (2), Dick Smith, N.Foice;
Conversions: D.Rutherford (2)

Oct 2 Bedford 8 Gloucester 11
Tries: P.Ford, N.Foice;
Conversion: D.Rutherford;
Penalty: D.Rutherford

Oct 6 Pontypool 12 Gloucester 3
Try: D.Christopher

Oct 9 Harlequins 14 Gloucester 5
Try: D.Owen;
Conversion: D.Ainge

Oct 16 Gloucester 14 Newport 13
Tries: N.Foice, R.Long, Dick Smith;
Conversion: G.White;
Penalty: G.White

Oct 23 Gloucester 5 Coventry 13
Try: N.Foice;
Conversion: B.Mace

Oct 30 Gloucester 14 Oxford University 3
Try: D.Owen;
Conversion: D.Rutherford;
Penalties: D.Rutherford (3)

Nov 6 Gloucester 0 Leicester 3

Nov 13 Gloucester 9 Moseley 28
Tries: N.Foice, G.Redding;
Penalty: M.Teague

Nov 17 Cambridge University 12 Gloucester 6
Tries: R.Morris, T.Hopson

Nov 20 Gloucester 6 Aberavon 6
Penalty: D.Rutherford;
Drop goal: D.Rutherford

Nov 27 Newbridge 11 Gloucester 6
Penalty: D.Ainge;
Drop goal: D.Ainge

Dec 4 Gloucester 9 Ebbw Vale 6
Tries: T.Hopson, R.Morris, J.Spalding

Dec 11 Gloucester 12 Bath 9

Tries: T.Hopson, N.Foice;
Penalties: D.Rutherford (2)

Dec 18 Coventry 6 Gloucester 3
Penalty: D.Ainge

Dec 27   Gloucester v Old Merchant Taylors - cancelled due to snow
Dec 28 Gloucester v Pontypool - cancelled due to snow

Jan 1 London Scottish 5 Gloucester 6
Try: P.Meadows;
Penalty: D.Ainge

Jan 8 Leicester 0 Gloucester 3
Try: C.Hannaford

Jan 13 Gloucester 25 Army 9
Tries: N.Foice (2), R.Morris, P.Meadows;
Conversions: D.Ainge (2);
Penalty: D.Ainge;
Drop goals: T.Hopson (2)

Jan 15 Gloucester v Wasps - cancelled due to snow

Jan 22 Cardiff 3 Gloucester 3
Penalty: D.Rutherford

Jan 29 Bristol 6 Gloucester 0

Feb 5 Gloucester 16 Stroud 0
Tries: J.Bayliss, P.Meadows, G.White;
Conversions: D.Rutherford (2);
Penalty: D.Rutherford

Feb 12 Bath v Gloucester - cancelled due to frost

Feb 19 Gloucester 12 Swansea 6
Try: J.Milner;
Penalties: D.Rutherford (3)

Feb 26 Aberavon 6 Gloucester 0

Mar 3 Northampton 8 Gloucester 8
Try: G.Redding;
Conversion: D.Rutherford;
Penalty: D.Rutherford

Mar 9 Ebbw Vale 3 Gloucester 8
Tries: J.Bayliss, N.Foice;
Conversion: G.White

Mar 12 Gloucester 23 R.A.F. 13
Tries: G.Redding (2), J.Bayliss, N.Foice, G.White, T.Hopson;
Conversion: P.Meadows;
Penalty: P.Meadows

Mar 19 Guy's Hospital 12 Gloucester 5

Try: Penalty try;
Conversion: P.Meadows

Mar 23 Bath 19 Gloucester 13
Tries: J.Bayliss (3);
Conversions: M.Booth (2)

Mar 26 Gloucester 14 Newbridge 12
Try: C.Hannaford;
Conversion: D.Rutherford;
Penalties: D.Rutherford (2);
Drop goal: T.Hopson

Mar 28 Newport 26 Gloucester 6
Try: G.White;
Penalty: D.Ainge

**Mar 29 Gloucester 0
French Universities 17**

Apr 2 Gloucester 3 Bridgend 6
Penalty: D.Ainge

Apr 7 Lydney 3 Gloucester 3
Penalty: D.Ainge

Apr 9 Gloucester 9 Headingley 16
Try: R.Long;
Penalties: D.Ainge (2)

Apr 11 Gloucester 32 Birkenhead Park 3
Tries: T.Hopson (2), J.Groves, A.Osman, J.Bayliss, G.Redding;
Conversions: D.Ainge (4);
Penalties: D.Ainge (2)

Apr 16 Gloucester 6 Harlequins 3
Penalty: D.Ainge;
Drop goal: T.Hopson

Apr 18 Gloucester 17 Cheltenham 6
Tries: M.Nicholls, C.Hannaford, G.White;
Conversion: D.Ainge;
Penalties: D.Ainge (2)

Apr 23 Redruth 6 Gloucester 12
Tries: T.Hopson, G.White;
Penalties: D.Ainge (2)

Apr 25 Penzance & Newlyn 11 Gloucester 6
Penalty: D.Ainge;
Drop goal: M.Booth

Apr 28 Stroud 0 Gloucester 3
Penalty: D.Ainge

Apr 30 Gloucester 18 Exeter 18
Tries: J.Groves, D.Christopher, Dick Smith, T.Hopson;
Conversions: D.Ainge (3)

J.Hickie T.Day A.D.Wadley(Hon.Treas) R.Collins R.R.Morris N.H.B.Duncalfe I.Jones P.K.Hawker F.Ewers S.F.Dangerfield C.A.Lynch T.Lane P.Ford
T.R.Tandy(Hon.Sec) J.Groves R.G.Pitt G.Edmunds A.Brinn N.Jackson R.G.Long H.Symonds C.N.Teague N.J.Foice M.Booth E.J.Stephens K.Grimshaw
G.Hudson(Hon.Team Sec)
F.D.H.Dawe(Hon.Fixture Sec) R.(Dick)Smith J.Fowke M.Nicholls Dr.A.Alcock(Pres) G.G.White(Capt) Rev.H.M.Hughes(Chairman) D.Rutherford
J.Bayliss D.B.W.Ainge A.Hudson(Vice-Pres).   (in front) J.Dix J.Spalding

Played 53 Won 24 Lost 24 Drawn 5
For 462 Against 570
Captain: Gary White

Gloucester United
Played 33 Won 9 Lost 23 Drawn 1
For 261 Against 426
Captain: Pete Hawker

Most appearances: A.Brinn 45, J.Groves 44,
Dick Smith 42, M.Nicholls 41, C.Teague 41,
R.Long 40, D.Ainge 38, N.Foice 36
Most tries: N.Foice, Dick Smith 8, J.Groves 7,
G.White 6, G.Mace, R.Pitt 5
Conversions: D.Ainge 19, D.Rutherford 11,
G.White, E.Stephens 2, T.Hopson, P.Meadows 1
Penalties: D.Ainge 27, D.Rutherford 12,
G.White 3, E.Stephens 2, G.Hook, M.Booth,
P.Meadows 1
Drop goals: D.Ainge 4, M.Booth 3, T.Hopson,
G.Mace, D.Rutherford 2, J.Groves,
E.Stephens 1

After several years wait, the new Social Club
was officially opened after the Wolfhounds
game on 22 September. It had cost £15,000, and
had a licensed bar and skittle alley.

This was a season that started brightly, but
largely due to a long run of injuries became
one of the worst seasons in the club's history.
At various times John Bayliss, Terry Hopson,
Mickey Booth, John Spalding, Tony Davies and
Dave Owen were missing for long periods. Don
Rutherford was not available until February.
Consequently, results suffered. On the road
there were heavy defeats at Newport, Cardiff,
and Newbridge. Even when the team played
well, pressure did not result in points. A good
example was at Northampton, where even the
home crowd conceded that Gloucester were
unlucky to lose 16-6. It was frustrating as
there were early successes; a good win over
Northampton at Kingsholm, and even better
a victory at Coventry where the fearsome
Midlanders pack was totally outplayed. In the
return game Gloucester could not quite force a
double, and the game was drawn. In October
Wellington, the New Zealand club team,
was beaten. But these were highlights in a
depressing season.

The forwards battled against the odds. Jackie
Fowke, Mike Nicholls, Colin Teague, Alan
Brinn, Roy Long, and Dick Smith (who played
in an England trial) managed to avoid most of
the injury plague. In the backs, wingers Nick
Foice and John Groves had good seasons. On
Boxing Day, a promising young winger, John
Dix, made his first team debut against Old
Merchant Taylors, and scored a try. Kingsholm
would get to know him well.

It was a tough season to be captain, but Gary
White never faltered, giving his all in the cause.
At the end of the season Don Rutherford, who
was already on the RFU's coaching committee
arranged special instructional sessions at
Kingsholm, involved with tactical skills, both
team and individual, theoretical and practical.
It was aimed at helping the team to adapt to a
more modern approach to the game.

Western Counties played the Australians at
Bristol. Dick Smith and Terry Hopson were in
the team, and Hopson kicked two penalties in
the 9-0 victory.

Sep 1 Gloucester 15 Clifton 6
Tries: G.Mace, N.Foice, T.Hopson;
Penalty: G.Hook,
Drop goal: G.Mace

Sep 3 Gloucester 16 Northampton 9
Tries: J.Groves (2), R.Morris;
Conversions: D.Ainge (2);
Penalty: D.Ainge

Sep 7 Stroud 6 Gloucester 3
Penalty: D.Ainge

Sep 10 Coventry 9 Gloucester 11
Tries: G.Mace, J.Spalding;
Conversion: D.Ainge;
Penalty: D.Ainge

Sep 15 Gloucester 24
Gloucestershire B 12
Tries: R.Long, N.Foice, G.White;
Conversions: D.Ainge (3);
Penalties: D.Ainge (3)

Sep 17 Gloucester 19 Moseley 23
Tries: Dick Smith, G.White, R.Pitt;
Conversions: G.White (2);
Penalties: G.White (2)

Sep 22 Gloucester 16 Wolfhounds 8
Tries: Dick Smith, R.Pitt, G.White, J.Groves;
Conversions: D.Ainge (2)

Sep 24 Bristol 15 Gloucester 3
Drop goal: D.Ainge

Sep 28 Cardiff 37 Gloucester 3
Try: N.Foice

Oct 1 Gloucester 9 Bedford 3
Try: N.Foice;
Penalty: D.Ainge;
Drop goal: J.Groves

Oct 6 Gloucester 8 Cheltenham 0
Tries: J.Groves, A.Brinn;
Conversion: D.Ainge

Oct 10 Ebbw Vale 13 Gloucester 0

Oct 13 Gloucester 9 Wellington (NZ) 6
Try: N.Foice;
Penalties: D.Ainge (2)

Oct 15 Newport 31 Gloucester 0

Oct 22 Gloucester 8 Old Blues 3
Tries: N.Foice, H.Symonds;
Conversion: D.Ainge

Oct 29 Oxford University 9 Gloucester 3
Drop goal: G.Mace

Nov 5 Gloucester 0 Leicester 3

Nov 12 Moseley 14 Gloucester 14
Tries: A.Davis, G.Mace;
Conversion: P.Meadows;
Penalty: P.Meadows;
Drop goal: M.Booth

Nov 19 Gloucester 9 Aberavon 8
Penalties: D.Ainge (3)

Nov 26 Newbridge 37 Gloucester 3
Penalty: G.White

Dec 3 Gloucester 6 Neath 9
Try: N.Foice;
Penalty: M.Booth

Dec 10 Bath 11 Gloucester 16
Tries: A.Davis, R.Pitt;
Conversions: D.Ainge (2);
Penalty: D.Ainge;

Drop goal: M.Booth

Dec 17 Gloucester 0 Coventry 0

Dec 24 Gloucester 11 Lydney 8
Tries: Dick Smith, P.Ford, J.Groves;
Conversion: D.Ainge

Dec 26 Gloucester 27
Old Merchant Taylors 3
Tries: Dick Smith (2), J.Dix, T.Hopson,
J.Groves, P.Ford;
Conversions: D.Ainge (3);
Penalty: D.Ainge

Dec 27 Gloucester 3 Pontypool 3
Drop goal: D.Ainge

Dec 31 Gloucester 11 Ebbw Vale 6
Try: G.Mace;
Conversion: D.Ainge;
Penalty: D.Ainge;
Drop goal: T.Hopson

Jan 7 Gloucester v London Scottish - cancelled
due to snow

Jan 14 Leicester 9 Gloucester 3
Penalty: D.Ainge

Jan 21 Wasps 0 Gloucester 3
Penalty: D.Ainge

Jan 28 Gloucester 8
Cambridge University 6
Try: T.Hopson;
Conversion: D.Ainge;
Penalty: D.Ainge

Feb 4 Gloucester 6 Bristol 14
Penalty: D.Ainge;
Drop Goal: T.Hopson

Feb 11 Gloucester 14 Bath 19
Try: J.Groves;
Conversion: D.Ainge;
Penalties: D.Ainge (3)

Feb 18 Swansea 14 Gloucester 8
Tries: R.Pitt, Dick Smith;
Conversion: T.Hopson

Feb 23 Gloucester 5 Army 14
Try: P.Ford;
Conversion: D.Rutherford

Feb 25 Aberavon 14 Gloucester 3
Penalty: D.Rutherford

Mar 4 Northampton 16 Gloucester 6
Penalties: D.Rutherford (2)

Mar 11 Gloucester 9 R.A.F. 3
Try: J.Dix;
Penalties: D.Rutherford (2)

Mar 16 Pontypool 19 Gloucester 3
Penalty: D.Ainge

Mar 18 Gloucester 3 Guy's Hospital 6
Try: R.Pitt

Mar 23 Lydney 13 Gloucester 16
Tries: Dick Smith, D.Ainge;
Conversions: D.Rutherford (2);
Penalty: D.Rutherford;
Drop goal: D.Rutherford

Mar 25 Gloucester 12 New Brighton 11
Tries: C.Hannaford, R.Morris, G.White,
D.Rutherford

Mar 27 Gloucester 21 Sale 14
Tries: C.Hannaford, Dick Smith, J.Dix;
Conversions: D.Rutherford (3);
Penalty: D.Rutherford;
Drop goal: D.Ainge

Mar 30 Clifton 6 Gloucester 6
Try: J.Spalding;
Penalty: D.Ainge

Apr 1 Gloucester 6 Cardiff 25
Penalties: D.Ainge (2)

Apr 3 Gloucester 19 Redruth 6
Tries: K.Grimshaw, G.Mace, H.Symonds;
Conversions: E.Stephens (2);
Penalties: E.Stephens (2)

Apr 5 Cheltenham 3 Gloucester 0

Apr 8 Neath 27 Gloucester 3
Penalty: D.Ainge

Apr 10 Gloucester 6 Newport 8
Penalties: D.Rutherford (2)

Apr 14 Gloucester 12 Harlequins 6
Penalties: D.Rutherford (2);
Drop goals: D.Rutherford, E.Stephens

Apr 19 Gloucester 21 Stroud 5
Tries: J.Dix, D.Rutherford, J.Bayliss, N.Foice,
G.White;
Conversions: D.Rutherford (3)

Apr 22 Penzance & Newlyn 3 Gloucester 3
Drop goal: M.Booth

Apr 24 Exeter 6 Gloucester 5
Try: G.White;
Conversion: D.Rutherford

1967-68

J.Haines M.Elway N.H.B.Duncalfe F.Ewers R.Morris L.Keck A.Kent T.Day I.Jones(Hon.Team Sec)
T.R.Tandy(Hon.Sec) A.Brinn M.Neal R.Collins R.Jardine A.Thomas J.Jarrett J.Fowke D.Owen M.Burton N.Jackson R.Cowlin R.J.Pitt J.Fryer J.Dix C.Lynch G.Dance
F.D.H.Dawe(Hon.Fixture Sec) T.H.Millington(Vice-Pres) J.Groves J.Bayliss M.H.Booth D.J.Rutherford(Capt) Dr.A.Alcock(Pres) R.(Dick)Smith G.White
M.Nicholls T.Palmer A.T.Voyce OBE(Vice-Pres) Rev.H.M.Hughes(Chairman)

Played 55 Won 23 Lost 25 Drawn 7
For 581 Against 520
Captain: Don Rutherford

Gloucester United
Played 33 Won 17 Lost 10 Drawn 6
For 367 Against 237
Captain: Mike Bayliss

Most appearances: A.Brinn 42, J.Groves 41,
J.Fowke 39, D.Owen 38, J.Bayliss 37
Most tries: J.Groves, G.White 10, N.Foice 8,
Dick Smith 7, R.Jardine 6
Most conversions: D.Rutherford 32,
E.Stephens 6
Most penalties: D.Rutherford 39, E.Stephens 13
Most drop goals: D.Rutherford 6, T.Palmer 5,
M.Booth 4

After many years of indecision floodlights were finally installed at Kingsholm, at a cost of £4,700. The first game to be played under the lights was against the Bosuns, an invitation XV, on 6 November. The previous home game under lights had been on the Spa in 1879.

Captain Don Rutherford changed the team's approach to the game. He introduced a far more rigorous and structured pattern to training. He also encouraged the players to express themselves, and play more running rugby. It was

quite revolutionary for Gloucester, and quickly produced results. Only three games in the first 13 were lost. There were wins over Coventry, Pontypool, Moseley (away) and Harlequins.

Thereafter, a number of injuries to key players affected results, because it was impossible to field a settled team. Dick Smith suffered an ankle injury which kept him out from Christmas until March. In addition, Gary White, Mike Burton, John Bayliss and Roy Morris were all injured at various times. The situation was so bad that Peter Ford came out of retirement to help out. As if all this was not enough, following a dispute on selection policy Terry Hopson left the club and joined Bath, playing against Gloucester at Kingsholm in March. However, he was back at Kingsholm for the start of the following season. It was not until late on that the early form was restored. From the end of March there were victories over Wasps, Neath and a win at Pontypool to complete the double, a game in which Don Rutherford made his last appearance for the club.

As always, the forwards performed to a high level all season. Gary White until injured, Alan Brinn, Dave Owen, Jackie Fowke and a young Nigel Jackson were to the fore. In the backs John Groves was always dangerous. A valuable recruit to the squad was Tom Palmer, who

played his county rugby for Cornwall. Versatile, he could play at full-back, centre or fly-half.

As usual Rutherford was a very reliable kicker, and in total scored 202 points. He was selected for the Barbarians Easter tour of South Wales, where he broke his arm for a second time, which ended his career. Although Peter Ford played a few games to help out because of the injury crisis, this was his final season after 507 appearances and 156 tries. Nick Foice left Gloucester to play for Cheltenham.

Dick Smith and Don Rutherford played for South of England against the New Zealanders at Bristol. Rutherford kicked a penalty.

Sep 2 Gloucester 18 Lydney 6
Tries: N.Foice, G.White, A.Brinn;
Penalties: E.Stephens (3)

Sep 6 Gloucester 14 Pontypool 3
Try: J.Bayliss;
Conversion: D.Rutherford;
Penalty: D.Rutherford
Drop goals: D.Rutherford, M.Booth

Sep 9 Gloucester 11 Coventry 9
Try: G.White;
Conversion: E.Stephens;
Penalties: E.Stephens (2)

Sep 13 Cheltenham 14 Gloucester 5
Try: R.Pitt;
Conversion: D.Rutherford

Sep 16 Moseley 11 Gloucester 14
Try: J.Dix;
Conversion: D.Rutherford;
Penalty: D.Rutherford;
Drop goals: D.Rutherford (2)

Sep 20 Cardiff 20 Gloucester 9
Try: J.Groves;
Penalties: D.Rutherford (2)

Sep 23 Gloucester 11 Bristol 12
Try: G.White;
Conversion: D.Rutherford;
Penalties: D.Rutherford (2)

Sep 30 Bedford 5 Gloucester 18
Tries: T.Hopson, M.Burton, J.Bayliss;
Conversions: D.Rutherford (3);
Drop goal: T.Hopson

Oct 2 Gloucester 12 Ebbw Vale 8
Try: N.Foice;
Penalties: D.Rutherford (3)

Oct 7 Bective Rangers 3 Gloucester 22
Tries: G.White, D.East, Dick Smith;
Conversions: D.Rutherford (2);
Penalty: D.Rutherford;
Drop goals: D.Rutherford, M.Booth

Oct 14 Gloucester 18 Harlequins 0
Tries: G.White, D.East;
Penalties: D.Rutherford (4)

Oct 21 Gloucester 13 Newport 13
Tries: J.Bayliss, Dick Smith;
Conversions: D.Rutherford (2);
Penalty: D.Rutherford

Oct 28 Gloucester 32 Old Blues 3
Tries: N.Foice (2), R.Morris, J.Bayliss, D.Owen,
J.Dix, penalty try;
Conversions: E.Stephens (4);
Penalty: E.Stephens

Nov 4 Leicester 9 Gloucester 6
Try: J.Groves;
Penalty: E.Stephens

Nov 6 Gloucester 34 Bosuns 8
Tries: M.Booth (2), N.Foice, T.Hopson,
G.White, J.Groves, J.Bayliss;
Conversions: J.Rutherford (5);
Drop goal: M.Booth

Nov 11 Gloucester 3 Moseley 6
Try: R.Jardine

**Nov 15 Cambridge University 9
Gloucester 3**
Try: N.Foice

Nov 18 Aberavon 11 Gloucester 3
Penalty: E.Stephens

Nov 25 Gloucester 9 Newbridge 11
Tries: R.Jardine, N.Foice;
Penalty: C.Wheatman

Nov 29 Gloucester 6 St.Luke's College 22
Tries: N.Foice, G.White

Dec 2 Gloucester 11 Oxford University 11
Try: R.Pitt;
Conversion: E.Stephens;
Penalty: E.Stephens;
Drop goal: M.Booth

Dec 6 Gloucester 27 Clifton 6
Tries: G.White, J.Groves, Dick Smith,
R.Jardine, R.Pitt;
Conversions: D.Rutherford (3)
Penalty: D.Rutherford;
Drop goal: D.Rutherford

Dec 9 Gloucester v Bath - cancelled

Dec 16 Coventry 8 Gloucester 3
Penalty: D.Rutherford

Dec 23 Gloucester 19 Northampton 3
Tries: R.Pitt, R.Morris, J.Groves;
Conversions: D.Rutherford (2);
Penalties: D.Rutherford (2)

**Dec 26 Gloucester 14
Old Merchant Taylors 8**
Tries: J.Dix (2), R.Jardine, Dick Smith;
Conversion: M.Booth

Dec 27 Gloucester 11 Stroud 3
Try: G.White;
Conversion: G.Hook;
Penalty: G.Hook;
Drop goal: D.Gent

Dec 30 Gloucester 6 Cardiff 21
Penalties: D.Rutherford (2)

Jan 6 London Scottish 16 Gloucester 6
Tries: G.White, M.Neal

Jan 13 Gloucester v Leicester - cancelled due
to frost

Jan 20 Gloucester 8 Plymouth Albion 0
Try: N.Jackson;
Conversion: D.Rutherford;

Penalty: D.Rutherford

Jan 27 Neath 14 Gloucester 0

Feb 8 Gloucester 8 Army 8
Try: N.Jackson;
Conversion: D.Rutherford;
Penalty: D.Rutherford

Feb 10 Bath 0 Gloucester 11
Try: A.Brinn;
Conversion: D.Rutherford;
Penalty: D.Rutherford;
Drop goal: D.Rutherford

**Feb 14 Gloucester 11
Loughborough Colleges 5**
Tries: M.Booth, J.Dix;
Conversion: D.Rutherford;
Penalty: D.Rutherford

Feb 16 Gloucester 3 Swansea 17
Drop goal: T.Palmer

Feb 24 Gloucester 6 Aberavon 6
Penalties: D.Rutherford (2)

Feb 28 Bristol 6 Gloucester 5
Try: N.Jackson;
Conversion: D.Rutherford

Mar 2 Northampton 18 Gloucester 8
Try: J.Groves;
Conversion: P.Meadows;
Penalty: P.Meadows

Mar 5 Gloucester 6 Bath 18
Try: J.Groves;
Penalty: D.Rutherford

Mar 9 Gloucester 6 R.A.F. 17
Tries: D.Gent, N.Jackson

Mar 13 Ebbw Vale 20 Gloucester 3
Drop goal: T.Palmer

Mar 16 Guy's Hospital 3 Gloucester 3
Drop goal: T.Palmer

Mar 21 Stroud 8 Gloucester 15
Try: D.Medcroft;
Penalties: D.Rutherford (4)

Mar 23 Gloucester 3 Saracens 3
Penalty: D.Rutherford

Mar 25 Newport 8 Gloucester 6
Tries: D.Rutherford, G.Robinson

Mar 27 Clifton 5 Gloucester 24
Tries: J.Groves, R.Jardine, Dick Smith;

Conversions: D.Rutherford (3);
Penalties: D.Rutherford (3)

Mar 30 Gloucester 23 Wasps 0
Tries: R.Jardine, M.Burton, R.Morris, J.Groves;
Conversion: D.Rutherford;
Penalties: D.Rutherford (2);
Drop goal: T.Palmer

Apr 1 Gloucester 3 Cheltenham 14
Try: R.Morris

Apr 6 Pontypool 11 Gloucester 16
Tries: J.Bayliss, T.Palmer, J.Groves;
Conversions: D.Rutherford (2);

Penalty: D.Rutherford

Apr 11 Lydney 0 Gloucester 9
Try: Dick Smith;
Penalties: C.Wheatman (2)

Apr 13 Gloucester 5 Headingley 30
Try: Dick Smith;
Conversion: C.Wheatman

Apr 15 Gloucester 3 Birkenhead Park 6
Penalty: J.Bayliss

Apr 20 Gloucester 15 Neath 11
Try: J.Spalding;

Penalties: E.Stephens (2), T.Palmer (2)

Apr 23 Newbridge 8 Gloucester 6
Penalty: E.Stephens;
Drop goal: T.Palmer

Apr 27 Penzance & Newlyn 6 Gloucester 6
Try: C.Teague;
Penalty: E.Stephens

Apr 29 Exeter 19 Gloucester 11
Try: A.Thomas;
Conversion: T.Palmer;
Penalties: T.Palmer (2)

1968-69

T.R.Tandy(Hon.Sec) J.Hickie A.D.Wadley(Hon.Treas) N.H.B.Duncalfe J.Haines A.Kent P.K.Hawker L.A.Keck I.Jones W.Cale F.Ewers P.J.Ford(Hon.Team Sec) T.Pritchard M.Elway
Dr.J.Neill T.Day R.J.Clewes K.Richardson R.Collins M.J.Nicholls J.Fowke M.J.Burton J.Haines R.G.Long K.Jarrett M.Potter D.Brooks D.East R.Gwilliam J.Spalding J.Fryer Rev.H.M.Hughes(Chairman)
F.D.H.Dawe(Hon.Fixture Sec) T.Palmer E.Stephens J.Bayliss R.(Dick)Smith(Capt) Dr.A.Alcock(Pres) A.Brinn J.Groves P.Kocerhan G.G.White A.T.Voyce O.B.E.(Vice-Pres)
J.T.Hopson M.H.Booth

Played 52 Won 32 Lost 15 Drawn 5
For 882 Against 532
Captain: Dick Smith

Gloucester United
Played 26 Won 16 Lost 8 Drawn 2
For 446 Against 287
Captain: Mike Bayliss

Most appearances: J.Groves 48, E.Stephens 43, Dick Smith 42, T.Palmer 41, M.Potter 40, R.Clewes, A.Brinn 35
Most tries: R.Clewes 24, J.Groves 17, G.White 15, Dick Smith, J.Bayliss 13, R.Gwilliam, T.Hopson 12
Most conversions: E.Stephens 66, M.Booth 6, T.Palmer 4

Most penalties: E.Stephens 56, T.Palmer 8
Most drop goals: T.Palmer 8, E.Stephens 3

The Club enjoyed what was, at that time, the best season ever with regard to the number of wins. A big factor in this success could be attributed to the phenomenal place kicking of Eric Stephens. He totalled 309 points, which broke the club record by a country mile. The total number of points scored was also easily a record. The scene was set with a huge 13-try beating of Lydney, and the team rarely looked back. There were wins over Bristol (away), Cardiff, Leicester, Northampton, Ebbw Vale and Wasps (away). In addition, there was a double over Pontypool for the second season running.

During the game at Bristol, there was the unusual sight of Jim Jarrett calling for a mark, and then coolly proceeding to drop a goal from 40 metres out. That was in the days when a mark could be called anywhere on the field. That drop goal seemed to inspire the team to fight on to an outstanding victory.

Playing in his first season, winger Bob Clewes made a big impact, and would continue to score prolifically for many seasons. John Groves on the other wing also scored heavily. Evergreen Gary White scored the most tries by a forward. Returning from his brief sojourn at Bath, Terry Hopson resumed his partnership with both Mickey Booth and John Spalding, to form the half-back combination. Tom Palmer was always reliable, starting the season at fly-half, he moved to centre later, to accommodate Hopson. Mike Burton, Mike Potter, Gary White, Alan Brinn and captain Dick Smith, gave sterling performances in the forwards.

An innovation was the introduction of the Midland Floodlit Alliance, all games being played mid-week, although this entailed shoe-horning extra games into an already crowded season.

Peter Meadows made his final two appearances for the first XV, but he would go on to captain the United from 1969-71. Roy Long who had first played in 1956 called time on his career. He had played in 339 games. John Groves, who made the most number of appearances in the season, returned to his old club Pontypridd, for the following campaign. He had made 159 appearances for Gloucester and scored 40 tries.

Sep 2 Gloucester 54 Lydney 6
Tries: G.White (2), J.Groves (2), J.Bayliss (2), R.Clewes (2), J.Jarrett, T.Palmer, M.Potter, R.Morris, Dick Smith;
Conversions: E.Stephens (4), T.Palmer (2);
Penalty: E.Stephens

Sep 5 Gloucester 30 Broughton Park 0
Tries: Dick Smith (2), R.Gwilliam, T.Palmer, R.Morris;
Conversions: E.Stephens (3);
Penalties: E.Stephens (3)

Sep 7 Gloucester 8 Moseley 8
Try: J.Spalding;
Conversion: E.Stephens;
Penalty: E.Stephens

Sep 12 Gloucester 19 Cheltenham 17
Tries: J.Groves, R.Gwilliam;
Conversions: E.Stephens (2);
Penalties: E.Stephens (2);
Drop goal: T.Palmer

Sep 14 Coventry 9 Gloucester 9
Penalty: E.Stephens;
Drop goals: T.Palmer (2)

Sep 19 Clifton 9 Gloucester 12
Penalties: E.Stephens (4)

Sep 21 Gloucester 20 Bective Rangers 6
Try: G.White;
Conversion: E.Stephens;
Penalties: E.Stephens (5)

Sep 25 Gloucester 15 Cardiff 6
Penalties: E.Stephens (5)

Sep 28 Bristol 6 Gloucester 9
Penalty: E.Stephens;
Drop goals: E.Stephens, J.Jarrett (from a mark)

Oct 2 Gloucester 15 Coventry 8
(Midland Floodlit Alliance)
Tries: Dick Smith, J.Bayliss, R.Clewes;
Penalties: T.Palmer (2)

Oct 5 Gloucester 21 Bedford 22
Tries: Dick Smith, R.Clewes, A.Brinn;
Conversions: M.Booth (3);
Penalty: Paul Butler
Drop goal: Paul Butler

Oct 10 Gloucester 16 Ebbw Vale 6
Tries: Dick Smith, J.Bayliss;
Conversions: T.Palmer (2);
Penalties: T.Palmer (2)

Oct 12 Harlequins 16 Gloucester 3
Try: R.Clewes

Oct 16 Gloucester 30 Bosuns 8
Tries: K.Richardson, M.Neal, J.Bayliss, M.Burton;
Conversions: E.Stephens (3);
Penalties: E.Stephens (3);
Drop goal: T.Palmer

Oct 19 Newport 29 Gloucester 0

Oct 26 Gloucester 59 Old Blues 0
Tries: R.Jardine (3), R.Clewes (3), T.Hopson (3), D.Brooks, J.Spalding, G.White, J.Groves;
Conversions: E.Stephens (9), M.Teague

Oct 30 Gloucester 19 Stroud 5
Tries: Dick Smith, T.Palmer, R.Jardine, R.Gwilliam;
Conversions: E.Stephens (2);
Penalty: E.Stephens

Nov 2 Gloucester 9 Leicester 3
Try: J.Spalding;
Penalties: E.Stephens (2)

Nov 9 Moseley 39 Gloucester 8
Try: C.Teague, R.Clewes;
Conversion: E.Stephens

Nov 16 Gloucester 11 Aberavon 12
Tries: Dick Smith, J.Bayliss;
Conversion: M.Booth;
Penalty: M.Booth

Nov 23 Newbridge 3 Gloucester 3
Try: J.Groves

Nov 27 Gloucester 9 St.Luke's College 9
Try: G.White;

Penalty: T.Palmer;
Drop goal: T.Palmer

Nov 30 Oxford University 23 Gloucester 3
Penalty: T.Palmer

Dec 7 Gloucester 15 Pontypool 8
Tries: J.Groves, R.Gwilliam, M.Potter, G.White;
Penalty: T.Palmer

Dec 14 Bath v Gloucester - cancelled due to frost

Dec 21 Gloucester 9 Coventry 14
Tries: J.Spalding, J.Bayliss;
Penalty: J.Spalding

Dec 26 Gloucester 42 Old Merchant Taylors 10
Tries: R.Gwilliam (5), J.Haines (2), T.Hopson (2), P.Butler, R.Clewes;
Conversions: T.Hopson (2), J.Spalding;
Penalty: T.Hopson

Dec 28 Gloucester v Newbridge - cancelled due to frost

Jan 4 Gloucester 11 London Scottish 12
Tries: T.Palmer, Paul Butler;
Conversion: J.Spalding;
Penalty: T.Palmer

Jan 11 Leicester 12 Gloucester 8
Try: J.Bayliss;
Conversion: E.Stephens;
Penalty: E.Stephens

Jan 18 Saracens v Gloucester - cancelled due to frost

Jan 25 Gloucester 27 Cambridge University 5
Tries: T.Hopson (2), R.Clewes, Dick Smith, J.Groves, T.Palmer;
Conversions: M.Booth (2), E.Stephens;
Penalty: E.Stephens

Feb 1 Gloucester 5 Bristol 6
Try: J.Bayliss;
Conversion: E.Stephens

Feb 7 Gloucester v Bath
Feb 13 Gloucester v Army
Feb 15 Swansea v Gloucester
Feb 19 Gloucester v Loughborough Colleges
Feb 22 Aberavon v Gloucester
All cancelled due to snow and/or frost

Feb 26 Cheltenham 3 Gloucester 6
(Midland Floodlit Alliance)

Tries: R.Clewes, J.Groves

Mar 1 Gloucester 16 Northampton 11
Tries: J.Groves (2), R.Clewes, T.Hopson;
Conversions: E.Stephens (2)

Mar 5 Gloucester 8 Bath 6
Try: Dick Smith;
Conversion: E.Stephens;
Penalty: E.Stephens

Mar 7 Gloucester 25 R.A.F. 8
Tries: J.Groves (2), D.Brooks;
Conversions: E.Stephens (2);
Penalties: E.Stephens (3)
Drop goal: M.Booth

Mar 12 Ebbw Vale 6 Gloucester 6
Try: Dick Smith;
Penalty: E.Stephens

Mar 15 Gloucester 24 Guy's Hospital 11
Tries: M.Neal, D.East, T.Hopson, Dick Smith,
R.Clewes, T.Palmer;
Conversions: E.Stephens (3)

Mar 19 Moseley 24 Gloucester 9
(Midland Floodlit Alliance)
Try: R.Clewes;
Penalty: E.Stephens;
Drop goal: T.Palmer

Mar 22 Gloucester 3 Newport 8
Try: R.Clewes

Mar 26 Gloucester 0 Leicester 6

(Midland Floodlit Alliance)

Mar 29 Wasps 14 Gloucester 22
Tries: M.Potter, A.Brinn, D.Brooks;
Conversions: E.Stephens (2);
Penalties: E.Stephens (2);
Drop goal: E.Stephens

Apr 3 Lydney 8 Gloucester 19
Tries: R.Clewes, T.Hopson, M.Booth;
Conversions: E.Stephens (2);
Penalties: E.Stephens (2)

Apr 5 Gloucester 25 New Brighton 9
Tries: R.Clewes (2), G.White, A.Brinn,
J.Bayliss;
Conversions: E.Stephens (2);
Penalties: E.Stephens (2)

Apr 7 Gloucester 20 Fylde 21
Tries: R.Gwilliam (2), M.Neal, R.Clewes;
Conversion: E.Stephens;
Penalty: E.Stephens
Drop goal: T.Palmer

Apr 12 Pontypool 6 Gloucester 15
Tries: T.Hopson, R.Clewes, R.Jardine;
Conversions: E.Stephens (3)

Apr 16 Cheltenham 5 Gloucester 16
Tries: K.Richardson, M.Potter, G.White;
Conversions: E.Stephens (2);
Penalty: E.Stephens

Apr 19 Gloucester 28 Sale 16
Tries: T.Palmer (2), Dick Smith, A.Brinn,

R.Clewes, T.Hopson;
Conversions: E.Stephens (2);
Penalty: E.Stephens;
Drop goal: T.Palmer

Apr 21 Bath 13 Gloucester 19
Tries: J.Peart, J.Bayliss, G.White, R.Gwilliam;
Conversions: E.Stephens (2);
Penalty: E.Stephens

Apr 23 Gloucester 12 Clifton 6
Tries: R.Clewes (2), G.White;
Penalty: E.Stephens

**Apr 26 Penzance & Newlyn 3
Gloucester 38**
Tries: J.Groves (4), A.Brinn, M.Potter;
Conversions: E.Stephens (4);
Penalties: E.Stephens (3);
Drop goal: T.Palmer

Apr 28 Plymouth Albion 12 Gloucester 8
Try: G.White;
Conversion: E.Stephens;
Penalty: E.Stephens

May 1 Stroud 13 Gloucester 27
Tries: M.Burton (2), A.Brinn, G.White;
Conversions: E.Stephens (3);
Penalties: E.Stephens (3)

May 3 Gloucester 37 Exeter 3
Tries: G.White (3), K.Richardson (2), J.Bayliss
(2), J.Groves;
Conversions: E.Stephens (5);
Penalty: E.Stephens

1969-70

**Played 57 Won 31 Lost 24 Drawn 1
Abandoned 1
For 761 Against 619
Captain: Dick Smith**

Gloucester United
Played 33 Won 19 Lost 13 Drawn 1
For 469 Against 370
Captain: Peter Meadows

Most appearances: R.Clewes 50, J.Spalding
49, M.Potter 48, M.Nicholls 44, D.Brooks 41
K.Richardson 39, G.White, R.Cowling 37
Most tries: R.Clewes 24, G.White 12,
D.Brooks 10, T.Hopson 8,
Most conversions: E.Stephens 29, T.Palmer,
J.Spalding 11, Paul Butler 8
Most penalties: E.Stephens 33, T.Palmer 13,
J.Spalding 10
Drop goals: T.Hopson 4, E.Stephens 3,
T.Palmer, R.Jardine, M.Booth 1

The playing record was a disappointment
following the success of the previous season.
Eric Stephens was injured and managed only
23 appearances, although he scored 178 points.
In his absence it fell to Tom Palmer and John
Spalding to take on the kicking role, and not
surprisingly they were not as accurate as the
excellent Stephens. Bob Clewes, in his second
season continued to run in lots of tries. With
Mickey Booth only playing a handful of games,
the half-back combination was Terry Hopson and
John Spalding. Ron Etheridge emerged as a very
promising full-back blessed with considerable
pace. After striving for several seasons, Mike
Nicholls became the regular hooker. Keith
Richardson made a move from the back-row to
prop, and quickly cemented his position. The
forwards as a whole were as tenacious as ever,
with Jim Jarrett, Robin Cowling, Nigel Jackson,
Mike Potter, Gary White and Dick Smith
working hard every week.

Although only a moderate season there were
some impressive performances. For a third
season running Pontypool were beaten home
and away. There were other good wins over
Ebbw Vale, Harlequins, Newport, Swansea, and
Bristol (away).

Terry Hopson had been in good form all season,
but a thigh injury kept him out for the start of
the 1970-71 campaign, and when making a
come back for the United in January 1971, he
broke his leg, which ended his career. So, this
was his final season playing for the first XV. He
had made 315 appearances and scored 103 tries.
His half-back partner Mickie Booth said of him,
"When he was on form he was a magnificent
player".

Jackie Fowke (267 games) and Ron Pitt (155)
retired at the end of the season

A.Brinn M.Elway J.Haines R.W.Collins P.Ford P.K.Hawker F.C.Ewers W.Cale Dr.T.E.Durkin J.Hickie T.Pritchard T.Day J.Fryer
D.C.Brooks K.Richardson J.Dix A.J.L.Fielding J.L.Fowke J.S.Jarrett D.W.Pegler M.J.Potter J.T.Hopson J.A.Horner T.Palmer R.J.Cowling J.A.Watkins
R.J.Clewes
T.Tandy M.J.Nicholls G.G.White A.T.Voyce(Pres) R.(Dick)Smith(Capt) Dr.A.Alcock(Life Vice-Pres) E.J.F.Stephens M.A.Burton Rev.H.M.Hughes
R.Etheridge J.H.Spalding

Gloucestershire made it to the final of the County Championship only to lose unexpectedly to Staffordshire. John Bayliss, Terry Hopson, Alan Brinn, Jim Jarrett and Dick Smith were the Gloucester players involved. Western Counties played South Africa, and Hopson, Brinn, Phil Hayward and Smith were in the team. Hayward and Brinn played in England trial games.

Sep 1 Gloucester 60
Philadelphia University 0
Tries: G.White (2), E.Stephens (2), R.Jardine (2), T.Palmer, Dick Smith, T.Hopson, J.Dix, M.Burton, J.Spalding, R.Clewes, M.Potter;
Conversions: E.Stephens (6), J.Spalding (3)

Sep 3 Cardiff 22 Gloucester 3
Penalty: J.Spalding

Sep 6 Gloucester 6 Broughton Park 11
Try: N.Jackson;
Penalty: E.Stephens

Sep 10 Cheltenham 15 Gloucester 17
Tries: R.Clewes, E.Stephens, G.White;
Conversion: E.Stephens;
Penalty: E.Stephens;
Drop goal: T.Hopson

Sep 13 Gloucester 9 Coventry 15
Penalties: E.Stephens (3)

Sep 16 Gloucester 16 Wolfhounds 6
Tries: G.White, E.Stephens, Dick Smith;
Conversions: E.Stephens (2);

Penalty: E.Stephens

Sep 20 Bective Rangers 3 Gloucester 13
Tries: R.Clewes, R.Cowling, T.Palmer;
Conversions: E.Stephens (2)

Sep 24 Newbridge 9 Gloucester 5 -
abandoned due to bad light and rain
Try: G.White;
Conversion: Paul Butler

Sep 27 Gloucester 8 Bristol 16
Try: T.Palmer;
Conversion: E.Stephens;
Penalty: E.Stephens

Oct 1 Gloucester 15 Ebbw Vale 11
Try: T.Hopson;
Penalties: E.Stephens (4)

Oct 4 Bedford 17 Gloucester 8
Try: T.Hopson;
Conversion: E.Stephens;
Penalty: E.Stephens

Oct 8 Gloucester 49 Stroud 14
Tries: D.Brooks (2), R.Clewes (2), Dick Smith, R.Morris, T.Palmer, M.Burton, A.Brinn, M.Potter;
Conversions: E.Stephens (6), J.Spalding (2);
Penalty: E.Stephens

Oct 11 Gloucester 14 Harlequins 6
Try: Dick Smith;
Conversion: T.Palmer;

Penalties: T.Palmer (3)

Oct 15 Gloucester 3 Bosuns 16
Penalty: T.Palmer

Oct 18 Gloucester 21 Newport 6
Tries: G.White, R.Morris, R.Clewes;
Conversions: T.Palmer (3);
Penalties: T.Palmer (2)

Oct 25 Gloucester 27 Old Blues 0
Tries: D.Brooks, J.Horner, K.Richardson, R.Morris;
Conversions: Paul Butler (3);
Penalty: Paul Butler;
Drop goals: J.Spalding, M.Booth

Oct 29 Gloucester 15 Clifton 3
Tries: T.Hopson, D.Brooks;
Penalties: Paul Butler, M.Booth;
Drop goal: T.Hopson

Nov 1 Leicester 15 Gloucester 12
Tries: J.Haines, M.Potter;
Penalty: T.Palmer;
Drop goal: T.Palmer

Nov 8 Moseley 14 Gloucester 17
Tries: D.Brooks, R.Jardine, J.Spalding;
Conversion: J.Spalding;
Penalty: J.Spalding;
Drop goal: R.Jardine

Nov 12 Gloucester 0 Cheltenham 6
(Midland Floodlit Alliance)

Nov 14 Aberavon 14 Gloucester 5
Try: A.J.L.Fielding;
Conversion: J.Spalding

**Nov 19 Cambridge University 23
Gloucester 19**
Tries: D.Brooks, Dick Smith, J.Spalding;
Conversions: Paul Butler, J.Spalding;
Penalties: J.Spalding (2)

Nov 22 Gloucester 13 Lydney 0
Tries: R.Morris (2), J.Horner;
Conversions: Paul Butler (2)

Nov 26 Gloucester 18 St.Luke's College 6
Tries: A.J.L.Fielding, M.Booth, R.Clewes,
J.Jarrett;
Conversions: T.Palmer (3)

**Nov 29 Gloucester 8
Oxford University 13**
Try: K.Richardson;
Conversion: Paul Butler;
Drop goal: T.Hopson

Dec 6 Pontypool 9 Gloucester 14
Tries: J.Jarrett (2), J.Dix;
Conversion: T.Palmer;
Penalty: T.Palmer

Dec 13 Gloucester 39 Bath 13
Tries: M.Potter (2), D.Brooks, R.Clewes, J.Dix,
J.Spalding, K.Richardson;
Conversions: T.Palmer (3);
Penalties: T.Palmer (4)

Dec 20 Coventry 20 Gloucester 9
Tries: R.Clewes, K.Richardson;
Penalty: T.Palmer

**Dec 26 Gloucester 16
Old Merchant Taylors 6**
Tries: D.Brooks, J.Bayliss, J.Spalding, R.Clewes;
Conversion: J.Spalding (2)

Dec 27 Gloucester 12 Pontypool 6
Tries: R.Clewes (2);
Penalties: E.Stephens (2)

Jan 3 London Scottish 32 Gloucester 3
Try: R.Morris

Jan 10 Gloucester 6 Leicester 8
Tries: G.White, J.Horner

Jan 17 Gloucester 6 Wasps 0
Tries: R.Clewes (2)

Jan 23 Bridgend 16 Gloucester 0

**Jan 27 Coventry 20 Gloucester 6
(Midland Floodlit Alliance)**
Try: J.Jarrett;
Drop goal: T.Hopson

Jan 31 Gloucester 11 Plymouth Albion 6
Tries: K.Richardson, J.Bayliss;
Conversion: Dick Smith;
Penalty: Dick Smith

Feb 4 Ebbw Vale 9 Gloucester 0

Feb 12 Gloucester v Army - cancelled due to
snow
Feb 14 Bath v Gloucester - cancelled due to
snow and frost

**Feb 18 Gloucester 14
Loughborough Colleges 3**
Tries: K.Richardson, M.Nicholls, R.Clewes,
G.White;
Conversion: R.Etheridge

Feb 21 Gloucester 19 Swansea 3
Tries: T.Hopson (3), R.Clewes;
Conversions: G.White (2);
Penalty: G.White

Feb 23 Gloucester 8 Newbridge 0
Tries: T.Hopson, R.Clewes;
Conversion: M.Booth

Feb 27 Gloucester 9 Aberavon 10
Tries: D.Brooks, J.Jarrett;
Penalty: Dick Smith

Mar 4 Leicester v Gloucester (Midland Floodlit
Alliance) - cancelled due to snow
Mar 7 Northampton v Gloucester - cancelled
due to snow

Mar 14 Gloucester 15 Richmond 16
Tries: M.Nicholls, A.J.L.Fielding, R.Clewes;
Penalties: J.Spalding (2)

Mar 18 Bristol 14 Gloucester 15
Tries: R.Clewes (2), P.Hayward;
Penalties: J.Spalding (2)

Mar 20 Gloucester 20 Guy's Hospital 6
Tries: J.Jarrett, R.Clewes, R.Etheridge,
A.J.L.Fielding, K.Richardson;
Conversion: J.Spalding;
Penalty: J.Spalding

Mar 26 Lydney 11 Gloucester 27
Tries: Dick Smith, J.Dix, G.White,

A.J.L.Fielding;
Conversions: E.Stephens (3);
Penalties: E.Stephens (3)

Mar 28 Gloucester 17 Headingley 3
Tries: J.Spalding, R.Clewes, Dick Smith,
R.Jardine;
Conversion: E.Stephens;
Penalty: E.Stephens

Mar 30 Gloucester 15 Birkenhead Park 3
Tries: J.Horner (2), G.White (2), A.J.L.Fielding

Mar 31 Stroud 14 Gloucester 6
Try: J.Dix;
Penalty: J.Spalding

Apr 4 Fylde 19 Gloucester 3
Try: M.Nicholls

Apr 10 Gloucester 3 Moseley 3
Try: A.Brinn

Apr 13 Newport 45 Gloucester 9
Penalties: E.Stephens (2);
Drop goal: E.Stephens (from a mark)

Apr 18 Sale 13 Gloucester 6
Try: J.Dix;
Penalty: E.Stephens

Apr 20 Gloucester 14 Cheltenham 6
Tries: J.Watkins, D.Brooks;
Conversion: E.Stephens;
Penalties: E.Stephens (2)

**Apr 25 Penzance & Newlyn 6
Gloucester 17**
Try: R.Clewes;
Conversion: E.Stephens;
Penalties: E.Stephens (4)

Apr 27 Redruth 9 Gloucester 14
Try: M.Bayliss;
Conversion: E.Stephens;
Penalties: E.Stephens (3)

Apr 28 Exeter 9 Gloucester 11
Try: G.White;
Conversion: E.Stephens;
Penalty: E.Stephens;
Drop goal: E.Stephens

May 2 Gloucester 16 Liverpool 20
Tries: R.Clewes, M.Potter;
Conversions: E.Stephens (2);
Penalty: E.Stephens;
Drop goal: E.Stephens (from a mark)

W.Cale A.D.Wadley(Hon.Treas) T.Pritchard N.H.B.Duncalfe H.King(Hon.Sec) P.J.Ford J.Haines M.Elway T.E.Durkin F.Ewers P.Hawker T.R.Tandy
J.Hickie R.R.Morris T.Day J.H.Spalding R.Collins K.R.Morris M.J.Potter D.W.Pegler A.Brinn J.S.Jarrett D.W.Owen R.(Dick)Smith M.A.Burton
R.Jardine R.J.Cowling R.G.Long(Team Sec) J.Fryer
F.D.H.Dawe(Hon. Fixture Sec) R.Etheridge J.A.Watkins J.Dix J.H.Haines Dr.A.Alcock M.J.Nicholls(Capt) A.T.Voyce OBE(Pres) J.A.Bayliss(Vice-Capt)
E.J.Stephens R.J.Clewes N.A.Jackson Rev.H.M.Hughes(Chairman)
M.Booth T.Palmer

Played 51 Won 35 Lost 12 Drawn 4
For 772 Against 382
Captain: Mike Nicholls

Gloucester United
Played 29 Won 13 Lost 16 Drawn 0
For 337 Against 346
Captain: Peter Meadows

Most appearances: M.Nicholls 51, R.Clewes 48, M.Burton 47, E.Stephens 46, R.Cowling 42, R.Etheridge, J.Haines 40, T.Palmer, 39, J.Bayliss 37, A.Brinn, M.Booth 36
Most tries: R.Clewes 33, R.Jardine 10, J.Dix, E.Stephens 9, J.Bayliss, T.Palmer 8
Conversions: E.Stephens 60, R.Etheridge, M.Booth 1
Penalties: E.Stephens 71, T.Palmer, Dick Smith, K.Richardson 1
Drop goals: M.Booth 4, T.Palmer, E.Stephens 1

An excellent season. The number of wins was the highest in the Club's history, as was the number of points scored. Eric Stephens' superb kicking provided 363 of those points, which was another club record. On the wing, Bob Clewes had an incredible season, scoring the most tries since 1905-06, when Arthur Hudson ran in 41.

In his first season as captain Mike Nicholls, at hooker, was an inspirational leader, who would take the Club to even greater success the following season. He had at his disposal an outstanding pack of forwards, with Robin

Cowling, and Mike Burton as his props, Alan Brinn and Jim Jarrett in the second row, John Haines, Mike Potter and the evergreen Dick Smith at the back. Unfortunately, Potter broke his collar bone in March, and played no further games. But Nicholls encouraged a more open style which resulted in some delightful back-play, not something the Cherry & Whites were necessarily noted for.

After the retirement of Terry Hopson, Mickey Booth forged a new half-back partnership with Cornishman Tom Palmer. Centres John Bayliss and Richard Jardine thrived on the service received and in turn gave plenty of ball to wingers Clewes and John Dix. Ron Etheridge continued in his role as an exciting attacking fullback.

An interesting feature of the game against Cheltenham in April was the fact that the Cheltenham team contained Bob White, Paul Tate, Bob Redwood, Phil Blakeway, Mike Curran and John Fidler who would in due course all play for Gloucester.

There was great deal of success against Welsh clubs. There was a cherished double over Newport, as well as wins over Pontypool (through a penalty by Dick Smith!), Aberavon, Newbridge (away), Bridgend and Cardiff. Against English clubs Leicester, Coventry and Northampton were defeated at Kingsholm, and Wasps were beaten away.

Gloucestershire reached the final of the Championship, only to lose to Surrey at Kingsholm. Eric Stephens scored the County's only points with a penalty. Other Gloucester players were Des Diamond, John Spalding, Robin Cowling, Alan Brinn, Nigel Jackson and Dick Smith. Western Counties played the Fijians, also at Kingsholm; Dick Smith scored a try; John Bayliss, John Spalding and Alan Brinn also played. Dick Smith yet again played in two England trial games, without further recognition.

Sep 2 Gloucester 26 Clifton 3
Tries: J.Dix (3), R.Etheridge, J.Jarrett, R.Clewes, T.Palmer;
Conversion: R.Etheridge;
Penalty: T.Palmer

Sep 5 Cheltenham 15 Gloucester 12
Tries: R.Jardine, N.Jackson, J.Bayliss;
Penalty: K.Richardson

Sep 9 Gloucester 3 Pontypool 0
Penalty: Dick Smith

Sep 12 Coventry 11 Gloucester 6
Penalty: E.Stephens;
Drop goal: E.Stephens

Sep 16 Gloucester 11 Moseley 6
Tries: M.Bayliss, J.Haines, R.Cowling;
Conversion: E.Stephens

Sep 19 Gloucester 20 Bective Rangers 12
Tries: J.Dix (2), R.Clewes, J.Spalding;
Conversion: E.Stephens,
Penalties: E.Stephens (2)

Sep 26 Bristol 18 Gloucester 0

Oct 3 Gloucester 11 Bedford 21
Tries: J.Bayliss, Dick Smith;
Conversion: E.Stephens;
Penalty: E.Stephens

Oct 7 Gloucester 13 Ebbw Vale 6
Tries: M.Nicholls, M.Burton;
Conversions: E.Stephens (2);
Penalty: E.Stephens

Oct 10 Harlequins 20 Gloucester 6
Penalties: E.Stephens (2)

Oct 14 Stroud 0 Gloucester 17
Tries: R. Jardine (3), R.Morris, R.Etheridge;
Conversion: E.Stephens

Oct 19 Newport 9 Gloucester 15
Penalties: E.Stephens (4);
Drop goal: M.Booth

Oct 24 Gloucester 44 Old Blues 9
Tries: J.Horner (2), R.Clewes, D.Ainge,
M.Booth, R.Jardine, R.Morris, G.White,
E.Stephens;
Conversions: E.Stephens (7);
Penalty: E.Stephens

Oct 31 Oxford University 6 Gloucester 8
Tries: R.Etheridge (2);
Conversion: E.Stephens

Nov 4 Gloucester 6 Newbridge 6
Penalties: E.Stephens (2)

Nov 7 Gloucester 25 Leicester 15
Tries: B.Clewes (2), Dick Smith (2);
Conversions: E.Stephens (2);
Penalties: E.Stephens (3)

Nov 14 Moseley 13 Gloucester 9
Penalties: E.Stephens (3)

Nov 21 Gloucester 9 Aberavon 3
Penalties: E.Stephens (3)

Nov 28 Gloucester 28 Lydney 3
Tries: D.Owen (2), J.Dix, R.Jardine, R.Clewes;
Conversions: E.Stephens, M.Booth;
Penalties: E.Stephens (3)

Dec 5 Newbridge 3 Gloucester 10
Tries: D.Owen, R.Clewes;
Conversions: E.Stephens (2)

Dec 12 Bath 0 Gloucester 0

Dec 19 Gloucester 11 Coventry 0
Try: D.Owen;
Conversion: E.Stephens;
Penalties: E.Stephens (2)

**Dec 26 Gloucester 50
Old Merchant Taylors 3**
Tries: J.Spalding (2), K.Richardson (2),
E.Stephens (2), J.Dix (2), D.Diamond (2),
R.Jardine, R.Etheridge, J.Gage, Dick Smith;
Conversions: E.Stephens (4)

Dec 28 Gloucester v Saracens - cancelled due
to unfit ground

Jan 2 Gloucester 19 London Scottish 6
Tries: R.Jardine (2), R.Clewes, A.Brinn;
Conversions: E.Stephens (2);
Penalty: E.Stephens

Jan 9 Leicester 17 Gloucester 15
Try: R.Clewes;
Penalties: E.Stephens (4)

Jan 16 Wasps 3 Gloucester 9
Try: R.Clewes;
Penalties: E.Stephens (2)

**Jan 23 Gloucester 20
Cambridge University 3**
Tries: T.Palmer (2), J.Bayliss, R.Clewes,
R.Jardine;
Conversion: E.Stephens;
Penalty: E.Stephens

Jan 30 Gloucester 12 Bridgend 11
Penalties: E.Stephens (4)

Feb 3 Gloucester 24 Saint Luke's College 6
Tries: J.Watkins (2), J.Dix;
Conversions: E.Stephens (3);
Penalties: E.Stephens (3)

Feb 6 Gloucester 23 Bristol 9
Tries: R.Clewes (3);
Conversion: E.Stephens;
Penalties: E.Stephens (3);
Drop goal: M.Booth

Feb 15 Gloucester 9 Bath 9
Try: J.Haines;
Penalties: E.Stephens (2)

Feb 20 Swansea 6 Gloucester 0

**Feb 24 Gloucester 11
Loughborough Colleges 10**
Tries: E.Stephens, R.Clewes;

Conversion: E.Stephens;
Penalty: E.Stephens

Feb 26 Aberavon 9 Gloucester 6
Try: R.Clewes;
Penalty: E.Stephens

Mar 8 Gloucester 25 Northampton 6
Tries: R.Clewes (2), T.Palmer, Dick Smith;
Conversions: E.Stephens (2);
Penalties: E.Stephens (2);
Drop goal: M.Booth

Mar 11 Gloucester 14 R.A.F. 5
Tries: R.Clewes (2), J.Bayliss;
Conversion: E.Stephens;
Penalty: E.Stephens

Mar 13 Richmond 19 Gloucester 11
Tries: D.Owen, M.Burton;
Conversion: E.Stephens;
Penalty: E.Stephens

Mar 17 Ebbw Vale 6 Gloucester 0

Mar 20 Gloucester 20 Guy's Hospital 6
Tries: R.Clewes (2), E.Stephens, R.Morris;
Conversion: E.Stephens;
Penalty: E.Stephens;
Drop goal: M.Booth

Mar 22 Clifton 3 Gloucester 20
Tries: R.Clewes (2), J.Spalding, E.Stephens;
Conversions: E.Stephens (4)

Mar 26 Gloucester 16 Newport 0
Tries: R.Clewes, T.Palmer;
Conversions: E.Stephens (2);
Penalties: E.Stephens (2)

Mar 31 Pontypool 3 Gloucester 3
Try: R.Clewes

Apr 3 Gloucester 15 Cardiff 6
Tries: A.Brinn, J.Watkins, M.Nicholls;
Penalties: E.Stephens (2)

Apr 8 Lydney 11 Gloucester 16
Tries: J.Watkins, R.Clewes, J.Bayliss;
Conversions: E.Stephens (2);
Penalty: E.Stephens

Apr 10 Gloucester 18 New Brighton 3
Tries: M.Booth, T.Palmer, M.Burton;
Conversions: E.Stephens (3);
Penalty: E.Stephens

Apr 12 Gloucester 17 Harrogate 6
Try: T.Palmer;
Conversion: E.Stephens;
Penalties: E.Stephens (4)

Apr 17 Gloucester 28 Sale 3
Tries: E.Stephens (2), J.Herniman, J.Bayliss,
R.Clewes;
Conversions: E.Stephens (2);
Penalties: E.Stephens (2);
Drop goal: T.Palmer

Apr 21 Gloucester 32 Cheltenham 3

Tries: A.Brinn (2), J.Watkins, J.Bayliss,
R.Clewes, R.Cowling, E.Stephens;
Conversions: E.Stephens (4);
Penalty: E.Stephens

**Apr 24 Penzance & Newlyn 3
Gloucester 14**
Tries: R.Clewes (2), J.Bayliss, R.Morris;
Conversion: E.Stephens

Apr 26 Plymouth Albion 16 Gloucester 0

Apr 30 Gloucester 35 Exeter 12
Tries: R.Clewes (2), N.Jackson (2), T.Palmer,
R.Morris;
Conversions: E.Stephens (4);
Penalties: E.Stephens (3)

1971-72

R.R.Morris R.Long R.Collins M.J.Potter M.Elway T.Pritchard J.Holder W.Cale N.H.B.Duncalfe P.J.Ford P.Hawker F.Ewers C.Pope C.A.R.Lankester
J.Hickie T.R.Tandy
H.C.King(Sec) J.A.Bayliss T.Palmer K.Richardson J.S.Jarrett A.Brinn N.Jackson J.Haines R.Jardine M.A.Burton R.J.Cowling Dr.T.Durkin
A.D.Wadley(Treas) J.Fryer S.T.Day
F.D.H.Dawe Dr.A.Alcock R.Smith M.H.Booth A.T.Voyce(Pres) M.J.Nicholls(Capt) R.J.Clewes J.Dix J.A.Watkins A.G.Hudson(Chairman) Canon
H.M.Hughes
J.Spalding J.Hargreaves E.J.F.Stephens R.Etheridge J.Horner R.Morris

Played 49 Won 37 Lost 9 Drawn 3
For 821 Against 414
Captain: Mike Nicholls

Gloucester United
Played 33 Won 23 Lost 7 Drawn 3
For 858 Against 334
Captain: Hal Symonds

Most appearances: J.Watkins 45, E.J.Stephens
44, R.Clewes 41, M.Nicholls 40,   J.Jarrett 39,
M.Booth 38, M.Potter 38
Most tries: R.Clewes 13, R.Jardine 10,
J.Watkins 9, J.Bayliss, D.Hargreaves 6
Conversions: E.J.Stephens 34, D.Hargreaves 11
Penalties: E.J.Stephens 102, D.Hargreaves 8,
R.White 2, T.Palmer 1
Drop goals: M.Booth 5, E.Stephens 2,
T.Palmer 1

The number of wins was the highest in the

Club's history. Eric Stephens scored 388 points,
beating the record he set a year earlier.

After the more carefree rugby played in the
previous season, Gloucester reverted to type,
and relied on the forwards to get and hold
possession, whilst the half-backs kicked for
position - "Ten Man Rugby".

Gloucester won the inaugural National Knock-
Out Competition. A lot of the credit for the
success must go to the inspiring captaincy
of Mike Nicholls. Without his whole hearted
leadership it is hard to see how the team would
have made it through to the final, when drawn
away from home in every round. In the first
two ties, Bath and Bristol were defeated. The
outstanding win was in the quarter-final against
London Welsh, the team which, at the time, was
the strongest in the country. Against Gloucester
they fielded eleven internationals including six

British Lions. Gloucester were given no chance,
but through sheer guts and determination the
game was won. Some of the players were seen to
be in tears after the final whistle, after one of the
greatest wins in the Club's history. The semi-
final was a bad-tempered affair at Coventry,
where the Cherry and Whites went through as
the away team in a drawn game in which no
tries were scored. The final was an anti-climax.
Moseley had a player sent off after five minutes.
Two other players had to leave the field injured,
(emphatically not through foul play) and so
finished the game with twelve men. The press
gave no credit to Gloucester and almost with
one voice condemned their approach of keeping
the ball tight.

A measure of the tenacity of this team is
illustrated by the fact that two days after the
draining semi-final against Coventry, Newport
were beaten at Rodney Parade to complete

a double over the Welsh club. The team was undefeated in all games at Kingsholm. Other notable achievements were a treble over Bath, and wins against Coventry, Ebbw Vale, Harlequins, Wasps, Newbridge, Bridgend (away), Swansea and Aberavon. There was another double over Pontypool, including a 29-0 win at Pontypool Park.

As usual, the foundation of the success of the team was in the forwards. The front row of Robin Cowling, Mike Nicholls and Mike Burton, was hardly ever bettered, and when coupled with a second row of Alan Brinn and Jim Jarrett or Nigel Jackson, to give extra shove, it gave time for the back row of John Watkins, Mike Potter and Dick Smith to break and harass the opposition. Whilst emphasis was always with the forwards, the backs also knew the way to the try-line, with Bob Clewes and Richard Jardine frequently scoring tries. Mickey Booth and Tom Palmer were a solid half-back pairing, whilst Eric Stephens was wonderfully reliable with his kicking.

The England selectors, recognising the strength of the Gloucester pack, awarded caps to Mike Burton and Alan Brinn. Burton played in all four of England's Championship games, and against South Africa. Brinn played against Wales, Ireland and Scotland.

After the triumph against Moseley, Mickey Booth decided to retire after a career which had commenced in 1956. He had played in 475 games, and kicked 41 drop goals, a Club record. Gary White, another long serving player also retired after 234 games, and 395 points including 82 tries. He would be captain of the United from 1972 to 1974.

Gloucestershire won the Championship, defeating Warwickshire 11-6 at Twickenham. Gloucester players in the team were Richard Jardine, Robin Cowling, Mike Burton, Alan Brinn, Dick Smith and Eric Stephens, who kicked a penalty.

(Value of try increased from 3 to 4 points)

Sep 4 Gloucester 26 Clifton 11
Tries: R.Clewes, J.Jarrett, M.Potter, E.J.Stephens;
Conversions: E.J.Stephens (2);
Penalties: E.J.Stephens (2)

Sep 8 Newbridge 6 Gloucester 3
Penalty: E.J.Stephens

Sep 11 Gloucester 16 Coventry 15
Try: R.White;

Penalties: E.J.Stephens (4)

Sep 15 Moseley 12 Gloucester 12
Penalties: E.J.Stephens (4)

Sep 18 Broughton Park 9 Gloucester 24
Tries: J.Watkins, T.Palmer;
Conversions: E.J.Stephens (2);
Penalties: E.J.Stephens (4)

Sep 25 Gloucester 12 Bristol 12
Try: N.Jackson;
Conversion: E.J.Stephens;
Penalties: E.J.Stephens (2)

Sep 30 Bath 3 Gloucester 12
(National K.O Competition)
Penalties: E.J.Stephens (4)

Oct 2 Bedford 3 Gloucester 13
Try: D.Hargreaves;
Penalties: E.J.Stephens (2), D.Hargreaves

Oct 6 Gloucester 16 Ebbw Vale 12
Try: R.Clewes;
Penalties: E.J.Stephens (4)

Oct 9 Gloucester 12 Harlequins 4
Try: J.Watkins;
Conversion: E.J.Stephens;
Penalties: E.J.Stephens (2)

Oct 13 Cheltenham 6 Gloucester 18
Tries: G.White (2), T.Palmer;
Penalties: E.J.Stephens (2)

Oct 16 Gloucester 18 Newport 0
Try: A.Brinn;
Conversion: E.J.Stephens;
Penalties: E.J.Stephens (4)

Oct 23 Gloucester v Stroud - cancelled due to county commitments

Oct 30 Gloucester 16 Oxford University 6
Try: R.Clewes;
Penalties: E.J.Stephens (4)

Nov 3 Pontypool 0 Gloucester 29
Tries: G.White (2), R.Clewes, Dick Smith, R.White;
Conversions: E.J.Stephens (3);
Penalty: E.J.Stephens

Nov 6 Leicester 31 Gloucester 9
Penalties: E.J.Stephens (3)

Nov 13 Gloucester 23 Moseley 10
Tries: J.Bayliss (2), J.Watkins, N.Jackson;
Conversions: D.Hargreaves (2);
Penalty: D.Hargreaves

Nov 17 Cambridge University 6
Gloucester 13
Try: J.Dix;
Penalties: E.J.Stephens (3)

Nov 20 Aberavon 7 Gloucester 6
Penalties: E.J.Stephens (2)

Nov 27 Gloucester 14 Lydney 3
Tries: R.Clewes, J.Herniman;
Penalties: R.White (2)

Dec 4 Saracens 20 Gloucester 12
Try: D.Owen;
Conversion: E.J.Stephens;
Penalty: E.J.Stephens;
Drop goal: M.Booth

Dec 8 Bristol 4 Gloucester 15
(National KO Competition)
Try: R.Clewes;
Conversion: E.J.Stephens;
Penalties: E.J.Stephens (3)

Dec 11 Gloucester 24 Bath 16
Tries: J.Bayliss, N.Jackson, E.J.Stephens;
Conversions: E.J.Stephens (3);
Penalties: E.J.Stephens (2)

Dec 18 Coventry 27 Gloucester 17
Tries: J.Jarrett, N.Jackson, R.Jardine;
Conversion: E.J.Stephens;
Penalty: E.J.Stephens

Dec 27 Gloucester 67
Old Merchant Taylors 3
Tries: D.Hargreaves (3), S.Clewes (3), Dick Smith (2), R.Jardine (2), A.Brinn, R.Clewes;
Conversions: D.Hargreaves (8);
Penalty: D.Hargreaves

Jan 1 London Scottish 7 Gloucester 6
Penalties: E.J.Stephens (2)

Jan 8 Gloucester v Leicester - cancelled due to South.West Group decider

Jan 15 Gloucester 28 Wasps 3
Tries: R.Jardine (2), D.Hargreaves, J.Watkins, R.Clewes;
Conversion: D.Hargreaves;
Penalties: D.Hargreaves (2)

Jan 22 Gloucester 16 Newbridge 6
Try: J.Watkins;
Penalties: E.J.Stephens (4)

Jan 29 Bridgend 0 Gloucester 6
Penalty: E.J.Stephens;
Drop goal: M.Booth

1971/72 National Knockout Competition Winning Team
R.Morris A.Brinn J.Herniman D.Owen N.Jackson J.Jarrett M.Burton R.Cowling
R.Smith E.Stephens J.Bayliss M.Nicholls(Capt) R.Etheridge T.Palmer J.Haines
R.Clewes M.Booth J.Watkins J.Dix R.White M.Potter (R.Jardine – absent)

Feb 2 Gloucester 23 St.Luke's College 14
Tries: R.Clewes (2), M.Burton;
Conversion: E.J.Stephens;
Penalties: E.J. Stephens (3)

Feb 4 Bristol 12 Gloucester 9
Try: J.Watkins;
Conversion: E.J.Stephens;
Penalty: E.J.Stephens

Feb 12 Bath 7 Gloucester 28
Tries: S.Clewes, R.Cowling, J.Watkins;
Conversions: E.J.Stephens (2);
Penalties: E.J.Stephens (3);
Drop goal: M.Booth

Feb 19 Gloucester 16 Swansea 10
Try: A.F.Parsloe;
Penalties: E.J.Stephens (3);
Drop goal: E.J.Stephens

Feb 23 Gloucester v Loughborough Colleges -
cancelled due to floodlight ban during miners'
strike.

Feb 26 Gloucester 12 Aberavon 9
Penalties: E.J.Stephens (4)

Mar 4 London Welsh 4 Gloucester 9
(National K.O Competition)
Try: M.Potter;
Conversion: E.J.Stephens;
Penalty: E.J.Stephens

Mar 11 Gloucester 17 Richmond 0
Tries: J.Bayliss, M.Nicholls;
Penalties: D.Hargreaves (3)

Mar 15 Gloucester 21 Cheltenham 3
Tries: R.Cowling, J.Dix, J.Bayliss;
Conversions: E.J.Stephens (3);
Penalty: E.J.Stephens

Mar 18 Guy's Hospital 13 Gloucester 33
Tries: R.Jardine (3), J.Dix, D.Hargreaves,
R.Clewes;
Conversions: E.J.Stephens (3);
Penalty: E.J.Stephens

Mar 25 Coventry 6 Gloucester 6
(National K.O Competition semi-final)
Penalty: E.J.Stephens;
Drop goal: E.J.Stephens

Mar 27 Newport 3 Gloucester 9

Try: J.Dix;
Conversion: E.J.Stephens;
Penalty: E.J.Stephens

Mar 30 Lydney 6 Gloucester 16
Tries: J.Watkins, D.Owen;
Conversion: E.J.Stephens;
Penalties: E.J.Stephens, T.Palmer

Apr 1 Gloucester 18 Headingley 6
Try: D.Owen;
Conversion: E.J.Stephens;
Penalties: E.J.Stephens (4)

Apr 3 Gloucester 29 Birkenhead Park 4
Tries: R.Clewes (2), R.Jardine (2), D.Pegler;
Conversions: E.J.Stephens (3);
Penalty: E.J.Stephens

Apr 4 Gloucester 16 Stroud 6
Try: R.Nicholls;
Penalties: E.J.Stephens (4)

Apr 8 Cardiff v Gloucester - cancelled due to
waterlogged pitch.

Apr 12 Ebbw Vale 27 Gloucester 3

Penalty: E.J.Stephens

Apr 15 Sale 3 Gloucester 12
Try: J.Bayliss;
Conversion: E.J.Stephens;
Penalty: E.J.Stephens (2)

Apr 17 Gloucester 16 Pontypool 4
Try: J.Watkins;

Penalties: E.J.Stephens (3);
Drop goal: M.Booth

Apr 19 Northampton 16 Gloucester 7
Try: F.Reed;
Penalty: E.J.Stephens

**Apr 22 Penzance-Newlyn 13
Gloucester 21**

Tries: J.Horner (2), S.Clewes;
Penalties: E.J.Stephens (3)

**Apr 29 Gloucester 17 Moseley 6
(National K.O Competition Final at
Twickenham)**
Tries: R.Morris, J.Dix;
Penalty: E.J.Stephens;
Drop goals: T.Palmer, M.Booth

1972-73

T.Tandy M.Elway W.Cale J.Haines T.Day P.Ford R.Morris R.Collins A.Lankester F.Ewers H.King T.Pritchard
J.Holder C.Pope T.Palmer D.Wadley(Hon.Treas) M.Nicholls R.Morris M.Burton K.Richardson J.Jarrett J.Fidler A.Brinn J.Watkins R.Cowling
E.Pinkney R.Long(Hon.Gen.Sec) Dr.T.Durkin D.Pegler J.Fryer H.Symonds Canon M.Hughes
D.Dawe(Hon.Fixture Sec) E.Stephens R.Smith R.Jardine Dr.A.Alcock(Life Vice-Pres) J.Bayliss(Capt) T.Voyce OBE(Pres) P.Butler R.Clewes J.Haines J.Dix
G.Hudson(Chairman)
J.Spalding R.Redwood

**Played 53 Won 36 Lost 15 Drawn 2
For 1145 Against 635
Captain: John Bayliss
Coach: Mickey Booth**

Gloucester United
Played 37 Won 28 Lost 8 Drawn 1
For 1209 Against 363
Captain: Gary White

Most appearances: R.Cowling 45, M.Nicholls 43, J.Spalding 40, R.Clewes 38, R.Jardine 37, A.Brinn, R.Fidler 35, M.Potter 34, J.Watkins, P.Butler 33
Most tries: J.Watkins 20, R.Clewes 17, J.Dix 14, R.White 11, R.Jardine 10
Conversions: P.Butler 61, E.Stephens 33
Penalties: P.Butler 66, E.Stephens 32
Drop goals: R.Redwood 3, R.Jardine, T.Palmer 1

Peter Butler took over from Eric Stephens as place-kicker, and turned out to be equally prolific scoring 324 points. Stephens, although playing in only 19 games still posted 170 points. Overall, over one thousand points were scored for the first time. In October, Mickey Booth was appointed as Gloucester's first coach.

New captain John Bayliss presided over another excellent season with regard to the number of wins, but a lot of the really big games were lost. In the National Knock-Out Competition, after beating Bath, the team lost to Bristol in the next round. Doubles were conceded to Newport and Bristol, and there were big defeats at Swansea and Aberavon. Among creditable results were the double over Newbridge, wins against Harlequins (away), Aberavon, Wasps (away), Northampton and Pontypool (away), and a draw against Cardiff. Front rowers, Robin Cowling and Mike Nicholls played in the lions' share of games, but their partner Mike Burton missed a lot of the season through injury. Keith

Richardson moved to the front to take his place and performed admirably. In the back row John Watkins just got better and better. He was top try scorer, touching down a hat-trick against Cheltenham and five in two games on the South-West tour at the end of the season. Bob Clewes and John Dix were dangerous try-scoring wings. At scrum-half John Spalding had a good campaign, partnering both Bob Redwood and Tom Palmer.

At the end of the season Gary Mace left the club after 15 years and 103 appearances, and went on to play for the very successful Matson team.

John Watkins won two England caps against New Zealand and Wales. Mike Burton played in an England trial game. Peter Butler kicked a conversion and two penalties and Mike Burton scored a try for Western Counties in a 12-39 loss to New Zealand at Kingsholm; Robin Cowling, John Bayliss, Alan Brinn, John Watkins and

Dick Smith also played. Tom Palmer scored a try and Peter Butler a penalty for the South & South-West against the North; John Bayliss, Mike Burton, Alan Brinn, John Watkins and Dick Smith also played.

Sep 2 Gloucester 14 Broughton Park 4
Tries: M.Potter, R.Clewes;
Penalties: E.Stephens (2)

Sep 6 Gloucester 31 Moseley 12
Tries: R.Redwood, G.Mace, J.Watkins, J.Bayliss, R.Clewes;
Conversions: P.Butler (4);
Penalty: P.Butler

Sep 9 Coventry 14 Gloucester 6
Penalties: P.Butler (2)

Sep 13 Gloucester 30 Abertillery 16
Tries: T.Palmer, J.Dix, J.Horner, M.Potter, R.Jardine;
Conversions: P.Butler (2);
Penalty: P.Butler;
Drop goal: T.Palmer

Sep 16 Ebbw Vale 14 Gloucester 22
Tries: J.Watkins (2), J.Dix;
Conversions: P.Butler (2);
Penalties: P.Butler (2)

Sep 20 Gloucester 26 British Police 3
Tries: J.Watkins, T.Palmer, R.Cowling, J.Bayliss;
Conversions: P.Butler (2);
Penalties: P.Butler (2)

Sep 23 Gloucester 9 Bristol 13
Penalties: P.Butler (3)

Sep 30 Gloucester 47 Bedford 13
Tries: R.Clewes (2), J.Bayliss (2), R.Jardine, Dick Smith, J.Spalding, J.Watkins;
Conversions: P.Butler (6);
Penalty: P.Butler

Oct 4 Stroud 10 Gloucester 35
Tries: R.White (2), J.Dix, M.Burton, J.Watkins, J.Haines;
Conversions: E.Stephens (4);
Penalty: E.Stephens

Oct 7 Gloucester 24 Newbridge 10
Tries: J.Dix, R.Jardine;
Conversions: P.Butler (2);
Penalties: P.Butler (4)

Oct 11 Gloucester 39 Cheltenham 0
Tries: J.Watkins (3), E.Pinkney (2), A.Brinn, J.Dix;
Conversions: P.Butler (4);

Penalty: P.Butler

Oct 14 Harlequins 0 Gloucester 13
Tries: J.Dix, P.Blakeway;
Conversion: P.Butler;
Penalty: P.Butler

**Oct 18 Gloucester 19
South Wales Police 4**
Tries: Dick Smith, M.Burton;
Conversion: P.Butler;
Penalty: P.Butler (3)

Oct 21 Newport 30 Gloucester 9
Penalties: E.Stephens (3)

Oct 28 Clifton v Gloucester - cancelled due to New Zealand game at Kingsholm

**Oct 31 Gloucester 16 Bath 0
(National K.O Competition)**
Tries: J.Watkins, A.Brinn, E.Pinkney;
Conversions: P.Butler (2)

Nov 4 Gloucester 13 Leicester 13
Try: A.Brinn;
Penalties: P.Butler (3)

Nov 11 Moseley 29 Gloucester 12
Try: J.Dix;
Conversion: E.Stephens;
Penalties: E.Stephens (2)

Nov 20 Gloucester 27 Aberavon 10
Tries: R.White, J.Dix;
Conversions: P.Butler (2);
Penalties: P.Butler (5)

Nov 25 Gloucester 19 Lydney 18
Tries: E.Pinkney, J.Fidler;
Conversion: E.Stephens;
Penalties: E.Stephens (3)

Dec 2 Oxford University 8 Gloucester 9
Try: R.Redwood;
Conversion: E.Stephens;
Penalty: E.Stephens

Dec 6 Cardiff v Gloucester - cancelled due to waterlogged pitch
Dec 9 Bath v Gloucester - cancelled due to waterlogged pitch

Dec 12 Gloucester 29 Southern Counties 7
Tries: R.Jardine, T.Palmer, Dick Smith, J.Dix, J.Watkins;
Conversions: P.Butler (3);
Penalty: P.Butler

Dec 16 Gloucester 18 Coventry 16
Penalties: P.Butler (6)

Dec 23 Gloucester 35 Saracens 3
Tries: J.Horner (2), R.Morris, R.Jardine, M.Burton;
Conversions: P.Butler (3);
Penalties: P.Butler (3)

**Dec 26 Gloucester 49
Old Merchant Taylors 9**
Tries: M.Burton (2), E.Stephens, R.Etheridge, R.Clewes, R.Morris, R.Jardine, Dick Smith, E.Pinkney;
Conversions: E.Stephens (5);
Penalty: E.Stephens

Jan 1 Gloucester 6 Bridgend 14
Penalties: P.Butler (2)

Jan 6 Gloucester 9 London Scottish 6
Try: J.Bayliss;
Conversion: P.Butler;
Penalty: P.Butler

**Jan 10 Bristol 16 Gloucester 11
(National K.O Competition)**
Tries: R.Jardine, R.Clewes;
Penalty: P.Butler

Jan 15 Leicester 20 Gloucester 12
Tries: Dick Smith, M.Potter;
Conversions: P.Butler (2)

Jan 20 Wasps 11 Gloucester 22
Tries: Dick Smith, R.Jardine;
Conversion: P.Butler;
Penalties: P.Butler (4)

**Jan 27 Gloucester 42
Cambridge University 0**
Tries: J.Bayliss (2), Dick Smith (2), R.Clewes, J.Dix, J.Spalding, R.Cowling;
Conversions: E.Stephens (5)

Feb 2 Bristol 4 Gloucester 3
Drop goal: R.Jardine

Feb 7 Gloucester 22 St.Luke's College 12
Tries: J.Bayliss, T.Palmer, E.Pinkney;
Conversions: E.Stephens (2);
Penalties: E.Stephens (2)

Feb 10 Gloucester 18 Bath 16
Tries: D.Hargreaves, J.Fidler;
Conversions: P.Butler (2);
Penalties: P.Butler (2)

Feb 17 Swansea 43 Gloucester 12
Tries: R.White (2), T.Palmer

**Feb 21 Gloucester 10
Loughborough Colleges 3**

Tries: R.White, E.Pinkney;
Conversion: E.Stephens

Feb 24 Aberavon 25 Gloucester 0

Mar 3 Gloucester 7 Northampton 3
Try: R.White;
Penalty: E.Stephens

Mar 10 Richmond 29 Gloucester 21
Tries: J.Haines, J.Spalding;
Conversions: E.Stephens (2);
Penalties: E.Stephens (3)

Mar 14 Pontypool 6 Gloucester 13
Tries: J.Dix, R,Jardine;
Conversion: E.Stephens;
Drop goal: R.Redwood

Mar 17 Gloucester 33 Guy's Hospital 13
Tries: J.Dix (2), E.Pinkney, J.Spalding;
Conversion: E.Stephens;
Penalties: E.Stephens (4);
Drop goal: R.Redwood

Mar 24 Gloucester 9 Newport 13
Penalies: E.Stephens (3)

Mar 28 Newbridge 18 Gloucester 23

Tries: R.Clewes (2), R.Jardine, J.Haines;
Conversions: P.Butler (2);
Penalty: P.Butler

Mar 31 Gloucester 24 Plymouth Albion 0
Tries: J.Watkins, J.Dix, A.Brinn;
Conversions: P.Butler (3);
Penalties: P.Butler (2)

Apr 2 Clifton 4 Gloucester 39
Tries: R.White (2), R.Clewes, J.Horner,
R.Redwood, P.Butler;
Conversions: P.Butler (3);
Penalties: P.Butler (3)

Apr 7 Gloucester 3 Cardiff 3
Penalty: P.Butler

Apr 11 Cheltenham 4 Gloucester 39
Tries: J.Spalding (2), D.Hargreaves, R.Morris,
R.Etheridge;
Conversions: P.Butler (5);
Penalties: P.Butler (3)

Apr 14 Exeter 15 Gloucester 18
Tries: R.Clewes, D.Hargreaves, J.Watkins,
M.Potter;
Conversion: E.Stephens

Apr 19 Lydney 12 Gloucester 32
Tries: J.Watkins (2), R.Clewes (2), R.White;
Conversions: P.Butler (3);
Penalties: P.Butler (2)

Apr 21 Gloucester 20 New Brighton 21
Tries: R.Etheridge, E.Stephens;
Penalties: E.Stephens (4)

Apr 23 Gloucester 21 Liverpool 24
Tries: A.Brinn, R.Morris, J.Haines;
Penalties: P.Butler (3)

Apr 25 Bath 16 Gloucester 7
Try: R.Clewes;
Drop goal: R.Redwood

Apr 28 Penzance & Newlyn 18 Gloucester 48
Tries: R.Clewes (2), J.Watkins (2), R.Etheridge
(2), R.White, J.Haines;
Conversions: P.Butler (5);
Penalties: P.Butler (2)

Apr 30 Camborne 9 Gloucester 70
Tries: J.Horner (3), J.Watkins (3), J.Haines (2),
J.Jarrett (2), R.Clewes, M.Burton;
Conversions: E.Stephens (8);
Penalties: E.Stephens (2)

1973-74

J.Holder M.Elway N.B.H.Duncalfe Capt.A.Lankester R.Collins P.Hawker P.Ford(Vice-Chairman) R.Morris(Vice-Pres) G.Edmunds(Hon.Team Sec)
D.Pegler W.Cale F.Ewers(Hon.Colts Sec) J.Haines T.Pritchard(Vice-Pres) T.Day(Vice-Pres)
H.Symonds C.Pope T.R.Tandy K.R.Morris P.Winnel J.S.Jarrett J.Fidler D.Owen K.Richardson M.J.Potter R.Smith J.A.Bayliss S.Dix T.Durkin(Hon.
Club Doctor) J.Horner J.Fryer
A.D.Wadley(Hon.Treas) J.Watkins R.Jardine P.J.Blakeway G.Hudson(Chairman) M.J.Nicholls(Capt) A.T.Voyce OBE(Pres) P.E.Butler R.G.Long(Hon.Sec)
R.J.Clewes T.Palmer Canon M.Hughes(Vice-Pres)
J.Spalding R.Etheridge

Played 54 Won 39 Lost 11 Drawn 4
For 1096 Against 570
Captain: Mike Nicholls
Coach: Gary White

Gloucester United
Played 35 Won 30 Lost 5
For 1024 Against 570
Captain: Eric Stephens

Most appearances: M.Nicholls 52, R.Clewes,
J.Spalding 46, P.Butler 45, A.Brinn 43, J.Haines
42, J.Fidler 39, D.Owen 35, K.Richardson 34,
J.Jarrett 33, R.Jardine 32, R.Etheridge 31
Most tries: R.Clewes 24, R.Etheridge 17,
R.White, R.Jardine 10, J.Haines 9, P.Butler 8
Conversions: P.Butler 57, E.Stephens 19,
N.Evans 1
Penalties: P.Butler 114 (still stands as Club
record), E.Stephens 11, D.Hargreaves 2,
N.Evans 1
Drop goals: R.Redwood 4, T.Palmer,
D.Hargreaves 1

In the Centenary season, with 39 wins, the
Club record was beaten, albeit from the high
number of 54 games played. For the second
season running, more than one thousand
points were scored. Peter Butler created a new
Club record by scoring 488 points, or 44% of
the total. Not only that, he scored another 64
for the County, and in all games totaled 574
points, just seven short of Sam Doble's world
record.

In the National Knock-Out Competition,
there was an unexpected home loss to London
Scottish. Only a few weeks earlier the Scottish
had been beaten 21-0 on their ground. Perhaps
it was thought that the win, especially as it
was at Kingsholm would be routine, but that
seems unlikely with Mike Nicholls as captain!
There were doubles over Moseley, Bath, and
most notably Leicester, with outstanding wins,
29-6 at Welford Road, and 27-10 at Kingsholm,
together with wins over Newbridge away,
Bristol, Wasps Swansea and Aberavon.

To celebrate the Centenary, Don Rutherford
assembled a powerful International XV to play
at Kingsholm. Gloucester put on a thrilling
performance to win 24-14. In February, the first
ever Sunday game was played at Kingsholm;
Bristol were the opponents, and admission was
by way of purchasing a programme.

As ever, the forwards lay the foundation for
victories. Mike Nicholls leadership was as
inspiring as ever. Alan Brinn, Jim Jarrett,
John Haines, John Fidler and Dave Owen all
had excellent seasons. Bob Clewes yet again

topped the try scorers, whilst Ron Etheridge
also enjoyed a particularly successful season.

The United had a great season under the
captaincy of Eric Stephens, winning 30 of 35
games played and scoring over one thousand
points. Eric still had time to play nine times for
the First XV, and chalk up 75 points. At the
end of the season, he decided to call time on his
illustrious career, having totaled 1559 points
from 221 games. Roy Morris also retired after
playing 228 games, whilst Robin Cowling,
after 216 appearances, moved on to Leicester,
where he had considerable success. Dave
Owen had originally intended to retire in 1972,
but could not resist a come-back, and finally
called it a day at the end of this season after
293 appearances.

In September, John Watkins helped England
to win away against New Zealand, and two
months later to beat Australia at Twickenham.
Mike Burton won England caps against France
and Wales. Gloucestershire won the County
Championship, with eleven Gloucester players
in the final: Peter Butler, Bob Clewes, John
Bayliss, Richard Jardine, Bob Redwood, Mike
Burton, Robin Cowling, Alan Brinn, John
Fidler, John Watkins and John Haines. South
& South-West Counties played the Australians
with Burton, Brinn, Fidler and Watkins in the
team, and Burton, Watkins and Butler played
against South-East & Metropolitan in the
Divisional Championship.

Sep 1 Broughton Park 33 Gloucester 24
Tries: R.Etheridge, R.Redwood;
Conversions: P.Butler (2);
Penalties: P.Butler (4)

Sep 5 Stroud 9 Gloucester 28
Tries: R.Redwood (2), R.Nicholls;
Conversions: P.Butler (2);
Penalties: P.Butler (4)

Sep 8 Gloucester 13 Coventry 8
Try: P.Butler;
Penalties: P.Butler (2);
Drop goal: R.Redwood

Sep 12 Gloucester 20
South Wales Police 14
Tries: R.White, R.Clewes;
Penalties: P.Butler (4)

Sep 15 Gloucester 25 Ebbw Vale 12
Tries: A.Brinn (2);
Conversion: P.Butler;
Penalties: P.Butler (4);
Drop goal: R.Redwood

Sep 18 Gloucester 6 Wolfhounds 3
Penalties: P.Butler (2)

Sep 22 Bristol 19 Gloucester 3
Penalty: P.Butler

Sep 24 Gloucester 9 Pontypool 9
Try: R.White;
Conversion: P.Butler;
Penalty: P.Butler

Sep 29 Bedford 37 Gloucester 15
Tries: R.Etheridge, M.Burton;
Conversions: P.Butler (2);
Penalty: P.Butler

Oct 3 Gloucester 24 International XV 14
(Centenary season celebration game)
Tries:K.Richardson, J.Haines, R.Jardine,
R.Redwood, P.Butler;
Conversions: P.Butler (2)

Oct 6 Gloucester 12 Saracens 10
Penalties: P.Butler (4)

Oct 10 Moseley 4 Gloucester 24
Tries: R.Morris, J.Watkins, J.Haines;
Conversions: P.Butler (3);
Penalties: P.Butler (2)

Oct 16 Cheltenham 0 Gloucester 13
Tries: R.Clewes, M.Nicholls;
Conversion: N.Evans;
Penalty: N.Evans

Oct 20 Newport 6 Gloucester 6
Penalties: D.Hargreaves (2)

Oct 27 Clifton 3 Gloucester 34
Tries: R.White, R.Etheridge, K.Richardson,
J.Jarrett;
Conversions: P.Butler (3);
Penalties: P.Butler (4)

Oct 31 Gloucester 49 Devizes 6
(National K.O Competition)
Tries: R.Clewes (4), R.White (2), R.Etheridge
(2), P.Butler;
Conversions: P.Butler (5);
Penalty: P.Butler

Nov 3 Leicester 6 Gloucester 29
Tries: R.Etheridge, J.Haines;
Penalties: P.Butler (7)

Nov 9 Gloucester 15 Moseley 13
Tries: J.Jarrett, J.Haines;
Conversions: E.Stephens (2);
Penalty: E.Stephens

Nov 14 Gloucester 18 British Police 12

Try: R.Clewes;
Conversion: P.Butler;
Penalties: P.Butler (4)

Nov 17 Aberavon 25 Gloucester 16
Tries: R.Clewes, P.Butler;
Conversion: P.Butler;
Penalties: P.Butler (2)

**Nov 21 Cambridge University 10
Gloucester 16**
Tries: R.Clewes (2), R.Jardine;
Conversions: E.Stephens (2)

Nov 24 Gloucester 27 London Irish 9
Tries: J.Dix, R.White, Dick Smith;
Conversions: E.Stephens (3);
Penalties: E.Stephens (3)

Dec 1 Gloucester 19 Oxford University 9
Try: R.Jardine;
Penalties: P.Butler (5)

Dec 8 Gloucester 18 Bath 8
Tries: M.Nicholls, R.Clewes, J.Watkins;
Penalties: P.Butler (2)

Dec 15 Coventry 20 Gloucester 4
Try: S.Dix

Dec 22 Newbridge 0 Gloucester 21
Tries: R.Redwood, R.Clewes, R.Jardine;
Conversions: P.Butler (3);
Penalty: P.Butler

**Dec 26 Gloucester 82
Old Merchant Taylors 12**
Tries: R.Etheridge (4), G.Pike (2), Dick Smith
(2), R.White (2), J.Dix (2), R.Redwood,
A.Brinn, E.Stephens;
Conversions: E.Stephens (11)

Dec 27 Gloucester 31 Lydney 3
Tries: R.Jardine, A.Brinn, R.Clewes,
K.Richardson, P.Butler;
Conversions: P.Butler (4);
Penalty: P.Butler

Dec 29 Gloucester 37 Exeter 10
Tries: R.Etheridge (4), J.Haines;
Conversions: P.Butler (4);
Penalties: P.Butler (3)

Jan 5 London Scottish 0 Gloucester 21
Tries: R.Clewes (2), J.Jarrett;
Conversions: P.Butler (3);

Penalty: P.Butler

Jan 12 Gloucester 27 Leicester 10
Tries: R.White (2), R.Clewes, S.Dix;
Conversion: E.Stephens;
Penalties: E.Stephens (2);
Drop goal: R.Redwood

Jan 19 Gloucester 23 Wasps 16
Tries: R.Etheridge, R.Redwood, R.Clewes;
Conversion: P.Butler;
Penalties: P.Butler (3)

Jan 26 Bridgend 17 Gloucester 16
Tries: J.Haines (2);
Conversion: P.Butler;
Penalties: P.Butler (2)

Feb 3 Gloucester 7 Bristol 3
Try: S.Dix;
Drop goal: R.Redwood

**Feb 9 Gloucester 9 London Scottish 12
(National K.O Competition)**
Penalties: P.Butler (3)

Feb 15 Gloucester 13 Swansea 0
Tries: J.Jarrett, K.Richardson;
Conversion: P.Butler;
Penalty: P.Butler

Feb 23 Gloucester 18 Aberavon 10
Penalties: E.Stephens (5);
Drop goal: D.Hargreaves

Mar 2 Northampton 17 Gloucester 15
Penalties: P.Butler (5)

Mar 9 Gloucester 33 Roundhay 0
Tries: S.Dix (3), R.Clewes, R.Jardine, P.Butler;
Conversions: P.Butler (3);
Penalty: P.Butler

Mar 13 Abertillery 12 Gloucester 12
Penalties: P.Butler (4)

Mar 16 Guy's Hospital 3 Gloucester 29
Tries: R.Clewes, R.Jardine, J.Dix, J.Spalding;
Conversions: P.Butler (2);
Penalties: P.Butler (3)

Mar 20 Gloucester 19 Cheltenham 8
Try: Dick Smith;
Penalties: P.Butler (5)

**Mar 27 Gloucester 21
Public School Wanderers 35**

Tries: R.Jardine, R.Etheridge, A.Brinn;
Penalties: P.Butler (3)

Mar 30 Gloucester 10 London Welsh 10
Try: R.Etheridge;
Penalties: P.Butler (2)

Apr 2 Bath 15 Gloucester 19
Tries: J.Dix, J.Haines;
Conversion: P.Butler;
Penalties: P.Butler (3)

Apr 6 Cardiff 20 Gloucester 10
Tries: R.Jardine, M.Potter;
Conversion: P.Butler

Apr 10 Gloucester 10 Newport 16
Try: P.Butler;
Penalties: P.Butler (2)

Apr 11 Lydney 6 Gloucester 15
Try: Dick Smith;
Conversion: P.Butler;
Penalties: P.Butler (3)

Apr 13 Gloucester 16 Headingley 3
Tries: R.Clewes, J.Horner;
Conversion: P.Butler;
Penalties: P.Butler (2)

Apr 15 Gloucester 50 Birkenhead Park 7
Tries: R.Clewes (3), J.Horner (3), R.Jardine,
Dick Smith, P.Winnell;
Conversions: P.Butler (4);
Penalties: P.Butler (2)

Apr 20 Sale 3 Gloucester 18
Try: P.Butler;
Conversion: P.Butler;
Penalties: P.Butler (3);
Drop goal: T.Palmer

Apr 26 Plymouth Albion 3 Gloucester 7
Try: R.Morris;
Penalty: P.Butler

**Apr 27 Penzance & Newlyn 13
Gloucester 21**
Tries: J.Dix, J.Haines;
Conversions: P.Butler (2);
Penalties: P.Butler (3)

Apr 29 Camborne 7 Gloucester 19
Tries: J.Dix, R.Clewes;
Conversion: P.Butler;
Penalties: P.Butler (3)

T.Pritchard M.Elway N.H.B.Duncalfe J.Haines C.Pope T.R.Tandy R.W.Collins P.J.Ford(Vice-Chairman) S.T.Day(Vice-Pres) J.A.Horner F.C.Ewers J.Hickey Dr.T.E.Durkin(Hon.Club Doctor)

R.G.Long(Hon.Sec) A.D.Wadley(Hon.Treas) J.W.G.Holder J.H.Haines M.A.Burton R.Jardine P.J.Winnel J.H.Fidler S.B.Boyle J.S.Jarrett J.A.Bayliss W.R.Morris(Vice-Pres) J.S.Fryer

F.D.H.Dawe(Hon.Fixture Sec) R.E.White J.Dix R.J.Clewes K.Richardson(Capt) A.T.Voyce(Pres) D.T.Crabbe F.C.Reed P.J.Blakeway P.E.Butler J.A.Watkins A.G.Hudson(Chairman)

E.A.Pinkney G.F.Hutchison R.R.Mogg M.Longstaff M.J.Nicholls R.Smith

Played 46 Won 32 Lost 14
For 954 Against 514
Captain: Keith Richardson
Coach: Gary White

Gloucester United
Played 37 Won 25 Lost 11 Drawn 1
For 855 Against 360
Captain: Dick Smith

Most appearances: K.Richardson 43, P.Butler, J.Dix 33, P.Kingston 32, J.Haines, E.Pinkney 31, J.Fidler, J.Watkins, 29, R.Jardine 28
Most tries: J.Dix 18, E.Pinkney 13, R.Clewes, R.Jardine 11, J.Watkins 9
Conversions: P.Butler 55, M.Longstaff 13, R.Correia 7, K.Richardson 1
Penalties: P.Butler 74, M.Longstaff 5, R.Correia 4, R.White 2
Drop goals: R.Redwood 4, R.Jardine 1

Another successful campaign, during which captain Keith Richardson missed only three games. There was an excellent start to the season with wins over Bristol, Harlequins, Leicester, Aberavon and Coventry. Kingsholm became a bit of a fortress, and the ground record was not surrendered until after Christmas, when Bridgend triumphed. This triggered a run of five successive defeats, but stability was restored, and there were later wins over Swansea (away) Northampton, Cardiff and Newport.

Although not quite so prolific as the previous season, Peter Butler was still very successful with his kicks. He scored 336 points for the Club, and 69 more for the County. In only his third full season Butler's all-round game improved so much that he was selected to go on England's summer tour to Australia, where he won his first cap, scoring a penalty and conversion. He was accompanied on the tour by Peter Kingston, Mike Burton and Phil Blakeway. The first two also won caps.

Alan Brinn and Dick Smith both passed the 500-appearances mark. It was quite remarkable that two players in one season would achieve this feat. Although Smith was United captain, he still made 12 appearances for the first XV, scoring four tries. John Dix topped the try scorers, but his brother Stuart was also in sparkling form scoring two tries against Bristol and a hat-trick against Northampton. He was soon in the County team and scored a try in the final. Eddie Pinkney scored the most tries amongst the forwards. Mike Longstaff demonstrated that as well as being a promising full-back, he was also a more than useful place kicker. In later seasons he would very successfully move to the back-row.

Two Gloucester stalwarts retired at the end of the season. Scrum-half John Spalding had made his first appearance way back in 1960 and played in 252 games. In September Tom Palmer

broke his ankle in the game against Stroud, which ended his Gloucester career, having made 211 appearances.

John Watkins played for England against France and Wales, whilst Mike Burton played against Scotland. John Bayliss captained Gloucestershire to victory in the Championship. beating Eastern Counties in the final at Kingsholm, where he was accompanied by Peter Butler, Richard Jardine, Stewart Dix, Peter Kingston, Mike Burton, Alan Brinn, John Fidler, John Watkins and John Haines. The regional South & South-West team, including Bayliss, Burton, Fidler, Watkins and Butler, played South-East & London.

Sep 7 Gloucester 31 Broughton Park 3
Tries: j.Haines (2), J.Jarrett, R.Jardine,
K.Richardson, J.Watkins;
Conversions: P.Butler (2);
Penalty: P.Butler

Sep 9 Gloucester 75 L'Aquilla (Italy) 0
Tries: R.Clewes (5), R.White (3), A.Brinn,
P.Kingston, P.Blakeway, R.Jardine, J.Dix,
J.Watkins
Conversions: P.Butler (8);
Penalty: P.Butler

Sep 11 Gloucester 17 Stroud 9
Tries: J.Dix, J.Haines, Penalties: R.White (2);
Drop goal: R.Jardine

Sep 14 Coventry 29 Gloucester 15
Try: P.Blakeway;
Conversion: P.Butler;
Penalties: P.Butler (3)

Sep 18 Gloucester 28 Abertillery 3
Tries: J.Watkins, R.Jardine;
Conversion: P.Butler;
Penalties: P.Butler (6)

Sep 21 Waterloo 3 Gloucester 17
Tries: R.Clewes, P.Butler, J.Haines;
Conversion: P.Butler;
Penalty: P.Butler

Sep 28 Gloucester 23 Bristol 12
Tries: S.Dix (2), J.Watkins;
Conversion: P.Butler;
Penalties: P.Butler (3)

Oct 5 Gloucester 15 Bedford 9
Try: J.Jarrett;
Conversion: P.Butler;
Penalties: P.Butler(3)

Oct 9 Gloucester 9 Moseley 6
Try: E.Pinkney;
Conversion: P.Butler;
Penalty: P.Butler

Oct 12 Gloucester 33 Harlequins 10
Tries: P.Kingston, J.Dix, R.Clewes, Dick Smith;
Conversions: P.Butler (4);
Penalties: P. Butler (3)

Oct 16 Gloucester 48 Cheltenham 0
Tries: Dick Smith (2), P.Kingston (2), J.Dix,
R.Clewes, E.Pinkney, J.Bayliss, N.Jackson;
Conversions: P.Butler (6)

**Oct 19 Gloucester 32
Plymouth Albion 15**
Tries: F.Reed, J.Dix, R.Redwood, R.Clewes,
R.Jardinne;
Conversions: P.Butler (3);
Penalties: P.Butler (2)

Oct 23 Newport 24 Gloucester 13
Tries: J.Haines, J.Dix;
Conversion: P.Butler;
Drop goal: R.Redwood

Oct 26 Clifton 0 Gloucester 12
Tries: R.Mogg, J.Dix, R.Etheridge

Nov 2 Gloucester 24 Leicester 7
Try: E.Pinkney;
Conversion: P.Butler;
Penalties: P.Butler (5);
Drop goal: R.Redwood

Nov 9 Moseley 29 Gloucester 14
Tries: J.Dix (2), Dick Smith;
Conversion: M.Longstaff

**Nov 13 Gloucester 21
St.Luke's College 3
(National K.O. Cup Competition)**
Tries: E.Pinkney, S.Dix;
Conversions: P.Butler (2);
Penalties: P.Butler (2);
Drop goal: R.Redwood

Nov 16 Gloucester 12 Aberavon 6
Try: R.Jardine;
Conversion: P.Butler;
Penalties: P.Butler (2)

Nov 23 London Irish v Gloucester - cancelled

**Nov 30 Oxford University 21
Gloucester 13**
Tries: J.Dix (2);
Conversion: P.Butler;
Penalty: P.Butler

Dec 7 Gloucester 23 Newbridge 19
Tries: S.Dix, E.Pinkney, M.Longstaff;
Conversion: M.Longstaff;
Penalties: M.Longstaff (2);
Drop goal: R.Redwood

Dec 14 Bath 12 Gloucester 7
Try: D.Crabbe;
Penalty: P.Butler

Dec 21 Gloucester 12 Coventry 3
Try: R.Gwilliam;
Conversion: P.Butler;
Penalties: P.Butler (2)

Dec 26 Gloucester 29 Lydney 10
Tries: J.Haines, D.Crabbe, S.Dix, J.Watkins,
M.Burton;
Conversions: M.Longstaff (3);
Penalty: M. Longstaff

Dec 28 Gloucester 15 Bridgend 18
Try: R.Mogg;
Conversion: P.Butler;
Penalties: P.Butler (3)

Jan 1 Gloucester 15 Nottingham 19
Try: J.Haines;
Conversion: P.Butler;
Penalties: P.Butler (3)

Jan 4   Gloucester 9 London Scottish 17
Penalties: P.Butler (3)

Jan 11 Leicester 18 Gloucester 4
Try: R.Mogg

Jan 18 Wasps 9 Gloucester 8
Tries: R.Mogg, J.Dix

Jan 22 Gloucester 19 Army 13
Try: D.Crabbe;
Penalties: P.Butler (5)

**Jan 25 Gloucester 31
Cambridge University 3**
Tries: J.Watkins (2), J.Bayliss, J.Haines;
Conversions: P.Butler (3);
Penalties: P.Butler (3)

Jan 28 Gloucester 18 St.Luke's College 9
Try: J.Dix;
Conversion: P.Butler;
Penalties: P.Butler (4)

Jan 31 Bristol 17 Gloucester 9
Try: E.Pinkney;
Conversion: P.Butler;
Penalty: P.Butler

**Feb 8 Moseley 10 Gloucester 7
(National K.O Cup Competition)**
Try: D.Crabbe;
Penalty: P.Butler

Feb 14 Swansea 6 Gloucester 15
Try: R.Jardine;
Conversion: P.Butler;
Penalties: P.Butler (3)

Feb 19 Gloucester v Loughborough Colleges -
cancelled
Feb 22 Gloucester v Aberavon - cancelled

Feb 25 Gloucester 28 Bath 3
Tries: R.Jardine (2), J.Watkins, E.Pinkney;
Conversions: P.Butler (3);
Penalties: P.Butler (2)

Mar 1 Gloucester 51 Northampton 10
Tries: S.Dix (3), K.Richardson, D.Crabbe,
J.Jarrett, S.Boyle, E.Pinkney, J.Watkins;
Conversions: P.Butler (3);
Penalties: P.Butler (3)

Mar 8 Richmond v Gloucester - cancelled
Mar 12 Pontypool v Gloucester - cancelled
Mar 15 Gloucester v Guy's Hospital - cancelled

Mar 19 Gloucester 49 Cheltenham 3
Tries: R.Mogg (2), J.Dix (2), J.Jarrett,
P.Blakeway, R.Clewes, P.Winnell;
Conversions: M.Longstaff (7);
Penalty: M.Longstaff

Mar 22 Saracens 30 Gloucester 0

Mar 29 Gloucester 19 New Brighton 13

Tries: E.Pinkney (2), R.Hutchinson;
Conversions: P.Butler (2);
Penalty: P.Butler

Mar 31 Gloucester 15 Fylde 12
Tries: M.Longstaff, R.White, R.Jardine;
Penalty: M.Longstaff

Apr 5 Gloucester 22 Cardiff 3
Tries: R.Clewes, E.Pinkney, D.Crabbe;
Conversions: P.Butler (2);

Penalties: P.Butler (2)
Apr 9 Gloucester 15 Newport 14
Try: M.Nicholls;
Conversion: P.Butler;
Penalties: P.Butler (3)

Apr 12 Ebbw Vale 24 Gloucester 10
Tries: J.Dix (2);
Conversion: M.Longstaff

**Apr 16 Gloucester 28
South Wales Police 9**

Tries: J.Dix, E.Pinkney, F.Reed;
Conversions: R.Correia (2);
Penalties: R.Correia (4)

Apr 19 Gloucester 30 Sale 12
Tries: R.Jardine (2), R.Mogg, E.Pinkney,
R.Etheridge;
Conversions: R.Correia (5)

Apr 25 Northern 9 Gloucester 14
Tries: P.Williams, R.Mogg, S.Boyle;
Conversion: K.Richardson

1975-76

T.Tandy A.Lankester P.Hawker R.Morris P.Ford R.Long(Hon.Sec) E.J.Stephens Dr.T.E.Durkin(Hon.Club Doctor) M.Elway
A.D.Wadley(Hon.Treas) K.Richardson J.Watkins J.Haines A.Brinn J.Fidler M.Potter R.Smith M.Curran T.Palmer Canon H.M.Hughes
J.Holder D.A.W.Dawe(Hon.Fixture Sec) D.Pointon R.Jardine R.Clewes A.G.Hudson(Chairman) M.Burton(Capt) P.Butler F.Read P.Kingston E.Pinkney
A.T.Voyce (inset) B.Vine J.Dix

Played 53 Won 34 Lost 16 Drawn 3
For 1105 Against 627
Captain: Mike Burton
Coach: Mike Nicholls

Gloucester United
Played 37 Won 24 Lost 12 Drawn 1
For 855 Against 351
Captain: Jerry Herniman

Most appearances: K.Richardson 48, J.Watkins
43, P.Butler, P.Kingston, B.Vine 41, J.Fidler 36,
M.Burton 35, R.Clewes 33, P.Winnell,
R.Mogg 32
Most tries: R.Clewes 32, B.Vine 13, J.Haines
12, J.Watkins 11, P.Williams 10
Conversions: P.Butler 68, R.Mogg, R.Correia 6,
D.Pointon 4, S.Boyle 2, K.Richardson 1
Penalties: P.Butler 70, R.Correia 4, D.Pointon,

R.Mogg 1
Drop goals: D.Pointon 3, P.Butler 2,

Another good season, this time with Mike
Burton as captain. Peter Butler accumulated
another 360 points for the club, and his
scoring for the County was quite remarkable,
accumulating 99 points out of 135 scored by
Gloucestershire in their seven matches. Bob
Clewes had a fantastic season scoring 32 tries,
more than double the next highest try scorer.
He achieved a hat-trick twice and no fewer than
four against Exeter. On the other wing John Dix
scored five tries in the Exeter game, when the
team total of 18 tries equalled the Club record.
New recruit Brian Vine from Lydney, made a big
impression in the centre, Richard Mogg greatly
improved his game on the wing and Chris
Williams a recruit from Headingley, quickly

settled at fly-half. Amongst the forwards,
Mike Burton, John Fidler, Alan Brinn and John
Watkins were outstanding.

The season started uncertainly with only
four wins in the first ten games. Results then
improved with away wins over Harlequins,
Leicester, Moseley and Bath before Christmas,
as well being the only English team to beat
Newport. In the second half of the season there
were successes against Bath (to complete the
double), Swansea and Northampton (away). It
was unusual to win so many games away from
Kingsholm, but the corollary was that there
were more home defeats than usual. There was
only one win in the John Player Cup before
a one-point defeat at Sale ended the club's
participation for the season.

Mike Potter, a great servant of the club retired at the end of the season having played in 224 games. He was a player who tended to be underrated, but it was he who had an outstanding game in the famous victory against London Welsh in the quarter-final of the National Knock-Out Competition in 1972, scoring Gloucester's only try. Another player from that game, Nigel Jackson also retired after 137 appearances. Dick Smith effectively retired after first appearing in 1958. He would re-appear for one game as a replacement in 1977, bringing his total of appearances to a remarkable 540, including 116 tries. In a similar way Mike Nicholls, arguably the best captain Gloucester ever had, retired in 1975, but played three more times in the following two seasons, and ended up playing in 434 games.

For the second season running John Bayliss captained the County to the title. Peter Butler, Bob Clewes, Chris Williams, Peter Kingston, John Watkins, John Fidler and Mike Burton also played in the final, and Butler scored all the points in the 24–9 victory over Middlesex with a try a conversion and six penalties. Western Counties played the Australians at Bristol with Butler, Williams, Burton, Fidler and Watkins in the team. Mike Burton won caps for England against Australia, Wales, Scotland, Ireland and France. Peter Butler and Chris Williams were capped against France.

Sep 3 Weston-S-Mare 3 Gloucester 37
Tries: J.Dix (2), R.Clewes (2), A.Brinn;
Conversions: P.Butler (4);
Penalties: P.Butler (3)

Sep 6 Broughton Park 18 Gloucester 26
Tries: R.Clewes (3), R.Jardine, P.Kingston;
Conversions: P.Butler (3)

**Sep 10 Gloucester 25
South Wales Police 10**
Tries: R.Clewes, J.Bayliss, E.Pinkney;
Conversions: P.Butler (2);
Penalties: P.Butler (2);
Drop goal: D.Pointon

Sep 13 Gloucester 13 Coventry 13
Try: R.Clewes;
Penalties: P.Butler (3)

Sep 18 Gloucester 20 Begles (France) 21
Tries: J.Bayliss, A.Brinn, E.Pinkney;
Conversion: P.Butler;
Penalties: P.Butler (2)

Sep 20 Fylde 31 Gloucester 3
Penalty: P.Butler

Sep 24 Stroud 9 Gloucester 30
Tries: R.Jardine, P.Williams, M.Burton, J.Hemmings;
Conversions: P.Butler (4);
Penalties: P.Butler (2)

Sep 27 Bristol 4 Gloucester 0

Oct 1 Gloucester 9 Moseley 22
Try: P.Williams;
Conversion: P.Butler;
Penalty: P.Butler

Oct 4 Bedford 18 Gloucester 10
Try: J.Dix;
Penalties: P.Butler (2)

Oct 8 Gloucester 31 British Police 6
Tries: P.Williams (2), Dick Smith, J.Dix;
Conversions: P.Butler (3);
Penalties: P.Butler (3)

Oct 11 Harlequins 13 Gloucester 24
Tries: R.White, R.Jardine, E.Pinkney;
Conversions: P.Butler (3);
Penalties: P.Butler (2)

Oct 15 Gloucester 40 Cheltenham 4
Tries: R.Mogg, R.Etheridge, S.Clewes, R.White, R.Correia, K.Richardson, F.Reed, E.Pinkney;
Conversions: R.Mogg (4)

Oct 18 Gloucester 17 Newport 13
Tries: P.Kingston, Dick Smith;
Penalties: P.Butler (3)

Oct 25 Gloucester 41 Clifton 0
Tries: S.Clewes (3), E.Pinkney (2), R.Moody, K.Richardson, M.Curran;
Conversions: R.Correia (3);
Penalty: R.Correia

Oct 29 Gloucester 12 Pontypool 19
Tries: P.Kingston, B.Vine;
Conversions: P.Butler (2)

Nov 1 Leicester 12 Gloucester 22
Tries: J.Bayliss, Dick Smith;
Conversion: P.Butler;
Penalties: P.Butler (4)

Nov 8 Gloucester 76 Exeter 6
Tries: J.Dix (5), R.Clewes (4), J.Haines (2), R.Etheridge (2), M.Curran, S.Clewes, R.Jardine, P.Winnell, R.Correia;
Conversions: R.Correia (2)

**Nov 12 Cambridge University 32
Gloucester 12**
Try: J.Watkins;

Conversion: P.Butler;
Penalties: P.Butler (2)

**Nov 15 Plymouth Albion 3 Gloucester 9
(John Player Cup)**
Try: J.Haines;
Conversion: P.Butler;
Penalty: P.Butler

Nov 22 Gloucester 7 London Irish 21
Try: J.Haines;
Penalty: R.Correia

**Nov 27 Gloucester 16
Loughborough Colleges 22**
Tries: J.Fidler, R.Mogg;
Conversion: R.Correia;
Penalties: R.Correia (2)

**Nov 29 Gloucester 23
Oxford University 6**
Tries: R.Clewes (2), P.Butler, J.Watkins;
Conversions: P.Butler (2);
Penalty: P.Butler

Dec 6 Moseley 18 Gloucester 26
Tries: K.Richardson, B.Vine;
Penalties: P.Butler (5);
Drop goal: P.Butler

Dec 13 Bath 15 Gloucester 18
Try: R.Clewes;
Conversion: P.Butler;
Penalties: P.Butler (4)

Dec 20 Coventry 18 Gloucester 15
Tries: R.Mogg, R.Jardine, J.Haines;
Penalty: R.Mogg

Dec 26 Gloucester 44 Lydney 7
Tries: R.Clewes (2), B.Vine, R.Mogg, P.Williams, J.Fidler, J.Watkins, J.Haines;
Conversions: P.Butler (6)

Dec 27 Gloucester 29 Newbridge 3
Tries: J.Haines (2), R.Jardine, R.Clewes;
Conversions: P.Butler (2);
Penalties: P.Butler (3)

Jan 1 Gloucester 17 Nottingham 3
Tries: J.Watkins, J.Haines, C.Williams;
Conversion: P.Butler;
Penalty: P.Butler

Jan 3 London Scottish 20 Gloucester 0

Jan 10 Gloucester 4 Leicester 9
Try: P.Williams

Jan 16 Gloucester 16 Wasps 6
Tries: K.Richardson, B.Vine;

Conversion: P.Butler;
Penalties: P.Butler (2)

Jan 20 Gloucester 15 Bristol 15
Try: J.Watkins;
Conversion: P.Butler;
Penalties: P.Butler (2);
Drop goal: D.Pointon

Jan 24 Gloucester 38 Army 8
Tries: B.Vine (3), D.Pointon (2), Dick Smith,
M.Potter;
Conversions: P.Butler (5)

Jan 28 Gloucester 23 St.Luke's College 16
Tries: R.Clewes (2), B.Vine, R.Jardine;
Conversions: P.Butler (2);
Penalty: P.Butler

Jan 31 Bridgend v Gloucester - cancelled due
to frost

Feb 7 Gloucester 32 Exeter 10
Tries: R.Clewes (2), B.Vine, R.Jardine, Dick
Smith;
Conversions: P.Butler (3);
Penalties: P.Butler (2)

Feb 14 Sale 16 Gloucester 15
(John Player Cup)
Try: R.Clewes;
Conversion: P.Butler;
Penalty: P.Butler;
Drop goals: P.Butler, D.Pointon

Feb 17 Gloucester 12 Bath 3
Tries: R.Clewes, R.Jardine, P.Kingston

Feb 20 Gloucester 33 Swansea 20
Tries: B.Vine (2), C.Williams;
Conversions: P.Butler (3);
Penalties: P.Butler (5)

Feb 28 Gloucester v Aberavon - cancelled due
to Aberavon playing a cup game

Mar 6 Northampton 3 Gloucester 20
Tries: J.Watkins, R.Clewes, J.Haines, S.Boyle;
Conversions: P.Butler (2)

Mar 10 Cheltenham 6 Gloucester 36
Tries: R.Clewes, B.Vine, C.Williams,
W.Birchley, S.Mills, J.Watkins, M.Potter;
Conversions: P.Butler (4)

Mar 13 Gloucester 18 Richmond 4
Try: P.Butler;
Conversion: P.Butler;
Penalties: P.Butler (4)

Mar 17 Newbridge 15 Gloucester 6
Try: R.Clewes;
Conversion: S.Boyle

Mar 20 Guy's Hospital 4 Gloucester 52
Tries: R.Clewes (2), J.Watkins (2), E.Pinkney
(2), R.Etheridge, D.Pointon, B.Vine, S.Clewes,
S.Boyle;
Conversions: R.Mogg (2), S.Boyle,
K.Richardson

Mar 24 Abertillery v Gloucester - cancelled
due to frost

Mar 27 Gloucester 11 Saracens 9

Tries: A.Brinn, Dick Smith;
Penalty: D.Pointon

Mar 31 Cardiff 32 Gloucester 4
Try: P.Williams

Apr 7 Newport 24 Gloucester 7
Try: R.Clewes;
Penalty: P.Butler

Apr 10 Gloucester 15 Ebbw Vale 12
Tries: P.Williams (2);
Conversions: P.Butler (2);
Penalty: P.Butler

Apr 15 Lydney 6 Gloucester 6
Try: J.Haines;
Conversion: P.Butler

Apr 17 Gloucester 27 Headingley 3
Tries: P.Williams (2), P.Pritchard, A.Brinn,
J.Watkins;
Conversions: P.Butler (2);
Penalty: P.Butler

Apr 19 Gloucester 28 Birkenhead Park 4
Tries: R.Clewes, A.Brinn, J.Fidler, J.Haines,
D.Pointon;
Conversions: D.Pointon (4)

Apr 24 Torquay Athletic 9 Gloucester 22
Tries: R.Clewes (2), Dick Smith;
Conversions: P.Butler (2);
Penalties: P.Butler (2)

May 1 Sale 3 Gloucester 13
Try: J.Watkins;
Penalties: P.Butler (3)

1976-77

Played 51 Won 35 Lost 14 Drawn 2
For 1147 Against 530
Captain: John Watkins

Gloucester United
Played 32 Won 23 Lost 9
For 704 Against 308
Captain: Jim Jarrett

Most appearances: R.Clewes 44, R.Mogg,
C.Williams, E.Pinkney, D.Pointon 39, J.Watkins
38, M.Burton 37, S.Boyle 33, P.Winnell 31,
P.Butler, S.Mills, J.Simonett 30
Most tries: R.Clewes 26, R.Mogg 20, E.Pinkney
18, J.Watkins 17, C.Williams 15, D.Pointon 11
Most conversions: P.Butler 59, J.Orwin 9,
R.Correia 8, D.Pointon 6
Most penalties: P.Butler 49, D.Pointon 11
Drop goals: D.Pointon 3, P.Butler 1

Captain John Watkins tried to introduce a more
running game. It certainly led to a big increase
in the number of tries scored, 185, which was a
club record. For the second season running the
club record of 18 tries in a game was equaled in
the 80-10 thrashing of Guy's Hospital. Scoring
was so free that the 1147 points scored was
another club record. Peter Butler, as usual, was
top points scorer with 272 points in the regular
season plus another 78 on the out-of-season
tour of North America. Bob Clewes was again
top try scorer, but Richard Mogg, increasingly
influential, also scored freely. Eddie Pinkney
was the top try scorer in the forwards. Peter
Kingston at scrum-half was injured in February,
but Paul Howell stepped in and was a more than
capable replacement, scoring eight tries. Dave
Pointon (centre), stepping in after Brian Vine
was injured early on, was soon at home, and

had a sequence of 23 successive appearances.
He was also a useful back-up place kicker.

John Bayliss (403 appearances and 92 tries)
retired after the end-of-season tour, having also
played 61 times for the County. Of Gloucester
players only "Bumps" Carpenter had appeared
in more. John Dix (217 games and 87 tries) also
effectively retired, although he made one more
appearance in the following season.

The best result of the campaign was the win over
Newport, the only English team to defeat the
Welsh club all season. At the end of the season
Bristol were beaten at the Memorial Ground by
an astonishing margin of 34-9. There were other
good away wins, at Coventry, Pontypool, Wasps
and Saracens. The John Player Cup campaign
started well with wins over Harlequins (away)

M.Elway T.Tandy C.Pope P.Ford R.Morris P.Hawker E.Stephens T.Palmer F.Ewers T.Pritchard W.Brinn
A.Lankester R.Long(Hon.Sec) D.Wadley(Hon.Treas) P.Kingston C.Williams S.Mills E.Pinkney S.Boyle P.Winnel J.Simonett A.Brinn M.Burton J.Haines
R.Etheridge Dr.T.Durkin (Hon.Club Doctor) M.Nicholls
R.Clewes F.Reed D.Pointon J.Watkins(Capt) T.Voyce(Pres) P.Butler B.Vine J.Cooke R.Jardine

and Bristol, but in the third round a long trip to Gosforth ended in defeat. Peter Butler missed several penalties in the windy conditions, but on one occasion, the Gloucester touch-judge signaled a kick had been successful, but his Gosforth counterpart did not agree. The referee disallowed the "score." Gosforth won 3-0 and went on to win the cup.

John Watkins captained the County to the Championship final only to lose to Lancashire. In the team with Watkins were Peter Butler, Bob Clewes, Richard Mogg, Chris Williams, Peter Kingston, Mike Burton and Steve Boyle.

After the end of the season there was a very successful tour of North America. All six games were won convincingly, and a total of 39 tries scored.

Sep 4 Gloucester 31 Broughton Park 6
Tries: P.Butler, B.Vine, C.Williams, J.Watkins;
Conversions: P.Butler (3);
Penalties: P.Butler (3)

Sep 8 Gloucester 23 Stroud 3
Tries: E.Pinkney (2), R.Clewes;
Conversion: P.Butler;
Penalties: P.Butler (3)

Sep 11 Coventry 11 Gloucester 12
Try: R.Mogg;
Conversion: P.Butler;
Penalties: P.Butler (2)

Sep 15 Gloucester 18 Newbridge 13
Tries: C.Williams, K.Richardson;
Conversions: P.Butler (2);
Penalties: P.Butler, G.Sargent

Sep 18 Gloucester 14 Waterloo 10
Tries: M.Burton, R.Mogg;
Penalty: G.Sargent;
Drop goal: D.Pointon

Sep 25 Gloucester 6 Bristol 9
Try: C.Williams;
Conversion: R.Correia

Sep 29 Cheltenham 7 Gloucester 62
Tries: P.Williams (3), R.Mogg (3), S.Clewes (2), S.Boyle (2), C.Williams, F.Reed;
Conversions: J.Orwin (7)

Oct 2 Gloucester 35 Bedford 14
Tries: J.Watkins (2), R.Clewes, S.Clewes, R.Jardine, S.Mills, E.Pinkney;
Conversions: J.Orwin (2);
Penalty: J.Orwin

Oct 6 Ebbw Vale 22 Gloucester 4
Try: R.Mogg

Oct 9 Gloucester 9 Harlequins 14
Penalties: D.Pointon (2), R.Correia

Oct 13 Pontypool 0 Gloucester 18
Tries: S.Clewes, E.Pinkney;
Conversions: C.Williams (2);
Penalties: C.Williams (2)

Oct 16 Newport 30 Gloucester 4
Try: R.Clewes

Oct 23 Gloucester 28 Clifton 0
Tries: P.Williams (2), R.Moody, R.Etheridge, J.Haines;
Conversion: D.Pointon;
Penalties: D.Pointon (2)

**Oct 27 Gloucester 47
South Wales Police 17**
Tries: R.Etheridge (2), R.Clewes, R.Jardine, R.Mogg, S.Mills, J.Watkins, E.Pinkney;
Conversions: D.Pointon (3);
Penalties: D.Pointon (3)

**Oct 30 Oxford University 13
Gloucester 24**
Try: S.Boyle;
Conversion: D.Pointon,
Penalties: D.Pointon (4), R.Mogg (2)

Nov 3 Gloucester 10 Bridgend 11
Tries: R.Mogg, A.Brinn;
Conversion: D.Pointon

Nov 6 Gloucester 14 Leicester 12
Tries: D.Pointon (2), R.Clewes;
Conversion: R.Light

**Nov 10 Gloucester 4
Cambridge University 4**
Try: G.Sargent

Nov 13 Stroud 10 Gloucester 8
Tries: L.Jones (2)

Nov 20 Gloucester 9 Aberavon 13
Penalties: P.Butler (3)

Nov 27 London Irish 16 Gloucester 7
Try: J.Dix;
Penalty: P.Williams

Dec 4 Harlequins 9 Gloucester 17
(John Player Cup)
Tries: E.Pinkney, S.Boyle, R.Clewes;
Conversion: P.Butler;
Penalty: P.Butler

Dec 11 Gloucester v Sale – cancelled due to frost
Dec 18 Gloucester v Coventry - cancelled due to frost

Dec 26 Gloucester 47 Lydney 10
Tries: R.Clewes (5), E.Pinkney (2), P.Kingston, K.Richardson;
Conversions: P.Butler (4);
Penalty: P.Butler

Jan 1 Gloucester 0 London Scottish 0

Jan 8 Leicester 10 Gloucester 25
Tries: E.Pinkney (2), C.Williams;
Conversions: P.Butler (2);
Penalties: P.Butler (2);
Drop goal: P.Butler

Jan 15 Wasps 6 Gloucester 32
Tries: J.Watkins (2), R.Jardine, D.Pointon, R.Mogg;
Conversions: P.Butler (3);
Penalties: P.Butler (2)

Jan 19 Gloucester 17 Army 8
Tries: W.Birchley (2), R.Clewes;
Conversion: R.Correia;
Penalty: R.Light

Jan 22 Moseley 28 Gloucester 0

Jan 29 Gloucester 26
Loughborough Colleges 3
Tries: C.Williams, J.Haines, D.Pointon, E.Pinkney, R.Moody;
Conversions: P.Butler (3)

Feb 4 Gloucester 26 St.Luke's College 3
Tries: R.Clewes (3), R.Moody, S.Boyle, E.Pinkney;
Conversion: P.Butler

Feb 12 Gloucester 12 Bristol 3
(John Player Cup)
Try: J.Watkins;
Conversion: P.Butler;
Penalties: P.Butler (2)

Feb 18 Swansea 11 Gloucester 6
Penalties: P.Butler (2)

Feb 26 Llanelli 57 Gloucester 16
Tries: D.Pointon, R.Light, J.Haines;
Conversions: P.Butler (2)

Mar 2 Gloucester 6 Newport 3
Penalties: P.Butler (2)

Mar 5 Gloucester 31 Northampton 6
Tries: C.Williams (3), R.Clewes, S.Mills, E.Pinkney;
Conversions: P.Butler (2);
Penalty: P.Butler

Mar 7 Gloucester 52 Cheltenham 0
Tries: J.Dix (3), R.Jardine (2), P.Howell (2), J.Watkins (2), J.Cook;
Conversions: P.Correia (6)

Mar 12 Gosforth 3 Gloucester 0
(John Player Cup)

Mar 16 Gloucester 51 Abertillery 4
Tries: J.Watkins (2), R.Clewes, D.Pointon, R.Jardine, R.Mogg, C.Williams, P.Howell, M.Burton;
Conversions: P.Butler (6);
Penalty: P.Butler

Mar 19 Gloucester 80 Guy's Hospital 10
Tries: R.Mogg (6), P.Williams (4), P.Howell (2), J.Watkins (2), S.Boyle (2), S.Mills, J.Simonett;
Conversions: C.Williams (2), P.Williams, R.Mogg

Mar 23 Gloucester 51 Bath 7
Tries: R.Clewes (2), D.Pointon, R.Jardine, R.Mogg, S.Mills, J.Watkins, E.Pinkney, J.Haines;
Conversions: P.Butler (6);
Penalty: P.Butler

Mar 26 Saracens 3 Gloucester 9
Try: R.Mogg;
Conversion: P.Butler;
Penalty: P.Butler

Mar 30 Newbridge 22 Gloucester 9
Penalties: P.Butler (3)

Apr 2 Gloucester 18 Cardiff 19
Penalties: P.Butler (6)

Apr 7 Lydney 6 Gloucester 18
Tries: C.Williams (2), E.Pinkney;
Conversions: P.Butler (3)

Apr 9 Gloucester 31 New Brighton 10

Tries: D.Pointon (2), R.Mogg, R.Clewes, A.Brinn, E.Pinkney;
Conversions: R.Mogg (2);
Penalty: R.Mogg

Apr 11 Gloucester 24 Fylde 12
Tries: R.Clewes (2);
Conversions: P.Butler (2);
Penalties: P.Butler (2);
Drop goals: D.Pointon (2)

Apr 16 Gloucester 37 Sale 9
Tries: R.Clewes, D.Pointon, J.Dix, P.Howell, M.Burton, V.Wooley;
Conversions: P.Butler (5)
Penalty: P.Butler

Apr 19 Nottingham 18 Gloucester 29
Tries: J.Watkins (2), S.Baker, R.Clewes;
Conversions: P.Butler (2);
Penalties: P.Butler (3)

Apr 23 Exeter 6 Gloucester 14
Tries: E.Pinkney, P.Williams;
Penalties: P.Butler (2)

Apr 27 Bristol 9 Gloucester 34
Tries: P.Howell (2), D.Pointon, R.Clewes;
Conversions: P.Butler (3);
Penalties: P.Butler (4)

Apr 30 Gloucester 42 Plymouth Albion 0
Tries: C.Williams (3), B.Vine, R.Mogg, R.Clewes, E.Pinkney, J.Watkins;
Conversions: P.Butler (5)

Out-of-Season Tour to North America

May 16 Columbus Area Select 11
Gloucester 57
Tries: J.Dix (3), R.Clewes (2), J.Watkins (2), E.Pinkney, P.Howell;
Conversions: P.Butler (9);
Penalty: P.Butler

May 19 Indianapolis Select 6
Gloucester 29
Tries: R.Clewes (2), J.Watkins, J.Simonett;
Conversions: P.Butler (2);
Penalties: P.Butler (3)

May 21 Michigan Select 0 Gloucester 46
Tries: M.Longstaff (2), R.Morris (2), R.Clewes, J.Watkins, P.Howell;
Conversions: P.Butler (6);
Penalties: P.Butler (2)

May 27 South Illinois Select 18
Gloucester 40
Tries: R.Etheridge (3), R.Light (2), S.Mills, J.Bayliss, K.Richardson, D.Pointon;

Conversions: R.Correia (2)

May 30 Midwest Select 4 Gloucester 28
Tries: E.Pinkney (3), R.Clewes, J.Watkins,

V.Woolley;
Conversions: P.Butler (2)

June 1 Chicago Lions 6 Gloucester 29

Tries: J.Watkins, M.Burton, P.Howell, J.Dix;
Conversions: P.Butler (2);
Penalties: P.Butler (3)

1977-78

J.Holder M.Elway T.Pritchard C.Pope M.Billington E.Stephens P.Hawker D.Wadley(Hon.Treas) N.Duncalfe T.Tandy(Hon.Sec)
R.Morris M.Nicholls P.Williams S.Mills C.Williams S.Boyle J.Simonett J.Fidler G.Sargent V.Wooley E.Pinkney Dr.T.Durkin(Hon.Club Doctor) Canon M.Hughes(Vice-Pres)
D.Dawe(Fixture Sec) D.Pointon B.Vine G.Hudson(Chairman) J.Watkins(Capt) T.Voyce(Pres) J.Haines R.Clewes P.Butler M.Burton
P.Howell P.Kingston R.Correia

Played 49 Won 38 Lost 11
For 993 Against 501
Captain: John Watkins

Gloucester United
Played 37 Won 30 Lost 6 D 1
For 946 Against 273
Captain: Alan Brinn

Most Appearances: J.Watkins 47, B.Vine 39,
J.Fidler 38, P.Butler 37, J.Simonett, R.Clewes 34,
M.Burton 30, R.Mogg 29, R.Jardine, S.Mills 28
Most tries: R.Clewes 19, R.Mogg 17,
J.Watkins 11
Most conversions: P.Butler 77, M.Longstaff 10
Penalties: P.Butler 66, R.Correia 6, M.Tunstall 5,
M.Longstaff 3
Drop goals: P.Butler 4, R.Jardine, D.Pointon,
P.Howell 1

A very successful season under the captaincy
of John Watkins. There was a victorious run in
the John Player Cup culminating in the final
at Twickenham, when Leicester were defeated.
The final was a tight affair, where for once
Dusty Hare had an off-day, missing five out
of six penalty attempts. Peter Butler was not
much better but did convert Richard Mogg's try
from the touch-line. In the second half Hare did

succeed with one kick, and near the end Leicester
would have scored but for a match saving tackle
from Richard Mogg. A remarkable feature of
the cup run was that the same 15 appeared in
every round. In the earlier rounds there was a
very satisfying win over the holders Gosforth.
Having narrowly lost at Gosforth the previous
season, Gloucester, at home, were not about
to let the same thing happen again. A raucous
crowd saw Gloucester lead 19-0, before two late
Gosforth tries made the score respectable. The
first of those was greeted by the Shed with a
rendition of, "Happy birthday to you".

Apart from the cup run there were other pleasing
wins, another over Leicester in a club game,
Coventry and Newport. In addition, there were
doubles over Bristol and Bath.

Peter Butler was again prolific, scoring 376
points, including 77 conversions, a club record
which would be equalled in 2001-02 by Ludovic
Mercier. Butler added another 75 points for
the County. Top try scorers Bob Clewes and
Richard Mogg, on the wings, took advantage
of the oceans of possession provided by the
dominant forwards, where John Watkins was
the top try scorer. Mike Longstaff, previously
full-back, re-emerged to play a few games in the

centre, but his time was yet to come as a back-
row forward.

At the end of the season Keith Richardson who
had made 281 appearances, and Eddie Pinkney
(134) retired. Pinkney had also scored 55 tries.

After the last game of the season, the John
Player Cup was paraded around Kingsholm.
There was a touching moment when John
Watkins handed the cup over to an emotional
Mike Burton, who had just played his last game
after announcing retirement. He had made 367
appearances. In fact, he would play one more
game as late as 1980.

In his last season Burton had won two more
caps playing against France and Wales. Richard
Jardine, Richard Mogg, Steve Boyle and John
Fidler played for England B against Romania
B. In the Divisional Championship, Mogg,
Boyle, Burton, Bob Clewes, Chris Williams,
Peter Kingston and Steve Mills all made
appearances. Gloucestershire lost in the final
of the Championship against North Midlands.
Peter Butler, Clewes, Burton, Williams, Paul
Howell, Mills, Fidler, Boyle and John Haines
were in the team.

Sep 3 Broughton Park 0 Gloucester 27
Tries: R.Mogg (2), R.Clewes;
Conversions: P.Butler (3);
Penalties: P.Butler (3)

Sep 9 Gloucester 27 Coventry 0
Tries: R.Jardine (2), E.Pinkney;
Conversions: P.Butler (3);
Penalties P.Butler (3)

Sep 14 Gloucester 40 Stroud 16
Tries: R.Mogg (2), S.Baker (2), P.Kingston,
R.Correia, M.Curran;
Conversions: P.Butler (3);
Penalties: P.Butler (2)

Sep 17 Fylde 12 Gloucester 30
Tries: R.Clewes, R.Mogg, F.Reed, J.Haines;
Conversions: P.Butler (4);
Penalties: P.Butler (2)

Sep 21 Gloucester 54 Cheltenham 4
Tries: V.Wooley (3), R.Etheridge (2), P.Kingston,
S.Mills, J.Simonett, J.Dix, J.Orwin;
Conversions: M.Longstaff (7)

Sep 24 Bristol 9 Gloucester 10
Try: R.Jardine;
Penalties: P.Butler (2)

Sep 27 Gloucester 15 Newbridge 10
Try: R.Clewes;
Conversion: R.Correia;
Penalties: R.Correia (3)

Oct 1 Bedford 33 Gloucester 6
Try: F.Reed;
Conversion: R.Correia

Oct 5 Gloucester 18 Pontypool 9
Penalties: P.Butler (6)

Oct 8 Harlequins 21 Gloucester 3
Penalty: R.Correia

Oct 12 Gloucester 21 St.Luke's College 3
Tries: D.Pointon, P.Tunstall, F.Reed, S.Boyle;
Conversion: R.Correia;
Penalty: R.Correia

Oct 15 Gloucester 16 Newport 6
Tries: R.Clewes, J.Haines;
Conversion: P.Butler;
Penalties: P.Butler (2)

**Oct 19 Gloucester 46
Loughborough Colleges 6**
Tries: J.Watkins (2), R.Clewes, R.Mogg,
J.Fidler, P.Howell, P.Wood;
Conversions: P.Butler (6);
Penalties: P.Butler (2)

Oct 22 Gloucester 15 Nottingham 13
Tries: R.Etheridge, P.Williams, P.Tunstall;
Penalty: R.Correia

**Oct 26 Gloucester 44
South Wales Police 0**
Tries: E.Pinkney (2), R.Clewes, D.Pointon,
C.Williams, S.Boyle, J.Watkins, P.Wood;
Conversions: P.Butler (6)

Oct 29 Gloucester 9 Oxford University 4
Penalties: M.Longstaff (3)

Nov 5 Leicester 28 Gloucester 15
Tries: S.Boyle, J.Haines;
Conversions: P.Butler (2);
Penalty: P.Butler

**Nov 9 Cambridge University 24
Gloucester 19**
Tries: P.Kingston, E.Pinkney;
Conversion: P.Butler;
Penalties: P.Butler (3)

**Nov 12 Gloucester 13
Plymouth Albion 20**
Try: J.Watkins;
Penalties: P.Tunstall (3)

Nov 17 Gloucester 25 Clifton 14
Tries: J.Haines, P.Kingston, R.Mogg, R.Clewes;
Conversions: P.Butler (3);
Penalty: P.Butler

Nov 22 Aberavon 14 Gloucester 12
Tries: P.Howell, R.Clewes;
Conversions: P.Butler (2)

Nov 26 Gloucester 6 London Irish 9
Penalties: P.Tunstall (2)

Dec 3 Moseley v Gloucester - cancelled

Dec 10 Gloucester 24 Bath 13
Try: P.Butler;
Conversion: P.Butler;
Penalties: P.Butler (5);
Drop goal: R.Jardine

Dec 17 Coventry 16 Gloucester 10
Try: K.Conway;
Penalty: P.Butler;
Drop goal: D.Pointon

Dec 21 Newport 17 Gloucester 0

Dec 26 Gloucester 41 Lydney 7
Tries: R.Mogg (3), J.Watkins (3), J.Delaney,
E.Rooney;
Conversions: P.Butler (3);
Penalty: P.Butler

Dec 31 Bridgend 50 Gloucester 0

Jan 2 Gloucester 21 Moseley 9
Tries: J.Watkins, C.Williams;
Conversions: P.Butler (2);
Penalties: P.Butler (2);
Drop goal: P.Butler

Jan 7 London Scottish 4 Gloucester 10
Try: P.Howell;
Penalty: P.Butler;
Drop goal: P.Butler

Jan 14 Gloucester 39 Leicester 6
Tries: R.Clewes (2). B.Vine (2), R.Mogg,
C.Williams, M.Burton;
Conversions: P.Butler (4);
Penalty: P.Butler

Jan 21 Gloucester 26 Wasps 12
Tries: G.Sargent (2), R.Mogg, R.Clewes;
Conversions: P.Butler (2);
Penalties: P.Butler (2)

**Jan 28 Gloucester 38 Lydney 6
(John Player Cup)**
Tries: R.Clewes (2), R.Mogg, S.Boyle,
V.Wooley;
Conversions: P.Butler (3);
Penalties: P.Butler (4)

Feb 3 Gloucester 17 Bristol 6
Tries: R.Clewes, J.Fidler, R.Mogg;
Conversion: P.Butler;
Penalty: P.Butler

Feb 11 Bath v Gloucester – cancelled due to
frost
Feb 13 Gloucester v Army – cancelled due to
frost
Feb 17 Gloucester v Swansea – cancelled due
to frost

**Feb 25 Gloucester 19 Gosforth 10
(John Player Cup)**
Tries: V.Wooley, S.Mills, C.Williams;
Conversions: P.Butler (2);
Penalty: P.Butler

Mar 3 Gloucester 34 St.Luke's College 4
Tries: M.Burton, R.Jardine, R.Mogg, P.Howell,
P.Butler;
Conversions: P.Butler (4);
Penalties: P.Butler (2)

Mar 6 Abertillery 12 Gloucester 6
Try: J.Delaney;
Conversion: M.Longstaff

**Mar 11 Wasps 3 Gloucester 13
(John Player Cup)**

Tries: V.Wooley, R.Mogg;
Conversion: P.Butler;
Penalty: P.Butler

Mar 15 Cheltenham 4 Gloucester 21
Try: J.Watkins;
Conversion: P.Butler;
Penalties: P.Butler (5)

Mar 23 Lydney 6 Gloucester 36
Tries: R.Jardine (2), J.Delaney, P.Howell,
M.Burton, S.Boyle;
Conversions: P.Butler (6)

Mar 25 Gloucester 33 Headingley 9
Tries: R.Clewes (2), C.Williams, P.Kingston,
F.Reed, S.Boyle;
Conversions: P.Butler (3);
Penalty: P.Butler

Mar 27 Gloucester 20 Birkenhead Park 0
Tries: P.Conway, J.Delaney, S.Mills,

M.Longstaff;
Conversions: M.Longstaff (2)

Apr 1 Harlequins 6 Gloucester 12
(John Player Cup Semi-final)
Try: R.Clewes;
Conversion: P.Butler;
Penalties: P.Butler (2)

Apr 8 Gloucester 16 Ebbw Vale 13
Tries: P.Howell, J.Watkins;
Conversion: P.Butler;
Penalty: P.Butler (2)

Apr 15 Gloucester 6 Leicester 3
(John Player Cup Final at Twickenham)
Try: R.Mogg;
Conversion: P.Butler

Apr 19 Bath 10 Gloucester 12
Try: J.Watkins;
Conversion: P.Butler;

Penalties: P.Butler (2)

Apr 22 Camborne 3 Gloucester 16
Tries: J.Delaney, P.Butler;
Conversion: P.Butler;
Penalty: P.Butler;
Drop goal: P.Butler

Apr 24 St.Ives 6 Gloucester 19
Tries: P.Williams, S.Baker;
Conversion: P.Butler;
Penalties: P.Butler (3)

Apr 25 Plymouth Albion 11 Gloucester 21
Tries: R.Clewes, J.Herniman;
Conversions: P.Butler (2);
Penalty: P.Butler;
Drop goals: P.Butler, P.Howell

Apr 29 Gloucester 12 Exeter 0
Tries: R.Clewes, P.Conway;
Conversions: P.Butler (2)

1978-79

T.Pritchard M.Elway A.D.Wadley(Hon.Treas) R.Collins A.Brinn P.J.Ford P.Hawker C.A.R.Lankester Canon H.M.Hughes(Vice-Pres) T.R.Tandy(Hon.Sec)
J.Holder M.Billington E.Rooney C.Williams R.Jardine S.Boyle J.Simonett P.Butler G.Sargent P.Williams A.Brooks S.Mills R.Etheridge
F.D.H.Dawe(Hon.Fixture Sec) B.Russell I.Wilkins D.Pointon A.T.Voyce(Pres) J.Watkins(Capt) A.G.Hudson(Chairman) R.Mogg R.Clewes L.Dick P.Wood
S.Baker P.Kingston

Played 48 Won 35 Lost 11 Drawn 2
For 798 Against 455
Captain: John Watkins

Gloucester United
Played 28 Won 23 Lost 5
For 695 Against 271
Captain: Jerry Herniman

Most appearances: R.Clewes, P.Wood 41,
J.Watkins 40, G.Sargent, S.Boyle 39,
A.Brookes 36,

R.Mogg 35, P.Butler, J.Simonett 33, S.Mills,
J.Orwin 32
Most tries: R.Clewes 20, R.Mogg 11, S.Boyle,
L.Dick 8
Conversions: P.Butler 30, B.Russell 10,
I.Wilkins 8, R.Clewes, G.Sargent 1
Penalties: P.Butler 65, B.Russell 10, I.Wilkins 5
Drop goals: P.Butler 4, B.Russell, D.Pointon 3

During the season Bob Clewes passed Arthur
Hudson's all-time record of 242 tries. Richard
Mogg made a successful move from wing

to centre. Although not quite so prolific as
usual Peter Butler still scored 279 points.
John Watkins, John Simonett and Paul Wood
provided a very reliable back-row, and the
second-row of Steve Boyle and John Orwin was
one of the best in the country.

After 19 seasons Alan Brinn retired having made
574 appearances, which is still the club record
and will probably stand for all time. Jim Jarrett
had effectively retired after captaining the
United in the 1976-77 season. But he returned

for one more game for the first XV to bring his total of appearances to 233. Chris Williams also moved on after making 101 appearances.

On the face of it the playing record looked impressive, but there was a disappointing exit from the John Player Cup at the first hurdle at home to Richmond. The game was drawn 3-3, but as no tries were scored Richmond qualified as the away team. The first half of the season was patchy, and by Christmas there had been nine defeats, but after that there were long winning sequences with 16 wins from 19 games. Over the season as a whole there were doubles over Coventry and Newport plus victories over Bristol (away), Aberavon, Northampton and Cardiff. There was also an excellent win in a special game against Taranaki of New Zealand, with captain John Watkins scoring a hat-trick of tries.

John Watkins, after three successive years as club captain, decided it was time to hand over the leadership to someone else. He had been a popular and hard-working captain, leading the club to 108 wins from 148 games.

Peter Kingston played for England against Ireland, France and Wales. South & South-West played against the All Blacks at Bristol. Peter Butler, Richard Mogg, Peter Kingston, John Watkins and Steve Mills were in the team.

Sep 2 Gloucester 33 Broughton Park 4
Tries: R.Clewes (3), P.Butler (2), E.Rooney, B.Vine;
Conversion: P.Butler;
Penalty: P.Butler

Sep 6 Stroud 3 Gloucester 13
Try: B.Vine;
Penalties: P.Butler (3)

Sep 9 Coventry 3 Gloucester 13
Try: R.Clewes;
Penalties: P.Butler (3)

Sep 13 Gloucester 6 Cheltenham 10
Penalties: P.Butler (2)

Sep 16 Waterloo 10 Gloucester 22
Tries: R.Mogg, C.Williams, S.Boyle;
Conversions: P.Butler (2);
Penalties: P.Butler (2)

Sep 20 Ebbw Vale 18 Gloucester 9
Try: R.Mogg;
Conversion: P.Butler;
Penalty: P.Butler

Sep 23 Gloucester 16 Bristol 16

Tries: C.Williams, P.Wood;
Conversion: P.Butler;
Penalties: P.Butler (2)

Sep 30 Gloucester 14 Bedford 10
Tries: R.Clewes, R.Mogg;
Penalties: P.Butler (2)

Oct 4 Pontypool 28 Gloucester 3
Penalty: P.Butler

Oct 7 Gloucester 28 Bucharest 30
Tries: R.Clewes, S.Boyle;
Conversion: P.Butler;
Penalties: P.Butler (6)

Oct 14 Gloucester 9 Harlequins 20
Penalties: B.Russell (2);
Drop goal: B.Russell

Oct 20 Newport 9 Gloucester 16
Tries: V.Wooley, G.Sargent;
Conversion: P.Butler;
Penalties: P.Butler (2)

**Oct 25 Gloucester 28
South Wales Police 0**
Tries: R.Jardine, L.Dick, S.Mills, A.Turton, J.Watkins;
Conversions: P.Butler (4)

Oct 28 Nottingham 24 Gloucester 8
Tries: P.Williams (2)

Nov 1 Clifton 13 Gloucester 32
Tries: R.Clewes (2), R.Jardine, P.Williams, J.Haines;
Conversions: P.Butler (3);
Penalties: P.Butler (2)

Nov 4 Gloucester 7 Leicester 9
Try: G.Sargent;
Penalty: P.Butler

**Nov 8 Gloucester 16
Cambridge University 10**
Tries: R.Clewes, R.Mogg, S.Boyle;
Conversions: R.Clewes, G.Sargent

Nov 11 Gloucester 13 Exeter 7
Tries: J.Delaney, J.Simonet;
Conversion: B.Russell;
Penalty: B.Russell

**Nov 15 Gloucester 46
Exeter University 20**
Tries: P.Howell (2), J.Delaney, R.Clewes, G.Sargent, V.Woolley, M.Teague;
Conversions: B.Russell (6);
Penalties: B.Russell (2)

Nov 18 Gloucester 15 Camborne 0
Tries: L.Dick (2), P.Howell;
Penalty: B.Russell

Nov 22 Gloucester 22 Aberavon 10
Tries: S.Boyle, J.Simonet;
Conversion: P.Butler;
Penalties: P.Butler (3);
Drop goal: P.Butler

Nov 25 London Irish 10 Gloucester 12
Try: A.Brookes;
Conversion: P.Butler;
Penalties: P.Butler (2)

Dec 2 Gloucester 19 Oxford University 4
Tries: J.Orwin, A.Turton;
Conversion: P.Butler;
Penalties: P.Butler (3)

**Dec 6 Gloucester 16
Loughborough Colleges 3**
Try: L.Dick;
Penalties: P.Butler (3);
Drop goal: P.Butler

Dec 8 Bath 20 Gloucester 10
Try: P.Wood;
Penalties: P.Butler (2)

Dec 15 Gloucester 19 Coventry 0
Tries: R.Clewes (2), P.Wood;
Conversions: P.Butler (2);
Penalty: P.Butler

**Dec 23 Gloucester 9
Glamorgan Wanderers 0**
Try: I.Wilkins;
Conversion: P.Butler;
Penalty: P.Butler

Dec 26 Gloucester 16 Lydney 7
Tries: P.Williams (2), R.Mogg (2)

Dec 30 Gloucester 12 Bridgend 16
Try: J.Watkins;
Conversion: P.Butler;
Penalties: P.Butler (2)

Jan 1 Moseley v Gloucester
Jan 6 Gloucester v London Scottish
Jan 13 Leicester v Gloucester
Jan 20 Wasps v Gloucester
Jan 27 Gloucester v Richmond (John Player Cup)
All cancelled due to frost and/or snow

Feb 2 Bristol 3 Gloucester 9
Penalties: P.Butler (2);
Drop goal: P.Butler

Feb 10 Gloucester 3 Richmond 3

(John Player Cup)
Drop goal: B.Russell

Feb 16 Swansea v Gloucester - cancelled

Feb 24 Gloucester 22 Plymouth Albion 13
Tries: P.Butler, P.Williams;
Conversion: P.Butler;
Penalties: P.Butler (3);
Drop goal: B.Russell

Feb 28 Gloucester 31 Abertillery 0
Tries: R.Clewes (2), G.Sargent, S.Baker,
P.Wood, J.Orwin;
Conversion: B.Russell (2);
Penalty: B.Russell

Mar 3 Gloucester 37 Northampton 4
Tries: G.Sargent, P.Wood, R.Mogg, S.Baker,
D.Pointon;
Conversions: P.Butler (4);
Penalties: P.Butler (3)

Mar 10 Richmond 7 Gloucester 3
Drop goal: B.Russell

**Mar 13 Gloucester 18
Taranaki (New Zealand) 6**
Tries: J.Watkins (3), S.Boyle;

Conversion: P.Butler

Mar 15 Cheltenham 0 Gloucester 12
Penalties: P.Butler (4)

Mar 24 Saracens 11 Gloucester 12
Penalties: P.Butler (3);
Drop goal: P.Butler

Mar 31 Plymouth Albion 10

Gloucester 32
Tries: R.Clewes (3), J.Simonet;
Conversions: P.Butler (2);
Penalties: P.Butler (3);
Drop goal: D.Pointon

Apr 2 Gloucester 11 Bath 3
Tries: R.Mogg, G.Sargent;
Penalty: P.Butler

Apr 7 Gloucester 6 Cardiff 3
Try: R.Clewes;
Conversion: P.Butler

Apr 12 Lydney 6 Gloucester 13
Tries: C.Williams, P.Wood;
Conversion: I.Wilkins;
Penalty: I.Wilkins

Apr 14 Gloucester 31 New Brighton 19
Tries: L.Dick (2), R.Clewes, R.Mogg,
R.Daldrey;
Conversions: I.Wilkins (4);
Penalty: I.Wilkins

Apr 16 Gloucester 22 Fylde 16
Tries: G.Sargent, S.Boyle;
Conversion: B.Russell;
Penalties: B.Russell (3);
Drop goal: D.Pointon

Apr 18 Newbridge 19 Gloucester 4
Try: J.Watkins

Apr 21 Gloucester 14 Sale 9
Tries: J.Watkins, L.Dick;
Penalties: I.Wilkins (2)

Apr 25 Gloucester 13 Newport 0
Tries: L.Dick, S.Boyle;
Conversion: I.Wilkins;
Penalty: I.Wilkins

Apr 28 Exeter 9 Gloucester 23
Tries: R.Mogg (2), R.Clewes, S.Boyle;
Conversions: I.Wilkins (2);
Drop goal: D.Pointon

1979-80

J.S.Jarrett M.Elway T.Day A.D.Wadley(Hon.Treas) R.Morris P.Ford A.Brinn E.Stephens R.Collins T.Durkin(Hon.Club Doctor) C.Pope T.Pritchard
T.Tandy(Hon.Sec) S.Mills A.Brooks F.Reed R.Mogg G.Sargent J.Herniman A.Turton J.Fidler S.Boyle M.Teague M.Preedy S.Ashmead D.Pointon J.Gadd J.Holder
D.Dawe(Hon.Fixture Sec) I.Wilkins P.Wood G.Hudson(Chairman) R.Clewes(Capt) Canon H.M.Hughes(Pres) P.Butler P.Tunstall J.Watkins
S.Baker C.Price B.Russdell P.Kingston

Played 50 Won 34 Lost 12 Drawn 4
For 884 Against 464
Captain: Bob Clewes

Gloucester United
Played 35 Won 25 Lost 8 Drawn 2
For 838 Against 369
Captain: Jerry Herniman

Most appearances: R.Clewes 50, R.Mogg
43, J.Watkins 41, P.Wood 40, D.Pointon 39,
A.Turton 38, P.Butler, S.Boyle 37, S.Baker 36,
S.Mills, D.Brookes 35
Most tries: S.Boyle 12, R.Clewes 11, P.Wood,
P.Tunstall 9
Conversions: P.Butler 37, B.Russell 10,
I.Wilkins 4, P.Ford, P.Tunstall 1
Penalties: P.Butler 69, B.Russell 11, I.Wilkins
7, P.Ford, P.Tunstall 2, C.Pryce 1
Drop goals: B.Russell 8, P.Butler, D.Pointon,
C.Pryce 2

Under the captaincy of Bob Clewes a more
expansive style of play was tried. Richard
Mogg was creative in the centre, but ironically
a forward, Steve Boyle, was the top try scorer.
He benefitted from tap penalties where his sheer
power took him across the try-line. Peter Butler
as usual scored heavily totaling 299 points.
Brian Russell took on the fly-half position from
the departed Chris Williams and was also a
sound place-kicker. Steve Baker became the
regular scrum-half, and scored some useful
tries. A young prop forward, Malcolm Preedy
made his first appearance in October and
quickly became a regular choice.

The John Player Cup campaign got off to a good
start with a draw at Richmond, which meant
Gloucester went through as the away team.
Coventry were beaten away, before a surprising
and disappointing home defeat to Rosslyn
Park, when the team just did not fire, ended
the club's hopes. There were good away wins at
Harlequins, Northampton and a second win at
Coventry. Newport were beaten at Kingsholm
and held to a draw at Rodney Parade. Other
notable home wins were against Leicester,
Bristol, Aberavon and Ebbw Vale.

Brian Vine who had played in 112 games, Ron
Etheridge (194) and Fred Reed (134) all retired
at the end of the season.

The most tragic event of the season was the death
of Tom Voyce, an icon of the Club and arguably
its greatest ever player. He won 27 England caps
from 1920-26, and revolutionised wing forward
play. At the end of his playing career, he went on
to the Club Committee, and in 1939 was elected
Chairman, a position he held until 1947. He was

a Vice-President until 1969, when he became
President, a position he held until 1979. He
served for many years on the County and RFU
committees, and was President of the RFU in
1960-61, the only Gloucester man to hold this
office.

There was an enjoyable out-of-season tour of
Canada in May for both the First XV and the
United.

Phil Blakeway was capped by England against
Ireland, France, Wales and Scotland. Steve
Boyle played for England 'B' against France
'B'. The County reached the final of the
Championship only to lose to Lancashire. Peter
Butler (conversion and three penalties), Bob
Clewes, Richard Mogg, Peter Kingston, Phil
Blakeway, Steve Mills, Gordon Sargent, John
Fidler and Paul Wood were in the team. Mogg
and Mills played for the South & South-West
against the All Blacks.

Sep 1 Broughton Park 9 Gloucester 16
Try: L.Dick;
Penalties: P.Butler (4)

Sep 5 Gloucester 22 Stroud 6
Tries: D.Brookes, J.Watkins, V.Wooley;
Conversions: P.Butler (2);
Penalties: P.Butler (2)

Sep 8 Gloucester 13 Coventry 13
Tries: S.Boyle, J.Watkins;
Conversion: I.Wilkins;
Penalty: I.Wilkins

Sep 12 Gloucester 16 Cheltenham 13
Try: S.Boyle;
Penalties: P.Butler (4)

Sep 15 Fylde 9 Gloucester 3
Penalty: P.Butler

Sep 19 Moseley 21 Gloucester 12
Try: J.Watkins;
Conversion: P.Butler;
Penalties: P.Butler (2)

Sep 22 Bristol 16 Gloucester 9
Penalties: P.Butler (3)

Sep 26 Gloucester 22
Glamorgan Wanderers 6
Tries: R.Mogg, M.Teague;
Conversion: P.Butler;
Penalties: P.Butler (4)

Sep 29 Bedford 4 Gloucester 9
Penalties: P.Butler (2);
Drop goal: D.Pointon

Oct 3 Gloucester 62 Clifton 0
Tries: P.Butler (2), R.Clewes (2), B.Russell,
R.Jardine, R.Mogg, S.Baker, D.Brookes,
A.Turton, J.Gadd, J.Herniman;
Conversions: P.Butler (4), B.Russell (3)

Oct 6 Gloucester 14 Pontypridd 22
Tries: S.Mills, D.Brookes, P.Wood;
Conversion: P.Butler

Oct 10 Abertillery 12 Gloucester 16
Tries: R.Mogg, S.Baker;
Conversion: P.Butler;
Penalty: P.Butler;
Drop goal: D.Pointon

Oct 13 Harlequins 6 Gloucester 15
Try: L.Dick;
Conversion: P.Ford;
Penalties: P.Ford (2);
Drop goal: B.Russell

Oct 17 Gloucester 9 Newbridge 9
Penalties: P.Butler (3)

Oct 20 Gloucester 31 Newport 12
Tries: S.Baker, D.Brookes, P.Wood;
Conversions: P.Butler (2);
Penalties: P.Butler (3);
Drop goals: P.Butler, B.Russell

Oct 24 Gloucester 18
South Wales Police 6
Tries: J.Watkins (2), L.Dick, R.Mogg;
Conversion: P.Butler

Oct 27 Gloucester 23 Nottingham 16
Tries: R.Clewes, L.Dick, S.Baker;
Conversion: B.Russell;
Penalties: B.Russell (3)

Nov 7 Cambridge University 13
Gloucester 25
Tries: R.Mogg, F.Reed;
Conversion: P.Butler;
Penalties: P.Butler (3);
Drop goals: B.Russell (2)

Nov 10 Gloucester 45 Plymouth Albion 3
Tries: F.Reed (2), P.Wood (2), B.Russell,
R.Clewes, P.Williams;
Conversions: B.Russell (4);
Penalties: B.Russell (3)

Nov 14 Gloucester 73
Exeter University 6
Tries: P.Tunstall (4), S.Baker (2), S.Boyle (2),
P.Williams (2), R.Clewes, J.Gadd, M.Longstaff,
J.Herniman
Conversions: P.Butler (7);
Penalty: P.Butler

Nov 21 Aberavon 12 Gloucester 6
Penalties: P.Butler (2)

Nov 24 Gloucester 3 London Irish 12
Penalty: P.Butler

Nov 28 Gloucester 15
Loughborough Colleges 8
Tries: I.Wilkins, A.Turton, J.Herniman;
Penalty: B.Russell

Dec 1 Gloucester 16 Oxford University 12
Tries: R.Clewes (2);
Conversion: P.Butler;
Penalties: P.Butler (2)

Dec 10 Gloucester 10 Bath 3
Try: R.Clewes;
Penalties: P.Butler (2)

Dec 15 Coventry 3 Gloucester 9
Try: B.Russell;
Conversion: B.Russell;
Penalty: B.Russell

Dec 22 Newport v Gloucester - cancelled

Dec 26 Gloucester 21 Lydney 3
Tries: I.Wilkins, C.Pryce, R.Mogg, F.Reed;
Conversion: I.Wilkins;
Penalty: C.Pryce

Dec 29 Bridgend 7 Gloucester 3
Drop goal: P.Butler

Jan 1 Gloucester v Moseley - cancelled

Jan 5 London Scottish 19 Gloucester 10
Tries: P.Wood, J.Watkins;
Conversion: P.Butler

Jan 12 Gloucester 20 Leicester 15
Tries: F.Reed, P.Tunstall;
Penalties: P.Butler (3);
Drop goal: B.Russell

Jan 19 Gloucester v Wasps - cancelled

Jan 26 Richmond 6 Gloucester 6
(John Player Cup)
Penalty: P.Butler;
Drop goal: B.Russell

Feb 2 Gloucester 15 Bristol 7
Penalties: P.Butler (5)

Feb 16 Gloucester 9 Swansea 12
Penalties: P.Butler (3)

Feb 23 Coventry 9 Gloucester 10
(John Player Cup)

Try: P.Tunstall;
Drop goals: B.Russell (2)

Feb 27 Newport 10 Gloucester 10
Tries: D.Pointon, S.Boyle;
Conversion: I.Wilkins

Feb 29 Northampton 3 Gloucester 12
Try: P.Tunstall;
Conversion: B.Russell;
Penalties: B.Russell (2)

Mar 8 Gloucester 3 Rosslyn Park 6
(John Player Cup)
Penalty: B.Russell

Mar 12 Gloucester 25 Aberavon 12
Tries: R.Clewes, S.Boyle, J.Gadd;
Conversions: P.Butler (2);
Penalties: P.Butler (3)

Mar 15 Exeter 3 Gloucester 10
Try: P.Tunstall;
Penalty: I.Wilkins;
Drop goal: C.Pryce

Mar 19 Gloucester 6 Pontypool 11
Penalties: P.Butler (2)

Mar 22 Gloucester 23 Saracens 3
Tries: P.Tunstall, S.Baker, P.Wood;
Conversion: P.Butler;
Penalties: P.Butler (3)

Mar 26 Bath 24 Gloucester 9
Try: S.Boyle;
Conversion: P.Butler;
Penalty: P.Butler

Mar 29 Orrell 6 Gloucester 10
Try: S.Boyle;
Penalties: P.Butler (2)

Apr 3 Lydney 0 Gloucester 13
Try: S.Boyle;
Penalties: I.Wilkins (3)

Apr 5 Gloucester 12 Headingley 7
Try: A.Turton;
Conversion: I.Wilkins;
Penalties: I.Wilkins (2)

Apr 7 Gloucester 51 Birkenhead Park 6
Tries: R.Clewes (2), R.Mogg, J.Delaney,
P.Kingston, S.Boyle, J.Watkins, P.Butler,
penalty try;
Conversions: P.Butler (6);
Penalty: P.Butler

Apr 12 Gloucester 29 Ebbw Vale 10
Tries: G.Sargent (3), S.Boyle, J.Orwin;

Conversions: P.Butler (3);
Drop goal: C.Pryce

Apr 19 Sale 11 Gloucester 16
Tries: P.Wood (2);
Conversion: P.Butler;
Penalties: P.Butler (2)

Apr 23 Cheltenham 10 Gloucester 13
Try: S.Ashmead;
Penalties: P.Butler (3)

Apr 26 Gloucester 36 Exeter 12
Tries: J.Orwin (3), P.Wood, S.Boyle, C.Pryce,
R.Mogg;
Conversion: P.Tunstall;
Penalties: P.Tunstall (2)

Out of Season Tour to Canada

May 12 Toronto Lions 16 Gloucester 33
Tries: J.Gadd (2), P.Wood (2), A.Brookes;
Conversions: P.Wood, C.Pryce;
Penalties: C.Pryce (2), P.Wood

May 12 Toronto Lions 'A' 4
Gloucester United 42
Tries: J.Delaney (5), P.Conway (2), P.Williams,
A.Durkin;
Conversions: B.Russell (3)

May 14 Toronto & District 9
Gloucester 45
Tries: G.Sargent, R.Clewes, J.Gadd, D.Pointon,
R.Etheridge, P.Wood;
Conversions: B.Russell (3)
Penalties: B.Russell (5)

May 18 Toronto Scottish 0 Gloucester 7
Try: F.Reed;
Penalty: C.Pryce

May 18 Toronto Scottish 'A' 6
Gloucester United 27
Tries: M.Longstaff (2), J.Herniman, P.Tunstall;
Conversions: P.Ford (2), A.Durkin (2);
Penalty: P.Ford

May 21 Niagra & District 6 Gloucester 19
Tries: R.Clewes, J.Haines;
Conversion: C.Pryce;
Penalties: C.Pryce (3)

May 21 Burlington 6
Gloucester United 33
Tries: P.Tunstall (2), J.Herniman, A.Durkin,
M.Longstaff;
Conversions: P.Ford (2);
Penalties: P.Ford (3)

T.R.Tandy(Hon.Sec) R.Smith(Coach) J.Bennett J.Jarrett R.Collins A.D.Wadley(Hon.Treas) T.Day M.Elway
A.Brooks P.Wood P.Blakeway P.Ford J.Gadd M.Teague J.Fidler S.Boyle J.Brain M.Longstaff M.Preedy P.Butler P.Conway R.Morris
J.Holder P.Kingston S.Ashmead A.G.Hudson(Chairman) S.Mills(Capt) Canon H.M.Hughes(Pres) P.Taylor R.Mogg R.Clewes V.Wooley
K.White S.Baker C.Pryce

Played 51 Won 37 Lost 12 Drawn 2
For 929 Against 555
Captain: Steve Mills
Coach: Dick Smith

Gloucester United
Played 37 Won 30 Lost 7
For 868 Against 310
Captain: Jerry Herniman

Most appearances: M.Teague 44, C.Pryce 43, P.Conway, S.Mills, S.Boyle 38, M.Longstaff 37. S.Baker 36, R.Clewes 34, P.Taylor 33, R.Mogg 31
Most tries: R.Clewes 18, P.Conway 17, S.Boyle 15, R.Mogg, M.Teague 9
Penalties: P.Butler 34, P.Ford 30, C.Pryce 5
Drop goals: P.Butler, C.Pryce 4, P.Ford, M.Longstaff 1

Under new coach Dick Smith, there were displays that showed what the team was capable of, but it sometimes felt as if the true potential of the side was not realized. A very promising John Player Cup campaign faltered at the quarter-final stage when Gloucester traveled to Richmond Athletic Ground to play London Scottish. The tie was drawn, but Scottish went through by virtue of scoring the only try of the game.

In October successive games were lost to Moseley and Newport, shipping 65 points in the process. Next up was a Wednesday evening

game at Pontypool, a prospect not for the faint-hearted. A new back-row of John Gadd, Mike Teague and Mike Longstaff played together for the first time. A superb performance resulted in a 17-15 victory, with Gadd scoring a try. This back-row would go on to be one of the best in the Club's long history. The confidence engendered by this win stimulated a sequence of eight consecutive wins including Aberavon and a sweeping 31-4 win over Leicester. Other good wins during the season were against Ebbw Vale (away), Harlequins, Newport, Bristol (away) and a double over Bath

Full-back Peter Butler was injured for a large part of the season, but still scored 166 points. Paul Ford, son of Peter, took over admirably. He proved to be a very good place-kicker, as well as scoring six tries, and totaled 223 points in all. There was a new half-back pairing in Colyn Pryce (a recruit from Lydney) and Steve Baker. Paul Taylor continued to be consistency itself in the centre, and as ever, Bob Clewes ran in the tries.

Phil Blakeway played for England against Wales, Scotland, Ireland and France. Gordon Sargent won a cap as a replacement against Ireland. The following players appeared for the South & South-West in the Divisional Championship: Richard Mogg, John Fidler, Steve Boyle, Phil Blakeway, Steve Mills, Gordon Sargent, Paul Taylor and John Gadd. Mogg, Boyle, Mills and Sargent played for England 'B'

against Ireland 'B'. The County lost in the final of the Championship to Northumberland at Kingsholm; Peter Butler, Paul Taylor, Richard Mogg, Peter Kingston, Gordon Sargent, John Fidler and Paul Wood were in the team.

Sep 6 Gloucester 24 Broughton Park 19
Tries: P.Conway, S.Boyle;
Conversions: P.Butler (2);
Penalties: P.Butler (4)

Sep 10 Stroud 6 Gloucester 31
Tries: R.Clewes (3), P.Conway;
Conversions: P.Butler (3);
Penalties: P.Butler (3)

Sep 13 Coventry 16 Gloucester 3
Penalty: P.Butler

Sep 17 Ebbw Vale 10 Gloucester 18
Try: P.Howell;
Conversion: P.Butler;
Penalties: P.Butler (2);
Drop goals: P.Butler (2)

Sep 20 Gloucester 12 Waterloo 10
Penalties: P.Butler (4)

Sep 24 Newbridge 18 Gloucester 9
Try: S.Boyle;
Conversion: P.Butler;
Penalty: P.Butler

Sep 27 Gloucester 6 Bristol 12

Penalties: P.Butler (2)

Sep 29 Cheltenham 6 Gloucester 20
Tries: P.Howell, G.Sargent, S.Boyle;
Conversion: C.Pryce;
Penalty: C.Pryce;
Drop goal: C.Pryce

Oct 4 Gloucester 32 Bedford 3
Tries: R.Mogg, P.Howell, P.Kingston, S.Boyle,
M.Teague;
Conversions: P.Butler (3);
Penalties: P.Butler (2)

Oct 8 Gloucester 23 Abertillery 10
Tries: R.Clewes, P.Conway, S.Boyle,
M.Longstaff;
Conversions: P.Butler (2);
Penalty: P.Butler

Oct 11 Gloucester 19 Harlequins 9
Try: M.Teague, P.Ford;
Conversion: P.Ford;
Penalties: P.Ford (3)

Oct 15 Gloucester 11 Moseley 27
Tries: P.Conway, M.Teague;
Penalty: P.Butler

Oct 18 Newport 38 Gloucester 6
Try: P.Ford;
Conversion: P.Ford

Oct 22 Pontypool 15 Gloucester 17
Tries: S.Parsloe, S.Boyle, J.Gadd;
Conversion: P.Ford;
Penalty: P.Ford

Oct 25 Nottingham 15 Gloucester 22
Tries: P.Conway, S.Parsloe, P.Tunstall, C.Pryce;
Conversions: P.Ford (3)

Oct 29 Gloucester 39 Clifton 0
Tries: R.Clewes (2), S.Baker (2), P.Conway,
G.Sargent, S.Boyle;
Conversions: P.Ford (4);
Penalty: P.Ford

Nov 1 Gloucester 31 Leicester 4
Tries: R.Mogg, P.Taylor, R.Clewes, J.Orwin,
M.Teague, M.Longstaff;
Conversions: P.Ford (2);
Drop goal: C.Pryce

Nov 5 Gloucester 16
Cambridge University 4
Tries: P.Ford, S.Boyle;
Conversion: P.Ford;
Drop goals: C.Pryce, M.Longstaff

Nov 8 Plymouth Albion 6 Gloucester 26

Tries: P.Williams, R.Clewes, J.Orwin,
M.Longstaff, J.Gadd;
Conversions: P.Ford (3)

Nov 12 Gloucester 19
South Wales Police 10
Tries: P.Conway, S.Boyle, P.Wood;
Conversions: P.Ford (2);
Penalty: P.Ford

Nov 18 Gloucester 15 Aberavon 13
Tries: R.Mogg, J.Gadd;
Conversions: P.Ford (2);
Penalty: P.Ford

Nov 22 London Irish 10 Gloucester 9
Penalties: P.Ford (3)

Nov 26 Gloucester 46
Loughborough Colleges 7
Tries: R.Mogg (4), S.Boyle (2), P.Ford (2),
P.Taylor;
Conversions: P.Ford (5)

Nov 29 Oxford University 3
Gloucester 27
Tries: R.Clewes (2), M.Teague (2), penalty try;
Conversions: P.Ford (2);
Penalty: P.Ford

Dec 3 Gloucester 56 Torquay Athletic 9
Tries: R.Clewes (2), P.Conway, P.Taylor,
M.Preedy, J.Brain, J.Gadd, M.Teague, P.Wood;
Conversions: P.Ford (7);
Penalties: P.Ford (2)

Dec 6 Pontypridd 34 Gloucester 14
Tries: P.Conway, M.Preedy;
Penalties: P.Ford (2)

Dec 15 Bath 0 Gloucester 19
Tries: P.Howell, P.Taylor, C.Pryce;
Conversions: P.Ford (2);
Penalty: P.Ford

Dec 20 Gloucester 25 Coventry 0
Tries: P.Conway (2), R.Clewes, S.Baker,
P.Williams;
Conversion: P.Ford;
Penalty: P.Ford

Dec 26 Gloucester 20 Lydney 6
Tries: P.Conway, P.Williams, M.Preedy;
Conversion: P.Butler;
Penalties: P.Butler (2)

Dec 27 Gloucester 13 Newport 11
Tries: C.Pryce, P.Ford;
Conversion: P.Ford;
Penalty: P.Ford

Jan 1 Moseley 6 Gloucester 16
Tries: G.Sargent, M.Teague;
Conversion: P.Ford;
Penalty: P.Ford;
Drop goal: C.Pryce

Jan 3 Gloucester 13 London Scottish 8
Try: R.Clewes;
Penalties: P.Ford (3)

Jan 10 Leicester 14 Gloucester 9
Try: P.Taylor;
Conversion: P.Ford;
Penalty: P.Ford

Jan 17 Wasps 19 Gloucester 9
Try: P.Conway;
Conversion: P.Ford;
Penalty: P.Ford

Jan 24 Southend 6 Gloucester 12
(John Player Cup)
Tries: P.Taylor, J.Gadd;
Conversions: P.Ford (2)

Feb 6 Bristol 0 Gloucester 7
Try: G.Sargent;
Penalty: P.Ford

Feb 14 Gloucester 15 Bath 10
Try: S.Boyle;
Conversion: P.Butler;
Penalties: P.Butler (2);
Drop goal: P.Butler

Feb 21 Swansea 20 Gloucester 7
Try: P.Tunstall;
Penalty: P.Butler

Feb 28 London Irish 13 Gloucester 22
(John Player Cup)
Tries: S.Boyle, R.Mogg, P.Conway;
Conversions: P.Butler (2);
Penalty: P.Butler;
Drop goal: P.Butler

Mar 3 Aberavon 12 Gloucester 9
Try: S.Baker;
Conversion: P.Butler;
Penalty: P.Butler

Mar 6 Gloucester 22 Northampton 7
Tries: R.Mogg, S.Boyle, P.Butler;
Conversions: P.Butler (2);
Penalties: P.Butler (2)

Mar 14 London Scottish 9 Gloucester 9
(John Player Cup)
Penalties: P.Butler (3)

Mar 18 Gloucester 12 Cheltenham 7

Try: P.Conway;
Conversion: P.Ford;
Penalty: P.Ford;
Drop goal: P.Ford

Mar 21 Gloucester 9 Orrell 0
Try: C.Pryce;
Conversion: P.Butler;
Penalty: P.Ford

Mar 28 Saracens 11 Gloucester 12
Tries: M.Longstaff, P.Butler;
Conversions: P.Butler (2)

Apr 4 Camborne 7 Gloucester 28
Tries: P.Conway, S.Baker, S.Boyle, J.Gadd;
Conversions: P.Ford (3);
Penalties: P.Ford (2)

Apr 11 Headingley 6 Gloucester 6
Try: J.Watkins;
Conversion: P.Ford

Apr 16 Lydney 13 Gloucester 23
Tries: R.Clewes (2), C.Pryce, M.Teague;
Conversions: P.Ford (2);
Penalty: P.Ford

Apr 18 Gloucester 29 New Brighton 21
Tries: R.Clewes, R.Lewis, K.White, J.Brain, J.Watkins;
Conversions: P.Ford (3);
Penalty: P.Ford

Apr 20 Gloucester 21 Fylde 13
Tries: R.Clewes, P.Conway;
Conversions: C.Pryce (2);
Penalties: C.Pryce (3)

Apr 25 Exeter 22 Gloucester 11
Tries: P.Tunstall, J.Fidler;
Penalty: C.Pryce

1981-82

T.R.Tandy(Hon.Sec) T.Pritchard M.Elway R.Collins J.Jarrett A.D.Wadley(Hon.Treas) A.Brinn C.A.R.Lankester A.C.Pope P.Hawker J.Bennett E.Stephens
R.Morris M.Longstaff M.Teague J.Brain S.Boyle A.Turton J.Fidler J.Orwin J.Gadd M.Preedy S.Parsloe L.Jones S.Ashmead M.Booth T.Day
R.Smith(Coach) A.Mitchell P.Ford P.Blakeway R.Clewes A.G.Hudson(Chairman) S.Mills(Capt) Canon H.M.Hughes(Pres) S.Baker R.Mogg P.Taylor
J.Holder M.Nicholls(Hon.Team Sec)
P.Pritchard K.White

Played 48 Won 41 Lost 3 Drawn 4
For 1045 Against 338
Captain: Steve Mills
Coach: Dick Smith

Gloucester United
Played 35 Won 31 Lost 4
For 763 Against 280
Captain: John Haines

Most appearances: M.Teague 43, S.Parsloe 42, S.Baker 41, S.Mills 40, J.Gadd, L.Jones 38, S.Boyle, M.Longstaff 36, P.Ford, P.Pritchard 34
Most tries: M.Teague 20, S.Boyle, P.Pritchard 15, J.Gadd 12
Conversions: P.Ford 47, A.Durkin 11, L.Jones 8, S.Parsloe 5, P.Butler 4, G.Thomas, P.Webb 3
Penalties: P.Ford 41, L.Jones 18, P.Butler 8, A.Durkin 7, G.Thomas, P.Webb 2, S.Parsloe 1
Drop goals: L.Jones 6

This was a marvelous season and the best in the Club's history, with 41 wins and only three losses. The team remained unbeaten at home. A total of 157 tries were scored as the emphasis was on playing flowing rugby. Phil Pritchard, playing on the wing was the top try scoring back, but even though there was a lot of open play a forward, Mike Teague, was the leading try scorer, with Steve Boyle not far behind. Peter Butler was absent for most of the season through injury, and Paul Ford consolidated his position at full-back, scoring 241 points including six tries. The back-row of Gadd, Teague and Longstaff was a menace to all opposing teams. The front five were formidable. The front row of Malcolm Preedy, Steve Mills and Phil Blakeway never took a step back, and with Steve Boyle and John Orwin in the second row the pack was seldom bettered. Les Jones, a fly-half from Matson, formed a potent half-back combination with Steve Baker.

Progress through the John Player Cup was smooth, and included a semi-final win at Coventry. Gloucester were firm favorites to win the final against Moseley at Twickenham, but for some reason failed to perform anywhere near the standard they had been showing all season. The game went to extra-time, and in a match of no tries, Paul Ford had to kick a penalty with two minutes of the extra period to go to save Gloucester's bacon. There was no provision for a replay and the cup was shared. The day after the final the team departed for a tour of South Africa.

Only three games were lost all season, a surprising defeat to Cambridge University, plus losses away to Newport and Bristol. For the rest it was more or less win after win. There were doubles over Coventry, Bath, and Moseley. Bristol, Pontypool and Newport were beaten at Kingsholm, together with away wins at Leicester, Neath and Northampton.

For a number of long serving Gloucester players this was their last season. Bob Clewes finished on 541 appearances; he had scored 286 tries, the most in the Club's history, a record which will probably stand for all time. Peter Butler ended his Gloucester career with 3006 points, the most by any Gloucester player, and 318 appearances; in addition he scored 654 points for the County, and went on to play a further season for Lydney. John Watkins, another of Gloucester's greats and Club captain for three seasons, retired after 389 games and 109 tries. John Haines also retired having played in 270 games; he was United captain in his final season. Richard Jardine made just one final appearance to finish on 314, accompanied by 91 tries.

Phil Blakeway played for England against Ireland, France and Wales. Richard Mogg, Mike Teague and John Gadd played for England 'B' against France 'B'. South & South-West played against the Australians at Kingsholm, with Blakeway (captain), Mogg, Teague, Steve Mills and Malcolm Preedy in the team.

Sep 5 New Brighton 4 Gloucester 58
Tries: P.Ford (3),S.Parsloe (2), S.Boyle (2), M.Teague (2), L.Jones, S.Mills, J.Gadd, penalty try;
Conversions: P.Ford (3)

Sep 9 Gloucester 22 Stroud 3
Tries: L.Jones, S.Boyle, J.Gadd;
Conversions: P.Ford (2);
Penalties: P.Ford (2)

Sep 12 Gloucester 21 Coventry 15
Tries: S.Boyle (2), S.Parsloe, M.Teague;
Conversion: P.Ford;
Penalty: P.Ford

Sep 16 Gloucester 25 Rosslyn Park 0
Tries: S.Parsloe, R.Mogg, P.Pritchard, J.Gadd;
Conversions: A.Durkin (3);
Penalty: A.Durkin

Sep 19 Gloucester 16 Pontypridd 12
Tries: M.Teague (2);
Conversion: A.Durkin;
Penalties: A.Durkin (2)

Sep 23 Gloucester 6 Newbridge 0
Penalties: A.Durkin, L.Jones

Sep 26 Bristol 12 Gloucester 6
Penalties: A.Durkin, L.Jones

Sep 30 Gloucester 19 Cheltenham 3

Tries: P.Pritchard, J.Orwin, M.Teague;
Conversions: A.Durkin (2);
Penalty: L.Jones

Oct 3 Bedford 9 Gloucester 19
Tries: A.Brookes, J.Gadd, P.Pritchard;
Conversions: A.Durkin, L.Jones;
Penalty: L.Jones

Oct 7 Gloucester 14 Pontypool 3
Tries: M.Preedy, S.Boyle;
Penalties: A.Durkin, L.Jones

Oct 10 Harlequins 3 Gloucester 3
Penalty: P.Ford

Oct 14 Gloucester 23 Ebbw Vale 0
Tries: P.Taylor, P.Howell, G.Sargent, J.Gadd:
Conversions: P.Ford (2);
Penalty: P.Ford

Oct 17 Gloucester 19 Newport 0
Tries: R.Mogg, S.Boyle: Conversion: P.Ford;
Penalties: P.Ford (3)

Oct 21 Clifton 3 Gloucester 36
Tries: M.Teague (3), S.Boyle (2), P.Pritchard, M.Longstaff;
Conversions: P.Ford (4)

Oct 24 Gloucester 20 Nottingham 7
Tries: P.Pritchard (2), J.Gadd;
Conversion: P.Ford;
Penalties: P.Ford (2)

**Oct 28 Gloucester 34
Loughborough Students 0**
Tries: R.Mogg, L.Jones, S.Baker, J.Gadd, M.Teague, M.Longstaff;
Conversions: P.Ford (5)

Oct 31 Gloucester 46 Oxford University 6
Tries: M.Teague (2), P.Taylor (2), P.Ford, P.Pritchard, S.Parsloe, R.Mogg, M.Preedy, S.Mills;
Conversions: P.Ford (2), L.Jones

Nov 4 Gloucester 24 South Wales Police 4
Tries: A.Durkin, P.Taylor, J.Gadd;
Penalties: L.Jones (3), A.Durkin

Nov 7 Leicester 9 Gloucester 12
Penalties: L.Jones (3);
Drop goal: L.Jones

**Nov 11 Cambridge University 20
Gloucester 12**
Tries: P.Williams, L.Jones;
Conversions: P.Ford (2)

Nov 14 Gloucester 58 Plymouth Albion 0

Tries: M.Teague (3), R.Clewes (2), G.Sargent (2), P.Pritchard, R.Ellis, D.Pointon, S.Baker, P.Kingston;
Conversions: P.Ford (5)

Nov 21 Broughton Park 7 Gloucester 13
Try: J.Watkins;
Penalties: P.Ford (3)

Nov 29 Gloucester 19 London Irish 6
Tries: S.Boyle, S.Mills, penalty try;
Conversions: L.Jones (2);
Penalty: L.Jones

Dec 5 Moseley 3 Gloucester 18
Tries: M.Teague, M.Longstaff, P.Taylor, L.Jones;
Conversion: P.Ford

Dec 9 Gloucester v Exeter University
Dec 12 Gloucester v Bath
Dec 19 Coventry v Gloucester
All cancelled due to frost or snow.

Dec 26 Gloucester 27 Lydney 7
Tries: L.Jones, G.Sargent, J.Brain, P.Conway;
Conversions: A.Durkin (3), L.Jones;
Penalty: L.Jones

Dec 28 Newport 29 Gloucester 10
Try: J.Bennett (2);
Conversion: P.Ford

Jan 1 Gloucester 27 Moseley 21
Tries: S.Boyle (2), L.Jones, M.Teague, P.Conway;
Conversions: L.Jones, A.Durkin;
Penalty: L.Jones

Jan 2 London Scottish 10 Gloucester 18
Tries: S.Parsloe, M.Teague;
Conversions: P.Ford (2);
Penalties: P.Ford (2)

Jan 9 Gloucester v Leicester - cancelled
Jan 16 Gloucester v Wasps - cancelled

**Jan 23 Gloucester 40 High Wycombe 6
(John Player Cup)**
Tries: J.Orwin (2), M.Teague, J.Gadd, S.Parsloe;
Conversions: P.Ford (4);
Penalties: P.Ford (3);
Drop goal: L.Jones

Jan 30 Bridgend 10 Gloucester 10
Try: P.Pritchard;
Penalties: P.Ford (2)

Feb 5 Gloucester 10 Bristol 3
Try: P.Ford;
Penalties: P.Ford (2)

Feb 13 Bath 6 Gloucester 12
Try: P.Taylor;
Conversion: P.Ford;
Penalties: P.Ford (2)

Feb 20 Neath 6 Gloucester 13
Try: S.Boyle;
Penalties: P.Ford (3)

Feb 27 Gloucester 34 Exeter 3
(John Player Cup)
Tries: P.Pritchard (3), S.Mills (2), S.Baker,
M.Longstaff;
Conversions: L.Jones (2), P.Ford

Mar 3 Northampton 7 Gloucester 14
Tries: P.Pritchard, S.Baker;
Penalties: P.Ford (2)

Mar 13 Gloucester 13 Sale 6
(John Player Cup)
Tries: M.Teague, P.Ford;
Conversion: P.Ford;
Penalty: P.Ford

Mar 20 Orrell 6 Gloucester 6
Penalty: P.Ford;
Drop goal: L.Jones

Mar 24 Cheltenham 0 Gloucester 23
Tries: R.Clewes, S.Boyle, G.Thomas, N.Price;
Conversions: S.Parsloe (2);
Penalty: S.Parsloe

Mar 27 Gloucester 30 Saracens 12
Tries: R.Clewes, S.Mills, R.Fatica, J.Gadd,
penalty tries (2);
Conversions: S.Parsloe (3)

Mar 30 Gloucester 21 Abertillery 7
Try: P.Conway;
Conversion: P.Butler;
Penalties: P.Butler (5)

Apr 3 Coventry 9 Gloucester 18
(John Player Cup semi-final)
Tries: S.Parsloe, P.Pritchard;
Conversions: P.Butler (2);
Penalties: P.Butler (2)

Apr 8 Lydney 11 Gloucester 12
Penalties: L.Jones (4)

Apr 10 Gloucester 34 Headingley 4
Tries: N.Price (2), R.Mogg, S.Baker, J.Watkins;
Conversions: G.Thomas (3), P.Webb;
Penalties: G.Thomas (2)

Apr 12 Gloucester 24 Birkenhead Park 12
Tries: P.Pritchard, J.Orwin;
Conversions: P.Webb (2);
Penalties: P.Webb (2), P.Ford (2)

Apr 17 Gloucester 40 Sale 0
Tries: J.Gadd (2), R.Clewes (2), L.Jones,
G.Sargent;
Conversions: P.Ford (5);

Penalty: P.Ford;
Drop goal: L.Jones

Apr 21 Gloucester 33 Bath 15
Tries: J.Orwin (2), S.Boyle;
Conversions: P.Ford (3);
Penalties: P.Ford (3);
Drop goals: L.Jones (2)

Apr 24 Gloucester 21 Exeter 7
Tries: N.Price (3), C.Dyke;
Conversion: P.Butler;
Penalty: P.Butler

May 1 Gloucester 12 Moseley 12
(John Player Cup Final at Twickenham)
Penalties: P.Ford (4)

Out-of-Season Tour of South Africa

May 4 Pretoria University 60 Gloucester 6
Try: S.Parsloe;
Conversion: P.Butler

**May 6 Bangor (Northern Ireland) 25
Gloucester 8**
Tries: R.Mogg, S.Boyle

May 8 Club of America 26 Gloucester 13
Try: P.Pritchard;
Drop goals: L.Jones (2), P.Butler

1982-83

Played 54 Won 24 Lost 25 Drawn 5
For 801 Against 692
Captain: Steve Mills
Coach: Dick Smith

Gloucester United
Played 35 Won 26 Lost 7 Drawn 2
For 914 Against 354
Captain: Paul Williams

Most appearances: N.Price 39, R.Mogg, S.Mills,
P.Wood 38, P.Ford, S.Baker 35, J.Brain 33
P.Pritchard, M.Teague, C.O'Donoghue 32
Most tries: R.Mogg 17, N.Price 10,
C.O'Donoghue 7
Conversions: P.Ford 32, G.Thomas, T.Smith 7,
C.Boon 5, M.Hamlin, L.Jones 1
Penalties: P.Ford 60, T.Smith 12, G.Thomas 11,
M.Hamlin, L.Jones 5
Drop goals: L.Jones 7, M.Hamlin 3, D.Pointon 2

Following the record breaking 1981-82 season,
this campaign was hugely disappointing. As
well as poor results there were rumblings of
discontent off the field. In the John Player

Cup the team fell at the first hurdle at home to
London Welsh, in a dismal display. Even worse,
qualification for the following season's cup
depended on finishing high enough in the South-
West Merit Table, and long before the end of the
season safety could not be reached. So, there was
no John Player Cup campaign to look forward to
in 1983-84. In such a campaign there were only
a few really good wins. Pontypridd and Wasps
were beaten on the road, whilst Bristol and
Harlequins were defeated at Kingsholm.

The pack was disrupted by suspensions and
injuries. John Orwin, John Gadd, Richard
Pascall and Mike Longstaff were all absent at
various points in the season. In the second-row
John Brain made encouraging progress. Steve
Boyle was in fine form all campaign and as
well as winning England caps he was selected
to tour New Zealand with the British Lions.
Richard Mogg was the best performing back
and was top try scorer. New winger Nick Price
was speedy and elusive. Paul Ford accumulated
another 256 points, and a young full-back, Tim
Smith, looked very promising for the future.

Adrian Turton left the club at the end of the
season having made 106 appearances.

An unusual occurrence was the televising of
the match against Moseley on 4 December. The
club celebrated the event by providing a new set
of jerseys.

Steve Boyle played for England against Wales,
Scotland and Ireland; Steve Mills played against
Wales. In a game against Fiji for which no caps
were awarded, John Gadd (2 tries) and Phil
Blakeway played. The South & South-West
also played Fiji; Blakeway was captain and
was accompanied by Steve Mills, John Orwin,
Steve Boyle and Mike Teague (2 tries). England
'B' played Ireland 'B' with Boyle, Teague and
Gadd in the team. Steve Boyle (try), Malcolm
Preedy, John Fidler and John Gadd were in the
Gloucestershire team which beat Yorkshire to
win the County Championship.

Sep 1 Stroud 21 Gloucester 16
Try: R.Mogg;
Penalties: P.Ford (4)

Sep 4 Gloucester 16 Swansea 23
Tries: S.Baker, S.Mills;
Conversion: P.Ford;
Penalties: P.Ford (2)

Sep 7 Gloucester 18 Lydney 12
Try: G.Thomas;
Conversion: L.Jones;
Penalties: L.Jones, G.Thomas;
Drop goals: L.Jones (2)

Sep 11 Coventry 12 Gloucester 10
Try: J.Gadd;
Penalty: P.Ford;
Drop goal: L.Jones

Sep 15 Rosslyn Park 17 Gloucester 9
Try: P.Taylor;
Conversion: M.Hamlin;
Drop goal: M.Hamlin

Sep 18 Pontypridd 6 Gloucester 10
Try: R.Mogg;
Penalties: L.Jones (2)

Sep 22 Newbridge 20 Gloucester 18
Try: J.Bennett;
Conversion: P.Ford;
Penalties: P.Ford (4)

Sep 25 Gloucester 16 Bristol 9
Try: R.Mogg;
Penalties: P.Ford (4)

Sep 29 Maesteg 20 Gloucester 6
Penalties: P.Ford (2)

Oct 2 Gloucester 12 Bedford 9
Penalties: P.Ford (2), L.Jones;
Drop goal: L.Jones

Oct 6 Pontypool 52 Gloucester 15
Penalties: P.Ford (5)

Oct 9 Gloucester 16 Harlequins 9
Try: P.Ford;
Penalties: P.Ford (4)

Oct 13 Ebbw Vale 45 Gloucester 18
Tries: S.Boyle, J.Woodhouse;
Conversions: P.Ford (2);
Penalties: P.Ford, L.Jones

Oct 16 Newport 10 Gloucester 6
Try: S.Boyle;
Conversion: P.Ford

Oct 20 Gloucester 40 Clifton 3
Tries: C.Dyke (4), R.Mogg (2), P.Pritchard;
Conversions: P.Ford (6)

Oct 27 Gloucester 28 Cheltenham 8
Tries: M.Teague (2), P.Pritchard,
C.O'Donoghue, D.Pointon;
Conversions: G.Thomas (4)

Oct 30 Oxford University 6 Gloucester 34
Tries: S.Parsloe, R.Mogg, J.Gadd, M.Teague,
P.Wood;
Conversions: P.Ford (4);
Penalties: P.Ford (2)

Nov 3 Gloucester 33
Cambridge University 9
Tries: P.Ford, C.O'Donoghue, N.Price,
D.Pointon, J.Bennett;
Conversions: P.Ford (2);
Penalties: P.Ford (3)

Nov 6 Gloucester 19
Glamorgan Wanderers 9
Try: R.Pascall;
Penalties: P.Ford (5)

Nov 10 Gloucester 17
Exeter University 10
Tries: N.Coyne, C.O'Donoghue;
Penalties: G.Thomas (3)

Nov 13 Plymouth Albion 6 Gloucester 3
Drop goal: D.Pointon

Nov 17 Llanelli 22 Gloucester 3
Penalty: G.Thomas

Nov 20 Gloucester 20 Broughton Park 6
Tries: G.Thomas, N.Price, S.Boyle;
Conversion: G.Thomas;
Penalties: G.Thomas (2)

Nov 24 Gloucester v South Wales Police -
cancelled

Nov 27 London Irish 15 Gloucester 12
Penalties: G.Thomas (3);
Drop goal: D.Pointon

Dec 2 Gloucester 10 Leicester 21
Try: M.Preedy;
Penalty: G.Thomas;
Drop goal: M.Hamlin

Dec 4 Gloucester 15 Moseley 13
Tries: R.Mogg, N.Price;
Conversions: P.Ford (2);
Penalty: P.Ford

Dec 8 Gloucester 35
Loughborough Students 3
Tries: N.Price (2), R.Mogg, S.Parsloe,
C.O'Donoghue, J.Bennett;
Conversions: P.Ford (4);

Penalty: P.Ford

Dec 11 Bath 21 Gloucester 12
Try: M.Teague;
Conversion: P.Ford;
Penalties: P.Ford (2)

Dec 18 Gloucester 3 Coventry 15
Penalty: P.Ford

Dec 27 Gloucester 70
Old Merchant Taylors 0
Tries: C.Boon (3), R.Mogg (2), C.O'Donoghue
(2), S.Baker (2), N.Scrivens (2), P.Taylor,
J.Gadd, J.Woodhouse;
Conversions: C.Boon (5), G.Thomas (2)

Dec 29 Gloucester 12 Newport 12
Penalties: P.Ford (3);
Drop goal: L.Jones

Jan 1 Gloucester 9 London Scottish 3
Try: P.Taylor;
Conversion: P.Ford;
Penalty: P.Ford

Jan 3 Moseley 6 Gloucester 6
Try: D.Spencer;
Conversion: P.Ford

Jan 8 Leicester 23 Gloucester 9
Try: W.Hall;
Conversion: P.Ford;
Penalty: P.Ford

Jan 15 Wasps 9 Gloucester 16
Tries: R.Mogg, P.Pritchard;
Conversion: P.Ford;
Penalties: P.Ford (2)

Jan 22 Gloucester 3 London Welsh 14
(John Player Cup)
Drop goal: L.Jones

Jan 29 Gloucester 4 Bridgend 10
Try: R.Mogg

Feb 5 Bristol 15 Gloucester 10
Try: W.Hall;
Penalties: P.Ford (2)

Feb 12 Gloucester 7 Bath 7
Try: N.Price;
Drop goal: L.Jones

Feb 19 Nottingham 7 Gloucester 3
Penalty: P.Ford

Feb 26 Liverpool 18 Gloucester 4
Try: J.Bennett

Mar 4 Gloucester 12 Northampton 10
Penalties: P.Ford (4)

Mar 12 Richmond 24 Gloucester 7
Try: J.Bennett;
Penalty: P.Ford

Mar 16 Gloucester 15 Abertillery 3
Penalties: T.Smith (5)

Mar 19 Gloucester 20 Orrell 3
Tries: N.Price, L.Jones, S.Baker;
Conversion: T.Smith;
Penalties: T.Smith (2)

Mar 24 Cheltenham 3 Gloucester 3
Penalty: T.Smith

Mar 27 Saracens 16 Gloucester 18
Tries: T.Smith, M.Teague;
Conversions: T.Smith (2);
Penalty: T.Smith;
Drop goal: M.Hamlin

Mar 30 Lydney 7 Gloucester 6
Try: R.Mogg;
Conversion: T.Smith

Apr 3 Gloucester 31 New Brighton 6
Tries: R.Mogg (3), P.Ford, J.Brain;
Conversions: P.Ford (4);
Penalty: P.Ford

Apr 5 Gloucester 22 Fylde 4

Tries: T.Smith, P.Taylor, R.Mogg, R.Phillips;
Conversions: T.Smith (3)

Apr 9 Gloucester 15 Neath 15
Penalties: T.Smith (4), M.Hamlin

Apr 16 Sale 26 Gloucester 8
Tries: C.O'Donoghue, N.Price

Apr 23 Exeter 13 Gloucester 11
Tries: N.Price (2);
Penalty: M.Hamlin

Apr 30 Waterloo 6 Gloucester 10
Try: P.Wood;
Penalties: T.Smith (2)

1983-84

T.Pritchard M.Elway A.Townsend R.Jardine T.Close R.Collins J.Jarrett P.Hawker J.Bennett T.Day D.Mountjoy D.Foyle B.Howells
A.Brinn E.Stephens T.R.Tandy(Hon.Sec) R.Smith(Coach) A.D.Wadley(Hon.Treas) P.Wood S.Mills J.Gadd R.Pascall J.Fidler S.Boyle J.Orwin P.Taylor
P.Blakeway R.Phillips F.Reed R.Morris R.Clewes
A.Mitchell J.Holder D.Morgan D.Spencer R.Mogg I.Smith Canon H.M.Hughes(Pres) G.Sargent(Capt) P.J.Ford(Chairman) P.Webb S.Baker K.White
M.Teague

Played 50 Won 33 Lost 16 Drawn 1
For 1045 Against 657
Captain: Gordon Sargent
Coach: Dick Smith

Gloucester United
Played 36 Won 25 Lost 9 Drawn 2
For 718 Against 382
Captain: Paul Williams

Most appearances: P.Taylor 47, D.Morgan 43,
N.Price, M.Hamlin 41, R.Mogg 39, S.Baker 38
D.Spencer 37, M.Teague 34, G.Sargent 33,
T.Smith 32, J.Gadd 31, J.Fidler 30
Most tries: N.Price 28, D.Morgan 26, D.Spencer
15, T.Smith 13, P.Taylor, M.Teague 10
Conversions: T.Smith 38, M.Hamlin 17, P.Webb,
P.Ford 8, S.Parsloe 6, R.Fowke 2, N.Price 1
Penalties: T.Smith 40, M.Hamlin, P.Webb 12,

P.Ford 5, S.Parsloe 3, R.Fowke 1
Drop goal: M.Hamlin 1

For the first time the players ran on to the field
from new changing rooms in the Grandstand,
after 78 years of running down the steps by the
entrance to the Shed from the changing rooms in
the Gymnasium (now the Lions Den).

The playing record was much improved on
the disappointing previous season, although
supporters were often perplexed by the team's
inconsistency. An example of this was when there
had been a fine win 16-3 away to Harlequins,
only to be followed four days later by defeat at
home to Newbridge 16-36, when the forwards
were completely outplayed. It was a particularly
poor season against the major Welsh clubs, but
there were doubles over Coventry and Moseley,

Leicester were beaten at Kingsholm and Bristol
at the Memorial Ground. However, Lydney
gained their first double over Gloucester since
the 1952-53 season.

On the plus side, the forwards were very
powerful and almost all were pressing for higher
honours. A particular tower of strength was
Mike Teague who produced one outstanding
performance after another. Dave Spencer also
had a fine season in the back-row. Wings Nick
Price and Derrick Morgan scored 54 tries
between them. Tim Smith amassed 248 points,
although his kicking lacked consistency, but
he was a full-back full of attacking flair. Mike
Hamlin and Steve Baker were the hard-working
half-backs. A recurring problem for the team
was an inability to turn possession into points.
Over and again Gloucester would dominate

in the first half, only to post too few points to see off the almost inevitable come-back by the opposition in the second-half. Good examples of this were the games at Kingsholm against Llanelli and Newport and at Welford Road against Leicester.

Veteran John Fidler played remarkably consistently at lock all through the campaign, at the end of which he announced his retirement after 288 games.

Phil Blakeway played for England against Ireland, France and Wales. John Gadd played in an England non-cap game against Canada. South & South-West played the New Zealanders at Bristol, with Phil Blakeway (captain), Richard Mogg, Malcolm Preedy, Steve Mills, Steve Boyle, John Orwin, Mike Teague and John Gadd in the team. The County again won the Championship beating Somerset 36-18 at Twickenham. Gloucester players were Mogg, Preedy, Mills, Blakeway, John Fidler, Orwin and Gadd.

Sep 1 Gloucester 26 Stroud 6
Tries: T.Smith, P.Pritchard, N.Price, J.Orwin;
Conversions: T.Smith (2);
Penalties: T.Smith (2)

Sep 3 Swansea 46 Gloucester 16
Tries: N.Price, R.Mogg, J.Gadd;
Conversions: T.Smith (2)

Sep 10 Gloucester 19 Coventry 14
Tries: R.Mogg (2), T.Smith;
Conversions: T.Smith (2);
Penalty: T.Smith

Sep 14 Gloucester 50 Launceston 0
Tries: D.Morgan (4), P.Tunstall (2), M.Teague (2), T.Smith;
Conversions: T.Smith (4);
Penalties: T.Smith (2)

Sep 17 Gloucester 24 Pontypridd 12
Tries: R.Mogg, M.Teague;
Conversions: T.Smith (2);
Penalties: T.Smith (4)

Sep 21 Gloucester 10 Cardiff 26
Try: N.Price;
Penalties: T.Smith (2)

Sep 24 Bristol 12 Gloucester 19
Tries: G.Sargent, N.Price;
Conversion: T.Smith;
Penalties: T.Smith (3)

Sep 27 Gloucester 7 Llanelli 7
Try: D.Spencer;

Penalty: T.Smith

Oct 1 Bedford 14 Gloucester 6
Try: D.Morgan;
Conversion: P.Webb

Oct 5 Gloucester 12 Pontypool 23
Try: R.Phillips;
Conversion: T.Smith;
Penalties: T.Smith (2)

Oct 8 Harlequins 3 Gloucester 16
Tries: D.Morgan (2), P.Taylor;
Conversions: P.Ford (2)

Oct 12 Gloucester 16 Newbridge 36
Tries: D.Spencer (2), S.Boyle;
Conversions: P.Ford (2)

Oct 15 Gloucester 3 Newport 7
Penalty: T.Smith

Oct 22 Clifton 6 Gloucester 49
Tries: N.Price (4), D.Spencer (4), D.Morgan;
Conversions: T.Smith (4), M.Hamlin;
Penalty: T.Smith

Oct 26 Abertillery 6 Gloucester 9
Penalties: T.Smith (3)

Oct 29 Gloucester 45
Oxford University 12
Tries: T.Smith (2), N.Price (2), S.Boyle (2), S.Baker, P.Taylor;
Conversions: M.Hamlin (5);
Penalty: M.Hamlin

Nov 2 Gloucester 33
Glamorgan Wanderers 3
Tries: D.Morgan (3), N.Price, M.Hamlin, T.Smith;
Conversions: T.Smith (3);
Penalty: M.Hamlin

Nov 5 Gloucester 30 Rosslyn Park 10
Tries: D.Spencer (2), J.Gadd, N.Price, S.Mills, T.Smith;
Conversions: T.Smith (3)

Nov 9 Gloucester 9 South Wales Police 13
Try: P.Wood;
Conversion: P.Webb;
Penalty: P.Webb

Nov 16 Gloucester 21 Cheltenham 16
Tries: P.Taylor, C.O'Donoghue;
Conversions: P.Ford (2);
Penalties: P.Ford (3)

Nov 19 Broughton Park 24 Gloucester 25
Tries: D.Morgan (2);

Conversion: P.Webb;
Penalties: P.Webb (5)

Nov 23   Gloucester v Exeter University - cancelled
Nov 26 Gloucester v London Irish - cancelled

Nov 30 Gloucester 23
Loughborough Colleges 9
Tries: N.Price (2), M.Hamlin, M.Teague;
Conversions: P.Ford (2);
Penalty: P.Ford

Dec 3 Leicester 30 Gloucester 20
Tries: P.Taylor, J.Orwin, M.Teague + penalty try;
Conversions: M.Hamlin (2)

Dec 7 Gloucester 14 Ebbw Vale 9
Tries: N.Price, S.Mills;
Penalty: M.Hamlin;
Drop goal: M.Hamlin

Dec 10 Gloucester 16 Bath 8
Tries: N.Price, R.Mogg;
Conversion: T.Smith;
Penalties: T.Smith (2)

Dec 17 Coventry 6 Gloucester 18
Tries: C.Dyke (2), N.Price, D.Spencer;
Conversion: T.Smith

Dec 21 Newport 16 Gloucester 3
Penalty: P.Ford

Dec 24 Gloucester 20 Plymouth Albion 15
Tries: D.Morgan, S.Boyle;
Penalties: T.Smith (4)

Dec 26 Gloucester 7 Lydney 15
Try: D.Morgan;
Penalty: T.Smith

Dec 31 Bridgend 32 Gloucester 15
Try: J.Bennett;
Conversion: R.Fowke;
Penalties: M.Hamlin (2), R.Fowke

Jan 2 Gloucester 10 Moseley 6
Tries: S.Baker, penalty try;
Conversion: R.Fowke

Jan 7 London Scottish 24 Gloucester 13
Try: D.Morgan;
Penalties: S.Parsloe (3)

Jan 14 Gloucester 22 Leicester 21
Tries: D.Morgan (2), N.Price (2);
Penalties: P.Webb (2)

Jan 21 Gloucester v Wasps - cancelled

Jan 28 Fylde 0 Gloucester 34
Tries: J.Orwin (2), D.Spencer (2), D.Morgan,
M.Hamlin, J.Bennett;
Conversions: P.Webb (3)

Feb 3 Gloucester v Bristol - cancelled

Feb 11 Bath 13 Gloucester 6
Penalties: M.Hamlin (2)

Feb 14 Gloucester 3 Auckland (NZ) 34
Penalty: M.Hamlin

Feb 17 Gloucester 23 Nottingham 9
Tries: N.Price, K.White, S.Boyle, S.Parsloe;
Conversions: M.Hamlin (2);
Penalty: P.Webb

Feb 25 Gloucester 20 Liverpool 4
Tries: P.Webb, M.Hamlin, J.Gadd, M.Teague;
Conversions: M.Hamlin, P.Webb

Mar 2 Northampton 17 Gloucester 14
Tries: M.Teague (2), T.Smith;
Conversion: M.Hamlin

Mar 10 Gloucester 28 Richmond 14
Tries: P.Taylor, D.Spencer, S.Mills;
Conversions: M.Hamlin (2);
Penalties: M.Hamlin (4)

Mar 17 Orrell 6 Gloucester 20
Tries: S.Boyle (2), L.Cummins, M.Hamlin;
Conversions: M.Hamlin (2)

Mar 21 Cheltenham 13 Gloucester 27
Try: J.Breeze;
Conversion: T.Smith;
Penalties: T.Smith (6);
Drop goal: R.Pinnell

Mar 24 Gloucester 36 Saracens 9
Tries: N.Price (2), J.Breeze (2), M.Teague (2),
J.Bennett, T.Smith;
Conversions: T.Smith (2)

Apr 4 Moseley 12 Gloucester 16
Tries: J.Bennett, N.Price, R.Mogg;
Conversions: T.Smith (2)

Apr 7 Launceston 9 Gloucester 50
Tries: N.Price (4), D.Morgan (2), R.Mogg (2),

P.Taylor (2), T.Smith;
Conversions: T.Smith, M.Hamlin, N.Price

Apr 14 Gloucester 15 Neath 9
Try: J.Orwin;
Conversion: T.Smith;
Penalties: T.Smith (3)

Apr 19 Lydney 12 Gloucester 8
Tries: R.Mogg, J.Gadd

Apr 21 Gloucester 19 Headingley 0
Tries: D.Morgan, M.Longstaff;
Conversion: P.Webb;
Penalties: P.Webb (3)

Apr 23 Gloucester 42 Birkenhead Park 0
Tries: T.Smith (2), P.Taylor, J.Breeze,
R.Wilmott, D.Spencer, S.Parsloe;
Conversions: T.Smith (2), S.Parsloe (2);
Penalties: T.Smith (2)

Apr 28 Gloucester 58 Exeter 9
Tries: D.Morgan (4), P.Taylor (2), T.Smith,
N.Price, R.Pascall, I.Smith, D.Spencer;
Conversions: S.Parsloe (4), T.Smith (3)

1984-85

Dr.H.Lister M.Elway R.Clewes B.Howells J.Beaman J.Jarrett R.Jardine J.Bennett R.Morris T.Day E.Stephens A.C.Pope D.Foyle M.Booth A.Townsend
D.Mountjoy T.Pritchard
P.Hawker G.Hudson A.D.Wadley(Hon.Treas) K.White S.Mills P.Jones M.Preedy N.Scrivens L.Cummins J.Brain M.Teague J.Bennett N.Price
T.R.Tandy(Hon.Sec) R.Rollaston R.Redwood A.Mitchell
D.Morgan M.Hamlin I.Smith T.Smith Canon H.M.Hughes(Pres) J.Orwin(Capt) P.J.Ford(Chairman) R.Ellis R.Mogg P.Taylor J.Breeze

Played 48 Won 32 Lost 15 Drawn 1
For 1105 Against 542
Captain: John Orwin
Coach: Bob Redwood

Gloucester United
Played 30 Won 19 Lost 8 Drawn 3
For 654 Against 292
Captain: Paul Wood

Most appearances: P.Taylor 43, J.Brain,

M.Hamlin 41, M.Hannaford 38, N.Price 36,
R.Mogg, R.Pascall 35,
T.Smith, I.Smith 34, D.Morgan, K.White 33,
J.Gadd 32
Most tries: N.Price 33, D.Morgan 29,
M.Hannaford 14, A.Richards, T.Smith 12
Conversions: T.Smith 61, P.Wickenden 13,
P.Ford 7, M.Hamlin 2, M.Evans 1
Penalties: T.Smith 54, P.Wickenden 11, P.Ford
9, M.Evans 3, M.Hamlin 2
Drop goals: M.Hamlin 2, R.Mogg, M.Evans 1

Under new coach Bob Redwood Gloucester
played a brand of expansive rugby. The result
was that wings Derrick Morgan and Nick Price
scored 62 tries between them. Another outcome
of this open play was that full-back Tim Smith
scored twelve tries. His place-kicking was much
more consistent than in the previous season and
he totaled 332 points. Marcus Hannaford had a
very good season at scrum-half, combining well
with Mike Hamlin. The forwards as ever were

tough with Richard Pascall, John Brain and Ian Smith always prominent.

There was a slow start to the season, when five out of eight games were lost, but then an improvement saw wins over Ebbw Vale (away), Harlequins and a thrashing of Leicester (37-15).

There was a good run in the John Player Cup, which included sweeping wins over Richmond, Saracens and Harlequins. The semi-final was at Kingsholm against Bath. Gloucester played all the rugby, but a dour Bath were on top in the scrums. Tim Smith scored all Gloucester's points with two tries and a penalty, but otherwise had an off day with the boot, missing six out of seven. The crucial point came with about 15 minutes to go. Good work by Mike Teague and Marcus Hannaford put Mike Hamlin away and he seemed certain to score under the posts. He was tackled just short, and although Smith scored his second try, it was by the touch-line and the vital conversion was missed. He missed another penalty attempt with a minute to go, so Gloucester lost by one point.

Although winning four more England caps, Phil Blakeway made only five appearances for Gloucester and retired at the end of the season, having played in 140 games. It was also Paul Ford's final season; he had appeared 120 times for the Club, and scored 804 points. Steve Boyle played in only seven games and retired after 303 appearances and 78 tries, a huge number for a second-row forward.

John Orwin won England caps against Romania, France, Scotland, Ireland and Wales, and Phil Blakeway against Romania, France, Scotland and Ireland; Mike Teague was a replacement against France. South & South-West played against the Australians at Exeter, with Steve Mills and John Orwin in the team, and included Orwin and Mike Teague against Romania at Kingsholm.

Sep 1 Gloucester 19 Swansea 20
Tries: N.Price, M.Longstaff;
Conversion: T.Smith;
Penalties: T.Smith (3)

Sep 5 Stroud 7 Gloucester 30
Tries: A.Richards (2), D.Morgan, M.Longstaff, G.Mann;
Conversions: P.Wickenden (2);
Penalties: P.Wickenden (2)

Sep 8 Coventry 6 Gloucester 10
Tries: A.Richards, G.Sargent;
Conversion: T.Smith

Sep 12 Gloucester 20 Maesteg 15
Tries: N.Price, J.Orwin;
Penalties: M.Hamlin (2), P.Wickenden (2)

Sep 15 Pontypridd 12 Gloucester 10
Try: J.Gadd;
Penalty: T.Smith;
Drop goal: M.Evans

Sep 19 Newbridge 17 Gloucester 9
Penalties: T.Smith (2);
Drop goal: M.Hamlin

Sep 22 Gloucester 9 Bristol 16
Try: A.Richards;
Conversion: M.Evans;
Penalty: M.Evans

Sep 26 Llanelli 20 Gloucester 6
Penalties: P.Wickenden (2)

Sep 29 Gloucester 16 Waterloo 4
Tries: J.Breeze, R.Pascall;
Conversion: P.Wickenden;
Penalties: P.Wickenden (2)

**Oct 3 Gloucester 30
Glamorgan Wanderers 21**
Tries: N.Price, M.Hannaford, J.Gadd, P.Wickenden;
Conversion: P.Ford;
Penalties: P.Ford (4)

Oct 6 Gloucester 22 Bedford 10
Tries: A.Richards (2), R.Ellis, M.Teague, M.Longstaff;
Conversion: P.Wickenden

Oct 10 Pontypool 19 Gloucester 3
Penalty: P.Ford

Oct 13 Gloucester 19 Harlequins 6
Tries: M.Hannaford (2), K.White;
Conversions: P.Ford (2);
Penalty: P.Ford

Oct 17 Ebbw Vale 15 Gloucester 24
Tries: A.Richards, R.Ellis, J.Gadd;
Conversions: P.Ford (3);
Penalties: P.Ford (2)

Oct 20 Newport 27 Gloucester 13
Tries: N.Price (2);
Conversion: P.Ford;
Penalty: P.Ford

Oct 27 Gloucester 36 Clifton 13
Tries: D.Morgan (3), N.Scrivens (2), R.Ellis, N.Price, L.Cummins;
Conversions: M.Hamlin (2)

Oct 31 Gloucester 33 Abertillery 6
Tries: N.Price (2), A.Richards (2), M.Preedy;
Conversions: T.Smith (2);
Penalties: T.Smith (3)

Nov 3 Rosslyn Park 12 Gloucester 34
Tries: N.Price, T.Smith, R.Ellis, P.Ford;
Conversions: T.Smith (3);
Penalties: T.Smith (4)

**Nov 7 Gloucester 32
South Wales Police 10**
Tries: D.Morgan (2), R.Ellis, N.Price, M.Hannaford;
Conversions: T.Smith (3);
Penalties: T.Smith (2)

**Nov 10 Plymouth Albion 12
Gloucester 20**
Tries: D.Morgan (2), T.Smith;
Conversion: T.Smith;
Penalties: T.Smith (2)

Nov 14 Gloucester 22 Cheltenham 15
Tries: D.Morgan (2), C.Dyke, I.Smith;
Penalties: M.Evans (2)

Nov 17 Gloucester 49 Broughton Park 3
Tries: M.Hannaford (2), T.Smith (2), J.Breeze, M.Teague, I.Smith, J.Bennett;
Conversions: T.Smith (4);
Penalties: T.Smith (3)

Nov 21 Gloucester 30 Exeter University 3
Tries: J.Breeze (2), A.Richards, T.Smith, M.Hamlin, R.Wood;
Conversions: T.Smith (3)

Nov 24 London Irish 19 Gloucester 16
Tries: M.Hamlin, N.Scrivens;
Conversion: T.Smith;
Penalties: T.Smith (2)

**Nov 28 Gloucester 41
Loughborough Students 10**
Tries: M.Hannaford (3), J.Breeze, P.Taylor, R.Mogg, M.Hamlin, P.Wickenden;
Conversions: P.Wickenden (3);
Penalty: P.Wickenden

Dec 1 Gloucester 37 Leicester 15
Tries: M.Hannaford (2), M.Hamlin, K.White, R.Pascall;
Conversions: T.Smith (4);
Penalties: T.Smith (3)

Dec 8 Bath 19 Gloucester 9
Penalties: T.Smith (2);
Drop goal: R.Mogg

Dec 15 Gloucester 58 Coventry 12

Tries: D.Morgan (4), N.Price (3), P.Taylor, J.Orwin, T.Smith;
Conversions: T.Smith (9)

Dec 22 Gloucester 6 Newport 6
Penalties: T.Smith (2)

Dec 26 Gloucester 25 Lydney 9
Tries: N.Price (2), T.Smith, D.Morgan;
Conversions: T.Smith (3);
Penalty: T.Smith

Dec 29 Gloucester 13 Bridgend 3
Try: N.Price;
Penalties: T.Smith (3)

Jan 1 Moseley 16 Gloucester 7
Try: J.Brain;
Penalty: T.Smith

Jan 5 Gloucester v London Scottish - cancelled

Jan 12 Leicester 27 Gloucester 6
Penalty: T.Smith;
Drop goal: M.Hamlin

Jan 19 Wasps v Gloucester - cancelled

Jan 26 Gloucester 29 Richmond 0
(John Player Cup)
Tries: N.Price, D.Morgan, R.Pascall, M.Hannaford, J.Bennett;
Conversions: T.Smith (3);
Penalty: T.Smith

Jan 31 Bristol 3 Gloucester 0

Feb 9 Gloucester v Bath - cancelled
Feb 16 Nottingham v Gloucester - cancelled

Feb 23 Gloucester 29 Saracens 3
(John Player Cup)
Tries: N.Price, D.Morgan, P.Taylor, L.Cummins, I.Smith;
Conversions: T.Smith (3);
Penalty: T.Smith

Mar 1 Gloucester 28 Northampton 10
Tries: N.Price (2), R.Mogg, L.Cummins, T.Smith;
Conversions: T.Smith (4)

Mar 9 Gloucester 31 Harlequins 12
(John Player Cup)
Tries: D.Morgan (2), N.Price;
Conversions: T.Smith (2);
Penalties: T.Smith (5)

Mar 15 Gloucester 25 Orrell 10
Tries: N.Price (2), D.Morgan, L.Cummins;
Penalties: T.Smith (3)

Mar 18 Cheltenham 3 Gloucester 25
Tries: R.Mogg (2), D.Morgan, N.Price, M.Teague;
Conversion: T.Smith;
Penalty: T.Smith

Mar 23 Gloucester 11 Bath 12
(John Player Cup Semi-Final)
Tries: T.Smith (2);
Penalty: T.Smith

Mar 29 Gloucester 17 Moseley 12

Tries: D.Morgan, N.Price, M.Hamlin;
Conversion: T.Smith;
Penalty: T.Smith

Apr 4 Lydney 3 Gloucester 12
Try: N.Price;
Conversion: T.Smith;
Penalties: T.Smith (2)

Apr 6 Gloucester 58 New Brighton 6
Tries: N.Price (6), D.Spencer (2), R.Ellis, P.Taylor;
Conversions: P.Wickenden (6);
Penalties: P.Wickenden (2)

Apr 8 Gloucester 45 Fylde 3
Tries: D.Morgan (3), R.Mogg (2), A.Richards (2), S.Mills, J.Bennett;
Conversions: T.Smith (3);
Penalty: T.Smith

Apr 13 Neath 15 Gloucester 9
Try: R.Mogg;
Conversion: T.Smith;
Penalty: T.Smith

Apr 20 Gloucester 13 Sale 16
Tries: D.Morgan, M.Hannaford;
Conversion: T.Smith;
Penalty: T.Smith

Apr 27 Exeter 9 Gloucester 59
Tries: D.Morgan (3), T.Smith (2), I.Smith, N.Price, M.Hannaford, R.Mogg, J.Brain, J.Bennett;
Conversions: T.Smith (6);
Penalty: T.Smith

1985-86

G.Hudson M.Elway T.Pritchard B.Howells A.Townsend A.Brinn R.Jardine P.Hawker J.Jarrett E.Stephens R.Collins T.Day D.Foyle D.Mountjoy A.C.Pope J.Fidler

Dr.T.Durkin R.Redwood(Coach) R.Clewes A.Mitchell R.Morris J.Breeze J.Beaman M.Longstaff N.Scrivens L.Cummings J.Etheridge J.Brain R.Pascall

J.Bennett T.Smith R.Mogg P.Taylor R.Rollaston M.Nicholls(Team Sec) T.R.Tandy(Hon.Sec)

J.Gadd P.Jones I.Smith D.Morgan Canon H.M.Hughes(Pres) J.Orwin(Capt) P.J.Ford(Chairman) M.Preedy M.Hamlin D.Spencer R.Maclean

M.Hannaford R.Phillips S.Artus K.White

Played 47 Won 33 Lost 14
For 1032 Against 517
Captain: John Orwin
Coach: Bob Redwood

Gloucester United
Played 30 Won 21 Lost 8 Drawn 1
For 695 Against 309
Captain: Paul Wood

Most appearances: P.Taylor 41, M.Hamlin 40, J.Gadd 36, J.Brain, T.Smith 35, R.Pascall 34 M.Hannaford, K.White 32, D.Morgan, R.Maclean 31, J.Breeze 30
Most tries: D.Morgan 27, J.Breeze 15, R.Mogg, P.Taylor, M.Hannaford 13, J.Gadd 12
Conversions: T.Smith 54, P.Wickenden 9, M.Hamlin 6, M.Evans 4, P.Lazenby 3
Penalties: T.Smith 48, S.Lazenby 6, P.Wickenden 5, M.Hamlin 2
Drop goals: M.Hamlin 3

In September a new club shop was opened, located by the side of the Worcester Street stand. It was run by Allan Townsend and Nick Price, with all profits going into the fund towards the end-of-season tour.

It was another season with plenty of wins, but yet again there was disappointment in the John Player Cup. The team approached their quarter-final contest against London Scottish at the Richmond Athletic Ground full of

confidence. Only a few weeks earlier Gloucester had won 37-13 on the same ground. But the Times neatly summed things up, "Gloucester's robust forwards had arrived with the intention of feasting on the carcass of a pack they had almost devoured on their last visit in January. This time, however, the exiles were much better prepared and the West Country side went away hungry." In fact, Gloucester scored two tries to one, and did make several strong forward rushes, but their cause was not helped when John Brain was sent off in the second-half for punching.

Elsewhere the team were the first winners of the John Smith Merit Table winning eight out of nine of the qualifying matches. The South-West Merit Table was also won. There was a coveted double over Leicester, and wins against Llanelli and Neath. Bristol were beaten at Kingsholm in consecutive weeks, one of the games being a cup tie.

Derrick Morgan was, by a distance the top try scorer. Tim Smith again scored the most points with 284. Captain John Orwin left the RAF and as a result was available for more games, although he was injured for most of March. Centre Ruari Maclean made a big impact in his first season.

A number of players played their last games for the Cherry & Whites this season - Steve Mills

(303 appearances), Steve Baker (216), John Orwin (205) and Paul Wood (176), who was also United captain from 1984-86.

In the Divisional Championship, Mike Hamlin, Kevin White, Richard Pascall and John Orwin played for South & South-West against London. Malcolm Preedy, Pascall and Orwin played against Midlands, and against North.

As soon as the season ended there was a short tour of Florida, USA, for the First XV and the United.

Sep 3 Exeter 13 Gloucester 36
Tries: M.Hannaford (2), R.Mogg, L.Cummins, I.Smith, M.Preedy;
Conversions: T.Smith (3);
Penalties: T.Smith (2)

Sep 7 Swansea 44 Gloucester 3
Penalty: T.Smith

Sep 11 Gloucester 28 Stroud 6
Tries: P.Tunstall, J.Breeze, M.Hamlin, S.Mills;
Conversions: T.Smith (3);
Penalties: T.Smith (2)

Sep 14 Gloucester 14 Coventry 18
Tries: P.Tunstall, P.Taylor, M.Hannaford;
Conversion: T.Smith

Sep 18 Glamorgan Wanderers 13 Gloucester 6
Try: M.Smith;
Conversion: T.Smith

Sep 21 Gloucester 53 Pontypridd 0
Tries: J.Gadd (2), J.Bennett (2), D.Spencer,
J.Orwin, M.Smith, R.Mogg, P.Taylor, J.Breeze;
Conversions: P.Wickenden (5);
Penalty: P.Wickenden

Sep 25 Gloucester 10 Newbridge 12
Try: I.Smith;
Penalties: P.Wickenden (2)

Sep 28 Gloucester 87 Exeter University 3
(John Player Cup)
Tries: R.Mogg (4), J.Breeze (3), M.Hannaford
(3), J.Bennett (3), P.Taylor (2), J.Gadd;
Conversions: P.Wickenden (4), M.Hamlin (3);
Penalties: P.Wickenden (2), M.Hamlin

Oct 2 Gloucester 27 Llanelli 12
Tries: S.Lazenby, P.Taylor, R.Mogg,
M.Hannaford, D.Spencer;
Conversions: M.Hamlin (2);
Penalty: M.Hamlin

Oct 5 Bedford 6 Gloucester 34
Tries: R.Mogg (2), S.Lazenby (2), M.Hamlin,
J.Gadd, I.Goslin;
Conversions: S.Lazenby (2), M.Hamlin

Oct 9 Gloucester 12 Pontypool 17
Penalties: S.Lazenby (4)

Oct 12 Harlequins 43 Gloucester 6
Penalty try;
Conversion: S.Lazenby

Oct 16 Gloucester 19 Ebbw Vale 22
Tries: B.Fowke (2), D.Burn;
Conversions: T.Smith (2);
Penalty: T.Smith

Oct 19 Gloucester 10 Newport 12
Try: D.Morgan;
Penalties: T.Smith (2)

Oct 26 Lewes 10 Gloucester 24
(John Player Cup)
Tries: D.Morgan (2), J.Breeze (2), J.Bennett;
Conversions: T.Smith (2)

Oct 30 Abertillery 0 Gloucester 13
Tries: D.Morgan, J.Breeze;
Conversion: T.Smith;
Penalty: T.Smith

Nov 2 Gloucester 25 Rosslyn Park 6
Tries: D.Morgan (2), P.Taylor, M.Hannaford;

Conversions: T.Smith (3);
Penalty: T.Smith

Nov 6 Gloucester 15 South Wales Police 14
Try: M.Hamlin;
Conversion: T.Smith;
Penalties: T.Smith (2);
Drop goal: M.Hamlin

Nov 9 Gloucester 15 Bath 11
Try: M.Hamlin;
Conversion: T.Smith;
Penalties: T.Smith (3)

Nov 13 Gloucester 18 Cheltenham 0
Tries: D.Morgan (2), T.Smith;
Penalties: T.Smith (2)

Nov 16 Broughton Park 7 Gloucester 18
Tries: D.Morgan (2), M.Longstaff, J.Orwin;
Conversion: M.Evans

Nov 23 Gloucester 44 London Irish 3
Tries: S.Long (2), J.Gadd (2), M.Longstaff (2),
J.Orwin, M.Hamlin;
Conversions: T.Smith (6)

Nov 30 Camborne 12 Gloucester 25
Tries: P.Taylor, M.Hannaford, J.Gadd;
Conversions: T.Smith (2);
Penalties: T.Smith (3)

Dec 7 Leicester 9 Gloucester 15
Try: M.Hannaford;
Conversion: T.Smith;
Penalties: T.Smith (3)

Dec 14 Launceston 12 Gloucester 24
Tries: D.Morgan, P.Taylor, R.Phillips, I.Smith,
J.Breeze;
Conversions: M.Evans (2)

Dec 21 Coventry 17 Gloucester 13
Try: T.Smith;
Penalties: T.Smith (3)

Dec 26 Gloucester 25 Lydney 0
Tries: T.Smith, M.Longstaff, L.Cummins,
J.Gadd, S.Artus;
Conversion: T.Smith;
Penalty: T.Smith

Jan 1 Gloucester 8 Moseley 3
Tries: J.Breeze (2)

Jan 4 London Scottish 13 Gloucester 37
Tries: J.Bennett (2), J.Breeze (2), D.Morgan,
M.Hannaford, M.Longstaff;
Conversions: T.Smith (3);
Penalty: T.Smith

Jan 11 Gloucester 15 Leicester 10
Tries: D.Morgan (2), J.Breeze;
Penalty: T.Smith

Jan 18 Gloucester 25 Wasps 13
Tries: J.Bennett, D.Morgan, M.Hamlin;
Conversions: T.Smith (2);
Penalties: T.Smith (3)

Jan 25 Gloucester 7 Bristol 4
(John Player Cup)
Try: T.Ford;
Penalty: T.Smith

Jan 31 Gloucester 21 Bristol 6
Try: M.Hamlin;
Conversion: T.Smith;
Penalties: T.Smith (5)

Feb 14 Gloucester v Nottingham – cancelled
due to frost

Feb 23 Truro 0 Gloucester 36
Tries: P.Taylor (2), J.Gadd, M.Teague, T.Ford,
D.Morgan, R.Maclean, P.Jones;
Conversions: T.Smith (2)

Mar 8 Saracens 6 Gloucester 13
(John Player Cup)
Try: M.Hannaford;
Penalties: T.Smith (3)

Mar 12 Bridgend 10 Gloucester 7
Try: D.Morgan;
Drop goal: M.Hamlin

Mar 15 Orrell 21 Gloucester 16
Tries: M.Hamlin, M.Hannaford, P.Taylor,
D.Morgan

Mar 17 Gloucester 52 Cheltenham 12
Tries: D.Morgan (3), R.Williams (2), J.Breeze,
M.Hamlin, I.Smith, T.Smith;
Conversions: T.Smith (5);
Penalties: T.Smith (2)

Mar 22 London Scottish 12 Gloucester 8
(John Player Cup Quarter-Final)
Tries: J.Gadd, T.Smith

Mar 27 Lydney 6 Gloucester 8
Tries: R.Mogg, R.Maclean

Mar 29 Gloucester 14 Headingley 7
Tries: T.Smith (2);
Penalties: T.Smith (2)

Mar 31 Gloucester 23 Birkenhead Park 11
Tries: T.Ford, N.Price, M.Smith, M.Evans;
Conversions: T.Smith, M.Evans;
Penalty: T.Smith

Apr 5 Moseley 18 Gloucester 7
Try: J.Gadd;
Drop goal: M.Hamlin

Apr 12 Gloucester 14 Neath 6
Tries: R.Mogg, J.Gadd;
Penalties: S.Lazenby (2)

Apr 19 Sale 15 Gloucester 29
Tries: D.Morgan (2), M.Hamlin (2), M.Teague;
Conversions: T.Smith (3);
Penalty: T.Smith

Apr 26 Gloucester 64 Exeter 0
Tries: D.Morgan (4), R.Mogg (2), P.Taylor (2),
R.Maclean, R.Phillips, J.Etheridge, M.Preedy;
Conversions: T.Smith (8)

May 3 Bath 22 Gloucester 9
Try: T.Smith;
Conversion: T.Smith;

Penalty: T.Smith
Tour of Florida, USA

May 10 Pelicans 12 Gloucester 48
Tries: M.Hamlin (2), T.Ford (2), R.Fowke (2),
R.Maclean (2), T.Smith;
Conversions: T.Smith (5), M.Hamlin

May 10 Tampa Bay 0 Gloucester United 51
Tries: S.Lomg (2), D.Burn (2), P.Wickenden,
A.Stanley, R.Pascall, J.Bennett;
Conversions: P.Wickenden (5);
Penalties: P.Wickenden (2);
Drop goal: P.Wickenden

May 13 Boca Raton 0 Gloucester 49
Tries: T.Ford (2), P.Wickenden, R.Maclean,
R.Phillips, M.Hannaford, M.Longstaff,
M.Hamlin, P.Taylor;
Conversions: P.Wickenden (5);

Penalty: P.Wickenden

**May 13 Fort Lauderdale 6
Gloucester United 52**
Tries: P.Tunstall (2), D.Morgan, M.Smith,
D.Burn, T.Smith, I.Smith, S.Artus, J.Bennett,
L.Cummins;
Conversions: T.Smith (6)

**May 17 University of Miami 9
Gloucester 40**
Tries: T.Smith (2), P.Taylor (2), M.Smith,
M.Teague, A.Stanley, penalty try;
Conversions: P.Wickenden (4)

**May 17 Miami Trident 18
Gloucester United 38**
Tries: T.Smith (3), L.Cummins, S.Artus,
I.Smith, R.Ellis, M.Longstaff;
Conversions: T.Smith (2), P.Wood

1986-87

**Played 47 Won 30 Lost 17
For 967 Against 589
Captain: Malcolm Preedy
Coach: Bob Redwood**

Gloucester United
Played 35 Won 33 Lost 0 Drawn 2
For 920 Against 284
Captain: Dave Pointon

Most Appearances: M.Hamlin 40, J.Breeze,
R.Pascall 37, M.Preedy 36, P.Taylor 35,
 I.Smith 34
J.Etheridge 32, K.Dunn 31, D.Morgan 27
Most Tries: J.Breeze 17, D.Morgan 16, N.Price
12, M.Hannaford 11, M.Teague, P.Taylor 10
Conversions: N.Marment 39, T.Smith 23,
P.Mansell 7, S.Lazenby 2, M.Hamlin 1
Penalties: N.Marment 32, T.Smith 12,

P.Mansell 4, M.Hamlin 1
Dropped Goals: M.Hamlin 4

The season began with a special fixture at
Cinderford to celebrate the start of the Forest
club's centenary season. During the season
The Cherry & Whites played some exciting
rugby at times, but the old problem of a lack of
consistency remained. The early season results
were far from promising, only four of the first 14
games being won. After that, things improved
including a famous win at Bath, then in their
full pomp. Bath were firm favorites, and had
won ten consecutive games. Played on a heavy
Recreation Ground, the exchanges were not
subtle. Bath got on top in scrum and line-out,
but an interception by scrum-half Richard
Williams turned the game. He kicked ahead,
but was obstructed resulting in a penalty try. In

the second-half the Gloucester forwards fought
back, and with Bath getting on the wrong side
of the referee Gloucester prevailed.

For the second season running there was a
double over Leicester. At Kingsholm Gloucester
won 41-6 although it must be said that the
Tigers were weakened by calls to the Midlands
Divisional Team. There was no such excuse at
Welford Road, Gloucester came back from a 0-9
deficit at half-time to score two tries, and inflict
Leicester's first home defeat of the season.

Malcolm Preedy was an inspirational leader,
but the forwards missed John Orwin who had
moved on to Bedford. Richard Pascall and
Mike Teague played magnificently throughout
the season. A loss of form on the part of Tim
Smith meant that Nick Marment took over as

the regular full-back and scored 202 points, but he lacked consistency with his place-kicking. Wings Jim Breeze and, inevitably, Derrick Morgan were the top try scorers. Gordon Sargent (204 appearances) and Mike Longstaff (164) ended their Gloucester careers this season.

Mention must be made of the magnificent season enjoyed by the United, under the leadership of Dave Pointon. They were unbeaten throughout the season, which, not surprisingly, was the best in the second XV's history.

In the Divisional Championship, Mike Hamlin and John Gadd played for South & South-West against London, and Gadd also played against the Midlands.

Sep 2 Cinderford 6 Gloucester 24
Tries: J.Breeze (3), D.Morgan, S.Lazenby;
Conversions: S.Lazenby (2)

Sep 6 Gloucester 4 Swansea 6
Try: M.Teague

Sep 10 Stroud 3 Gloucester 24
Tries: L.Cummins, I.Smith, R.Williams, T.Smith;
Conversion: T.Smith;
Penalties: T.Smith (2)

Sep 15 Coventry 19 Gloucester 11
Tries: J.Gadd, L.Cummins;
Penalty: T.Smith

**Sep 17 Gloucester 34
Glamorgan Wanderers 13**
Tries: J.Breeze (2), N.Price, R.Williams, A.Stanley, R.Mogg, K.Dunn;
Conversions: N.Marment (3)

Sep 20 Pontypridd 18 Gloucester 9
Try: D.Morgan;
Conversion: T.Smith;
Penalty: T.Smith

Sep 22 Gloucester 16 Munster 28
Tries: R.Williams, N.Marment;
Conversion: N.Marment;
Penalties: N.Marment (2)

Sep 27 Gloucester 3 Bristol 12
Penalty: T.Smith

Oct 1 Llanelli 25 Gloucester 16
Tries: D.Morgan, R.Pascall;
Conversion: T.Smith;
Penalties: T.Smith (2)

Oct 4 Gloucester 22 Bedford 12
Tries: J.Breeze, P.Taylor, R.Maclean,

R.Williams;
Conversions: T.Smith (3)

Oct 8 Pontypool 26 Gloucester 16
Tries: D.Morgan, J.Breeze, R.Pascall;
Conversions: T.Smith (2)

Oct 11 Gloucester 10 Harlequins 16
Try: D.Morgan;
Penalties: T.Smith (2)

Oct 15 Gloucester 7 Ebbw Vale 9
Try: K.Dunn;
Penalty: P.Mansell

Oct 18 Newport 34 Gloucester 21
Tries: P.Taylor, M.Hamlin, J.Breeze;
Conversions: P.Mansell (3);
Penalty: P.Mansell

Oct 25 Gloucester 37 Plymouth Albion 15
Tries: D.Morgan (2), P.Taylor, R.Mogg, R.Williams, K.Dunn, I.Smith;
Conversions: P.Mansell (3);
Penalty: P.Mansell

Nov 1 Rosslyn Park 6 Gloucester 16
Tries: M.Teague, P.Taylor;
Conversion: N.Marment;
Penalties: N.Marment (2)

Nov 5 Gloucester 20 South Wales Police 9
Tries: B.Fowke, R.Pascall, penalty try;
Conversion: N.Marment;
Penalties: N.Marment (2)

Nov 8 Newbridge 16 Gloucester 13
Tries: R.Mogg, J.Breeze;
Conversion: N.Marment;
Drop goal: M.Hamlin

Nov 12 Gloucester 36 Cheltenham 13
Tries: M.Teague (3), J.Breeze, R.Williams, R.Phillips;
Conversions: N.Marment (3);
Penalties: N.Marment (2)

Nov 15 Gloucester 32 Broughton Park 6
Tries: K.Dunn (2), I.Smith, L.Cummins, M.Smith, M.Hamlin;
Conversion: N.Marment;
Penalties: N.Marment (2)

Nov 22 London Irish 6 Gloucester 24
Tries: I.Smith, N.Marment, M.Smith, J.Breeze, L.Gardner;
Conversions: N.Marment (2)

Nov 26 Bath 9 Gloucester 12
Try: penalty try;
Conversion: N.Marment;

Penalty: N.Marment;
Drop goal: M.Hamlin

Nov 29 Gloucester 32 Camborne 3
Tries: N.Price (2), M.Hannaford, L.Cummins, J.Gadd, G.Mann;
Conversion: N.Marment;
Penalties: N.Marment (2)

Dec 6 Gloucester 41 Leicester 6
Tries: N.Price (2), P.Taylor (2), J.Breeze, J.Gadd, M.Hamlin, N.Marment;
Conversions: N.Marment (3);
Penalty: N.Marment

Dec 13 Launceston 3 Gloucester 19
Tries: N.Price, M.Hannaford, penalty try;
Conversions: N.Marment (2);
Penalty: N.Marment

Dec 20 Gloucester 33 Coventry 6
Tries: M.Teague (2), R.Williams, R.Morgan, L.Gardner, K.Dunn;
Conversions: N.Marment (3);
Penalty: N.Marment

Dec 26 Gloucester 25 Lydney 9
Tries: L.Gardner (2), L.Cummins, J.Breeze;
Conversions: T.Smith (3);
Penalty: T.Smith

Dec 27 Gloucester 15 Newport 29
Tries: C.Guest, J.Breeze;
Conversions: N.Marment (2);
Penalty: N.Marment

Jan 1 Moseley 15 Gloucester 10
Try: K.Dunn;
Penalties: N.Marment (2)

Jan 3 Gloucester 15 London Scottish 9
Try: N.Marment;
Conversion: N.Marment;
Penalties: N.Marment (3)

Jan 10 Leicester 12 Gloucester 14
Tries: L.Gardner (2);
Penalty: M.Hamlin;
Drop goal: M.Hamlin

Jan 17 Wasps v Gloucester - cancelled

**Jan 24 West Hartlepool 12 Gloucester 16
(John Player Cup)**
Tries: R.Williams, P.Taylor;
Conversion: N.Marment;
Penalties: N.Marment (2)

Jan 31 Gloucester 20 Bridgend 17
Tries: P.Taylor, N.Price, M.Teague;
Conversion: M.Hamlin;

Penalties: N.Marment (2)

Feb 6 Bristol 17 Gloucester 10
Try: J.Gadd;
Penalties: N.Marment (2)

Feb 14 Gloucester 18 Old Reigatians 6
(John Player Cup)
Tries: J.Breeze (2), R.Williams;
Penalties: T.Smith (2)

Feb 21 Nottingham v Gloucester - cancelled

Feb 28 Orrell 16 Gloucester 10
(John Player Cup)
Try: K.Dunn;
Penalties: N.Marment (2)

Mar 6 Gloucester 17 Northampton 6
Tries: M.Hamlin (2), N.Marment;
Conversion: N.Marment;
Penalty: N.Marment

Mar 14 Richmond 6 Gloucester 23
Tries: P.Taylor, M.Hamlin, M.Hannaford,
R.Pascall;
Conversions: N.Marment (2);
Penalty: N.Marment

Mar 16 Cheltenham 0 Gloucester 46
Tries: R.Maclean (2), N.Price (2), T.Smith (2),
D.Morgan, M.Hannaford, J.Bennett, I.Smith;
Conversions: T.Smith (3)

Mar 21 Gloucester 31 Orrell 3
Tries: M.Teague (2), M.Hannaford (2),
P.Taylor, D.Morgan;
Conversions: T.Smith (2);
Drop goal: M.Hamlin

Mar 28 Saracens 7 Gloucester 10
Tries: D.Morgan, K.Dunn;
Conversion: T.Smith

Apr 3 Gloucester 8 Moseley 25
Tries: M.Hannaford, N.Marment

Apr 11 Neath 35 Gloucester 6
Try: J.Breeze; Conversion: T.Smith

Apr 16 Lydney 14 Gloucester 17
Tries: D.Morgan (2), L.Cummins;
Conversion: P.Mansell;
Penalty: P.Mansell

Apr 18 Gloucester 42 New Brighton 4
Tries: M.Hannaford (2), P.Ashmead (2),
D.Morgan, N.Price, A.Stanley, P.Wallace;
Conversions: T.Smith (5)

Apr 20 Gloucester 38 Fylde 10
Tries: R.Mogg (2), M.Hannaford (2), N.Price,
A.Stanley, N.Marment;
Conversions: N.Marment (5)

Apr 25 Exeter 12 Gloucester 44
Tries: D.Morgan (3), L.Cummins (3),
R.Morgan , N.Price, R.Pascall;
Conversions: N.Marment (4)

1987-88

T.Day(Vice-Pres) B.Howells T.Close J.Beaman P.Hawker A.Brinn J.Jarrett R.Jardine K.Richardson(Coach) R.Collins E.Stephens M.Booth
M.Nicholls(Hon.Team Sec) R.Morris(Vice-Pres) K.Dunn C.Dyke A.Stanley N.Marment J.Etheridge N.Scrivens R.Pascall M.Teague J.Bennett T.Smith
A.Mitchell R.Redwood(Coach)
J.Breeze R.Phillips D.Spencer G.Mann P.Ford(Chairman) M.Hannaford(Capt) H.M.Hughes(Pres) R.Mogg T.Preedy D.Morgan R.Maclean
J.Roberts M.Hamlin

Played 47 Won 32 Lost 12 Drawn 3
For 973 Against 591
Captain: Marcus Hannaford
Coach: Keith Richardson
Courage League: Played 10 Won 6 Lost 3
Drawn 1
For 206 Against 121
Position: 5th

Gloucester United

Played 35 Won 26 Lost 6 Drawn 3
For 817 Against 383
Captain: Dave Pointon

Most appearances: J.Breeze, M.Preedy 36,
M.Hamlin 35, M.Hannaford 34, I.Smith 32,
K.Dunn, N.Scrivens 30, R.Pascall 29,
D.Morgan, D.Cummins 26
Most Tries: J.Breeze 25, D.Morgan,
M.Hannaford 15, P.Ashmead 12

Conversions: T.Smith 31, N.Marment,
P.Mansell 19, A.Broady 9, M.Hamlin 4
Penalties: T.Smith 22, N.Marment 18,
P.Mansell 12, M.Hamlin, A.Broady 1
Dropped goals: M.Hamlin 5

This was the first season of national leagues.
There were 12 teams in "National One" as it
was called then, and Gloucester finished in
mid table. The league game against Leicester

(Champions) was never played. In general, the new competition did not encourage adventurous rugby, and many games were arm wrestles of attrition among the forwards. An exception was the very first league game Gloucester played, which was against Coventry when six tries were scored. And another was the final league game against Sale, when no fewer than 11 tries were dotted down.

The John Player Cup campaign did not last long. After a good win against Orrell, a very disappointing loss at home to Wasps (which doubled up as a league/cup game) ended interest. The fact was that on a very muddy Kingsholm the Wasps forwards outplayed the Gloucester pack in the loose and scrum. In those conditions that was all it needed. It was particularly galling because only a few weeks before Wasps had been defeated comfortably enough at Kingsholm in a club game.

The season opened with a rare win at Swansea, and a few weeks later Bristol were defeated at the Memorial Ground. There was a double over Newport and home wins against Leicester and Neath. Jim Breeze was by a distance the top try scorer. Early in the season against Stroud, Derrick Morgan scored four tries, the second of which was his 100th for the club. A return to form saw Tim Smith competing for the full-back position with Nick Marment. Paul Taylor missed a lot of the season with knee problems, but Damian Cummins stepped up to fill his place in the centre, and made an immediate impact.

Although having effectively retired in 1985, Peter Kingston came on as a replacement for one game to bring his final tally to 181 appearances. Dave Pointon who had made 167 appearances also retired, having also captained the United team with great success for two seasons.

Mike Hamlin, Richard Pascall and John Brain played in all three of the South & South-West's Divisional Championship games.

Sep 5 Swansea 6 Gloucester 19
Tries: J.Bennett, M.Hannaford, N.Marment;
Conversions: N.Marment (2);
Drop goal: M.Hamlin

Sep 9 Gloucester 46 Stroud 9
Tries: D.Morgan (4), M.Hamlin (2), J.Breeze, I.Smith;
Conversions: N.Marment (4);
Penalties: N.Marment (2)

**Sep 12 Gloucester 39 Coventry 3
(Courage League)**
Tries: J.Bennett (2), D.Morgan, R.Maclean, J.Breeze, N.Marment;
Conversions: N.Marment (3);
Penalties: N.Marment (3)

Sep 16 Glamorgan Wanderers 22 Gloucester 13
Tries: D.Morgan, M.Hannaford;
Conversion: N.Marment;
Penalty: N.Marment

Sep 19 Gloucester 26 Pontypridd 19
Tries: D.Morgan, M.Hannaford, K.Dunn;
Conversion: P.Mansell;
Penalties: P.Mansell (4)

Sep 23 Gloucester 35 Exeter 0
Tries: T.Ruck (2), J.Roberts, L.Gardner, K.Hopson, A.Stanley, K.Jeavons;
Conversions: P.Mansell, A.Broady;
Penalty: P.Mansell

**Sep 26 Bristol 16 Gloucester 21
(Courage League)**
Tries: D.Spencer, I.Smith, J.Breeze;
Conversions: N.Marment (3);
Penalty: N.Marment

Oct 3 Bedford 12 Gloucester 10
Try: N.Marment;
Penalties: N.Marment (2)

Oct 7 Gloucester 8 Pontypool 10
Tries: M.Hannaford, P.Taylor

Oct 14 Ebbw Vale 17 Gloucester 14
Tries: D.Morgan, J.Breeze, I.Smith;
Conversion: P.Mansell

Oct 17 Gloucester 16 Newport 0
Tries: D.Morgan, I.Smith;
Conversion: P.Mansell;
Penalties: M.Marment (2)

**Oct 24 Gloucester 17 Nottingham 9
(Courage League)**
Tries: D.Morgan, J.Breeze, J.Bennett;
Conversion: N.Marment;
Penalty: N.Marment

**Oct 31 Waterloo 16 Gloucester 6
(Courage League)**
Penalties: N.Marment (2)

Nov 4 Gloucester 27 South Wales Police 6
Tries: K.Dunn (2), P.Ashmead, D.Morgan, L.Cummins;
Conversions: T.Smith (2);
Penalty: T.Smith

Nov 7 Gloucester 16 Rosslyn Park 6
Tries: N.Price (2), P.Ashmead;
Conversions: T.Smith (2)

Nov 11 Gloucester 27 Cheltenham 3
Tries: M.Hannaford (2), D.Spencer, N.Price;
Conversion: N.Marment;
Penalties: N.Marment (3)

Nov 14 Gloucester 28 Newbridge 13
Tries: J.Bennett (3), K.Dunn, D.Morgan, N.Marment;
Conversions: N.Marment (2)

Nov 21 Harlequins 9 Gloucester 9 (Courage League)
Try: J.Bennett;
Conversion: N.Marment;
Penalty: M.Hamlin

Nov 28 Gloucester 17 London Irish 3
Tries: N.Beytell, C.Dee, J.Breeze;
Conversion: N.Marment;
Penalty: N.Marment

**Nov 30 Gloucester 9 Bath 16
(Courage League)**
Try: P.Ashmead;
Conversion: T.Smith;
Penalty: T.Smith

Dec 5 Leicester 19 Gloucester 12
Tries: J.Breeze (2);
Conversions: T.Smith (2)

Dec 12 Plymouth Albion 4 Gloucester 10
Try: N.Price;
Penalties: T.Smith (2)

Dec 19 Coventry 17 Gloucester 6
Penalties: T.Smith (2)

Dec 21 Newport 6 Gloucester 16
Tries: P.Ashmead, M.Hamlin, T.Smith;
Conversions: T.Smith (2)

Dec 26 Lydney 3 Gloucester 9
Try: S.Cuff;
Conversion: T.Smith;
Penalty: T.Smith

**Jan 1 Gloucester 18 Moseley 12
(Courage League)**
Tries: G.Mann (2), J.Breeze, D.Morgan;
Conversion: T.Smith

Jan 2 London Scottish 8 Gloucester 8
Tries: J.Breeze (2)

Jan 9 Gloucester 30 Leicester 16
Tries: M.Hannaford (2), R.Maclean (2), D.Morgan, M.Teague;

Conversions: T.Smith (3)

Jan 16 Gloucester 22 Wasps 13
Tries: D.Morgan, P.Ashmead, I.Smith;
Conversions: T.Smith (2);
Penalties: T.Smith (2)

Jan 23 Gloucester 19 Orrell 9
(John Player Cup)
Tries: J.Breeze, M.Hannaford;
Conversion: T.Smith;
Penalties: T.Smith (3)

Jan 30 Gloucester 24 Cross Keys 12
Tries: J.Breeze, A.Stanley, D.Spencer,
R.Maclean;
Conversion: T.Smith;
Penalties: T.Smith (2)

Feb 5 Gloucester 10 Bristol 13
Tries: M.Preedy, J.Breeze;
Conversion: T.Smith

Feb 13 Gloucester 13 Wasps 24
(Courage League & John Player Cup)
Tries: M.Hannaford, D.Cummins;
Conversion: T.Smith;
Penalty: T.Smith

Feb 20 Bath 26 Gloucester 26
Tries: M.Hamlin, P.Ashmead, R.Maclean;
Conversion: T.Smith;
Penalties: T.Smith (2);
Drop goals: M.Hamlin (2)

Feb 27 Gloucester 25
Liverpool St Helens 21
Tries: R.Mogg, M.Hannaford, J.Brain, I.Smith;
Conversions: T.Smith (3);
Penalty: T.Smith

Mar 4 Northampton 12 Gloucester 13
Tries: J.Breeze, T.Smith;
Conversion: T.Smith;
Penalty: T.Smith

Mar 12 Gloucester 44 Richmond 12
Tries: R.Mogg (2), J.Breeze (2), D.Cummins (2),
R.Maclean, I.Smith;
Conversions: T.Smith (6)

Mar 16 Cheltenham 3 Gloucester 21
Tries: L.Gardner, C.Dee, A.Kitchen;
Conversions: P.Mansell (3);
Penalty: P.Mansell

Mar 19 Orrell 9 Gloucester 13
(Courage League)
Try: J.Breeze;
Penalties: T.Smith (3)

Mar 23 Bridgend 18 Gloucester 8
Tries: R.Smith, M.Hannaford

Mar 26 Gloucester 26 Saracens 24
Tries: J.Breeze (2), K.Dunn, A.Stanley, penalty
try;
Conversions: M.Hamlin (3)

Mar 31 Gloucester 23 Lydney 12
Tries: P.Taylor, M.Hamlin, R.Phillips,
P.Ashmead;
Conversions: P.Mansell (2);
Penalty: P.Mansell

Apr 2 Moseley 10 Gloucester 19
Tries: J.Breeze, M.Hannaford, P.Ashmead;
Conversions: A.Broady (2);
Drop goal: M.Hamlin

Apr 4 Gloucester 47 Birkenhead Park 7
Tries: J.Breeze (2), P.Ashmead (2), S.Davies,
N.Price, J.Roberts, R.Phillips;
Conversions: A.Broady (6);
Penalty: A.Broady

Apr 9 Gloucester 35 Neath 19
Tries: P.Mansell, J.Breeze, R.Maclean, R.Mogg;
Conversions: P.Mansell (2);
Penalties: P.Mansell (4);
Drop goal: M.Hamlin

Apr 16 Gloucester 61 Sale 7
(Courage League)
Tries: M.Hannaford (2), P.Ashmead (2),
J.Breeze, R.Maclean, R.Mogg, R.Pascall,
N.Scrivens, I.Smith, P.Mansell;
Conversions: P.Mansell (6), M.Hamlin;
Penalty: P.Mansell

Apr 23 Llanelli 60 Gloucester 12
Tries: M.Hamlin (2);
Conversions: P.Mansell (2)

1988-89

A.Mitchell M.Elway A.C.Pope B.Howells T.Close A.Townsend R.Collins E.Stephens P.Hawker R.Rollaston F.Reed(Hon.Team Sec) K.Richardson(Coach) M.Booth J.Fidler
R.Redwood T.Day(Vice-Pres) T.R.Tandy(Hon.Gen.Sec) N.Price R.Phillips B.Clark J.Brain J.Etheridge N.Scrivens M.Teague J.Gadd A.Stanley T.Smith R.Morris(Vice-Pres) B.Glanville
K.Dunn D.Cummins I.Smith M.Preedy J.Jarrett(Vice-Chairman) R.Hannaford(Capt) H.M.Hughes(Pres.) P.Ashmead R.Dogg J.Breeze N.Marment L.Gardiner M.Hamlin

Played 45 Won 34 Lost 10 Drawn 1
For 1030 Against 524
Captain: Marcus Hannaford
Coach: Keith Richardson
Courage League: Played 11 Won 7 Lost 3 Drawn 1
For 215 Against 112
Position: 2nd

Gloucester United
Played 34 Won 24 Lost 8 Drawn 2
For 698 Against 421
Captain: Dave Spencer

Most appearances: M.Hamlin 38 (36 starts + 2 as replacement), M.Hannaford 35, J.Etheridge 34, N.Scrivens, R.Mogg 33, D.Cummins, T.Smith 32, N.Price 31, M.Preedy 30
Most tries: N.Price 18, J.Breeze 17, T.Smith 11, M.Hannaford 8, R.Mogg 7
Conversions: T.Smith 58, N.Marment 21, M.Hamlin, J.Roberts 1
Penalties: T.Smith 62, N.Marment 18
Drop goals: M.Hamlin 3, M.Preedy 1

This was a pretty successful season, but without any trophies to display at the end of it. The team finished as runners-up to Bath in the Courage League, and reached the semi-final of the Pilkington Cup before narrowly losing, in a dour game at Kingsholm in front of 10,000, to the same team. The only other home defeat was to Bristol in a league game, although there was a win at the Memorial Ground. For the second season running there was a double over Newport, including a 42-6 win at Kingsholm, which was at that time the biggest win ever against the Welsh team. The Times said, "Newport were run ragged by an energetic and skillful Gloucester performance". Leicester were beaten 28-0 in a league game. The Times again enthused about Gloucester: "Their dynamic driving and tidy rucking reduced Leicester to stumbling ineffectiveness." The other notable thing about the Leicester game was that Gloucester scored seven tries, and none were converted! There were also wins against Pontypool (away), Bridgend and Bath.

Tim Smith, fully returned to form, had a wonderful season scoring 346 points, including 11 tries. Only wings Jim Breeze and Nick Price scored more tries. Price scored his 100th try when he touched down the first of two against Bridgend. Although only playing in 15 games, Nick Marment still scored 116 points. Mike Teague's form throughout was outstanding. With Kevin Dunn as regular hooker, Kevin White made only six appearances and retired at the end of the season after 165 games. Two promising players - Dave Sims and Tony Windo - scored tries on their debut against Cheltenham

in November. A lot more would be heard about them in future seasons.

Mike Teague played for England against Scotland, Ireland, France and Wales, and in a non-cap test against Romania. For England B, Richard Pascall and Kevin Dunn (try) played against France B, John Etheridge and Kevin Dunn (try) against Italy B, and Mike Hamlin (penalty) against Spain.

Malcolm Preedy (try), Kevin Dunn and Richard Pascall played for South-West Division against Australia. In the Divisional Championship, Richard Pascall, Malcolm Preedy and Mike Teague (two tries) played in all three games, Kevin Dunn in two, and Ian Smith was a replacement in one.

Sep 3 Gloucester 35 Swansea 13
Tries: J.Breeze, R.Maclean, J.Gadd, M.Teague, I.Smith;
Conversions: T.Smith (3);
Penalties: T.Smith (2);
Drop goal: M.Hamlin

Sep 6 Stroud 0 Gloucester 34
Tries: R.Temple (2), C.Dee, N.Matthews, P.Wallace, J.Bennett;
Conversions: N.Marment (2);
Penalties: N.Marment (2)

Sep 10 Gloucester 37 Moseley 9
(Courage League)
Tries: D.Cummins (2), M.Teague, M.Hamlin, R.Maclean,
Conversions: T.Smith (4);
Penalties: T.Smith (3)

Sep 17 Pontypridd 18 Gloucester 25
Tries: N.Marment (2), J.Gadd;
Conversins: T.Smith (2);
Penalties: T.Smith (3)

Sep 20 Gloucester 44 Clifton 9
Tries: N.Matthews (3), J.Breeze, R.Temple, P.Ashmead, J.Bennett;
Conversions: N.Marment (5);
Penalties: N.Marment (2)

Sep 24 Bath 19 Gloucester 9
(Courage League)
Penalties: T.Smith (3)

Sep 27 Exeter 18 Gloucester 14
Tries: M.Hannaford, R.Mogg;
Penalties: N.Marment (2)

Oct 1 Gloucester 25 Bedford 16
Tries: T.Smith, J.Breeze, R.Temple;
Conversions: T.Smith (2);

Penalties: T.Smith (3)

Oct 8 Gloucester 19 Wasps 3
(Courage League)
Tries: D.Cummins, N.Scrivens;
Conversion: T.Smith;
Penalties: T.Smith (3)

Oct 12 Gloucester 21 Ebbw Vale 10
Tries: T.Smith, A.Stanley, P.Ashmead, N.Marment;
Conversion: T.Smith;
Penalty: T.Smith

Oct 15 Newport 15 Gloucester 19
Try: I.Smith;
Penalties: T.Smith (5)

Oct 22 Liverpool St Helens 9
Gloucester 31 (Courage League)
Tries: M.Hamlin (2), G.Mann (2), R.Mogg;
Conversions: T.Smith (4);
Penalty: T.Smith

Oct 29 Newbridge 17 Gloucester 10
Try: N.Price;
Penalties: N.Marment (2)

Nov 2 Gloucester 45 South Wales Police 7
Tries: J.Breeze (2), R.Mogg (2), J.Etheridge (2), M.Hannaford, K.White, D.Cummins;
Conversions: N.Marment (3);
Penalty: N.Marment

Nov 9 Gloucester 48 Cheltenham 3
Tries: J.Breeze, R.Temple, D.Prestajeskyj, N.Matthews, L.Gardner, A.Windo, D.Sims, A.Stanley, N.Marment;
Conversions: N.Marment (6)

Nov 12 Rosslyn Park 8 Gloucester 26
(Courage League)
Tries: R.Mogg, J.Gadd, R.Pascall, M.Teague;
Conversions: N.Marment (2);
Penalties: N.Marment (2)

Nov 19 Gloucester 10 Bristol 11
(Courage League)
Tries: M.Hamlin, M.Teague;
Conversion: T.Smith

Nov 26 Waterloo 15 Gloucester 15
(Courage League)
Try: M.Hamlin;
Conversion: T.Smith;
Penalties: T.Smith (3)

Dec 3 Leicester 19 Gloucester 13
Try: D.Morgan;
Penalties: T.Smith (2);
Drop goal: M.Hamlin

Dec 10 Gloucester 28 Plymouth Albion 22
Tries: T.Smith (2), N.Price (2);
Conversions: T.Smith (2), M.Hamlin;
Penalties: T.Smith (2)

Dec 17 Coventry 14 Gloucester 30
Tries: J.Breeze, A.Windo, J.Brain, P.Ashmead, B.Clarke;
Conversions: T.Smith (5)

Dec 19 Gloucester 42 Newport 6
Tries: N.Price, M.Hannaford, N.Scrivens, J.Gadd, I.Smith;
Conversions: T.Smith (5);
Penalties: T.Smith (4)

Dec 26 Gloucester 21 Lydney 10
Tries: J.Breeze (2), K.Dunn, P.Wallace;
Conversion: N.Marment;
Penalty: N.Marment

Dec 31 Gloucester 17 Bridgend 12
Tries: N.Price (2);
Penalties: N.Marment (3)

Jan 2 Moseley 23 Gloucester 3
Penalty: T.Smith

Jan 7 Gloucester 20 London Scottish 12
Tries: T.Smith, I.Smith, J.Gadd;
Conversion: T.Smith;
Penalties: T.Smith (2)

Jan 14 Gloucester 28 Leicester 0
(Courage League)
Tries: J.Breeze (2), M.Hannaford, M.Hamlin, N.Price, K.Dunn, M.Teague

Jan 18 Pontypool 13 Gloucester 23
Tries: N.Price (3), T.Smith;
Conversions: T.Smith (2);
Penalty: T.Smith

Jan 21 Gloucester 37 Blackheath 0
Tries: D.Morgan (3), D.Cummins (2), J.Breeze, T.Smith;
Conversions: T.Smith (3);
Penalty: T.Smith

Jan 28 Brixham 4 Gloucester 28
(Pilkington Cup)
Tries: N.Price (3), T.Smith, N.Scrivens;
Conversion: T.Smith;
Penalties: T.Smith (2)

Feb 3 Bristol 13 Gloucester 15
Penalties: N.Marment (3);
Drop goals: M.Hamlin, M.Preedy

Feb 11 Gloucester 19 Waterloo 16
(Pilkington Cup)
Tries: T.Smith (2), K.Dunn;
Conversions: T.Smith (2);
Penalty: T.Smith

Feb 17 Gloucester 18 Bath 12
Try: I.Smith;
Conversion: T.Smith;
Penalties: T.Smith (4)

Feb 25 Wakefield 13 Gloucester 28
(Pilkington Cup)
Tries: N.Price (2), M.Hannaford;
Conversions: T.Smith (2);
Penalties: T.Smith (4)

Mar 3 Gloucester 29 Northampton 12
Tries: J.Breeze (2), M.Hannaford, B.Clarke, A.Stanley;
Conversions: T.Smith (3);
Penalty: T.Smith

Mar 11 Harlequins 26 Gloucester 11
(Courage League)

Tries: J.Breeze (2);
Penalty: T.Smith

Mar 15 Cheltenham 19 Gloucester 16
Tries: N.Marment, J.Brain, P.Ashmead;
Conversions: N.Marment (2)

Mar 18 London Irish 19 Gloucester 32
Tries: M.Hannaford (2), N.Scrivens, B.Clarke, J.Gadd, R.Mogg;
Conversions: T.Smith (4)

Mar 25 Gloucester 3 Bath 6
(Pilkington Cup Semi-Final)
Penalty: T.Smith

Mar 27 Gloucester 42 Fylde 15
Tries: N.Price, C.Dee, J.Roberts, J.Hawker, D.Sims, A.Stanley, G.Keyse;
Conversions: T.Smith (6), J.Roberts

Apr 1 Headingley 9 Gloucester 12
Tries: N.Price, R.Mogg, K.Dunn

Apr 8 Orrell 6 Gloucester 16
(Courage League)
Tries: N.Price, I.Smith;
Conversion: T.Smith;
Penalties: T.Smith (2)

Apr 15 Sale 7 Gloucester 19
Tries: T.Smith, J.Breeze;
Conversion: T.Smith;
Penalties: T.Smith (3)

Apr 22 Gloucester 13 Nottingham 6
(Courage League)
Try: K.Dunn;
Penalties: T.Smith (3)

Apr 28 Lydney 10 Gloucester 0

1989-90

Played 47 Won 34 Lost 11 Drawn 2
For 1122 Against 622
Captain: Mike Hamlin
Coach: Keith Richardson
League record: Played 11 Won 8 Lost 2 Drawn 1
For 214 Against 139
Position: 2nd

Gloucester United
Played 33 Won 25 Lost 7 Drawn 1
For 817 Against 375
Captain: Dave Spencer

Most appearances: R.Mogg, N.Scrivens 37, M.Hamlin, D.Morgan 33, I.Smith 32,

M.Preedy 31, K.Dunn 30 (29 + 1 as rep), R.Pascall 30 (29 + 1)
Most tries: D.Morgan 19, R.Mogg 17, K.Dunn 13, T.Smith, M.Hamlin 10
Conversions: T.Smith 44, N.Marment 27, P.Mansell 9, M.Hamlin 4
Penalties: T.Smith 47, N.Marment 14, P.Mansell 3
Drop goals: M.Hamlin 4, N.Matthews 2

With two weeks of the season remaining, Gloucester appeared to be in line for a double - the Courage League title and the Pilkington Cup. The final league game was at Nottingham, and a win would mean the title was Gloucester's.

A large Cherry & White contingent travelled to the game only to see Gloucester outplayed by an inspired Nottingham. This was particularly galling as the same team was beaten at the same venue only a few weeks before in a Pilkington Cup game. Wasps beat Saracens on the same day, and the title was theirs'.

There was still the Pilkington Cup. In the event the team was blown away by Bath to the tune of 48-6! To turn the knife in the wound, John Gadd was sent off, but the game was long gone by then. It was a heart-breaking end to a season which had promised so much. It also illustrated how different Bath's preparation for the final

T.Pritchard M.Elway B.Howells E.Stephens J.Beaman R.Jardine J.Fidler A.Brinn A.Townsend P.Hawker T.Day(Vice-Pres)
F.Reed(Hon.Team Sec) A.Mitchell K.Dunn R.Phillips P.Ashmead M.Preedy B.Clark R.Pascall M.Teague N.Marment J.Breeze J.Hawker D.Cummins
T.R.Tandy(Hon.Gen.Sec) K.Richardson(Coach)
J.Holder I.Smith R.Mogg P.Ford(Chairman) M.Hamlin(Capt) H.M.Hughes(Pres) D.Morgan M.Hannaford T.Smith
L.Gardiner D.Caskie

had been. They had no chance of winning the league and so had rested players before the final. In addition, the team travelled to London the day before the final and so were fully rested. Gloucester travelled on the day and were caught in a traffic jam on the M4!

Apart from the depressing end, the season had been a triumph. Well over 1,000 points were scored, with Tim Smith contributing 269 of those, and Nick Marment 120. Derrick Morgan and evergreen Richard Mogg were the top try scorers. The forwards were as formidable as ever, with, Richard Pascall, Kevin Dunn, Nigel Scrivens and John Brain having excellent seasons. Mike Teague made only ten appearances, having missed the first half of the season due to a shoulder injury. Skipper Mike Hamlin and Marcus Hannaford were the dependable half-backs.

The campaign opened with an encouraging victory at Swansea. As the season progressed there were doubles over Bristol and Leicester, and a particularly satisfying win against Bath in the league game at Kingsholm. The Bath match was an abrasive, bad-tempered affair, and after several warnings to both teams for rough play, Bath's Gareth Chilcott was sent off. The league win at Leicester ended the Tigers 13-month ground record. Gloucester were at their best, cutting down all the Tigers attempts to win the game through their backs, and Leicester ended up well beaten.

At the end of the season John Etheridge having made 118 appearances moved on to Northampton. Jim Breeze (178 appearances, 90 tries) and Paul Taylor (283 and 59 tries) ended their Gloucester careers.

Mike Teague played for England against France, Wales and Scotland. In the Divisional Championship, Richard Pascall, Kevin Dunn, John Etheridge and Dave Sims (try) played in all three South & South-West games; Mike Hamlin and Mike Teague in two; and Ian Smith in one.

Sep 2 Swansea 29 Gloucester 32
Tries: D.Morgan (2), R.Mogg, M.Hannaford, I.Smith;
Conversions: T.Smith (3);
Penalties: T.Smith (2)

Sep 5 Gloucester 36 Stroud 8
Tries: C.Guest (2), G.Keyse, J.Hawker, M.Roberts, A.Curtis, L.Gardner, P.Jones;
Conversions: N.Marment (2)

Sep 9 Moseley 12 Gloucester 16 (League)
Try: J.Gadd;
Penalties: T.Smith (3);
Drop goal: M.Hamlin

Sep 13 Gloucester 18 Cheltenham 13
Tries: J.Etheridge, J.Hawker;
Conversions: N.Marment (2);
Penalties: N.Marment (2)

Sep 16 Gloucester 15 Pontypridd 10
Try: M.Hamlin;
Conversions: T.Smith;
Penalties: T.Smith (2);
Drop goal: M.Hamlin

Sep 20 Clifton 19 Gloucester 27
Tries: A.Curtis, G.Keyse, D.Spencer;
Conversions: N.Marment (3);
Penalties: N.Marment (3)

Sep 23 Gloucester 13 Bath 6 (League)
Try: K.Dunn;
Penalties: T.Smith (3)

Sep 27 Gloucester 37 Exeter 8
Tries: D.Morgan (3), D.Cummins, J.Breeze, N.Scrivens, B.Clark, T.Smith;
Conversion: T.Smith;
Penalty: T.Smith

Sep 30 Gloucester 13 Pontypool 20
Tries: T.Smith (2);
Conversion: T.Smith;
Penalty: T.Smith

Oct 4 Gloucester 68 British Police 15
Tries: D.Morgan (3), J.Etheridge (2), R.Mogg (2), J.Gadd (2), K.Dunn, J.Breeze, L.Gardner, I.Smith, T.Smith;
Conversions: T.Smith (5), M.Hamlin

Oct 11 Gloucester 43 Exeter University 4
Tries: N.Matthews (2), A.Curtis, C.Dee, G.Richards, J.Hawker, P.Ashmead, A.Stanley, D.Sims;
Conversions: P.Mansell (2);
Penalty: P.Mansell

Oct 14 Wasps 29 Gloucester 4 (League)
Try: J.Gadd

Oct 18 Ebbw Vale 10 Gloucester 38
Tries: K.Dunn (2), D.Morgan, J.Breeze,
M.Hamlin, N.Scrivens, I.Smith;
Conversions: P.Mansell (5)

Oct 21 Gloucester 31 Newport 10
Tries: D.Morgan, T.Smith, K.Dunn, D.Caskie,
R.Mogg, I.Smith;
Conversions: T.Smith (2);
Penalty: T.Smith

Oct 28 Gloucester 37 Bedford 6 (League)
Tries: D.Morgan (2), D.Caskie (2), N.Marment,
J.Brain, B.Clark, M.Hamlin;
Conversion: M.Hamlin;
Penalty: T.Smith

Nov 3 Gloucester 19 Newbridge 13
Tries: B.Clark (2), P.Ashmead;
Conversions: T.Smith (2);
Penalty: T.Smith

Nov 8 Gloucester 6 South Wales Police 8
Penalties: P.Mansell (2)

**Nov 11 Gloucester 41 Rosslyn Park 12
(League)**
Tries: D.Morgan (3), N.Price (2), M.Hannaford,
J.Hawker, T.Smith;
Conversions: M.Hamlin (2), T.Smith;
Penalty: T.Smith

Nov 18 Bristol 6 Gloucester 13 (League)
Tries: N.Marment, R.Pascall;
Conversion: N.Marment;
Penalty: N.Marment

**Nov 25 Gloucester 21 Saracens 21
(League)**
Tries: D.Morgan, M.Hamlin, J.Breeze,
M.Hannaford;
Conversion: N.Marment;
Penalty: N.Marment

Dec 2 Gloucester 19 Leicester 13
Tries: A.Windo, J.Gadd, penalty try;
Conversions: N.Marment (2);
Penalty: N.Marment

Dec 9 Plymouth Albion 9 Gloucester 31
Tries: P.Ashmead (2), L.Gardner, J.Hawker,
R.Mogg;
Conversions: N.Marment (4);
Drop goal: N.Matthews

Dec 16 Gloucester 37 Coventry 9
Tries: N.Marment, N.Matthews, A.Windo,
P.Ashmead, M.Hannaford, R.Mogg;

Conversions: N.Marment (2);
Penalties: N.Marment (3)

Dec 23 Newport 10 Gloucester 10
Try: J.Breeze;
Penalties: T.Smith (2)

Dec 26 Gloucester 8 Lydney 4
Tries: K.Dunn, W.Birchley

Dec 30 Bridgend 18 Gloucester 9
Try: R.Phillips;
Conversion: T.Smith;
Drop goal: M.Hamlin

Jan 1 Gloucester 33 Moseley 4
Tries: N.Price (2), I.Smith, K.Dunn, T.Smith,
M.Hamlin;
Conversions: T.Smith (3);
Penalty: T.Smith

Jan 6 London Scottish 4 Gloucester 19
Tries: R.Mogg, D.Caskie, D.Morgan;
Conversions: T.Smith (2);
Penalty: T.Smith

Jan 13 Leicester 16 Gloucester 26 (League)
Tries: M.Hannaford (2), R.Mogg, J.Brain;
Conversions: T.Smith (2);
Penalties: T.Smith (2)

Jan 20 Blackheath 12 Gloucester 19
Tries: I.Smith, R.Mogg, M.Hamlin;
Conversions: T.Smith (2);
Penalty: T.Smith

**Jan 27 Wasps 19 Gloucester 23
(Pilkington Cup)**
Tries: J.Gadd, J.Breeze, R.Mogg;
Conversion: T.Smith;
Penalties: T.Smith (3)

Feb 3 Gloucester 19 Bristol 6
Tries: M.Hamlin (2), R.Mogg;
Conversions: T.Smith (2);
Penalty: T.Smith

**Feb 10 Gosforth 15 Gloucester 26
(Pilkington Cup)**
Tries: M.Hamlin, J.Gadd, J.Breeze, K.Dunn;
Conversions: T.Smith (2);
Penalties: T.Smith (2)

Feb 17 Bath 12 Gloucester 9
Penalties: T.Smith (3)

**Feb 24 Nottingham 16 Gloucester 26
(Pilkington Cup)**
Tries: K.Dunn, D.Morgan, M.Teague, R.Mogg;
Conversions: T.Smith (2);

Penalty: T.Smith;
Drop goal: M.Hamlin

**Mar 10 Gloucester 24 Harlequins 9
(League)**
Tries: K.Dunn;
Conversion: T.Smith;
Penalties: T.Smith (6)

Mar 13 Cheltenham 9 Gloucester 29
Tries: D.Sims (2), P.Taylor, N.Price, P.Jones;
Conversions: N.Marment (3);
Drop goal: N.Matthews

Mar 17 Gloucester 27 Llanelli 28
Tries: R.Mogg (2), L.Gardner, P.Ashmead;
Conversions: N.Marment (4);
Penalty: N.Marment

**Mar 24 Northampton 12 Gloucester 17
(Pilkington Cup Semi-final)**
Tries: M.Teague, D.Morgan;
Penalties: T.Smith (3)

Mar 31 Gloucester 16 Orrell 10 (League)
Tries: I.Smith, N.Price;
Conversion: T.Smith;
Penalties: T.Smith (2)

Apr 7 Gloucester 10 Richmond 12
Try: R.Mogg;
Penalties: N.Marment (2)

Apr 12 Lydney 26 Gloucester 20
Tries: A.Curtis, M.Roberts, J.Hawker, L.Beck;
Conversions: P.Mansell (2)

Apr 14 Gloucester 28 Headingley 9
Tries: R.Mogg (2), K.Dunn (2), A.Curtis (2),
D.Spencer

Apr 16 Gloucester 84 Birkenhead Park 0
Tries: T.Smith (3), N.Marment (3), P.Ashmead
(2), D.Caskie, C.Dee, J.Roberts, Roger Fowke,
J.Brain, J.Gadd, A.Deacon, A.Stanley;
Conversions: T.Smith (7), N.Marment (3)

Apr 21 Gloucester 16 Sale 21
Tries: M.Hamlin, I.Smith;
Conversion: T.Smith;
Penalties: T.Smith (2)

**Apr 28 Nottingham 12 Gloucester 3
(League)**
Penalty: T.Smith

**May 5 Bath 48 Gloucester 6
(Pilkington Cup Final at Twickenham)**
Try: K.Dunn;
Conversion: T.Smith

1990-91

T.Pritchard M.Elway A.Townsend T.Day(Vice-Pres) T.Close R.Collins E.Stephens A.Brinn J.Jarrett J.Beaman R.Jardine R.Morris(Vice-Pres)
D.Foyle(Hon.Memb.Sec) R.Clewes T.Tandy(Hon.Gen.Sec)
A.Mitchell D.Wadley(Hon.Treas) A.Stanley R.Phillips N.Marment D.Spencer N.Scrivens P.Miles D.Sims M.Teague N.Price S.Morris M.Preedy
D.Morgan J.Hawker F.Reed(Hon.Team Sec) K.Richardson(Coach) M.Nicholls(Hon.Fixture Sec)
K.Dunn L.Gardiner I.Smith M.Hannaford H.M.Hughes(Pres) M.Hamlin(Capt) P.Ford(Chairman) J.Perrins T.Smith P.Ashmead D.Caskie

Played 43 Won 32 Lost 11
For 1252 Against 414
Captain: Mike Hamlin
Coach: Keith Richardson
League: Played 12 Won 6 Lost 6
For 207 Against 163
Position: 6th

Gloucester United
Played 34 Won 29 Lost 5 Drawn 0
For 1147 Against 365
Captain: Dave Spencer

Most appearances: M.Hamlin 36, D.Sims 28 (27 start + 1 rep), T.Smith, N.Marment 27, D.Caskie, P.Jones, N.Scrivens 25, K.Dunn 24 (23+1), I.Smith 23, M.Hannaford 22
Most tries: N.Marment 17, J.Perrins 13, D.Morgan, D.Spencer 12, P.Ashmead 11
Conversions: T.Smith 54, M.Roberts 34, N.Marment 14, M.Hamlin 6
Penalties: T.Smith 36, M.Roberts 8, M.Hamlin 5, N.Marment 3
Drop goals: M.Hamlin, N.Matthews 1

Older supporters will remember the old "Tump" at the western end of Kingsholm. It was just that, a grassy knoll, with a very old scoreboard. By September 1990 the area was transformed, and 14 hospitality boxes had been erected at the cost of over £400,000.

Although the playing record was similar to the previous season, it was ultimately disappointing. There was a slip of four places in the league, and only one win in the Pilkington Cup before Harlequins won at Kingsholm at the next stage. However, 1252 points were scored, a club record which was not beaten until 2001-02. As usual

Tim Smith was the heaviest scorer totaling 232 points. Newcomer Martin Roberts scored 108 points in only ten games, and Nick Marment was the third player to top one hundred with 105 points. Having moved successfully from full-back to wing Marment topped the try scorers. Mike Teague was absent for several games due to international commitments. In the front-row Malcolm Preedy came under increasing pressure due to the excellent form of Pete Jones.

There were good wins against Newport, Aberavon, and Northampton (away). Bristol and Leicester were beaten at Kingsholm, but the more important league games, both away, were lost.

Several players made their final appearances this season. John Gadd's career was ended by injury, after playing in 284 games. He had scored 64 tries. Dave Spencer moved on to Lydney after 115 games. Two players went on to play for Bedford; John Brain having played 253 games and Richard Pascall 258.

Gloucester United under the captaincy of Dave Spencer had a fantastic season, scoring well over a thousand points, and winning the inaugural Midland & West Merit Table for Second XVs.

Mike Teague played in all four of England's tests in the International Championship scoring tries against Wales and Ireland. In the Divisional Championship only two games were played by the South & South-West. Mike Teague and Mike Hamlin played in both. Ian Smith captained Scotland 'B' against Ireland 'B'.

Sep 1 Gloucester 4 Swansea 14

Try: M.Hannaford

Sep 4 Gloucester 64 Clifton 3
Tries: D.Spencer (3), A.Stanley (2), K.Dunn (2), P.Miles, L.Gardner, J.Perrins, R.Phillips, N.Marment
Conversions: N.Marment (5);
Penalty: N.Marment;
Drop goal: N.Matthews

Sep 8 Neath 17 Gloucester 10
Tries: D.Spencer, A.Stanley;
Conversion: T.Smith

Sep 11 Stroud 0 Gloucester 48
Tries: D.Spencer (2), A.Curtis, R.Mogg, R.Phillips, A.Deacon, A.Stanley, penalty try;
Conversions: M.Roberts (5);
Penalties: M.Roberts (2)

Sep 15 Pontypridd 15 Gloucester 38
Tries: D.Morgan (3), N.Marment;
Conversions: T.Smith (2);
Penalties: T.Smith (6)

Sep 22 Leicester 18 Gloucester 6 (League)
Penalties: T.Smith (2)

Sep 26 Newport 15 Gloucester 10
Tries: A.Curtis, D.Caskie;
Conversion: T.Smith

Sep 29 Gloucester 45 Ebbw Vale 3
Tries: N.Marment, S.Morris, R.Mogg, D.Morgan, M.Hamlin, L.Gardner, R.Phillips, N.Scrivens, P.Ashmead
Conversions: T.Smith (3);
Penalty: T.Smith

Oct 3 Gloucester 46 Exeter University 0
Tries: B.Clark (3), A.Curtis (2), C.Dee, A.Windo, K.Dunn, P.Miles, A.Stanley, M.Roberts;
Conversion: M.Roberts

Oct 6 Gloucester 30 Moseley 12 (League)
Tries: D.Morgan (2), D.Cummins, N.Marment, M.Hannaford;
Conversions: T.Smith (2);
Penalties: T.Smith (2)

Oct 13 Gloucester 72 Plymouth Albion 3
Tries: D.Caskie (3), N.Marment (3), P.Ashmead (2), D.Morgan, L.Gardner, K.Dunn, D.Spencer, I.Smith, T.Smith;
Conversions: T.Smith (8)

Oct 16 Gloucester 45 Cheltenham 0
Tries: S.Morris (2), P.Miles, N.Matthews, A.Windo, D.Parry, S.Davis, M.Roberts;
Conversions: M.Roberts (5);
Penalty: M.Roberts

Oct 20 Wasps 14 Gloucester 9 (League)
Penalties: T.Smith (3)

Oct 27 Gloucester 22 Nottingham 6 (League)
Tries: M.Teague (2), L.Gardner, D.Spencer;
Conversions: T.Smith (3)

Oct 31 Gloucester 59 South Wales Police 4
Tries: D.Cummins (2), N.Matthews (2), A.Windo, L.Gardner, R.Phillips, N.Scrivens, T.Smith, penalty try
Conversions: T.Smith (7), M.Hamlin;
Penalty: T.Smith

Nov 3 Gloucester 28 Bristol 6
Tries: N.Marment, R.Phillips, P.Ashmead, L.Gardner, N.Scrivens, D.Caskie;
Conversions: T.Smith (2)

Nov 11 Rosslyn Park 17 Gloucester 12 (League)
Try: D.Cummins;
Conversion: T.Smith;
Penalties: T.Smith (2)

Nov 17 Gloucester 21 Saracens 16 (League)
Tries: P.Ashmead (2), D.Morgan, C.Dee;
Conversion: T.Smith;
Penalty: T.Smith

Nov 24 Gloucester 52 Broughton Park 0 (Pilkington Cup)
Tries: D.Morgan, N.Marment, D.Cummins, I.Smith, P.Ashmead, D.Sims, M.Hamlin, T.Smith, penalty try
Conversions: T.Smith (8)

Dec 1 Gloucester 18 Leicester 15
Tries: C.Guest, D.Morgan;
Conversions: N.Marment (2);
Penalties: N.Marment (2)

Dec 8 Rugby v Gloucester - cancelled

Dec 15 Coventry 7 Gloucester 26
Tries: P.Ashmead (2), M.Preedy, N.Matthews, N.Marment;
Conversions: N.Marment (3)

Dec 22 Exeter 9 Gloucester 36
Tries: N.Marment (2), J.Perrins (2), N.Price (2), M.Hamlin;
Conversions: M.Hamlin (4)

Dec 26 Gloucester 39 Lydney 9
Tries: C.Dee (2), L.Beck, D.Spencer, P.Miles, D.Parry, D.Sims;
Conversions: M.Roberts (3), M.Hamlin
Penalty: M.Roberts

Dec 29 Gloucester 20 Bridgend 7
Tries: J.Hawker, M.Hamlin;
Penalties: M.Hamlin (4)

Jan 1 Moseley 10 Gloucester 20
Tries: S.Morris, D.Parry, J.Perrins;
Conversion: T.Smith;
Penalties: T.Smith, M.Hamlin

Jan 5 Gloucester 17 London Scottish 10
Tries: D.Spencer, N.Scrivens, A.Windo;
Conversion: T.Smith;
Penalty: T.Smith

Jan 12 Liverpool-St.Helens 7 Gloucester 26 (League)
Tries: J.Perrins (2), D.Spencer, I.Smith;
Conversions: T.Smith (2);
Penalties: T.Smith (2)

Jan 19 Gloucester 38 Blackheath 4
Tries: N.Price (2), J.Perrins, D.Cummins, I.Smith, C.Guest, S.Morris, N.Marment;
Conversions: N.Marment (3)

Jan 26 Gloucester 13 Harlequins 15 (Pilkington Cup)
Tries: N.Marment, M.Hamlin;
Conversion: T.Smith;
Penalty: T.Smith

Feb 2 Newbridge v Gloucester - Cancelled
Feb 9 Gloucester v Bath - Postponed

Feb 15 Gloucester 20 Newport 3
Tries: M.Hannaford, T.Smith;
Penalties: T.Smith (4)

Feb 23 Gloucester 18 Richmond 8
Tries: D.Caskie (2), N.Marment, penalty try;
Conversion: T.Smith

Mar 1 Pontypool 21 Gloucester 24
Tries: S.Morris (2), N.Price;
Conversions: T.Smith (3);
Penalties: T.Smith (2)

Mar 9 Northampton 6 Gloucester 7 (League)
Try: P.Jones;
Penalty: T.Smith

Mar 12 Lydney 3 Gloucester 38
Tries: J.Perrins (2), N.Matthews (2), R.Mogg, K.Dunn, P.Ashmead;
Conversions: M.Roberts (5)

Mar 15 Gloucester 36 Aberavon 6
Tries: N.Marment (2), R.Phillips, R.Williams, L.Beck, N.Price;
Conversions: T.Smith (3);
Penalties: T.Smith (2)

Mar 23 Gloucester 9 Orrell 16 (League)
Try: P.Miles;
Conversion: N.Marment;
Penalty: T.Smith

Mar 30 Gloucester 54 New Brighton 6
Tries: D.Morgan (2), N.Price (2), P.Miles (2), J.Perrins, M.Hamlin, N.Scrivens, G.Fenwick, penalty try
Conversions: G.Fenwick (5)

Apr 1 Gloucester 30 Fylde 3
Tries: J.Perrins (3), M.Teague, S.Devereux, M.Hamlin;
Conversions: M.Roberts (3)

Apr 6 Gloucester 15 Bath 17 (League)
Try: M.Hannaford;
Conversion: T.Smith;
Penalties: T.Smith (3)

Apr 13 Bristol 15 Gloucester 12 (League)
Tries: R.Phillips, P.Miles;
Conversions: T.Smith (2)

Apr 16 Cheltenham 3 Gloucester 58
Tries: I.Morgan (2), C.Dee (2), D.Spencer, D.Sims, A.Windo, M.Roberts, P.Miles, A.Curtis, J.Hawker
Conversions: M.Roberts (7)

Apr 20 Bath 32 Gloucester 19
Tries: M.Hamlin, M.Roberts; onversion: M.Roberts;
Penalties: M.Roberts (2);

Drop goal: M.Hamlin

Apr 27   Gloucester 38   Harlequins 19
(League)

Tries: I.Smith (2), C.Dee (2), P.Ashmead,
D.Sims;
Conversions: M.Roberts (4);
Penalties: M.Roberts (2)

1991-92

J.Holder M.Elway D.Foyle(Hon.Memb.Sec) B.Howells T.Close G.Hudson(Vice-Pres) J.Beaman E.Stephens R.Jardine T.Day(Vice-Pres) C.Pope
T.Pritchard I.Wright M.Nicholls(Hon.Fixture Sec) F.Reed(Hon.Team Sec)
A.Mitchell D.Wadley(Hon.Treas) R.Phillips P.Jones M.Hannaford A.Stanley S.Masters N.Scrivens P.Miles D.Sims A.Deacon B.Fowke A.Windo
M.Hamlin N.Marment D.Cummins J.Hawker B.Glanville K.Richardson(Club Coach)
N.Matthews K.Dunn L.Gardiner T.Smith P.Ford(Chairman) I.Smith(Capt) H.M.Hughes(Pres) S.Morris D.Caskie I.Morgan J.Perrins

Played 38 Won 27 Lost 10 Drawn 1
For 793 Against 469
Captain: Ian Smith
Coach: Keith Richardson
League: Played 12 Won 7 Lost 4 Drawn 1
For 193 Against 168
Position: 4th

Gloucester United
Played 32 Won 30 Lost 1 Drawn 1
For 909 Against 304
Captain: Andrew Stanley

Most appearances: J.Perrins 29, D.Caskie 27,
N.Scrivens , S.Masters 26, T.Smith 25,
S.Morris 24,
P.Ashmead 22, I.Smith, R.Phillips, D.Sims 21
Most tries: S.Morris 13, J.Perrins 11, R.Fowke,
P.Ashmead 7, D.Caskie, S.Masters 6
Conversions: T.Smith 32, M.Roberts 13,
N.Marment 4, M.Hamlin, G.Fenwick 1
Penalties: T.Smith 48, M.Roberts 14,
N.Marment, M.Hamlin 5, G.Fenwick 2
Drop goals: N.Matthews 3, T.Smith,
M.Hamlin 2

This was another season which promised much,
then faltered. Until well into the second half
of the season the team were in the hunt for the
Division 1 title, but three losses in four games
saw the end of the challenge. In the Pilkington
Cup there was a heartbreaking loss to Bath in

the semi-final at Kingsholm. Leading 18-15 with
three minutes of extra-time to go, Gloucester
were almost there, but two Bath tries ended the
Cherry & White's hopes.

A unique feature of the season were the games
against an England XV (including Mike Teague)
and Irish President's XV in successive weeks,
providing warm-up games for the England and
Ireland squads before the start of the World
Cup. The win over the Irish was remarkable
as the selection was effectively the full Ireland
team, which finished up well beaten. One of
Gloucester's great wins, the one-point victory
would have been greater had Gloucester taken
all their chances.

There were doubles over Leicester and Bristol.
Newport were defeated 42-4, the biggest ever
win over that club, and Cardiff were beaten at
The Arms Park for the first time since 1935.

Ian Smith was an inspirational captain, and
thoroughly deserved recognition by the Scotland
selectors. Neil Matthews showed huge promise
at fly-half, where he displaced longstanding
Mike Hamlin. Dave Sims made further progress
as did hooker John Hawker. Also, in the front
row Andy Deacon and Tony Windo made steady
progress. Simon Morris was in fine form all
season and was the Club's top try scorer. As
usual Tim Smith was top points scorer with 222.

Several players ended their Gloucester careers
this season. Richard Mogg, a member of the "500
Club" called it a day after 513 appearances and
170 tries, Malcolm Preedy (313 appearances),
Nick Price (228 and 128 tries), both retired,
whilst Nigel Scrivens (232) went on to play for
London Welsh, Nick Marment (114) departed
for Bedford, and Kevin Dunn (156) for Wasps.

The United, with Andrew Stanley now captain,
only lost one game all season and retained the
Midland & West Merit Table title for Second
XVs.

In the World Cup Mike Teague played against
New Zealand and Italy in the pool games,
France in the quarter-final, Scotland in the semi-
final and Australia in the final. Ian Smith played
for Scotland against England, Ireland and Wales.
Pete Jones came on as a replacement for Scotland
against Wales. In the Divisional Championship
Neil Matthews and John Hawker played in all
three games, Dave Sims and Paul Ashmead in
two, Simon Morris and Bob Phillips in one, and
Ian Sanders was a replacement in one.

In May the Club had a short out-of-season tour
of North America

Sep 3 Gloucester 54 Stroud 6
Tries: D.Morgan (3), S.Morris (2), I.Smith (2),
P.Miles, S.Masters, D.Caskie;

Conversions: T.Smith (4)
Penalties: T.Smith (2)

Sep 7 Swansea 18 Gloucester 14
Tries: S.Masters, P.Ashmead, R.Phillips;
Conversion: T.Smith

Sep 14 Gloucester 4 England XV 34
Try: D.Morgan

Sep 21 Gloucester 14 Ireland XV 13
Tries: S.Morris, J.Perrins;
Penalties: T.Smith (2)

Sep 28 Gloucester 15 Neath 20
Tries: J.Hawker (2), I.Smith;
Penalty: T.Smith

Oct 2 Gloucester 43 Moseley 0
Tries: M.Preedy, T.Smith, D.Kearsey, R.Fowke,
C.Dee, I.Smith, D.Caskie;
Conversions: T.Smith (6);
Penalty: T.Smith

Oct 5 Gloucester 33 Exeter 10
Tries: R.Fowke (2), D.Kearsey, P.Glanville,
C.Dee, J.Perrins;
Conversions: T.Smith (3);
Penalty: T.Smith

Oct 11 Newport 25 Gloucester 12
Try: J.Perrins;
Conversion: G.Fenwick;
Penalties: G.Fenwick (2)

Oct 19 Leicester 12 Gloucester 22
Tries: P.Ashmead, N.Scrivens;
Conversion: T.Smith;
Penalties: T.Smith (3);
Drop goal: M.Hamlin

Oct 29 Lydney 13 Gloucester 19
Try: D.Malpas;
Penalties: M.Roberts (4), M.Hamlin

Nov 1 Cardiff 6 Gloucester 11
Tries: J.Perrins, S.Masters;
Penalty: T.Smith

Nov 4 Gloucester 36 Cheltenham 3
Tries: M.Preedy (2), R.Mogg (2), A.Curtis,
L.Beck, N.Price, T.Smith;
Conversions: T.Smith (2)

Nov 9 Gloucester 14 Bath 12
Tries: J.Perrins (2);
Penalties: N.Marment (2)

Nov 16 Gloucester 21 Leicester 3 (League)
Tries: D.Caskie, R.Phillips;
Conversions: T.Smith (2);

Penalties: T.Smith (3)

Nov 23 Rugby 16 Gloucester 19 (League)
Tries: P.Miles, S.Morris;
Conversion: T.Smith;
Penalties: T.Smith (3)

**Nov 30 Rugby 3 Gloucester 23
(Pilkington Cup)**
Tries: J.Perrins, N.Matthews, P.Ashmead;
Conversion: T.Smith;
Penalties: T.Smith (2);
Drop goal: T.Smith

Dec 7 Plymouth Albion 13 Gloucester 36
Tries: R.Fowke (2), J.Perrins, S.Morris,
D.Caskie, L.Beck;
Conversions: M.Roberts (3);
Penalties: M.Roberts (2)

**Dec 21 Nottingham 3 Gloucester 14
(League)**
Tries: S.Masters, S.Morris;
Penalties: T.Smith (2)

Dec 26 Gloucester 28 Lydney 10
Tries: J.Rogers (2), A.Curtis, D.Malpas, L.Beck,
S.Devereux;
Conversions: M.Roberts (2)

Dec 28 Bridgend 8 Gloucester 6
Penalties: M.Roberts (2)

**Jan 4 Gloucester 12 Rosslyn Park 9
(League)**
Try: P.Ashmead;
Conversion: T.Smith;
Penalties: T.Smith (2)

Jan 11 Saracens 12 Gloucester 12 (League)
Penalties: T.Smith (4)

Jan 17 Gloucester 42 Newport 4
Tries: S.Morris (3), J.Perrins, D.Caskie,
D.Cummins, M.Hamlin;
Conversions: M.Roberts (4);
Penalties: M.Roberts (2)

Jan 31 Gloucester 26 Pontypridd 10
Tries: A.Stanley, M.Hannaford, J.Hawker,
N.Scrivens;
Conversions: T.Smith (2);
Penalties: T.Smith (2)

**Feb 8 Gloucester 20 London Scottish 7
(Pilkington Cup)**
Tries: J.Hawker, N.Matthews, P.Ashmead;
Conversion: T.Smith;
Penalties: T.Smith (2)

Feb 14 Bristol 7 Gloucester 19

Tries: D.Cummins, P.Ashmead, penalty try;
Conversions: N.Marment (2);
Penalty: N.Marment

**Feb 22 Orrell 16 Gloucester 25
(Pilkington Cup)**
Tries: J.Perrins, D.Caskie, S.Morris;
Conversions: T.Smith (2);
Penalties: T.Smith (2);
Drop goal: N.Matthews

Feb 29 Bath 29 Gloucester 9 (League)
Try: M.Hannaford;
Conversion: T.Smith;
Drop goal: N.Matthews

Mar 6 Gloucester 13 Pontypool 8
Tries: A.Deacon, R.Fowke;
Conversion: M.Hamlin;
Penalty: N.Marment

**Mar 14 Gloucester 10 Northampton 17
(League)**
Try: J.Hawker;
Penalties: T.Smith (2)

**Mar 25 Gloucester 22 London Irish 15
(League)**
Tries: J.Perrins, P.Ashmead, S.Morris;
Conversions: N.Marment (2);
Penalty: N.Marment;
Drop goal: M.Hamlin

Mar 28 Orrell 18 Gloucester 12 (League)
Penalties: M.Hamlin (4)

**Apr 4 Gloucester 18 Bath 27
(Pilkington Cup Semi-final)**
Penalties: T.Smith (4);
Drop goals: T.Smith, N.Matthews
Extra time was played. The score after 80
minutes was 15-15.

Apr 11 Gloucester 29 Bristol 15 (League)
Tries: S.Morris (2), N.Scrivens, S.Masters,
D.Sims;
Conversions: T.Smith (3);
Penalty: T.Smith

Apr 14 Clifton 10 Gloucester 16
Try: A.Curtis;
Penalties: T.Smith (4)

Apr 18 Gloucester 15 Wasps 10 (League)
Try: L.Gardner;
Conversion: M.Roberts;
Penalties: M.Roberts (3)

Apr 20 Gloucester 37 Birkenhead Park 6
Tries: A.Stanley (2), D.Malpas, P.Beech,
R.Mogg, C.Dee, R.Fowke;

Conversions: M.Roberts (3)
Penalty: M.Roberts

**Apr 25 Harlequins 21 Gloucester 18
(League)**
Try: S.Masters;
Conversion: T.Smith;
Penalties: T.Smith (4)

North America Tour

**May 19 Old Blue (New York) 8
Gloucester 14**
Tries: J.Perrins, M.Hamlin, S.Morris;
Conversion: M.Hamlin

**May 23 Washington 12 Gloucester 28
(Boston Tournament)**

Tries: P.Ashmead, R.West, S.Morris, R.Fowke,
D.Caskie, D.Morgan;
Conversions: M.Hamlin (2)

**May 25 Vancouver 0 Gloucester 23
(Boston Tournament)**
Tries: R.Fowke (2), S.Morris, N.Marment;
Conversions: M.Hamlin (2);
Penalty: M.Hamlin

1992-93

J.Holder M.Elway C.Pope B.Howells T.Close J.Jarrett K.Richardson(Coach) J.Beaman A.Townsend E.Stephens(Team Sec) P.Williams
A.Mitchell T.Pritchard D.Wadley(Sec) P.Holford A.Windo A.Deacon M.Roberts S.Devereux D.Sims R.Fowke P.Ashmead A.Stanley P.Jones J.Perrins
A.Brinn R.Morris
D.Cummins R.Phillips D.Morgan M.Hannaford Canon M.Hughes(Pres) I.Smith(Capt) P.Ford(Chairman) T.Smith D.Caskie D.Kearsey I.Morgan

**Played 38 Won 28 Lost 10
For 852 Against 429
Captain: Ian Smith
Coach: Keith Richardson**
League: Played 12 Won 6 lost 6
For 173 Against 151
Position: 5th

Gloucester United
Played 36 Won 30 Lost 3 Drawn 3
For 1202 Against 420
Captain: Andrew Stanley

Most appearances: D.Sims 27, D.Caskie 26, S.Morris 25 (24 starts + 1 rep), T.Smith, R.West 23, R.Fowke, P.Jones 22, M.Roberts, 21, R.Phillips 21 (20+1)
Most tries: R.Fowke, S.Morris, T.Smith 9, M.Roberts 7, J.Perrins 6
Conversions: M.Roberts 25, P.Beech 14, T.Smith 9, P.Morris 6, J.Merchant 2
Penalties: M.Roberts 24, T.Smith 18, P.Beech 9, J.Merchant 3

The team was hit by a plague of injuries. Marcus Hannaford and Laurie Beck were injured at the start of the campaign, so there was no recognised scrum-half available for selection. At various points of the season Neil Matthews and Derrick Morgan were side-lined. This coupled with retirements and the departure of several players pre-season made it a difficult campaign.

Of the first five league games, four were lost, including a particularly dispiriting 6-21 loss at home to West Hartlepool. Relegation became a possibility, especially as four teams were to be relegated, but a late season rally removed that fear and the final position was mid-table respectability. There were good wins against Bath (away), Northampton (away), Bristol and Harlequins.

Due to the injuries some players had to play out of position; Tim Smith played on the wing and Damian Cummins at fly-half on occasions. There were opportunities for new players to make their mark, such as England Under 21 selection Paul Beech, and wingers Paul Holford and Mark Nicholson. It was a break-through season for Martin Roberts. He had an extended run at full-back and his accomplished place kicking, coupled with seven tries saw him total 157 points. Tim Smith missed several games through injury but still scored 117 points. It was notable that equal top try scorer was Bobby Fowke from the back-row of the forwards.

There was an exit from the Pilkington Cup at the first stage, a journey to Newcastle/Gosforth resulting in defeat.

In a fabulous season when a record 1202 points were scored, the United side won the Second XV Championship for the third season in a row.

In the Divisional Championship, Simon Morris was the club's sole representative, playing in all three games. He scored three tries against the North.

In August 1992, the club took part in a Euro Trophy in Leiden, Holland.

In May 1993 the inaugural Worthington National Tens Competition was staged at Kingsholm. Gloucester won the trophy beating Harlequins 29-0 in the final.

Note: The value of a try was increased to 5 points this season

Sep 1 Lydney 3 Gloucester 21
Tries: A.Windo, R.Fowke, M.Roberts;
Conversions: M.Roberts (3)

Sep 5 Gloucester 10 Blackheath 7
Tries: R.Phillips, P.Ashmead

Sep 8 Stroud 0 Gloucester 18
Tries: P.Miles, C.O'Donoghue;
Conversion: J.Merchant;
Penalties: J.Merchant (2)

Sep 12 Gloucester 17 Sale 11
Tries: J.Perrins, M.Roberts;
Conversions: M.Roberts (2);
Penalty: M.Roberts

Sep 19 London Scottish 8 Gloucester 3 (League)
Penalty: T.Smith

Sep 26 Leicester 22 Gloucester 21 (League)
Tries: D.Morgan, M.Hannaford;
Conversion: T.Smith;
Penalties: T.Smith (3)

Oct 3 Gloucester 21 Rugby 12 (League)
Tries: D.Morgan, penalty try;
Conversion: T.Smith;
Penalties: T.Smith (3)

Oct 17 Goucester 38 Bristol 11
Tries: R.Phillips (2), N.Matthews, J.Hawker, J.Perrins, I.Smith;
Conversion: T.Smith;
Penalties: T.Smith (2)

Oct 24 Wasps 14 Gloucester 9 (League)
Penalties: T.Smith (3)

Oct 31 Gloucester 6 West Hartlepool 21 (League)
Penalties: T.Smith, N.Matthews

Nov 3 Cheltenham 3 Gloucester 37
Tries: P.Holford, A.Deacon, G.Reayer, D.Cummins;
Conversion: M.Roberts;
Penalties: M.Roberts (5)

Nov 7 Pontypool 10 Gloucester 24
Tries: D.Cummins, J.Davis, D.Morgan, M.Roberts;
Conversions: M.Roberts (2)

Nov 13 Gloucester 31 Transvaal 11
Tries: S.Morris, M.Hannaford, penalty try;

Conversions: M.Roberts (2);
Penalties: M.Roberts (4)

Nov 14 Moseley 5 Gloucester 34
Tries: P.Holford, P.Glanville, J.Perrins, G.Mann, P.Beech;
Conversions: P.Beech (3);
Penalty: P.Beech

Nov 21 Gloucester 19 Saracens 5 (League)
Tries: R.West, D.Morgan;
Penalties: M.Roberts (3)

**Nov 24 Gloucester 62
Exeter University 15**
Tries: G.Reayer (2), G.Mann (2), T.Smth, J.Perrins, I.Morgan, J.Davis, R.Fowke, P.Morris;
Conversions: P.Morris (6)

**Nov 28 Newcastle/Gosforth 13
Gloucester 10 (Pilkington Cup)**
Try: A.Windo;
Conversion: M.Roberts;
Penalty: M.Roberts

Dec 5 Gloucester 36 Leicester 13
Tries: P.Miles (2), A.Windo, R.Fowke, S.Devereux, M.Roberts;
Conversions: M.Roberts (3)

Dec 12 Exeter 21 Gloucester 18
Penalties: M.Roberts (6)

Dec 19 Coventry 12 Gloucester 19
Tries: R.Fowke, D.Kearsey, J.Perrins;
Conversions: M.Roberts (2)

Dec 22 Neath 23 Gloucester 14
Tries: P.Ashmead, R.Phillips;
Conversions: M.Roberts (2)

Dec 26 Gloucester v Lydney - cancelled
Jan 2 Gloucester v Moseley - cancelled

Jan 9 London Irish 6 Gloucester 18 (League)
Tries: M.Roberts, penalty try;
Conversion: M.Roberts;
Penalties: M.Roberts (2)

Jan 15 Gloucester 19 Nottingham 3
Tries: P.Ashmead, D.Cummins, M.Roberts;
Conversions: M.Roberts (2)

Jan 23 Gloucester 10 Rosslyn Park 3
Try: S.Morris;
Conversion: M.Roberts;
Penalty: M.Roberts

Jan 30 Sale 19 Gloucester 17

Tries: G.Mann, T.Smith, D.Caskie;
Conversion: M.Roberts

Feb 5 Gloucester 42 Newport 7
Tries: T.Smith (3), P.Ashmead (2), D.Morgan, M.Hannaford;
Conversions: M.Roberts (2);
Penalty: M.Roberts

Feb 12 Gloucester 0 Bath 20 (League)

Feb 23 Gloucester 49 Clifton 3
Tries: S.Devereux (2), R.Fowke (2), A.Stanley (2), P.Morris, A.Windo;
Conversions: P.Beech (3)
Penalty: P.Beech

Feb 27 Gloucester 24 Richmond 15
Tries: D.Caskie, S.Morris, M.Roberts, P.Glanville;
Conversions: P.Beech, T.Smith

Mar 2 Newport 16 Gloucester 20
Tries: J.Merchant, I.Morgan, G.Mann;
Conversion: P.Beech;
Penalty: P.Beech

Mar 5 Gloucester 42 Bridgend 15
Tries: S.Morris (2), T.Smith, P.Holford, P.Miles, L.Beck;
Conversions: T.Smith (2), P.Beech;
Penalties: P.Beech (2)

Mar 13 Northampton 16 Gloucester 21 (League)
Tries: S.Morris, P.Holford;
Conversion: P.Beech;
Penalties: T.Smith (2), P.Beech

Mar 27 Gloucester 8 Orrell 13 (League)
Try: T.Smith;
Penalty: T.Smith

Apr 3 Bristol 9 Gloucester 22 (League)
Tries: T.Smith, D.Caskie, R.Phillips;
Conversions: P.Beech (2);
Penalty: P.Beech

Apr 10 Gloucester 25 Benneton Treviso 15
Tries: S.Morris, J.Davis, R.Fowke;
Conversions: P.Beech (2);
Penalties: P.Beech (2)

Apr 12 Gloucester 25 Fylde 8
Tries: J.Perrins, G.Reayer, C.Dee, A.Windo;
Conversion: J.Merchant;
Penalty: J.Merchant
Apr 17 Bath 16 Gloucester 17
Tries: R.Fowke, S.Morris, P.Glanville;
Conversion: T.Smith

Apr 24 Gloucester 25 Harlequins 5 (League)
Tries: R.Fowke, S.Morris, T.Smith;
Conversions: T.Smith (2);
Penalties: T.Smith (2)

Leiden, Holland (Euro Trophy)

Aug 14 Cascais (Portugal) 21 Gloucester 50
Tries: P.Ashmead (2), I.Smith (2), D.Morgan, D.Sims, D.Caskie, S.Devereux;

Conversions: T.Smith (5)

Aug 15 Bridgend 22 Gloucester 12 (Final)
Tries: S.Morris, R.Fowke;
Conversion: T.Smith

1993-94

J.Fider T.Pritchard P.Ford M.Elway A.Mitchell T.Close A.Townsend J.Beaman R.Collins D.Foyle T.Day R.Clewes F.Reed
R.Morris J.Hawker A.Stanley A.Windo A.Deacon S.Devereux P.Miles D.Sims R.West M.Nicholls P.Glanville D.Cummings J.Perrins M.Nicholson
R.Fowke E.Stephens K.Richardson(Coach)
S.Morris P.Jones B.Fenley D.Caskie T.Smith M.Hughes(Pres) I.Smith(Capt) A.Brinn(Chairman) P.Holford D.Kearsey I.Morgan P.Beech

Played 41 Won 22 Lost 17 Drawn 2
For 849 Against 610
Captain: Ian Smith
Director of Rugby: Barry Corless
Coach: Keith Richardson
League: Played 18 Won 6 Lost 10 Drawn 2
For 247 Against 356
Position: 8th

Gloucester United
Played 31 Won 29 Lost 2
For 990 Against 269

Most appearances: D.Sims 29 (27 starts + 2 rep),
B.Fenley 27 (26+1), D.Cummins 27 (26+1),
T.Smith, D.Caskie, I.Smith 26
Most tries: P.Holford 9, A.Sharp 8, M.Nicholson
7, B.Fenley, P.Miles, S.Morris, A.Windo 6,
Conversions: T.Smith 28, P.Beech 13, J.Merchant
7, M.Roberts, A.Johnson 4, G.Fenwick 1
Penalties: T.Smith 31, M.Roberts 11,
A.Johnson 8, P.Beech 7, J.Merchant 3, G.Fenwick
2, S.Cattermole 1
Drop goals: D.Cummins 3, P.Beech 2,
A.Johnson, T.Smith 1

An innovation saw Barrie Corless recruited
to be the club's first Director of Rugby. Keith
Richardson retained his post as Coach.
Corless had had some success in restoring
Northampton's fortunes, and much was expected
of him. However, the season could hardly have
started more depressingly. The first two league
games against Wasps and West Hartlepool
were drawn, but there followed four successive
defeats. Especially concerning was a lack of
spirit in a humiliating 46-17 defeat at Bath.

It was just as well that there was a short revival
of three wins on the trot, because in the second
half of the season five of the last seven games
were lost and the team finished with only the
two relegated clubs below them. In fact, safety
was only achieved in the penultimate game when
Orrell were beaten at Kingsholm.

Tim Smith who scored 161 points in all games,
saved the situation on several occasions, most
notably at London Irish when he scored all the
points with four penalties and a drop goal. Other
key players throughout were Paul Holford who
scored the most tries, Dave Sims, Don Caskie,
Damian Cummins and Ian Smith.

Gloucester reached the quarter-final of the
Pilkington Cup before losing disappointingly
at home to Orrell. Morale was not helped when
Keith Richardson left the club at the end of the
season to join Harlequins, as their coach.

Derrick Morgan moved on to Cheltenham after
248 games and 160 tries. Bob Phillips had made
191 appearances, before moving to Pontypool,
and Jeremy Bennett made his final and 115th
appearance in September.

Ian Smith played for Scotland against Ireland and
France and was a replacement against England.
Paul Holford and Dave Sims were replacements
when the South & South-West played New
Zealand at Redruth. In the Divisional
Championship Dave Sims and Paul Holford
played in two games. Holford scored a try against
London. Richard West played in one game.

For the fourth season running the United won the
Midlands & South-West Merit Table for second
XVs; a quite remarkable performance.

On 2 May 1994 the second Worthington National
Tens competition was again held at Kingsholm.
Again, Gloucester reached the final, but this time
lost to Bristol. On 8 May the Club travelled to
Ireland to play in the Kinsale Sevens, and won
the tournament, beating Old Belvedere 37-7 in
the final.

Sep 1 Lydney 3 Gloucester 0

Sep 2 Casale 10 Gloucester 45
Tries: M.Nicholson (2), P.Holford, P.Ashmead,
I.Smith, R.Fowke, J.Merchant;
Conversions: T.Smith (3), P.Beech, J.Merchant

Sep 4 Gloucester 34 Blackheath 14
Tries: P.Glanville, P.Jones, A.Martin, L.Beck,
A.Johnson;
Conversions: A.Johnson (3);

Penalty: A.Johnson

Sep 4 Benetton Treviso 18 Gloucester 13
Try: D.Caskie;
Conversion: T.Smith;
Penalties: T.Smith, P.Beech

Sep 11 Gloucester 9 Wasps 9 (League)
Penalties: T.Smith (2);
Drop goal: D.Cummins

Sep 14 Gloucester 15 Cheltenham 11
Penalties: J.Merchant (2), P.Beech;
Drop goal: P.Beech (2)

**Sep 18 Newcastle/Gosforth 12
Gloucester 12 (League)**
Penalties: T.Smith (2), P.Beech (2)

**Sep 25 Gloucester 14 Leicester 23
(League)**
Try: P.Holford;
Penalties: T.Smith (2), P.Beech

Oct 2 Bath 46 Gloucester 17 (League)
Tries: D.Cummins, P.Holford;
Conversions: T.Smith, P.Beech;
Penalty: P.Beech

Oct 5 Gloucester 39 Stroud 8
Tries: A.Windo, R.Baxter, D.Morgan,
I.Morgan, P.Bell, P.Miles;
Conversions: M.Roberts (3);Penalty:
M.Roberts

**Oct 9 Gloucester 9 London Irish 10
(League)**
Penalties: M.Roberts (3)

Oct 16 Gloucester 16 Cardiff 5
Try: T.Smith;
Conversion: M.Roberts;
Penalties: M.Roberts (3)

**Oct 19 Gloucester 11
South African Barbarians 15**
Try: D.Sims;
Penalties: M.Roberts, A.Johnson

Nov 6 Nottingham 26 Gloucester 14
Try: J.Hawker;
Penalties: M.Roberts (3)

**Nov 13 Bristol 16 Gloucester 12
(League)**
Penalties: A.Johnson (4)

**Nov 20 Gloucester 19 Northampton 14
(League)**
Try: A.Deacon;
Conversion: A.Johnson;

Penalties: A.Johnson (2), T.Smith (2)

Nov 27 Gloucester 19 Sale 16
Tries: B.Fenley, P.Bell, A.Martin;
Conversions: J.Merchant (2)

Dec 4 Orrell 6 Gloucester 10 (League)
Try: A.Johnson;
Conversion: T.Smith;
Penalty: T.Smith

**Dec 11 Gloucester 24 Harlequins 20
(League)**
Tries: A.Windo, A.Deacon, B.Fenley,
M.Nicholson;
Conversions: T.Smith (2)

**Dec 18 Nottingham 9 Gloucester 29
(Pilkington Cup)**
Tries: A.Windo, P.Miles, M.Nicholson;
Conversion: T.Smith;
Penalties: T.Smith (3);
Drop goal: A.Johnson

Dec 22 Newport 36 Gloucester 14
Tries: P.Beech, J.Merchant;
Conversions: P.Beech (2)

Dec 27 Gloucester 22 Lydney 3
Tries: G.Keyse, P.Glanville, B.Maslen;
Conversions: P.Beech, J.Merchant;
Penalty: P.Beech

Jan 1 Moseley 3 Gloucester 20
Tries: M.Nicholson, P.Miles;
Conversions: T.Smith (2);
Penalties: T.Smith (2)

Jan 8 Wasps 29 Gloucester 18 (League)
Tries: B.Fenley, penalty try;
Conversion: T.Smith;
Penalties: T.Smith (2)

**Jan 15 Gloucester 15
Newcastle/Gosforth 9 (League)**
Tries: P.Holford, penalty try;
Conversion: T.Smith;
Penalty: T.Smith

**Jan 22 Gloucester 11 Northampton 6
(Pilkington Cup)**
Try: P.Holford;
Penalties: T.Smith (2)

**Jan 29 Leicester 28 Gloucester 8
(League)**
Try: D.Sims;
Penalty: T.Smith

Feb 4 Gloucester 24 Pontypool 5
Tries: A.Sharp, J.Davis, J.Merchant;

Conversions: J.Merchant (3);
Penalty: J.Merchant

Feb 12 Gloucester 6 Bath 16 (League)
Penalty: T.Smith;
Drop goal: D.Cummins

**Feb 26 Gloucester 3 Orrell 10
(Pilkington Cup)**
Penalty: T.Smith

Mar 5 Gloucester 41 London Scottish 17
Tries: M.Nicholson (2), B.Fenley, A.Windo,
A.Deacon, T.Smith;
Conversions: T.Smith (4);
Penalty: T.Smith

Mar 9 Gloucester 79 Exeter University 5
Tries: P.Miles (3), S.Morris (3), M.Bedney (2),
P.Ashmead (2), I.Morgan, J.Davis, G.Keyse
Conversions: P.Beech (7)

**Mar 12 London Irish 12 Gloucester 15
(League)**
Penalties: T.Smith (4);
Drop goal: T.Smith

Mar 16 Bridgend 21 Gloucester 17
Tries: A.Windo, D.Kearsey, G.Fenwick;
Conversion: G.Fenwick

Mar 26 Gloucester 6 Bristol 24 (League)
Penalties: G.Fenwick (2)

Apr 2 Gloucester 50 Portuguese XV 0
Tries: A.Sharp (2), J.Perrins, S.Morris,
B.Fenley, P.Glanville, M.Nicholls, T.Smith;
Conversions: T.Smith (5)

**Apr 9 Northampton 19 Gloucester 3
(League)**
Drop goal: D.Cummins

Apr 13 Clifton 7 Gloucester 8
Try: M.Hamlin;
Penalty: S.Cattermole

Apr 16 Gloucester 78 Torquay Athletic 6
Tries: P.Holford (4), A.Sharp (3), G.Keyse (2),
M.Hamlin (2), I.Smith, S.Morris, T.Smith
Conversions: T.Smith (4)

Apr 23 Gloucester 30 Orrell 25 (League)
Tries: A.Sharp (2), S.Morris, B.Fenley;
Conversions: T.Smith (2);
Penalties: T.Smith (2)

**Apr 30 Harlequins 38 Gloucester 20
(League)**
Tries: I.Smith, A.Windo, D.Kearsey;
Conversion: P.Beech;
Penalty: T.Smith

J.Holder M.Elway C.Pope M.Nicholls T.Close J.Fidler J.Beaman R.Collins A.Townsend R.Clewes T.Day D.Foyle
A.Mitchell D.Wadley(Treas/Sec) R.Morris A.Powles A.Windo P.Glanville M.Nicholls D.Sims R.West S.Devereux M.Teague M.Roberts S.Morris
P.Holford P.Ashmead V.Wooley(Coach) E.Stephens(Team Sec)
M.Kimber B.Fenley P.Jones T.Smith A.Brinn(Chairman) A.Deacon(Capt) M.Hughes(Pres) L.Osborne I.Smith D.Caskie J.Hawker

Played 35 Won 17 Lost 17 Drawn 1
For 851 Against 612
Captain: Andy Deacon
Director of Rugby: Barrie Corless (until February 1995)
Coach: Viv Wooley
League games: Played 18 Won 6 Lost 11
Drawn 1
For 269 Against 336
Position: 7th

Gloucester United
Played 31 Won 26 Lost 5
For 1093 Against 526
Captain: Bobby Fowke

Most appearances: B.Fenley 30 (28 starts + 2rep), A.Deacon 29, M.Kimber 28, P.Holford, L.Osborne, D.Sims 27 (26+1), S.Morris 23, J.Hawker, R.West 20
Most tries: P.Ashmead 13, P.Holford 12, S.Morris 10
Conversions: L.Osborne 21, M.Mapletoft 18, M.Kimber 7, T.Smith, M.Roberts, P.Hart 3, S.Cattermole, M.Hamlin 2
Penalties: M.Mapletoft 26, L.Osborne 19, T.Smith 5, M.Hamlin 2
Drop goals: M.Kimber 8, L.Osborne 1

After a successful pre-season tour of South Africa, there was an air of optimism that Barrie Corless' second season in charge would produce a better set of results. It did not happen. Five of the first seven league games were lost. Even then there was only a slight improvement. Form was erratic, and Corless did not seem to be capable of motivating the players. In February Corless was relieved of his post, ironically his last game was a win over Leicester. Viv Wooley was left in charge for the rest of the season. There was a particularly humiliating loss at Orrell, which must rank as one of Gloucester's worst ever away displays. In the end although finishing seventh from ten, Gloucester only had one more point than relegated Northampton. Equally depressing was the exit from the Pilkington Cup by ten clear points, to second division Wakefield. Things were not helped by a long injury list. At various times Mark Mapletoft, John Hawker, Ashley Johnson, Andy Deacon, Mark Nicholson, Simon Morris and Don Caskie were all unavailable.

One of Barrie Corless's successes was to recruit Mark Mapletoft from Rugby. Although only making 16 appearances due to injury, he still scored 124 points, hinting at the goal kicking skills which would prove so effective in future seasons. In Mapletoft's absence Lee Osborne took on kicking duties and totalled 122 points. Promising young hooker Phil Greening captained England Colts. In top form all season was Dave Sims and he was awarded the captaincy for the 1995-96 season. Top try scorer this season was Paul Ashmead, who at the end of campaign left to play for Rugby, after making 158 appearances. Marcus Hannaford only appeared once and retired having played in 255 games. Mike Hamlin also played in one game to bring his appearances to 345. He had scored a total of 561 points. He went on to play for Coney Hill. After playing for Moseley for two seasons, Mike Teague returned to Kingsholm for one final campaign, and retired at the age of 35, having made 306 appearances.

Ian Smith played for Scotland in two internationals against Argentina. Richard West played for England 'A' against Natal. In the Divisional Championship Dave Sims, Simon Morris and Paul Holford played in all three games, with Holford scoring against the North. John Hawker played in two games, and Pete Glanville in one.

It had been a difficult season, but further challenges were just over the horizon. Professional rugby was approaching.

Sep 3 Gloucester 44 Lydney 0
Tries: S.Morris (2), P.Holford, B.Maslen, D.Sims, S.Cattermole;
Conversions: L.Osborne (2), M.Mapletoft, S.Cattermole;
Penalties: M.Mapletoft (2)

Sep 6 Stroud 7 Gloucester 63
Tries: C.Raymond (3), S.Devereux (2), A.Sharp (2), P.Ashmead (2), A.Windo, L.Beck;
Conversions: M.Roberts (3), S.Cattermole

Sep 10 Wasps 45 Gloucester 8 (League)
Try: S.Morris;
Penalty: M.Mapletoft

Sep 17 Gloucester 48 West Hartlepool 12 (League)
Tries: S.Morris (3), P.Holford (2), T.Smith, M.Mapletoft;
Conversions: M.Mapletoft (5);
Penalty: M.Mapletoft

Sep 24 Leicester 16 Gloucester 6 (League)
Penalty: M.Mapletoft;
Drop goal: M.Kimber

Oct 1 Gloucester 10 Bath 15 (League)
Try: T.Smith;
Conversion: M.Mapletoft;
Penalty: M.Mapletoft

Oct 8 Sale 16 Gloucester 14 (League)
Try: T.Smith;
Penalties: M.Mapletoft (2);
Drop goal: M.Kimber

Oct 15 Gloucester 19 Bristol 17 (League)
Try: D.Sims;
Conversion: M.Mapletoft;
Penalties: M.Mapletoft (4)

Oct 22 Northampton 9 Gloucester 6 (League)
Penalties: M.Mapletoft (2)

Oct 29 Gloucester 9 Orrell 6 (League)
Penalties: M.Mapletoft (2);
Drop goal: M.Kimber

Nov 5 Harlequins 10 Gloucester 14 (League)
Tries: P.Holford (2);
Conversions: L.Osborne (2)

Nov 8 Cardiff 20 Gloucester 17
Tries: I.Morgan, D.Sims, L.Osborne;
Conversion: M.Mapletoft

Nov 19 Gloucester 7 Canterbury (NZ) 70
Try: S.Devereux;
Conversion: M.Kimber

Nov 25 Gloucester 45 Bridgend 0
Tries: L.Osborne (2), P.Ashmead, B.Fenley,
M.Cornwell, M.Kimber + penalty try;
Conversions: M.Kimber (5)

Nov 30 Gloucester 36 Clifton 12
Tries: G.Keyse (2), J.Perrins (2), P.Miles,
M.Cornwell;
Conversions: P.Hart (3)

Dec 3 Bedford 16 Gloucester 14
Tries: M.Kimber, B.Maslen;
Conversions: L.Osborne (2)

Dec 9 Gloucester 73 Coventry 3
Tries: P.Ashmead (4), S.Devereux (2), P.Holford,
A.Windo, M.Kimber, B.Fenley, D.Sims;
Conversions: M.Mapletoft (6);
Penalties: M.Mapletoft (2)

Dec 13 Cheltenham 14 Gloucester 25

Tries: R.Fidler, P.Greening, G.Keyse;
Conversions: M.Hamlin (2);
Penalties: M.Hamlin (2)

Dec 17 Wakefield 19 Gloucester 9 (Pilkington Cup)
Penalties: M.Mapletoft (2);
Drop goal: M.Kimber

Dec 26 Lydney 5 Gloucester 14
Try: R.Saltmarsh;
Penalties: L.Osborne (2);
Drop goal: L.Osborne

Dec 31 Gloucester 35 Moseley 6
Tries: P.Greening, P.Holford, T.Smith,
M.Teague, B.Fenley;
Conversions: L.Osborne (2);
Penalty: L.Osborne;
Drop goal: M.Kimber

Jan 7 Gloucester 16 Wasps 21 (League)
Try: M.Mapletoft;
Conversion: M.Mapletoft;
Penalties: M.Mapletoft (3)

Jan 14 West Hartlepool 22 Gloucester 21 (League)
Tries: M.Teague, P.Ashmead;
Conversion: M.Mapletoft;
Penalties: M.Mapletoft (2);
Drop goal: M.Kimber

Jan 20 Gloucester 72 Exeter 5
Tries: D.Caskie (3), P.Ashmead (2), B.Fenley,
S.Morris, B.Maslen, M.Teague, M.Cornwell,
P.Holford, M.Kimber;
Conversions: L.Osborne (6)

Feb 4 Rugby 33 Gloucester 28
Tries: P.Ashmead (2), S.Morris, L.Osborne;
Conversion: T.Smith;
Penalties: L.Osborne (2)

Feb 12 Gloucester 9 Leicester 3 (League)
Penalties: L.Osborne (3)

Feb 26 Gloucester 35 Waterloo 16
Tries: D.Caskie (2), D.Sims, B.Fenley, S.Morris;
Conversions: L.Osborne (2);
Penalties: L.Osborne, T.Smith

Mar 4 Bath 19 Gloucester 19 (League)
Try: P.Holford;
Conversion: L.Osborne;
Penalties: L.Osborne (2);
Drop goals: M.Kimber (2)

Mar 11 Gloucester 21 Northern Transvaal 31
Tries: P.Glanville, S.Morris;

Conversion: L.Osborne;
Penalties: L.Osborne (3)

Mar 17 Gloucester 44 Newport 19
Tries: T.Smith, H.Brown, M.Roberts, P.Miles,
C.Dee, R.Saltmarsh;
Conversions: T.Smith (2), M.Mapletoft,
M.Kimber;
Penalties: T.Smith, M.Mapletoft

Mar 25 Gloucester 8 Sale 20 (League)
Try: P.Holford;
Penalty: L.Osborne

Apr 8 Bristol 21 Gloucester 17 (League)
Tries: P.Holford (2), M.Teague;
Conversion: L.Osborne

Apr 15 Gloucester 14 Northampton 13 (League)
Try: D.Sims;
Penalties: T.Smith (3)

Apr 22 Orrell 43 Gloucester 14 (League)
Try: P.Ashmead;
Penalties: L.Osborne (3)

Apr 29 Gloucester 17 Harlequins 28 (League)
Tries: M.Cornwell (2);
Conversions: L.Osborne (2);
Penalty: L.Osborne

Pre-Season Tour of South Africa

Aug 6 Hamilton 27 Gloucester 23
Tries: P.Ashmead, B.Fenley, P.Holford,
M.Nicholls;
Drop goal: T.Smith

Aug 9 Milnerton 11 Gloucester 38
Tries: S.Morris (2), P.Holford (2);
Conversions: M.Mapletoft (3);
Penalties: P.Mapletoft (3);
Drop goal: S.Cattermole

Aug 12 Belville 7 Gloucester 41
Tries: T.Smith (3), P.Holford (2), P.Glanville;
Conversions: M.Mapletoft (4);
Drop goal: S.Cattermole

Aug 16 Stellenbosch University 9 Gloucester 26
Tries: P.Holford (2), R.West;
Conversion: M.Mapletoft;
Penalties: M.Mapletoft (2);
Drop goal: L.Osborne

1995-96

R.Collins J.Holder T.Pritchard C.Pope A.Townsend T.Close A.Mitchell E.Stephens J.Beaman H.Davie R.Clewes D.Foyle T.Heale
R.Morris D.Wadley(Sec/Treas) M.Peters R.Rolleston(Physio) A.Powles P.Glanville M.Lloyd A.Deacon P.Miles R.Fidler C.Raymond M.Roberts
A.Windo W.Bullock A.Stanley Canon M.Hughes J.Fidler(Team Sec) M.Teague(Team Manager) R.Hill(Dir of Coaching)
P.Greening L.Osborne S.Benton D.Caskie T.Smith T.Day(Pres) D.Sims(Capt) A.Brinn(Chairman) J.Hawker I.Smith B.Fenley M.Kimber P.Holford

Played 34 Won 17 Lost 16 Drawn 1
For 758 Against 643
Captain: Dave Sims
Director of Coaching: Richard Hill
League games: Played 18 Won 6 Lost 12
For 275 Against 370
Position: 8th

Gloucester United
Played 31 Won 23 Lost 8
For 742 Against 456
Captain: Andrew Stanley

Most appearances: M.Kimber 26, P.Holford,
M.Roberts, D.Sims 25, D.Caskie 22,
L.Osborne 21 (15 starts + 6 rep),
C.Raymond 21 (20+1), A.Deacon 19 (17+2),
P.Glanville 19 (18+1)
Most tries: P.Holford 8, M.Cornwell,
M.Peters 6, D.Caskie 5
Conversions: G.Fenwick 19,
L.Osborne 9, T.Smith 7, M.Mapletoft 5,
M.Kimber, A.Saverimuto 3, P.Hart 1
Penalties: T.Smith 26, G.Fenwick 12,
M.Mapletoft 9, L.Osborne 8, M.Kimber 7,
A.Saverimuto 2, A.Windo 1
Drop goals: M.Kimber 11, P.Hart, T.Smith 1

On 27 August 1995, just before the season opened
it was announced that Rugby Union would go
"open", in other words players could be paid. In
fact, it has to be said that this only recognised
what had been happening for several years all
around the rugby world. The RFU said that
there would be one year's moratorium so that
clubs could prepare. Following the departure of
Barrie Corless, a chief executive, Mike Coley
was appointed to run the commercial side of
the club. Richard Hill was made Director of

Coaching in the autumn of 1995.
On the field the Cherry and Whites struggled.
Nine of the first ten league games were lost.
There was a brief revival as Richard Hill's
influence started to make an impression, but
by April relegation was a real possibility. Bath,
who would win the league, visited Kingsholm to
find that Gloucester were rent by injuries. Seven
players were unavailable. The match was played
on a Wednesday under floodlights, which seem
to produce a strange magic at Kingsholm. In
front of 10,000 the depleted team tore into Bath.
After only four minutes Scott Benton broke
and gave a scoring chance to Paul Holford who
crossed in the corner. Tim Smith converted from
the touch-line, and later kicked three penalties.
Gloucester played like heroes to triumph 16-10.

By the time of the last game, it appeared to be
a straight shoot-out between Gloucester and
Saracens for the second relegation spot (West
Hartlepool having lost all their games). The
forwards saw them home. In the event it was
decided that there would be no relegation as the
league was to be extended! Nevertheless, it had
been a big scare and it was realised that changes
had to be made if the club was to survive as a
major force in the new professional world. Hill
demanded much higher levels of fitness, and
attendance to basics, but it was at last dawning
that the club could no longer rely on local players
alone to maintain a place at the highest level.

Captain, Dave Sims, led by example and was
ably supported by Phil Greening, and Pete
Glanville up front, whilst Bruce Fenley and then
Scott Benton were both live-wire scrum-halves.
Mark Mapletoft was missing through injury for
most of the season and was greatly missed.

Two players, Tim Smith and Simon Morris left
at the end of the season to play for the ambitious
Worcester. Smith had made 351 appearances and
scored 2703 points, whilst Morris played in 114
games. Damian Cummins (174 appearances)
also called time on his Gloucester career.

Dave Sims played for England 'A' against the
'A' teams of France, Italy and Ireland. Phil
Greening played against France 'A'. In the
Divisional Championship, Paul Holford,
Greening and Pete Glanville played in all three
games. Glanville scored a try against the North.
Bruce Fenley played in two matches, scoring a
try against the Midlands. Tony Windo and Dave
Sims played in one game. Rob Fidler was a
replacement in two games, and Ed Pearce in one.

Sep 2 Gloucester 39 Wakefield 12
Tries: I.Smith (2), R.Fidler, A.Martin, L.Beck;
Conversions: L.Osborne (4);
Penalty: L.Osborne;
Drop goal: M.Kimber

Sep 9 Gloucester 17 Sale 22 (League)
Try: D.Sims;
Penalties: L.Osborne (3);
Drop goal: T.Smith

Sep 16 Bath 37 Gloucester 11 (League)
Try: P.Holford;
Penalty: L.Osborne;
Drop goal: M.Kimber

**Sep 23 West Hartlepool 19 Gloucester 27
(League)**
Tries: P.Holford (2), D.Sims, A.Deacon;
Conversions: M.Kimber (2);

Penalty: M.Kimber

Sep 30 Gloucester 14 Leicester 27 (League)
Try: P.Holford;
Penalties: M.Kimber (3)

Oct 7 Orrell 21 Gloucester 3 (League)
Penalty: T.Smith

Oct 14 Gloucester 15 Wasps 26 (League)
Penalties: T.Smith (4);
Drop goal: M.Kimber

Oct 21 Bristol 22 Gloucester 16 (League)
Try: M.Kimber;
Conversion: T.Smith;
Penalties: T.Smith (3)

Oct 28 Gloucester 13 Harlequins 24 (League)
Try: B.Fenley;
Conversion: T.Smith;
Penalties: T.Smith (2)

Nov 4 Saracens 19 Gloucester 16 (League)
Try: A.Windo;
Conversion: T.Smith;
Penalties: T.Smith (2);
Drop goal: M.Kimber

Nov 11 Sale 21 Gloucester 13 (League)
Tries: D.Sims, P.Miles;
Penalty: T.Smith

Nov 14 Gloucester 27 Cheltenham 20
Tries: M.Cornwell, M.Peters, A.Stanley;
Conversions: G.Fenwick (3);
Penalties: G.Fenwick (2)

Nov 17 Gloucester 63 Bedford 15
Tries: M.Cornwell (3), M.Nicholson, J.Perrins, C.Hannaford, M.Lloyd, H.Brown, P.York;
Conversions: G.Fenwick (9)

Nov 22 Clifton 12 Gloucester 45
Tries: P.York (2), M.Kimber (2), A.Deacon, D.Caskie, M.Cornwell;
Conversions: G.Fenwick (5)

Dec 2 Gloucester 34 Vaal Triangle (SA) 10

Tries: T.Smith, D.Caskie, M.Cornwell, M.Peters, S.Benton, P.Miles;
Conversions: T.Smith (2)

Dec 9 Moseley 31 Gloucester 5
Try: C.Dee

Dec 15 Coventry 8 Gloucester 8
Try: A.Windo;
Penalty: A.Windo

Dec 23 Gloucester 47 Walsall 0 (Pilkington Cup)
Tries: P.Glanville (2), D.caskie (2), P.Holford, A.Deacon, P.Miles, T.Beim;
Conversions: T.Smith, P.Hart
Drop goal: P.Hart

Jan 6 Gloucester 17 West Hartlepool 16 (League)
Try: T.Beim;
Penalties: T.Smith (3), L.Osborne

Jan 13 Bristol 14 Gloucester 31
Tries: A.Stanley, M.Roberts, M.Lloyd, S.Devereux;
Conversion: M.Kimber;
Penalties: M.Kimber (2)
Drop goal: M.Kimber

Jan 20 Waterloo 28 Gloucester 42
Tries: M.Peters (4), D.Caskie, C.Mulraine;
Conversions: A.Saverimutto (3);
Penalties: A.Saverimutto (2)

Feb 10 Nottingham 10 Gloucester 36 (Pilkington Cup)
Tries: C.Raymond (2), L.Osborne, M.Lloyd, penalty try;
Conversions: L.Osborne (4);
Penalty: M.Kimber

Feb 17 Gloucester 27 Orrell 0 (League)
Tries: M.Roberts, A.Windo;
Conversion: G.Fenwick;
Penalties: G.Fenwick (4);
Drop goal: M.Kimber

Feb 24 Gloucester 22 Wasps 9 (Pilkington Cup)

Tries: D.Sims, M.Lloyd;
Penalties: G.Fenwick (2);
Drop goals: M.Kimber (2)

Mar 2 Gloucester 23 Swansea 33
Tries: H.Conradie, B.Fenley, P.Bell;
Conversion: L.Osborne;
Penalties: L.Osborne (2)

Mar 5 Gloucester 39 Army 31
Tries: P.Holford (2), M.Mapletoft, R.West, C.Mulraine;
Conversions: M.Mapletoft (4);
Penalties: M.Mapletoft (2)

Mar 19 Lydney 21 Gloucester 12
Penalties: T.Smith (4)

Mar 23 Bath 19 Gloucester 10 (Pilkington Cup Semi-Final)
Try: S.Benton;
Conversion: M.Mapletoft;
Drop goal: M.Kimber

Mar 30 Wasps 21 Gloucester 10 (League)
Penalty try;
Conversion: G.Fenwick;
Penalty: G.Fenwick

Apr 6 Gloucester 18 Bristol 14 (League)
Penalties: G.Fenwick (3), M.Mapletoft (2);
Drop goal: M.Kimber

Apr 10 Gloucester 16 Bath 10 (League)
Try: P.Holford;
Conversion: T.Smith;
Penalties: T.Smith (3)

Apr 13 Harlequins 33 Gloucester 19 (League)
Tries: T.Smith, C.Raymond;
Penalties: T.Smith (3)

Apr 24 Leicester 28 Gloucester 6 (League)
Penalties: M.Mapletoft (2)

Apr 27 Gloucester 17 Saracens 10 (League)
Try: A.Windo;
Penalties: M.Mapletoft (3);
Drop goal: M.Kimber

1996-97

Played 42 Won 23 Lost 18 Drawn 1
For 1053 Against 1003
Captain: Dave Sims
Director of Coaching: Richard Hill
Premiership: Played 22 Won 11 Lost 10 Drawn 1
For 476 Against 589
Position: 7th

Gloucester United
Played 25 Won 20 Lost 5
For 889 Against 541

Most appearances: M.Mapletoft, A.Windo, R.Fidler 33 (32 starts + 1 rep), D.Sims 32 (31+1), S.Devereux 29, S.Benton,

P.Greening 28, M.Lloyd, A.Deacon 27
Most tries: M.Mapletoft 18, M.Lloyd 13, A.Saverimutto, A.Lumsden 10
Conversions: M.Mapletoft 61, A.Morris 8, M.Kimber 6, L.Osborne 2, N.Paisley 1
Penalties: M.Mapletoft 77, A.Morris 5, M.Kimber 1

J.Fidler T.Day C.Stephenson R.Rolleston M.Potter J.Beaman J.Jarrett E.Stephens M.Warner J.Milner M.Nicholls R.Clewes D.Foyle J.Brain
W.Nicholls A.Mitchell D.Wadley A.Saverimutto T.Woodman A.Windo P.Vickery E.Pearce R.Fidler S.Devereux M.Roberts P.Glanville C.Emmerson
L.Beck D.Caskie T.Curtis R.Hill(Dir of Coaching)
E.Anderson A.Stanley A.Deacon N.Carter P.Greening R.Collins(Pres) D.Sims(Capt) A.Brinn(Chairman) S.Benton M.Mapletoft A.Lumsden C.Catling
A.Metcalfe

Drop goals: M.Mapletoft 5, C.Catling 1

This was the first season after the sport went open, and payment of players became permissible. The old "First Division" became the "Premiership". Captain Dave Sims became the club's first professional player, signing a contract in May 1996. He certainly earned his money, as the team got off to what was becoming the usual dreadful start. The first league game was an awful drubbing away to Harlequins. Richard Hill had selected what was in effect a second fifteen, and the result was inevitable. He owned up to his mistake, but the next four league games were all lost. Thankfully the players kept faith with Hill and there followed a splendid run of seven wins on the trot, which ensured Premiership survival.

A good cup run ended at the semi-final stage to Leicester. Two weeks later the Tigers were back at Kingsholm for an evening league game. As against Bath in the previous season, a mid-week game under the lights inspired Gloucester and in a magnificent game, a last-minute Phil Greening try, when he was driven over by the inspired forwards, brought the scores level at 30-30. Mapletoft converted from the touch-line to huge cheers. A nail biting few minutes of injury time followed but the team emerged victorious. A jubilant pitch invasion followed. Tom Walkinshaw, a keen rugby fan was clearly impressed, for only a few weeks later he announced a £3 million investment in the club. Gloucester was at last embracing the new professional era.

This season saw Gloucester's first taste of European Rugby, with only moderate success.

The Anglo-Welsh Competition was not a success and was abandoned mid-season.

Mark Mapletoft topped all categories and scored a total of 458 points in the season, the most since Peter Butler's 488 in 1973-74. In October against Ebbw Vale he scored 34 points, a club record. Chris Catling was a potent attacking full-back. As demonstrated against Leicester, the forwards were capable of stirring performances. There was a rock-solid front row of Andy Deacon, Phil Greening and Tony Windo, which laid the foundation. Rob Fidler, Dave Sims, Simon Devereux and Pete Glanville were all outstanding.

Ian Smith only played a few games and retired at the end of the season after 336 appearances. He would later go on to coach at Moseley. Several other players also made their last Gloucester appearances. Long serving prop Pete Jones who first played in 1982 had made 189 appearances, whilst Andrew Stanley who made his first appearance in 1985, also retired. He had made 146 appearances and captained the United for five seasons. Paul Holford (107 appearances) departed for Worcester. Hooker John Hawker (144) retired, as did Don Caskie (201).

Mark Mapletoft played for England against Argentina and kicked a penalty. Phil Greening was a replacement against Italy. The club had several players who appeared for England 'A'. Dave Sims played against Argentina, Scotland 'A' and France 'A'. Chris Catling, Rob Fidler and Mapletoft (2 conversions and 2 penalties) played against South Africa 'A'. Against Ireland 'A' Mapletoft scored a try, 4 conversions and 2 penalties, whilst Scott Benton scored a try.

Mapletoft was a replacement against France 'A' and kicked a conversion.

Aug 23 Gloucester 15 Pontypridd 5
Tries: S.Edwards, M.Mapletoft;
Conversion: M.Mapletoft;
Penalty: M.Mapletoft

Aug 31 Harlequins 75 Gloucester 19 (Premiership)
Tries: L.Osborne, M.Lloyd, C.Mulraine;
Conversions: L.Osborne (2)

Sep 7 Gloucester 12 Sale 16 (Premiership)
Penalties: M.Mapletoft (4)

Sep 11 Newbridge 17 Gloucester 26 (Anglo-Welsh Comp.)
Tries: C.Mulraine, M.Mapletoft;
Conversions: M.Mapletoft (2);
Penalties: M.Mapletoft (4)

Sep 14 Saracens 41 Gloucester 11 (Premiership)
Try: M.Lloyd;
Penalties: M.Mapletoft (2)

Sep 21 Gloucester 29 Bath 45 (Premiership)
Tries: A.Deacon, D.Sims, P.Greening;
Conversion: M.Mapletoft;
Penalties: M.Mapletoft (4)

Sep 28 Leicester 32 Gloucester 14 (Premiership)
Try: E.Anderson;
Penalties: M.Mapletoft (3)

Oct 2 Gloucester 64 Dunvant 16

(Anglo-Welsh Comp.)
Tries: R.York (3), A.Lumsden (2), M.Peters (2),
A.Saverimutto, S.Benton, M.Mapletoft;
Conversions: M.Mapletoft (7)

**Oct 6 Gloucester 28 Wasps 23
(Premiership)**
Tries: A.Saverimutto, C.Catling;
Penalties: M.Mapletoft (6)

**Oct 12 Gloucester 59 Ebbw Vale 7
(European Conference)**
Tries: M.Mapletoft (4), S.Devereux,
A.Saverimutto, E.Anderson, A.Lumsden +
Penalty try;
Conversions: M.Mapletoft (7)

**Oct 16 Gloucester 10 Begles Bourdeaux
17 (European Conference)**
Try: Penalty try;
Conversion: M.Mapletoft;
Penalty: M.Mapletoft

**Oct 19 Swansea 62 Gloucester 12
(European Conference)**
Penalties: A.Morris (4)

**Oct 27 Gloucester 9 Bourgoin 24
(European Conference)**
Penalties: M.Mapletoft (3)

**Nov 2 London Irish 13 Gloucester 29
(European Conference)**
Tries: A.Lumsden (2), P.Greening (2),
A.Saverimutto;
Conversions: M.Mapletoft (2)

Nov 5 Gloucester 32 Combined Services 7
Tries: P.Holford (3), M.Lloyd (2), M.Cornwell;
Conversion: N.Paisley

**Nov 9 West Hartlepool 14 Gloucester 23
(Premiership)**
Tries: A.Lumsden, M.Mapletoft;
Conversions: M.Mapletoft (2);
Penalties: M.Mapletoft (3)

**Nov 16 Orrell 3 Gloucester 49
(Premiership)**
Tries: A.Saverimutto (2), S.Benton, A.Windo,
A.Lumsden, M.Peters;
Conversions: M.Mapletoft (5)
Penalties: M.Mapletoft (3)

Nov 19 Gloucester 33 R.A.F 7
Tries: I.Smith, E.Anderson, P.Holford, P.Vickery,
S.Pearman;
Conversions: A.Morris (4)

Nov 23 Wakefield 29 Gloucester 24
Tries: S.Pearman, L.Beck, K.Wilkinson;

Conversions: A.Morris (3);
Penalty: A.Morris

**Nov 30 Gloucester 76 Newbridge 0
(Anglo-Welsh Comp.)**
Tries: M.Mapletoft (3), C.Catling (2), M.Lloyd
(2), A.Saverimutto (2), S.Devereux, D.Sims,
M.Peters
Conversions: M.Mapletoft (8)

**Dec 7 Gloucester 29 London Irish 19
(Premiership)**
Tries: S.Benton, M.Roberts;
Conversions: M.Mapletoft (2);
Penalties: M.Mapletoft (4);
Drop goal: M.Mapletoft

**Dec 10 Ebbw Vale 15 Gloucester 22
(Anglo-Welsh Comp.)**
Tries: W.Bullock, P.Glanville, J.Hawker;
Conversions: M.Kimber (2);
Penalty: M.Kimber

Dec 14 Moseley 22 Gloucester 7
Try: M.Peters;
Conversion: A.Morris

**Dec 21 Gloucester 55 Leeds 20
(Pilkington Cup)**
Tries: M.Lloyd (2), M.Mapletoft (2), D.Sims,
S.Benton, P.Glanville;
Conversions: M.Mapletoft (4);
Penalties: M.Mapletoft (4)

**Jan 11 London Irish 20 Gloucester 21
(Premiership)**
Tries: R.Fidler, P.Glanville;
Conversion: M.Mapletoft;
Penalties: M.Mapletoft (2);
Drop goal: M.Mapletoft

**Jan 18 Gloucester 37 West Hartlepool 10
(Premiership)**
Tries: M.Lloyd (3), M.Mapletoft, A.Windo;
Conversions: M.Mapletoft (3);
Penalty: M.Mapletoft
Drop goal: M.Mapletoft

**Jan 25 Gloucester 18 Bristol 12
(Pilkington Cup)**
Tries: A.Windo, S.Benton;
Conversion: M.Mapletoft;
Penalties: M.Mapletoft (2)

Feb 8 Gloucester 30 Orrell 0 (Premiership)
Tries: M.Mapletoft (2), M.Lloyd, M.Peters;
Conversions: M.Mapletoft (2);
Penalties: M.Mapletoft (2)

**Feb 18 Bristol 18 Gloucester 13
(Premiership)**

Tries: P.Glanville;
Conversion: M.Mapletoft;
Penalties: M.Mapletoft;
Drop goal: C.Catling

**Feb 22 Wakefield 21 Gloucester 25
(Pilkington Cup)**
Tries: M.Peters, Penalty tries (2);
Conversions: M.Mapletoft (2);
Penalties: M.Mapletoft (2)

**Mar 4 Gloucester 19 Northampton 6
(Premiership)**
Try: S.Benton;
Conversion: M.Mapletoft;
Penalties: M.Mapletoft (4)

**Mar 9 Wasps 36 Gloucester 10
(Premiership)**
Try: C.Catling;
Conversion: M.Mapletoft;
Penalty: M.Mapletoft

Mar 14 Bedford 58 Gloucester 19
Tries: N.Matthews, A.Saverimutto,
C.Emmerson;
Conversions: M.Kimber (2);

Mar 18 Gloucester 29 Army 36
Tries: L.Beck, R.Ward, W.Gay, H.Dawson,
M.Kimber;
Conversions: M.Kimber (2)

**Mar 29 Gloucester 13 Leicester 26
(Pilkington Cup Semi-Final)**
Try: C.Catling;
Conversion: M.Mapletoft;
Penalties: M.Mapletoft (2)

Apr 5 Gloucester 9 Saracens 6 (Premiership)
Penalty: M.Mapletoft;
Drop goal: M.Mapletoft (2)

**Apr 8 Gloucester 32 Leicester 30
(Premiership)**
Tries: A.Lumsden, P.Greening;
Conversions: M.Mapletoft (2);
Penalties: M.Mapletoft (6)

Apr 12 Sale 52 Gloucester 12 (Premiership)
Tries: M.Mapletoft, A.Lumsden;
Conversion: M.Mapletoft

**Apr 19 Gloucester 11 Harlequins 27
(Premiership)**
Try: S.Benton;
Penalties: M.Mapletoft (2)

**Apr 26 Gloucester 20 Bristol 20
(Premiership)**
Tries: M.Lloyd, N.Carter;

Conversions: M.Mapletoft (2);
Penalties: M.Mapletoft (2)

Tries: A.Deacon, M.Mapletoft, A.Saverimutto;
Penalties: M.Mapletoft (2)

Tries: A.Lumsden, C.Catling;
Conversion: M.Mapletoft;
Penalties: M.Mapletoft (5)

**Apr 30 Bath 71 Gloucester 21
(Premiership)**

**May 3 Northampton 25 Gloucester 27
(Premiership)**

1997-98

L.Beck T.Woodman N.Carter A.Windo S.Devereux M.Roberts N.Osman C.Emmerson C.Fortey A.Deacon
R.Hill(Dir of Coaching) P.Balsom(Fitness Advisor) P.Vickery M.Lloyd A.Gibbs D.Sims M.Cornwell R.Fidler R.Ward E.Pearce J.Brain(Coach)
J.Fidler(Team Manager)
N.McCarthy I.Sanders P.Saint-André P.Greening A.Lumsden P.Glanville(Capt) M.Mapletoft S.Benton C.Catling R.Tombs R.Saint-André T.Fanolua

**Played 38 Won 23 Lost 14 Drawn 1
For 1050 Against 847
Owner: Tom Walkinshaw
Captain: Pete Glanville
Director of Rugby: Richard Hill**
Premiership: Played 22 Won 11 Lost 10 drawn 1
For 512 Against 528
Position: 7th

Gloucester United
Played 20 Won 8 Lost 11 Drawn 1
For 514 Against 517
Captain: Andrew Stanley

Most appearances: R.Tombs 34, N.Carter 34
(33 starts + 1 rep), M.Mapletoft 32 (31+1),
T.Fanolua 32, P.Glanville 30, R.Fidler 29,
C.Catling, A.Windo 28, S.Devereux 28 (26+2)
Most tries: T.Fanolua 14, P.St.Andre 12,
M.Mapletoft 9, N.Osman 7
Conversions: M.Mapletoft 63, S.Ward 10,
A.Morris, T.Fanolua 4, N.Osman 2
Penalties: M.Mapletoft 78, A.Morris 2,
T.Fanolua, S.Ward 1
Drop goals: M.Mapletoft 6

For the start of the season the ground capacity
had been increased to 10,800 due to the
construction of more hospitality boxes and a
temporary stand on the grandstand side of the
ground.

The season started with a greatly enhanced
back division. There were exciting signings
including Phillipe St.Andre the France captain
on the wing, and in the centre internationals
Terry Fanolua from Samoa and Australian
Richard Tombs. The first game started with
a bang as St.Andre scored two glorious tries
against Bristol. Nevertheless, four of the first
six Premiership games were lost. The team then
settled and finished comfortably in mid-table.
Away form was disappointing with only two
victories. There were satisfying doubles over
Northampton and Bristol.

Promising early victories in the European
Challenge Cup ended with a heavy defeat
in Paris to Stade Francais. There was some
consolation though with the winning of the
Cheltenham & Gloucester Cup. Not every team
took the competition seriously. A very weak
Leicester were thrashed at Welford Road 53-15
in the semi-final, before Bedford were beaten in
the final.

Mark Mapletoft scored a total of 423 points,
275 of them in league games. With St.Andre,
Fanolua and Tombs in the backs, more tries
should have been scored, but when the going got
tough the team seemed to revert to type and hope
the forwards would get them out of trouble. And

it was true that the first choice eight was solid.
But reserve strength was not as strong as some
other Premiership clubs. There were several
promising young players, but it was difficult to
find your feet in the very competitive top flight.
In the back-row Steve Ojomoh made immediate
impact after his signing from Bath. Indeed, the
complete back-row of Ojomoh, Simon Devereux
and skipper Pete Glanville had a very good
season. A young local lad, Andy Hazell made a
single appearance off the bench.

Phil Vickery was capped by England against
Wales. Phillipe St.Andre won France caps
against Argentina, Italy (try), Romania (try),
and in two tests against South Africa. England
'A' had a full programme and several Gloucester
players figured. Against New Zealand Scott
Benton scored a try. Vickery, Dave Sims and
Rob Fidler also played, and Mark Mapletoft
was a replacement. Mark Mapletoft scored
four penalties against France 'A'. Also in the
team were Brian Johnson, Chris Catling and
Rob Fidler. Catling, Johnson and Mapletoft
played against Wales 'A', with the latter scoring
four penalties. Catling, Johnson and Fidler also
featured against Scotland 'A', whilst against
Ireland 'A' Phil Greening played; Fidler scored
a try

**Aug 24 Gloucester 35 Bristol 13
(Premiership)**
Tries: P.St.Andre (2), A.Windo, R.Fidler;
Conversions: M.Mapletoft (3);
Penalties: M.Mapletoft (3)

**Aug 30 Leicester 33 Gloucester 16
(Premiership)**
Try: M.Mapletoft;
Conversion: M.Mapletoft;
Penalties: M.Mapletoft (2);
Drop goal: M.Mapletoft

**Sep 7 Gloucester 43 Petrarca Padova 10
(European Conference)**
Tries: P.Glanville (3), R.St.Andre, P.St.Andre,
C.Emmerson;
Conversions: M.Mapletoft (5);
Penalty: M.Mapletoft

**Sep 13 Gloucester 18 Toulon 15
(European Conference)**
Penalties: M.Mapletoft (4);
Drop goals: M.Mapletoft (2)

**Sep 21 Beziers 27 Gloucester 29
(European Conference)**
Tries: A.Windo, P.Glanville, P.Greening;
Conversion: M.Mapletoft;
Penalties: M.Mapletoft (4)

**Sep 28 Toulon 16 Gloucester 13
(European Conference)**
Try: P.Greening;
Conversion: M.Mapletoft;
Penalties: M.Mapletoft (2)

**Oct 4 Gloucester 38 Beziers 17
(European Conference)**
Tries: P.St.Andre (2), M.Mapletoft, C.Catling;
Conversions: M.Mapletoft (3);
Penalties: M.Mapletoft (4)

**Oct 12 Petrarca Padova 16 Gloucester 29
(European Conference)**
Tries: N.Osman, A.Windo, P.St.Andre,
R.Tombs, S.Benton;
Conversions: T.Fanolua (2)

**Oct 19 Gloucester 29 London Irish 7
(Premiership)**
Tries: T.Fanolua, R.Tombs, P.Glanville, penalty
try;
Conversions: M.Mapletoft (3);
Penalty: M.Mapletoft

**Oct 26 Saracens 42 Gloucester 24
(Premiership)**
Tries: R.Tombs (2), T.Fanolua, M.Mapletoft;
Conversions: M.Mapletoft, N.Osman

**Nov 2 Gloucester 16 Harlequins 17
(Premiership)**
Try: T.Fanolua;
Conversion: M.Mapletoft;
Penalties: M.Mapletoft (3)

**Nov 8 Stade Francais 53 Gloucester 22
(European Conference Quarter-Final)**
Tries: N.Osman, A.Lumsden, penalty try;
Conversions: T.Fanolua (2);
Penalty: T.Fanolua

**Nov 15 West Hartlepool 13 Gloucester
35 (C&G Cup)**
Tries: N.Osman (2), R.St.Andre, A.Gibbs,
M.Roberts;
Conversions: S.Ward (5)

**Nov 21 Northampton 30 Gloucester 5
(C&G Cup)**
Try: M.Cornwell

Dec 6 Gloucester 88 Fylde 0 (C&G Cup)
Tries: T.Fanolua (3), A.Lumsden (2), R.Jewell
(2), S.Benton (2), C.Catling, N.McCarthy,
P.Glanville, S.Devereux, M.Mapletoft;
Conversions: M.Mapletoft (9)

**Dec 14 Newcastle 37 Gloucester 27
(Premiership)**
Tries: C.Catling, R.Jewell, penalty try;
Conversions: M.Mapletoft (3);
Penalties: M.Mapletoft (2)

**Dec 27 Gloucester 26 Richmond 20
(Premiership)**
Tries: T.Fanolua, A.Lumsden, B.Johnson;
Conversion: M.Mapletoft;
Penalties: M.Mapletoft (3)

Dec 30 Sale 24 Gloucester 24 (Premiership)
Tries: P.Vickery, penalty try;
Conversion: M.Mapletoft;
Penalties: M.Mapletoft (4)

**Jan 3 London Welsh 18 Gloucester 34
(Tetley's Bitter Cup)**
Tries: R.Jewell (2), M.Cornwell, D.Sims,
M.Mapletoft + penalty try;
Conversions: M.Mapletoft, N.Osman

**Jan 11 Wasps 26 Gloucester 20
(Premiership)**
Tries: T.Fanolua, C.Fortey, N.Carter;
Conversion: M.Mapletoft;
Penalty: M.Mapletoft

**Jan 18 Bristol 13 Gloucester 14
(Premiership)**
Try: R.Fidler;
Penalties: M.Mapletoft (3)

**Jan 25 Northampton 30 Gloucester 11
(Tetley's Bitter Cup)**
Try: M.Lloyd;
Penalties: M.Mapletoft (2)

**Feb 1 Gloucester 32 Leicester 25
(Premiership)**
Tries: M.Mapletoft, S.Benton;
Conversions: M.Mapletoft (2);
Penalties: M.Mapletoft (6)

**Feb 6 Gloucester 48 Wakefield 7
(C&G Cup)**
Tries: I.Sanders (2), C.Emerson, R.Ward,
S.Devereux, M.Lloyd, N.Osman;
Conversions: S.Ward (5)
Penalty: S.Ward

Feb 11 Bath 47 Gloucester 3 (Premiership)
Penalty: M.Mapletoft

**Feb 14 Gloucester 20 Northampton 15
(Premiership)**
Tries: A.Lumsden, T.Fanolua;
Conversions: M.Mapletoft (2);
Penalties: M.Mapletoft (2)

**Feb 20 Gloucester 39 Richmond 27
(C&G Cup)**
Tries: N.Osman (2), R.Tombs, A.Deacon,
R.Ward;
Conversions: A.Morris (4);
Penalties: A.Morris (2)

**Feb 28 Gloucester 20 Bedford 32
(Friendly. Not included in season records)**
Tries: D.Sims, penalty try;
Conversions: M.Mapletoft (2);
Penalties: M.Mapletoft (2)

**Mar 11 Gloucester 22 Wasps 15
(Premiership)**
Tries: R.Fidler, B.Johnson, R.Tombs;
Conversions: M.Mapletoft (2);
Penalty: M.Mapletoft

**Mar 15 Gloucester 38 Saracens 15
(Premiership)**
Tries: S.Benton, R.Fidler, B.Johnson, A.Windo;
Conversions: M.Mapletoft (3);
Penalties: M.Mapletoft (4)

**Mar 21 Leicester 15 Gloucester 53
(C&G Cup Semi-Final)**
Tries: T.Fanolua (3), P.St.Andre (2), A.Lumsden,
D.Sims;
Conversions: M.Mapletoft (6);
Penalties: M.Mapletoft (2)

**Mar 24 London Irish 23 Gloucester 19
(Premiership)**

Try: S.Devereux;
Conversion: M.Mapletoft;
Penalties: M.Mapletoft (3);
Drop goal: M.Mapletoft

Mar 29 Harlequins 36 Gloucester 16 (Premiership)
Penalty try;
Conversion: M.Mapletoft;
Penalties: M.Mapletoft (3)

Apr 3 Gloucester 33 Bedford 25 (C&G Cup Final played at Northampton)
Tries: T.Fanolua, R.Ward, M.Mapletoft + penalty try;
Conversions: M.Mapletoft (2);

Penalty: M.Mapletoft;
Drop goals: M.Mapletoft (2)

Apr 11 Gloucester 27 Newcastle 29 (Premiership)
Tries: P.St.Andre, S.Ojomoh;
Conversion: M.Mapletoft;
Penalties: M.Mapletoft (5)

Apr 18 Gloucester 27 Bath 17 (Premiership)
Tries: P.St.Andre, R.Fidler;
Conversion: M.Mapletoft;
Penalties: M.Mapletoft (5)

Apr 25 Richmond 33 Gloucester 22

(Premiership)
Tries: P.St.Andre, M.Mapletoft, S.Ojomoh;
Conversions: M.Mapletoft (2);
Penalty: M.Mapletoft

May 2 Gloucester 31 Sale 19 (Premiership)
Tries: N.McCarthy, T.Fanolua, B.Johnson, P.St. Andre;
Conversions: M.Mapletoft (4);
Penalty: M.Mapletoft

May 17 Northampton 22 Gloucester 24 (Premiership)
Tries: M.Mapletoft, B.Johnson;
Conversion: M.Mapletoft;
Penalties: M.Mapletoft (4)

1998-99

A.Deacon S.Mannix M.Worsley R.Tombs S.Devereux N.Osman P.Vickery N.Carter T.Woodman L.Beck
J.Brain(Asst Coach) A.Lumsden B.Johnson C.Fortey E.Pearce R.Ward R.Fidler M.Cornwell P.Glanville A.Windo A.Dawling R.Hill(Dir of Rugby)
J.Fidler(Team Manager)
P.Greening S.Ojomoh C.Catling M.Mapletoft D.Sims(Capt) N.McCarthy S.Benton T.Fanolua P. Saint-André

Played 34 Won 16 lost 17 Drawn 1
For 766 Against 780
Owner: Tom Walkinshaw
Director of Rugby: Richard Hill
From February 1999: Phillipe St.Andre
Captain: Dave Sims
Premiership: Played 26 Won 9 Lost 16 Drawn 1
For 554 Against 643
Position: 10th

Gloucester United
Played 23 Won 15 Lost 7 Drawn 1
For 663 Against 526

Most appearances: N.Carter 31 (28+3reps), S.Ojomoh 30 (29+1), C.Fortey 27 (13+14), R.Tombs 28 D.Sims 27 (19+8), C.Catling 25

(24+1), T.Woodman 24 (19+5), S.Mannix 24 (22+2)
Most tries: C.Catling, P.St.Andre 9, R.Tombs, M.Mapletoft 7
Conversions: M.Mapletoft 22, S.Mannix 19, M.Kimber 5, S.Ward 1
Penalties: M.Mapletoft 56, S.Mannix 21, M.Kimber 3, S.Ward 2, T.Fanolua 1
Drop goal: I.Sanders 1

The temporary stand which had been installed for the start of the previous season was taken down and replaced by more hospitality boxes three storeys high.

Tom Walkinshaw increased his stake in the club to 98% following overwhelming support from members at a special meeting in July 1998.

At the time he had ambitions to increase the capacity of Kingsholm to 20,000.

For once the season got off to a bright start, the first three Premiership games all being won. All too soon a familiar pattern began to emerge, with wins at home, but defeats away from Kingsholm. By the turn of the season home games were also turning into defeats. In February after a loss to Harlequins Richard Hill was sacked as coach, and Phillipe St.Andre took his place. St.Andre found the pressure of playing and coaching debilitating and only appeared in three more games before the end of the season. But results did not improve. There were four more consecutive Premiership losses before the final game against Northampton was won. Thankfully, The Cheltenham and Gloucester cup was won for the second season running against the same opponents, Bedford, in the final. In the Tetley's Bitter Cup the semi-final was reached, where Wasps were victorious and they would go on to win the final.

Neil McCarthy won an England cap, being a replacement against Ireland. Trevor Woodman won no fewer than seven England 'A' caps. Terry Fanolua won caps for Samoa. Mark Mapletoft again scored heavily compiling 256 points, and played for England 'A'. But the arrival of Simon Mannix meant that Mapletoft rotated between fly-half and fullback. His form suffered, and wanting to play only at No.10, in July 1999 he signed for Saracens. He had accumulated 1323 points from 111 games.

Although Dave Sims was club captain, he was put on the transfer list at the end of the season as a cost cutting exercise, and after 256 appearances went on to play for Worcester. Popular prop Tony Windo also left to play for Worcester. Other exits were Phil Greening to Sale and Scott Benton to Leeds. Simon Devereux started the season in good form but against Bedford in November he badly dislocated his ankle. Despite intensive treatment, the injury proved serious enough to end his playing career after 136 appearances.

Sep 5 Gloucester 29 London Irish 22 (Premiership)
Tries: M.Mapletoft, penalty try;
Conversions: M.Mapletoft (2);
Penalties: M.Mapletoft (5)

Sep 12 Richmond 22 Gloucester 25 (Premiership)
Tries: M.Mapletoft (2), P.St.Andre;
Conversions: M.Mapletoft (2);
Penalties: M.Napletoft (2)

Sep 20 Gloucester 36 West Hartlepool 3 (Premiership)
Tries: R.Tombs (2), C.Catling, S.Ojomoh, P.St.Andre;
Conversions: M.Mapletoft (4);
Penalty: M.Mapletoft

Sep 26 Bath 21 Gloucester 16 (Premiership)
Tries: P.St.Andre, S.Mannix;
Penalties: M.Mapletoft (2)

Oct 3 Gloucester 12 Wasps 13 (Premiership)
Penalties: M.Mapletoft (4)

Oct 10 Swansea 27 Gloucester 16

(Friendly-not included in season records)
Try: A.Hazell;
Conversion: S.Mannix;
Penalties: M.Mannix (3)

Oct 17 Gloucester 41 Newcastle 32 (Premiership)
Tries: C.Catling (3), A.Lumsden, P.St.Andre;
Conversions: S.Mannix (2);
Penalties: S.Mannix (4)

Oct 20 Harlequins 39 Gloucester 7 (Premiership)
Penalty try;
Conversion: S.Mannix

Oct 25 Gloucester 29 London Scottish 16 (Premiership)
Tries: P.St.Andre, A.Dawling;
Conversions: S.Mannix (2);
Penalties: S.Mannix (5)

Oct 31 Northampton 22 Gloucester 8 (Premiership)
Try: A.Lumsden;
Penalty: S.Mannix

Nov 7 Gloucester 31 Bedford 21 (Premiership)
Tries: C.Fortey, S.Ojomoh, C.Catling;
Conversions: M.Mapletoft (2);
Penalties: M.Mapletoft (4)

Nov 15 Cardiff 17 Gloucester 9 (Friendly: not included in season records)
Penalties: M.Mapletoft (3)

Nov 21 Gloucester 28 Saracens 27 (Premiership)
Tries: R.Tombs (2), T.Fanolua;
Conversions: S.Mannix (2);
Penalties: S.Mannix (3)

Dec 12 Sale 26 Gloucester 10 (Premiership)
Try: P.St.Andre;
Conversion: S.Mannix;
Penalty: S.Mannix

Dec 19 Gloucester 18 Leicester 23 (Premiership)
Tries: M.Mapletoft, B.Johnson;
Conversion: M.Mapletoft;
Penalties: M.Mapletoft (2)

Dec 27 Wasps 23 Gloucester 9 (Premiership)
Penalties: M.Mapletoft (2), T.Fanolua

Jan 2 Gloucester 23 Bath 7 (Premiership)

Tries: C.Catling (2), T.Fanolua;
Conversion: M.Mapletoft;
Penalties: M.Mapletoft (2)

Jan 5 London Scottish 24 Gloucester 13 (Premiership)
Try: M.Mapletoft;
Conversion: M.Mapletoft;
Penalties: M.Mapletoft (2)

Jan 9 Gloucester 31 Worcester 17 (Tetley's Bitter Cup)
Tries: C.Fortey, S.Ojomoh, M.Mapletoft, P.St.Andre;
Conversion: M.Mapletoft;
Penalties: M.Mapletoft (3)

Jan 16 Gloucester 24 Richmond 24 (Premiership)
Tries: S.Benton, penalty try;
Conversion: M.Mapletoft;
Penalties: M.Mapletoft (4)

Jan 23 Leicester 23 Gloucester 16 (Premiership)
Try: R.Tombs;
Conversion: M.Mapletoft;
Penalties: M.Mapletoft (3)

Jan 30 Gloucester 31 Henley 9 (Tetley's Bitter Cup)
Tries: T.Fanolua (2), S.Mannix (2), R.Greenslade-Jones;
Conversions: S.Mannix (3)

Feb 7 London Irish 42 Gloucester 20 (Premiership)
Tries: N.Carter, S.Benton, P.St.Andre;
Conversion: M.Mapletoft;
Penalty: M.Mapletoft

Feb 13 Gloucester 20 Harlequins 31 (Premiership)
Tries: T.Beim, penalty try;
Conversions: M.Mapletoft (2);
Penalties: M.Mapletoft (2)

Feb 21 Gloucester 27 Leeds 9 (C&G Cup)
Tries: B.Johnson (2), C.Catling, M.Davis;
Conversions: M.Mannix (2);
Penalty: S.Mannix

Feb 27 Gloucester 15 Harlequins 13 (Tetley's Bitter Cup)
Penalties: M.Mapletoft (5)

Mar 7 Waterloo 8 Gloucester 18 (C&G Cup)
Tries: R.Greenslade-Jones, A.Eustace, B.Johnson;

Penalty: S.Ward

**Mar 14 West Hartlepool 33
Gloucester 32 (Premiership)**
Tries: N.Carter, T.Beim, S.Ojomoh,
M.Mapletoft, penalty try;
Conversions: M.Mapletoft (2)
Penalty: M.Mapletoft

Mar 17 Gloucester 25 Cardiff 30
(Friendly: not included in season's records)
Tries: L.Beck, R.Greenslade-Jones, R.Stott;
Conversions: M.Kimber (2);
Penalties: M.Kimber (2)

Mar 21 Gloucester 45 Sale 37
(C&G Cup)
Tries: C.Fortey, A.Harris, R.Ward, A.Eustace,
M.Kimber, penalty try;
Conversions: M.Kimber (3)
Penalties: M.Kimber (3)

Mar 27 Bedford 19 Gloucester 15

(Premiership)
Tries: M.Cornwell, P.St.Andre;
Conversion: S.Mannix;
Penalty: S.Mannix

Apr 4 Wasps 35 Gloucester 21
(Tetley's Bitter Cup Semi-Final)
Drop goal: I.Sanders;
Penalties: M.Mapletoft (6)

Apr 9 Gloucester 24 Bedford 9
(C&G Cup Final at Northampton)
Tries: E.Pearce (2), D.Sims, penalty try;
Conversions: M.Kimber (2)

Apr 25 Newcastle 39 Gloucester 15
(Premiership)
Tries: M.Davis, T.Beim;
Conversion: S.Mannix;
Penalty: M.Mapletoft

May 1 Gloucester 24 Sale 34
(Premiership)

Tries: T.Woodman, R.Tombs;
Conversion: M.Mapletoft;
Penalties: M.Mapletoft (4)

May 4 Gloucester 37 Swansea 10
(Friendly: Not included in season records)
Tries: S.Mannix, A.Windo, S.Morgan,
E.Moncrieff;
Conversions: E.Moncrieff (4);
Penalties: E.Moncrieff (3)

May 7 Saracens 26 Gloucester 10
(Premiership)
Try: A.Eustace;
Conversion: S.Ward;
Penalty: S.Ward

May 15 Gloucester 43 Northampton 31
(Premiership)
Tries: S.Mannix, C.Catling, N.Carter,
R.Tombs;
Conversions: S.Mannix (4);
Penalties: S.Mannix (5)

1999-2000

M.Kimber A.Lumsden T.Glassie R.Stott A.Eustace E.Pearce P.Glanville J.Djoudi R.Tombs I.Sanders
P.Finch(Fitness Coach) E.Archer(Fitness Coach) T.Beim C.Catling R.Ward R.Fidler M.Cornwell P.Vickery B.Johnson S.Mannix P. Saint-André(Head Coach) J.Fidler(Team Admin Manager)
S.Ojomoh E.Moncrieff L.Beck A.Hazell C.Fortey K.Jones(Capt) T.Woodman A.Deacon A.Powles J. Ewens C.Yates

**Played 31 Won 21 Lost 9 Drawn 1
For 901 Against 655
Owner: Tom Walkinshaw
Director of Rugby: Phillipe St.Andre
Captain: Kingsley Jones**
Premiership: Played 22 Won 15 Lost 7
For 628 Against 490
Position: 3rd

Gloucester United
Played 9 Won 7 Lost 2

For 311 Against 202

Most appearances: C.Yates 28 (24 starts + 4 as
rep.), R.Fidler 26 (25+1), J.Ewens 26 (24+2),
C.Catling 27 (25+2), S.Mannix 25 (24+1),
S.Ojomoh 25 (22+3)
Most tries: C.Catling 10, B.Johnson,
E.Moncrieff 9, T.Beim 7, T.Glassie 6
Conversions: S.Mannix 42, T.Fanolua 12,
B.Hayward 2, E.Moncrieff 1
Penalties: S.Mannix 69, T.Fanolua 9,
B.Hayward, E.Moncrieff, M.Kimber 2

Dropped goals: S.Mannix 3, E.Moncrieff 1

Phillipe St.Andre's first full season as Director
of Rugby was a good one, with the club rising
up the Premiership to third. Of the first twelve
Premiership clashes ten were won, and it
seemed possible that Gloucester could win the
Premiership title.   This period included the
World Cup which had weakened many teams,
with Gloucester affected less than some. After
January a decline set in and five of the last
eleven Premiership fixtures were lost, not good

enough to sustain a title challenge. However, finishing third guaranteed Heineken Cup rugby in the following season, for the first time. In the Tetley's Bitter Cup there was a welcome win over Bath and a thrashing of Orrell, but the run ended in the quarter-final against London Irish. The last game of the Premiership season was again away to the Irish. A brilliant game ended in victory for Gloucester 42-40. In the European Shield things looked promising before the only loss away to Biarritz stopped progress at the group stage.

Simon Mannix scored a total of 282 points in the Premiership, and 315 in all games. Australian scrum-half Elton Moncrieff proved to be a shrewd acquisition, and scored nine tries. Thanks to St.Andre the acquisition of All Black legend Ian Jones, who scored a try on his first appearance, was a master stroke. He quickly became a Shed favourite through his always giving 100% to the cause. With Rob Fidler, the pair formed a formidable second row. Another newcomer, Junior Paramore was also loved by the fans. It was a pity that due to injury he could not start his Gloucester career until January. It was soon apparent why he had been signed. Paramore, Kingsley Jones and Steve Ojomoh formed an excellent back-row.

Phil Vickery played for England against Ireland, France, Wales and Italy. Trevor Woodman was a replacement against Ireland and Italy, whilst Neil McCarthy also came off the bench against Italy. Terry Fanolua won further caps for Samoa. Pete Glanville who had missed a lot of the 1998-99 season through a cruciate ligament injury, had to admit defeat when breaking down again with the same problem in January 2000, which ended his career. He had made 145 appearances and scored 21 tries.

Aug 10 Begles Bourdeaux 11 Gloucester 19
(Friendly: not included in season record)
Try: B.Johnson;
Conversion: E.Moncrieff;
Penalties: S.Mannix (3), E.Moncrieff

Aug 28 Gloucester 31 Edinburgh Reivers 13
(Friendly: not included in season record)
Tries: T.Glassie, R.Jewell, J.Ewens;
Conversions: S.Mannix (2);
Penalties: S.Mannix (4)

Sep 11 Gloucester 31 Newcastle 16
(Premiership)
Tries: E.Moncrieff (2), S.Mannix;
Conversions: S.Mannix (2);
Penalties: S.Mannix (4)

Sep 26 Wasps 30 Gloucester 26

(Premiership)
Tries: T.Beim, A.Deacon, R.Tombs;
Conversion: S.Mannix;
Penalties: S.Mannix (3)

Oct 1 Gloucester 34 Leicester 6
(Premiership)
Tries: C.Catling, R.Tombs, I.Sanders, penalty try;
Conversions: S.Mannix (4);
Penalties: S.Mannix (2)

Oct 10 Bath 33 Gloucester 20
(Premiership)
Try: R.Tombs;
Penalties: S.Mannix (5)

Oct 15 Gloucester 24 Harlequins 23
(Premiership)
Tries: T.Beim, C.Catling;
Conversion: S.Mannix;
Penalties: S.Mannix (4)

Oct 30 Northampton 9 Gloucester 25
(Premiership)
Tries: R.Tombs, C.Yates, S.Mannix;
Conversions: S.Mannix, E.Moncrieff;
Penalties: E.Moncrieff (2)

Nov 5 Gloucester 35 Sale 14
(Premiership)
Tries: C.Catling (2), E.Moncrieff, T.Fanolua;
Conversions: S.Mannix (3);
Penalties: S.Mannix (3)

Nov 14 Gloucester 22 Saracens 19
(Premiership)
Try: T.Beim;
Conversion: S.Mannix;
Penalties: S.Mannix (5)

Nov 20 Gloucester 22 Biarritz 13
(European Shield)
Tries: B.Johnson, I.Jones;
Penalties: S.Mannix (2), M.Kimber (2)

Nov 28 Spain 19 Gloucester 42
(European Shield)
Tries: B.Johnson (2), K.Jones, T.Glassie, R.Jewell, C.Catling;
Conversions: T.Fanolua (3);
Penalties: T.Fanolua (2)

Dec 4 Bristol 25 Gloucester 38
(Premiership)
Tries: C.Yates, K.Jones, T.Beim, B.Hayward;
Conversions: S.Mannix (3);
Penalties: S.Mannix (3);
Drop goal: S.Mannix

Dec 11 Bridgend 29 Gloucester 29

(European Shield)
Tries: J.Ewens, T.Fanolua, I.Sanders, penalty try;
Conversions: S.Mannix (3);
Penalty: S.Mannix

Dec 18 Gloucester 23 Bridgend 6
(European Shield)
Tries: J.Ewens, M.Cornwell, B.Johnson;
Conversion: T.Fanolua;
Penalties: T.Fanolua (2)

Dec 26 Gloucester 40 London Irish 15
(Premiership)
Tries: C.Catling, S.Ojomoh, S.Mannix, K.Jones, E.Pearce, T.Fanolua;
Conversions: S.Mannix (2);
Penalties: S.Mannix (2)

Dec 30 Bedford 6 Gloucester 18
(Premiership)
Tries: E.Moncrieff, penalty try;
Conversion: S.Mannix;
Penalties: S.Mannix (2)

Jan 3 Gloucester 13 Bath 6
(Tetley's Bitter Cup)
Penalty try;
Conversion: B.Hayward;
Penalties: B.Hayward (2)

Jan 8 Gloucester 47 Spain 7
(European Shield)
Tries: T.Glassie (2), T.Fanolua, B.Johnson, J.Djoudi;
Conversions: T.Fanolua (3), S.Mannix (2);
Penalties: S.Mannix (2), T.Fanolua (2)

Jan 15 Biarritz 39 Gloucester 25
(European Shield)
Tries: T.Glassie (2), R.Tombs, N.McCarthy;
Conversion: T.Fanolua;
Penalty: T.Fanolua

Jan 22 Gloucester 29 Bristol 23
(Premiership)
Tries: C.Yates, penalty try;
Conversions: S.Mannix (2);
Penalties: S.Mannix (5)

Jan 25 Saracens 35 Gloucester 21
(Premiership)
Tries: R.Tombs, S.Ojomoh, E.Moncrieff;
Penalty: S.Mannix;
Drop goal: S.Mannix

Jan 29 Gloucester 54 Orrell 12
(Tetley's Bitter Cup)
Tries: M.Cornwell (2), T.Glassie, J.Djoudi, A.Deacon, B.Johnson, J.Paramore, R.Jewell;
Conversions: T.Fanolua (4);

Penalties: T.Fanolua (2)

**Feb 12 Sale 13 Gloucester 31
(Premiership)**
Tries: T.Beim (2), J.Paramore;
Conversions: S.Mannix (2);
Penalties: S.Mannix (4)

**Feb 26 London Irish 34 Gloucester 18
(Tetley's Bitter Cup)**
Tries: T.Beim, J.Ewens;
Conversion: S.Mannix;
Penalties: S.Mannix (2)

**Mar 11 Gloucester 11 Northampton 35
(Premiership)**
Try: R.Jewell;
Penalties: S.Mannix (2)

**Mar 25 Harlequins 24 Gloucester 38
(Premiership)**

Tries: B.Johnson (2), T.Woodman, C.Yates;
Conversions: S.Mannix (3);
Penalties: S.Mannix (4)

**Apr 8 Gloucester 16 Bath 36
(Premiership)**
Tries: I.Jones, R.Jewell;
Penalty: S.Mannix;
Drop goal: S.Mannix

**Apr 18 Leicester 24 Gloucester 13
(Premiership)**
Try: B.Hayward;
Conversion: B.Hayward;
Penalties: B.Hayward (2)

**Apr 22 Gloucester 26 Wasps 12
(Premiership)**
Tries: B.Johnson, J.Ewens;
Conversions: S.Mannix (2);

Penalties: S.Mannix (4)

**Apr 30 Newcastle 36 Gloucester 28
(Premiership)**
Tries: C.Catling, A.Deacon;
Penalties: S.Mannix (5);
Drop goal: E.Moncrieff

**May 6 Gloucester 60 Bedford 16
(Premiership)**
Tries: E.Moncrieff (4), T.Fanolua, C.Yates,
C.Catling, A.Hazell;
Conversions: S.Mannix (7);
Penalties: S.Mannix (2)

**May 20 London Irish 40 Gloucester 42
(Premiership)**
Tries: A.Powles (2), C.Catling (2), R.Jewell,
A.Eustace, M.Cornwell;
Conversions: S.Mannix, B.Hayward;
Penalty: S.Mannix

2000-01

A.Gomarsall A.Deacon C.Fortey C.Catling R.Greenslade-Jones O.Azam K.Jones F.Schisano T.Woodman T.Beim
E.Archer(Conditioning Coach) R.Jewell J.Paramore J.Boer E.Pearce M.Cornwell R.Ward A.Eustace S.Ojomoh C.Yates P.Finch(Conditioning Coach)
I.Sanders H.Gregoire-Mazzocco A.Powles P.Vickery I.Jones(Capt) R.Fidler J.Ewens R.Todd S.Mannix
E.Moncrieff B.Hayward S.Sanchez A.Hazell J.Little(inset)

Played 33 Won 16 Lost 16 Drawn 1
For 738 Against 761
Owner: Tom Walkinshaw
Director of Rugby: Phillipe St.Andre
Captains: Ian Jones and Kingsley Jones
Premiership: Played 22 Won 10 Lost 12
For 473 Against 526
Position: 7th

Gloucester United

Played 8 Won 6 Lost 2
For 290 Against 204

Most appearances: T.Fanolua 29 (28
starts+1rep.), R.Fidler 28 (26+2), J.Boer 28
(25+3), A.Gomarsall 28 (21+7), C.Yates 27
(21+6), J.Paramore 27 (24+3), S.Ojomoh 27
(17+10)
Most tries: T.Beim 11, J.Little 8, F.Shisano 5
Conversions: S.Mannix 20, B.Hayward 16,

T.Fanolua 4, E.Moncrieff 3, A.Gomarsall 2
Penalties: S.Mannix 74, B.Hayward 23,
E.Moncrieff 8, A.Gomarsall 6, T.Fanolua 3
Drop goals: E.Moncrieff 2

This was the first season that Gloucester
played in the Heineken Cup, surprising many
by reaching the semi-final. Premiership form
was uneven. Pre-season was difficult and when
the season proper began there were already a

number of injuries. The first game resulted in a drubbing from Saracens, and the first three games at Kingsholm were all lost. The fourth home game was against Harlequins. Simon Mannix scored all 27 points for Gloucester to create a club record with nine penalties. In all games he would total 267 points. Captain Ian Jones was finding the cares of leadership were undermining his form, so he stood down in favour of Kingsley Jones. Phillipe St.Andre made another major signing from the Southern Hemisphere, Jason Little the multi-capped Australian centre, and World Cup winner. In his first appearance he scored two tries, and in his second scored a try at Llanelli in a Heineken Cup game. It looked as if Little would be a great acquisition. However, an injury to Simon Mannix meant that Little had to take over at fly-half. His form suffered and never really recovered. He left the club at the end of the season to join Bristol.

Form throughout the season was inconsistent. There were heavy defeats to Saracens and Wasps, but good home wins over Leicester, Bristol and London Irish, as well as an outstanding Tetley's Bitter Cup win in November at Bath, where Tom Beim had a fine game. The win at Bath was an exception; the perennial problem of Gloucester away from Kingsholm persisted. If league form was frustrating, the club's first experience of Heineken Cup rugby was a revelation. There was a double over Llanelli. At Kingsholm in a very tight game, Elton Moncrieff mis-cued a drop goal attempt, only for the ball to strike a Llanelli player and go over the bar to win the game. Much against expectation Cardiff were beaten in the quarter-final, but against Leicester in the semi-final, played at Vicarage Road, Watford, the team were a trifle unlucky to lose.

Olivier Azam, Jake Boer, Andy Gomarsall, James Simpson-Daniel, Robert Todd, Jon Goodridge and James Forrester all made their debuts in this season, laying the foundation of the formidable team of the next few seasons.

Shed favourite Steve Ojomoh, retired at the end of the season. He had made exactly 100 appearances. Ian Jones announced his retirement, but re-appeared in Wasps colours the following season.

Phil Vickery won six England caps against Australia, Argentina, South Africa, Wales, Italy and Scotland. Trevor Woodman was a replacement against Wales and Italy.

**Aug 20 Saracens 50 Gloucester 20
(Premiership)**
Tries: S.Simon, C.Yates;

Conversions: B.Hayward (2);
Penalties: B.Hayward (2)

**Aug 26 Gloucester 18 Sale 19
(Premiership)**
Tries: J.Boer, F.Shisano;
Conversion: B.Hayward;
Penalties: B.Hayward (2)

**Sep 2 Rotherham 23 Gloucester 29
(Premiership)**
Tries: F.Shisano (3), R.Jewell;
Conversions: B.Hayward (3);
Penalty: B.Hayward

**Sep 6 Newcastle 18 Gloucester 19
(Premiership)**
Tries: A.Hazell, J.Ewens;
Penalties: B.Hayward (3)

**Sep 9 Gloucester 21 Bath 22
(Premiership)**
Tries: A.Gomarsall, B.Hayward;
Conversion: A.Gomarsall;
Penalties: A.Gomarsall (2), B.Hayward

**Sep 16 Wasps 43 Gloucester 23
(Premiership)**
Tries: T.Beim, C.Yates;
Conversions: S.Mannix (2);
Penalties: S.Mannix (3)

**Sep 23 Gloucester 27 Harlequins 23
(Premiership)**
Penalties: S.Mannix (9)

**Sep 30 Gloucester 38 Bristol 16
(Premiership)**
Tries: J.Little (2), P.Vickery, O.Azam;
Conversions: S.Mannix (3);
Penalties: S.Mannix (4)

**Oct 6 Llanelli 20 Gloucester 27
(Heineken Cup)**
Tries: J.Little, A.Hazell;
Conversion: A.Gomarsall;
Penalties: S.Mannix (3), T.Fanolua (2)

**Oct 15 Gloucester 52 Roma 12
(Heineken Cup)**
Tries: T.Beim (5), F.Shisano;
Conversions: T.Fanolua (3), E.Moncrieff (2);
Penalties: E.Moncrieff (4)

**Oct 21 Gloucester 22 Colomiers 22
(Heineken Cup)**
Penalty try;
Conversion: E.Moncrieff;
Penalties: E.Moncrieff (4), T.Fanolua

Oct 28 Colomiers 30 Gloucester 19

(Heineken Cup)
Try: C.Catling;
Conversion: S.Mannix;
Penalties: S.Mannix (4)

**Nov 4 Bath 18 Gloucester 24
(Tetley's Bitter Cup)**
Tries: M.Cornwell, T.Beim, B.Hayward;
Conversions: B.Hayward (3);
Penalty: B.Hayward

**Nov 11 Gloucester 13 Leicester 25
(Tetley's Bitter Cup)**
Penalty try;
Conversion: B.Hayward;
Penalties: B.Hayward (2)

**Nov 18 Gloucester 16 Saracens 15
(Premiership)**
Try: T.Beim;
Conversion: B.Hayward;
Penalties: B.Hayward (3)

**Nov 25 Gloucester 26 London Irish 6
(Premiership)**
Tries: K.Jones, T.Beim;
Conversions: S.Mannix (2);
Penalties: S.Mannix (4)

**Dec 2 Leicester 31 Gloucester 28
(Premiership)**
Tries: A.Deacon, C.Yates, J.Paramore;
Conversions: B.Hayward (2);
Penalties: B.Hayward (3)

**Dec 16 Northampton 34 Gloucester 15
(Premiership)**
Penalties: S.Mannix (4);
Drop goal: E.Moncrieff

**Dec 23 Gloucester 28 Newcastle 13
(Premiership)**
Tries: T.Beim, J.Little, M.Cornwell;
Conversions: S.Mannix (2);
Penalties: S.Mannix (3)

**Dec 27 Gloucester 12 Northampton 15
(Premiership)**
Tries: T.Fanolua, S.Mannix;
Conversion: T.Fanolua

**Jan 6 Bristol 18 Gloucester 9
(Premiership)**
Penalties: S.Mannix (3)

**Jan 13 Gloucester 28 Llanelli 27
(Heineken Cup)**
Penalty try;
Conversion: S.Mannix;
Penalties: S.Mannix (6);
Drop goal: E.Moncrieff

Jan 20 Roma 29 Gloucester 38
(Heineken Cup)
Tries: J.Ewens, J.Little;
Conversions: S.Mannix (2);
Penalties: S.Mannix (8)

Jan 27 Gloucester 21 Cardiff 15
(Heineken Cup Quarter-Final)
Penalties: S.Mannix (6), B.Hayward

Feb 6 Harlequins 21 Gloucester 19
(Premiership)
Try: R.Greenslade-Jones;
Conversion: B.Hayward;
Penalties: S.Mannix (2), B.Hayward (2)

Feb 10 Gloucester 3 Wasps 28
(Premiership)
Penalty: B.Hayward

Feb 24 Bath 50 Gloucester 16
(Premiership)
Try: C.Catling;
Conversion: S.Mannix;
Penalties: S.Mannix (3)

Mar 10 Gloucester 50 Rotherham 17
(Premiership)
Tries: T.Beim, C.Catling, M.Cornwell,
J.Simpson-Daniel, J.Little,
R.Todd, penalty try;
Conversions: S.Mannix (5), B.Hayward;
Penalty: S.Mannix

Mar 17 Sale 16 Gloucester 24
(Premiership)
Tries: J.Little (2);
Conversion: S.Mannix;
Penalties: S.Mannix (4)

Mar 31 Gloucester 22 Leicester 13
(Premiership)
Tries: I.Jones, A.Gomarsall;
Penalties: A.Gomarsall (4)

Apr 15 London Irish 35 Gloucester 10
(Premiership)
Try: J.Forrester;
Conversion: B.Hayward;
Penalty: B.Hayward

Apr 21 Leicester 19 Gloucester 15
(Heineken Cup Semi-Final at Northampton)
Penalties: S.Mannix (5)

Apr 29 Wasps 18 Gloucester 6
(Zurich Championship Play-off)
Penalties: S.Mannix (2)

2001-02

Played 35 Won 25 Lost 10
For 1295 Against 677
Owner: Tom Walkinshaw
Director of Rugby: Phillipe St.Andre until
Feb 2002, then Nigel Melville
Captain: Phil Vickery
Premiership: Played 22 Won 14 Lost 8
For 692 Against 485
Position: 3rd

Most appearances: J.Paramore 33 (29 starts
+ 4 reps), T.Fanolua 32 (28+4), C.Fortey 32
(15+17), L.Mercier 31 (30+1), D.O'Leary 31
(30+1), R.Fidler 31 (27+4), J.Boer 30 (26+4)
Most tries: J.Simpson-Daniel 15, J.Forrester 14,
D.O'Leary, J.Paramore 13, T.Fanolua 12
Conversions: L.Mercier 77, H.Paul 33,
A.Gomarsall 2
Penalties: L.Mercier 96, H.Paul 9
Drop goals: L.Mercier 17

During the summer of 2001 a little-known
Ludovic Mercier, who played for Aurillac, in
France at D2 level was recruited. Another close
season recruit was Rugby League star Henry
Paul.

The total points scored in the season (1295)
was a club record. Gloucester won the Zurich
Championship Final against Bristol at
Twickenham, with Ludovic Mercier scoring
23 points. Mercier, in his first season was also
breaking records. His 508 points in the season
was a club record, unlikely to be ever bettered,
and his 77 conversions equalled Peter Butler's
record (1977-78). Mercier also kicked 17 drop
goals, which equalled Willie Jones record set in
1947-48. In Premiership games Mercier scored
334 points, another club record. Indeed, it was
an incredible season for Mercier.

The other major signing Henry Paul, perhaps
never fully met expectations following his

glittering rugby league career. But there were
occasions when his skills shone through, he was
best when a delayed pass would put a colleague
through into space. He also demonstrated that
he was a very competent place kicker. The
England selectors were certainly impressed and
he won his first England cap as a replacement
against France. Phil Vickery won caps against
Ireland and France, and in the summer of 2001,
Terry Fanolua added seven more to his collection
of Samoan caps.

At home the team was almost unbeatable, apart
that is, from a heavy defeat to Leicester, who were
the eventual Premiership champions. However,
yet again, away form was poor, which may have
contributed to the surprise sacking of Phillipe
St.Andre. Ironically his last game in charge was
an away win at the Stoop against Harlequins.
Nigel Melville replaced St.Andre, and towards
the end of the season three successive away
games in the Premiership were won.

In the European Shield, Gloucester waltzed through the pool stage, with huge wins over Caerphilly and Gran Parma. Ebbw Vale were dispatched in the quarter-final, to leave a game against Sale in the semi-final at Northampton. At the end, the ultra-reliable Mercier had the chance to win the game with a penalty, but missed.

James Simpson-Daniel, who in his first season had made only six appearances, soon consolidated his place with some sparkling tries. James Forrester, although a back-row forward, ran like a back, and scored only one try fewer than Simpson-Daniel. Junior Paramore became a Shed favourite, in the same way as his cousin Terry Fanolua. Local boy, Andy Hazell, having broken through in the previous season, had a frustrating time with niggling injuries. Also in the back-row, Jake Boer was a tower of strength. Another crowd favourite Ollie Azam, through consistent performances. eventually displaced Chris Fortey from the hooker spot. A very promising winger, Marcel Garvey, made his debut this season, scoring a try on his debut.

Sep 1 Gloucester 22 Northampton 9
(Premiership)
Try: J.Paramore;
Conversion: L.Mercier;
Penalties: L.Mercier (5)

Sep 8 Saracens 34 Gloucester 30
(Premiership)
Tries: O.Azam, D.O'Leary;
Conversion: L.Mercier;
Penalties: L.Mercier (6)

Sep 15 Gloucester 18 Leicester 40
(Premiership)
Penalties: L.Mercier (6)

Sep 22 Sale 21 Gloucester 44
(Premiership)
Tries: T.Woodman, D.Yachvilli, T.Fanolua, F.Puchiarello;
Conversions: L.Mercier (3);
Penalties: L.Mercier (3);
Drop goals: L.Mercier (3)

Sep 29 Gloucester 34 La Rochelle 15
(Parker Pen, European Shield)
Tries: J.Paramore, C.Fortey, J.Ewens;
Conversions: L.Mercier (2);
Penalties: L.Mercier (4);
Drop goal: L.Mercier

Oct 6 GRAN Parma 5 Gloucester 48
(Parker Pen, European Shield)
Tries: J.Forrester (2), J.Simpson-Daniel (2),

O.Azam, C.Stoica;
Conversions: L.Mercier (4), A.Gomarsall (2);
Penalties: L.Mercier (2)

Oct 13 Gloucester 33 Harlequins 7
(Premiership)
Tries: D.Albenese, J.Paramore, penalty try;
Conversions: L.Mercier (3);
Penalties: L.Mercier (3);
Drop goal: L.Mercier

Oct 21 London Irish 19 Gloucester 15
(Premiership)
Penalties: L.Mercier (5)

Oct 27 Gloucester 98 Caerphilly 14
(Parker Pen, European Shield)
Tries: J.Simpson-Daniel (3), J.Forrester (3), J.Boer (2), T.Fanolua, J.Goodridge, D.O'Leary, F.Pucciarello, K.Sewabu, M.Cornwell, H.Paul;
Conversions: H.Paul (10);
Penalty: H.Paul

Nov 3 Caerphilly 16 Gloucester 47
(Parker Pen, European Shield)
Tries: R.Todd, C.Fortey, J.Paramore, D.Yachvilli, J.Ewens;
Conversions: L.Mercier (5);
Penalties: L.Mercier (4)

Nov 10 Gloucester 51 Bristol 17
(Premiership)
Tries: C.Catling, C.Fortey, A.Hazell, J.Paramore, A.Gomarsall, J.Simpson-Daniel;
Conversions: L.Mercier (5), H.Paul;
Penalties: L.Mercier (3)

Nov 18 Newcastle 18 Gloucester 16
(Premiership)
Try: A.Gomarsall;
Conversion: L.Mercier;
Penalties: L.Mercier (3)

Nov 23 Gloucester 43 Wasps 13
(Premiership)
Tries: O.Azam (2), J.Boer, penalty try;
Conversions: L.Mercier (3), H.Paul; ;
Penalties: H.Paul (2), L.Mercier;
Drop goals: L.Mercier (2)

Dec 1 Gloucester 58 Leeds 17
(Premiership)
Tries: J.Simpson-Daniel (2), M.Garvey, D.O'Leary, R.Todd, A.Eustace, H.Paul, L.Mercier;
Conversions: L.Mercier (5), H.Paul;
Penalties: L.Mercier (2)

Dec 8 Bath 12 Gloucester 9
(Premiership)
Penalty: L.Mercier;

Drop goals: L.Mercier (2)

Dec 16 Bristol 23 Gloucester 37
(Powergen Cup)
Tries: J.Forrester (3), T.Fanolua, M.Garvey;
Conversions: H.Paul (3);
Penalties: H.Paul (2)

Dec 29 Gloucester 29 Newcastle 25
(Premiership)
Tries: A.Eustace, T.Fanolua, D.O'Leary;
Conversion: H.Paul;
Penalties: H.Paul (4)

Jan 5 Gloucester 99 GRAN Parma 0
(Parker Pen, European Shield)
Tries: D.O'Leary (5), K.Sewabu (2), J.Ewens, H.Paul, D.Albenese, J.Forrester, T.Fanolua, A.Hazell, C.Stuart-Smith, J.Paramore;
Conversions: H.Paul (12)

Jan 12 La Rochelle 12 Gloucester 36
(Parker Pen, European Shield)
Tries: C.Fortey, A.Hazell, D.O'Leary;
Conversions: L.Mercier (2), H.Paul;
Penalties: L.Mercier (3)
Drop goals: L.Mercier (2)

Jan 20 London Irish 25 Gloucester 10
(Powergen Cup)
Try: A.Gomarsall;
Conversion: L.Mercier;
Penalty: L.Mercier

Jan 25 Gloucester 46 Ebbw Vale 11
(Parker Pen, European Shield)
Tries: D.O'Leary, J.Simpson-Daniel, J.Boer, J.Forrester;
Conversions: L.Mercier (4);
Penalties: L.Mercier (6)

Feb 9 Gloucester 29 London Irish 22
(Premiership)
Tries: O.Azam, T.Fanolua;
Conversions: L.Mercier (2);
Penalties: L.Mercier (5)

Feb 23 Harlequins 6 Gloucester 18
(Premiership)
Tries: A.Azam, D.Albenese;
Conversion: L.Mercier;
Penalties: L.Mercier (2)

Mar 9 Gloucester 42 Sale 14
(Premiership)
Tries: A.Gomarsall, J.Forrester, J.Paramore, J.Simpson-Daniel, F.Pucciarello;
Conversions: L.Mercier (4);
Penalties: L.Mercier (3)

Mar 16 Leicester 27 Gloucester 10

(Premiership)
Try: L.Mercier;
Conversion: L.Mercier;
Penalty: L.Mercier

Mar 30 Gloucester 36 Saracens 13
(Premiership)
Tries: R.Todd, T.Fanolua, A.Gomarsall;
Conversions: L.Mercier (2), H.Paul;
Penalties: L.Mercier (5)

Apr 10 Wasps 44 Gloucester 9
(Premiership)
Penalties: L.Mercier (3)

Apr 13 Northampton 58 Gloucester 21
(Premiership)
Tries: K.Sewabu, J.Paramore;
Conversion: L.Mercier;
Penalties: L.Mercier (2);
Drop goal: L.Mercier

Apr 21 Bristol 40 Gloucester 41
(Premiership)
Tries: J.Paramore (2), K.Sewabu, A.Gomarsall,

P.Vickery;
Conversions: L.Mercier (2);
Penalties: L.Mercier (2);
Drop goals: L.Mercier (2)

Apr 28 Sale 28 Gloucester 27
(Parker Pen, European Shield Semi-Final
played at Northampton
Tries: T.Fanolua (2), J.Forrester;
Conversions: L.Mercier (3);
Penalty: L.Mercier;
Drop goal: L.Mercier

May 4 Gloucester 68 Bath 12
(Premiership)
Tries: J.Simpson-Daniel (3), T.Fanolua (2),
J.Paramore, R.Todd, P.Collazo, H.Paul;
Conversions: L.Mercier (7);
Penalties: L.Mercier (2);
Drop goal: L.Mercier

May 12 Leeds 17 Gloucester 50
(Premiership)
Tries: J.Simpson-Daniel (2), J.Forrester,
J.Paramore, T.Woodman, D.O'Leary,

K.Sewabu;
Conversions: L.Mercier (6);
Penalty: L.Mercier

May 18 Gloucester 60 Newcastle 9
(Zurich Championship)
Tries: R.Todd, J.Forrester, L.Mercier, T.Beim,
J.Paramore, D.O'Leary, H.Paul, P.Vickery,
T.Fanolua
Conversions: L.Mercier (4), H.Paul (2);
Penalty: L.Mercier

June 2 Sale 11 Gloucester 33
(Zurich Championship Semi-Final)
Tries: K.Sewabu, A.Gomarsall, T.Beim;
Conversions: L.Mercier (3);
Penalties: L.Mercier (3);
Drop goal: L.Mercier

June 8 Gloucester 28 Bristol 23
(Zurich Championship Final at
Twickenham)
Try: J.Boer;
Conversion: L.Mercier;
Penalties: L.Mercier (7)

2002-03

M.Garvey J.Goodridge J.Frape J.Simpson-Daniel T.Beim T.Delport J.Boer P.Buxton M.Irish D.Murray C.Stuart-Smith
K.Owen(Sports Therapist) N.Allen(Physio) A.Lamb(Kit Man) W.Diesel(Head Physio) P.Glanville(Team Manager) R.Fidler A.Eustace E.Pearce M.Cornwell
J.Forrester C.Catling D.O'Leary N.Cox S.Amor D.Ryan(Coach) N.Melville(Dir of Rugby) D.Ellis(Defensive Coach) E.Archer(Fitness & Conditioning
Coach) R.Todd T.Woodman H.Paul C.Fortey P.Vickery(Capt) A.Hazell A.Gomarsall L.Mercier P.Collazo

Played 33 Won 25 Lost 6 Drawn 2
For 1003 Against 634
Owner: Tom Walkinshaw
Director of Rugby: Nigel Melville
Coach: Dean Ryan
Captain: Phil Vickery
Premiership: Played 22 Won 17 Lost 3 Drawn 2
For 617 Against 396
Position: 1st

Gloucester United

Played 5 Won 3 Lost 2
For 119 Against 46

Most appearances: T.Fanolua 31, L.Mercier
31 (30 starts + 1 rep.), J.Boer 30, A.Gomarsall
30 T.Delport 30 (26+4), H.Paul 30 (28+2),
O.Azam 30 (26+4)
Most tries: J.Boer 14, M.Garvey 13, J.Forrester
12, T.Fanolua 10, L.Mercier 9
Conversions: L.Mercier 74, H.Paul 11
Penalties: L.Mercier 64, H.Paul 12, S.Amor 3

Drop goals: L.Mercier 3, A.Gomarsall 1

Immediately after Gloucester had played
Harlequins in the first game of the season, new
captain Phil Vickery was interviewed, and did
not seem impressed with his team's performance,
although they had won by six points, away from
home. This signalled that Vickery was going to
make sure that the Cherry and Whites would be
expected to perform to a high level every week.
As the season progressed, he could not have

been disappointed.

Gloucester topped the Premiership by 15 clear points, but in the first season when play-offs decided the champion club, lost in the final to Wasps, and so won nothing. As the table topping team Gloucester qualified for the final whilst Wasps had to play a semi-final against Northampton, and the following week Bath in the final of the European Shield. Thus, Wasps were battle hardened, whilst Gloucester had gone three weeks without a game. It showed, and Wasps thrashed the Cherry and Whites in the final. But Gloucester did win the Powergen Cup before a crowd of 75,000 at Twickenham, defeating Northampton 40-22, in a thrilling game. The team had earned their place in the final, following a titanic struggle against Leicester in the semi-final played at Northampton. For nearly the whole season, Gloucester carried all before them. The problem with away games was solved, and only three Premiership games were lost away from Kingsholm. Kingsholm was a fortress and remained unconquered all season.

Things looked very promising in the Heineken Cup. There was an outstanding victory over Munster at Kingsholm, and when the return fixture was played, Gloucester only had to avoid losing by more than 26 points to qualify for the quarter-finals. But in the "Miracle game" at Thomond Park, Gloucester were overwhelmed by Irish passion to lose to a last minute Ronan O'Gara conversion, and elimination.

Ludovic Mercier was again prolific scoring 394 points in all games, and 255 in the Premiership alone. Jake Boer scored the most tries and was voted Zurich Premiership player of the season. In his first season Marcel Garvey had only made four appearances as a replacement, but on his first start, in the first game of the season, scored a try against Harlequins and never looked back. He had searing pace and penetration. Fellow wing James Simpson-Daniel missed several games through injury, but was always a threat when fit. New recruit, South African, Thinus Delport was a fine attacking full-back full of pace. With Terry Fanolua, Robert Todd and Henry Paul also in the backs, Gloucester had probably the most dynamic three-quarter line in the Premiership. At scrum-half Andy Gomarsall was as dependable as ever. He won an England cap against France, and was on the bench against Wales. Simpson-Daniel was also a replacement against Wales, and started against Italy, scoring a try. Trevor Woodman was a replacement against both Scotland and Ireland.

Woodman missed the middle of the season through injury, but was part of the team which won the Powergen Final. Argentinian Rodrigo Roncero stepped in to replace Woodman and did an admirable job. Phil Vickery was effective as ever, and Shed favourite Ollie Azam was magic in the loose, but erratic with his throws into the line-out. It was to the dismay of the fans when it was announced that Azam was to return to France to play for Montferrand. James Forrester was again in dynamic form in the back-row.

At the end of the season two other players moved to France; Ed Pearce to Montferrand and Chris Catling to Beziers, whilst Rob Fidler moved to arch-rivals Bath.

Aug 31 Harlequins 19 Gloucester 25 (Premiership)
Tries: M.Garvey, J.Paramore, T.Woodman;
Conversions: L.Mercier, H.Paul;
Penalties: H.Paul (2)

Sep 7 Gloucester 44 Sale 8 (Premiership)
Tries: J.Forrester (2), H.Paul, T.Beim, T.Delport, J.Boer;
Conversions: L.Mercier (4);
Penalties: L.Mercier (2)

Sep 15 Newcastle 19 Gloucester 22 (Premiership)
Try: J.Paramore;
Conversion: L.Mercier;
Penalties: H.Paul (3), L.Mercier (2)

Sep 21 Gloucester 45 Bristol 18 (Premiership)
Tries: M.Garvey (3), J.Boer, J.Paramore, L.Mercier;
Conversions: L.Mercier (3);
Penalties: L.Mercier (3)

Sep 28 Bath 21 Gloucester 21 (Premiership)
Tries: H.Paul, J.Forrester;
Conversion: H.Paul;
Penalties: L.Mercier (2), H.Paul

Oct 5 Gloucester 44 Saracens 14 (Premiership)
Tries: O.Azam (2), T.Fanolua, J.Boer, L.Mercier;
Conversions: L.Mercier (5);
Penalties: L.Mercier (3)

Oct 12 Gloucester 35 Munster 16 (Heineken Cup)
Tries: J.Boer (2), M.Garvey, L.Mercier;
Conversions: L.Mercier (3);
Penalties: L.Mercier (3)

Oct 18 Viadana 28 Gloucester 80 (Heineken Cup)
Tries: J.Simpson-Daniel (3), T.Fanolua (3), H.Paul (2), R.Roncero, J.Boer, J.Forrester, M.Garvey
Conversions: L.Mercier (10)

Oct 26 Wasps 23 Gloucester 16 (Premiership)
Try: T.Fanolua;
Conversion: L.Mercier;
Penalties: L.Mercier (2), H.Paul

Nov 2 Gloucester 18 Northampton 9 (Premiership)
Penalties: L.Mercier (5);
Drop goal: A.Gomarsall

Nov 10 London Irish 19 Gloucester 40 (Premiership)
Tries: A.Eustace, J.Paramore, J.Forrester, J.Boer, R.Roncero;
Conversions: L.Mercier (3);
Penalties: L.Mercier (3)

Nov 15 Leicester 20 Gloucester 15 (Premiership)
Tries: J.Boer, T.Fanolua;
Conversion: H.Paul;
Penalty: H.Paul

Nov 24 Gloucester 28 Leeds 10 (Premiership)
Tries: J.Boer, J.Paramore, R.Todd;
Conversions: L.Mercier (2);
Penalties: L.Mercier (3)

Nov 30 Gloucester 25 London Irish 20 (Premiership)
Tries: J.Boer, J.Paramore, penalty try;
Conversions: L.Mercier (2);
Penalties: L.Mercier (2)

Dec 8 Gloucester 33 Perpignan 16 (Heineken Cup)
Tries: M.Garvey (2), L.Mercier;
Conversions: L.Mercier (3);
Penalties: L.Mercier (4)

Dec 14 Perpignan 31 Gloucester 23 (Heineken Cup)
Tries: J.Boer, L.Mercier;
Conversions: L.Mercier (2);
Penalties: L.Mercier (3)

Dec 21 Gloucester 35 Exeter 6 (Powergen Cup)
Tries: C.Catling (2), J.Boer, P.Buxton, D.O'Leary;
Conversions: H.Paul (5)

Dec 28 Northampton 13 Gloucester 16
(Premiership)
Try: O.Azam;
Conversion: L.Mercier;
Penalties: L.Mercier (2);
Drop goal: L.Mercier

Jan 4 Gloucester 24 Wasps 17
(Premiership)
Tries: M.Cornwell (2), H.Paul;
Penalties: H.Paul (2), L.Mercier

Jan 11 Gloucester 64 Viadana 16
(Heineken Cup)
Tries: J.Paramore (2), R.Todd (2), M.Garvey,
J.Forrester, T.Beim, O.Azam, J.Simpson-Daniel,
C.Collins
Conversions: L.Mercier (7)

Jan 18 Munster 33 Gloucester 6
(Heineken Cup)
Penalties: L.Mercier (2)

Jan 25 Gloucester 51 Saracens 20
(Powergen Cup)
Tries: T.Delport (2), J.Forrester (2), T.Fanolua,
A.Gomarsall, A.Eustace, R.Roncero;
Conversions: L.Mercier (3), H.Paul;
Penalty: L.Mercier

Feb 2 Saracens 22 Gloucester 29
(Premiership)
Tries: T.Fanolua, L.Mercier;
Conversions: L.Mercier (2);
Penalties: L.Mercier (4);
Drop goal: L.Mercier

Feb 8 Gloucester 29 Bath 16
(Premiership)
Tries: O.Azam, M.Garvey;
Conversions: L.Mercier (2);
Penalties: L.Mercier (5)

Mar 1 Gloucester 16 Leicester 11
(Powergen Cup Semi-Final at Northampton)
Tries: M.Garvey, T.Delport;
Penalties: L.Mercier (2);

Mar 16 Bristol 21 Gloucester 38
(Premiership)
Tries: J.Forrester (3), A.Hazell, L.Mercier,
M.Garvey;
Conversions: L.Mercier (4)

Apr 5 Gloucester 40 Northampton 22
(Pilkington Cup Final at Twickenham)
Tries: J.Simpson-Daniel (2), J.Forrester,
M.Garvey;
Conversions: L.Mercier (4);
Penalties: L.Mercier (3)
Drop goal: L.Mercier

Apr 12 Gloucester 25 Newcastle 23
(Premiership)
Tries: A.Hazell, T.Delport, T.Woodman;

Conversions: L.Mercier (2);
Penalties: L.Mercier (2)

Apr 18 Sale 30 Gloucester 30
(Premiership)
Tries: T.Fanolua, J.Boer, L.Mercier;
Conversions: L.Mercier (2), H.Paul;
Penalties: L.Mercier (3)

Apr 26 Gloucester 29 Harlequins 11
(Premiership)
Tries: J.Boer, J.Simpson-Daniel, H.Paul,
L.Mercier;
Conversions: L.Mercier (3);
Penalty: H.Paul

May 4 Leeds 30 Gloucester 23
(Premiership)
Tries: D.O'Leary, T.Beim;
Conversions: H.Paul (2);
Penalties: S.Amor (3)

May 10 Gloucester 31 Leicester 13
(Premiership)
Tries: T.Delport, T.Beim, A.Gomarsall,
T.Fanolua;
Conversions: L.Mercier (4);
Penalty: L.Mercier

May 31 Wasps 39 Gloucester 3
(Zurich Premiership Final at Twickenham)
Penalty: L.Mercier

2003-04

D.MacRae C.Collins H.Paul P.Johnstone S.Brotherstone A.Hazell J.Goodridge A.Deacon
N.Allen(Physio) R.Meir(Skills & Conditioning Coach) K.Owen(Sports Therapist) Dr.R.MacKay M.Garvey A.Page J.Frape A.Eustace M.Cornwell A.Brown
P.Buxton M.Foster N.Melville(Dir of Rugby) D.Ryan(Coach) E.Archer(Fitness & Conditioning Coach) A.Lamb(Kit Manager) D.Pointon(Technical Analyst)
S.Amor T.Woodman R.Todd P.Vickery J.Boer J.Paramore J.Forrester C.Fortey B.Davies

Played 31 Won 20 Lost 11
For 764 Against 617
Owner: Tom Walkinshaw
Director of Rugby: Nigel Melville
Coach: Dean Ryan
Captain: Jake Boer
Premiership: Played 22 Won 14 Lost 8
For 491 Against 412
Position: 4th

Gloucester United
Played 11 Won 6 Lost 5
For 410 Against 367

Most appearances: A.Brown 31, H.Paul 29, J.Boer 29, A.Eustace 29 (16 starts + 13 reps), M.Cornwell 29 (15+14), C.Fortey 28 (26+2), R.Todd 28 (21+7), P.Buxton 28 (20+8)
Most tries: J.Simpson-Daniel 14, M.Garvey 10, T.Fanolua, J.Goodridge, J.Paramore, R.Todd 5
Conversions: H.Paul 52, D.McRae 8
Penalties: H.Paul 75, D.McRae 3
Drop goals: D.McRae 4, H.Paul 1

Gloucester slipped to fourth in the Premiership largely due to a poor run through November and December, so that by Christmas wins and losses were equal. The second half of the season was much more successful, with superb away wins to complete doubles over Leicester and Saracens. In the Heineken Cup there were five wins in the group stage, the only defeat being at Thomond Park against Munster. However, at the quarter-final stage, Wasps were overwhelming winners.

Phil Vickery, Andy Gomarsall and Trevor Woodman all missed the early season because of World Cup duties. Against Northampton in November Woodman made his return, and received a tremendous ovation as he came on as a replacement and duly scored a scorching try. The return of the World Cup contingent certainly strengthened the team. Not only the England players but Rodrigo Roncero who had been playing for Argentina, Thinus Delport for South Africa, and Terry Fanolua for Samoa, ensured that Gloucester had a formidable fifteen. They moved up to third in the Premiership, but long-term injuries to Delport, James Forrester and Vickery took their toll. And a final day league defeat to Bath meant that Gloucester missed the play-offs. However, a fourth finish ensured Heineken Cup rugby for the following season. Kingsholm was still a fortress. The home defeat to Bath in November was the first since September 2001, and there would only be one more for the rest of the season, ironically the very next game against London Irish in the Powergen Cup!

With the departure of Ludovic Mercier, Henry Paul took over the kicking duties and had great success, scoring 352 points in all games. James Simpson-Daniell and Marcel Garvey were amongst the best wingers in the country and scored 24 tries between them. The acquisition of Australian fly-half Duncan McRae proved to be a shrewd move, as did Alex Brown who had played several successful seasons with Bristol in the second row. Jake Boer was a very popular and inspirational captain, and with Forrester, Junior Paramore and Andy Hazell formed a very effective back-row. A very promising young prop, Nick Wood, made his first appearance.

Phil Vickery, Trevor Woodman and Andy Gomarsall all played for England in the World Cup, with Vickery playing in all seven games and captaining his country against Uruguay, Woodman playing in five, and Gomarsall in four. Vickery and Woodman were the props in the defeat of Australia in the final. They also played in all the Six Nations internationals, and Gomarsall played against Italy and Scotland. Henry Paul was a replacement against Italy and Scotland, and James Simpson-Daniel came off the bench against Ireland. Woodman (136 appearances) also signed a contract to play for Sale and left at the end of the season. Junior Paramore (116 appearances) also left, and after exactly 300 appearances veteran Andy Deacon decided to call it a day.

Off the field 6,500 season tickets were sold, which was a record, and eight of the Club's eleven Premiership games were 11,000 sell-outs. At the end of the season planning permission was granted for a new 2,500 seated stand to take the ground capacity to 12,500. Other good news at the end of the season was that Olivier Azam was to return from France.

Sep 13 Gloucester 22 Rotherham 8
(Premiership)
Try: R.Teague;
Conversion: H.Paul;
Penalties: H.Paul (5)

Sep 20 London Irish 16 Gloucester 10
(Premiership)
Try: J.Paramore;
Conversion: H.Paul;
Penalty: H.Paul

Sep 27 Gloucester 30 Saracens 7
(Premiership)
Tries: J.Goodridge (2), J.Simpson-Daniel, J.Forrester;
Conversions: H.Paul (2);
Penalties: H.Paul (2)

Oct 5 Newcastle 42 Gloucester 22
(Premiership)
Tries: J.Goodridge, J.Simpson-Daniel, J.Boer;
Conversions: H.Paul (2);
Penalty: H.Paul

Oct 11 Gloucester 24 Leicester 3
(Premiership)
Tries: M.Garvey, R.Todd;
Conversion: H.Paul;
Penalties: H.Paul (4)

Oct 18 Harlequins 0 Gloucester 16
(Premiership)
Try: R.Todd;
Conversions: H.Paul;
Penalties: H.Paul (3)

Oct 25 Gloucester 24 Leeds 19
(Premiership)
Tries: J.Simpson-Daniel (2), J.Forrester;
Conversions: H.Paul (3);
Penalty: H.Paul

Nov 1 Northampton 30 Gloucester 17
(Premiership)
Tries: J.Forrester (2), A.Hazell;
Conversion: H.Paul

Nov 8 Gloucester 14 Bath 20
(Premiership)
Try: M.Garvey;
Penalties: H.Paul (3)

Nov 15 Gloucester 29 London Irish 35
(Powergen Cup)
Tries: S.Amor, H.Paul;
Conversions: H.Paul (2);
Penalties: H.Paul (5)

Nov 21 Wasps 21 Gloucester 12
(Premiership)
Penalties: H.Paul (4)

Nov 29 Gloucester 28 Northampton 20
(Premiership)
Tries: M.Garvey, J.Simpson-Daniel, T.Woodman;
Conversions: H.Paul (2);
Penalties: H.Paul (3)

Dec 6 Benneton Treviso 12 Gloucester 33
(Heineken Cup)
Tries: J.Paramore (2), J.Simpson-Daniel, A.Eustace;
Conversions: H.Paul (2);
Penalties: H.Paul (3)

Dec 13 Gloucester 49 Bourgoin 13
(Heineken Cup)
Tries: J.Simpson-Daniel (2), A.Eustace, H.Paul, M.Garvey, T.Fanolua;

Conversions: H.Paul (5);
Penalties: H.Paul (3)

Dec 21 Leeds 22 Gloucester 18 (Premiership)
Penalties: H.Paul (6)

Dec 27 Gloucester 18 Harlequins 17 (Premiership)
Tries: J.Simpson-Daniel, T.Woodman;
Conversion: H.Paul;
Penalties: H.Paul (2)

Jan 3 Leicester 18 Gloucester 28 (Premiership)
Tries: D.McRae, A.Brown, J.Paramore;
Conversions: H.Paul (2);
Penalty: H.Paul;
Drop goals: D.McRae (2)

Jan 10 Gloucester 22 Munster 11 (Heineken Cup)
Try: J.Simpson-Daniel;
Conversion: H.Paul;
Penalties: H.Paul (4);
Drop goal: H.Paul

Jan 17 Munster 35 Gloucester 14 (Heineken Cup)
Try: J.Goodridge;
Penalties: H.Paul (3)

Jan 24 Bourgoin 18 Gloucester 37 (Heineken Cup)
Tries: M.Garvey, J.Simpson-Daniel, D.McRae,

H.Paul;
Conversions: H.Paul (4);
Penalties: H.Paul (3)

Jan 31 Gloucester 42 Benneton Treviso 11 (Heineken Cup)
Tries: P.Buxton, J.Simpson-Daniel, R.Todd, M.Garvey, J.Goodridge, penalty try;
Conversions: H.Paul (6)

Feb 7 Gloucester 36 Newcastle 12 (Premiership)
Tries: R.Todd, M.Garvey, D.McRae, J.Forrester, T.Fanolua;
Conversions: H.Paul (4);
Penalty: H.Paul

Feb 14 Gloucester 38 Sale 12 (Premiership)
Tries: R.Roncero (2), J.Boer, J.Paramore, penalty try;
Conversions: D.McRae (5);
Penalty: D.McRae

Feb 22 Rotherham 21 Gloucester 35 (Premiership)
Tries: T.Fanolua (2), J.Forrester (2);
Conversions: D.McRae (3);
Penalties: D.McRae (2);
Drop goal: D.McRae

Mar 26 Sale 38 Gloucester 20 (Premiership)
Tries: A.Brown, D.Du Preez;
Conversions: H.Paul (2);

Penalties: H.Paul (2)

Apr 3 Saracens 8 Gloucester 16 (Premiership)
Try: M.Garvey;
Conversion: H.Paul;
Penalties: H.Paul (3)

Apr 11 Wasps 34 Gloucester 3 (Heineken Cup Quarter-Final)
Penalty: H.Paul

Apr 18 Gloucester 28 London Irish 13 (Premiership)
Tries: C.Fortey, J.Simpson-Daniel, H.Paul;
Conversions: H.Paul (2);
Penalties: H.Paul (2);
Drop goal: D.McRae

May 1 Gloucester 28 Wasps 25 (Premiership)
Tries: J.Simpson-Daniel, M.Garvey, A.Hazell;
Conversions: H.Paul (2);
Penalties: H.Paul (3)

May 8 Bath 41 Gloucester 7 (Premiership)
Try: D.Du Preez;
Conversion: H.Paul

May 15 Gloucester 44 Sale 35 (Wild Card Play Off)
Tries: A.Hazell, T.Fanolua, M.Garvey, R.Todd;
Conversions: H.Paul (3);
Penalties: H.Paul (6)

2004-05

Played 33 Won 16 Lost 16 Drawn 1
For 650 Against 692
Owner: Tom Walkinshaw
Director of Rugby: Nigel Melville
Coach: Dean Ryan

Captain: Jake Boer
Premiership: Played 22 Won 10 Lost 11 Drawn 1
For 407 Against 487
Position: 6th

Gloucester United
Played 10 Won 5 Lost 5
For 270 Against 310

Most appearances: P.Buxton 33 (19 starts +

14 reps), A.Balding 32 (26+6), J.Goodridge 31, A.Eustace 30 (26+4), T.Fanolua 29 (28+1), A.Brown 28 (27+1), J.Boer 28 (27+1)
Most tries: M.Garvey, T.Fanolua 8, J.Simpson-Daniel 6, J.Forrester 5
Conversions: H.Paul 28, S.Amor, B.Davies 4, D.McRae 3
Penalties: H.Paul 55, D.McRae 8, S.Amor 4, B.Davies 3
Drop goals: D.McRae 5, H.Paul 2, S.Amor, B.Davies 1

New faces at the club included Terry Sigley, Adam Balding, James Bailey, Mefin Davies, South African Christo Bezuidenhout, and making just two appearances, a very promising Ollie Morgan. Ollie Azam was also back from France.

The start to the season was excellent with six wins out of the first seven Premiership fixtures. Unfortunately, there were only four more victories in the rest of the campaign. Consistency, or the lack of it was a problem. A good win was too often followed by a poor display. A factor in the tail-off was the number of injuries suffered during the autumn. Several were injured during the October Heineken Cup game against Ulster, and then at various times James Simpson-Daniel, Duncan McRae, Terry Sigley, Ollie Azam and Gary Powell were all absent. The early season momentum was never regained. The last three Premiership matches were all lost including a 33-15 defeat at Kingsholm to lowly Leeds. At the end of the season the Club parted company with Nigel Melville, Dean Ryan taking his place as Head Coach, and Bryan Redpath was appointed his assistant.

In the Heineken Cup there was the injury strewn win over Ulster and a double over Cardiff, but hopes of progress out of the pool stage ended when Stade Francais won 27-0 at Kingsholm, the first time the Club had been "nilled" since 1993. The team reached the semi-final of the Powergen Cup, with a game at home against Bath. The contest was very tight and at 80 minutes the scores were tied at 19 apiece. However, in extra-time Bath winger, Andy Williams chased his own kick ahead to score the winning try. Yet another semi-final loss at home to Bath!

Henry Paul scored 242 points in all games, and had a sound season in the centre partnering Terry Fanolua. Jon Goodridge was an attacking full-back who started more games than anybody else. Although Ollie Azam was back, he was one of the several injured players, and when Mefin Davies arrived from Wales he took over

as first choice hooker. Davies played in all Wales' Six Nations Internationals. For England, Andy Hazell started against Wales and was a replacement against France, Scotland and Italy. Phil Vickery started against France and was a replacement against Wales. James Forrester also came off the bench against Wales to win his first cap. In the summer of 2005 Terry Fanolua would win yet more caps for Samoa.

Scrum-half Andy Gomarsall (130 appearances) played his last season at Kingsholm and moved on to Worcester. Chris Fortey (181) broke his ankle in November against Sale. This was his last game for Gloucester and in the summer like Gomarsall signed for the Warriors. Summer recruit Peter Richards was a direct replacement for Gomarsall. Ludovic Mercier returned from France. An exciting signing in Mike Tindall made the promise of the coming season alluring.

At the end of the season director of rugby Nigel Melville left the club, and Dean Ryan became head coach. Bryan Redpath was appointed as his assistant.

Sep 5 Leeds 16 Gloucester 21 (Premiership)
Tries: T.Fanolua, J.Simpson-Daniel;
Conversion: H.Paul;
Penalties: H.Paul (2);
Drop goal: D.McRae

Sep 11 Gloucester 23 London Irish 16 (Premiership)
Tries: O.Azam, J.Boer, A.Hazell;
Conversion: H.Paul;
Penalties: H.Paul (2)

Sep 18 Northampton 12 Gloucester 18 (Premiership)
Tries: O.Azam, M.Garvey;
Conversion H.Paul;
Penalty: H.Paul;
Drop goal: D.McRae

Sep 25 Gloucester 31 Newcastle 17 (Premiership)
Tries: M.Garvey, A.Brown, J.Simpson-Daniel;
Conversions: H.Paul (2);
Penalties: H.Paul (3), D.McRae

Oct 2 Bath 29 Gloucester 14 (Premiership)
Try: J.Goodridge;
Penalties: H.Paul (2);
Drop goal: D.McRae

Oct 9 Gloucester 29 Harlequins 23 (Premiership)
Tries: T.Fanolua (2), H.Paul, J.Simpson-Daniel;

Conversions: H.Paul (3);
Penalty: H.Paul

Oct 16 Worcester 13 Gloucester 18 (Premiership)
Tries: H.Paul, J.Goodridge;
Conversion: H.Paul;
Penalty: H.Paul;
Drop goal: D.McRae

Oct 23 Stade Francais 39 Gloucester 31 (Heineken Cup)
Tries: J.Simpson-Daniel (2), J.Forrester;
Conversions: H.Paul (2);
Penalties: H.Paul (4)

Oct 30 Gloucester 55 Ulster 13 (Heineken Cup)
Tries: D.McRae (2), C.Bezuidenhout, J.Simpson-Daniel, A.Balding, M.Garvey;
Conversions: H.Paul (5)
Penalties: H.Paul (4);
Drop goal: H.Paul

Nov 6 Leicester 28 Gloucester 13 (Premiership)
Try: H.Paul;
Conversion: H.Paul;
Penalties: H.Paul (2)

Nov 12 Gloucester 17 Wasps 27 (Premiership)
Tries: A.Balding, S.Amor;
Conversions: S.Amor (2);
Penalty: S.Amor

Nov 21 Saracens 14 Gloucester 9 (Premiership)
Penalties: S.Amor (3)

Nov 26 Gloucester 24 Sale 14 (Premiership)
Tries: M.Garvey, T.Fanolua, J.Goodridge, J.Parkes;
Conversions: S.Amor (2)

Dec 4 Gloucester 23 Cardiff Blues 19 (Heineken Cup)
Tries: T.Fanolua (2), J.Bailey;
Conversion: H.Paul;
Penalties: H.Paul (2)

Dec 11 Cardiff Blues 16 Gloucester 23 (Heineken Cup)
Tries: M.Garvey, J.Goodridge;
Conversions: H.Paul (2);
Penalties: H.Paul (3)

Dec 18 Leicester 13 Gloucester 20 (Powergen Cup)
Tries: N.Mauger, penalty try;

Conversions: H.Paul (2);
Penalties: H.Paul (2)

**Dec 27 Wasps 33 Gloucester 20
(Premiership)**
Try: J.Forrester;
Penalties: H.Paul (5)

**Jan 2 Gloucester 13 Leicester 28
(Premiership)**
Tries: N.Mauger, A.Eustace;
Penalty: H.Paul

**Jan 7 Ulster 14 Gloucester 12
(Heineken Cup)**
Penalties: H.Paul (3);
Drop goal: S.Amor

**Jan 16 Gloucester 0 Stade Francais 27
(Heineken Cup)**

**Jan 22 Gloucester 21 Bristol 0 (Powergen
Cup)**
Tries: A.Gomarsall, A.Brown;
Conversion: H.Paul;
Penalties: H.Paul (3)

**Jan 29 Gloucester 28 Worcester 16
(Premiership)**
Tries: S.Kiole, A.Gomarsall, T.Sigley;
Conversions: H.Paul (2);
Penalties: H.Paul (2);
Drop goal: D.McRae

**Feb 5 Harlequins 38 Gloucester 9
(Premiership)**
Penalties: H.Paul (3)

**Feb 19 Gloucester 17 Bath 16
(Premiership)**
Try: S.Kiole;
Penalties: H.Paul (3);
Drop goal: B.Davies

**Feb 27 Newcastle 27 Glloucester 27
(Premiership)**
Tries: M.Garvey, A.Gomarsall, T.Fanolua,
L.Narraway;
Conversions: H.Paul (2);
Drop goal: H.Paul

**Mar 6 Gloucester 19 Bath 24
(Powergen Cup Semi-Final)**
Try: S.Kiole;
Conversion: H.Paul;
Penalties: H.Paul (4)

**Mar 12 Gloucester 18 Northampton 26
(Premiership)**
Tries: M.Garvey, N.Mauger;
Conversion: B.Davies;
Penalties: H.Paul (2)

**Mar 26 London Irish 12 Gloucester 13
(Premiership)**
Try: M.Garvey;

Conversion: B.Davies;
Penalties: B.Davies (2)

**Apr 9 Gloucester 15 Leeds 33
(Premiership)**
Tries: J.Forrester, N.Wood;
Conversion: D.McRae;
Penalty: D.McRae

**Apr 15 Sale 35 Gloucester 17
(Premiership)**
Tries: P.Buxton, penalty try;
Conversions: B.Davies (2);
Penalty: B.Davies

**Apr 30 Gloucester 13 Saracens 14
(Premiership)**
Try: O.Morgan;
Conversion: D.McRae;
Penalties: D.McRae (2)

**May 8 Gloucester 23 Newcastle 16
(Zurich Wild Card)**
Tries: J.Forrester (2), A.Balding;
Conversion D.McRae;
Penalties: D.McRae (2)

**May 14 Saracens 24 Gloucester 16
(Zurich Wild Card Final at Twickenham)**
Tries: B.Davies, A.Eustace;
Penalties: D.McRae (2)

2005-06

Played 34 Won 22 Lost 11 Drawn 1
For 996 Against 542
Owner: Tom Walkinshaw
Head Coach: Dean Ryan
Captain: Adam Balding
Premiership: Played 22 Won 11 Lost 10 Drawn 1
For 483 Against 385
Position: 5th

Gloucester United
Played 13 Won 8 Lost 5
For 374 Against 266

Most appearances: L.Mercier 34 (26 starts +
8 reps), A.Eustace 33 (22+11), P.Buxton 30
(25+5), M.Foster 28, P.Richards 28 (21+7),
M.Davies 28 (23+5)
Most tries: J.Simpson-Daniel 18, P.Richards
12, M.Foster 10, J.Forrester 8
Conversions: L.Mercier 58, R.Lamb 14,
D.McRae 6, S.Amor 4
Penalties: L.Mercier 68, R.Lamb 16,
M.Tindall 2, S.Amor 1
Drop goals: L.Mercier 2

A new stand at the Worcester Street end of the
stadium greeted spectators for the start of the
season.

In August, for the first time in the Club's
history, Gloucester won the Middlesex Sevens
tournament, beating Wasps in the final.

This was expected to be a season of transition
under new coach Dean Ryan. However,
silverware was won in the shape of the European
Challenge Cup. The final against London Irish,
played at the Stoop Memorial Ground, was
an exciting affair. Well into the second half
following tries from James Simpson-Daniel,

Mark Foster and Andy Hazell, Gloucester led
by 12 points. But two Irish tries levelled the
scores at 31 apiece. Barry Everitt missed the
conversion which would have won the game. In
extra-time Everitt put London Irish ahead with a
penalty, but with only a few minutes left James
Forrester kicked ahead, and showing great pace
touched the ball down just inside the dead ball
line. Even then Everitt could have won the match
but missed with a penalty and a drop goal
attempt. Earlier in the same competition there
was a club record score of 106 points against
Steaua Buceresti. As well there were huge wins
against Toulon both home and away.

In the Premiership, a top four finish seemed
likely until four games in-a-row were lost in the
Spring. The final chance to qualify for the play-
offs depended on beating Wasps at Kingsholm
in the last game of the season. Young Ryan Lamb
showed great attacking flair and confidence,
starting a run from his own 22 which resulted in
a try. At one point Gloucester led 32-23, but two
tries in the last ten minutes won it for Wasps.

All season the Cherry & Whites played an
exhilarating open style of rugby. There was
a big win at Bristol, and there was victory in
the first home game of the season over Sale the
eventual champions. With backs like Simpson-
Daniel, Mike Tindall, Anthony Allen and Mark
Foster, and with Ollie Morgan at full-back, the
team often ran the opposition off their feet. With
the emergence of Ryan Lamb, it seemed likely
that he would, in future, be putting pressure
on regular fly-half Ludovic Mercier, who had
returned having played two seasons for Pau.
Mercier's place kicking was again excellent, and
he scored 336 points.

Mike Tindall played for England in both the
autumn internationals and all the Six Nations
Tests; Phil Vickery in both the autumn games
against Australia and New Zealand and James
Simpson-Daniel scored a try playing against
Italy. Peter Richards would win two caps on the
summer tour of Australia.

There were some departures. Henry Paul left
after playing in seven early season games
and having made 116 appearances. Half-
way through the season Phil Vickery (155
appearances) left to play for Wasps. At the end of
the season Kingsholm favourite Terry Fanolua
departed after 226 appearances and 60 tries,
to play for French club Brive. After playing in
219 games Mark Cornwell left to play a season
for Birmingham/Solihull. Marcel Garvey (95
appearances) left to pursue his career with
Worcester.

With the Club returning to the Heineken Cup for
the 2006-07 season Dean Ryan appeared to have
recruited wisely. He signed Marco Bortolami,
the world class Italian forward, England star Ian
Balshaw, and Cornish Pirates second-row Will
James. These players joined a young squad that
was promising much.

Sep 4 Worcester 15 Gloucester 15
(Premiership)
Penalties: L.Mercier (4);
Drop goal: L.Mercier

Sep 10 Gloucester 21 Sale 18
(Premiership)
Tries: O.Azam, penalty try;
Conversion: L.Mercier;
Penalties: L.Mercier (3)

Sep 18 Bristol 9 Gloucester 41
(Premiership)
Tries: J.Forrester (2), H.Thomas, J.Goodridge;
Conversions: L.Mercier (3);
Penalties: L.Mercier (5)

Sep 24 Gloucester 28 Northampton 24
(Premiership)
Tries: P.Richards, J.Boer, J.Simpson-Daniel;
Conversions: L.Mercier (2);
Penalties: L.Mercier (3)

Oct 1 Gloucester 23 Ospreys 7
(Powergen Cup)
Tries: J.Simpson-Daniel, H.Paul;
Conversions: L.Mercier (2);
Penalties: L.Mercier (3)

Oct 9 Bristol 6 Gloucester 34
(Powergen Cup)
Tries: J.Simpson-Daniel (2), P.Buxton,
M.Cornwell;
Conversions: L.Mercier (4);
Penalties: L.Mercier (2)

Oct 15 Bath 18 Gloucester 16
(Premiership)
Try: R.Thirlby;
Conversion: L.Mercier;
Penalties: L.Mercier (3)

Oct 22 Bayonne 10 Gloucester 26
(European Challenge Cup)
Tries: H.Thomas, A.Hazell, M.Foster;
Conversion: L.Mercier;
Penalties: L.Mercier (3)

Oct 29 Gloucester 106 Steuea Bucuresti 3
(European Challenge Cup)
Tries: J.Simpson-Daniel (4), R.Thirlby (2),
M.Garvey (2), L.Narraway, H.Thomas,
N.Wood, A.Allen, A.Hazell, A.Eustace,
J.Forrester, penalty try;
Conversions: L.Mercier (10), S.Amor (3)

Nov 5 Gloucester 27 Newcastle 20
(Premiership)
Tries: J.Forrester, P.Richards;
Conversion: L.Mercier;
Penalties: L.Mercier (5)

Nov 12 Leicester 25 Gloucester 20
(Premiership)
Tries: A.Allen, O.Morgan;
Conversions: L.Mercier (2);
Penalties: L.Mercier (2)

Nov 20 London Irish 25 Gloucester 10
(Premiership)
Try: P.Richards;
Conversion: L.Mercier;

Penalty: L.Mercier

Nov 26 Gloucester 19 Saracens 8
(Premiership)
Tries: M.Foster, J.Bailey;
Penalties: L.Mercier (2);
Drop goal: L.Mercier

Dec 3 Bath 21 Gloucester 12
(Powergen Cup)
Penalties: L.Mercier (4)

Dec 10 Toulon 3 Gloucester 74
(European Challenge Cup)
Tries: M.Foster (2), J.Boer (2), P.Richards (2),
M.Garvey, M.Tindall, G.Powell, J.Forrester;
Conversions: L.Mercier (6), D.McRae (3);
Penalties: L.Mercier (2)

Dec 17 Gloucester 66 Toulon 5
(European Challenge Cup)
Tries: J.Boer (2), J.Simpson-Daniel (2),
A.Brown, G.Powell, A.Balding, P.Richards,
N.Wood, J.Forster
Conversions: L.Mercier (5), D.McRae (3)

Dec 26 Wasps 32 Gloucester 25
(Premiership)
Tries: L.Mercier, J.Bailey, penalty try;
Conversions: L.Mercier (2);
Penalties: L.Mercier (2)

Dec 31 Gloucester 31 Leeds 7
(Premiership)
Tries: J.Simpson-Daniel (2),
L.Mercier penalty try;
Conversions: L.Mercier (4);
Penalty: L.Mercier

Jan 8 Saracens 9 Gloucester 19
(Premiership)
Try: P.Richards;
Conversion: L.Mercier;
Penalties: L.Mercier (4)

Jan 14 Steuea Bucuresti 13 Gloucester 27
(European Challenge Cup)
Tries: J.Boer, R.Elloway, P.Richards, penalty
try;
Conversions: L.Mercier, S.Amor;
Penalty: S.Amor

Jan 21 Gloucester 32 Bayonne 19
(European Challenge Cup)
Tries: G.Powell (2), M.Tindall, O.Morgan;
Conversions: L.Mercier (3);
Penalties : L.Mercier (2)

Jan 28 Gloucester 9 London Irish 13
(Premiership)
Penalties: L.Mercier (3)

Feb 10 Gloucester 34 Leicester 16
(Premiership)
Tries: J.Bailey, M.Foster, penalty try;
Conversions: L.Mercier (2);
Penalties : L.Mercier (5)

Feb 19 Newcastle 9 Gloucester 13
(Premiership)
Try: T.Fanolua;
Conversion: L.Mercier;
Penalties: L.Mercier (2)

Feb 25 Gloucester 15 Bath 18
(Premiership)
Tries: J.Bailey, M.Foster;
Conversion: L.Mercier;
Penalty: L.Mercier

Mar 11 Northampton 21 Gloucester 20
(Premiership)
Tries: P.Richards, penalty try;
Conversions: L.Mercier (2);
Penalties: L.Mercier (2)

Mar 25 Gloucester 15 Bristol 20
(Premiership)
Tries: J.Simpson-Daniel, A.Allen;
Conversions: L.Mercier;
Penalty: L.Mercier

Apr 1 Gloucester 46 Brive 13
(European Challenge Cup Quarter Final)
Tries: J.Forrester (2), P.Richards (2), M.Tindall,
A.Hazell, J.Simpson-Daniel;
Conversions: R.Lamb (4)
Penalty: R.Lamb

Apr 8 Sale 18 Gloucester 15
(Premiership)
Penalties: R.Lamb (5)

Apr 15 Gloucester 27 Worcester 16
(Premiership)
Tries: M.Foster (2), J.Simpson-Daniel;
Penalties: R.Lamb (2), M.Tindall (2)

Apr 22 Gloucester 31 Worcester 23
(European Challenge Cup Semi Final)
Tries: J.Simpson-Daniel, A.Allen, M.Foster;
Conversions: R.Lamb (2);
Penalties: R.Lamb (3), L.Mercier

Apr 30 Leeds 7 Gloucester 31
(Premiership)
Tries: M.Tindall, A.Hazell, P.Richards,
J.Simpson-Daniel;
Conversions: R.Lamb (4);
Penalty: R.Lamb

May 6 Gloucester 32 Wasps 37
(Premiership)

Tries: A.Allen (2), R.Lamb, J.Bailey;
Conversions: R.Lamb (3);
Penalties: R.Lanb (2)

**May 21 Gloucester 36 London Irish 34
(after extra time)
(European Challenge Cup Final at Stoop
Memorial Ground)**

Tries: M.Foster, A.Hazell, J.Simpson-Daniel,
J.Forrester;
Conversions: L.Mercier, R.Lamb
Penalties: L.Mercier (2), R.Lamb (2)

2006-07

**Played 33 Won 21 Lost 10 Drawn 2
For 861 Against 687
Owner: Tom Walkinshaw
Head Coach: Dean Ryan
Captain: Marco Bortolami**
Premiership: Played 22 Won 15 Lost 5 Drawn 2
For 531 Against 404
Position: 1st

Gloucester United
Played 10 Won 4 Lost 6
For 207 Against 284

Most appearances: P.Buxton 30, R.Lawson
29 (13 starts, 16 reps), O.Azam 28 (19+9),
A.Allen 27 (26+1), P.Richards 27 (18+9),
N.Wood 26 (20+6), M.Davies 26 (13+13)
Most tries: A.Allen 9, M.Foster 8, P.Richards,
J.Forrester, J.Bailey 6
Conversions: W.Walker 36, L.Mercier,
R.Lamb 15
Penalties: W.Walker 43, R.Lamb 26, L.Mercier
19, B.Davies 1
Drop goals: W.Walker 3, R.Lamb 1

Another outstanding season saw Gloucester top
the Premiership, but yet again they tripped on
the final step. Having despatched Saracens 50-9
in the play-off, Leicester were the opponents in
the Twickenham final. Gloucester were torn to
pieces by Alesana Tuilagi. The Cherry & Whites
cause was not helped by injuries. Missing from
the final were inspirational captain Marco
Bortolami with a knee injury and Mike Tindall
with a broken leg. After only 15 minutes
replacement captain, Pete Buxton had to come
off with a broken hand. However, it would have

taken an exceptional team to have matched the
Tigers on the day. It was a disappointing end to
a season during which the young team played
some lovely rugby.

In Premiership games the club remained
unbeaten at home. Indeed, the only home defeat
was to Agen in the Heineken Cup. One of the
most satisfying wins was against Leicester,
who were leading 19-11 at half-time and looking
ominously in control. However, in the second
half Andy Hazell scored a try and Willie Walker
kicked four penalties to see the team home.

There were mixed fortunes in the Heineken Cup.
Defeat in the first contest in Ireland against
Leinster immediately put the team under
pressure, and losing both games to Agen ensured
that the pool stage was as far as Gloucester were
going to go. However, the final game was the
return match against Leinster. The Cherry &
Whites put on a forward display which the older
fans would have loved. Early on a rolling maul
ended with the referee awarding a penalty try.
Leinster fought back and by the hour led 10-7,
but late tries from Christian Califano and Mark
Foster saw Gloucester home, and thoroughly
deserving their victory.

New arrivals were Marco Bortolami (who was
made captain), Ian Balshaw, Willie Walker,
Christian Califano, Rory Lawson, Will James
and Carlos Nieto. Willie Walker scored a
total of 220 points. All these players quickly
settled and made valuable contributions.
This coupled with the already present James
Simpson-Daniel, Mike Tindall, Mark Foster,

Peter Richards and Ryan Lamb made for a
scintillating back division, whilst Ollie Azam,
Alex Brown, Pete Buxton, Andy Hazell and the
emerging Luke Narraway ensured the forwards
were as formidable as ever. Gloucester's
final Premiership game of the season was a
"home" game against Bristol played at Ashton
Gate, because of the construction of the new
grandstand at Kingsholm. James Forester
scored a try, but soon after suffered an injury
which, in the end, terminated his career after
136 appearances.

Ludovic Mercier left the Club at the end of the
season. He had scored a total of 1325 points in
105 games. Jake Boer returned to South Africa,
although he would return to help out when the
team was injury stricken in the 2009-10 season.

Gloucester players were well represented at
international level. Ollie Morgan, Ian Balshaw,
Anthony Allen, Peter Richards, Andy Hazell,
and Mike Tindall all won England caps, whilst
Rory Lawson played for Scotland, and Marco
Bortolami was captain of Italy.

**Sep 2 Gloucester 24 Bath 19
(Premiership)**
Tries: J.Adams, O.Morgan;
Conversion: W.Walker;
Penalties: W.Walker (4)

**Sep 9 Harlequins 21 Gloucester 31
(Premiership)**
Tries: P.Richards, O.Azam, J.Forrester;
Conversions: W.Walker (2);
Penalties: W.Walker (4)

**Sep 16 Leicester 27 Gloucester 27
(Premiership)**
Tries: J.Forrester, A.Allen;
Conversion: W.Walker;
Penalties: W.Walker (2), B.Davies;
Drop goals: W.Walker (2)

**Sep 23 Gloucester 28 Northampton 7
(Premiership)**
Tries: J.Forrester, A.Hazell, J.Adams;
Conversions: L.Mercier (2);
Penalties: L.Mercier (3)

**Sep 29 Ospreys 49 Gloucester 19
(EDF Cup)**
Try: P.Richards;
Conversion: L.Mercier;
Penalties: L.Mercier (4)

**Oct 7 Gloucester 63 Bristol 25
(EDF Cup)**
Tries: J.Goodridge (2), J.Bailey, J.Forrester,
R.Lawson, R.Lamb, P.Richards, M.Foster;
Conversions: L.Mercier (7);
Penalties: L.Mercier (3)

**Oct 13 Worcester 24 Gloucester 33
(Premiership)**
Tries: J.Adams, A.Allen, I.Balshaw;
Conversions: R.Lamb (3);
Penalties: R.Lamb (4)

**Oct 21 Leinster 37 Gloucester 20
(Heineken Cup)**
Tries: M.Foster, J.Adams;
Conversions: R.Lamb (2);
Penalties: R.Lamb (2)

**Oct 28 Gloucester 26 Agen 32
(Heineken Cup)**
Tries: A.Allen (2), O.Azam;
Conversion: W.Walker;
Penalties: R.Lamb (3)

**Nov 4 Gloucester 21 Saracens 12
(Premiership)**
Tries: R.Keil (2);
Conversion: W.Walker;
Penalties: W.Walker (2), L.Mercier

**Nov 10 London Irish 11 Gloucester 22
(Premiership)**
Tries: J.Bailey, R.Lawson, J.Simpson-Daniel;
Conversions: W.Walker (2);
Penalty: W.Walker

**Nov 18 Gloucester 27 Wasps 21
(Premiership)**
Tries: J.Bailey, A.Allen;
Conversion: W.Walker;
Penalties: W.Walker (5)

**Nov 24 Bristol 14 Gloucester 12
(Premiership)**
Penalties: W.Walker (4)

Dec 2 Gloucester 30 Bath 12 (EDF Cup)
Tries: J.Merriman, A.Balding, W.Walker,
penalty try;
Conversions: W.Walker (2);
Penalties: W.Walker (2)

**Dec 9 Gloucester 38 Edinburgh 22
(Heineken Cup)**
Tries: M.Tindall, O.Azam, J.Simpson-Daniel,
M.Foster, A.Allen;
Conversions: W.Walker (2);
Penalties: W.Walker, R.Lamb;
Drop goal: W.Walker

**Dec 17 Edinburgh 14 Gloucester 31
(Heineken Cup)**
Tries: L.Narrawy, M.Tindall, A.Allen,
O.Morgan;
Conversions: W.Walker (3), R.Lamb;
Penalty: R.Lamb

Dec 22 Gloucester v Newcastle (Premiership) -
postponed due to fog

**Dec 26 Wasps 33 Gloucester 12
(Premiership)**
Tries: A.Allen, R.Lawson;
Conversion: R.Lamb

**Jan 1 Gloucester 15 London Irish 3
(Premiership)**
Tries: O.Morgan, I.Balshaw;
Conversion: W.Walker;
Penalty: W.Walker

**Jan 6 Sale 20 Gloucester 19
(Premiership)**
Try: J.Simpson-Daniel;
Conversion: R.Lamb;
Penalties: R.Lamb (4)

**Jan 12 Agen 26 Gloucester 18
(Heineken Cup)**
Tries: P.Richards, I.Balshaw;
Conversion: R.Lamb;
Penalties: R.Lamb (2)

**Jan 19 Gloucester 19 Leinster 13
(Heineken Cup)**
Tries: C.Califano, M.Foster, penalty try;
Conversions: W.Walker, R.Lamb

**Jan 27 Gloucester 44 Sale 24
(Premiership)**
Tries: R.Lamb, I.Balshaw, O.Azam,
M.Bortolami, O.Morgan;
Conversions: L.Mercier (3), R.Lamb (2)

Penalties: L.Mercier, R.Lamb;
Drop goal: R.Lamb

**Feb 18 Saracens 24 Gloucester 22
(Premiership)**
Try: A.Brown;
Conversion: L.Mercier;
Penalties: L.Mercier (5)

**Feb 24 Gloucester 33 Worcester 19
(Premiership)**
Tries: P.Buxton, M.Foster, J.Bailey;
Conversions: R.Lamb (2), L.Mercier;
Penalties: R.Lamb (2), L.Mercier (2)

**Mar 3 Northampton 5 Gloucester 7
(Premiership)**
Try: J.Simpson-Daniel;
Conversion: W.Walker

**Mar 11 Gloucester 28 Leicester 24
(Premiership)**
Tries: A.Hazell, P.Richards;
Penalties: W.Walker (6)

**Mar 17 Gloucester 34 Harlequins 25
(Premiership)**
Tries: N.Wood, J.Bailey, J.Forrester, M.Foster;
Conversions: W.Walker (4);
Penalties: W.Walker (2)

**Mar 24 Gloucester 24 Newcastle 18
(Premiership)**
Tries: J.Forrester, J.Boer, R.Lamb;
Conversions: W.Walker (3);
Penalty: W.Walker

**Apr 7 Bath 21 Gloucester 21
(Premiership)**
Tries: W.James, J.Bailey;
Conversion: R.Lamb;
Penalties: R.Lamb (3)

**Apr 13 Newcastle 19 Gloucester 12
(Premiership)**
Penalties: R.Lamb (3), W.Walker

**Apr 28 Gloucester 35 Bristol 13
(Premiership)** ("Home" game played at
Ashton Gate)
Tries: W.Walker, M.Foster, J.Boer, A.Hazell;
Conversions: W.Walker (3);
Penalties: W.Walker (3)

**May 5 Gloucester 50 Saracens 9
(Premiership Play Off Semi-Final)**
Tries: P.Richards, L.Narraway, A.Allen,
M.Foster, A.Hazell, C.Califano penalty try;
Conversions: W.Walker (6);
Penalty: W.Walker

May 12 Leicester 44 Gloucester 16
(Premiership Final at Twickenham)
Try: R.Lamb;

Conversion: W.Walker;
Penalties: W.Walker (3)

2007-08

Played 33 Won 21 Lost 11 Drawn 1
For 820 Against 596
Owner: Tom Walkinshaw
Head Coach: Dean Ryan
Captain: Pete Buxton
Premiership: Played 22 Won 15 Lost 7
For 551 Against 377
Position: 1st

Gloucester United
Played 7 Won 1 Lost 6
For 133 Against 302

Most appearances: A.Allen 30 (29 starts + 1
rep), L.Narraway 30 (21+9), A.Strokosch 29
(21+8), A.Titterrell 29 (14+15), J.Simpson-
Daniel 28 (27+1), O.Azam 27 (16+11),
P.Buxton 27 (22+5)
Most tries: J.Simpson-Daniel 15, L.Vainikolo
11, R.Lamb, A.Qera, I.Balshaw 8, A.Allen,
O.Azam 6
Conversions: R.Lamb 41, W.Walker 13,
C.Paterson 10
Penalties: R.Lamb 42, W.Walker 19,
C.Paterson 6
Drop goals: R.Lamb, W.Walker 1

The new grandstand was erected during the
summer of 2007, and completed in time for the
start of the new season. It brought the ground
capacity up to more than 16,000.

For the second season running, and the third
time in six seasons Gloucester topped the
Premiership, but this time did not even make the
play-off final, losing at home to Leicester in the
semi-final. The Tigers triumphed by way of an
Andy Goode drop goal in the very last minute.
So yet again a marvellous season ended in anti-
climax. But there was much to be pleased about.
There were outstanding Premiership wins,
including a very satisfying win at Welford Road
against Leicester, where the home fans, fully
aware that the game was lost, were streaming
away through the exits long before the end.
However, the Tigers had their revenge in the
return game, when Gloucester suffered their
first home Premiership defeat since May 2006.

But the last two matches of the regular season
demonstrated the Cherry & Whites at their
best. The current European Champions, Wasps,
were beaten on their own patch. Tries from Ollie
Morgan, James Simpson-Daniel and Mike
Tindall were enough for victory, and Wasps
were denied even a losing bonus point when
Ryan Lamb kicked a last-minute penalty. The
next game against Bath illustrated how a low
scoring game can still be exciting. In the first
half Simpson-Daniel scored a glorious try. It
was the only one of the game, and the second
half was scoreless, but the excitement never
abated. It was a game of rugby that was a credit
to both teams. Simpson-Daniel had been at his
best all season and was the top try scorer. He
was also named the Premiership Player of the
Season.

In the Heineken Cup, five out of the six group
games were won, including doubles over Ulster
and Bourgoin. In the away tie with Ulster,
Gloucester had the bonus point try in the bag
after only 25 minutes. But in the quarter-final
against Munster, the performance was very
disappointing, not helped by Chris Paterson
missing a series of easy kicks.

A recruit from rugby league, Lesley Vainikolo,
who had been a star playing for Bradford Bulls,
had an amazing debut scoring five tries against
Leeds, and was soon capped by England. As
well as Vainikolo, Ian Balshaw, James Simpson-
Daniel, Mike Tindall and Luke Narraway all
won England caps, whilst Alasdair Strokosch
and Chris Paterson played for Scotland, Will
James for Wales and Marco Bortolami for Italy.

Young Ryan Lamb had a satisfying season
scoring 251 points. When he was not available
his spot was taken ably by Willie Walker,
another consistent place kicker. Jack Adams
showed promise in the centre. Akapusi Qera,
who had played for Fiji in the World Cup made a
big impression. Much was expected from multi-
capped Chris Paterson, but for some reason he
did not fire, was never a regular selection, and
left at the end of the season. Two young players
started their Gloucester careers, and much more
would be heard from them as the seasons passed
- Charlie Sharples and Henry Trinder.

Sep 16 Leeds 24 Gloucester 49

(Premiership)
Tries: L.Vainikolo (5), J.Simpson-Daniel,
I.Balshaw, A.Allen;
Conversions: R.Lamb (3);
Penalty: R.Lamb

**Sep 23 Saracens 31 Gloucester 38
(Premiership)**
Tries: A.Allen, R.Lamb, L.Narraway,
O.Morgan;
Conversions: R.Lamb (3);
Penalties: R.Lamb (4)

**Sep 29 Gloucester 29 Worcester 7
(Premiership)**
Tries: J.Simpson-Daniel, O.Azam, M.Tindall;
Conversion: R.Lamb;
Penalties: R.Lamb (3);
Drop goal: R.Lamb

**Oct 6 Leicester 17 Gloucester 30
(Premiership)**
Tries: L.Lloyd, W.Walker, penalty try;
Conversions: W.Walker (3);
Penalties: W.Walker (3)

**Oct 13 Gloucester 31 Sale 12
(Premiership)**
Tries: L.Lloyd (2), O.Morgan;
Conversions: R.Lamb (2);
Penalties: R.Lamb (4)

**Oct 21 London Irish 15 Gloucester 10
(Premiership)**
Try: I.Balshaw;
Conversion: C.Paterson;
Penalty: C.Paterson

**Oct 27 Gloucester 18 Newcastle 18
(EDF Cup)**
Tries: J.Simpson-Daniel (2);
Conversion: W.Walker;
Penalties: C.Paterson, W.Walker

**Nov 4 Wasps 29 Gloucester 26 (EDF
Cup)**
Tries: R.Lawson, O.Morgan, O.Azam,
I.Balshaw;
Conversions: R.Lamb (3)

**Nov 9 Ulster 14 Gloucester 32
(Heineken Cup)**
Tries: L.Vainikolo, M.Tindall, R.Lamb,
J.Simpson-Daniel, I.Balshaw;
Conversions: R.Lamb (2);
Penalty: R.Lamb

**Nov 16 Gloucester 26 Ospreys 18
(Heineken Cup)**
Tries: A.Allen, J.Simpson-Daniel;
Conversions: R.Lamb, C.Paterson;

Penalties: R.Lamb (3), C.Paterson

**Nov 24 Gloucester 27 Harlequins 25
(Premiership)**
Tries: L.Vainikolo (2), M.Tindall;
Conversions: C.Paterson (3);
Penalties: C.Paterson (2)

**Nov 30 Newport Gwent Dragons 11
Gloucester 13 (EDF Cup)**
Try: G.Delve;
Conversion: C.Paterson;
Penalties: W.Walker (2)

**Dec 7 Bourgoin 7 Gloucester 31
(Heineken Cup)**
Tries: J.Simpson-Daniel, R.Lamb, A.Titterrell,
A.Allen;
Conversions: R.Lamb (4);
Penalty: R.Lamb

**Dec 15 Gloucester 51 Bourgoin 27
(Heineken Cup)**
Tries: R.Lamb, I.Balshaw, L.Vainikolo, A.Qera,
G.Delve, W.Walker;
Conversions: R.Lamb (6);
Penalties: R.Lamb (3)

**Dec 23 Newcastle 13 Gloucester 20
(Premiership)**
Tries: I.Balshaw, O.Azam;
Conversions: R.Lamb (2);
Penalties: R.Lamb (2)

**Dec 29 Gloucester 27 Bristol 0
(Premiership)**
Tries: L.Lloyd (2), O.Azam, J.Simpson-Daniel;
Conversions: R.Lamb (2);
Penalty: R.Lamb

Jan 4 Bath 10 Gloucester 5 (Premiership)
Try: C.Paterson

**Jan 12 Ospreys 32 Gloucester 15
(Heineken Cup)**
Tries: R.Lamb, R.Lawson;
Conversion: C.Paterson;
Penalty: R.Lamb

**Jan 20 Gloucester 29 Ulster 21
(Heineken Cup)**
Tries: A.Qera (2), I.Balshaw, A.Strokosch,
L.Narraway;
Conversions: C.Paterson (2)

**Jan 26 Gloucester 18 Wasps 17
(Premiership)**
Penalties: R.Lamb (6)

**Feb 9 Gloucester 13 Leicester 20
(Premiership)**
Try: O.Azam;

Conversion: W.Walker;
Penalties: W.Walker (2)

**Feb 17 Bristol 29 Gloucester 26
(Premiership)**
Tries: J.Simpson-Daniel, J.Adams, A.Allen;
Conversion: C.Paterson;
Penalties: W.Walker (2), C.Paterson

**Feb 23 Gloucester 28 Newcastle 20
(Premiership)**
Tries: J.Simpson-Daniel, A.Qera, J.Bailey;
Conversions: W.Walker (2);
Penalties: W.Walker (3)

**Mar 1 Harlequins 30 Gloucester 25
(Premiership)**
Tries: J.Simpson-Daniel, I.Balshaw, J.Adams,
A.Allen;
Conversion: W.Walker;
Penalty: W.Walker

**Mar 8 Gloucester 34 London Irish 14
(Premiership)**
Tries: J.Adams, N.Wood, M.Foster, A.Titterrell;
Conversions: W.Walker (4);
Penalties: W.Walker (2)

**Mar 14 Sale 22 Gloucester 16
(Premiership)**
Penalty try;
Conversion: W.Walker;
Penalties: W.Walker (3)

**Mar 29 Worcester 17 Gloucester 14
(Premiership)**
Tries: L.Vainikolo, R.Lawson;
Conversions: R.Lamb (2)

**Apr 5 Gloucester 3 Munster 16
(Heineken Cup Quarter-Final)**
Penalty: R.Lamb

**Apr 12 Gloucester 39 Saracens 15
(Premiership)**
Tries: R.Lamb (2), A.Qera, J.Simpson-Daniel,
L.Vainikolo, R.Lawson;
Conversions: R.Lamb (3);
Penalty: R.Lamb

**Apr 19 Gloucester 39 Leeds 16
(Premiership)**
Tries: A.Qera (3), R.Lamb, O.Azam;
Conversions: R.Lamb (4);
Penalties R.Lamb (2)

**May 4 Wasps 17 Gloucester 25
(Premiership)**
Tries: J.Simpson-Daniel, M.Tindall, O.Morgan;
Conversions: R.Lamb (2);
Penalties: R.Lamb (2)

May 10 Gloucester 8 Bath 6
(Premiership)
Try: J.Simpson-Daniel;
Penalty: R.Lamb

May 18 Gloucester 25 Leicester 26
(Premiership Play-off Semi-Final)
Try: J.Simpson-Daniel;
Conversion: R.Lamb;

Penalties: R.Lamb (5);
Drop goal: W.Walker

2008-09

Played 33 Won 19 Lost 14
For 680 Against 656
Owner: Tom Walkinshaw
Head Coach: Dean Ryan
Captain: Mike Tindall
Premiership: Played 22 Won 12 Lost 10
For 435 Against 448
Position: 6th

Gloucester United
Played 7 Won 4 Lost 3
For 193 Against 202

Most appearances: O.Azam 30 (22 starts +
8 reps), A.Brown 29 (27+2), O.Barkley 28
(20+8), R.Lawson 28 (18+10), N.Wood 26
(19+7), R.Lamb 26 (18+8)
Most tries: I.Balshaw 11, L.Vainikolo,
O.Morgan 8, J.Simpson-Daniel 6, M.Foster 5
Conversions: R.Lamb, O.Barkley 18, W.Walker
4, C.Spencer 2
Penalties: O.Barkley 49, R.Lamb 17, W.Walker
8, C.Spencer 2
Dropped goals: R.Lamb 4, W.Walker 2

For most of the season the team was fighting for
top place in the Premiership, only to fall away
at the very end. The last four games were all
lost, including a double conceded to Worcester.
The net result was not even a play-off place, but
mid-table sixth, which did at least guarantee
Heineken Cup qualification for the following

season. A good run in the EDF Energy Cup
took Gloucester to a semi-final, played at the
Ricoh Stadium, Coventry, and a fine win over
the Ospreys, the highlight being a marvellous
length of the field try by Ian Balshaw, playing in
what turned out to be his final game. And so to
Twickenham for the final against Cardiff Blues,
in front of 54,000 spectators. It was a disaster
with Cardiff running up 50 points. Fly-half
Nicky Robinson, who would join Gloucester the
following season had a great game.

The season had promised so much. In only the
second game Bath were defeated at the Rec for
the first time since leagues began in 1987-88.
There were more notable wins, particularly
at Kingsholm, and there were doubles over
Bath and Saracens. Lesley Vainikolo was in
great form running in eight tries before injury
in January ended his season. But the Club's
away form was not good - a win at Bristol in
December proved to be the last of the season. A
long injury list, with Andy Hazell, Pete Buxton
and Will James absent at various times, took
the momentum out of the league season. The
Heineken Cup campaign ended in the pool
stage, thanks to two losses to Cardiff Blues.

Ollie Barkley, who had left Bath to come to
Kingsholm scored 188 points. Although trying
his best the move was not a great success; he
lasted just the one season, then returned to Bath.

Greg Somerville, the most capped All Black of
all time arrived in December to form a solid
front-row with Nick Wood and Ollie Azam.
Alex Brown was consistency personified in the
second row and manged to avoid the injury bug.
Club captain Mike Tindall was another player
to miss games through injury, although he did
appear for England in four of the Six Nations
tests. Marco Bortolami was again captain of
Italy, and he was accompanied by Carlos Nieto
in all the Six Nations games. Rory Lawson
played for Scotland, as did Alasdair Strokosch
who appeared in all their matches.

At the end of the season Ryan Lamb left for
London Irish, Anthony Allen for Leicester, and
Ian Balshaw to France to play for Biarritz.

Sep 7 Gloucester 8 Leicester 20
(Premiership)
Try: O.Morgan;
Penalty: R.Lamb

Sep 13 Bath 17 Gloucester 21
(Premiership)
Tries: W.Walker, L.Narraway;
Conversion: W.Walker;
Penalties: W.Walker (2);
Drop goal: W.Walker

Sep 20 Gloucester 24 Harlequins 20
(Premiership)

Tries: O.Morgan, A.Strokosch;
Conversion: W.Walker;
Penalties: W.Walker (2), O.Barkley;
Drop goal: W.Walker

Sep 26 Sale 23 Gloucester 9
(Premiership)
Penalties: O.Barkley (3)

Sep 30 Gloucester 39 Newcastle 23
(Premiership)
Tries: I.Balshaw (3), J.Simpson-Daniel (2);
Conversion: W.Walker;
Penalties: O.Barkley (4)

Oct 4 Gloucester 24 Wasps 19
(EDF Cup)
Tries: W.Walker, L.Vainikolo;
Conversion: W.Walker;
Penalties: W.Walker (3);
Drop goal: R.Lamb

Oct 11 Gloucester 22 Biarritz 10
(Heineken Cup)
Try: J.Simpson-Daniel;
Conversion: O.Barkley;
Penalties: O.Barkley (4), R.Lamb

Oct 19 Cardiff Blues 37 Gloucester 24
(Heineken Cup)
Tries: I.Balshaw (2), O.Morgan;
Conversions: O.Barkley (3);
Penalty: O.Barkley

Oct 25 Gloucester 25 Newport Gwent
Dragons 20 (EDF Cup)
Tries: L.Vainikolo (2), I.Balshaw, S.Lawson;
Conversion: O.Barkley;
Penalty: O.Barkley

Nov 2 Newcastle 10 Gloucester 11
(EDF Cup)
Try: A.Satala;
Penalties: O.Barkley (2)

Nov 16 Saracens 21 Gloucester 25
(Premiership)
Tries: A.Allen, O.Morgan, L.Vainikolo;
Conversions: R.Lamb (2);
Penalties: R.Lamb (2)

Nov 21 Gloucester 39 Bristol 10
(Premiership)
Tries: P.Buxton (2), R.Lamb, O.Morgan,
A.Brown;
Conversions: R.Lamb (4);
Penalty: R.Lamb;
Drop goal: R.Lamb

Nov 29 Gloucester 33 Northampton 10
(Premiership)
Tries: I.Balshaw, O.Barkley, L.Narraway,
L.Vainikolo;
Conversions: R.Lamb (2);
Penalties: R.Lamb (3)

Dec 6 Calvisano 17 Gloucester 40
(Heineken Cup)
Tries: R.Lamb, M.Bortolami, M.Tindall,
M.Foster, L.Narraway penalty try;
Conversions: O.Barkley (5)

Dec 13 Gloucester 48 Calvisano 5
(Heineken Cup)
Tries: L.Vainikolo (2), M.Watkins (2), M.Foster,
L.Narraway;
Conversions: R.Lamb (6);
Penalties: R.Lamb (2)

Dec 20 London Irish 42 Gloucester 12
(Premiership)
Penalties: R.Lamb (3), W.Walker

Dec 27 Bristol 10 Gloucester 29
(Premiership)
Tries: M.Tindall (2), O.Morgan, L.Vainikolo;
Conversions: R.Lamb (2), O.Barkley;
Penalty: R.Lamb

Jan 3 Gloucester 22 Saracens 16
(Premiership)
Try: O.Morgan;
Conversion: O.Barkley;
Penalties: O.Barkley (5)

Jan 11 Newcastle 10 Gloucester 7
(Premiership)
Try: R.Lawson;
Conversion: O.Barkley

Jan 18 Gloucester 12 Cardiff Blues 16
(Heineken Cup)
Penalties: O.Barkley (4)

Jan 23 Biarritz 24 Glloucester 10
(Heineken Cup)
Try: J.Simpson-Daniel;
Conversion: O.Barkley;
Penalty: O.Barkley

Jan 31 Gloucester 23 London Irish 21
(Premiership)
Try: I.Balshaw;
Penalties: O.Barkley (6)

Feb 14 Gloucester 24 Sale 17

(Premiership)
Tries: A.Satala, M.Foster;
Conversion: O.Barkley;
Penalties: O.Barkley (3);
Drop goal: R.Lamb

Feb 21 Harlequins 14 Gloucester 9
(Premiership)
Penalties: O.Barkley (3)

Feb 28 Gloucester 36 Bath 27
(Premiership)
Tries: J.Simpson-Daniel (2), C.Sharples,
R.Lawson;
Conversions: O.Barkley, C.Spencer;
Penalties: O.Barkley (3), C.Spencer

Mar 7 Leicester 24 Gloucester 10
(Premiership)
Try: I.Balshaw;
Conversion: O.Barkley;
Penalty: O.Barkley

Mar 14 Gloucester 24 Wasps 22
(Premiership)
Tries: O.Morgan, I.Balshaw, A.Qera;
Penalties: O.Barkley (3)

Mar 22 Worcester 14 Gloucester 10
(Premiership)
Penalty try;
Conversion: C.Spencer;
Penalty: C.Spencer

Mar 28 Gloucester 17 Ospreys 0
(EDF Semi-Final at Coventry)
Try: I.Balshaw;
Penalties: R.Lamb (3;
Drop goal: R.Lamb

Apr 4 Northampton 40 Gloucester 22
(Premiership)
Tries: N.Wood, W.James, M.Foster;
Conversions: R.Lamb (2);
Penalty: O.Barkley

Apr 18 Cardiff Blues 50 Gloucester 12
(EDF Final at Twickenham)
Tries: M.Foster, penalty try;
Conversion: O.Barkley

Apr 21 Gloucester 6 Worcester 13
(Premiership)
Penalties: O.Barkley (2)

Apr 25 Wasps 34 Gloucester 3
(Premiership)
Penalty: O.Barkley

Played 35 Won 17 Lost 17 Drawn 1
For 755 Against 757
Owner: Tom Walkinshaw
Head Coach: Brian Redpath
Captain: Gareth Delve
Premiership: Played 22 Won 10 Lost 11 Drawn 1
For 470 Against 457
Position: 7th

Gloucester United
Played 9 Won 1 Lost 7 Drawn 1
For 144 Against 372

Most appearances: N.Robinson 32 (28 starts + 4 reps), J.Simpson-Daniel 30 (28+2), R.Lawson 29 (25+4), A.Qera 28 (21+7), T.Molenaar 27 (19+8), S.Lawson 28 (19+9), A.Eustace 27 (12+15)
Most tries: J.Simpson-Daniel 13, C.Sharples, A.Qera 10, L.Vainikolo 6
Conversions: N.Robinson 38, T.Taylor 7, F.Burns 5
Penalties: N.Robinson 69, F.Burns 11, C.Spencer 4, T.Taylor 2
Drop goals: N.Robinson, F.Burns 2

The season started with a new Head Coach. Dean Ryan was replaced by Nigel Melville. A disappointing season in the Premiership was largely down to yet another season of poor away form, only two games being won. The autumn period was most difficult due to international calls and a host of injuries. However, home form remained good throughout and Gloucester were unbeaten at Kingsholm from early November onwards. In February there were two superb

displays of running rugby in very muddy conditions at Kingsholm. James Simpson-Daniel scored a hat trick of tries against Harlequins, and six tries in all were scored in the 46-6 victory. Then two weeks later Sale were similarly thrashed 47-3, when seven tries were scored.

The Heineken Cup campaign was not helped by two early defeats to Biarritz and Glasgow, but a double over the Dragons and return game wins over Glasgow and Biarritz meant that Gloucester were parachuted down into the Challenge Cup, only to lose heavily to Wasps. The Anglo-Welsh Cup got off to a terrible start, the first two matches being lost, but successive wins over Worcester, Harlequins and Cardiff Blues, put the campaign back on track. The win against Harlequins was remarkable for a magnificent fight back from 20-0 down after 25 minutes. Tim Taylor in his first start scored a try and three conversions, the last winning the game at the very end. Cardiff Blues were beaten in Wales in the semi-final, so it meant that Gloucester played Northampton in the final at Worcester. It was a close contest, but for the second season running the final was lost, with the Saints coming out on top in the end.

A seventh-place finish in the Premiership would usually mean qualification for the Heineken Cup in 2010-11, but Cardiff Blues' victory over Toulon in the final of the Challenge Cup meant that Scarlets instead of Gloucester would qualify.

In his first season Nicky Robinson scored 304 points, and formed a fruitful half-back partnership with scrum-half Rory Lawson who was made captain of Scotland. For a change Simpson-Daniel had an injury free season and was top try scorer. Charlie Sharples established his place on the other wing. In the centre a new recruit from Bath, Eliota Fuimaono-Sapolu, also impressed, and won caps playing for Samoa. Injuries were a problem for several players, affecting Mike Tindall, Andy Hazell, Marco Bortolami (who returned to Italy at the end of the season), Alex Brown, Will James and Ollie Azam. The problem was so acute that Jake Boer returned from South Africa to help out, which boosted his total appearances to 190. Two very promising youngsters, Jonny May and Freddie Burns made their first appearances, the latter scoring 74 points including five tries. After 245 games Adam Eustace left Gloucester for Northampton.

As well as Rory Lawson, Alasdair Strokosch and Alasdair Dickinson won Scotland caps. Despite injuries Mike Tindall still added another cap against France to his list, and as ever, Marco Bortolami captained Italy. Akapusi Qera and Apo Satala won caps playing for Fiji.

Sep 6 Gloucester 24 Bath 5
(Premiership)
Tries: J.Simpson-Daniel (2), N.Robinson;
Conversions: N.Robinson (3);
Penalty: N.Robinson

Sep 13 London Irish 40 Gloucester 10

(Premiership)
Try: C.Sharples;
Conversion: N Robinson;
Penalty: N.Robinson

Sep 19 Gloucester 14 Northampton 27
(Premiership)
Try: A.Qera;
Penalties: N.Robinson (3)

Sep 27 Saracens 19 Gloucester 16
(Premiership)
Try: R.Lawson;
Conversion: N.Robinson;
Penalties: N.Robinson (3)

Oct 4 Leeds 10 Gloucester 26
(Premiership)
Tries: O.Azam, J.Simpson-Daniel, M.Tindall;
Conversion: N.Robinson;
Penalties: N.Robinson (3)

Oct 9 Gloucester 19 Newport Gwent Dragons 17 (Heineken Cup)
Try: A.Qera;
Conversion: N.Robinson;
Penalties: N.Robinson (4)

Oct 17 Biarritz 42 Gloucester 15
(Heineken Cup)
Tries: T.Voyce, J.Boer;
Conversion: F.Burns;
Penalty: N.Robinson

Oct 24 Gloucester 6 Wasps 35
(Premiership)
Penalties: C.Spencer (2)

Oct 30 Sale 28 Gloucester 23
(Premiership)
Tries: T.Voyce, G.Somerville, W.James;
Conversion: N.Robinson;
Penalty: N.Robinson;
Drop goal: N.Robinson

Nov 3 Gloucester 5 Australia 36
(Friendly – not included in season records)
Try: F.Burns

Nov 8 Gloucester 25 Cardiff Blues 26
(LV Cup)
Tries: A.Eustace, G.Delve;
Penalties: C.Spencer (2), F.Burns (2)
N.Robinson

Nov 15 Wasps 21 Gloucester 14
(LV Cup)
Tries: F.Burns (2);
Conversions: F.Burns (2)

Nov 20 Gloucester 12 Leicester 9

(Premiership)
Penalties: F.Burns (2);
Drop goals: F.Burns (2)

Nov 28 Harlequins 35 Gloucester 29
(Premiership)
Tries: C.Sharples (2), G.Delve;
Conversion: N.Robinson;
Penalties: N.Robinson (2), F.Burns (2)

Dec 5 Gloucester 25 Newcastle 13
(Premiership)
Try: C.Sharples;
Conversion: N.Robinson;
Penalties: N.Robinson (5);
Drop goal: N.Robinson

Dec 11 Glasgow Warriors 33
Gloucester 11 (Heineken Cup)
Try: C.Sharples;
Penalties: N.Robinson (2)

Dec 20 Gloucester 19 Glasgow Warriors 6
(Heineken Cup)
Tries: C.Sharples, A.Brown;
Penalties: N.Robinson (3)

Dec 27 Bath 24 Gloucester 8
(Premiership)
Try: A.Dickinson;
Penalty: N.Robinson

Jan 2 Gloucester 13 Worcester 13
(Premiership)
Tries: A.Qera, D.Attwood;
Penalty; N.Robinson

Jan 16 Gloucester 23 Biarritz 8
(Heineken Cup)
Tries: L.Vainikolo, T.Molenaar;
Conversions: N.Robinson (2);
Penalties: N.Robinson (3)

Jan 24 Newport Gwent Dragons 23
Gloucester 32 (Heineken Cup)
Tries: A.Qera (3), penalty try;
Conversions: N.Robinson (3);
Penalties: N.Robinson (2)

Jan 30 Gloucester 17 Worcester 5
(LV Cup)
Tries: A.Qera, F.Burns;
Conversions: N.Robinson (2);
Penalty: N.Robinson

Feb 7 Harlequins 29 Gloucester 31
(LV Cup)
Tries: J.Simpson-Daniel (2), T.Taylor,
T.Molenaar, T.Voyce;
Conversions: T.Taylor (3)

Feb 13 Gloucester 46 Harlequins 6
(Premiership)
Tries: J.Simpson-Daniel (3), T.Molenaar,
T.Voyce, L.Vainikolo;
Conversions: N.Robinson (3), T.Taylor (2);
Penalties: N.Robinson (2)

Feb 20 Leicester 33 Gloucester 11
(Premiership)
Try: J.May;
Penalties: N.Robinson (2)

Feb 27 Gloucester 47 Sale 3
(Premiership)
Tries: L.Vainikolo (2), N.Robinson, J.Simpson-
Daniel, A.Hazell, A.Qera, penalty try;
Conversions: N.Robinson (4), T.Taylor (2)

Mar 7 Wasps 24 Gloucester 19
(Premiership)
Try: M.Tindall;
Conversion: N.Robinson;
Penalties: N.Robinson (2), T.Taylor (2)

Mar 14 Cardiff Blues 18 Gloucester 29
(LV Cup Semi-Final)
Tries: J.Simpson-Daniel (3), F.Burns;
Conversions: N.Robinson (3);
Penalty: N.Robinson

Mar 21 Northampton 30 Gloucester 24
(LV Cup Final at Worcester)
Tries: A.Qera, penalty try;
Conversion: N.Robinson;
Penalties: N.Robinson (4)

Mar 27 Gloucester 19 Leeds 0
(Premiership)
Try: N.Robinson;
Conversion: N.Robinson;
Penalties: N.Robinson (4)

Mar 31 Newcastle 25 Gloucester 13
(Premiership)
Try: T.Taylor;
Conversion: N.Robinson;
Penalties: N.Robinson (2)

Apr 3 Gloucester 29 Saracens 28
(Premiership)
Tries: C.Sharples (2);
Conversions: F.Burns (2);
Penalties: F.Burns (5)

Apr 11 Wasps 42 Gloucester 26
(Amlin Cup Quarter-Final)
Tries: A.Eustace, C.Sharples;
Conversions: N.Robinson (2);
Penalties: N.Robinson (4)

Apr 17 Northampton 38 Gloucester 23

(Premiership)
Tries: D.Attwood, C.Sharples;
Conversions: N.Robinson (2);
Penalties: N.Robinson (3)

Apr 24 Gloucester 34 London Irish 20 (Premiership)
Tries: L.Vainikolo, J.Simpson-Daniel, A.Dickinson;
Conversions: N.Robinson (2);
Penalties: N.Robinson (5)

May 8 Worcester 22 Gloucester 23 (Premiership)
Tries: A.Qera, S.Lawson, L.Vainikolo;
Conversion: N.Robinson;
Penalties: N.Robinson (2)

2010-11

Copyright Martin Bennett

Played 35 Won 23 Lost 11 Drawn 1
For 991 Against 617
Owner: Tom Walkinshaw (died December 2010)
Head Coach: Bryan Redpath
Captains: Mike Tindall and Luke Narraway
Premiership: Played 22 Won 14 Lost 7 Drawn 1
For 528 Against 452
Position: 3rd

Gloucester United
Played 11 Won 3 Lost 8
For 201 Against 269

Most appearances: N.Wood 32 (25 starts + 7 reps), L.Narraway 31 (26+5), A.Brown 30 (22+8), O.Azam 30 (14+16), C.Sharples 29 (25+4), E.Fuimaono-Sapolu 28 (27+1)
Most tries: C.Sharples 18, H.Trinder 13, J.Simpson-Daniel 12, L.Vainikolo 9, J.May 8
Conversions: N.Robinson 38, F.Burns 32, T.Taylor 18, R.Mills 1
Penalties: N.Robinson 40, F.Burns 21, T.Taylor 5

Gloucester won silverware for the first time since 2006, getting to the LV Cup Final for the third season running, but this time winning

in style against Newcastle. They also got to the Premiership Semi-Finals, losing away to Saracens. Kingsholm was a fortress, all 11 league games were won there, and the only home defeat was to La Rochelle in the Amlin Cup, days after the death of Tom Walkinshaw, so if the players were distracted it was eminently understandable.

The season had not started well, with a defeat at Exeter, who were playing their first ever Premiership game, and were full value for their win. Leeds were only beaten by a point, followed by another loss to London Irish. After that wins were more frequent than losses. From January there was a run of eleven successive victories in all competitions. In April there was a remarkable game at Welford Road against Leicester which consisted of ten tries equally shared in a 41-41 draw. Third position in the Premiership secured a semi-final play-off against Saracens, which was only narrowly lost to a late penalty. Despite winning four out of six games in the group stage of the Amlin Cup, the team did not qualify for the quarter-finals. The LV Cup campaign did not get off to a good start with defeat against the Dragons, but all subsequent matches were won, including a dominating performance in the final

against Newcastle.

Several of the younger players matured this season. Freddie Burns, Dave Lewis, Jonny May, Charlie Sharples and Henry Trinder all became regulars, and formed a potent back division. But perhaps Samoan international centre, Eliota Fuimaono-Sapolu, playing in his second season deserved the highest accolade with a series of match-winning performances, including a superb display in the LV final. In the forwards newcomers Jim Hamilton and Brett Deacon made a good impression.

The Club had to deal with regular absentees during the autumn internationals and the Six Nations, but were honoured that Mike Tindall and Luke Narraway captained England, as did Rory Lawson for Scotland. Dave Attwood won two England caps in the autumn internationals, whilst the two Alasdairs, Dickinson and Strokosch, plus Scott Lawson won further caps for Scotland. Akapusi Qera won caps for Fiji.

Mike Tindall was Club captain, but injury meant he did not play for Gloucester after early January. Luke Narraway took over to lead the team for the rest of the season. Nicky Robinson who scored 216 points in all games, announced in February that he would be leaving at the end of the season to join Wasps. Freddie Burns who would take over at fly-half scored 147 points. Perennial favourite Ollie Azam, who had made 240 appearances, was not retained at the end of the campaign and was appointed forwards coach at Toulon to serve under Phillipe St.Andre. Dave Attwood was another departure and went to Bath.

Sep 4 Exeter 22 Gloucester 10 (Premiership)
Tries: J.Simpson-Daniel, T.Taylor

Sep 11 Gloucester 22 Leeds 21 (Premiership)
Tries: E.Fuimaono-Sapolu, A.Dickinson, L.Narraway;
Conversions: N.Robinson (2);
Penalty: N.Robinson

Sep 19 London Irish 23 Gloucester 16 (Premiership)
Try: L.Vainikolo;
Conversion: T.Taylor;
Penalties: N.Robinson (3)

Sep 25 Gloucester 22 Wasps 20 (Premiership)
Try: E.Fuimaono-Sapolu;
Conversion: T.Taylor;
Penalties: T.Taylor (3), N.Robinson (2)

Oct 1 Bath 3 Gloucester 18 (Premiership)
Tries: N.Robinson, L.Vainikolo;
Conversion: N.Robinson;
Penalties: N.Robinson (2)

Oct 8 Agen 26 Gloucester 19 (Amlin Cup)
Try: S.Lawson;
Conversion: N.Robinson;
Penalties: N.Robinson (4)

Oct 16 Gloucester 90 Rovigo 7 (Amlin Cup)
Tries: J.May (3), J.Simpson-Daniel (2), O.Morgan (2), L.Vainikolo (2), A.Hazell, H.Trinder, C.Sharples, F.Burns, penalty try;
Conversions: F.Burns (9), N.Robinson

Oct 23 Gloucester 33 Harlequins 26 (Premiership)

Tries: D.Lewis, C.Sharples, B.Deacon;
Conversions: N.Robinson (3);
Penalties: N.Robinson (4)

Oct 30 Gloucester 19 Leicester 12 (Premiership)
Try: L.Vainikolo;
Conversion: N.Robinson;
Penalties: N.Robinson (4)

Nov 4 Newport Gwent Dragons 18 Gloucester 12 (LV Cup)
Tries: L.Vainikolo penalty try;
Conversion: F.Burns

Nov 13 Gloucester 36 Saracens 10 (LV Cup)
Tries: H.Trinder (2), J.Simpson-Daniel, C.Sharples, O.Azam;
Conversions: T.Taylor (4);
Penalty: T.Taylor

Nov 21 Newcastle 12 Gloucester 6 (Premiership)
Penalties: F.Burns (2)

Nov 27 Gloucester 19 Saracens 13

2010-11 LV Cup Winners. Copyright Martin Bennett

(Premiership)
Try: C.Sharples;
Conversion: N.Robinson;
Penalties: N.Robinson (4)

**Dec 12   La Rochelle 6   Gloucester 13
(Amlin Cup)**
Try: J.Simpson-Daniel;
Conversion: N.Robinson;
Penalties: F.Burns (2)

**Dec 19   Gloucester 18   La Rochelle 24
(Amlin Cup)**
Tries: L.Vainikolo (2), F.Burns;
Penalty: N.Robinson

**Jan 1   Leeds 15   Gloucester 13
(Premiership)**
Try: J.Simpson-Daniel;
Conversion: F.Burns;
Penalties: F.Burns (2)

**Jan 8   Gloucester 37   Exeter 23
(Premiership)**
Tries: R.Lawson, O.Morgan, J.Simpson-Daniel,
C.Sharples, A.Qera;
Conversions: F.Burns (2), T.Taylor
Penalties: F.Burns (2)

**Jan 15   Rovigo 7   Gloucester 55
(Amlin Cup)**
Tries: T.Taylor (2), J.Simpson-Daniel (2),
H.Trinder (2), M.Cox, J.May;
Conversions: F.Burns (3), T.Taylor (3);
Penalty: F.Burns

**Jan 20   Gloucester 60   Agen 7
(Amlin Cup)**
Tries: J.Simpson-Daniel (2), H.Trinder (2),
F.Burns, O.Morgan, T.Voyce, L.Narraway;
Conversions: F.Burns (5), T.Taylor (2);
Penalties: F.Burns (2)

Jan 30   Leeds 16   Gloucester 30 (LV Cup)
Tries: L.Vainikolo, T.Voyce, N.Wood,
T.Molenaar;
Conversions: N.Robinson, F.Burns;

Penalties: N.Robinson, F.Burns

**Feb 5   Gloucester 41   London Irish 8
(LV Cup)**
Tries: C.Sharples (2), T.Molenaar, J.Hamilton,
O.Morgan, A.Qera, penalty try;
Conversions: N.Robinson (2), F.Burns

**Feb 13   Wasps 9   Gloucester 10
(Premiership)**
Try: J.Simpson-Daniel;
Conversion: N.Robinson;
Penalty: N.Robinson

**Feb 18   Gloucester 23   London Irish 9
(Premiership)**
Tries: L.Narraway, A.Qera;
Conversions: N.Robinson (2);
Penalties: N.Robinson (3)

**Feb 26   Northampton 16   Gloucester 18
(Premiership)**
Tries: J.May (2);
Conversion: N.Robinson;
Penalties: N.Robinson (2)

**Mar 5   Gloucester 34   Bath 22
(Premiership)**
Tries: T.Voyce (2), H.Trinder, P.Doran-Jones;
Conversion: N.Robinson;
Penalties: N.Robinson (4)

**Mar 13   Gloucester 45   Newport Gwent
Dragons 17 (LV Cup Semi-Final)**
Tries: C.Sharples (4), N.Robinson, A.Hazell,
E.Fuimaono-Sapolu;
Conversions: N.Robinson (5)

**Mar 20   Gloucester 34   Newcastle 7
(LV Cup Final)** played at Northampton
Tries: T.Voyce, C.Sharples, E.Fuimaono-Sapolu,
D.Dawidiuk;
Conversions: N.Robinson (4);
Penalties: N.Robinson (2)

Mar 26   Harlequins 53   Gloucester 15

(Premiership)
Tries: H.Trinder, T.Molenaar;
Conversion: N.Robinson;
Penalty: N.Robinson

**Apr 2   Gloucester 34   Newcastle 9
(Premiership)**
Tries: H.Trinder, J.May, F.Burns, R.Lawson;
Conversions: T.Taylor (3), F.Burns;
Penalties: F.Burns (2)

**Apr 8   Sale 36   Gloucester 31
(Premiership)**
Tries: T.Molenaar, J.May, penalty try;
Conversions: F.Burns, T.Taylor;
Penalties: F.Burns (3), T.Taylor

**Apr 16   Leicester 41   Gloucester 41
(Premiership)**
Tries: E.Fuimaono-Sapolu (2), O.Morgan,
A.Hazell, T.Molenaar;
Conversions: F.Burns (5);
Penalties: F.Burns (2)

**Apr 19   Gloucester 27   Northampton 15
(Premiership)**
Tries: T.Molenaar, C.Sharples, O.Azam;
Conversions: F.Burns (2), N.Robinson;
Penalties: F.Burns (2)

**Apr 24   Saracens 35   Gloucester 12
(Premiership)**
Tries: J.Simpson-Daniel, H.Trinder;
Conversion: R.Mills

**May 7   Gloucester 68   Sale 17
(Premiership)**
Tries: C.Sharples (3), H.Trinder (2), J.Simpson-
Daniel, S.Lawson, R.Lawson, D.Lewis,
N.Robinson;
Conversions: N.Robinson (7), T.Taylor (2)

**May 15   Saracens 12   Gloucester 10
(Premiership Play-Off Semi-Final)**
Try: N.Robinson;
Conversion: N.Robinson;
Penalty: N.Robinson

2011-12

**Played 32 Won 13 Lost 18 Drawn 1
For 694 Against 722
Owner: Walkinshaw Family Trust
Head Coach: Bryan Redpath (resigned April
2012)
Captain: Luke Narraway**
Premiership: Played 22 Won 8 Lost 13 Drawn 1
For 456 Against 507
Position: 9th

Gloucester United
Played 6 Won 4 Lost 2
For 155 Against 128

Most appearances: R.Harden 29 (25 starts +
4 replacements), F.Burns 29 (24+5), P.Buxton
28 (18+10), C.Sharples 27 (26+1), J.May 27
(22+5), D.Dawidiuk 25 (14+11), N.Wood 24
(22+2), A.Qera 24 (19+5)
Most tries: C.Sharples, J.May 10, J.Simpson-

Daniel 6, O.Morgan, A.Qera 5
Conversions: F.Burns 36, T.Taylor 8, R.Mills 3,
M.Tindall 1
Penalties: F.Burns 63, T.Taylor 17, R.Mills 4,
M.Tindall 1
Drop goal: F.Burns 1

A very frustrating season. A run of three
Premiership victories in a row in February
aroused hopes of finishing in a play-off position.

Copyright Martin Bennett

However, the last six league games were all lost, including three at Kingsholm and Bryan Redpath resigned from his position of Head Coach. A few weeks later he would re-emerge for a game at Kingsholm as Director of Rugby at Sale. Many of the losses throughout the season were narrow, and a depressing number of those were where winning positions were surrendered in the last few minutes. The finishing position of ninth was a poor return considering the talent available in the squad. Overall, the percentage of wins was the lowest since the 1960-61 season.

It was always going to be a difficult season considering the number of players away representing their countries in the World Cup. Redpath needed the rest of his squad to be fit. Unfortunately, skipper Luke Narraway and centre Tim Molenaar missed the start of the season. They were soon joined by Andy Hazell, Alex Brown, James Simpson-Daniel and in his first season Tom Savage. Perhaps the most upsetting of all was Ollie Morgan. He was in fine form and scored two tries against Wasps on Boxing Day. Two games later and playing against Worcester he picked up a bad knee injury, which proved to be career ending after 131 appearances. This all meant that a young team had to take a lot on their shoulders. Perhaps this explained the inconsistent form, and the loss of so many games in the last few minutes. But there were exceptional wins - in the Heineken Cup, after coming close to winning in France, Toulouse were defeated at Kingsholm in a superb performance, some thought the best they had ever seen by a Gloucester team, and there was a double over Bath.

With the departure of Nicky Robinson, Freddie Burns became first choice at No.10 and scored

279 points in all matches. In the game against Toulouse he kicked four conversions and two penalties. The Times said, "Two of Gloucester's tries came from high kicks by Burns and he also helped to create another with a touch of running brilliance."

Captain Luke Narraway announced mid-season that he was leaving at the end of the campaign to play in France for Perpignan after 162 appearances. Another unfortunate departure was that of Eliota Fuimaono-Sapolu, who, after contract negotiations broke down, signed to play in Japan. Others who left were Scott Lawson to London Irish and Rory Lawson (148 appearances) to Newcastle. Lesley Vainikolo, after never really re-capturing his early promise, departed for La Rochelle, and Alasdair Strokosch for Perpignan.

Charlie Sharples was capped by England. Scott Lawson, Jim Hamilton, Rory Lawson and Alasdair Strokosch all won further caps for Scotland. Eliota Fuimaono-Sapolu won caps playing for Samoa in the World Cup, as did Akapusi Qera for Fiji and Sione Kalamafoni for Tonga.

Sep 4 Northampton 26 Gloucester 24 (Premiership)
Tries: J.May, C.Sharples;
Conversion: T.Taylor;
Penalties: T.Taylor (2), F.Burns;
Drop goal: F.Burns

Sep 10 Gloucester 29 Worcester 8 (Premiership)
Tries: J.May, T.Voyce;
Conversions: T.Taylor, F.Burns;
Penalties: T.Taylor (4), F.Burns

Sep 17 Harlequins 42 Gloucester 6 (Premiership)
Penalties: F.Burns (2)

Sep 24 Gloucester 23 Bath 6 (Premiership)
Tries: D.Dawidiuk, C.Sharples;
Conversions: T.Taylor, F.Burns;
Penalties: T.Taylor (3)

Oct 1 Gloucester 33 London Irish 30 (Premiership)
Tries: T.Voyce, D.Dawidiuk, penalty try;
Conversions: T.Taylor (3);
Penalties: T.Taylor (3), F.Burns

Oct 8 Sale 13 Gloucester 11 (Premiership)
Try: H.Trinder;
Penalties: T.Taylor (2)

Oct 15 Gloucester 58 Sale 27 (LV Cup)
Tries: L.Vainikolo, J.May, L.Narraway, R.Lawson, C.Sharples, F.Burns, S.Lawson;
Conversions: F.Burns (6), T.Taylor;
Penalties: F.Burns (3)

Oct 21 Leicester 40 Gloucester 14 (LV Cup)
Tries: D.Murphy, L.Vainikolo;
Conversions: F.Burns (2)

Oct 29 Gloucester 17 Saracens 19 (Premiership)
Try: O.Morgan;
Penalties: F.Burns (2), T.Taylor (2)

Nov 5 Exeter 19 Gloucester 24 (Premiership)
Tries: A.Qera, O.Morgan, F.Burns;
Conversions: F.Burns (3);

Penalty: F.Burns

**Nov 12 Toulouse 21 Gloucester 17
(Heineken Cup)**
Tries: C.Sharples, H.Trinder;
Conversions: F.Burns (2);
Penalty: F.Burns

**Nov 19 Gloucester 9 Harlequins 28
(Heineken Cup)**
Penalties: F.Burns (3)

**Nov 26 Gloucester 14 Leicester 19
(Premiership)**
Try: L.Narraway;
Penalties: F.Burns (3)

**Dec 2 Newcastle 26 Gloucester 25
(Premiership)**
Tries: O.Morgan, J.Simpson-Daniel, S.Lawson;
Conversions: F.Burns (2);
Penalties: F.Burns (2)

**Dec 10 Connacht 10 Gloucester 14
(Heineken Cup)**
Try: J.Simpson-Daniel;
Penalties: F.Burns (3)

**Dec 17 Gloucester 23 Connacht 19
(Heineken Cup)**
Tries: T.Taylor, J.May;
Conversions: T.Taylor, F.Burns;
Penalties: F.Burns (2), T.Taylor

**Dec 26 Gloucester 39 Wasps 10
(Premiership)**
Tries: O.Morgan (2), J.May (2), L.Narraway,
H.Trinder;
Conversions: F.Burns (3);
Penalty: F.Burns

**Jan 1 Saracens 15 Gloucester 15
(Premiership)**
Penalties: F.Burns (5)

**Jan 7 Worcester 21 Gloucester 15
(Premiership)**
Tries: C.Sharples, J.May;
Conversion: F.Burns;
Penalty: F.Burns

**Jan 14 Harlequins 20 Gloucester 14
(Heineken Cup)**
Try: J.Simpson-Daniel;
Penalties: F.Burns (3)

**Jan 20 Gloucester 34 Toulouse 24
(Heineken Cup)**
Tries: J.May (2), A.Qera, C.Sharples;
Conversions: F.Burns (4);
Penalties: F.Burns (2)

**Jan 28 Gloucester 40 Cardiff Blues 3
(LV Cup)**
Tries: J.Simpson-Daniel (2), P.Buxton,
T.Molenaar, A.Hazell;
Conversions: R.Mills (3);
Penalties: R.Mills (3)

**Feb 4 London Irish 23 Gloucester 15
(LV Cup)**
Tries: I.Clark (2);
Conversion: M.Tindall;
Penalty: M.Tindall

**Feb 11 Gloucester 27 Northampton 24
(Premiership)**
Tries: C.Sharples, D.Dawidiuk;
Conversion: F.Burns;
Penalties: F.Burns (5)

**Feb 18 Bath 11 Gloucester 14
(Premiership)**

Try: N.Wood;
Penalties: F.Burns (2), R.Mills

**Feb 25 Gloucester 29 Harlequins 23
(Premiership)**
Tries: C.Sharples, J.May, A.Qera;
Conversion: F.Burns;
Penalties: F.Burns (4)

**Mar 4 Leicester 36 Gloucester 3
(Premiership)**
Penalty: F.Burns

**Mar 24 Gloucester 27 Exeter 28
(Premiership)**
Tries: J.Simpson-Daniel, N.Runciman, F.Burns;
Conversions: F.Burns (3);
Penalties: F.Burns (2)

**Apr 1 Wasps 26 Gloucester 24
(Premiership)**
Tries: S.Lawson, C.Sharples, A.Qera;
Conversions: F.Burns (3);
Penalty: F.Burns

**Apr 14 Gloucester 20 Newcastle 29
(Premiership)**
Try: A.Qera;
Penalties: F.Burns (5)

**Apr 21 Gloucester 19 Sale 24
(Premiership)**
Try: C.Sharples;
Conversion: F.Burns;
Penalties: F.Burns (4)

**May 5 London Irish 52 Gloucester 18
(Premiership)**
Tries: T.Voyce (2);
Conversion: F.Burns;
Penalties: F.Burns (2)

2012-13

**Played 33 Won 19 Lost 13 Drawn 1
For 810 Against 719
Owner: Walkinshaw Family Trust
Director of Rugby: Nigel Davies
Captain: Jim Hamilton**
Premiership: Played 22 Won 12 Lost 9 Drawn 1
For 515 Against 481
Position: 5th

Gloucester United
Played 6 Won 4 Lost 2
For 209 Against 140
Captain: Peter Buxton

Most appearances: D.Murphy 32 (10 starts
+ 22 reps), T.Savage 30 (26+4), D.Robson

29 (19+10), S.Kalamafoni 29 (26+3), A.Qera
29 (24+5), N.Wood 29 (20+9), M.Tindall 28
(21+7)
Most tries: J.May 10, S.Monahan 7, A.Qera,
C.Sharples, H.Trinder 6, B.Morgan 5
Conversions: F.Burns 37, R.Cook 7, D.Robson
2, M.Tindall, B.Burns, R.Mills 1
Penalties: F.Burns 86, R.Cook 12,
B.Twelvetrees 10, B.Burns 2, T.Taylor, R.Mills 1
Drop goal: F.Burns 1

Under the new leadership of Nigel Davies, the
former coach at Scarlets, Gloucester enjoyed
a much better season than the end of the last
might have suggested would be possible.
Heineken Cup competition was guaranteed for

2013-14, and with a little more consistency a
play-off place would have been achieved.

The season got off to a disappointing start with
a home defeat to Northampton, but seven of the
next eight games were won with the other drawn.
For most of the season a play-off place seemed
quite possible. There was an improvement in
away form with good wins at Northampton
and London Irish. But in the end fifth was a
decent reward for a much-altered squad. New
recruits Billy Twelvetrees, Ben Morgan, Shane
Monahan, Huia Edmonds, Sione Kalamafoni,
Rob Cook, Martin Thomas and Jimmy Cowan
all had to settle in. The team proved very difficult
to beat, taking at least a losing bonus point from

Copyright Martin Bennett

every Premiership fixture bar one.

There was an excellent start to the Amlin Cup campaign, with all six group games being won, including away wins in France against Mont de Marsan and Bourdeaux-Begles. It was disappointing to lose at Kingsholm to Biarritz in the quarter-final.

Freddie Burns scored 350 points, which was the most since Ludovic Mercier's 394 in the 2002-03 season. Freddie also scored a brilliant kick and catch try against Leicester at Kingsholm, and he won two England caps in the autumn internationals. With Dan Robson at scrum-half, Gloucester had a skilled half back pairing. There was an outstanding signing from the Championship in the shape of Sione Kalamafoni, who had a barnstorming season and was voted the Club's Player of the Season. Another acquisition from the Championship was Rob Cook who settled in well, and was another dependable place kicker. No.8 Ben Morgan made a big impression in his first season. Jonny May was hampered by injury but was still top try scorer with ten from only 16 appearances. In November, against Harlequins, James Simpson-Daniel was yet again injured and was unable to play for the rest of the season. Even worse, Alex Brown suffered a career ending injury in the first game of the season after 233 appearances.

In his first season at Gloucester Billy Twelvetrees won four England caps in the Six Nations, and Club captain Jim Hamilton won further Scotland caps. It was a surprise when he announced with one year left on his contract that he was to leave and play for Montpellier.

Peter Buxton, who captained the United for the season, but still appeared in several games for the first XV, retired at the end of the season to take up a post as Senior Academy Manager. He had played 270 times for the Club.

Sep 1 Gloucester 19 Northampton 24 (Premiership)
Try: penalty try;
Conversion: F.Burns;
Penalties: F.Burns (4)

Sep 8 London Irish 31 Gloucester 40 (Premiership)
Tries: B.Morgan, J.Simpson-Daniel, A.Qera;
Conversions: F.Burns (2);
Penalties: F.Burns (7)

Sep 15 Worcester 16 Gloucester 16 (Premiership)
Try: H.Trinder;
Conversion: F.Burns;
Penalties: B.Twelvetrees (2), F.Burns

Sep 22 Gloucester 29 Wasps 22 (Premiership)
Tries: J.Simpson-Daniel, S.Kalamafoni;
Conversions: F.Burns (2);
Penalties: F.Burns (5)

Sep 30 London Welsh 25 Gloucester 31 (Premiership)
Tries: S.Monahan, T.Savage, S.Knight;
Conversions: F.Burns (2);
Penalties: F.Burns (3), B.Twelvetrees

Oct 6 Gloucester 16 Bath 10 (Premiership)

Try: R.Cook;
Conversion: F.Burns;
Penalties: F.Burns (2);
Drop goal: F.Burns

Oct 11 Mont de Marsan 6 Gloucester 11 (Amlin Cup)
Try: I.Clark;
Penalties: T.Taylor, B.Twelvetrees

Oct 18 Gloucester 25 Bordeaux Begles 13 (Amlin Cup)
Tries: C.Sharples (2), W.James, B.Twelvetrees;
Conversion: B.Twelvetrees;
Penalty: B.Twelvetrees

Oct 27 Gloucester 27 Leicester 21 (Premiership)
Tries: C.Sharples, F.Burns, A.Qera;
Conversions: F.Burns (3);
Penalties: F.Burns (2)

Nov 3 Harlequins 28 Gloucester 25 (Premiership)
Try: B.Twelvetrees;
Conversion: F.Burns;
Penalties: F.Burns (6)

Nov 9 Ospreys 33 Gloucester 27 (LV Cup)
Tries: Y.Thomas, D.Murphy, penalty try;
Conversions: D.Robson (2), B.Burns;
Penalties: B.Burns (2)

Nov 13 Gloucester 31 Fiji 29 (Friendly not included in season records)
Tries: penalty tries (2), M.Cox, K.Britton;
Conversions: D.Robson (4);

Penalty: D.Robson

**Nov 17 Gloucester 46 London Welsh 20
(LV Cup)**
Tries: B.Morgan (3), A.Qera, K.Britton,
S.Monahan;
Conversions: F.Burns (4), R.Cook;
Penalties: F.Burns (2)

**Nov 24 Gloucester 29 Sale 3
(Premiership)**
Tries: A.Qera, penalty try;
Conversions: F.Burns (2);
Penalties: F.Burns (5)

**Dec 2 Saracens 28 Gloucester 23
(Premiership)**
Tries: D.Murphy, A.Qera;
Conversions: B.Twelvetrees (2);
Penalties: B.Twelvetrees (3)

**Dec 8 London Irish 22 Gloucester 29
(Amlin Cup)**
Tries: F.Burns, D.Murphy;
Conversions: F.Burns (2);
Penalties: F.Burns (5)

**Dec 15 Gloucester 47 London Irish 3
(Amlin Cup)**
Tries: S.Monahan (4), R.Cook, D.Robson;
Conversions: F.Burns (4);
Penalties: F.Burns (3)

**Dec 22 Gloucester 18 Exeter 16
(Premiership)**
Penalties: F.Burns (6)

**Dec 29 Leicester 17 Gloucester 12
(Premiership)**
Penalties: F.Burns (4)

**Jan 5 Gloucester 12 London Irish 18
(Premiership)**
Penalties: F.Burns (4)

**Jan 11 Bourdeaux Begles 26 Gloucester 31
(Amlin Cup)**
Try: D.Dawidiuk;
Conversion: F.Burns;
Penalties: F.Burns (8)

**Jan 19 Gloucester 36 Mont de Marsan 16
(Amlin Cup)**
Tries: J.May (2), H.Trinder (2), C.Sharples;
Conversion: B.Twelvetrees;
Penalties: B.Twelvetrees (2), F.Burns

**Jan 26 Northampton 26 Gloucester 7
(LV Cup)**
Try: R.Mills;
Conversion: R.Mills
Feb 2 Gloucester 5 Bath 32 (LV Cup)
Try: H.Edmonds

**Feb 9 Northampton 11 Gloucester 27
(Premiership)**
Tries: J.May (2);
Conversion: R.Cook;
Penalties: R.Cook (5)

**Feb 17 Wasps 33 Gloucester 29
(Premiership)**
Tries: D.Robson, M.Tindall, R.Mills,
C.Sharples;
Conversions: R.Cook (2), M.Tindall;
Penalty: R.Cook

**Feb 22 Gloucester 29 Worcester 23
(Premiership)**
Tries: H.Trinder, penalty try;
Conversions: R.Cook (2);

Penalties: R.Cook (4), R.Mills

**Mar 1 Bath 31 Gloucester 25
(Premiership)**
Tries: J.May (2), H.Trinder;
Conversions: R.Cook, F.Burns;
Penalties: R.Cook (2)

**Mar 23 Gloucester 15 London Welsh 14
(Premiership)**
Penalties: F.Burns (5)

**Mar 29 Gloucester 17 Harlequins 15
(Premiership)**
Tries: J.May, A.Qera;
Conversions: F.Burns (2);
Penalty: F.Burns

**Apr 4 Gloucester 31 Biarritz 41
(Amlin Cup Quarter Final)**
Tries: S.Monahan, M.Tindall, H.Edmonds;
Conversions: F.Burns (2);
Penalties: F.Burns (4)

**Apr 12 Sale 32 Gloucester 9
(Premiership)**
Penalties: F.Burns (3)

**Apr 20 Gloucester 28 Saracens 23
(Premiership)**
Tries: J.May (2), B.Morgan;
Conversions: F.Burns (2);
Penalties: F.Burns (3)

**May 4 Exeter 40 Gloucester 39
(Premiership)**
Tries: J.May, C.Sharples, H.Trinder, R.Cook,
F.Burns;
Conversions: F.Burns (4);
Penalties: F.Burns (2)

2013-14

**Played 33 Won 13 Lost 20
For 646 Against 749
Owner: Walkinshaw Family Trust
Director of Rugby: Nigel Davies
Captain: Tom Savage**
Premiership: Played 22 Won 8 Lost 14
For 440 Against 539
Position: 9th

Gloucester United
Played 5 Won 2 Lost 3
For 115 Against 110

Most appearances: Rob Cook 30 (27 starts + 3 reps), Elliot Stooke 29 (23+6), Matt Kvesic 29 (27+2), Freddie Burns 28 (22+6), Yann Thomas 28 (9+19), Dan Robson 26 (11+15), Charlie

Sharples 25 (22+3)
Most Tries: Jonny May 12, Charlie Sharples 8, Rob Cook and Shane Monahan 6
Conversions: Freddie Burns 22, Rob Cook 13, B.Twelvetrees 6, J.Bentley, B.Burns 1
Penalties: Freddie Burns 34, Billy Twelvetrees 23, Rob Cook 11, J.Bentley 1
Drop goal: F.Burns 1

In a pre-season boost to morale the Club won the Premiership Sevens title beating Leicester in the final.

After the previous campaign's promise, this one was hugely disappointing, and, following the final day defeat to Worcester, resulted in Nigel Davies being removed from his post. The

forwards could find no platform for most of the season and clubs had no fear of coming to Kingsholm. It was the first time that Gloucester had lost more league games at home than wins in the entire history of the leagues which commenced in 1987-88. The pattern was set from the first game of the season when Sale won at Kingsholm. There were a few highlights with excellent away wins at Northampton and Perpignan, but too often there were agonisingly narrow defeats. In the Heineken Cup, Edinburgh were defeated at Murrayfield, but the following week the result was reversed at Kingsholm. Two losses to Munster meant that Gloucester qualified only for the quarter-final of the Amlin Challenge Cup which resulted in defeat to Wasps. The season's frustrations were

Copyright Martin Bennett

encapsulated perfectly in the late season home game against Bath. In front of a full house the team was on the brink of a morale boosting win when, at the very end, Bath were awarded a match winning penalty try to win by a single point. The last straw was the loss at Worcester, again by one point, in the final game. Worcester won for only the second time in their league campaign.

James Simpson-Daniel was in good form when, in November against Newcastle, he dislocated and fractured an ankle. There was optimism that he would return in due course, but the damage proved to be so bad that in September he announced his retirement. Injuries had dogged his career. He had scored 119 tries in 272 appearances. He was one of those players who caused an anticipatory frisson of excitement every time he took possession of the ball.

Although Freddie Burns scored 164 points, he had an overall loss of form, and his kicking percentages fell to such an extent that on some occasions Billy Twelvetrees or Rob Cooke took over the place-kicking duties. Rumours of a move to Leicester surfaced, which later proved to have substance. It was a sad end to his Gloucester career. He had scored 1009 points in 125 games.

Matt Kvesic was a new signing from Worcester and he settled in well. Ben Morgan also had a good season and won further England caps. Elliot Stooke broke through with a series of fine displays to become a regular in the second row. With the arrival of Kvesic, Akapusi Qera found his opportunities limited and left mid-season after 138 appearances to play for Toulouse. Stooke's arrival prompted Will James (169) to retire at the end of the season. Andy Hazell only

played a handful of games before announcing his retirement after making 263 appearances. In July 2014 Mike Tindall (178) also took leave on his illustrious career. The two Tongans, Sione Kalamafoni and Lua Lokotui won caps for their country.

A number of new signings, including John Afoa and James Hook, and the appointment of David Humphreys as the new Director of Rugby, gave hope that the following season might see a revival of fortunes.

Sep 7 Gloucester 16 Sale 22
(Premiership)
Try. H.Trinder,
Conversion: F.Burns;
Penalties: F.Burns (3)

Sep 15 Saracens 44 Gloucester 12
(Premiership)
Penalties: F.Burns (4)

Sep 21 Gloucester 26 Northampton 24
(Premiership)
Tries: C.Sharples, B.Twelvetrees, E.Stooke;
Conversion: F.Burns;
Penalties: F.Burns (2), B.Twelvetrees

Sep 29 Newcastle 16 Gloucester 22
(Premiership)
Tries: R.Cook, J.May;
Penalties: F.Burns (4)

Oct 6 Gloucester 12 Exeter 29
(Premiership)
Tries: M.Thomas, J.May;
Conversion: F.Burns

Oct 12 Gloucester 27 Perpignan 22
(Heineken Cup)

Tries: J.May, J.Cowan;
Conversion: B.Twelvetrees;
Penalties: B.Twelvetrees (5)

Oct 19 Munster 26 Gloucester 10
(Heineken Cup)
Try: C.Sharples;
Conversion: J.Bentley;
Penalty: J.Bentley

Oct 25 Bath 15 Gloucester 13
(Premiership)
Try: F.Burns;
Conversion: F.Burns;
Penalties: F.Burns (2)

Nov 2 Gloucester 30 Wasps 32
(Premiership)
Tries: R.Cook (2), S.Knight, S.Kalamafoni;
Conversions: F.Burns (2);
Penalties: F.Burns (2)

Nov 9 Northampton 33 Gloucester 6
(LV Cup)
Penalties: F.Burns (2)

Nov 12 Gloucester 40 Japan 5
(Friendly not included in season records)
Tries: C.Sharples (3), J.Simpson-Daniel,
S.Reynolds, M.Cox;
Conversions: R.Cook (5)

Nov 16 Gloucester 20 Newcastle 3
(LV Cup)
Tries: R.Cook, M.Tindall;
Conversions: F.Burns (2);
Penalties: F.Burns (2)

Nov 23 Harlequins 28 Gloucester 19
(Premiership)
Tries; B.Twelvetrees (2), J.May;

Conversions: F.Burns (2)

Nov 29 Gloucester 17 Leicester 22 (Premiership)
Tries: F.Burns, J.May;
Conversions: F.Burns, R.Cook;
Penalty: B.Twelvetrees

Dec 8 Edinburgh 12 Gloucester 23 (Heineken Cup)
Tries: M.Thomas (2), R.Cook;
Conversion: F.Burns;
Penalties: F.Burns (2)

Dec 15 Gloucester 10 Edinburgh 16 (Heineken Cup)
Penalty try;
Conversion: F.Burns;
Penalty: F.Burns

Dec 22 Gloucester 12 Worcester 6 (Premiership)
Penalties: B.Twelvetrees (4)

Dec 29 London Irish 19 Gloucester 22 (Premiership)
Try: J.May;
Conversion: B.Twelvetrees;
Penalties: B.Twelvetrees (4), F.Burns

Jan 4 Gloucester 8 Saracens 29 (Premiership)
Try: M.Cox;
Penalty: B.Twelvetrees

Jan 11 Gloucester 7 Munster 20 (Heineken Cup)
Try: C.Sharples;
Conversion: F.Burns

Jan 19 Perpignan 18 Gloucester 36 (Heineken Cup)
Tries: S.Monahan (2), J.May, C.Sharples, B.Morgan;
Conversions: F.Burns (4);
Drop goal: F.Burns

Jan 24 Llanelli Scarlets 13 Gloucester 7 (LV Cup)
Try: B.Burns;
Conversion: B.Burns

Feb 1 Gloucester 36 Wasps 5 (LV Cup)
Tries: H.Trinder (2), M.Cox (2), D.Murphy;
Conversions: R.Cook (4);
Penalty: R.Cook

Feb 7 Sale 24 Gloucester 19 (Premiership)
Tries: M.Thomas, C.Sharples;
Penalties: F.Burns (3)

Feb 16 Leicester 11 Gloucester 8 (Premiership)
Try: C.Sharples;
Penalty: R.Cook

Feb 22 Gloucester 25 Harlequins 20 (Premiership)
Tries: S.Kalamafoni, M.Kvesic, D.Murphy;
Conversions: R.Cook (2);
Penalties: R.Cook (2)

Mar 1 Northampton 39 Gloucester 13 (Premiership)
Try: H.Trinder;
Conversion: F.Burns;
Penalties: F.Burns (2)

Mar 22 Gloucester 40 Newcastle 33 (Premiership)
Tries: S.Kalamafoni, J.Hudson, J.May, M.Tindall, R.Cook;
Conversions: R.Cook (3);
Penalties: R.Cook (3)

Mar 29 Exeter 13 Gloucester 14 (Premiership)
Try: C.Sharples;
Penalties: R.Cook (3)

Apr 6 Wasps 36 Gloucester 24 (Amlin Cup Quarter-Final)
Tries: J.May, G.Evans, M.Thomas;
Conversions: R.Cook (3);
Penalty: R.Cook

Apr 12 Gloucester 17 Bath 18 (Premiership)
Try: H.Trinder;
Penalties: B.Twelvetrees (4)

Apr 19 Wasps 38 Gloucester 30 (Premiership)
Tries: J.May, H.Edmonds, F.Burns;
Conversions: B.Twelvetrees (3);
Penalties: B.Twelvetrees (3)

May 3 Gloucester 38 London Irish 30 (Premiership)
Tries: S.Monahan (3), S.Kalamafoni, C.Sharples;
Conversions: F.Burns, B.Twelvetrees;
Penalties: F.Burns (3)

May 10 Worcester 28 Gloucester 27 (Premiership)
Tries: J.May (2), S.Monahan, B.Morgan;
Conversions: F.Burns (2);
Penalty: F.Burns

2014-15

Played 37 Won 22 Lost 14 Drawn 1
For 991 Against 802
Owner: Walkinshaw Family Trust
Director of Rugby: David Humphreys
Captain: Billy Twelvetrees
Premiership: Played 22 Won 9 Lost 12 Drawn 1
For 553 Against 575
Position: 9th

Gloucester United
Played 6 Won 2 Lost 3 Drawn 1
For 150 Against 169

Most Appearances: R.Moriarty 32 (13 starts + 19 reps), Y.Thomas 32 (11+21), T.Savage 31 (30+1), C.Sharples 30, J.Hook 30 (28+2), J.Afoa 30 (28+2)

Most tries: C.Sharples 11, J.May, H.Purdy 9, D.Robson 8
Conversions: G.Laidlaw 40, J.Hook 19, B.Burns 10, A.Thomas 7, R.Cook 3
Penalties: G.Laidlaw 63, J.Hook 22, A.Thomas 14, B.Burns 6, B.Twelvetrees 5
Drop goal: B.Twelvetrees 1

In August 2014, Gloucester won the Premiership Sevens title for the second year running. This time Newport Gwent Dragons were beaten in the final.

Gloucester started the season proper with a new coaching regime led by David Humphreys as Director of Rugby with Laurie Fisher as Head Coach. A whole raft of new players arrived at

Kingsholm including Greg Laidlaw, James Hook, John Afoa, Henry Purdy, Richard Hibbard, Steve McColl, Mark Atkinson, Tom Palmer, Aled Thomas, Jacob Rowan and Mariano Galarza.

With so many new players. It was clear the team would take time to settle. Even so the opening game was a shock, losing by a margin of 47 points at Northampton. In the second game there was a second half rally from 6-17 down to beat Sale. There followed big wins over London Welsh and Leicester, sandwiched between narrow defeats to Exeter and Saracens, and the pattern was set. As the campaign carried on further new talent was uncovered. Henry Purdy, Callum Braley, Ross Moriarty and Billy Burns,

Copyright Martin Bennett

who were all England U20 World Champions, broke through. In the New Year there was a superb win at Exeter, followed by a last-minute penalty by James Hook to beat Saracens at Kingsholm. But overall the Premiership season proved to be a disappointment, with the finishing position being unchanged and only one more game won.

It was in the Amlin Challenge Cup that Gloucester hit the heights. All six group games were won and Connacht defeated in the quarter-final, setting up a plum game against Exeter in the semi-final. A fine display ensured the win and the Cherry & Whites first appearance in a final since 2011. The game was at the Twickenham Stoop against Edinburgh, and thousands of Gloucester supporters cheered the team home, not without some fears, when in the second half Billy Meakes was sent off, and for a time there were only 13 Gloucester players on the field. But for once the team ran the clock down cleverly, aided by some fine tactical kicking by Greg Laidlaw. For this particular season winning the Challenge Cup did not lead to an automatic Champions Cup qualification. Consequently, a play-off against Connacht was won, which meant Bourdeaux-Begles were the opponents in the "home" final at Worcester, Kingsholm not being available due to a concert. The match was lost to a last-minute drop goal.

The club was well represented on the international stage, with Billy Twelvetrees, Mariano Galarza, Jonny May, James Hook, Sione Kalamafoni, Lua Lokotui, David Halaifonua, Greg Laidlaw, Richard Hibbard and Ben Morgan all winning caps for their respective countries.

Sep 5   Northampton 53 Gloucester 6 (Premiership)
Penalties: J.Hook, G.Laidlaw

Sep 13   Gloucester 34 Sale 27 (Premiership)
Tries: J.May, R.Cook, penalty try;
Conversions: G.Laidlaw (2);
Penalties: G.Laidlaw (5)

Sep 19   Gloucester 22   Exeter 25 (Premiership)
Tries: J.May, D.Murphy, S.Kalamafoni;
Conversions: G.Laidlaw, J.Hook;
Penalty: J.Hook

Sep 26   London Welsh 10   Gloucester 46 (Premiership)
Tries: M.Atkinson (2), H.Purdy, C.Sharples, J.May penalty try;
Conversions: G.Laidlaw (4), J.Hook
Penalties: G.Laidlaw, B.Twelvetrees

Oct 4   Gloucester 33   Leicester 16 (Premiership)
Tries: N.Wood, C.Sharples, J.May;
Conversions: G.Laidlaw (3);
Penalties: G.Laidlaw (4)

Oct 11   Saracens 28   Gloucester 21 (Premiership)
Tries: R.Cook, T.Savage;
Conversion: G.Laidlaw;
Penalties: G.Laidlaw (3)

Oct 16   Gloucester 55   Brive 0

(European Challenge Cup)
Tries: C.Sharples (3), J.Hook, D.Dawidiuk, D.Robson penalty try;
Conversions: G.Laidlaw (3), R.Cook (3), J.Hook;
Penalties: G.Laidlaw (2)

Oct 25   Oyonnax 15   Gloucester 25 (European Challenge Cup)
Try: M.Kvesic;
Conversion: G.Laidlaw;
Penalties: G.Laidlaw (6)

Nov 1   Exeter 28   Gloucester 27 (LV Cup)
Tries: G.Evans, B.Meakes, Y.Thomas;
Conversions: A.Thomas (3);
Penalties: A.Thomas (2)

Nov 9   London Welsh 9   Gloucester 18 (LV Cup)
Penalties: A.Thomas (6)

Nov 14   Gloucester 15   Harlequins 22 (Premiership)
Penalties: B.Twelvetrees (4), A.Thomas

Nov 21   Newcastle 20   Gloucester 10 (Premiership)
Try: J.Afoa;
Conversion: B.Burns;
Penalty: B.Burns

Nov 30   London Irish 9   Gloucester 21 (Premiership)
Tries: S.McColl, H.Purdy;
Conversion: G.Laidlaw;
Penalties: G.Laidlaw (3)

Dec 7   Gloucester 35   Zebre 10
(European Challenge Cup)
Tries: S.McColl, M.Kvesic, J.Hook,
M.Atkinson;
Conversions: B.Burns (2), G.Laidlaw;
Penalties: G.Laidlaw (3)

Dec 13   Zebre 16   Gloucester 32
(European Challenge Cup)
Tries: S.McColl, H.Purdy, C.Sharples,
B.Morgan;
Conversions: J.Hook (3);
Penalties: J.Hook, B.Burns

Dec 20   Gloucester 16   Bath 39
(Premiership)
Try: D.Robson;
Conversion: J.Hook;
Penalties: G.Laidlaw (3)

Dec 28   Gloucester 23   Wasps 30
(Premiership)
Tries: J.May, M.Kvesic;
Conversions: G.Laidlaw (2);
Penalties: G.Laidlaw (3)

Jan 3   Exeter 25   Gloucester 26
(Premiership)
Tries: T.Savage, B.Morgan;
Conversions: G.Laidlaw (2);
Penalties: G.Laidlaw (3);
Drop goal: B.Twelvetrees

Jan 9   Gloucester 24   Saracens 23
(Premiership)

Tries: D.Robson, C.Braley;
Conversion: J.Hook;
Penalties: J.Hook (4)

Jan 17   Gloucester 33   Oyonnax 3
(European Challenge Cup)
Tries: B.Burns, J.May, M.Atkinson, D.Robson,
penalty try;
Conversions: G.Laidlaw (4)

Jan 22   Brive 20   Gloucester 31
(European Challenge Cup)
Tries: M.Kvesic (2), D.Robson, penalty try;
Conversions: J.Hook (4);
Penalty: J.Hook

Jan 31   Gloucester 32   Ospreys 25
(LV Cup)
Tries: A.Thomas, O.Thorley, D.Thomas
penalty try;
Conversions: B.Burns (3);
Penalties: B.Burns, A.Thomas

Feb 7   Gloucester 25   Harlequins 7
(LV Cup)
Tries: D.Thomas, J.Rowan, S.Reynolds;
Conversions: A.Thomas (2);
Penalties: A.Thomas (2)

Feb 13   Leicester 18   Gloucester 15
(Premiership)
Penalties: J.Hook (5)

Feb 21   Gloucester 48   London Welsh 10
(Premiership)

Tries: H.Purdy (2), R.Moriarty, C.Sharples,
M.Kvesic, S.Puafisi;
Conversions: J.Hook (6);
Penalties: J.Hook (2)

Mar 1   Wasps 32   Gloucester 21
(Premiership)
Tries: R.Moriarty, H.Purdy;
Conversion: J.Hook;
Penalties: J.Hook (3)

Mar 7   Gloucester 33   Northampton 33
(Premiership)
Tries: C.Sharples, R.Hibbard, D.Murphy;
Conversions: G.Laidlaw (3);
Penalties: G.Laidlaw (4)

Mar 29   Sale 23   Gloucester 6
(Premiership)
Penalties: J.Hook (2)

Apr 3   Gloucester 14   Connacht 7
(European Challenge Cup Quarter-Final)
Tries: C.Sharples, B.Meakes;
Conversions: G.Laidlaw (2)

Apr 11   Harlequins 29   Gloucester 26
(Premiership)
Tries: B.Meakes, C.Sharples, D.Robson;
Conversions: G.Laidlaw;
Penalties: G.Laidlaw (3)

Apr 18   Gloucester 30   Exeter 19
(European Challenge Cup Semi-Final)
Tries: B.Meakes, T.Savage, J.May;

2014-15 European Challenge Cup Champions (Copyright Martin Bennett)

Conversions: G.Laidlaw (3);
Penalties: G.Laidlaw (2), J.Hook

Apr 25 Gloucester 42 Newcastle 40 (Premiership)
Tries: B.Twelvetrees (2), D.Robson, H.Purdy, B.Burns;
Conversions: B.Burns (4);
Penalties: B.Burns (3)

May 1 Gloucester 19 Edinburgh 13 (European Challenge Cup Final played at Stoop Memorial Ground)
Try: B.Twelvetrees;
Conversion: G.Laidlaw;
Penalties: G.Laidlaw (4)

May 9 Gloucester 35 London Irish 13 (Premiership)
Tries: J.May, D.Thomas, H.Purdy;
Conversion: G.Laidlaw;

Penalties: G.Laidlaw (6)

May 16 Bath 50 Gloucester 30 (Premiership)
Tries: S.McColl (2), D.Robson, D.Thomas;
Conversions: A.Thomas (2);
Penalties: A.Thomas (2)

May 24 Gloucester 40 Connacht 32 (Champions Cup Play-off)
Tries: R.Moriarty, C.Sharples, B.Meakes, D.Dawidiuk, J.May;
Conversions: G.Laidlaw (3);
Penalties: G.Laidlaw (2), J.Hook

May 31 Gloucester 22 Bordeaux Begles 23 (Champions Cup Play-off Final Played at Worcester)
Try: H.Purdy;
Conversion: G.Laidlaw;
Penalties: G.Laidlaw (5)

Gloucester-Hartpury Women

The Gloucester-Hartpury women's team was formed at the start of this season, under the jurisdiction of Gloucester Rugby, but in partnership with Hartpury University and Hartpury College. In this first season, they played friendly matches and competed in the Junior Cup, which they won.

Junior Cup results:
16 Nov Bideford 25 Gloucester-Hartpury 19
14 Dec Windsor 12
Gloucester-Hartpury 34
25 Jan Newbury 10 Gloucester-Hartpury 29
8 Feb Old Leamington 12
Gloucester-Hartpury 31
7 Mar Gloucester-Hartpury 24
Teddington Antlers 0
11 Apr Gloucester-Hartpury 50
Kendal Wasps 3

2015-16

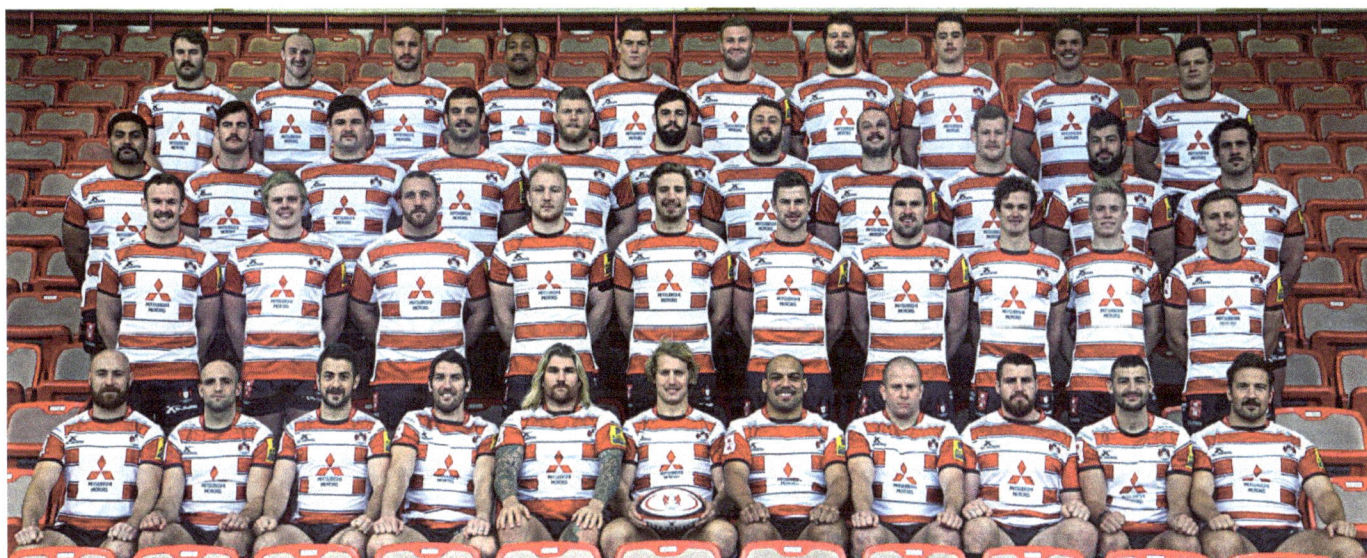

Copyright Martin Bennett

Played 29 Won 16 Lost 12 Drawn 1
For 601 Against 532
Owner: Walkinshaw Family Trust. From January 2016: Martin St Quinton
Director of Rugby: David Humphreys
Captain: Billy Twelvetrees
Premiership: Played 22 Won 10 Lost 11 Drawn 1
For 429 Against 423
Position: 8th

Gloucester United
Played 5 Won 3 Lost 1 Drawn 1
For 112 Against 69

Most appearances: M.Kvesic 26 (22 starts, 4 reps), T.Savage 26 (22+4), B.Twelvetrees 25

(24+1), J.Hook 22, R.Hibbard 22, R.Cook 22 (17+5), J.Rowan 22 (9+13), Y.Thomas 22 (7+15)
Most tries: S.McColl 6, J.Hook 5, R.Cook 4, H.Trinder 4, B.Morgan 4
Conversions: G.Laidlaw 20, J.Hook 9, B.Twelvetrees 4, B.Burns 2
Penalties: G.Laidlaw 37, J.Hook 25, B.Twelvetrees 20, B.Burns 5

A very frustrating season. In the Premiership one more game was won than the previous season, and the finishing position was one better. At times the team played with great spirit, as in the wins over Wasps and Exeter at home and Bath away, but in too many others performances were disappointing and

culminated in the quarter-final of the Challenge Cup, with a dismal performance against the Dragons. Players joining the club included Jeremy Thrush, Paddy McAllister, Willi Heinz and Tom Marshall.

The season started on a bright note when, for the first time since 2009, the initial match was won. In the victory at Newcastle Billy Twelvetrees kicked nine penalties, to equal the club record, and scored 29 points, the most by any Gloucester player in a Premiership match. The season progressed reasonably well, and following the win over Wasps in March, it seemed that a sixth or even higher finish was possible. Unfortunately, it was at that point the season unravelled. Only two of the last eight games were won, which saw exit from Europe and a slippage to eighth in the Premiership. In that sequence there were losses to three of the bottom four teams in the Premiership

The Challenge Cup campaign had run extremely smoothly. All six group games were won, and there was considerable confidence that Dragons, not in the best of form, would be beaten, especially at Kingsholm. The actual performance was depressing, and the Welsh region were well worth their surprise victory.

It must be said that a crippling injury list made consistency difficult to maintain. Billy Burns, Tom Marshall, Jonny May, Henry Purdy, Charlie Sharples and Henry Trinder were all missing for lengthy periods. All were backs, and it made it more difficult to put points on the board, especially during that run-in at the end of the season. Even with the injuries the team produced some outstanding wins, but also lost too many others in the last few minutes, having done all the hard work.

James Hook had a good season. He was instrumental in the win at Bath, kicking all Gloucester's points with five penalties. His tactical kicking was of the highest order, and he pinned Bath back, so that they could not mount meaningful attacks. There was a remarkable game at Twickenham against Harlequins in front of 70,000 spectators. Ten tries were shared evenly. Henry Trinder scored two tries, but his injury curse struck again as he limped in from the 22 to score his second.

Greg Laidlaw, Jonny May, James Hook, Sione Kalamafoni, Mariano Galarza, Ben Morgan and David Halaifonua all won international recognition.

At the end of the season Nick Wood retired having made 277 appearances, the most of any Gloucester player in the professional era.

Oct 16 Newcastle 27 Gloucester 39
(Premiership)
Tries: C.Sharples, M.Kvesic;
Conversion: B.Twelevetrees;
Penalties: B.Twelvetrees (9)

Oct 23 Gloucester 15 Saracens 17
(Premiership)
Penalties: B.Twelvetrees (5)

Oct 31 Gloucester 24 Worcester 22
(Premiership)
Tries: D.Halaifonua, R.Hibbard, S.Kalamafoni;
Penalties: B.Twelvetrees (3)

Nov 8 Wasps 23 Gloucester 3
(Premiership)
Penalty: G.Laidlaw

Nov 14 Gloucester 23 Zebre 10
(European Challenge Cup)
Tries: H.Purdy, R.Moriarty, S.McColl;
Conversion: B.Burns;
Penalties: B.Burns (2)

Nov 17 Gloucester 14 Barbarians 62
(Friendly not included in season record)
Tries: D.Thomas, penalty try;
Conversions: L.Evans (2)

Nov 19 La Rochelle 20 Gloucester 33
(European Challenge Cup)
Tries: B.Morgan, S.McColl, C.Sharples;
Conversions: B.Twelvetrees (2), G.Laidlaw;
Penalties: G.Laidlaw (4)

Nov 27 Northampton 15 Gloucester 3
(Premiership)
Penalty: B.Twelvetrees

Dec 4 Gloucester 23 Sale 19
(Premiership)
Tries: S.Kalamafoni (2), R.Cook;
Conversion: G.Laidlaw;
Penalties: B.Twelvetrees (2)

Dec 10 Worcester 22 Gloucester 34
(European Challenge Cup)
Tries: H.Purdy (2), R.Cook, S.McColl, B.Twelvetrees;
Conversions: G.Laidlaw (3);
Penalty: G.Laidlaw

Dec 17 Gloucester 27 Worcester 13
(European Challenge Cup)
Tries: G.Laidlaw, M.Kvesic;
Conversion: G.Laidlaw;
Penalties: G.Laidlaw (5)

Dec 27 Harlequins 39 Gloucester 39
(Premiership)
Tries: H.Trinder (2), J.Thrush, J.Hook, R.Cook;
Conversions: G.Laidlaw (4);
Penalties: G.Laidlaw (2)

Jan 2 Gloucester 27 London Irish 14
(Premiership)
Tries: M.Kvesic, B.Burns;
Conversion: J.Hook;
Penalties: J.Hook (5)

Jan 9 Exeter 19 Gloucester 10
(Premiership)
Try: C.Sharples;
Conversion: B.Burns;
Penalty: G.Laidlaw

Jan 16 Gloucester 20 La Rochelle 10
(European Challenge Cup)
Tries: R.Cook, B.Twelvetrees;
Conversions: G.Laidlaw (2);
Penalties: G.Laidlaw (2)

Jan 23 Zebre 11 Gloucester 14
(European Challenge Cup)
Try: M.Atkinson;
Penalties: B.Burns (3)

Jan 30 Gloucester 18 Leicester 19
(Premiership)
Tries: J.Hook, B.Morgan;
Conversion: J.Hook;
Penalties: J.Hook (2)

Feb 5 Bath 11 Gloucester 15
(Premiership)
Penalties: J.Hook (5)

Feb 13 Gloucester 28 Harlequins 6
(Premiership)
Tries: R.Hook, B.Morgan, S.McColl;
Conversions: R.Hook (2);
Penalties: R.Hook (3)

Feb 20 Saracens 25 Gloucester 12
(Premiership)
Penalties: J.Hook (4)

Feb 27 Gloucester 32 Newcastle 6
(Premiership)
Tries: J.Hook, B.Meakes, R.Moriarty, T.Savage;
Conversions: J.Hook (2), B.Twelvetrees;
Penalties: J.Hook (2)

Mar 5 Gloucester 13 Wasps 10
(Premiership)
Try: R.Hibbard;
Conversion: G.Laidlaw;
Penalties: G.Laidlaw (2)

Mar 12 Worcester 28 Gloucester 20
(Premiership)
Tries: J.Hook, B.Meakes;
Conversions: R.Hook (2);
Penalties: R.Hook (2)

Mar 20 London Irish 23 Gloucester 18
(Premiership)
Tries: L.Ludlow, H.Trinder;
Conversion: J.Hook;
Penalties: J.Hook (2)

Mar 26 Gloucester 12 Bath 17
(Premiership)
Penalties: G.Laidlaw (4)

Apr 2 Leicester 35 Gloucester 30
(Premiership)

Tries: S.McColl, H.Trinder, P.McAllister;
Conversions: G.Laidlaw (3);
Penalties: G.Laidlaw (3)

Apr 9 Gloucester 21 Newport Gwent Dragons 23 (ECC Quarter-Final)
Tries: S.McColl, B.Morgan;
Conversion: G.Laidlaw;
Penalties: G.Laidlaw (3)

Apr 15 Gloucester 16 Exeter 9 (Premiership)
Try: O.Thorley;
Conversion: G.Laidlaw;
Penalties: G.Laidlaw (3)

Apr 29 Sale 11 Gloucester 12 (Premiership)
Penalties: G.Laidlaw (4)

May 7 Gloucester 20 Northampton 28 (Premiership)

Tries: L.Evans, R.Moriarty;
Conversions: G.Laidlaw (2);
Penalties: G.Laidlaw (2)

Gloucester-Hartpury Women

The RFU placed Gloucester-Hartpury in the Women's Championship Midlands 2 league, where they finished in second place.

13 Sep Gloucester-Hartpury 36 Worcester Warriors II 22 (League)
20 Sep Gloucester-Hartpury 45 Shelford 17 (League)
27 Sep Bridgnorth v Gloucester-Hartpury (League – Away Walk Over)
11 Oct Gloucester-Hartpury 10 Lichfield Green 12 (League)
18 Oct Birmingham Moseley 5 Gloucester-Hartpury 29 (League)
1 Nov Gloucester-Hartpury 92 Buckingham Swans 0 (League)

8 Nov Deeping Devils 7 Gloucester-Hartpury 33 (League)
22 Nov Birkenhead Park 10 Gloucester-Hartpury 59 (Intermediate Cup)
29 Nov Shelford 15 Gloucester-Hartpury 47 (League)
13 Dec Gloucester-Hartpury 67 Bridgnorth 7 (League)
10 Jan Lichfield Green 24 Gloucester-Hartpury 0 (League)
17 Jan Gloucester-Hartpury 34 Birmingham Moseley 0 (League)
24 Jan Buckingham Swans 5 Gloucester-Hartpury 41 (League)
31 Jan Worcester Warriors II 30 Gloucester-Hartpury 29 (League)
7 Feb Gloucester-Hartpury 29 Birmingham Moseley 0 (intermediate Cup)
21 Feb Gloucester-Hartpury v Deeping Devils (League – Home Walk Over)

Some results missing

2016-17

Copyright Martin Bennett

Played 35 Won 16 Lost 16 Drawn 3
For 939 Against 793
Owner: Martin St Quinton
Director of Rugby: David Humphreys
Captain: Greg Laidlaw
Premiership: Played 22 Won 7 Lost 13 Drawn 2
For 533 Against 537
Position: 9th

Gloucester United
Played 8 Won 6 Lost 2
For 199 Against 191

Most appearances: T.Savage 31 (28 starts + 3 rep), R.Hibbard 30 (27+3), C.Sharples 29 (25+4), B.Twelvetrees 28 (19+9), B.Burns 27 (26+1), J.Rowan 27 (22+5)
Most tries: M.Scott 13, J.May 12, C.Sharples 9, H.Purdy 7, T.Marshall, D.Halaifonua 6
Conversions: G.Laidlaw 28, B.Burns 27, J.Hook 16, B.Twelvetrees 13, L.Evans 6
Penalties: B.Burns 26, G.Laidlaw 23, J.Hook 9, B.Twelvetrees 4, L.Evans 1

A dreadfully frustrating season. In the league, there were only seven wins, the fewest by Gloucester since the start of the Premiership, and the team finished ninth for the third time in four seasons. The pattern was set from the first game against Leicester when a 24-point lead was squandered. Time and again Gloucester lost from winning positions, and a disastrous defeat to Harlequins in March led to the resignation of head coach Laurie Fisher. The European Challenge Cup offered a chance to turn the season round, following a brilliant win away to La Rochelle in the semi-final. Although Gloucester led 10-0 early on, the final was lost to the superior Stade Francais team.

Frustration started straight away against Leicester. Early in the second half the team was leading 31-7, only to concede an amazing 31 points to lose. The team was infuriatingly unpredictable. There was an excellent win away at Sale for the second season running, only to lose the next game at Kingsholm to Newcastle, who won away for the first time since October 2014. The first Premiership win at Kingsholm did not come until November, but it was worth waiting for, when five tries were scored against Wasps. At Exeter with 10 minutes to go the Cherry & Whites led 27-13, but in the end had to settle for a draw. Later in the season matches against Northampton, Harlequins and Newcastle were all lost in the last few minutes.

In the Challenge Cup, Gloucester won five of the six group games, spoilt only by a heavy defeat at La Rochelle. Cardiff Blues were despatched in the quarter-final, which meant that there was another visit to France to play La Rochelle again. The team was given little chance considering the margin of defeat in the first game, to say nothing of the fact that the French were unbeaten at home, and nine points clear at the top of their league. In one of Gloucester's finest hours, the home team's colours were lowered in a tour de force from Billy Burns who scored all Gloucester's points with a try, conversion and three penalties. The final was against Stade Francais, and although Gloucester led 10-0 early on, Stade were worthy winners.

In his first season Matt Scott was the top try scorer. In his first game he scored a brace against Leicester. He quickly formed centre partnerships with Billy Twelvetrees and Mark Atkinson. Jonny May ran in almost as many tries as Scott, and it was a blow when it was announced that he was leaving to play for Leicester. Billy Burns made swift progress and scored 147 points. He displaced James Hook at fly-half, which may have precipitated the latter's departure. Another disappointing departure was that of skipper Greg Laidlaw for Clermont Auvergne. Darren Dawidiuk, Yann Thomas, Matt Kvesic and Sione Kalamafoni were other departees.

International caps were won by Greg Laidlaw, Jonny May, David Halaifonua, Sione Kalamafoni and Matt Scott.

**Sep 2 Gloucester 31 Leicester 38
(Premiership)**
Tries: M.Scott (2), C.Sharples, H.Purdy;
Conversions: G.Laidlaw (4);
Penalty: G.Laidlaw

**Sep 9 Worcester 23 Gloucester 23
(Premiership)**
Tries: M.Scott, H.Purdy;
Conversions: G.Laidlaw (2);
Penalties: G.Laidlaw (3)

**Sep 16 Sale 13 Gloucester 26
(Premiership)**
Tries: J.Afoa, C.Sharples;
Conversions: G.Laidlaw (2);
Penalties: G.Laidlaw (4)

**Sep 24 Gloucester 13 Newcastle 18
(Premiership)**
Try: R.Moriarty;
Conversion: B.Burns;
Penalties: B.Burns, G.Laidlaw

**Oct 1 Gloucester 6 Bath 15
(Premiership)**
Penalties: G.Laidlaw, J.Hook

**Oct 8 Exeter 27 Gloucester 27
(Premiership)**
Tries: M.Scott, C.Sharples, B.Morgan;
Conversions: G.Laidlaw (3);
Penalties: G.Laidlaw, B.Twelvetrees

**Oct 15 Bayonne 27 Gloucester 47
(European Challenge Cup)**
Tries: M.Atkinson (2), M.Scott, B.Twelvetrees, J.May, T.Savage;
Conversions: J.Hook (4);
Penalties: J.Hook (3)

**Oct 22 Gloucester 37 Treviso 8
(European Challenge Cup)**
Tries: L.Ludlow, J.May, M.Scott, C.Braley;
Conversions: G.Laidlaw (3), J.Hook;
Penalties: G.Laidlaw (3)

**Oct 28 Northampton 23 Gloucester 20
(Premiership)**
Tries: J.Rowan, C.Sharples;
Conversions: G.Laidlaw (2);
Penalties: G.Laidlaw (2)

**Nov 5 Gloucester 36 Saracens 32
(Anglo-Welsh Cup)**
Tries: D.Halaifanoua (2), J.Mullis, D.Thomas, H.Purdy penalty try;
Conversions: L.Evans (3)

**Nov 12 Northampton 19 Gloucester 13
(Anglo-Welsh Cup)**
Tries: O.Thorley, D.Thomas;
Penalty: B.Burns

**Nov 19 Gloucester 36 Wasps 18
(Premiership)**
Tries: R.Hibbard, M.Atkinson, M.Scott, C.Sharples, H.Purdy;
Conversions: J.Hook (4);
Penalty: J.Hook

**Nov 27 Saracens 24 Gloucester 20
(Premiership)**
Tries: B.Morgan, B.Burns;
Conversions: J.Hook (2);
Penalties: J.Hook (2)

**Dec 3 Gloucester 26 Bristol 18
(Premiership)**
Tries: M.Scott, W.Heinz, H.Purdy, penalty try;
Conversions: J.Hook (3)

**Dec 8 Gloucester 35 La Rochelle 14
(European Challenge Cup)**
Tries: M.Atkinson, J.Hohneck, O.Thorley, M.Scott;
Conversions: G.Laidlaw (3);
Penalties: G.Laidlaw (3)

**Dec 17 La Rochelle 42 Gloucester 13
(European Challenge Cup)**
Try: J.Afoa;
Conversion: B.Burns;
Penalties: B.Burns (2)

**Dec 27 Harlequins 28 Gloucester 24
(Premiership)** Played at Twickenham
Tries: G.Evans, J.Hook, M.Matu'u;
Conversions: G.Laidlaw (2), B.Burns;
Penalty: G.Laidlaw

**Jan 1 Gloucester 12 Northampton 13
(Premiership)**
Penalties: B.Burns (4)

**Jan 7 Gloucester 55 Worcester 19
(Premiership)**
Tries: M.Scott (2), J.May, J.Rowan, J.Afoa, J.Hohneck, C.Sharples;
Conversions: B.Twelvetrees (4), G.Laidlaw (3);
Penalty: G.Laidlaw, B.Burns

**Jan 14 Benneton Treviso 0 Gloucester 41
(European Challenge Cup)**
Tries: R.Hibbard (2), J.Hook, M.Scott, D.Halaifonua, B.Twelvetrees;
Conversions: G.Laidlaw (2), B.Burns (2);
Penalty: G.Laidlaw

**Jan 21 Gloucester 64 Bayonne 19
(European Challenge Cup)**
Tries: W.Heinz (3), L.Ludlow, J.May, D.Dawidiuk, A.Symonds, H.Purdy, J.Hohneck, C.Braley;
Conversions: B.Burns (6), B.Twelvetrees

**Jan 27 Bath 17 Gloucester 17
(Anglo-Welsh Cup)**
Tries: D.Dawidiuk, B.Vellacott;

Conversions: J.Hook (2);
Penalty: J.Hook

Feb 4 Gloucester 24 Newport Gwent Dragons 13 (Anglo-Welsh Cup)
Tries: C.Orr, H.Trinder, B.Vellacott;
Conversions: L.Evans (3);
Penalty: L.Evans

Feb 11 Leicester 34 Gloucester 9 (Premiership)
Penalties: B.Burns (3)

Feb 17 Gloucester 31 Saracens 23 (Premiership)
Tries: T.Marshall, J.Thrush, R.Hibbard;
Conversions: B.Burns (2);
Penalties: B.Burns (3), B.Twelvetrees

Feb 26 Wasps 35 Gloucester 22 (Premiership)
Tries: J.Hook, D.Halaifonua, M.Scott;
Conversions: B.Twelvetrees (2);
Penalty: B.Twelvetrees

Mar 4 Gloucester 27 Harlequins 30 (Premiership)
Tries: C.Sharples (2), D.Halaifonua;
Conversions: B.Burns (3);
Penalties: B.Burns (2)

Mar 24 Bristol 14 Gloucester 3 (Premiership)
Tries: C.Sharples, B.Burns, L.Ludlow, J.May;
Conversions: B.Burns (3);
Penalties: B.Burns (2)

Apr 1 Gloucester 46 Cardiff Blues 26 (European Challenge Cup Quarter-final)
Tries: T.Marshall (2), J.May, R.Moriarty,

H.Purdy, M.Atkinson;
Conversions: B.Twelvetrees (4), B.Burns;
Penalties: B.Twelvetrees, B.Burns

Apr 7 Newcastle 16 Gloucester 14 (Premiership)
Tries: T.Marshall, J.May;
Conversions: B.Twelvetrees (2)

Apr 15 Gloucester 39 Sale 30 (Premiership)
Tries: T.Marshall (2), R.Hibbard, H.Trinder, B.Twelvetrees;
Conversions: B.Burns (4);
Penalties: B.Burns (2)

Apr 22 La Rochelle 14 Gloucester 16 (European Challenge Cup Semi-Final)
Try: B.Burns;
Conversion: B.Burns;
Penalties: B.Burns (3)

April 30 Bath 44 Gloucester 20 (Premiership)
Tries: J.May (2), D.Halaifonua;
Conversion: G.Laidlaw;
Penalty: J.Hook

May 6 Gloucester 20 Exeter 34 (Premiership)
Tries: J.May (2), L.Ludlow;
Conversion: G.Laidlaw;
Penalty: G.Laidlaw

May 12 Stade Francais 25 Gloucester 17 (European Challenge Cup Final at Murrayfield)
Tries: J.May, R.Moriarty;
Conversions: B.Burns (2);
Penalty: B.Burns

Gloucester-Hartpury Women

In Women's Championship Midlands 2, Gloucester-Hartpury women won their league, going through the season unbeaten, and were losing finalists in the Intermediate Cup.

11 Sep Birmingham Moseley 0 Gloucester-Hartpury 95 (League)
25 Sep Shelford 0 Gloucester-Hartpury 82 (League)
9 Oct Gloucester-Hartpury 63 Bletchley 15 (League)
23 Oct Gloucester- Hartpury 99 Buckingham Swans 5 (League)
20 Nov Loughborough Town 13 Gloucester-Hartpury 26 (Intermediate Cup)
11 Dec Gloucester-Hartpury 66 Olney 0 (League - counted as both home and away result)
15 Dec Worcester Warriors II 3 Gloucester-Hartpury 55 (League)
8 Jan Gloucester-Hartpury 86 Shelford 7 (League)
15 Jan Bletchley 0 Gloucester- Hartpury 15 (League)
5 Feb Sheffield 7 Gloucester-Hartpury 50 (Intermediate Cup)
19 Feb Buckingham Swans 7 Gloucester-Hartpury 59 (League)
26 Feb Hove 13 Gloucester-Hartpury 47 (Intermediate Cup)
4 Mar Gloucester-Hartpury 71 Worcester Warriors II 12 (League)
12 Mar Gloucester-Hartpury 17 Trojans 9 (Intermediate Cup)
19 Mar Gloucester-Hartpury v Birmingham Moseley – (League - Home Walk Over)
1 Apr Gloucester-Hartpury 19 West Park Leeds 32 (Intermediate Cup Final)

2017-18

Played 35 Won 19 Lost 15 Drawn 1
For 972 Against 891
Owner: Martin St Quinton
Director of Rugby: David Humphreys
Head Coach: Johan Ackermann
Captain: Willi Heinz
Premiership: Played 22 Won 11 Lost 10 Drawn 1
For 490 Against 597
Position: 7th

Gloucester United
Played 8 Won 3 Lost 5
For 172 Against 274
Captain: Charlie Beckett

Most appearances: B.Twelvetrees 32 (22 starts + 10 rep.), L.Ludlow 31 (24+7), J.Hohneck 31

(20 + 11), B.Burns 29 (24 +5), T.Savage 29 (19 + 10), J.Afoa 28 (23 + 5)
Most tries: H.Trinder 11, O.Thorley 10, B.Vellacott 7, J.Woodward, M.Atkinson, H.Purdy, C.Braley 6
Conversions: B.Twelvetrees 48, O.Williams 26, B.Burns 23, L.Evans 3
Penalties: B.Twelvetrees 26, O.Williams 5, B.Burns 3, L.Evans 1

Under the new leadership of Johan Ackermann Gloucester seemed to have fresh flair and determination. Seven out of the first ten Premiership games were won, and the team was sitting third. Unfortunately, only four of the remaining 12 games were won, and seventh was the final position, although this

was the highest finish since 2013. The final of the European Challenge Cup was lost to a 78th minute penalty, but Gloucester qualified for the Champions Cup by playing in the final. New players included Jason Woodward, Ruan Ackermann, Ed Slater, Fraser Balmain, Gareth Denman, Owen Williams, James Hanson and Val Rapava-Ruskin.

The season got off to an inspiring start when the defending champions Exeter, were beaten in a thrilling game at Kingsholm. Three of the next four Premiership games were lost, relieved only by a very tight win over Worcester, and there were visions of yet another false dawn. But the team settled into an understanding of the game Johan Ackermann wanted them to

Copyright Martin Bennett

play, and there was a sense of mutual respect between squad and coach. There was a good run to the turn of the season, and if the second half was not quite so successful, qualification for the Champions cup for the first time in six years was still a good return.

Yet again there was a good run in the Challenge Cup. In the group stage, the only failure was conceding a double to Pau. That meant there was a trip to Ireland in the quarter-final to play Connacht. A close contest went Gloucester's way, as did the semi-final without much trouble against Newcastle. In the final against Cardiff Blues the team led 20-6 at half-time, but finally lost to a penalty in the 78th minute.

Billy Twelvetrees scored 184 points in all games, and Gloucester were well blessed with two other reliable kickers in Owen Williams, a recruit from Leicester, and Billy Burns. The former Bristol player, Jason Woodward proved to be a penetrating, attacking full-back, and the head coach's son, Ruan, soon settled in the back-row. Another backrower to burst through was Jake Polledri who won caps for Italy. The previous season's leading try scorer, Matt Scott was injured for most of the season, and finally departed for Leicester. Billy Burns had another good season, but was another who left, after 100 appearances, signing for Ulster. After giving four seasons' graft in the front-row, and 104 appearances, All Black John Afoa moved down the A38 to Bristol, and Richard Hibbard (100 appearances), returned to Wales to play for Dragons. Motu Matu'u was capped by Samoa.

**Sep 1 Gloucester 28 Exeter 21
(Premiership)**
Tries: J.Thrush (2), B.Morgan, J.Woodward;
Conversions: B.Burns (3), B.Twelvetrees

**Sep 9 Harlequins 28 Gloucester 17
(Premiership)**
Tries: F.Clarke, J.Rowan;
Conversions: B.Burns, B.Twelvetrees;
Penalty: B.Burns

**Sep 16 Leicester 24 Gloucester 10
(Premiership)**
Try: J.Hohneck;
Conversion: B.Twelvetrees;
Penalty: B.Twelvetrees

**Sep 22 Gloucester 24 Worcester 19
(Premiership)**
Tries: O.Thorley (2), B.Twelvetrees;
Conversions: B.Burns (3);
Penalty: B.Burns

**Sep 29 Sale 57 Gloucester 10
(Premiership)**
Try: J.Afoa;
Conversion: B.Burns;
Penalty: B.Burns

**Oct 7 Gloucester 29 Northampton 24
(Premiership)**
Tries: H.Trinder (2), B.Twelvetrees,
J.Woodward, W.Heinz;
Conversions: O.Williams (2)

**Oct 12 Pau 27 Gloucester 21 (European
Challenge Cup)**
Tries: H.Purdy, R.Ackerman, B.Vellacott;
Conversions: O.Williams (3)

**Oct 19 Gloucester 61 Agen 16
(European Challenge Cup)**
Tries: B.Vellacott (2), H.Purdy, H.Trinder,
O.Williams, T.Savage, J.Polledri, B.Morgan,
R.Hibbard
Conversions: B.Burns (6), O.Williams (2)

**Oct 29 Bath 21 Gloucester 22
(Premiership)**
Tries: W.Heinz (2), E.Slater;
Conversions: O.Williams (2);
Penalty: O.Williams

**Nov 4 Leicester 26 Gloucester 24
(Anglo/Welsh Cup)**
Tries: P.McAllister, B.Vellacott, T.Hudson;
Conversions: L.Evans (3);
Penalty: L.Evans

**Nov 11 Gloucester 47 London Irish 7
(Anglo/Welsh Cup)**
Tries: W.Heinz, V.Rapava-Ruskin, T.Hudson,
J.Thrush, H.Trinder, C.Braley, J.Polledri;
Conversions: B.Twelvetrees (4), B.Burns (2)

**Nov 17 Gloucester 23 Saracens 17
(Premiership)**
Tries: O.Thorley, T.Hudson;
Conversions: B.Twelvetrees (2);
Penalties: B.Twelvetrees (3)

**Nov 24 Newcastle 7 Gloucester 29
(Premiership)**
Tries: A.Symons, J.Thrush, H.Purdy,
G.Denman;
Conversions: B.Twelvetrees (3);
Penalty: B.Twelvetrees

**Dec 2 Gloucester 39 London Irish 15
(Premiership)**
Tries: B.Burns (2), L.Ludlow, J.Polledri,
H.Purdy;
Conversions: B.Twelvetrees (4);
Penalties: B.Twelvetrees (2)

**Dec 9 Zebre 26 Gloucester 33
(European Challenge Cup)**
Tries: O.Thorley (2), R.Ackermann,

O.Williams, R.Hibbard;
Conversions: O.Williams (4)

**Dec 16 Gloucester 69 Zebre 12
(European Challenge Cup)**
Tries: O.Thorley (4), D.Halaifonua (2),
F.Clarke, W.Safe, C.Sharples, C.Orr, M.Tatu'u;
Conversions: B.Twelvetrees (6), O.Williams

**Dec 23 Wasps 49 Gloucester 24
(Premiership)**
Tries: W.Heinz, M.Atkinson, T.Marshall,
F.Clarke;
Conversions: B.Twelvetrees (2)

**Dec 30 Gloucester 20 Sale 16
(Premiership)**
Tries: D.Halaifonua, B.Vellacott;
Conversions: B.Twelvetrees (2);
Penalties: B.Twelvetrees (2)

**Jan 6 Northampton 22 Gloucester 19
(Premiership)**
Tries: J.Hanson, J.Afoa, penalty try;
Conversion: O.Williams

**Jan 12 Agen 24 Gloucester 45
(European Challenge Cup)**
Tries: H.Purdy (2), C.Braley, J.Woodward,
M.Atkinson, E.Slater;
Conversions: O.Williams (6);
Penalty: O.Williams

**Jan 19 Gloucester 24 Pau 34
(European Challenge Cup)**
Tries: J.Thrush, C.Braley, J.Polledri;
Conversions: B.Twelvetrees (3);
Penalty: B.Twelvetrees

**Jan 26 Gloucester 43 Ospreys 20
(Anglo/Welsh Cup)**
Tries: R.Hibbard, M.Atkinson, C.Braley,
O.Thorley, H.Trinder, B.Morgan, M.Scott;
Conversions: B.Burns (4)

**Feb 3 Newcastle 31 Gloucester 19
(Anglo/Welsh Cup)**
Tries: B.Vellacott, G.Evans, M.Scott;
Conversions: O.Williams (2)

**Feb 10 Gloucester 24 Leicester 17
(Premiership)**
Tries: H.Trinder (2), M.Scott;
Conversions: B.Twelvetrees (3);
Penalty: B.Twelvetrees

**Feb 17 Worcester 25 Gloucester 15
(Premiership)**
Tries: H.Trinder, M.Scott;

Conversion: B.Burns;
Penalty: B.Twelvetrees

**Feb 24 Gloucester 25 Wasps 25
(Premiership)**
Tries: R.Hibbard, C.Sharples, H.Trinder;
Conversions: B.Twelvetrees (2);
Penalties: B.Twelvetrees (2)

**Mar 3 Gloucester 20 Newcastle 21
(Premiership)**
Tries: J.Woodward, D.Halaifonua, M.Atkinson,
L.Ludlow

**Mar 24 London Irish 29 Gloucester 33
(Premiership)**
Tries: T.Marshall (2), J.Hanson, M.Atkinson,
L.Ludlow;
Conversions: B.Twelvetrees (2), B.Burns (2)

**Mar 31 Connacht 28 Gloucester 33
(European Challenge Cup Quarter-Final)**
Tries J.Afoa, H.Trinder, J.Hanson, T.Marshall;
Conversions: O.Williams (2);
Penalties: O.Williams (2), B.Twelvetrees

**Apr 8 Exeter 46 Gloucester 10
(Premiership)**
Try: C.Braley;
Conversion: O.Williams;
Penalty: O.Williams

**Apr 14 Gloucester 37 Harlequins 9
(Premiership)**
Tries: C.Braley, J.Polledri, J.Woodward,
R.Ackermann;
Conversions: B.Twelvetrees (4);
Penalties: B.Twelvetrees (3)

**Apr 20 Gloucester 33 Newcastle 12
(European Challenge Cup Semi-Final)**
Tries: T.Marshall, M.Matu'u, B.Burns,
B.Vellacott;
Conversions: B.Twelvetrees (2);
Penalties: B.Twelvetrees (3)

**Apr 28 Gloucester 20 Bath 43
(Premiership)**
Tries: E.Slater, J.Woodward;
Conversions: B.Twelvetrees (2);
Penalties: B.Twelvetrees (2)

**May 5 Saracens 62 Gloucester 12
(Premiership)**
Tries: T.Seabrook, D.Halaifonua;
Conversion: B.Twelvetrees

May 11 Cardiff Blues 31 Gloucester 30

(European Challenge Cup Final at Bilbao)
Tries: H.Trinder, M.Atkinson, J.Hanson;
Conversions: B.Twelvetrees (3);
Penalties: B.Twelvetrees (3)

Gloucester-Hartpury Women

Tyrrells Premier 15s
Played 20 Won 11 Lost 8 Drawn 1
For 598 Against 487
Position 4th

Following England's victory in the 2014 Women's Rugby World Cup, Gloucester-Hartpury Women were awarded a franchise in the first season of the new women's topflight league, the Tyrrells Premier 15s. Essentially this meant moving up two divisions, but they finished fourth and qualified for the play-offs, only to lose to Saracens.

**Sep 16 Darlington Mowden Park 3
Gloucester-Hartpury 32**
Sep 23 Gloucester-Hartpury 26 Wasps 22
**Sep 30 Gloucester-Hartpury 29 Richmond
0**
Oct 7 Bristol 29 Gloucester-Hartpury 20
**Oct 21 Worcester 0
Gloucester-Hartpury 43**
**Oct 28 Gloucester-Hartpury 7
Saracens 33**
**Nov 4 Harlequins 39
Gloucester-Hartpury 12**
**Nov 11 Gloucester-Hartpury 29
Firwood Waterloo 22**
**Dec 2 Loughborough Lightning 43
Gloucester-Hartpury 33**
**Dec 9 Gloucester-Hartpury 24
Darlington Mowden Park 38**
Dec 16 Wasps 37 Gloucester-Hartpury 17
**Jan 14 Richmond 15
Gloucester-Hartpury 37**
Jan 20 Gloucester-Hartpury 34 Bristol 17
**Feb 3 Gloucester-Hartpury 80
Worcester 0**
**Feb 17 Saracens 29
Gloucester-Hartpury 29**
**Mar 3 Gloucester-Hartpury 40
Harlequins 36**
**Mar 10 Firwood Waterloo 10
Gloucester-Hartpury 44**
**Mar 24 Gloucester-Hartpury 36
Loughborough Lightning 8**
**Apr 7 Gloucester-Hartpury 0
Saracens 62 (Play-off)**
**Apr 14 Saracens 45
Gloucester-Hartpury 26 (Play-off)**

Copyright Martin Bennett

Played 33 Won 17 Lost 15 Drawn 1
For 786 Against 814
Owner: Martin St Quinton
Director of Rugby: David Humphreys
Head Coach: Johan Ackermann
Captain: Willi Heinz
Premiership: Played 22 Won 13 Lost 8 Drawn 1
For 587 Against 515
Position: 3rd

Gloucester United
Played 10 Won 3 Lost 7
For 225 Against 404

Most appearances: J.Hohneck 29 (24 starts + 5 as rep.), B.Twelvetrees 28 (26+2), C.Braley 28 (12+16), F.Balmain 27 (25+2), B.Morgan 27 (24+3), E.Slater 27 (24+3), F.Clarke 27 (13+14)
Most tries: C.Sharples 10, J.Woodward 8, M.Banahan, B.Morgan 7, R.Ackermann, O.Thorley 6
Conversions: B.Twelvetrees 52, D.Cipriani 11, L.Evans 6, O.Williams 2, C.Chapman 1
Penalties: B.Twelvetrees 26, D.Cipriani 15, O.Williams 3, L.Evans 1

A new hybrid pitch had been installed at Kingsholm during the summer, which ensured that there would be no more muddy matches in the future.

An encouraging season, consolidating the progress made under Johan Ackermann's leadership. In the Premiership, Gloucester rose four places to third, and qualified for the play-offs, for the first time in eight years. Danny Cipriani had an outstanding season and was made the Rugby Players Association Premiership Player of the Season. Besides

Cipriani other newcomers included Matt Banahan, Franco Marais, Gerbrandt Grobler, Jaco Kriel and Franco Mostert.

From the start the influence of Cipriani was obvious. Many tries were scored due to his instinctive timing of a break or devastating pass to set up a try. A particular beneficiary was Charlie Sharples who had a run of scoring seven tries in four games. In October Wasps were beaten at home for the first time since 2011. Against Leicester at Kingsholm Ollie Thorley scored two superb tries, the second of which was reckoned by many to be one of the best ever seen at Kingsholm. Later in the season there were great wins away to Harlequins, who were completely outplayed, and in a thrilling match at Northampton where there were eleven tries, six by Gloucester, with Mark Atkinson scoring a hat-trick. It was the first win at Franklins Gardens since 2013. In April the team came back from 0-17 down to defeat Bath at Kingsholm. Saracens handed out a lesson in the play-off semi-final, but it did not detract from a most encouraging season, which gave much promise for the future.

There were mixed fortunes in the Champions Cup. The French champions, Castres, were beaten at Kingsholm in the first round, but in the second at Thomond Park against Munster, Cipriani was sent off for a head high tackle. Gloucester fought magnificently, and scored three second half tries. This was backed up in the next round with a fine performance at Exeter who were completely outplayed. Unfortunately, a week later Exeter turned the tables at Kingsholm in a Premiership game.

Gloucester's hopes evaporated after a very poor

performance against Munster in the return match. In the final pool game, at Castres, the Cherry & Whites had only to kick the ball into touch with the clock in the red for a famous win, but for some reason kicked downfield, only for the ball to be run back by Castres, to secure the win with a try.

A very young Louis Rees-Zammit made two appearances and showed promise. Billy Twelvetrees had a good season with the boot totalling 182 points. Mark Atkinson seemed to improve with every season. Jake Polledri won more caps for Italy, and Mariano Galarza won one more for Argentina, although only appearing twice for Gloucester. Motu Matu'u won three further caps for Samoa.

Departures included Tom Savage after 193 appearances to play in Japan, Henry Purdy to Coventry and Ben Vellacott to Wasps.

Sep 1 Gloucester 27 Northampton 16 (Premiership)
Tries: J.Hanson, C.Sharples;
Conversion: B.Twelvetrees;
Penalties: B.Twelvetrees (5)

Sep 8 Bath 31 Gloucester 31 (Premiership)
Tries: R.Ackermann (2), C.Braley, M.Banahan;
Conversions: B.Twelvetrees (4);
Penalty: B.Twelvetrees

Sep 14 Gloucester 35 Bristol 13 (Premiership)
Tries: C.Sharples (2), G.Grobler, E.Slater, M.Banahan;
Conversions: B.Twelvetrees (2);

Penalties: B.Twelvetrees (2)

**Sep 23 Saracens 38 Gloucester 15
(Premiership)**
Tries: M.Atkinson, C.Sharples;
Conversion: B.Twelvetrees;
Penalty: B.Twelvetrees

**Sep 29 Gloucester 25 Harlequins 27
(Premiership)**
Tries: C.Sharples (2), D.Cipriani;
Conversions: D.Cipriani (2);
Penalties: D.Cipriani (2)

**Oct 6 Wasps 21 Gloucester 35
(Premiership)**
Tries: C.Sharples (2), B.Vellacott, L.Ludlow;
Conversions: D.Cipriani (3);
Penalties: D.Cipriani (3)

**Oct 14 Gloucester 19 Castres 14
(Heineken Champions Cup)**
Try: C.Braley;
Conversion: D.Cipriani;
Penalties: D.Cipriani (4)

**Oct 20 Munster 36 Gloucester 22
(Heineken Champions Cup)**
Tries: J.Woodward, G.Grobler, B.Morgan;
Conversions: B.Twelvetrees (2);
Penalty: D.Cipriani

**Oct 27 Gloucester 31 Wasps 7
(Premiership Rugby Cup)**
Tries: C.Terry, B.Vellacott, L.Evans, D.Coetzer,
J.Mullis;
Conversions: L.Evans (2), C.Chapman

**Nov 2 Bristol 21 Gloucester 13
(Premiership Rugby Cup)**
Penalty try (7pts - conversion kick not required
from this season);
Penalties: O.Williams (2)

**Nov 9 Gloucester 14 Northampton 12
(Premiership Rugby Cup)**
Tries: M.Banahan, G.Grobler;
Conversions: B.Twelvetrees (2)

**Nov 17 Gloucester 36 Leicester 13
(Premiership)**
Tries: O.Thorley (2), J.Woodward, M.Banahan,
F.Balmain;
Conversions: D.Cipriani (3), B.Twelvetrees;
Penalty: D.Cipriani

**Nov 24 Exeter 23 Gloucester 6
(Premiership)**
Penalties: D.Cipriani (2)

Dec 1 Gloucester 36 Worcester 16

(Premiership)
Tries: O.Thorley (2), J.Hanson, C.Sharples,
F.Clarke, J.Visagie;
Conversions: B.Twelvetrees (3)

**Dec 8 Exeter 19 Gloucester 27 (Heineken
Champions Cup)**
Tries: W.Heinz, J.Visagie, B.Morgan;
Conversions: D.Cipriani (2), B.Twelvetrees;
Penalties:
D.Cipriani(2)

**Dec 15 Gloucester 17 Exeter 29
(Heineken Champions Cup)**
Tries: J.Woodward (2), T.Hudson;
Conversion: B.Twelvetrees

**Dec 23 Newcastle 17 Gloucester 20
(Premiership)**
Tries: E.Slater, B.Morgan;
Conversions: B.Twelvetrees (2);
Penalties: B.Twelvetrees (2)

**Dec 29 Gloucester 15 Sale 30
(Premiership)**
Tries: J.Visagie, M.Banahan;
Conversion: B.Twelvetrees;
Penalty: B.Twelvetrees

**Jan 5 Leicester 34 Gloucester 16
(Premiership)**
Try: G.Evans;
Conversion: B.Twelvetrees;
Penaltes: B.Twelvetrees (3)

**Jan 11 Gloucester 15 Munster 41
(Heineken Champions Cup)**
Tries: O.Thorley, F.Balmain;
Conversion: B.Twelvetrees;
Penalty: B.Twelvetrees

**Jan 19 Castres 24 Gloucester 22
(Heineken Champions Cup)**
Tries: H.Trinder, B.Vellacott, O.Williams;
Conversions: O.Williams (2);
Penalty: O.Williams

**Feb 4 Bath 52 Gloucester 0
(Premiership Cup)**

**Feb 14 Gloucester 24 Exeter 17
(Premiership)**
Tries: J.Woodward, W.Heinz, B.Morgan;
Conversions: B.Twelvetrees (3);
Penalty: B.Twelvetrees

**Feb 22 Gloucester 30 Saracens 24
(Premiership)**
Tries: B.Morgan (2), E.Slater;
Conversions: B.Twelvetrees (3);
Penalties: B.Twelvetrees (3)

**Mar 1 Bristol 28 Gloucester 24
(Premiership)**
Tries: J.Woodward, T.Marshall, O.Thorley;
Conversions: B.Twelvetrees (3);
Penalty: B.Twelvetrees

**Mar 10 Harlequins 7 Gloucester 29
(Premiership)**
Tries: J.Woodward, R.Ackermann, T.Marshall,
D.Cipriani;
Conversions: B.Twelvetrees (3);
Penalty: B.Twelvetrees

**Mar 23 Gloucester 27 Wasps 14
(Premiership)**
Tries: W.Heinz, R.Ackermann, J.Polledri;
Conversions: B.Twelvetrees (3);
Penalties: B.Twelvetrees (2)

**Apr 7 Northampton 31 Gloucester 40
(Premiership)**
Tries: M.Atkinson (3), R.Ackermann, E.Slater,
F.Marais;
Conversions: B.Twelvetrees (5)

**Apr 13 Gloucester 27 Bath 23
(Premiership)**
Tries: J.Hohneck, R.Ackermann, H.Purdy,
T.Seabrook;
Conversions: B.Twelvetrees (2);
Penalty:
B.Twelvetrees

**April 29 Worcester 27 Gloucester 20
(Premiership)**
Tries: H.Purdy (2), W.Heinz;
Conversion: B.Twelvetrees;
Penalty: B.Twelvetrees

**May 4 Gloucester 28 Newcastle 19
(Premiership)**
Tries: J.Woodward, D.Cipriani, C.Sharples,
M.Banahan;
Conversions: B.Twelvetrees (4)

**May 18 Sale 46 Gloucester 41
(Premiership)**
Tries: B.Vellacott (2), T.Seabrook, M.Banahan,
L.Ludlow, D.Coetzer;
Conversions: L.Evans (4);
Penalty: L.Evans

**May 25 Saracens 44 Gloucester 19
(Premiership Semi-Final Play-Off)**
Tries: B.Morgan, R.Dreyer, L.Ludlow;
Conversions: B.Twelvetrees (2)

Gloucester-Hartpury Women

Tyrrells Premier 15s
Played 18 Won 8 Lost 9 Drawn 1

For 584 Against 470
Position: 5th

Most tries: Kelly Smith 24, Ellie Underwood 14, Emily Wood 11
Most conversions: Ellie Underwood 19, Mary-Ann Gittings 17

**Sep 8 Gloucester-Hartpury 24
Harlequins 38**
Tries: S.Acheson (2), E.Wood, K.Smith;
Conversions: M-A.Gittings (2)

**Sep 15 Darlington Mowden Park 14
Gloucester-Hartpury 57**
Tries: M-A.Gittings (2), K.Smith, Z.Aldcroft, G.Bradley, T.Bricknell, T.Heard, E.Underwood, C.Gill;
Conversions: M-A.Gittings (6)

Sep 22 Bristol 43 Gloucester-Hartpury 5
Try: B.Blackburn

**Sep 29 Gloucester-Hartpury 40
Loughborough Lightning 41**
Tries: E.Underwood (2), K.Smith (2), M-A. Gittings, B.Blackburn;
Conversions: M-A.Gittings (5)

**Oct 13 Firwood Waterloo 10
Gloucester-Hartpury 43**
Tries: K.Smith (3), E.Wood (2), B.Blackburn, E.Underwood;

Conversions: M-A.Gittings (4)

Oct 20 Gloucester-Hartpury 67 Worcester 3
Tries: K.Smith (3), E.Underwood (3), S.Williams, C.Large, E.Wood, E.Sing, S.Acheson;
Conversions: D.Fahey (4), E.Sing (2)

**Oct 28 Saracens 48
Gloucester-Hartpury 24**
Tries: E.Underwood (2), K.Smith, D.Hywel;
Conversions: E.Underwood (2)

**Nov 3 Gloucester-Hartpury 34
Richmond 15**
Tries: K.Smith (2), D.Hywel, E.Underwood, E.Wood, H.Fisher;
Conversions: E.Underwood (2)

**Nov 24 Wasps 26
Gloucester-Hartpury 10**
Tries: S.Williams, S.Tandy

**Dec 1 Gloucester-Hartpury 64
Darlington Mowden Park 0**
Tries: K.Smith (3), Z.Aldcroft (3), E.Wood (2), S.Powell-Hughes, S.Bennett, E.Underwood, S.Nicholas;
Conversions: C.Large (2)

Dec 8 Gloucester-Hartpury 53 Bristol 7
Tries: T.Heard (2), S.Acheson (2), K.Smith (2), E.Wood, C.Large, E.Underwood;
Conversions: E.Underwood (2), C.Large,

T.Heard

**Dec 15 Loughborough Lightning 29
Gloucester-Hartpury 10**
Tries: C.Large, E.Wood

**Dec 22 Gloucester-Hartpury 52
Firwood Waterloo 20**
Tries: N.Hunt (2), D.Hywel (2), E.Underwood, T.Bricknell, B.Lewis, E.Wood;
Conversions: E.Underwood (5), N.Hunt

**Jan 12 Worcester 7
Gloucester-Hartpury 27**
Tries: K.Smith (4), N.Hunt;
Conversion: E.Underwood

**Jan 19 Gloucester-Hartpury 28
Saracens 34**
Tries: T.Heard (2), D.Hywel, T.Bricknell;
Conversions: E.Underwood (4)

**Jan 27 Richmond 26
Gloucester-Hartpury 26**
Tries: S.Powell-Hughes (2), B.Randall, E.Febrey;
Conversions: E.Underwood (3)

**Mar 23 Gloucester-Hartpury 20
Wasps 47**
Tries: K.Smith (2), E.Wood, E.Underwood

**Mar 30 Harlequins 62
Gloucester-Hartpury 0**

2019-20

Copyright Martin Bennett

Played 32 Won 10 Lost 22
For 756 Against 788
Owner: Martin St Quinton
Director of Rugby: David Humphreys (until June 2020)

Head Coach: Johan Ackermann (until June 2020)
Captain: Willi Heinz
Premiership: Played 22 Won 8 Lost 14
For 515 Against 513

Position: 7th

Gloucester United
Played 5 Won 2 Lost 3
For 123 Against 129

Most appearances: B.Twelvetrees 28 (18 starts + 10 as replacement), R.Ackermann 27 (24+3), L.Ludlow 27 (22+5), J.Simpson 25 (13+12), M.Atkinson 23 (19+4), F.Balmain 23 (17+6), O.Thorley 22, V.Rapava-Ruskin 22 (18+4), L.Rees-Zammit 21 (17+4)
Most tries: L.Rees-Zammit 15, O.Thorley 11, J.Simpson 9, T.Marshall 7
Conversions: B.Twelvetrees 40, D.Cipriani 17, L.Evans 9, G.Barton 1
Penalties: B.Twelvetrees 19, D.Cipriani 4, O.Williams, L.Evans 3

A truly unprecedented season was totally disrupted by the Coronavirus pandemic. It started on time in September 2019, but did not finish until October 2020, with a walkover in the last match. In the summer, which turned out to be mid-season, Johan Ackermann, David Humphreys and Rory Teague left from the coaching and management side, to be replaced by George Skivington, Alex King and Dom Waldouck. The finishing position of seventh in the Premiership was a drop of four from the previous season. Over the whole campaign 68% of games were lost, which by a distance was the worst in the Club's long history. It was very disappointing after the promise of the previous season. On the bright side, Ollie Thorley, who won an England cap, was the Premiership's top try scorer with eleven, and Gloucester qualified for the Champions Cup. Willi Heinz also won England caps, and Jake Polledri won more for Italy. He had become a Kingsholm favourite and was voted player of the season.

In the pre-season period Gloucester won the Plate at the Premiership 7s competition. Because of the World Cup, the season proper began with four rounds of Premiership Cup games, all of which were lost, but Louis Rees-Zammit showed his potential with a glorious try against Bath. The Premiership campaign got off to a good start with two wins, but these were followed by three consecutive losses, and the season never really recovered. The loss to Saracens was disappointing. Sarries had just had 35 league points deducted and arrived without most of their World Cup players, but still won comfortably. Although losing at Northampton, Rees-Zammit again demonstrated his genius when he became the youngest player to score a hat-trick of Premiership tries. In the New Year there were four Premiership defeats on the trot before lockdown in March caused a five-month break in proceedings. By the time the season restarted in August, a completely new coaching team was in place. There were big wins over Worcester and Leicester; in the latter Ollie Thorley scored four tries in the first half, only the third time this had happened in Premiership history. There was a

depressing loss at Bath, where, with 60 minutes gone, Gloucester were leading 20-3, but then imploded, conceding 28 points.

It was not a vintage year for Gloucester in the Champions Cup with only two wins in the six rounds. At Connacht the team was leading 24-13 with four minutes to go, but still managed to lose.

The form that Danny Cipriani had shown in the previous season seemed to desert him, and he was in no way as effective as before. The recruitment of Scottish international Chris Harris was a sound investment, and the emergence of Louis Rees-Zammit and Ollie Thorley on the wings gave hope of better things to come. Callum Braley, who had broken through into the Italy team, left at the end of the season to play for Benneton. In July 2020, Josh Hohneck decided to return with his family to New Zealand.

George Skivington took on the coaching role during lockdown and was faced with a monumental task to turn the club round with brand new staff, but Tim Taylor stayed put and carried on as backs coach.

Sep 21 Gloucester 29 London Irish 49 (Premiership Cup)
Tries: L.Evans, J.Morris, A.Hinkley, L.Rees-Zammit;
Conversions: L.Evans (2), G.Barton;
Penalty: L.Evans

Sep 27 Bristol 20 Gloucester 17 (Premiership Cup)
Tries: J.Simpson, M.Banahan, G.Grobler;
Conversion: L.Evans

Oct 5 Harlequins 40 Gloucester 31 (Premiership Cup)
Tries: J.Simpson, A.Hinkley, T.Seabrook, G.Grobler, B.Twelvetrees;
Conversions: B.Twelvetrees (3)

Oct 11 Gloucester 24 Bath 26 (Premiership Cup)
Tries: L.Rees-Zammit, J.Kriel, C.Chapman, J.Morris;
Conversions: L.Evans (2)

Oct 19 Sale 16 Gloucester 18 (Premiership)
Tries: T.Marshall, M.Atkinson;
Conversion: B.Twelvetrees;
Penalties: B.Twelvetrees (2)

Oct 26 Gloucester 25 Wasps 9 (Premiership)
Tries: J.Simpson (2), T.Marshall (2);
Conversion: B.Twelvetrees;

Penalty: B.Twelvetrees

Nov 2 Leicester 16 Gloucester 13 (Premiership)
Try: J.Simpson;
Conversion: B.Twelvetrees;
Penalties: B.Twelvetrees (2)

Nov 9 Gloucester 12 Saracens 21 (Premiership)
Tries: T.Marshall, L.Ludlow;
Conversion: B.Twelvetrees

Nov 15 Gloucester 20 Toulouse 25 (Champions Cup)
Tries: J.Simpson (2);
Conversions: D.Cipriani (2);
Penalties: D.Cipriani (2)

Nov 24 Montpelier 30 Gloucester 27 (Champions Cup)
Tries: C.Braley, M.Banahan, J.Simpson;
Conversions: B.Twelvetrees (2), L.Evans;
Penalties: B.Twelvetrees (2)

Dec 1 Harlequins 23 Gloucester 19 (Premiership)
Tries: O Thorley (2), B.Morgan;
Conversions: D.Cipriani (2)

Dec 8 Gloucester 26 Connacht 17 (Champions Cup)
Tries: T.Marshall (2), L.Rees-Zammit, J.Polledri;
Conversions: D.Cipriani (3)

Dec 14 Connacht 27 Gloucester 24 (Champions Cup)
Tries: M.Atkinson (2), G.Grobler, L.Ludlow;
Conversions: B.Twelvetrees (2)

Dec 20 Gloucester 36 Worcester 3 (Premiership)
Tries: L.Rees-Zammit (2), R.Ackermann, C.Harris, B.Morgan;
Conversions: D.Cipriani (4);
Penalty: D.Cipriani

Dec 28 Northampton 33 Gloucester 26 (Premiership)
Tries: L.Rees-Zammit (3), C.Harris;
Conversions: D.Cipriani (3)

Jan 4 Gloucester 29 Bath 15 (Premiership)
Tries: J.Woodward, F.Clarke, G.Grobler, R.Ackermann;
Conversions: B.Twelvetrees (2), D.Cipriani
Penalty: B.Twelvetrees

Jan 11 Gloucester 29 Montpellier 6 (Champions Cup)

Tries: W.Heinz, L.Rees-Zammit, B.Morgan, T.Gleave;
Conversions: B.Twelvetrees (3);
Penalty: B.Twelvetrees

Jan 19 Toulouse 35 Gloucester 14 (Champions Cup)
Tries: L.Rees-Zammit, J.Woodward;
Conversions: B.Twelvetrees (2)

Jan 25 Bristol 24 Gloucester 16 (Premiership)
Try: F.Clarke;
Conversion: B.Twelvetrees;
Penalties: O.Williams (3)

Feb 14 Gloucester 15 Exeter 26 (Premiership)
Tries: J.Polledri, L.Rees-Zammit;
Conversion: B.Twelvetrees;
Penalty: B.Twelvetrees

Feb 22 London Irish 24 Gloucester 20 (Premiership)
Tries: C.Chapman, O.Thorley, L.Rees-Zammit;
Conversion: B.Twelvetrees;
Penalty: B.Twelvetrees

Feb 28 Gloucester 17 Sale 23 (Premiership)
Tries: B.Twelevtrees, F.Balmain;
Conversions: B.Twelvetrees (2);
Penalty: B.Twelvetrees

March 7 Wasps 39 Gloucester 22 (Premiership)
Tries: T.Marshall, B.Twelvetrees, O.Thorley, L.Evans;
Conversion: B.Twelvetrees

Aug 15 Worcester 15 Gloucester 44 (Premiership)
Tries: O.Thorley (2), J.Singleton, L.Rees-Zammit, J.Woodward, S.Varney;
Conversions: B.Twelvetrees (4);
Penalties: B.Twelvetrees (2)

Aug 21 Gloucester 24 Bristol 33 (Premiership)
Tries: F.Balmain, C.Harris, S.Varney;
Conversions: B.Twelvetrees (2), D.Cipriani;
Penalty: B.Twelvetrees

Aug 26 Saracens 36 Gloucester 20 (Premiership)
Tries: S.Varney, H.Walker, L.Rees-Zammit;
Conversion: L.Evans;
Penalty: L.Evans

Aug 30 Gloucester 46 Leicester 30 (Premiership)

Tries: O.Thorley (4), J.Simpson, C.Harris, L.Evans;
Conversions: B.Twelvetrees (4);
Penalty: B.Twelvetrees

Sept 5 Gloucester 36 London Irish 23 (Premiership)
Tries: L.Evans, O.Thorley, L.Rees-Zammit, J.Stanley, S.Varney;
Conversions: L.Evans (2), B.Twelvetrees (2);
Penalty: L.Evans

Sept 9 Exeter 35 Gloucester 22 (Premiership)
Tries: M.Banahan (2), J.Gray;
Conversions: B.Twelvetrees (2);
Penalty: B.Twelvetrees

Sep 14 Gloucester 15 Harlequins 28 (Premiership)
Tries: J.Polledri, M.Alemanno;
Conversion: D.Cipriani;
Penalty: D.Cipriani

Sep 22 Bath 31 Gloucester 20 (Premiership)
Tries: C.Harris, M.Banahan;
Conversions: B.Twelvetrees (2);
Penalties: B.Twelvetrees (2)

Oct 4 Gloucester 20 Northampton 0 (Premiership)
A season which had started on 21 September 2019, ended well over a year later in bizarre fashion, as Northampton could not raise a team due to Coronavirus infections and injuries, so the game was awarded to Gloucester.

Gloucester-Hartpury Women

Tyrrells Premier 15s
Played 12 Won 8 Lost 4
For 362 Against 210
Position 4th

Most tries: Ellie Underwood, Kelly Smith 9, Natasha Hunt, Mia Venner 5
Most conversions: Lleucu George 14, Ellen Murphy 8

Sep 21 Firwood Waterloo 7 Gloucester-Hartpury 48
Tries: E.Underwood (2), K.Jones, B.Randall, K.Ingram, C.Large, S.Powell-Hughes, Z.Aldcroft;
Conversions: E.Murphy (3), L.George

Sep 28 Gloucester-Hartpury 22 Wasps 19
Tries: C.Powell, K.Smith, B.Lewis, S.Powell-Hughes;
Conversion: E.Murphy

Oct 5 Harlequins 39 Gloucester-Hartpury 12
Tries: Z.Aldcroft, E.Sing;
Conversion: N.Hunt

Oct 12 Gloucester-Hartpury 31 Richmond 12
Tries: K.Smith (2), C.Powell, E.Febrey, penalty try;
Conversions: E.Murphy (2)

Oct 19 Gloucester-Hartpury 53 Worcester 0
Tries: M.Venner (3), K.Smith (2), N.Hunt, T.Copson, R.Lund, E.Wood;
Conversions: N.Hunt (2), L.George (2)

Oct 26 Saracens 15 Gloucester-Hartpury 7
Try: E.Mills;
Conversion: L.George

Nov 30 Gloucester-Hartpury 60 Darlington Mowden Park 12
Tries: K.Smith (2), E.Underwood (2), R.Lind, M.Venner, E.Perry, C.Large, N.Hunt, C-M. Manns;
Conversions: L.George (3), E.Murphy (2)

Dec 7 Bristol 24 Gloucester-Hartpury 53
Tries: E.Underwood (2), T.Tauasosi, K.Dougan, C.Large, C.Hale, L.George, Z.Aldcroft, N.Hunt;
Conversions: L.George (4)

Dec 14 Gloucester-Hartpury 17 Loughborough Lightning 36
Tries: E.Underwood, B.Lewis, N.Hunt;
Conversion: L.George

Dec 21 Wssps 17 Gloucester-Hartpury 22
Tries: K.Smith, T.Tauasosi, E.Underwood;
Conversions: L.George (2);
Penalty: L.George

Jan11 Gloucester-Hartpury 17 Harlequins 29
Tries: R.Lund, C.Powell;
Conversions: E.Underwood, E.Sing;
Penalty: E.Underwood

Jan 18 Richmond 0 Gloucester-Hartpury 20
Tries: K.Smith, M.Venner, E.Underwood, N.Hunt
No games were played after mid-January 2020 due to the Coronavirus pandemic

Photographs (left to right, top to bottom):

Ruan Ackermann — Back Row; Matias Alemanno — Lock; Ollie Atkins — Lock; Mark Atkinson — Centre; Fraser Balmain — Prop; Giorgi Kveseladze — Centre; Lewis Ludlow — Back Row; Jonny May — Winger; Ben Morgan — Back Row; Kyle Moyle — Fullback

Matt Banahan — Winger; Santiago Carreras — Fullback; Charlie Chapman — Scrum Half; Freddie Clarke — Back Row; Alex Craig — Lock; Seb Nagle-Taylor — Back Row; Jake Polledri — Back Row; Val Rapava-Ruskin — Prop; Louis Rees-Zammit — Winger; Jordy Reid — Back Row

Lloyd Evans — Fly Half; Val Ford-Robinson — Prop; Corne Fourie — Prop; Matt Garvey — Lock; Jamie Gibson — Back Row; Tom Seabrook — Centre; Alex Seville — Prop; Charlie Sharples — Winger; Joe Simpson — Scrum Half; Jack Singleton — Hooker

Todd Gleave — Hooker; Chris Harris — Centre; Will Heinz — Scrum Half; Tom Hudson — Fullback; Ciaran Knight — Prop; Ed Slater — Lock; Santiago Socino — Hooker; Jack Stanley — Prop; Ollie Thorley — Winger; Henry Trinder — Centre

Billy Twelvetrees — Centre; Stephen Varney — Scrum Half; Henry Walker — Hooker; Jason Woodward — Fullback

George Skivington — Head Coach; Alex King — Attack Coach; Dom Waldouck — Defence Coach; Trevor Woodman — Assistant Coach; Tim Taylor — Assistant Coach; Dan Tobin — Head of Performance; Eoin Power — Head of Medical; Will Carvalho — Performance Chef; Shaun Bullock — Kit Manager; Peter Walton — Head of Academy; Tom Reynolds — Lead Analyst

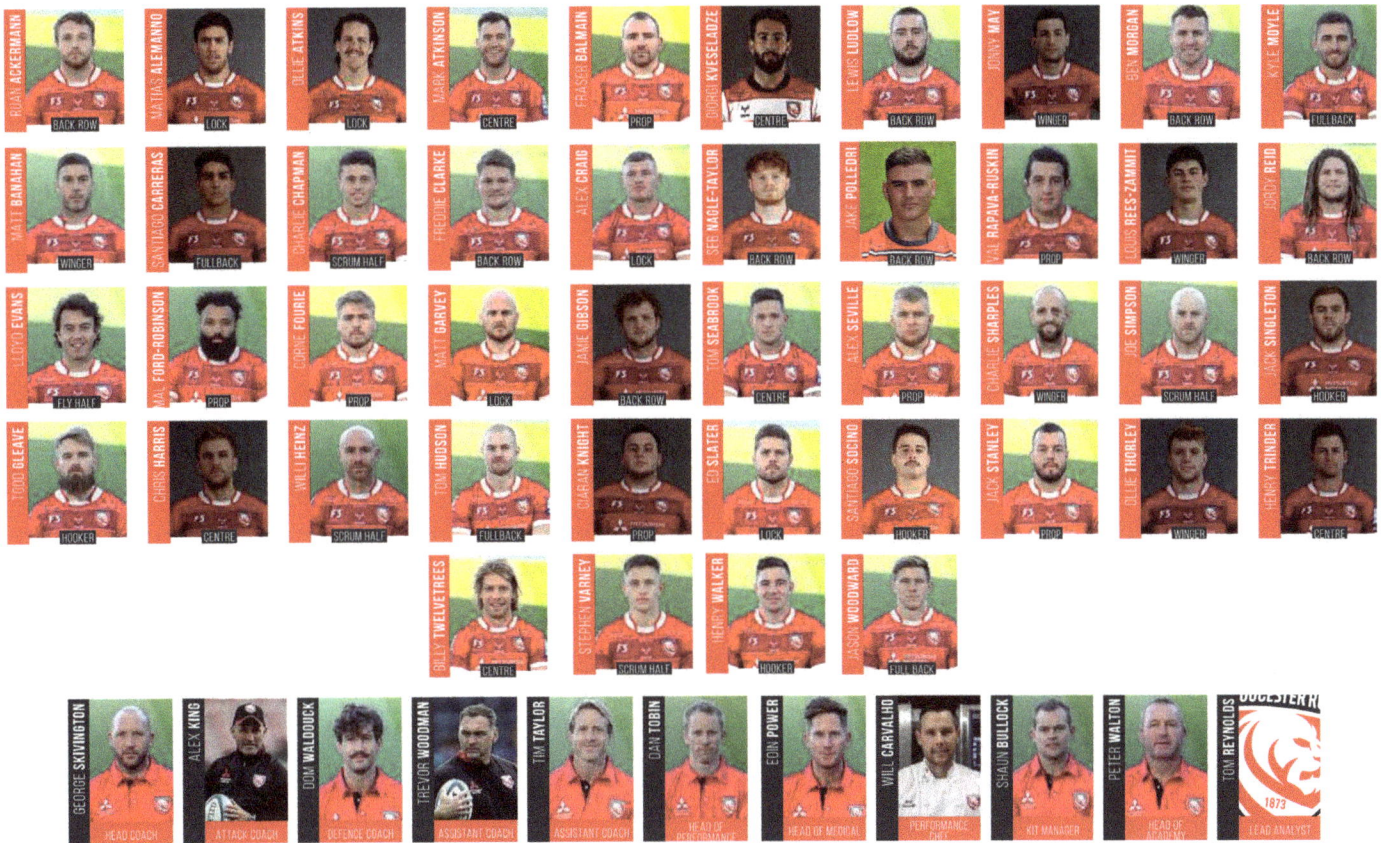

Copyright Martin Bennett

Played 25 Won 8 Lost 17
For 514 Against 634
Owner: Martin St Quinton
Head Coach: George Skivington
Captain: Lewis Ludlow
Premiership: Played 22 Won 7 Lost 15
For 450 Against 518
Position: 11th

Gloucester United
Played 1 Lost 1
For 19 Against 36

Most appearances: J.Ford-Robinson 23 (4 starts + 19 reps), L.Ludlow 21, R.Ackermann 20, B.Twelvetrees 19 (14+5), A.Craig 18 (8+10), K.Moyle 18 (13+5) M.Atkinson, E.Slater 17, J.Reid 17 (16+1)
Most tries: S.Carreras, L.Rees-Zammit 6, W.Heinz 5, J.Hanson, E.Slater, C.Chapman 3
Conversions: B.Twelvetrees 20, G.Barton 12, L.Evans 10, J.Morris 2
Penalties: B.Twelvetrees 18, G.Barton 10, L.Evans 7
A season played in empty stadia (except for a handful of matches) began late while the previous season was finished, and for Gloucester it started with a series of losses. Just when fortunes began to turn, and the possibility of qualification for the Champions Cup became real, the last two games were cancelled due to a Covid outbreak in the Gloucester camp. Only 23 games were played in the whole season, the lowest since 1939-40. On the bright side both centre Chris Harris and winger Louis Rees-Zammit were selected to tour South Africa with the British & Irish Lions. Both players were fixtures for Scotland and Wales respectively.

The first Premiership game was a heavy defeat at Leicester, but in the second a fine display swept Wasps away. There then followed a run of eight successive defeats, the Club's worst ever sequence in league games. Several were lost in the dying minutes. That disastrous sequence ended with a stimulating win away to Wasps, where for once it was Gloucester's turn to win at the death thanks to a Billy Twelvetrees penalty. This was despite playing with 14 men for three-quarters of the game after Ollie Thorley had been red-carded. In a late season revival three of the last four games were won, including a record win at Northampton. However, Covid struck the squad and the final two matches had to be conceded without taking the field. This meant that the finishing position left the team with only Worcester below them in the table.

In a reduced format, there were only three games played in the Champions Cup. A shadow team was taken to Lyon with a predictable outcome. Next up were Ulster at Kingsholm. In a thrilling encounter, Gloucester led 24-10, only to concede 24 points without reply. But with time running out, Gloucester were awarded a penalty try, and won the game after 85 minutes, when newcomer George Barton scored a try, his first for the Club. This was one of the few games where limited spectators were allowed; the attendance was 2,000. The chance of any further progress in the competition ended with defeat at La Rochelle.

Ollie Thorley was in fine form on the wing all season and was rewarded with an England cap. Jake Polledri was a regular for Italy, but a bad injury against Scotland would side line him for two years. Second row Alex Craig was spotted by the Scottish selectors and won two caps. Argentinian international duo Santiago Carreras and Matias Alemmano made a big impression in the back three and second row respectively, and both won four caps in the autumn internationals. Val Rapava-Ruskin became more and more influential at prop, as did Ruan Ackermann as No 8. Scrum-half Willi Heinz, who had been captain for the previous three seasons was still troubled by injuries, and at the end of the season left for Worcester after 172 appearances, which would have been many more but for injury. Centre Henry Trinder departed after 172 appearances to Brittany to play for Vannes in French D2.

Nov 21 Leicester 38 Gloucester 15 (Premiership)
Tries: J.Hanson, J.Simpson;
Conversion: B.Twelvetrees;
Penalty: B.Twelvetrees

Nov 28 Gloucester 40 Wasps 24 (Premiership)
Tries: J.Singleton, M.Garvey, J.Simpson, J.Woodward, B.Twelvetrees;
Conversions: B.Twelvetrees (3)
Penalties: B.Twelvetrees (3)

Dec 6 Gloucester 24 Harlequins 34 (Premiership)
Tries: J.Hanson (2), E.Slater;
Conversions: J.Morris (2), B.Twelvetrees;
Penalty: B.Twelvetrees

Dec 13 Lyon 55 Gloucester 10 (Champions Cup)
Try: S.Nagle-Taylor;
Conversion: G.Barton;
Penalty: G.Barton

Dec 19 Gloucester 38 Ulster 34 (Champions Cup)
Tries: penalty tries (2), L.Rees-Zammit, M.Atkinson, G.Barton;
Conversions: L.Evans (3);
Penalty: L.Evans

Dec 26 Exeter 28 Gloucester 20 (Premiership)
Tries: T.Venner (2);
Conversions: L.Evans (2);
Penalties: L.Evans (2)

Jan 2 Gloucester 19 Sale 23 (Premiership)
Tries: F.Balmain, l.Rees-Zammit;
Penalties: L.Evans (3)

Jan 9 Newcastle 22 Gloucester 10 (Premiership)
Try: J.May;
Conversion: L.Evans;
Penalty: L.Evans

Jan 30 Gloucester 26 Northampton 31 (Premiership)
Tries: W.Heinz, M.Alemanno;

Conversions: B.Twelvetrees (2);
Penalties: B.Twelvetrees (4)

Feb 6 London Irish 32 Gloucester 26 (Premiership)
Tries: A.Craig (2), H.Trinder, M.Atkinson;
Conversions: B.Twelvetrees (3)

Feb 12 Gloucester 17 Bristol 18 (Premiership)
Tries: S.Carreras (2), O.Thorley;
Conversion: B.Twelvetrees

Feb 19 Bath 16 Gloucester 14 (Premiership)
Try: L.Ludlow;
Penalties: B.Twelvetrees (3)

Feb 27 Gloucester 22 Worcester 14 (Premiership)
Tries: B.Twelvetrees, M.Alemanno, T.Seabrook;
Conversions: B.Twelvetrees (2);
Penalty: G.Barton

Mar 6 Wasps 19 Gloucester 20 (Premiership)
Tries: S.Socino, C.Harris;
Conversions: G.Barton (2);
Penalties: G.Barton, B.Twelvetrees

Mar 13 Gloucester 14 Leicester 20 (Premiership)
Tries: S.Carreras, E.Slater;
Conversions: G.Barton (2)

Mar 20 Harlequins 59 Gloucester 24 (Premiership)
Tries: C.Chapman (2), F.Clarke;
Conversions: G.Barton (3);
Penalty: G.Barton

Mar 26 Gloucester 34 Exeter 18 (Premiership)
Tries: H.Walker (2), C.Chapman, penalty try;
Conversions: C.Barton (3);
Penalties: G.Barton (2)

Apr 2 Gloucester 16 La Rochelle 27 (Champions Cup)
Try: R.Ackermann;
Conversion: G.Barton;
Penalties: G.Barton (3)

Apr 17 Sale 25 Gloucester 22 (Premiership)
Tries: J.May, S.Carreras, W.Heinz;
Conversions: B.Twelvetrees (2);
Penalty: G.Barton

Apr 24 Gloucester 35 Newcastle 24 (Premiership)

Tries: W.Heinz (2), L.Rees-Zammit, R.Ackermann, L.Evans;
Conversions: L.Evans (4), B.Twelvetrees

May 8 Northampton 7 Gloucester 31 (Premiership)
Tries: L.Rees-Zammit (2), E.Slater, J.Singleton;
Conversion: B.Twelvetrees;
Penalties: B.Twelvetrees (3)

May 17 Bristol 39 Gloucester 7 (Premiership)
Try: S.Carreras;
Conversion: B.Twelvetrees

May 28 Gloucester 30 London Irish 28 (Premiership)
Tries: S,Carreras, W.Heinz, K.Moyle, L.Rees-Zammit;
Conversions: B.Twelvetrees (2);
Penalties: B.Twelvetrees (2)

Jun 5 Gloucester v Bath (Premiership)
Cancelled due to Coronavirus outbreak in Gloucester squad. Bath 4 pts, Gloucester 2 pts.

Jun 12 Worcester v Gloucester (Premiership)
The final game of the season was also cancelled due to the Coronavirus outbreak. Worcester 4pts, Gloucester 2 pts.

Gloucester-Hartpury Women

Allianz Premier 15s
Played 18 Won 10 Lost 8
For 433 Against 339
Position: 5th

Most tries: Ellie Underwood 10, Zoe Aldcroft, Emily Wood 6, Kelly Smith, Hannah Jones 5
Most conversions: Emma Sing 17, Daisy Fahey 11

Oct 10 Gloucester-Hartpury 34 Exeter 14
Tries: Z.Aldcroft (2), K.Smith, S.Bonar, H.Jones, D.Fahey;
Conversions: E.Underwood, D.Fahey

Oct 17 Loughborough Lightning 32 Gloucester-Hartpury 26
Tries: H.Jones, S.Powell-Hughes, M.Venner, E.Wood;
Conversions: N.Hunt (2), E.Sing

Nov 7 Gloucester-Hartpury 5 Saracens 43
Try: E.Wood

Nov 14 Bristol 3 Gloucester-Hartpury 28

Tries: H.Jones, B.Blackburn, D.Fahey, S.Bonar;
Conversion: L.George;
Penalties: L.George (2)

Nov 21 Gloucester-Hartpury 17 Sale 14
Tries: B.Lewis, H.Jones;
Conversions: L.George, D.Fahey;
Penalty: L.George

Nov 28 Gloucester-Hartpury 5
Harlequins 22
Try: S.Powell-Hughes

Dec 6 Worcester 7
Gloucester-Hartpury 15
Tries: K.Jones, E.Wood;
Conversion: D.Fahey;
Penalty: D.Fahey

Dec 19 Wasps 29 Gloucester-Hartpury 17
Tries: S.Powell-Hughes, B.Blackburn;
Conversions: L.George (2);
Penalty: L.George

Jan 9 Gloucester-Hartpury 21
Loughborough Lightning 29
Tries: S.Pinnock, E.Wood, penalty try;
Conversions: D.Fahey, E.Sing

Feb 6 Sale 7 Gloucester-Hartpury 26
Tries: Name withheld, K.Jones, E.Underwood,
B.Blackburn;
Conversions: D.Fahey (3)

Feb 14 Saracens 36
Gloucester-Hartpury 10
Tries: K.Smith, E.Wood

Feb 27 Gloucester-Hartpury 36 Bristol 0
Tries: N.Hunt (2), E.Underwood (2), H.Jones,
K.Smith;
Conversions: D.Fahey (3)

Mar 6 Harlequins 28
Gloucester-Hartpury 15
Tries: N.Hunt, R.Lund, E.Sing

Mar 13 Gloucester-Hartpury 74

Darlington Mowden Park 7
Tries: E.Underwood (4), E.Sing (3), S.Tandy (2),
E.Wood, D.Fahey, R.Lund;
Conversions: E.Sing (6), D.Fahey

Mar 20 Gloucester-Hartpury 28
Worcester 24
Tries: Z.Aldcroft (3), K.Smith;
Conversions: E.Sing (4)

Mar 27 Darlington Mowden Park 7
Gloucester-Hartpury 38
Tries: E.Perry, K.Smith, C-M.Manns,
C.Powell, E.Underwood, R.Lock;
Conversions: E.Sing (3), E.Mundy

Apr 17 Gloucester-Hartpury 20 Wasps 25
Tries: E.Underwood, B.Blackburn, R.Lund;
Conversion: E.Sing;
Penalty: E.Sing

May 8 Exeter 8 Gloucester-Hartpury 18
Tries: Z.Aldcroft, E.Underwood;
Conversion: E.Sing;

2021-22

Copyright Martin Bennett

Played 35 Won 20 Lost 14 Drawn 1
For 1097 Against 784
Owner: Martin St Quinton
Head Coach: George Skivington
Captain: Lewis Ludlow
Premiership: Played 24 Won 13 Lost 10
Drawn 1
For 685 Against 525
Position: 5th

Most appearances: F.Clarke 29 (27 starts +
2 rep.), B.Meehan 28 (19+9), L.Ludlow 27,
R.Ackermann 26 (24+2), J.Clement 26 (9+17),
A.Hastings 25 (21+4), J.Singleton 25 (21+4),
F.Balmain 25 (18+7), B.Twelvetrees 25 (16+9),
C.Chapman 25 (10+15), A.Davidson 25
(9+16), S.Socino 25 (9+16), J.Ford-Robinson
25 (5+20)
Most Tries: L.Rees-Zammit 12, J.Singleton 11,

B.Morgan 9, S.Socino 9, C.Harris 8, O.Thorley
6, J.Clement 6
Conversions: A.Hastings 60, L.Evans 27,
G.Barton 14, B.Twelvetrees 6
Penalties: A.Hastings 27, L.Evans 6, G.Barton
3, B.Twelvetrees 3
Drop goals: A.Hastings 2

After only three seasons the hybrid playing

surface at Kingsholm was replaced by a fully artificial one.

With coach George Skivington in charge for a second season, and his methods starting to take effect, and with captain, Lewis Ludlow leading by example from the front, the team rose six places in the Premiership to finish just outside the play-offs. The rolling maul was so efficient that few sides knew how to neutralise it. The result was that 22 tries were scored by hookers. In fact, in all, 141 tries were scored, the most since 1990-91, and the total points at 1097 was the highest since 2001-02. Gloucester was the only team to achieve the double over Saracens. Other doubles were gained over Bath and Newcastle.

Although the first two Premiership games were lost, there was a new spirit in the team. Of the next twelve league games nine resulted in wins and only one loss. Away form had been transformed, and there was a 40-20 win at Bath. The scores against Bath were quite remarkable. Ten tries were scored in the league game at Kingsholm and eleven in the Premiership Cup, making a total of 175 points scored against the old rivals in the three matches. In the course of the double over Saracens, there was the first away win since 2008. In the Northampton game at Kingsholm, the Saints were leading 27-14, only for Louis Rees-Zammit to come on as a replacement and score a glorious try, which sparked off a stirring revival. The other side of the coin was demonstrated at the Stoop, where Gloucester were leading 24-7 at half-time only to lose 28-24.

The team showed good form through the group stages of the Challenge Cup, only to come up against Saracens in the quarter-final, when Gloucester were completely outplayed. In the Premiership Cup the Cherry & Whites reached the semi-final and a home game against Worcester. The Warriors turned up with a full-strength squad, and prevailed against the young Gloucester team, despite a brave fight by what was essentially an Academy squad.

Adam Hastings soon found his feet at fly-half, and quickly formed an effective half-back pairing with another newcomer, Ben Meehan. Against Sale in October Hastings kicked the first drop goal by a Gloucester player since January 2015. Ruan Ackermann had a superb season in the back-row, and there was speculation that he could be picked for the England squad, having qualified through residence. Ollie Thorley and Louis Rees-Zammit were a constant threat, and Santiago Carreras contributed spiky competitiveness with silky skills.

Lewis Ludlow won his first two England caps in the summer of 2021, captaining the team. Mark Atkinson won his first England cap, whilst Louis Rees-Zammit was a regular for Wales, and Chris Harris for Scotland. Adam Hastings was also capped for Scotland; Santiago Carreras, Santiago Socino, and Matias Alemanno won Argentina caps. Steven Varney won more Italy caps. Giorgi Kveseladze (Georgia), Kirill Gotovtsev (Russia) were other internationals.

Charlie Sharples who had played his first game back in 2008, had intended this to be his last season. However, due to a shoulder injury he did not make any appearances, and announced his retirement in February. He had played in 273 games and scored 88 tries.

With a new optimism and players buying into George Skivington's vision, the next season promised the possibility of even more success.

Sep 18 Northampton 34 Gloucester 20
(Premiership)
Tries: O.Thorley, J.Reid, J.May;
Conversion: B.Twelvetrees;
Penalty: B.Twelvetrees

Sep 24 Gloucester 26 Leicester 33
(Premiership)
Tries: F.Balmain, R.Ackermann, M.Atkinson, J.Clement;
Conversions: L.Evans (2), A.Hastings

Oct 2 Worcester 23 Gloucester 31
(Premiership)
Tries: B.Morgan, J.Woodward, C.Harris;
Conversions: A.Hastings (2);
Penalties: A.Hastings (4)

Oct 9 Gloucester 33 Sale 32
(Premiership)
Tries: L.Rees-Zammit (2), B.Morgan, J.Singleton;
Conversions: A.Hastings (2);
Penalties: A.Hastings (2)
Drop goal: A.Hastings

Oct 17 London Irish 25 Gloucester 25
(Premiership)
Tries: B.Morgan (2), L.Rees-Zammit;
Conversions: A.Hastings (2);
Penalties: A.Hastings (2)

Oct 23 Gloucester 29 Newcastle 20
(Premiership)
Tries: V.Rapava-Ruskin, J.May;
Conversions: L.Evans (2);
Penalties: L.Evans (5)

Oct 29 Gloucester 13 Exeter 16

(Premiership)
Try: J.Singleton;
Conversion: A.Hastings;
Penalties: A.Hastings

Nov 12 Gloucester 71 Bath 10
(Premiership Cup)
Tries: B.Morgan (3), J.Clement (2), K.Moyle, L.Ludlow, R.Ackermann, A.Davidson, F.Balmain, J.Morris;
Conversions: L.Evans (8)

Nov 20 Gloucester 45 Exeter 19
(Premiership Cup)
Tries: A.Morgan (2), H.Taylor, J.Morris, G.Barton, J.Reeves;
Conversions: L.Evans (5), B.Twelvetrees;
Penalty: L.Evans

Nov 26 Wasps 33 Gloucester 35
(Premiership)
Tries: B.Twelvetrees (2), J.May, J.Clement;
Conversions: A.Hastings (3);
Penalties: A.Hastings (3)

Dec 3 Gloucester 27 Bristol 10
(Premiership)
Tries: J.Singleton, C.Harris, C.Chapman, penalty try;
Conversion: A.Hastings;
Penalty: A.Hastings

Dec 10 Lyon 19 Gloucester 13
(European Challenge Cup)
Try: C.Jordan;
Conversion: B.Twelvetrees;
Penalties: B.Twelvetrees (2)

Dec 17 Gloucester 54 Benetton 25
(European Challenge Cup)
Tries: J.Singleton, B.Meehan, J.Reid, M.Alemanno, S.Varney, J.May, J.Clement, penalty try
Conversions: A.Hastings (4), L.Evans (2)

Dec 26 Bath 20 Gloucester 40
(Premiership)
Tries: C.Harris (2), J.Singleton, F.Balmain, K.Moyle, penalty try;
Conversions: A.Hastings (4)

Dec 29 Worcester 27 Gloucester 21
(Premiership Cup)
Tries: T.Seabrook, S.Blake, A.Morgan;
Conversions: G.Barton (3)

Jan 2 Gloucester 17 Harlequins 20
(Premiership)
Tries: R.Ackermann, S.Socino;
Conversions: A.Hastings, L.Evans;
Penalty: A.Hastings

Jan 8 Saracens 24 Gloucester 25 (Premiership)
Tries: F.Balmain, J.Singleton, L.Ludlow;
Conversions: A.Hastings (2);
Penalties: A.Hastings (2)

Jan 22 Gloucester 68 Perpignan 19 (European Challenge Cup)
Tries: J.Reid (2), L.Ludlow, K.Moyle, S.Socino, M.Atkinson, S.Varney, L.Rees-Zammit, J.Singleton, C.Harris;
Conversions: A.Hastings (5), L.Evans (4)

Jan 29 Newcastle 22 Gloucester 32 (Premiership)
Tries: V.Rapava-Ruskin, S.Carreras, L.Ludlow, O.Thorley, L.Rees-Zammit;
Conversions: A.Hastings, L.Evans;
Penalty: A.Hastings

Feb 4 Gloucester 24 London Irish 7 (Premiership)
Tries: R.Ackermann (2), O.Thorley;
Conversions: L.Evans (2), A.Hastings;
Penalty: A.Hastings

Feb 12 Exeter 24 Gloucester 15 (League)
Tries: F.Clarke, S.Carreras, C.Chapman

Feb 26 Leicester 35 Gloucester 23 (Premiership)
Tries: O.Thorley, H.Elrington;
Conversions: A.Hastings, G.Barton;
Penalties: A.Hastings (3)

Mar 5 Gloucester 35 Northampton 30 (Premiership)
Tries: H.Elrington, L.Rees-Zammit, T.Seabrook, A.Craig, penalty try;
Conversions: A.Hastings (4)

Mar 12 Sale 26 Gloucester 24 (Premiership)
Tries: S.Socino (2), C.Chapman, L.Hillman-Cooper;
Conversions: G.Barton (2)

Mar 25 Gloucester v Worcester (Premiership)
With five hours to go before kick-off, Worcester called the game off due to illness, injuries and Covid. Match awarded to Gloucester (20-0) with five points.

Mar 30 Bristol 15 Gloucester 43 (Premiership Cup)
Tries: H.Walker (2), J.Morris, J.Bartlett, F.Thomas, A.Morgan;
Conversions: G.Barton (5);
Penalty: G.Barton

Apr 2 Gloucester 21 Wasps 27 (Premiership)
Tries: K.Moyle, penalty try;
Penalties: A.Hastings (3)

Apr 9 Dragons 21 Gloucester 26 (European Challenge Cup)
Tries: S.Socino (3), L.Rees-Zammit;
Conversions: B.Twelvetrees (2), G.Barton

Apr 16 Gloucester 31 Northampton 21 (European Challenge Cup)
Tries: O.Thorley, V.Rapava-Ruskin, M.Alemanno, S.Socino;
Conversions: A.Hastings (4);
Penalty: A.Hastings

Apr 22 Bristol 29 Gloucester 28 (Premiership)
Tries: C.Chapman, L.Rees-Zammit, C.Harris, J.Singleton;
Conversions: A.Hastings (4)

Apr 27 Gloucester 25 Worcester 39 (Premiership Cup Semi-Final)
Tries: C.Jordan, J.Morris, A.Morgan;
Conversions: G.Barton (2);
Penalties: G.Barton (2)

Apr 30 Gloucester 64 Bath 0 (Premiership)
Tries: L.Rees-Zammit (2), C.Harris, S.Carreras, B.Morgan, M.Atkinson, L.Ludlow, B.Meehan, M.Alemanno, J.Ford-Robison;
Conversions: A.Hastings (7)

May 6 Gloucester 15 Saracens 44 (European Challenge Cup Quarter-Final)
Tries: J.Singleton, L.Rees-Zammit;
Conversion: B.Twelvetrees;
Penalty: A.Hastings

May 21 Harlequins 28 Gloucester 24 (Premiership)
Tries: B.Morgan, F.Clarke, C.Harris;
Conversions: A.Hastings (3);
Drop goal: A.Hastings

June 4 Gloucester 54 Saracens 7 (Premiership)
Tries: J.Singleton (2), J.Reid, S.Carreras, O.Thorley, S.Socino, J.Clement, L.Rees-Zammit;
Conversions: A.Hastings (7)

Gloucester-Hartpury Women

Allianz Premier 15s
Played 18 Won 9 Lost 8 Drawn 1
For 541 Against 327
Position: 6th

Most tries: Ellie Underwood 16, Connie Powell 9, Rachel Lund, Sisilia Tuipulota, Emma Sing 7
Most conversions: Emma Sing 43
Most penalties: Emma Sing 10

Sep 4 Gloucester-Hartpury 84 Darlington Mowden Park 0
Tries: E.Underwood (3), K.Smith (2), M.Isaac (2), K.Jones, S.Tandy, G.Brock, E.Sing, N.Hunt, C.Powell,
Conversions: E.Sing (4), R.Wilkins (2);
Penalty: E.Sing (scorers of two conversions unknown)

Sep 11 Gloucester-Hartpury 17 Bristol 24
Tries: C.Powell, K.Smith;
Conversions: E.Sing (2);
Penalty: E.Sing

Sep 18 Sale 21 Gloucester-Hartpury 45
Tries: E.Underwood (2), C.Powell (2), Z.Aldcroft, E.Sing, penalty try;
Conversions: E.Sing (4)

Oct 2 Gloucester-Hartpury 18 Harlequins 21
Tries: K.Smith (2);
Conversion: E.Sing;
Penalties: E.Sing (2)

Oct 10 Wasps 34 Gloucester-Hartpury 25
Tries: N.Hunt, B.Lewis, E.Underwood;
Conversions: E.Sing (2);
Penalties: E.Sing (2)

Nov 27 Gloucester-Hartpury 21 Saracens 24
Tries: R.Lund, C.Powell, T.Heard;
Conversions: E.Sing (3)

Dec 4 Gloucester-Hartpury 31 Loughborough Lightning 33
Tries: C.Powell, R.Lund, B.Lewis, E.Underwood, S.Tuipulotu;
Conversions: E.Sing (3)

Dec 11 Exeter 8 Gloucester-Hartpury 10
Tries: Z.Aldcroft, K.Smith

Dec 19 Worcester 10 Gloucester-Hartpury 36
Tries: Z.Aldcroft (2), S.Tuipulotu (2), R.Lund, E.Sing;
Conversions: E.Sing (3)

Jan 8 Bristol 14 Gloucester-Hartpury 36
Tries: E.Underwood (2), S.Tuipulotu, G.Brock, R.Lund, E.Sing;
Conversions: E.Sing (3)

Jan 15 Gloucester-Hartpury 17 Sale 3
Tries: R.Lund, C.Powell, K.Sommer;
Conversion: E.Sing

**Jan 29 Harlequins 26
Gloucester-Hartpury 12**
Tries: C.Powell, B.Blackburn;
Conversion: E.Sing

Feb 5 Gloucester-Hartpury 32 Exeter 36
Tries: G.Crabb, H.Jones, C.Powell,
S.Tuipulotu;
Conversions: E.Sing (3);
Penalties: E.Sing (2)

**Feb 26 Loughborough Lightning 19
Gloucester-Hartpury 19**
Tries: S.Tuipulotu, E.Underwood, H.Jones;
Conversions: E.Sing (2)

**Mar 5 Gloucester-Hartpury 15
Worcester 12**
Tries: B.Lewis, S,Tuipulotu;
Conversion: E.Sing;
Penalty: E.Sing

**Mar 13 Saracens 35
Gloucester-Hartpury 20**
Tries: A.Maude, A.Caplice, E.Underwood;
Conversion: D.Fahey;

Penalty: D.Fahey

May 7 Gloucester-Hartpury 36 Wasps 7
Tries: N.Hunt, N.Jones, R.Lund,
E.Underwood, E.Sing;
Conversions: E.Sing (4);
Penalty: E.Sing

**May 14 Darlington Mowden Park 0
Gloucester-Hartpury 67**
Tries: E.Underwood (4), L.George, B.Lewis,
Z.Aldcroft, K.Lake, R.Lund, E.Sing, L.Scott;
Conversions: E.Sing (6)

2022-23

Copyright Martin Bennett

**Played 30 Won 13 Lost 17
For 699 Against 811
Owner: Martin St Quinton
Head Coach: George Skivington
Captain: Lewis Ludlow
Premiership
Played 20 Won 7 Lost 13
For 435 Against 504
Position: 10th**

Gloucester United
Played 1 Won 1
For 45 Against 33

Most appearances: L.Ludlow 24, F.Clarke 24 (22 starts + 2 reps), C.Jordan 22 (6+16), M.Alemanno 21 (20+1), C.Harris 20, S.Carreras 20, L.Evans 20 (16+4), B.Twelvetrees 19 (9+10)
Most tries: S.Socino 7, S.Blake 6, Louis Rees-Zammit, O.Thorley, R.Rapava-Ruskin,

J.Reeves, J.May 5
Most conversions: A.Hastings 22, G.Barton 21, S.Carreras 15
Most penalties: S.Carreras 8, A.Hastings 6

Whilst Gloucester-Hartpury Women won the Allianz Premier 15s, for Gloucester Rugby, the campaign was disappointing. For much of the season the team was well in contention for a play-off place. But a very poor run of six losses on the trot, including successive defeats to the bottom two clubs Newcastle and Bath, resulted in a drop to 10th in the table. Much of the decline can be explained by a long injury list. Adam Hastings was absent for much of the campaign after being injured playing for Scotland against Fiji in the autumn. Then, in his come-back game against Leicester on Christmas Eve he damaged a shoulder which required surgery. He made it back for the last two games of the season. Mark Atkinson managed just three games

before his season ended, but his place was filled by name-sake Seb Atkinson who was signed after the demise of the Worcester Warriors; his performances became more authoritative as he gained experience, and he became a keen attacking threat. Hookers Jack Singleton and Santiago Socino were both injured. Not only that, but George McGuigan a mid-season signing from Newcastle took up the hooking berth for five games before he too was injured. Youngster Seb Blake had to slot in at hooker and did a very good job. Ruan Ackermann was injured playing against La Rochelle and that ended his season.

After being absent through injury for two years Jake Polledri tried to make a come-back, but facing competition from a powerful back row, he could only make three appearances in the Premiership Cup, one in the Challenge Cup and as a replacement in one Premiership game, before announcing in March that he would be moving to Italy to play for Zebre.

In the Champions Cup there was a good double over Bordeaux-Begles, and qualification for the last 16. This entailed a journey to La Rochelle to face the champions. In what was perhaps the best performance of the season the team was extremely unlucky to lose to a try at the death.

It was the first season since 1965-66 when no player scored more than 100 points.

Louis Rees-Zammit, Chris Harris, Matias Alemanno, Santiago Carreras and Santiago Socino won international caps.

After 11 seasons, 274 appearances and 980 points, Billy Twelvetrees ended his Gloucester career in order to play the following season with Ealing Trailfinders. Jordy Reid also left to play for the same club, whilst Tom Seabrook departed for Northampton. Ben Morgan retired having made 187 appearances and scoring 38 tries.

Sep 11 Gloucester 27 Wasps 21 (Premiership) *
Tries: L.Rees-Zammit, C.Chapman, F.Clarke, penalty try;
Conversion: A.Hastings;
Penalty: A.Hastings
*Result later expunged due to Wasps entering administration.

Sep 21 Gloucester 49 Worcester 21 (Premiership Cup) *
Tries: J.Reeves (2), F.Thomas (2), A.Clark, J.Clement, T.Seabrook;
Conversions: G.Barton (7)
* Result later expunged due to Worcester entering administration.

Sep 24 Saracens 41 Gloucester 39 (Premiership)
Tries: V.Rapava-Ruskin (2), A.Tuisue, C.Harris, A.Hastings;
Conversions: A.Hastings (3);
Penalty: A.Hastings

Sep 28 Bath 15 Gloucester 29 (Premiership Cup)
Tries: J.Reeves (2), J.Polledri, K.Moyle;
Conversions: G.Barton (3);
Penalty: G.Barton

Oct 1 Gloucester v Worcester (Premiership) Game cancelled due to Worcester entering administration

Oct 8 Bath 17 Gloucester 21 (Premiership)

Tries: M.Alemanno (2), S.Socino;
Conversions: A.Hastings (3)

Oct 15 Gloucester 31 Bristol 28 (Premiership)
Tries: V.Rapava-Ruskin (2), J.Reid, F.Clarke;
Conversions: A.Hastings (4);
Penalty: A.Hastings

Oct 21 London Irish 21 Gloucester 22 (Premiership)
Tries: S.Socino (2), R.Ackermann;
Conversions: A.Hastings (2);
Drop goal: A.Hastings

Oct 28 Gloucester 38 Exeter 21 (Premiership)
Tries: L.Rees-Zammit, S.Carreras, C.Chapman, R.Ackermann, L.Ludlow, S.Socino;
Conversions: A.Hastings (4)

Nov 5 Sale 27 Gloucester 17 (Premiership)
Tries: S.Socino, J.Morris, F.Clarke;
Conversion: L.Evans

Nov 12 Gloucester 21 Newcastle 27 (Premiership)
Tries: T.Seabrook, C.Jordan, penalty try;
Conversions: G.Barton (2)

Nov 19 Gloucester 38 Bristol 31 (Premiership Cup)
Tries: J.Morris (2), S.Atkinson, H.Walker, J.Clement, S.Blake;
Conversions: G.Barton (4)

Nov 25 Harlequins 21 Gloucester 12 (Premiership)
Tries: B.Morgan, S.Socino;
Conversion: S.Carreras

Dec 3 Gloucester 34 Northampton 19 (Premiership)
Tries: S.Carreras, J.Singleton, C.Harris, F.Balmain;
Conversions: S.Carreras (4);
Penalties: S.Carreras (2)

Dec 4 Exeter 50 Gloucester 33 (Premiership Cup)
Tries: B.Meehan, S.Blake, J.Morris, A.Morgan, J.Reeves;
Conversions: G.Barton (4)

Dec 10 Gloucester 22 Bordeaux Begles 17 (Champions Cup)
Tries: S.Varney, S.Socino, A.Tuisue, C.Chapman;
Conversion: S.Carreras

Dec 16 Leinster 57 Gloucester 0 (Champions Cup)

Dec 24 Leicester 28 Gloucester 13 (Premiership)
Tries: A.Tuisue, J.May;
Penalty: A.Hastings

Dec 31 Gloucester 8 London Irish 6 (Premiership)
Try: M.Alemanno;
Penalty: S.Carreras

Jan 6 Gloucester 16 Saracens 19 (Premiership)
Try: O.Thorley;
Conversion: S.Carreras;
Penalties: S.Carreras (3)

Jan 14 Gloucester 14 Leinster 49 (Champions Cup)
Tries: Penalty tries (2)

Jan 21 Bourdeaux Begles 17 Gloucester 26 (Champions Cup)
Tries: G.McGuigan (2), A.Tuisue;
Conversion: G.Barton;
Penalties: G.Barton (3)

Jan 28 Exeter 24 Gloucester 17 (Premership)
Tries: J.May, V.Rapava-Ruskin;
Conversions: B.Twelvetrees (2), S.Carreras;
Penalty: S.Carreras

Feb 17 Gloucester 28 Harlequins 26 (Premiership)
Tries: S.Blake, O.Thorley, S.Carreras, L.Rees-Zammit;
Conversions: S.Carreras (4)

Feb 25 Northampton 41 Gloucester 34 (Premiership)
Tries: S.Blake (2), J.Ford-Robinson (2), O.Thorley, M.Alemanno;
Conversions: B.Twelvetrees (2)

Mar 12 Gloucester 5 Leicester 26 (Premiership)
Try: J.May

Mar 24 Newcastle 17 Gloucester 12 (Premiership)
Tries: S.Blake, O.Thorley;
Conversion: S.Carreras

Apr 1 La Rochelle 29 Gloucester 26 (Champions Cup)
Tries: C.Harris, F Clarke, L.Rees-Zammit;
Conversion: B.Twelvetrees;

Penalties: B.Twelvetrees (3)

**Apr 14 Gloucester 24 Bath 33
(Premiership)**
Tries: S.Varney, S.Carreras, S.Atkinson;
Conversions: S.Carreras (3);
Penalty: S.Carreras

**Apr 22 Gloucester 22 Sale 25
(Premiership)**
Tries: L.Ludlow, L.Rees-Zammit, J.May;
Conversions: A.Hastings (2);
Penalty: A.Hastings

**May 6 Bristol 36 Gloucester 21
(Premiership)**
Tries: O.Thorley, J.May, penalty try;
Conversions: A.Hastings (2)

Gloucester-Hartpury Women

Allianz Premier 15s
Played 20 Won 18 Lost 2
For 799 Against 284
Position: 1st & Champions

Most tries: Ellie Underwood 15, Rachel Lund
11, Sarah Beckett 10, Sophie Bridger 9
Most conversions: Emma Sing 25, Lleucu
George 21

Undoubtedly the great achievement of the
season was the capturing of the Allianz Premier
15s title by Gloucester-Hartpury women. They
beat Exeter in the final at "Queensholm" in
front of nearly 10,000 spectators. It was a fine
example of top-class rugby from two well
matched teams.

**Nov 19 Exeter 17
Gloucester-Hartpury 25**
Tries: S.Bridger, N.Hunt, R.Lund;
Conversions: E.Sing (2);
Penalty: E.Sing (2)

Nov 26 Gloucester-Hartpury 36 Bristol 5
Tries: N.Jones (2), E.Underwood (2), M.Venner,
E.Sing;
Conversions: E.Sing (3)

Dec 3 Wasps 3 Gloucester-Hartpury 67
Tries: E.Underwood (3), G.Crabb (3),
E.Goulden (2), S.Beckett, R.Lund, B.Lewis;
Conversions: L.George (5), E.Underwood

**Dec 10 Saracens 7
Gloucester-Hartpury 53**
Tries: E.Underwood (2), K.Jones, N.Hunt,
R.Lund, S.Bridger, B.Lewis, S.Tuipulotu,
penalty try;
Conversions: E.Sing (3)

**Dec 18 Gloucester-Hartpury 61
Darlington Mowden Park 0**
Tries: R.Lund (2), S.Beckett, J.Isherwood,
N.Hunt, E.Gilbert, A.Matthews, C.Cooney,
Z.Aldcroft, S.Else, H.Jones;
Conversions: E.Goulden (3)

**Jan 7 University of Worcester 5
Gloucester-Hartpury 52**
Tries: N.Jones (2), S.Beckett (2), S.Tuipulotu
(2), Z.Aldcroft, E.Sing;
Conversions: E.Sing (5), N.Jones

**Jan 14 Gloucester-Hartpury 46
Loughborough Lightning 12**
Tries: E.Underwood (2), N.Hunt (2), E.Sing,
S.Tuipulotu, R.Lund, H.Jones;
Conversions: E.Sing (3)

**Jan 22 Harlequins 22
Gloucester-Hartpury 33**
Tries: R.Lund, H.Jones, B.Lewis, Z.Alscroft,
S.Monaghan;
Conversions: E.Sing (3), L.George

Copyright Martin Bennett

Jan 28 Gloucester-Hartpury 41 Sale 7
Tries: C.Powell (2), N.Jones, E.Underwood,
K.Jones, Z.Aldcroft, S.Tandy;
Conversions: E.Goulden (3)

Feb 4 Bristol 17 Gloucester-Hartpury 19
Tries: E.Sing, R.Lund, E.Underwood;
Conversions: E.Sing (2)

Feb 18 Gloucester-Hartpury v Wasps
Gloucester/Hartpury awarded home walk-over.

**Feb 25 Gloucester-Hartpury 27
Saracens 36**
Tries: S.Bridger (2), R.Lund (2), penalty try

**Mar 4 Darlington Mowden Park 0
Gloucester-Hartpury 60**
Tries: C.Powell (2), M.Venner (2), P.Hendy,
S.Bridger, S.Else, B.Blackburn, E.Goulden,
N.Hunt;

Conversions: L.George (4), C.Powell

**Mar 11 Gloucester-Hartpury 50
University of Worcester 12**
Tries: K.Jones (2), S.Bridger, M.Venner,
S.Beckett, E.Goulden, S.Lillicrap, C.Hale;
Conversions: L.George (5)

**May 14 Loughborough Lightning 26
Gloucester-Hartpury 40**
Tries: B.Lewis (2), E.Underwood (2), N.Hunt,
N.Jones;
Conversions: E.Sing (5)

**May 21 Gloucester-Hartpury 67
Harlequins 14**
Tries: S.Monoghan (2), E.Sing (2), K.Jones,
M.Muir, T.Heard, M.Venner, S.Bridger,
E.Underwood, C.Powell;
Conversions: E.Sing (4), L.George (2)

May 27 Sale 14 Gloucester-Hartpury 48
Tries: S.Beckett (3), E.Underwood, S.Bridger,
K.Jones, C.Powell, L.Neumann;
Conversions: L.George (4)

Jun 3 Gloucester-Hartpury 19 Exeter 58
Tries: S.Bridger, L.Neumann, S.Tuipulotu;
Conversions: E.Goulden (2)

**Jun 10 Gloucester-Hartpury 21
Bristol 12 (Play-off Semi-final)**
Tries: S.Beckett, K.Jones, R.Lund;
Conversions: E.Sing (3)

**Jun 24 Gloucester-Hartpury 34
Exeter 19 (Premier 15s Final)**
Tries: K.Jones, R.Lund, S.Beckett, L.Neumann,
penalty try;
Conversions: E.Sing (2);
Penalty: E.Sing